The

PORTABLE
MBA
DESK
REFERENCE

AN ESSENTIAL BUSINESS
COMPANION

The Portable MBA Series

The portable MBA Series provides managers, executives, professionals, and students with a "hands-on," easy-to-access overview of the ideas and information covered in a typical Masters of Business Administration program. The published and forthcoming books in the program are:

Published

The Portable MBA (0-471-61997-3, cloth; 0-471-54895-2, paper) Eliza G. C. Collins and Mary Anne Devanna

The Portable MBA Desk Reference (0-471-57681-6) Paul A. Argenti

The Portable MBA in Finance and Accounting (0-471-53226-6) John Leslie Livingstone

The Portable MBA in Management (0-471-57379-5) Allan R. Cohen

The Portable MBA in Marketing (0-471-54728-X) Alexander Hiam and Charles Schewe

New Product Development: Managing and Forecasting for Strategic Success (0-471-57226-8) Robert J. Thomas

Real-Time Strategy: Improving Team-Based Planning for a Fast-Changing World (0-471-58564-5) Lee Tom Perry, Randall G. Stott, and W. Norman Smallwood

Forthcoming

The Portable MBA in Economics (0-471-59526-8) Philip K. Y. Young and John McCauley

The Portable MBA in Entrepreneurship (0-471-57780-4) William Bygrave

The Portable MBA in Global Business Leadership (0-471-30410-7) Noel Tichy, Michael Brimm, and Hiro Takeuchi

The Portable MBA in Strategy (0-471-58498-3) Liam Fahey and Robert Randall

Analyzing the Balance Sheet (0-471-59191-2) John Leslie Livingstone

Information Technology and Business Strategy (0-471-59659-0) N. Venkatraman and James E. Short

Negotiating Strategically (0-471-1321-8) Roy Lewicki and Alexander Hiam

The New Marketing Concept (0-471-59576-4) Frederick E. Webster

Psychology for Leaders (0-471-59538-1) Dean Tjosvold and Mary Tjosvold

Total Quality Management: Strategies and Techniques Proven at Today's Most Successful Companies (0-471) Arnold Weimerskirch and Stephen George

The

PORTABLE
MBA
DESK
REFERENCE

AN ESSENTIAL BUSINESS
COMPANION

Paul A. Argenti, Editorial Director

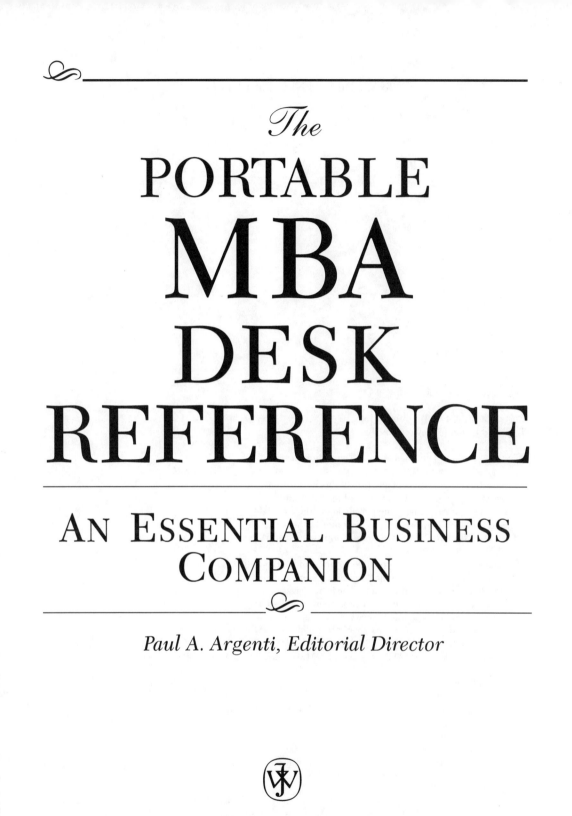

JOHN WILEY & SONS, INC.

New York • Chichester • Brisbane • Toronto • Singapore

To My Parents, Nick and Elenora

Text design by Lee Goldstein.

This text is printed on acid-free paper.

ISBN 0-471-57681-6

The Portable MBA desk reference / Paul Argenti, editorial director.
     p.   cm.
  Includes index.
  ISBN 0-471-57681-6 (cloth)
  1. Business—Handbooks, manuals, etc. 2. Business information
services—United States—Handbooks, manuals, etc. I. Argenti, Paul A.
HF5356.P67 1994
650—dc20   93-32666

Printed in the United States of America

10 9 8 7 6 5 4 3 2 1

Contents

∼ Appendices 605

Board of Experts

The information in the *Portable MBA Desk Reference* has been reviewed by a panel of experts from both academia and professional practice. The members of the Board of Experts are:

Edward I. Altman, Max L. Heine Professor of Finance, New York University; author of *Corporate Financial Distress*.

Tony Antin, independent consultant, formerly Director of Advertising at *Reader's Digest*.

Alvin Arnold, author of *The Arnold Encyclopedia of Real Estate*.

William Bygrave, Hamilton Professor of Entrepreneurship, Babson College; editor of *The Portable MBA in Entrepreneurship* and coauthor of *Venture Capital at the Crossroads*.

Joan Canning, Business Reference Librarian, Brooklyn Public Library.

Allan R. Cohen, Academic Vice-President, Babson College; editor of *The Portable MBA in Management* and coauthor of *Managing for Excellence* and *Influence without Authority*.

Karmen N. T. Crowther, Librarian, University of Tennessee; author of *Researching Your Way to a Good Job*.

David J. Curry, Professor of Marketing, University of Cincinnati; author of *The New Marketing Research Systems: How to Use Strategic Database Information for Better Marketing Decisions*.

Jeff Davidson, certified management consultant; author of numerous books including *Getting New Clients* and *Marketing on a Shoestring*.

Don Debelak, author of *How to Bring a Product to Market for Less Than $5000*.

Cristopher Engholm, author of *When Business East Meets Business West: The Guide to Practice and Protocol in the Pacific Rim* and the forthcoming *Asia and Japan Business Information Sourcebook*.

Liam Fahey, editor of *Planning Review*, coeditor of *The Portable MBA in Strategy* (forthcoming), and *Winning in the New Europe: Taking Advantage of the Single Market*.

Michael Fetters, certified public accountant; Chairperson, Accounting and Law Division, Babson College.

Richard Freierman, coauthor of *Corporate Realities and Environmental Truths: Strategies for Leading Your Business in the Environmental Era*.

Leonard Fuld, President and founder, Fuld & Company, Inc., a firm specializing in gathering competitor intelligence; author of *Competitor Intelligence: How to Get It, How to Use It* and *Monitoring the Competition*.

Robert Gaston, author of *Finding Private Venture Capital for Your Firm: A Complete Guide*.

Introduction: How to Use the Portable MBA Desk Reference

It's not enough to be an accountant and just know accounting. Or to be a marketer and just know marketing. Or, for that matter, to be a manager and just know management. In today's business environment, as companies downsize, streamline, grow, and reorganize, executives, managers, entrepreneurs, and even students are expected to become *de facto* experts in all areas of business. Production managers have to know about marketing; financial planners have to know about corporate strategy; and accountants have to know about both monetary and human costs. The key to this knowledge is information. That information is here, in *The Portable MBA Desk Reference*.

For information to have value, it has to be accessible. If you can't find something immediately, the information might just as well not exist. Ease and speed of access are the two characteristics that make *The Portable MBA Desk Reference* *the* standard business reference for practitioners and students of business. *The Portable MBA Desk Reference* is unique, both in the nature of the information that it contains and in the way its contents are organized to provide users with easy access to the data they seek.

Part One: A-to-Z Reference of Essential Business Topics

The first section of the *Desk Reference*, A-to-Z Reference of Essential Business Topics, is an alphabetical listing of hundreds of phrases, rules, principles, theories, laws, trends, formulas, and strategies related to the practice of business. These listings are drawn from eight major business disciplines: accounting, economics, finance, international business, management, manufacturing, marketing, and strategy. Entries include a wide-ranging collection of topics such as "double declining balance depreciation," "cost of capital," "total quality management," "just-in-time," and "conjoint analysis." The A-to-Z Reference goes beyond the simple definitions that might be found in a more conventional business reference. Each entry begins with a concise definition, then goes on to include a description, discussion, or practical example of the topic at hand.

There is a strong emphasis on the business impact of the topics included in the A-to-Z Reference section. It is not enough to simply understand the definition of concepts such as "last in, first out (LIFO)" or "return on investment (ROI)." You need to know how they affect a business, the decisions made by its managers and employees, and its bottom line. The A-to-Z Reference, with its clear examples and comprehensive discussions, explains all aspects of these important subjects.

To give you an idea of the range of material covered in Part I, here are a few additional examples:

- News reports frequently refer to "leading economic indicators." The entry for *leading, coincident, and lagging indexes* explains what these indicators are, describes the government agencies that issue them, and explains the components of each.

- You've heard of S corporations and their potential tax advantages. The *S Corporation* entry explains precisely what an S corporation is and how a small business can qualify for S status.

- Business is rife with not only buzzwords but buzz phrases. What exactly are *benchmarking, activity-based costing, countertrade,* and *debt-equity swaps*? Part I provides a convenient way to find out.

- There are innumerable tools of financial analysis to help manage a business more efficiently. In Part I, the most important ones are explained with detailed, worked-out examples.

For additional explanation and elaboration, each entry in Part I, where appropriate, includes cross references to other topics covered within this section.

Part Two: Sources of Business Information

Sometimes, it's easy enough to know the basics about a topic, such as *business plans, market research,* or *new product development.* But sometimes you need much more information—for example, when you have to actually write a business plan, conduct market research, or develop a new product. When you do, you'll want to consult Sources of Business Information, the second section of the *Desk Reference.*

The Sources of Business Information section is designed to give you the quickest and easiest route to the information you need—whether it's by telephone request to a government agency or professional association or by computer interface with an electronic database. It lists and describes (alphabetically by title) hundreds of books, databases, online services, periodicals, professional groups, government agencies, and research groups that offer current, detailed, and practical information on almost any business issue. Individual listings are organized under 48 broad headings, each focusing on a specific business topic such as economic data, accounting, the job market, and so on. Each listing offers a brief description of the source, name of author(s), publisher's name, and date/frequency of publication.

The uses to which you can put the Sources of Business Information section are many and varied:

- If you have to do a strategic marketing plan that analyzes the demographics for a new product line, look through the "Demographics, Marketing Data, and Market Research" section for a description of the sources that will provide you with the information you need.

- That same strategic plan also needs your assessment of how the long- and short-term economic picture affects your product line. Go to the "Economic Data, Trends, and Projections" section to find the best sources for that information.

- Perhaps you want to begin exporting your product line internationally. The "Export-Import" section shows where to get information on how to do this and also provides a breakdown of some of the many resources offered by the United States Department of Commerce.

- Finally, say you want to sell your product by direct mail. The "Direct Marketing" section show where to get the right prospect lists to make your campaign work.

A "Directory of Publishers, Vendors, and Databases" at the end of Part II provides addresses, phone numbers, and FAX numbers to enable users of the *Desk Reference* to locate and request information from the various sources easily.

Appendices

The Appendices present a compendium of useful business facts, figures, and lists. Some can help you pinpoint opportunities such as the list of *Inc.* magazine's 500 fastest growing private companies. And some will help you in your quest for more information. Say you want to export your new product line of personal computers to Poland. The Appendices include two lists to help you out. The list of "Industry Specialists of the International Trade Administration of the Department of Commerce" tells you who can provide you with specific information about exporting your product and how to reach them. Second, the list of "Country Desk Specialists" (also from the International Trade Administration) will provide you with information on just about every country of the world, from Afghanistan to Zimbabwe.

In short, you can consult *The Portable MBA Desk Reference* on nearly any subject and feel confident that either the information you need will be there, or the *Desk Reference* will tell you exactly where to go get it. We believe it will become one of your most frequently used business tools.

Part I
An A-to-Z Reference of Essential Business Topics

Part II
Sources of Business Information

Appendices

An A-to-Z Reference of Essential Business Topics

HOW TO USE
THE A-TO-Z REFERENCE

The A-to-Z Reference of Essential Business Topics provides a concise, comprehensive, and convenient source of business information. Entries are included on the basis of their practical application to business. Any phrase, rule, principle, theory, formula, law, or strategy likely to affect or influence a businessperson's professional life or be useful to him or her is listed and explained here.

The A-to-Z Reference covers eight major business disciplines: accounting, economics, finance, international business, management, manufacturing, marketing, and strategy. Entries are arranged alphabetically, and cross-referenced terms are printed in boldface italics. Cross references include the standard "see" and "see also" as well as "compare to," an innovative feature that allows consideration of similar topics in order to see how they might differ from, relate to, or interact with one another.

Entries in the A-to-Z Reference section were chosen with an eye toward considering their strategic impact on a business and its operations. In addition to providing a straightforward definition, many entries go on to discuss practical examples and possible uses for the topics covered. A number of entries were also chosen based on their value as "reminders" of useful ratios and formulas, such as "current ratio," "return on assets," and "inventory turnover."

Together, the entries in the A-to-Z Reference section combine to form a complete, accurate, and practical resource that can be used in any business situation.

The entries in Part I are arranged alphabetically; following is a list of the entries arranged by business topic.

Entries Arranged by Business Topic

Accounting and Finance

absorption costing
accelerated cost recovery system (ACRS)
accelerated depreciation
account
accountant
accounting change
accounting equation
accounting period
accounting rate of return (ARR)
accounts payable
accounts receivable
accounts receivable turnover
accrual accounting
accrued expense
accumulated benefit obligation
accumulated depreciation
acid test ratio
activity-based costing
additional paid-in capital
adverse opinion
affiliated company
allowance for bad debts
ALPHA
American Depository Receipts (ADRs)
American Stock Exchange (AMEX)
amortization
annual percentage rate (APR)
annual report
annuity
arbitrage
arithmetic return
arm's-length transaction
asset
asset-backed securities
asset turnover
asset value business valuation method
audit
audit option
Auditing Standards Board (ASB)

average cost method
backorder
balance sheet
The Bank for International Settlements (BIS)
banker's acceptance (BA)
Barron's confidence index
basis points
bearer bond
bellwether
best effort
beta
big six
blank check offerings
blind pool offerings
blue chip
bond
bond buyback
bond valuation
bond yield
book value
book value per share
bookkeeping
borrowing base
breakeven analysis
call feature
capital
capital asset
capital asset pricing model (CAPM)
capital flight
capital lease
capital market theory
capital markets
capital stock
capital structure
capitalization ratio
capitalize
carrying costs
cash basis accounting
cash dividend
cash equivalent
cash flow
cash-to-current liabilities ratio
central bank
change in accounting estimate
change in accounting principle

future value
future value of an annuity
generally accepted accounting
    principles (GAAP)
globalization
going private
going public
goodwill
gross profit
hard currency
held companies
income from continuing operations
income statement
incremental cost
indexing
indirect cost
intangible asset
interest rates
internal rate of return
inventory
inventory turnover
investment
journal entry
junk bonds
Keogh plan
last-in, first-out (LIFO)
leverage
leveraged buyout (LBO)
leveraging
LIFO liquidation
LIFO reserve
limited partnership
liquidity
London Interbank Offered Rate
    (LIBOR)
long bond
lower of cost or market
marginal cost
marginal revenue
market risk
market risk premium
matching principle
materiality
merger
minimum lease payments

minimum pension liability
money center banks
money markets
National Association of Securities
    Dealers Automated Quotation
    System (NASDAQ)
net income
net present value (NPV)
noncurrent asset
noncurrent liability
nonmarket risk
note payable
note receivable
off-balance sheet
offshore financial center
operating expenses
operating income
operating lease
option
paid-in capital in excess of par value
par value
penny stocks
percentage of completion method
performance bond
pink sheets
pooling of interests
preferred stock
prepaid expense
present value
present value of an annuity
price/earnings (P/E) ratio
prime rate
private placements and limited
    exempt offerings
privately held company
pro forma
profit margin
projected benefit obligation (PBO)
publicly held company
purchase method
qualified opinion
quality of earnings
quarterly report
rate of return
raw materials inventory

Economics

cartel
central bank
cost–benefit analysis
demand
discount rate
employment
exchange rates
externality
federal reserve
fiscal policy
foreign exchange
forward contract
gross domestic product (GDP)
hard currency
housing starts and residential
    construction
industrial policy
interest rates
International Monetary Fund
investment
labor force
Leading, Coincident, and Lagging
    Indexes (LCLg)
marginal cost
marginal cost–marginal revenue rule
monetarism
monetary aggregates
monetary policy
money center banks
opportunity cost
perfect competition
personal consumption expenditures
price controls
prime rate
production function
productivity
saving
shortage
shut-down situation
soft currency
spending multiplier
supply
surplus
trade deficit
unemployment rate
value-added tax (VAT)

International Business

balance of payments
balance of trade
The Bank for International
    Settlements (BIS)
Berne Convention (for the Protection
    of Literary and Artistic Works of
    1886)
capital flight
cartel
central bank
coproduction
countertrade
debt/equity swaps
development banks
dumping
Edge Act
Eurobond
Eurocurrency
Eurodollar
European Community (EC)
exchange rates
Eximbank's City-State Agency
    Cooperation Program
Export/Import Bank (Eximbank)
Foreign Credit Insurance Association
    (FCIA)
foreign currency translation
foreign direct investment
foreign exchange
foreign sales corporations
forward contract
General Agreement on Tariffs and
    Trade (GATT)
global marketing
globalization
industrial policy
industrial production
International Monetary Fund
keiretsu
letter of credit (L/C)
London Interbank Offered Rate
    (LIBOR)
North American Free Trade
    Agreement (NAFTA)

offshore financial center
Organization for Economic
  Cooperation and Development
  (OECD)
Organization of Petroleum Exporting
  Countries (OPEC)
parallel trade
regional banks
Section 936
tax haven
trade credit (international)
trade deficit
trade finance
venture capital

Management

action research
active listening
alternative work schedules
Americans with Disabilities Act
annual report
attribution theory
benchmarking
business process reengineering
Chapter 7
Chapter 11
coaching
cognitive dissonance
concurrent engineering
conjoint analysis
coproduction
copyright
corporate culture
cost-benefit analysis
cost center
cost leadership
cost-plus pricing
decentralization
decision making
decision support system
decision tree
defensiveness
defined benefit pension plan
defined contribution pension plan
Delphi analysis

diversification
economies of scale
economies of scope
employee discharge
employee stock ownership plan
  (ESOP)
empowerment
environment
environments matrix
ERG Theory
ethical frameworks
expectant theory
expert system
externality
401 (k) plan
functional organizational design
fundamental interpersonal relations
  orientation (FIRO)
group norms
groups
human resources management
incentive plans
incremental cost
indirect cost
informal organizational structure
intellectual property
interdependence
job depth
job enlargement
job enrichment
job range
job satisfaction
joint venture
Keogh plan
leadership
learning
learning curve
leveraged buyout (LBO)
limited partnership
management by objectives (MBO)
management control systems
management information systems
  (MIS)
Maslow's Hierarchy of Needs
matrix structure
merger

mission statement
Myers-Briggs Type Indicator (MBTI)
new product development
observational research
organizational environments
outsourcing
power
privately held company
profit center
publicly held company
quality circle
quality of work life (QWL)
regression analysis
research validity, external
research validity, internal
response time
reward systems
role conflict
S Corporation
scientific management
self-concept
self-managed work teams
sexual harassment
span of control
spin-offs
stock option
stock split
stockout
synergy
T-groups
team building
technology transfer
total quality management (TQM)
transformation process

Manufacturing

ABC classification system
acceptance sampling
age discrimination
aggregate plan
artificial intelligence
automated storage and retrieval
    system (AS/RS)
automatic guided vehicle system
    (AGVS)

automation
autonomation
backlog
backward scheduling
balance delay
bar code
benchmarking
bill of material (BOM)
blanket purchase order
bottleneck
breakeven analysis
buffer stock
business process reengineering
capacity
cellular production
chase demand
computer-aided design (CAD)
computer-aided engineering (CAE)
computer-aided manufacturing (CAM)
computer-integrated manufacturing
    (CIM)
concurrent engineering
control charts
critical path method (CPM)
critical ratio analysis
cycle
cycle counting
cycle time
design capacity
design for manufacturability
direct numerical control (DNC)
dispatching
economic order quantity
economies of scale
effective capacity
efficiency
engineering change order (ECO)
expediting
finite loading
flexible manufacturing system (FMS)
flow process system
forward scheduling
Gantt Chart
group technology
inputs
inventory forms

inventory functions
job process system
Johnson's Rule for Dual Workstations
just-in-time (JIT)
kanban
learning curve
level production
line balancing
loading
make-to-order
make-to-stock
manufacturing requirements
  planning (MRPII)
marginal cost
master production schedule
materials requirements planning
  (MRP)
methods time measurement
newsboy problem
numerical control (NC)
periodic inventory review system
process control
production plan
program evaluation and review
  technique (PERT)
quality circle
queue time
response time
rough cut capacity planning
runout method
sequencing
setup costs
shop floor control
single sourcing
slack
spoilage
time study
two-bin system
type I error
type II error

Marketing

A-B split
accordion fold

ad response
advertising
advertising agency
advertising frequency
afternoon drive time
alternate weeks (A/W)
area of dominant influence
  (ADI)
art director
automatic merchandising
available market
behavioral response
behavioral segmentation
body copy
brand
brand awareness
brand extension
brand mark
brand name
brand switching matrix
bundling
buyer power
buying decision process
buying roles
camera-ready
cannibalization
casual research
cherry picking
cold call
column inch
commission
commodity
comparison advertising
complementary products
conjoint analysis
consignment
consumer adoption process
consumer market
consumer motivation
copy
cost leadership
cost per thousand (CPM)
cost plus pricing
demand forecasting
demographic segmentation
derived demand

descriptive research
differentiated marketing
differentiation
diffusion of innovation curve
direct marketing
discretionary income
display advertisement
distribution channels
dumping
durable goods
emotional appeal
events marketing
experimental research
exploratory research
financial public relations
focus group interview
font
Four Ps
freelance
generic appeal
generic product
ghost shopper
global marketing
government market
horizontal marketing strategy
image advertising
independent demand
industrial market
insertion order
latent market
list broker
makegood
marginal revenue
market
market life-cycle
market segmentation
market share
marketing control systems
marketing mix
marketing myopia
marketing orientation
marketing plan
marketing research
mass marketing
media buyer
micro markets

modified rebuy
morning drive time
new product development
new task
nondurable good
observational research
omnibus panel
opinion leaders
organizational buying
original equipment manufacturer
penetrated market
perceived value pricing
percentage of sales
personal communications channels
point of purchase (POP) advertising
potential market
preference segments
price elasticity of demand
primary data
private label
product attributes
product, augmented
product concept
product life-cycle
product maturity
product mix
product positioning
psychographic segmentation
public relations (PR)
public service advertisement
"pull" strategy
purchasing high and low involvement
"push" strategy
reach
reference group
regression analysis
relationship marketing
repeat rate
research validity, external
research validity, internal
reseller market
response rate
response time
rollout market entry
sales promotions
sampling frame

secondary data
self-liquidator
served market
share of voice
skimming
stockout
storyboard
straight rebuy
target return pricing
telemarketing
television rating
television share
test market
trademark
undifferentiated marketing
utility
variable pricing
volume segmentation
word-of-mouth advertising

Strategy

backward integration
barriers to entry
barriers to exit
better-off test
cash cow
competitive advantage
competitor analysis
coproduction
core competence
corporate strategy

cost-of-entry test
cost-plus pricing
decentralization
Delphi analysis
diversification
environment
environments matrix
externality
first mover
five forces model
focus strategy
forward integration
fragmented industry
generic competitive strategies
growth/market share matrix
harvesting
horizontal integration
industry attractiveness test
joint venture
mission statement
organizational environments
profit impact of market stategies
   (PIMS)
seven-S framework
strategic business unit
strategic planning
supplier power
SWOT analysis
synergy
technology transfer
value chain
vertical integration

AAAA *See American Association of Advertising Agencies*

AAF *See American Advertising Federation*

A-B split In direct mail, a method of generating a random sample of research subjects by dividing a list of names into two equal groups on an every-other-name basis.

    This method allows researchers to avoid sampling errors that might occur if they used the names in the order in which they appeared.

EXAMPLE: A telemarketer selling portable computers wants to test two sales strategies to see which performs better. She has an alphabetical list of 500 companies and plans to call the head of purchasing at each. If she tries sales approach A on the first 250 names and sales approach B on the second half, her results may be flawed. Technology companies, for example, are more likely to have portables already, and many of these companies begin with the letter C (for "computer"). To eliminate this potential bias, she divides her list into two by every other name. Now, by comparing the sales generated by each approach, she can decide which strategy to use in the future.

ABC classification system A method of organizing and managing *inventory* according to cost and usage; also called ABC analysis or distribution by value.

    In most companies, a relatively small number of items account for a large portion of a company's inventory. Thus this fraction of line items gives rise to the largest segment of inventory carrying costs. By implementing an ABC classification system, managers can instead track and control the most expensive or frequently used inventory. The ABC classifications are:

    (A) High value items—the 15 to 20 percent of the items that make up approximately 75 percent of the total inventory value.

    (B) Medium value items—the 20 to 40 percent of the items that make up approximately 15 percent of the total inventory value.

    (C) Low value items—the 40 to 50 percent of the items that make up approximately 10 percent of the total inventory value.

Usually, the A inventory items are identified first, then the C items, and whatever is left is classified as the B items. ABC classification should be based on the total dollar investment in individual inventory items.

EXAMPLE: An expensive item, if used infrequently, might cause a small amount of the annual inventory cost and be classified as a C item, whereas an inexpensive item, if used regularly, might constitute a large portion of the inventory investment and be classified as an A item.

Once a company's inventory is classified as A, B, or C, the management of each class can be differentiated in order to increase control and decrease costs.

EXAMPLE: A items have the most detailed records, with a great deal of attention paid to order quantities and reorder points. B items might have less frequent updating of records, order quantities, and reorder points. C items might have very simple records, or no records at all, and might simply be routinely ordered at the beginning of each year. Essentially, the time saved by not actively managing the C items can be used in tightening control over the A items.

ABO *See accumulated benefit obligation*

absorption costing An accounting method required for all external reporting, including annual reports, Security and Exchange Commission (SEC) filings, and interim reports to shareholders.

Under this method, both *variable* manufacturing costs, such as utilities and raw material expenses, and *fixed* manufacturing costs, such as factory overhead and insurance, are added to the value of the inventory on hand—that is, these costs are now part of inventory and are considered assets until the inventory is sold.

All *nonmanufacturing* costs, such as selling and general administrative expenses, are treated as expenses, which means they are charged against sales revenue in the period in which the revenue is earned. Absorption costing is also called the full-cost method, because the full cost of producing a product or service is attributed to (that is, absorbed by) those products or services.

Absorption costing is frequently compared with *variable,* or *direct, costing,* in which only the variable costs of manufacturing a product are included in the costs of inventory, and fixed costs are considered periodic expenses. In other words, absorption costing treats both fixed and variable costs as assets; variable costing treats variable costs as assets and fixed costs as expenses.

Management sometimes uses the variable costing method for internal analysis. Depending on the volume of sales relative to production, absorption costing can yield a higher reported income, because it incorporates fixed costs into inventory, thereby removing them from the cost of goods sold.

EXAMPLE: Comparison of absorption and variable costing if sales volume is less than production volume.

	Absorption costing	Variable costing
	(unit cost = $60: $40 variable, $20 fixed)	(unit cost = $40: $40 variable)
Sales (80 units @ $100)	$8,000	$8,000
Cost of goods sold:		
Beginning inventory	$ 0	$ 0
Cost of goods produced		
(100 units)	6,000	4,000
Available for sale	6,000	4,000
Less: Ending inventory		
(20 units)	1,200	800
Cost of goods sold	4,800	3,200
Gross margin	3,200	4,800
Less: Period costs:		
Production overhead		2,000 (100 units × $20 fixed cost)
Selling and administrative	2,800	2,800
Total period costs	2,800	4,800
Income before taxes	$ 400	$ 0

Three relationships always hold between absorption costing and variable costing:

(1) If sales volume is equal to production volume, both systems report the same income.

(2) If sales volume is greater than production volume, resulting in a decrease in the amount of inventory on hand at the end of a period, absorption costing reports a lower income than variable costing.

(3) If sales volume is less than production volume, resulting in an increase in the amount of inventory on hand at the end of a period, absorption costing reports a higher income than variable costing.

See also *fixed cost, variable cost.*

accelerated cost recovery system (ACRS) In corporate finance, a method of calculating *depreciation* for tax purposes.

Congress created ACRS in 1981; it was later modified by the Tax Reform Act of 1986. ACRS encourages investment by allowing companies to take greater depreciation deductions in the early years of an *asset*'s life and thus realize greater tax savings. Under ACRS:

(1) Depreciation deductions are not based on the individual useful life of a particular asset. Rather, assets are grouped into eight different property classes, determined by their useful economic lives, or asset depreciation range (ADR) midpoint lives. If a new piece of equipment has a useful life of 4 years, for example, it falls into the 3-year ACRS property class.

(2) *Salvage value* is not incorporated into the calculation of depreciation deductions.

(3) If a company uses **straight-line depreciation,** it can follow the *half-year convention*—that is, it can deduct half the normal straight-line depreciation in the first year. This rule allows companies to stretch out, rather than accelerate, depreciation and thereby report more income on their *income statements.*

EXAMPLE: A company buys a new piece of equipment that falls under the 3-year property class and costs $6,000. If it uses the half-year convention, the company can deduct only $1,000 in the first and fourth year of the asset's life ($6,000/3 years = $2,000; $2,000/2 = $1,000). The following table shows the deductions available both under the half-year convention and under standard ACRS procedure.

Year	Straight-line (half-year) depreciation	Cost	×	ACRS %	=	ACRS deduction
1	$1,000	$6,000	×	33.3%	=	$1,998
2	2,000	6,000	×	44.5%	=	2,670
3	2,000	6,000	×	14.8%	=	888
4	1,000	6,000	×	7.4%	=	444
	$6,000			100%		$6,000

With the exception of the half-year convention, ACRS 3-, 5-, 7-, and 10-year property classes are subject to **double declining balance depreciation.** The 15- and 20-year classes use a variation on the double declining balance method called the 150 percent declining balance method. The remaining two property classes (depreciable over 27.5 and 31.5 years) use straight-line depreciation. *See also accelerated depreciation, double declining balance depreciation, straight-line depreciation.*

accelerated depreciation An accounting method that recognizes higher amounts of *depreciation* in the early years of a *fixed asset*'s life and lower amounts in later years.

Some office equipment—a computer, say—is more efficient and productive in the years immediately following its purchase. As it gets older, maintenance costs and inefficiency increase, or the computer becomes obsolete. Since the benefits an asset provides decline over time, the *matching concept* dictates that depreciation should be higher in the early years of an asset's life and decline over time as well. Because accelerated depreciation gives businesses the tax benefit of writing off larger depreciation charges in the early years of an asset's life, it is frequently used in tax reporting to the Internal Revenue Service. When it comes to financial reporting, however, companies can choose the depreciation method that suits them best. *See also **depreciation, amortization**. Compare to **double declining balance depreciation, straight-line depreciation, sum-of-the-years'-digits method**.*

acceptable quality level (AQL)   The actual percentage, specified by management, of goods in a lot of incoming materials that a company will allow to be defective and still accept the lot as "good."

In a defect detection environment, a percentage of incoming material may be defective and the incoming lot may be accepted as "good." Management may allow an AQL of one-half of 1 percent. This means in a lot of 1000 units as many as 5 may be defective and the lot is still accepted. This method is normally used in cases where the lot size is very large and 100 percent inspection is impossible or very costly. Setting an AQL allows incoming inspection to be conducted by random sampling. A sample size is computed along with an acceptance number. The incoming lot is inspected by taking a sample of n units. If the number of defects found exceeds the calculated acceptance number, c, the *entire lot* is rejected. This is a tradeoff situation, accepting a small percentage defective to allow sampling as opposed to 100 percent inspection. *See also **type I error**.*

acceptance sampling   A statistical tool that uses a cumulative binomial probability distribution in setting up sampling parameters; sometimes called single sampling.

Often incoming lots are so large that complete inspection is impractical. Acceptance sampling allows the individual to statistically determine a sample size, n, and an acceptance number, c. Since sampling involves risk of making the wrong decision on the basis of sample results, acceptance sampling allows us to limit the probability of making the typical sampling errors, which are rejecting a "good" lot or accepting a "bad" lot on the basis of sample information. A sample of n units is inspected. If more than c defects are found, the entire lot is rejected. Acceptance sampling allows companies to sample extremely large lots with very small samples and make the correct decision within reasonable probabilities.

EXAMPLE: A company purchasing light bulbs cannot afford the time to test an incoming lot of 1,000. Therefore, it sets an *acceptable quality level* of one percent. It specifies a five percent α (alpha) risk—or *type I error* (a 95 percent probability of *accepting* a good lot). By using a cumulative binomial distribution, it determines a sample size of 50 and an acceptance number of 2. The relevant attribute is simply whether the bulbs work or not. If a sample of 50 is drawn and three bulbs are found defective, the lot is rejected.

accordion fold A back-and-forth type of fold in which a piece of paper has at least two parallel folds that allow it to open like an accordion; the entire sheet of paper can then be unfolded with a single pull.

Accordion folds are frequently used in brochures and direct-mail advertising. Because they require no binding or staples, they're usually less expensive to print and mail. The decision to use an accordion fold for a project depends on both the advertiser's budget and the appropriateness of the copy for the format.

account A systematic grouping that illustrates the effect of transactions and other events on particular *balance sheet* or *income statement* items.

Accounts, which are usually expressed in terms of money, are maintained in a ledger and allow a company to collect and organize each of the different factors that affect its business. Companies maintain a separate account for each asset, liability, revenue, expense, and stockholders' equity item. *See also chart of accounts.*

account executive (AE) Person in an advertising agency who serves as the liaison between the agency and one or more of its clients.

An agency, depending on its size, may have several AEs. The account executive analyzes problems and develops a marketing strategy with the client; coordinates research, copy, and media activities; and supervises the production of all advertising. In large agencies, the account executive reports to the account supervisor, who in turn reports to the vice-president of account services. In smaller agencies, the AE reports directly to, or can even serve as, the vice-president of account services.

accountant A person who performs accounting services.

The duties of an accountant range from preparing tax returns and financial statements to auditing financial records and developing financial plans. Accountants frequently specialize in a particular area, such as cost accounting, taxes, or auditing. An accountant is distinguished from a bookkeeper by the degree of professional skills he or she brings to a job. Bookkeepers usually *record* transactions into various accounts and ledgers, whereas accountants *analyze* these accounts in order to determine their financial impact on a company.

accounting change A change in any of three areas: (1) accounting principles, such as a new method of *depreciation*; (2) accounting estimates, such as the useful life of an *asset*; or (3) a different reporting entity, such as a merger or takeover.

Usually, a company must show the effects of these changes in its financial statements, so readers can make credit and investment decisions based on comparable, up-to-date information. Several factors can prompt accounting changes. *Financial Accounting Standards Board (FASB)* pronouncements or new IRS regulations frequently mandate changes in accounting principles. Companies often justify changes in accounting estimates by pointing to altered circumstances—more wear and tear of factory equipment than the company initially anticipated, for instance. A need to combine and reconcile two different accounting systems, as in a merger or acquisition, motivates a business to adopt a new reporting entity.

accounting equation The formula that expresses the dual nature of accounting: *Assets = Liabilities + Owners' Equity.*

The accounting equation is based on the idea that every business transaction has a dual effect on the company's *accounts.* When a company makes a sale for $100, for example, it receives $100 in cash and gives up $100 of its product or service.

EXAMPLE: Jimmy Jones is starting a new business and opens a bank account with $50,000 of his own money. The business now has an asset, $50,000 cash (the first aspect of this transaction). Jones also has a claim of $50,000 against this asset (the second aspect). In other words,

$$\text{Assets (cash)} = \text{Owners' equity}$$

$$\$50,000 \quad = \quad \$50,000$$

If the company then borrows $25,000 from the bank, its accounting records will change in two ways: (1) Cash will increase by $25,000 and (2) the business will have incurred a liability of $25,000:

Assets		Liabilities and owners' equity	
Cash	$75,000	Loan	$25,000
Total assets	$75,000	Owners' equity	$50,000
		Total liabilities and owners' equity	$75,000

See also *bookkeeping.*

accounting period The length of time covered by a business's financial statements.

Accounting periods can be any length of time but are usually annual, quarterly, or monthly. Companies with annual accounting periods can choose to be on either a calendar year or a fiscal year. The annual fiscal accounting period for the Campbell Soup Company, for example, begins in August. Selecting an accounting period can be an important managerial decision, particularly in highly seasonal industries such as toy retailing, where most sales occur at Christmas and huge returns come in January. Setting the beginning of the accounting period on January 1, then, could distort the picture of the toy retailer's revenue.

accounting rate of return (ARR) In corporate finance, a method of measuring the potential profitability of an investment.

ARR is calculated by dividing net income by the amount (or average amount) of the investment.

$$\frac{\text{Net income}}{\text{Investment}} = \text{ARR}$$

When ARR is used as a decision-making tool, the investment with the higher rate of return should be selected.

EXAMPLE: A company is considering the following investment in new plant equipment that will increase capacity and provide an annual cash flow of $2,000.

Initial investment	$13,000
Estimated life	25 years
Cash inflows per year	$2,000
Annual depreciation (straight-line method)	$520

The accounting rate of return for this investment is

$$\frac{\$2,000 - \$520}{\$13,000} = .1138, \text{ or } 11.38\%$$

If the average investment (usually assumed as one-half of the initial investment) is used, the accounting rate of return is

$$\frac{\$2,000 - \$520}{\$6,500} = .2277, \text{ or } 22.77\%$$

ARR has these advantages. It's simple to calculate, easy to understand, and gives some sense of the expected profitability of an investment. Financial managers and project analysts frequently use it to compare the potential profitability of different investment opportunities.

Disadvantages of ARR include a failure to recognize the time value of money and its use of accounting data rather than cash-flow information. *Compare to* **internal rate of return.**

accounts payable An obligation to pay for goods or services that have been purchased on credit from suppliers.

Accounts payable is a **current liability** on the **balance sheet.**

accounts receivable The amount owed to a company from customers who purchased goods or services on credit.

Accounts receivable is a **current asset** on the **balance sheet.**

accounts receivable turnover A ratio that shows how long a company holds its **receivables** before collecting them.

The lower the turnover rate, the longer a company holds its receivables—which in most cases means that they are less likely to be collected. Accounts receivable turnover is calculated by dividing sales by average **accounts receivable.**

$$\frac{\text{Sales}}{\text{Average accounts receivable}}$$

EXAMPLE: A company racks up sales of $200,000, its beginning-of-year accounts receivable total $50,000, and its end-of-year accounts receivable come to $30,000. Therefore, its average accounts receivable equal $40,000. (Average accounts receivable is calculated by adding accounts receivable at the beginning of the year to accounts receivable at the end of the year and dividing by 2.)

$$\frac{\$50,000 + \$30,000}{2} = \$40,000$$

The company's accounts receivable turnover comes to

$$\frac{\$200,000}{\$40,000} = 5 \text{ times}$$

This ratio means that the company collected five times its average amount of accounts receivable in the past year; put another way, the company requires an average of 2.4 months (12 months divided by 5) to collect an account receivable.

accrual accounting An accounting method that recognizes revenue when it is earned, without regard to when cash is collected, and recognizes expenses when they are incurred, regardless of when cash is paid to meet an obligation.

If a company makes a sale on credit, it recognizes revenue, even though it has not yet received cash for its product or service. By the same token, any salaries that remain unpaid at the end of an *accounting period* are recognized as expenses. Under the accrual method, companies measure income for an accounting period as the difference between the revenues and expenses recognized in that period. Accrual accounting is the only method permitted for corporations under *generally accepted accounting principles (GAAP)*.

accrued expense Those expenses incurred, but not yet paid, at the end of an *accounting period*; also called accrued *liabilities*.

EXAMPLE: A company purchases $5,000 worth of office supplies on credit on December 29 and its accounting period ends on December 31. It shows the $5,000 as an accrued expense on the *balance sheet* for the year.

accumulated benefit obligation (ABO) The *present value* of the amount a company would owe to its pension plan if its eligible employees retired today.

See also projected benefit obligation, minimum pension liability.

accumulated depreciation In accounting, the total *depreciation* to date on a particular *asset.*

EXAMPLE: A company purchased a delivery truck for $12,000 in January 1990. The truck had an expected life of 10 years and an expected *salvage value* of $2,000. Under *straight-line depreciation* (*see also double declining balance depreciation, sum-of-the-years'-digits method*) the annual depreciation charge would come to $1,000 ($12,000 less $2,000 salvage value = $10,000 divided by 10 years of expected life, or $1,000). In January 1993, the accumulated depreciation on the truck would total $3,000 ($1,000 for 1990, 1991, and 1992).

ACI *See Advertising Council Inc.*

acid test ratio A test of a company's ability to pay its liabilities; also called quick ratio.

The ratio is calculated by dividing the current assets that are most easily converted into cash (cash, *marketable securities,* and *accounts receivable*) by *current liabilities.*

$$\frac{\text{Cash} + \text{Marketable securities} + \text{Accounts receivable}}{\text{Current liabilities}}$$

The acid test ratio is identical to the *current ratio*, with this exception: Some *current assets*—namely, inventory and prepaid expenses—are not included in the numerator. Inventory is omitted, because a company might not be able to convert it quickly or easily to cash. Prepaid expenses are excluded for the same reason. Since these expenses can't be converted into cash, they can't be used to help pay current liabilities.

As a rule, the acid test ratio should equal at least 1. That means for every dollar in current liabilities, the company has $1 in quick assets.

EXAMPLE: A company has $5,000 in marketable securities, $4,000 in accounts receivable, $1,500 in cash, and $9,000 in current liabilities. Its acid test ratio is

$$\frac{\text{Quick assets}}{\text{Current liabilities}} = \frac{\$10,500}{\$\ 9,000} = 1.17$$

That means the company has $1.17 of quick assets for every dollar in current liabilities.

Companies can compare their acid test ratio for any one year with the ratios of previous years and with competitors' in order to highlight any trends.

acquisition   *See business combination*

ACRS   *See accelerated cost recovery system*

action research   A process for instigating and managing change through the systematic collection of data and the selection of an appropriate course of action based on that data.

There are five steps to action research: diagnosis, analysis, feedback, action, and evaluation.

The diagnosis stage of action research is roughly analogous to a physician's initial examination. The change agent—usually an outside consultant—reviews records, interviews employees, questions managers, and so on in order to "get a feel" for the organization. This process gives the change agent some rough idea about the company's general problems and their possible solutions.

The data gathered during the diagnostic phase is then analyzed. Analysis should show exactly which problems people feel are important, and what patterns those problems follow within the company. In the end, analysis should show primary concerns, problem areas, and possible actions.

Action research necessarily involves the participation and feedback of the affected parties, so it is important to share the information found in steps one and two. This allows employees to understand the problems within the company and help develop plans for making any needed changes.

Once all the affected parties have had a chance to offer their feedback, specific actions are taken to correct the problems.

Once the change has been undertaken, it is important to implement a program of evaluation by which the effectiveness of the action plan can be compared with the initial data gathered during diagnosis.

Action research has two important advantages over more traditional (that is, authoritarian) change actions. First, because action research relies so heavily on employee input and feedback, it effectively reduces resistance to change. Frequently, employee involvement can even increase the speed of change. Second, action research is problem focused. This may make sense intuitively, but in many cases, change actions are solution centered; in other words, the change agent has some solution in mind—for instance, *alternative work schedules* or job sharing—that he or she attempts to fit to a problem.

active listening Listening with (1) intensity, (2) acceptance, (3) empathy, and (4) a willingness to assume responsibility for understanding the speaker's complete message.

The human brain is able to comprehend a speaking rate of about four times that of the average speaker. This can lead to a certain amount of daydreaming on the part of the listener. An active listener dismisses these daydreams and focuses intensely on what the speaker is saying. The "spare brain time" can be used to summarize and integrate what the speaker has said.

Demonstrating acceptance requires that the active listener consider the speaker's message objectively and not make any judgments about its content until the speaker is finished. This is no simple trick. It is very easy to be distracted by a speaker's message, especially when it creates some controversy or disagreement. When this happens, it is only natural to begin considering mental arguments to counter what is being said. Of course, while these arguments are being formulated, it is very easy to miss the rest of the speaker's message.

Empathy requires an understanding of what the speaker is trying to communicate—not what the listener wants to understand. The listener must suspend his or her thoughts and feelings and try to step into the speaker's world. This makes it more likely that the speaker's message will be interpreted as it was intended.

The final component of active listening is assuming responsibility for completeness. In other words, the listener must follow up and be sure to get the full meaning of the speaker's message. There are two techniques that help to ensure completeness: asking questions and listening for feelings as well as content.

activity-based costing An accounting method that assigns identifiable costs and allocates common costs to specific product lines or business segments; also known as product-line costing.

By using this method, a company can determine the profitability or profit contribution that each activity, segment, and product line brings to the company as a whole.

EXAMPLE: In 1991, the *income statement* for ABC Corp. was as follows:

Sales		$1,000
Cost of sales		600
Gross profit		$ 400
Selling expenses	$100	
Administrative expenses	200	
Total operating expenses	300	
Net profit	$100	

In the next year, when the company introduced a new product, its income statement was as follows:

Sales		$1,200
Cost of sales		800
Gross profit		400
Selling expenses	$200	
Administrative expenses	300	
Total operating expense	500	
Net profit (loss)	(100)	

If the company now assigns the activity costs of developing and bringing the new product to market, the income statement reads as follows:

	Old products	New products	Total
Sales	$1,000	$200	$1,200
Cost of sales	600	200	800
Gross profit	400	0	400
Selling expenses	100	100	200
Administrative expenses	200	100	300
Total operating expense	300	200	500
(loss)	100	(200)	(100)

The statement shows that the *activity* of bringing the new product to market adversely affected the company by $200 in the first year.

AD *See art director*

ad response A measurement of consumer reaction to an advertisement.

Marketers can measure response by testing the consumers' recall, recognition, or awareness of an ad or by actual purchase behavior. One simple way of measuring response is to count the number of coupons clipped from a newspaper advertisement and returned to a particular store. In more complex programs, marketers issue identification cards to grocery store customers who agree to have their exposure to television and newspaper *advertising* monitored. The customers show their cards each time they make a purchase, and the store tracks their buying patterns through electronic scanning technology. By analyzing buying patterns after customers are exposed to their ads, advertisers can determine whether the advertising did, in fact, influence people to buy their products.

additional paid-in capital In accounting, the excess amount over *par value* that shareholders pay for a company's stock; usually treated as a donation.

The amount a company pays to buy back its *treasury stock* is treated as a reduction to additional paid-in capital. Additional paid-in capital is shown in the *stockholders' equity* section of the *balance sheet.*

EXAMPLE: A company issues 10,000 shares of stock with a par value of $5 at a price of $7 per share. The additional paid-in capital then comes to $20,000 (10,000 shares × $2). At the end of the company's *accounting period,* the stockholders' equity section of the balance sheet would show an increase of $20,000 in additional paid-in capital.

ADI *See area of dominant influence*

adverse opinion An auditor's unfavorable report on a company's financial statements when the company does not accurately represent its financial position, results of operation, or changes in financial position or does not conform to *generally accepted accounting principles (GAAP).*

An adverse opinion is rare, and the auditor must justify his or her conclusions in an audit report. *See also audit, audit opinion. Compare to qualified opinion, unqualified opinion.*

advertising Any printed or broadcast message sent and paid for by an identified organization to a *target market* via mass media, including television, radio, newspapers, magazines, direct mail, billboards, and transit cards.

In the print media, such as newspapers and magazines, the message is called an advertisement. When the message is broadcast on radio or television, it is called a commercial, or spot. Advertising is designed to inform, persuade, and remind. It can be an effective *marketing* tool and is frequently used in conjunction with *public relations, sales promotions,* and personal selling strategies in a ***marketing mix.*** Advertising can take any number of forms, from a 30-minute television "infommercial" to a sign on the side of a bus to a flyer tucked under the windshield wiper of a parked car.

Advertising Age A weekly advertising trade publication that covers the ***marketing*** industry and the business issues that affect it, including government actions that have an impact on the media, advertisers, and advertising agencies.

The magazine, which has a circulation of nearly 90,000, enjoys a wide readership in the advertising and marketing industry and is sold at newsstands and through subscriptions. *See also* ***Adweek.***

advertising agency A company that specializes in the service of producing advertising campaigns and strategies to help clients target and promote their products.

There are three types of advertising agencies: full-service, specialty service, and in-house.

Full-service advertising agencies offer their clients creative services, ***public relations, marketing research,*** promotion advice, media buying, and publicity. Most full-service agencies charge a 15 percent commission on all media purchases they make for a client. For large accounts, this commission is the only compensation the agency receives, unless it also provides ***public relations*** and publicity. For these services, the client usually pays on a dollar fee basis, since no media charges are involved.

Specialty service agencies offer only one or two of the services that full-service agencies provide. Many agencies supply only research, copy, or media. Frequently, specialty service agencies, sometimes referred to as boutique agencies, operate within a single industry, such as fashion or health care. Some agencies also function as wholesale media buyers and offer a more efficient, less expensive method of buying television or radio time.

An in-house agency is an advertising agency that is actually part of a client company; the marketing company thus has its own advertising agency. In-house agencies can perform any number of advertising services, although the company may still use outside agencies for certain projects.

Advertising Council Inc. (ACI) A volunteer organization made up of distinguished figures in advertising and the media.

ACI is dedicated to producing and distributing national public-service advertising campaigns (*see* ***public-service advertisement***). Established as the War Advertising Council during World War II, the organization adopted a strictly nonpolitical stance and worked to encourage public support for war bonds, blood donations, and the enlisting of women into the armed forces. The ACI is funded entirely from the donations of businesses, advertising firms, and the media. Since its founding, the total value of time and space donated to the ACI exceeds $10 billion. Slogans from past campaigns include "Drinking and driving can kill a friendship" for the U.S. Department of Transportation and "A mind is a terrible thing to waste" for the United Negro College Fund. *See also **American Advertising Federation, American Association of Advertising Agencies, American Marketing Association.***

advertising frequency The number of times an average prospect is exposed to an advertisement within a specified time period.

EXAMPLE: *Business Week* magazine has 775,200 readers. If, during the month of May, an ad reaches 100,000 of them once, 300,000 of them twice, 200,000 three times, and the remaining 175,200 four times, its frequency is

$$\frac{(100{,}000 \times 1) \times (300{,}000 \times 2) + (200{,}000 \times 3) + (175{,}200 \times 4)}{775{,}200}$$

or 2.6.

Ads in magazines can have a high frequency, as in our example, through repeated readings as well as through pass-ons. The repetition of a commercial on television or radio also provides greater frequency, or intensity of exposure. High-frequency advertising is an effective strategy when customers need to be continually reminded of a product—for example, when competition is strong; when the advertisement has a complicated sales message; when the product is in a frequently purchased category, such as soap; when brand loyalty is weak; or when consumers are hesitant to adopt the *brand* or category.

Adweek A weekly trade magazine that focuses on *advertising agencies* and the campaigns they produce.

The magazine, which has seven regional editions, has a circulation of about 75,000 and is available on newsstands or through subscription. *See also **Advertising Age.***

AE *See account executive*

affiliated company In accounting, a company that owns less than a majority of the *common stock* of another company.

Two companies that are both *subsidiaries* of the same third company are also considered affiliates. Taco Bell restaurants and Frito-Lay are affiliated, for example, since they are both owned by Pepsico. Frequently, affiliated companies will share the same management.

afternoon drive time In radio advertising, the time segment between 3:00 P.M. and 7:00 P.M.

Afternoon drive time is an important period for radio advertisers, because it allows them to reach one of the largest audiences of the day: commuters on their way home from work. For radio broadcasters, afternoon drive time and morning drive time (6:00 A.M. to 10:00 A.M.) are considered prime time, since together they account for the largest listening audience. *See also morning drive time.*

age discrimination
Any negative actions in hiring, training, promotions, health benefits, discipline, compensation, or termination taken against an individual on the basis of age.

In most cases, age discrimination is directed at older people, age 55 and up. In 1967, age discrimination was prohibited by the Age Discrimination in Employment Act (ADEA). Originally, the act was enforced by the Department of Labor and protected job applicants and employees between 40 and 60 years old. By 1979, protection had been extended to the age of 70, and the authority to enforce the act was given to the Equal Employment Opportunity Commission (EEOC). The following year, the number of age discrimination cases tripled.

The ADEA applies to private employers with 20 or more employees, employment agencies, labor unions with 25 or more members, and governmental agencies. In 1986, the Omnibus Budget Reconciliation Act included an amendment to the ADEA that removed the upper age limit of 70 years; many feel that this action was strictly ceremonial, because recent trends and studies have shown that employees are retiring earlier than in past years.

In 1987, the EEOC released a policy position on age harassment, based on the logic that age harassment is related to age discrimination in the same way that sexual harassment is related to sex discrimination. Prohibited actions include (1) remarks that link a person's performance, health, attendance record, and similar job-related issues to his or her age; (2) jokes about a person's age; (3) derogatory terms, such as old man, codger, and gramps; and (4) any derogatory remarks about a person's age.

There are two legal theories that can be used to argue a case of age discrimination. The first is *disparate treatment,* in which the employer's actions were intentional and result in differential working conditions for older employees. The second is *disparate impact,* in which the employer's actions, intentional or not, result in differential working conditions for older employees.

Most age discrimination cases are based on disparate treatment. Proving age discrimination with this theory requires that employer intent be established by either direct or indirect evidence. Direct evidence is actual, documented employer actions and policies, such as a mandatory retirement age, or the refusal to hire employees past a certain age. Indirect evidence regarding an employer's motivation in an age discrimination case is usually inferred from statistical data that shows consistent evidence of less favorable treatment of older employees, such as hiring, advancement, and salary increases. Indirect evidence can also be inferred from comments, such as

"We didn't think an old guy like you would mind," implying that age was a factor in employer treatment of older employees.

In cases of age discrimination, five basic defenses can be used.

(1) *Bona fide occupational qualification (BFOQ):* The unique requirements of a job necessitate the establishment of age criteria. In 1985, this defense was used successfully in a New Jersey case in which police officers faced a mandatory retirement age of 55. The employer showed that physical endurance (a requirement of the job) decreased after age 55. As a result, the court found no evidence of age discrimination. The definition of the exact job requirements facing older employees is frequently very narrow, and the courts are often reluctant to accept BFOQ defenses.

(2) *Bona fide seniority system:* The differential treatment of older employees is justified on the basis of an established seniority system rather than age. For example, if an employer has a promotions policy based on the length of time that an employee has worked at a company, it can be used as a defense against an employee who claims to have been passed over because of an age-related issue. Essentially, the employer argues that the older employee was treated according to the seniority system, as would any other employee, regardless of age.

(3) *Good cause:* The differential treatment of an older employee is based on individual factors and violations of company policies rather than age discrimination. Cases involving the good cause defense usually involve demotion, disciplinary actions, and discharge. Examples of good cause include falsification, theft, chronic absenteeism, poor judgment, and so on. Employers must provide evidence of the particular issues at hand, such as performance appraisals, discipline reports, and counseling sessions.

(4) *Factor other than age (FOA):* The differential treatment of an employee is based on individual circumstances other than age. When using this defense, employers must clearly justify the action taken against an employee. Justifications can include violation of company policy, poor performance, layoffs, and so on. Once the employer has established FOA justification, the employee must show that the FOA is really a rationalization for age discrimination.

(5) *Business necessity:* Conditions are present in particular businesses that necessitate the implementation of policies that discriminate against older employees. For example, a clothing store that caters to a youthful customer might argue that it is necessary to hire only younger sales personnel. The strength of this defense lies in the employer's ability to prove that employing other than older workers is key to the survival of a business.

aggregate plan A preliminary schedule of a company's operations designed to satisfy long-term demand at minimum cost.

Aggregate plans are developed by comparing a company's production capabilities with projected sales. From this comparison, managers can develop a business strategy that includes a production plan, purchasing plan, budgets, and work-force changes. This level of planning allows managers to minimize the short-sighted effects of daily scheduling where, for example, small shipments of materials may be ordered and workers laid off during one month only to have to order more material and hire extra workers the next month. By using an aggregate plan to forecast resource use in the long term, short-term changes in requirements can be minimized with a considerable cost savings.

The key to minimizing short-term variations is to work with grouped, or aggregate, units (such as total number of machine hours, materials, and finished goods or services) without distinguishing between the minor differences between them. For example, a toy manufacturer that makes dolls, games, and puzzles should create an aggregate plan based on the total number of "units" produced, projected sales of those units, and the materials that they require.

Generally, an aggregate plan serves as a rough guideline for managing production. There will always be small deviations, but as a whole, the plan should give a clear strategy for meeting day-to-day changes in demand. There are two broad types of aggregate plans: *level production* and *chase demand.* Although neither is widely used on its own, they both give some insight into the options available.

A level production aggregate plan sets production at a constant level over the planning period in order to stabilize the work force. Inventories act as shock absorbers and fluctuate as demand varies. This increases inventory costs but offers steady employment with few overtime expenses. In a service company, where there is usually no way to stockpile inventories, a level production plan requires a constant, but poorly utilized, work force in order to meet peak demand.

A chase demand aggregate plan calls for quick response changes in the level of output in order to match demand as closely as possible. This minimizes inventories but may involve changes in the work force. In a service company, a chase demand aggregate plan requires the use of overtime, split shifts, temporary workers, and part-time workers. *See also chase demand, level production.*

AGVS *See automatic guided vehicle system*

AI *See artificial intelligence*

AICPA *See American Institute of Certified Public Accountants*

allowance for bad debts A provision a company makes for uncollectible *accounts receivable*.

On a *balance sheet*, net receivables—the amount that a company realistically expects to collect—is calculated by reducing accounts receivable by the allowance for bad debt. If accounts receivable are $150,000 and the allowance for bad debt equals $10,000, the *current asset* section of the balance sheet would read as follows:

Accounts receivable	$150,000
Less: allowance for bad debts	10,000
Net receivables	$140,000

In reviewing a company's financial statements, it is important to note both the amount of the allowance for bad debts in relation to accounts receivable and whether it has changed in recent years. In the example we just gave, the allowance for bad debt comes to about 6 percent of total accounts receivable ($10,000 divided by $150,000). At first glance, this ratio seems reasonable. But say the company had traditionally set aside 12 percent of its total accounts receivable as an allowance for bad debt. In that case, one could argue that management is attempting to artificially inflate the company's net receivables.

alpha A mathematical expression of the nonmarket or internal risk (such as the rate of growth of earnings per share) used for valuing a security.

Alpha (α) is in contrast to another mathematical expression, beta (β), which measures the risk inherent in total market volatility as expressed by market indexes and averages. When beta and the expected market return are kept at zero, alpha can be used to measure a projected rise in a given stock's price. For instance, alpha of 1.15 means the stock price should rise 15 percent. It is calculated by multiplying a stock's beta by the difference between the market return of an index or average and a risk-free return, as with a U.S. Treasury security.

When applied to mutual funds, alpha measures the relationship between the fund's performance and its beta over a three-year period.

The London Stock Exchange uses the term "alpha" to describe stocks that in the United States are considered *blue-chip* stocks. Alpha stocks represent about 80 percent of the trading value on the London exchange and are under more stringent trading regulations than either beta or gamma stocks.

alternate weeks (A/W) A media strategy in which a radio station, television station, or newspaper runs a commercial or print advertisement for one week, skips a week, then runs it again for a week; also called flighting.

The A/W strategy allows advertisers to pay for only two weeks of exposure, even though their advertisement runs over a three-week period.

alternative work schedules   A method of increasing worker flexibility by offering one of a number of different job scheduling options.

Three of the most popular options are flextime, a compressed workweek, and job sharing.

Flextime allows employees some discretion over when they come and go from the workplace. Employees must work a set number of hours each week, but they are allowed to vary those hours, within certain limits. In a flextime system, the work day consists of a core time, six hours in most cases, surrounded on either side by a flexibility band.

EXAMPLE: In company XYZ, the core time might be 9:00 A.M. to 3:00 P.M.—not including a one-hour lunch break—although office hours are actually 6:00 A.M. to 6:00 P.M. Each employee must be present during the six-hour core time but is free to schedule the other two hours either at the beginning or the end of the day.

Flexible hours	Core time	Lunch	Core time	Flexible hours
6 A.M.	9 A.M.	12 noon 1 P.M.	3 P.M.	6 P.M.

For example, Jane Doe might be a "morning person." She gets up at 5:00 A.M. and is ready to go to bed right after the 7:00 news. A person like Jane might benefit from a policy of flextime, which would allow her to come to the office early, say 6:30 A.M., work a full eight hours, and leave work at 3:30 P.M.

The advantages of flextime are that it reduces absenteeism, increases *productivity*, reduces overtime, and increases employee autonomy and responsibility—factors that can increase employee *job satisfaction.* Flextime's major disadvantage is that it cannot be applied to every job. For example, it does not work for salespeople, receptionists, or other jobs where employees must be available at predetermined times.

The compressed workweek gives employees a 40-hour week by allowing them to work four 10-hour days rather than the traditional five-day, 8-hours-a-day program. This gives employees more leisure time and allows them to commute to and from work at non-rush-hour times. Proponents of the 4-40 program argue that it can increase employee morale, reduce absenteeism, increase productivity, and aid in the recruitment of new employees. In one study, employees were given a compressed workweek for six months. At the end of the study, although some employees complained of fatigue at the end of the day, 78 percent wanted to keep the new schedule.

Job sharing is a relatively recent work-scheduling development. It allows two or more employees to split a full-time job. For example, one person might work from 8:00 A.M. to noon with another person doing the same job from 1:00 P.M. to 5:00 P.M. A variation on this schedule might be to have two employees work alternate full days. Job sharing allows a company to take advantage of the talents of two different people within the same function. It also gives the company the opportunity to hire skilled workers, such as retirees or women with small children, who might not be available full-time.

AMA   *See American Marketing Association*

American Advertising Federation (AAF)   A national association of people in the advertising industry committed to maintaining standards for truthful and responsible advertising.

Founded in 1967 through the merger of the Advertising Federation of America and the Advertising Association of the West, the AAF's roots go back to 1905. In that year, a number of local advertising clubs formed a national association, which established committees to ensure truth in advertising. These committees led directly to the establishment of the Better Business Bureau. The AAF was also influential in establishing the Federal Trade Commission (FTC). *See also Advertising Council Inc., American Association of Advertising Agencies, American Marketing Association.*

American Association of Advertising Agencies   The national association of leading U.S. *advertising agencies.*

The Four A's, as it is called, was founded in 1917 to help regulate the advertising industry by monitoring advertising practices and setting standards. Potential members must file an application to join; any agency judged to be unethical is rejected. The AAAA is divided into three regions—Eastern, Central, and Western—and its members place more than 80 percent of all national advertising. The organization sponsors the AAAA Educational Foundation, which offers grants and fellowships for graduate work in advertising. It also provides a group insurance and pension plan for member agencies. *See also Advertising Council Inc., American Advertising Federation, American Marketing Association.*

American Depositary Receipts (ADRs)   Certificates that represent shares in a foreign company.

These certificates are denominated in U.S. dollars and can be purchased and sold on American exchanges or over the counter. ADRs may be purchased through a stockbroker, an ADR mutual fund, or directly from a depositary bank.

The leading American depositaries are Bank of New York, with 51 percent of the market, J. P. Morgan, with 27 percent, and Citibank, with about 20 percent. About 900 foreign firms had ADRs going into 1992, with the number projected to increase about 10 to 15 percent annually for the next few years.

The mechanics of ADRs are relatively simple. Foreign companies place shares on deposit in the trust account of a New York bank (one of those previously mentioned). The bank, in turn, issues certificates representing receipts for these shares (called "depositary receipts"). These receipts are listed and traded on U.S. exchanges and over-the-counter markets just like ordinary common shares.

It is virtually impossible to tell the difference between ADR transactions and those involving common shares of American companies. The stock certificate looks approximately the same, broker commissions are identical, and, of course, the transaction is denominated in U.S. dollars. Stock quotes and analyses for listed ADRs appear in *Standard and Poor's Stock Guide, The Wall Street Journal,* and *Value Line,* just like those of American companies.

The advantages of ADRs over investing through foreign stock exchanges are as follows:

- ADRs pay dividends in dollars.
- Settlement costs that apply in some foreign markets are totally eliminated.
- Financial reports are in English, and even though underlying accounting assumptions vary from American standards, at least the reports are readable.
- The trading inconveniences and custodial fees associated with buying shares on foreign exchanges are eliminated.

American Institute of Certified Public Accountants (AICPA) A national organization of *certified public accountants.*

The AICPA develops standards for its members and offers advice both to members and to such governmental agencies as the *Securities and Exchange Commission (SEC).*

American Marketing Association (AMA) The national society of marketing professionals.

Headquartered in Chicago, the AMA was founded in 1915 by the merger of the American Marketing Society and the National Association of Marketing Teachers. The organization's objective is to promote honest and ethical marketing. In addition to publishing *Marketing News* and *The Journal of Marketing Research,* the AMA offers various books, pamphlets, and marketing bibliographies. *See also Advertising Council Inc., American Advertising Federation, American Association of Advertising Agencies.*

American Stock Exchange (AMEX) The second-largest exchange in the United States.

Listing requirements are more lenient than the New York Stock Exchange (NYSE), making the AMEX more attractive to smaller companies. The minimum listing requirements are as follows:

- Publicly held shares: 300,000
- Market value of $2.5 million for those shares

- Annual pre-tax net income of $750,000
- Total minimum number of shareholders 900, of which 600 must own 100 shares or more
- Net assets of $4 million

However, delisting steps are similar to those of the NYSE and occur under two conditions:

(1) At the request of the AMEX with approval from the SEC, or
(2) At the request of the company, which must be supported by a vote of two-thirds of the shareholders; furthermore, less than 10 percent of individual investors can vote "no."

The Americans with Disabilities Act A federal law banning discrimination against people with disabilities.

On July 20, 1990, then president George Bush fulfilled a campaign promise by signing into law the Americans with Disabilities Act (ADA), regarded by many as the most sweeping piece of legislation since the Civil Rights Act of 1964.

The new law will require changes in the way businesses and public facilities operate. Some of these changes will be physical and will cost money; others will involve adopting new attitudes toward people with disabilities.

The ADA extends civil rights protection to people with disabilities that are parallel to those established by the federal government for women and minorities. It is essentially an amalgam of two major civil rights statutes: the Civil Rights Act of 1964 and the Rehabilitation Act of 1973. The ADA uses the framework of Titles II and VII of the Civil Rights Act of 1964 for coverage and enforcement, and the framework of the Rehabilitation Act of 1973 for defining disability and determining what constitutes discrimination.

But whereas the Rehabilitation Act prohibited only those doing business with the federal government or receiving federal financial assistance from discriminating against qualified individuals with handicaps (the term used under that law), the ADA reaches into the private sector as well, affecting both large and small businesses.

Another significant difference between the ADA and its predecessor laws is that the ADA does not merely prohibit discrimination, as does Title VII of the Civil Rights Act, but imposes additional affirmative obligations upon businesses to accommodate the needs of people with disabilities and to promote their economic independence.

Since enacting the Rehabilitation Act of 1973, Congress has passed several other statutes prohibiting discrimination against individuals with disabilities. In addition to the federal laws, more that 40 states have their own laws protecting individuals with disabilities. The scope of protection under these laws varies greatly on such issues as coverage of private sector employers, the number of employers covered, and the obligation to make reasonable accommodation.

In congressional hearings on the ADA, former attorney general Richard Thornburgh argued that this new law weaves together the torn patchwork of existing federal and state legislation regarding people with disabilities and closes gaps in coverage.

Certain key terms are not defined in the law itself, so Congress directed the Equal Employment Opportunity Commission to issue comprehensive regulations clarifying the employment provisions of Title I in the ADA, and the attorney general of the United States to issue comprehensive regulations interpreting the public accommodations provisions of Title III in the ADA. These regulations are extremely useful in interpreting the ADA.

Title I: Employment. A key provision of the ADA is the prohibition of discrimination against individuals with disabilities in public- and private-sector employment. Title VII of the Civil Rights Act of 1964 opened the doors of American business to minorities and women. Title I of the ADA offers the same promise to qualified individuals with disabilities. It requires employers to take immediate action to provide "reasonable accommodations" to both employees and job applicants for a broad range of mental and physical disabilities.

Title II: State and local governments and public services. This title prohibits public entities from discriminating against qualified individuals with disabilities or excluding them from participating in their services, programs, or activities. The ADA's guarantee of full participation in the mainstream of American life is illusory if accessible transportation is not available; hence, most of Title II's provisions deal with transportation provided to the general public via bus, rail, taxis, and limousines. Aircraft are excluded.

All new public buses must be accessible to persons with disabilities. Transit authorities must provide supplementary or special services to those who cannot use fixed-route bus services. New over-the-road buses, new rail vehicles, and all new rail stations must be accessible. Existing rail systems must have one accessible car per train within the next five years.

Title III: Public accommodations and services operated by private entities. Title III prohibits discrimination against individuals with disabilities in the full and equal enjoyment of the goods, services, facilities, and privileges of any place of public accommodation. It requires that the above benefits be offered "in the most integrated setting appropriate to the needs of the individual," except when the individual poses a direct threat to the health or safety of others.

Public accommodations include a broad range of entities, from airports to zoos. They extend to sales, rental, and service establishments as well as educational institutions, recreational facilities, and social service centers. Title III requires public accommodations to modify their policies and procedures and to provide auxiliary aids to disabled people unless doing so would fundamentally alter the nature of the organization or cause an undue burden. All newly constructed and substantially renovated buildings must be readily accessible to people with disabilities. Existing facilities must be made accessible if changes are "readily achievable."

Title IV: Telecommunications. Title IV ensures that individuals with disabilities will be able to communicate electronically. It requires that, within three years, telephone companies must provide telecommunications relay services that enable hearing- and speech-impaired individuals to communicate with hearing individuals through the use of telecommunications devices for the deaf (TDD) and other nonvoice terminal devices.

Title V: Miscellaneous provisions. In general, this title delineates the ADA's relationship to other laws, outlines insurance issues, and explains how each title in the act will be implemented. Title V prohibits retaliation against individuals who try to enforce their own rights under the ADA and amends the Rehabilitation Act of 1973 to exclude current users of alcohol and drugs from its coverage. It provides that nothing in the ADA shall be construed to apply to a lesser standard than the standards set in any other federal or state law as long as the previous law provides greater or equal protection. (*Source:* Jeffrey Allen, *Complying with the ADA*, Copyright © 1993 John Wiley & Sons, Inc. Reprinted with permission.)

amortization   The process of allocating the portion of an *intangible asset*'s value that has been consumed during the current period against revenues.

Like *depreciation,* amortization recognizes that every asset is reduced in value through use.

EXAMPLE: Say a bakery pays $10,000 for an oven that it estimates will be able to bake 500,000 loaves of bread over its useful life. Say, too, that the oven will have no *salvage value* after the 500,000 loaves are baked. Under those circumstances, the value of the oven is reduced by $0.02 ($10,000 divided by 500,000 loaves) each time a loaf of bread comes out of it. When this same reasoning is applied to an *intangible asset,* such as a patent or *copyright,* it is called amortization.

As an asset is reduced in value, the cost is listed on a company's *income statement.* Estimating the useful life of an intangible asset is something of an art. A patented manufacturing process, for example, might become obsolete in a matter of months, or it could have a useful life of many years. *Generally accepted accounting principles* (GAAP) state that the amortization of an intangible asset cannot exceed 40 years and that it must be done on a straight-line basis.

annual percentage rate (APR)   A measure of the true cost of credit.

APR shows, as a percentage, the ratio of the finance charge to the average amount of credit used during the term of a loan. There are four ways to calculate APR for installment loans: (1) the actuarial method, (2) the direct-ratio method, (3) the constant-ratio method, and (4) the N-ratio method.

Lenders usually use the actuarial method. It gives the most accurate results, but it relies on complicated calculations that are best performed on a computer. Essentially, the actuarial method is the interest calculated, at a fixed rate, on the unpaid balance of the principal of a loan, with each payment allocated first to interest, then to the remaining principal.

The direct-ratio method is much simpler than the actuarial method, but it tends to slightly understate the APR. The direct-ratio formula is

$$\frac{6MC}{3P(N+1) + C(N+1)} = \text{APR}$$

where:

M = number of payment periods per year
N = number of scheduled payments
C = finance charges
P = original proceeds

The constant-ratio method also gives a fairly good approximation of APR, although it tends to *overstate* the rate. The constant-ratio formula is

$$\frac{2MC}{P(N+1)} = \text{APR}$$

In most cases, the N-ratio method approximates APR more precisely than either the constant-ratio or direct-ratio method. The N-ratio formula is

$$\frac{M(95N+9)C}{12N(N+1)(4P+C)} = \text{APR}$$

EXAMPLE: A company borrows $1,000, which it must repay in 12 equal payments of $92. The finance charge comes to $104. The APR under each of the four methods is calculated as follows.

Actuarial method: The APR under this method, as calculated by computer, is 18.67 percent.

Direct-ratio method:

$$\frac{6 \times 12 \times \$104}{3 \times \$1,000(12+1) + \$104(12+1)} = 0.1856, \qquad \text{or } 18.56\%$$

Constant-ratio method:

$$\frac{2 \times 12 \times \$104}{\$1,000(12+1)} = 0.192, \qquad \text{or } 19.20\%$$

N-ratio method:

$$\frac{12\,[(95 \times 12) + 9] \times 104}{12 \times 12 \times 13 \times [4(\$1,000) + \$104]} = 0.1866, \qquad \text{or } 18.66\%$$

The Consumer Credit Protection Act requires lenders to disclose both the annual percentage rate and the dollar amount of the finance charge to borrowers, so they can make meaningful comparisons between different loans.

annual report A detailed statement that a company prepares at the end of its reporting year; the reporting year can be either on a calendar or fiscal basis.

Annual reports contain a company's *income statement, balance sheet, statement of cash flows, statement of shareholders' equity, management's discussion and analysis of operations,* notes to the financial statements, *audit opinion,* and other selected data. The *Financial Accounting Standards Board (FASB)* also requires that companies include in their annual reports operations in different industries, export sales, foreign operations, major customers, and government contracts. The annual report is read and analyzed by stockholders, investors, creditors, analysts, employees, and other interested parties.

annuity A contract sold by life insurance companies that guarantees periodic payments to the buyer (annuitant) at a future point in time, usually upon retirement.

There are two general types of annuities: fixed and variable. With a fixed annuity, all future payments are of equal amounts. With a variable annuity, payments vary according to the value of the underlying investments that make up the annuity. An annuity, either fixed or variable, that continues indefinitely is called a perpetuity. *See also future value of an annuity, present value of an annuity.*

APR *See annual percentage rate*

arbitrage The process of simultaneously buying a security, currency, or commodity on one market and selling it in another.

Price differences between the two markets give the arbitrageur his or her profit.

EXAMPLE: Stock X trades on the London Stock Exchange for $10.00 per share and on the New York Stock Exchange for $10.50 per share. A broker buys 10,000 shares of the stock in London and simultaneously sells 10,000 shares in New York. The arbitrage profit is calculated as follows:

$$(X_b - X_a) \times Q = \pi$$

where:

X_b = the price of the higher-priced security

X_a = the price of the lower-priced security

Q = quantity

π = arbitrage profit

$$(\$10.50 - \$10.00) \times 10{,}000 = \$5{,}000$$

So the arbitrage profit comes to $5,000.

This transaction—and others like it—increases the demand for the stock (and therefore its price) on the London Exchange, while it lowers the demand for the stock (and the price) on the New York Stock Exchange. This evening-out process continues until the price of the stock is the same on both exchanges. Because arbitrage tends to equalize prices in this way, the arbitrageur must act on opportunities quickly.

area of dominant influence (ADI) A geographic area made up of all counties that receive radio and television signals from stations in a particular market.

The Arbitron Ratings Company first put counties into different ADIs in 1965. Arbitron did a county-by-county study of television and radio habits to determine which stations people tuned in to in any particular county. In areas that received signals from stations in two different cities, the company determined which stations were more frequently listened to or watched. If, for example, people in Midpoint City watched or listened to stations from City X more than stations from City Y, Arbitron would designate Midpoint as part of City X's ADI.

The Federal Communications Commission (FCC) adopted the ADI as a standard definition in the radio and television industries. National advertisers use ADI to define both budget amounts and sales and distribution territories when they create marketing plans.

arithmetic return A measure of investment return over either a single time period or multiple periods.

Arithmetic return is calculated by taking the average of a series of one-period returns. The formula for arithmetic return is

$$\frac{1}{n} \times \sum r_i = \text{Arithmetic return}$$

where:

$\sum$ = sum

n = number of time periods

r_i = return of each single holding period

EXAMPLE: A company invests in a non-dividend-paying stock that triples in price during one time period (t) and then returns to its original price at the end of the following period.

	$t = 0$	$t = 1$	$t = 2$
Price (end of period)	$50	$150	$50

The holding period returns for periods 1 and 2 are calculated as follows:

$$\frac{\text{Current income} + \text{Capital gain (or loss)}}{\text{Purchase price}} = \text{Holding period return}$$

period 1 $\dfrac{\$0 + (\$150 - \$50)}{\$50} = 200\%$

period 2 $\dfrac{0 + (\$50 - \$150)}{\$150} = -66.6\%$

The arithmetic return can then be calculated:

$$\frac{200\% + (-66.6\%)}{2} = 66.6\%$$

The stock's arithmetic average return, then, is the average of the 200 percent return during period 1 and the negative 66.6 percent return at the end of period 2, or positive 66.6 percent. Although the arithmetic average return can be helpful in tracking successive rates of return, it can be misleading when used for extended multiperiod calculations because it does not incorporate the **time value of money**. In these cases, the **geometric average return** might be more appropriate.

arm's length transaction A business transaction at market-established prices between two unrelated parties.

Intercompany sales (as between a parent company and a subsidiary) are considered to be arm's length if the prices, terms, and conditions are identical to those offered in the general marketplace. Many tax laws relate to the disallowance of deductions or adjustments to business valuations (for estate taxes) if business transactions between related parties do not conform to market conditions. Examples of transactions not considered as arm's length include

- Sales from a subsidiary to a parent company at cost
- Rent charged a subsidiary by a parent at substantially less than market rates
- Loans from shareholders at interest rates less than market rates

- Loans from corporations to shareholders at no interest or at interest rates less than market rates

ARR *See accounting rate of return*

art director (AD)   Person in an advertising agency responsible for the overall look and design of a client's advertisements.

Art directors, who usually report to an agency's *creative director,* supervise a staff of artists and designers that actually put the advertisements together. Art directors are frequently teamed with copywriters for particular projects. If, for example, the agent's client is a candy company bringing a new product to market, the art director and copywriter would together create the theme, copy, and look for the introductory campaign. Once the client approves these elements, the art director passes them on to the agency's staff of designers, which produces the final ads.

artificial intelligence   A computer system designed to have the ability to learn and reason like a human being.

In order to do this, artificial intelligence systems work with symbols rather than data. Because of this orientation, artificial intelligence systems use rules, procedures, and networks rather than calculations and algorithms. By manipulating symbols through these procedures, artificial intelligence systems can reason deductively, make assumptions, and learn from their mistakes. This makes them well suited for handling decisions in cases where information may change but the process is relatively constant. The technology for artificial intelligence is still developing, but it will be easily adapted to tasks such as processing paperwork or making airline reservations.

ASB   *See Auditing Standards Board*

AS/RS   *See automated storage and retrieval system*

asset   An economic resource of a company.

Assets include money, land, buildings, property and property rights, and machinery. There are two broad types of assets: *tangible assets* and *intangible assets*. Tangible assets, such as a machine or building, can be seen and felt. Intangible assets, such as patent rights and *goodwill,* have no physical substance. An asset, to be considered as such, must meet three conditions: (1) It must provide future economic benefits that can be reasonably estimated, (2) it must be controlled by its owner, and (3) it must be the result of a previous event or transaction (the *purchase* of a factory building, for instance). Assets are classified as current or noncurrent on the *balance sheet.* An asset is current if its future economic benefit will be realized in one year or less. Inventory is an example of a current asset. An asset is noncurrent if its future economic benefit will be realized in more than one year. Machinery, for example, is a noncurrent asset.

asset turnover In accounting, a ratio that measures the *productivity* of a company's assets.

As a rule, the asset turnover ratio relates a company's total average assets to annual sales, as follows:

$$\frac{\text{Sales}}{\text{Total average assets}} = \text{Asset turnover}$$

Average assets are calculated by adding total assets at the beginning of the year to total assets at the end of the year and dividing by 2.

Asset turnover can also be used to measure the productivity of specific assets, such as inventory turnover or *accounts receivable* turnover. In this case, inventory or receivables numbers are substituted for total average assets.

Asset turnover ratios can then be compared to industry standards to determine how a company compares to its competitors.

asset value business valuation method A method for determining the valuation of business equity interests.

The asset value method assumes that all or a significant portion of a company's assets could be liquidated readily if so desired. Such an assumption makes this a favorite method of secured lenders for assessing the value of collateralized assets. Small businesses also frequently look to this method as a starting point from which to make plus and minus adjustments. In this case, book value, not liquidation value, is normally used as an expression of net asset value.

The IRS also uses the asset value method to value *employee stock owner-ship plans* (ESOPs), special recapitalizations, and other situations involving tax impacts.

The fundamental problem with using the asset value approach is that it looks at business assets as valuable in themselves, without regard to their impact on a going concern. Except in rare cases where investments in businesses are made for the express purpose of liquidating the company, the only real value in business assets lies in their ability to enhance the company's earning power.

In general, valuations relating to mergers, the acquisition or sale of companies or equity interests, and other purely business purposes employ other methods that more properly reflect future benefits to investors.

asset-backed securities A securitized obligation used extensively by subsidiaries of multinationals to finance long-term export orders from developing countries.

These securities are used primarily because the underdevelopment of local banking systems and government export-credit institutions precludes straightforward export credit. Many of these securities are issued and traded on foreign exchanges in emerging capital markets. Some longer-term export orders also securitize debt issues on American exchanges.

Export order-backed securities attract investors for several reasons:

- Interest rates run one to three percentage points higher than market rates (and sometimes more).
- Active trading on booming local exchanges offers a good potential for capital gains.
- Many issues carry secondary guarantees from such multilateral agencies as the World Bank's Multilateral Investment Guarantee Agency (MIGA), local development banks, or home-country government-backed export-credit agencies.

attitudes A person's feelings toward other people, things, or activities.

Attitudes tend to last for a relatively long time, and can be either positive or negative. Attitudes have a great deal of influence on a person's behavior within an organization. There are three basic components to attitudes: affective, cognitive, and conative. The affective component is the emotional response created by the object of the attitude. The affective component of an attitude usually involves feelings such as happiness, sadness, like, dislike, love, and hate. The cognitive components of an attitude involve the system of beliefs that a person has about a particular object. For example, a person might believe that his co-workers are inefficient, that his managers are rigid, and that the people in the marketing department are flakes. These beliefs are developed over time, and are difficult to change, even when they are clearly shown to be false. The conative component of an attitude is the behavior that a person exhibits toward the object. For example, an employee with a positive attitude toward her job is likely to arrive on time, stay late, and perform tasks with enthusiasm. This is not to say that knowledge of a person's attitudes can result in predictions of his or her behavior. Rather, the conative component simply suggests that there is a strong link between the two.

Understanding employee attitudes is a key aspect to *human resources management*. The most popular way to measure attitudes is through a confidential survey (called survey feedback). For example, workers might be asked to strongly agree, agree, remain neutral, disagree, or strongly disagree with a series of statements such as "My supervisor assigns tasks fairly within my department." Attitude surveys are usually given to a number of employees in order to obtain an overall measure of group or department attitudes. Attitudes can also be measured through a series of interviews. Since this method does not provide the anonymity of a survey, employees are often reluctant to air their more negative feelings. For this reason, many companies use outside parties to perform the interviews.

Once attitudes have been measured, management might want to change them. Since attitudes are the result of a number of learning experiences and influences, both positive and negative, it is important to use these experiences and influences to effect change. For example, say a company's employees feel that management is not concerned with their long-term careers because outside candidates, rather than current employees, are frequently hired for managerial positions. This attitude might be changed if the company creates a policy of hiring from its own ranks. In creating this policy, it is important to be aware of both the affective and cognitive components that make up the existing attitude. The program should be introduced by a manager who elicits a positive emotional response from the workers. A trusted and well-liked manager is likely to have more success changing employee attitudes than a manager who is disliked and viewed with suspicion. The program must also live up to its promises. If, after several months, no current employees have been promoted to management positions, employees will realize, via the cognitive component of their attitudes, that the program is simply paying lip service to their concerns. If this happens, the negative attitude will be reinforced rather than changed.

attractiveness test *See industry attractiveness test*

attribution theory A behavioral theory that attempts to explain how people observe behavior and its causes.

The attribution theory states that there are two types of causes for any particular behavior: external and internal. Externally caused behavior is the result of outside factors. Internally caused behavior is under the personal control of the individual. For example, if an employee is late returning from a lunch break because of a traffic accident, his or her lateness might be seen as externally caused. If, however, the employee is late from lunch because he or she had stopped at a tavern and lost track of time, the tardiness might be seen as internally caused.

The decision as to whether a particular behavior is externally or internally caused is based on three factors: consistency, consensus, and distinctiveness.

Consistency is the extent to which a person acts in the same way at different times. For example, if a particular employee is usually late returning from lunch, an observer might attribute the behavior to internal causes. If the employee is seldom late, the behavior might be attributed to external causes.

Consensus is the extent to which other people in the same situation act in the same way. If everyone in a particular department is late coming back from lunch (high consensus), an observer might attribute the behavior to internal causes, such as poor morale. If most of the people in the department come back from lunch on time (low consensus), the observer might attribute the behavior to external causes.

Distinctiveness is the extent to which a person acts the same way in different situations. Does the employee usually arrive late in the morning? Does he or she leave early? Do co-workers complain that the employee is a "slacker"? If this is the case, the situation has low distinctiveness and the behavior might be internally attributed. If the lateness is not unusual, it shows low distinctiveness and might be attributed to internal causes; if the lateness is unusual, it might be attributed to external causes.

audit An examination of a company's compliance with accounting standards and policies.

There are four types of audits: financial, internal, management, and compliance. In a financial audit, an independent *certified public accountant* examines a company's accounting records and procedures, and then gives an *audit opinion*. In an internal audit, an internal auditor investigates a company's procedures to make certain that they meet corporate policies. A management audit, as its name suggests, examines management's efficiency. Finally, a compliance audit determines whether a company is following specific rules and regulations. *See also audit opinion, adverse opinion, qualified opinion, unqualified opinion.*

audit opinion A report given by an independent *certified public accountant* that states the auditor's opinion as to the reasonableness of a company's financial statement.

See adverse opinion, qualified opinion, unqualified opinion.

Auditing Standards Board (ASB) The authoritative branch of the *American Institute of Certified Public Accountants* (AICPA) that creates and interprets generally accepted auditing standards through its Statements on Auditing Standards.

automated storage and retrieval system (AS/RS) A computerized system of storage racks with vehicles that load and unload the racks automatically.

automatic guided vehicle system (AGVS) A transportation system that automatically sends materials (via pallet trucks, carts, conveyor belts, and the like) to predetermined destinations without the aid of an operator.

automatic merchandising Sales made through a vending machine.

Automatic merchandising allows around-the-clock sales in heavily trafficked locations, such as taverns, college dormitories, office buildings, and factories. Beverage and cigarette distributors account for 70 percent of all automatic merchandising.

Vending machines can also expand a marketer's distribution at locations—restrooms, libraries, and hospitals, for instance—that the marketer couldn't otherwise use. Automatic merchandising does have drawbacks, however, including the vending machines' high repair and service costs. Moreover, perishable goods must be replaced often, and vending machines are especially vulnerable to vandalism and burglary. To compensate for these *operating expenses*, vending machine marketers must price products relatively high.

automation The mechanical replacement of human sensing skills.

Automation is different from mechanization, which is the replacement of human physical labor.

EXAMPLE: A CNC (computer numerically controlled) metal cutting machine will drill, plane, and ream aluminum. This is automation, the substitution of machinery for human labor and skills. The process of continuous measurement and comparison to specifications is a benefit of the process of automation. Another example is the automatic door opener; it senses the presence of an object and opens the door.

autonomation The automatic shutdown of a machine, process, or line due to the detection of some defect or abnormality.

available market In marketing, those consumers who have interest in a particular product or service, access to it, and enough income to buy it.

The key word in this definition is *interest*. The available market, in other words, is not the same as the *potential market*, which consists of all those who potentially have interest in a given product or service.

EXAMPLE: In the razor blade market, all women and men who have reached puberty and are showing hair growth make up the potential market for companies such as Gillette, Schick, and Bic. Men and women who choose not to shave, however—that is, those who have no interest in shaving—would not be part of the *available* market for these shaving technology companies.

Identifying the available market helps marketers understand precisely where sales are being generated. *Compare to **penetrated market**, **potential market**, **served market***.

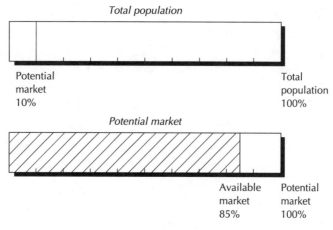

Available Market

average cost method A method of *inventory valuation* that uses the average cost of the goods on hand to determine both the value of *inventory* on the *balance sheet* and the *cost of goods sold* on the *income statement*.

EXAMPLE: During the year, a company makes the following purchases:

January	100 units @ $70 =	$ 7,000
March	200 units @ $80 =	16,000
April	50 units @ $90 =	4,500
July	100 units @ $100 =	10,000
October	100 units @ $110 =	11,000
Total goods available for sale: 550		$48,500

So the average cost for each unit of inventory comes to $88.18 ($48,500 divided by 550 units). If *ending inventory* on December 31 is 175 units, the company enters it on the *balance sheet* as follows:

$$175 \times \$88.18 = \$15,432$$

Cost of goods sold is calculated in a similar manner:

Total goods purchased	550 units
Ending inventory	175 units
Units sold	375 units

Cost of goods sold: 375 × $88.18 = $33,068

The average cost method is a compromise between the *first-in, first-out* (FIFO) or *last-in, first-out* (LIFO) methods of inventory valuation. *See also first-in, first-out* (FIFO), *inventory valuation, last-in, first-out* (LIFO).

B

backlog Any customer orders that have been received and booked but are either not produced or in process; also called the order board or open orders.

    Backlogs are based on a scheduling heuristic, usually first-come, first-serve, and they generally occur because an item may not be stocked or is built to customer specifications. Large items, such as mainframe computers or aircraft, are frequently backlogged.

backorder A customer order that was unfillable at the time it was placed.

    Backorders are usually the result of out-of-stock situations. A company has backorders when its *inventory* is mismanaged or demand has not been estimated accurately.

backward integration A strategy in which a company creates a competitive advantage by controlling the supply of its raw materials.

    For example, the De Beers diamond company has actively pursued backward integration by contracting for about 80 percent of the diamond supply in the Western hemisphere. Backward integration strategies can take a number of forms. The James River Corporation significantly reduced costs (and increased return on equity) by purchasing used paper machines for very low prices and converting them to produce its own products.

    Although backward integration can be an effective strategy, it is by no means sustainable. For example, if a major new diamond source is discovered, De Beers might lose its control of the market. Backward integration can also be threatened directly by competitors. Many of James River's competitors have begun purchasing used paper machines, which has greatly increased their price. This higher price makes them a less attractive purchase, which limits James River's growth.

backward scheduling In manufacturing, a technique of scheduling where the due dates of orders are the driving force.

    Jobs with the longest due date are scheduled to be completed exactly when they are needed. Jobs are loaded into workstations in the reverse of their processing order within those stations. If the job with the latest due date is required in eight hours and the last operation on that job is in workstation 1, and 2 hours are needed in that station, the scheduler would begin by scheduling that job during hours 7 and 8 in station 1. Scheduling begins from the due date and moves backward to the current time.

A backward schedule quickly reveals if all jobs can be completed within due dates. It also identifies bottlenecks and idle time at workstations.

EXAMPLE: Two customers enter a print shop with rush orders. The first order involves printing, collating, and binding. The second job involves printing, tabbing, and binding. The print shop has a third order in a semi-finished stage with only tabbing and binding to be done. This third order is also due out today. The first customer needs the job done in 8 hours. The second job must be done in 6 hours, and the third customer is coming in 4 hours to pick up the completed job. All jobs have a sequence involving printing, collating, tabbing, and binding. Consider each operation as a workstation; they are designated as follows:

$$\begin{array}{rcl}
\text{Printing} &=& \text{Workstation 1} \\
\text{Collating} &=& \text{Workstation 2} \\
\text{Tabbing} &=& \text{Workstation 3} \\
\text{Binding} &=& \text{Workstation 4}
\end{array}$$

Job	Hour due	Required processing (in order)
X	8	2 hours at station 1, 1 hour at 2, 1 hour at 3, 1 hour at 4
Y	6	2 hours at station 1, 2 hours at 3, 2 hours at 4
Z	4	2 hours at station 3, 2 hours at 4

Looking at the schedule, we begin with job X because it is not needed for 8 hours. We begin the scheduling in the fourth workstation because that is the last operation to be completed, and we schedule hour 8 in that workstation.

Hours:	1	2	3	4	5	6	7	8
Station 1	*Y	Y		*X	X			
Station 2						*X		
Station 3	*Z	Z	*Y	Y			*X	
Station 4			*Z	Z	*Y	Y		*X

* Indicates a changeover for the next job.

A look at the schedule shows the semi-finished job (Z) being completed "just in time" with the first job (X) not having to start until 5 hours before promised. Job Y gets done when needed. The blank spaces show the work centers as idle. Thus we see 50 percent use of station 1, 12.5 percent use of station 2, and 62.5 percent use of both stations 3 and 4. The shop average is 46.88 percent utilization based on 15 work hours used in all four stations.

We assumed that there was no significant move time between work-stations. If binding took place in another building and it took half an hour to move an order to binding, orders Y and Z would both be late because half an hour would have to be added to the operation time.

Another complication can be setup time. If we make the problem more realistic and say that each workstation requires $\frac{1}{4}$ of an hour changeover from the previous job, then jobs Y and Z would be late and X would have to be started earlier. Changeovers are indicated with asterisks.

An obvious advantage of this scheduling approach is identification of capacity used, bottlenecks, and efficiency of plant use.

balance delay A measure of inefficiency of a production line derived from looking at three production factors: cycle time, the total task time, and the number of workstations in the line.

Cycle time is the amount of time that can be spent at a workstation before having to move to the next workstation. Assigned tasks performed at that workstation must be completed in that cycle time. Cycle time is determined by dividing daily production time by daily demand.

The total task time is simply the summation of all times of all tasks needed to produce a unit of output. The number of workstations needed is total task time divided by the cycle time. The resulting value is rounded *up* to the next highest *whole* number. Efficiency is now calculated as follows:

Efficiency = Total task time/(Number of workstations × Cycle time)

EXAMPLE: A company produces 200 units per day.

(1) The cycle time is (8 hours × 60 min/hr)/200 units = 2.4 minutes. The most time a unit can spend at a workstation is 2.4 minutes.

(2) Total task time is 6.0 minutes.

(3) Number of workstations = 6.0/2.4 = 2.5 workstations.

(4) Rounding 2.5 to 3, efficiency = 6.0/(3 × 2.4) = .8333, or 83 percent efficiency. With three workstations and a cycle time of 2.4 minutes, 7.2 minutes of time are available to complete 6.0 minutes of work.

(5) Balance delay = 1 − efficiency, or 17 percent.

(6) Adding more workstations decreases efficiency. A fourth workstation decreases efficiency to 6/(4 × 2.4) = 63 percent.

balance of payments A summary of the official statement of international transactions between U.S. residents and residents of foreign nations.

In effect, this depicts the U.S. international trade and capital positions. The concept of the balance of payments has changed since the early 1970s, when the foreign exchange value of the U.S. dollar ceased to have a fixed relationship with other currencies and began floating.

During the 1960s the balance of payments accounts underwent several changes in definition. With the advent of flexible exchange rates in the 1970s two major accounts emerged, which represent the two major categories of international transactions. The first account is the *current account*, which contrasts exports of goods and services with imports of goods and services. These are short-term payments that represent the flow of goods and services on an ongoing basis. The second account is the *capital account*, which contrasts the inflow of capital—direct investment and long-term lending by foreigners—with the outflow of capital—direct investment by U.S. residents abroad and long-term lending to foreigners.

In general, a current account deficit induces a capital account surplus, and a current account surplus induces a capital account deficit. Thus, the current account is of greater importance, at least in terms of cause and response. A capital account outflow (deficit) is a response to a current account surplus, and vice versa. Otherwise, the exchange rate shows what must change to offset any imbalance.

The table below presents data for the merchandise trade deficit, the current account, and the capital account for the 1980–1992 period in billions of dollars.

	Merchandise trade balance	Current account	Capital account
1980	− 25.5	2.3	− 28.9
1981	− 28.0	5.0	− 31.1
1982	− 36.5	− 11.4	− 29.9
1983	− 67.1	− 43.6	24.5
1984	−112.5	− 98.8	72.8
1985	−122.2	−121.7	96.9
1986	−145.1	−147.5	132.1
1987	−159.6	−163.5	167.6
1988	−127.0	−126.7	126.8
1989	−115.7	−101.1	98.7
1990	−108.9	− 90.4	43.1
1991	− 73.4	− 3.7	4.8
1992	− 96.3	− 53.7	63.0

balance of trade   The net difference between the dollar value of a country's imports and exports over a period of time.

A country's current account reflects a currency drain when imports exceed exports and a currency surplus when exports exceed imports. Although the balance of trade plays an important role in establishing national trade policies, it has little effect on a company's fortunes, other than as a long-term indicator of currency stability.

balance sheet
A statement representing a company's financial position at a specific date, usually at the end of an accounting period; also called a statement of financial position.

The balance sheet, which presents a picture at one point in time of a company's financial standing, shows a company's resources, the amount it owes creditors, and ownership value. Balance sheets categorize a company's assets, liabilities, and stockholders' equity according to the following formula:

$$Assets = Liabilities + Shareholders'\ equity$$

On every balance sheet, the amount of total assets will equal the combined amounts of liabilities and share-owners' equity.

EXAMPLE:

Consolidated Balance Sheets
Wal-Mart Stores, Inc. and Subsidiaries
(Amounts in thousands)

	1991	1990
Assets		
Current Assets:		
Cash and cash equivalents	$ 13,014	$ 12,790
Receivables	305,070	155,811
Recoverable costs from sale/leaseback	239,867	78,727
Inventories (LIFO)	5,808,416	4,428,073
Prepaid expenses	48,408	37,215
TOTAL CURRENT ASSETS	6,414,775	4,712,616
Property, plant, and equipment, at cost:		
Land	833,344	463,110
Buildings and improvements	1,764,155	1,227,519
Fixtures and equipment	2,037,476	1,441,752
Transportation equipment	63,237	57,215
	4,698,212	3,189,596
Less accumulated depreciation	974,060	711,763
Net property, plant, and equipment	3,724,152	2,477,833
Property under capital leases	1,298,452	1,212,169
Less accumulated amortization	310,565	259,943
Net property under capital leases	987,887	952,226
Other assets and deferred charges	262,101	55,809
TOTAL ASSETS	$11,388,915	$8,198,484

Consolidated Balance Sheets
Wal-Mart Stores, Inc. and Subsidiaries (cont.)
(Amounts in thousands)

	1991	1990
Liabilities and Shareholders' Equity		
Current liabilities:		
Commercial paper	$ 395,179	$ 184,774
Accounts payable	2,651,315	1,826,720
Accrued liabilities:		
Salaries	189,535	157,216
Other	539,020	473,677
Accrued federal and state income taxes	184,512	179,049
Long-term debt due within one year	6,394	1,581
Obligations under capital leases		
due within one year	24,459	22,298
TOTAL CURRENT LIABILITIES	3,990,414	2,845,315
Long-term debt	740,254	185,152
Long-term obligations under capital leases	1,158,621	1,087,403
Deferred income taxes	134,102	115,053
Shareholders' equity:		
Common stock (shares outstanding,		
1,142,282 in 1991 and 566,153 in 1990)	114,228	56,614
Capital in excess of par value	415,586	180,465
Retained earnings	4,835,710	3,728,482
TOTAL SHAREHOLDERS' EQUITY	5,365,524	3,965,561
TOTAL LIABILITIES		
AND SHAREHOLDERS' EQUITY	$11,388,915	$8,198,484

In the Wal-Mart balance sheet, total assets for 1991 equal $11,388,915,000, as do total liabilities and shareholders' equity. At the end of the year, Wal-Mart also had $6,414,775,000 in current assets, $4,698,212,000 in noncurrent assets, $974,060,000 in accumulated depreciation, $3,990,414,000 in current liabilities, and $5,365,524,000 in shareholders' equity.

Bank for International Settlements (BIS) A consortium bank founded to coordinate the collection and rescheduling of German reparations after World War I.

No longer involved with settlements, the BIS has survived as sort of an international financial ombudsman, a central bank for the central banks of its 10 member countries. With consensus approval from its member central banks, the BIS sets standards for the global banking system.

In the late 1980s, the Bank for International Settlements recognized that overextended loan portfolios had resulted in the deterioration of capital ratios of banks throughout the world. In 1988 it moved to correct this untenable situation by issuing minimum standards for the capital/asset ratios of banks with significant operations outside their local markets. These guidelines stated that by January 1, 1993, banks must have a minimum capital/assets ratio of 8 percent. Confirmed by the U.S. Comptroller of the Currency, these guidelines were a major factor in slowing U.S. bank lending to businesses and consumers.

banker's acceptance (BA) A time draft countersigned or "accepted" by a bank.

Both documentary and clean BAs are used extensively in export trade to evidence that bank credit has been extended. Banker's acceptances can be discounted; that is, when they are presented by the drawer, the bank actually pays less than the face amount of the draft. This reflects the market discount plus the bank's acceptance commission. In the past, BAs have not been used widely in the United States, although with the increasing number of foreign banks doing business in this country who do use BAs, competitive forces undoubtedly will encourage American banks to meet the challenge.

Banks charge a very low discount rate for BAs, making this instrument the least costly of practically any form of trade credit. However, to compensate for the low discount rate, issuing banks charge an acceptance fee ranging from 0.5 to 2 percent per annum of the face amount of the L/C for handling the transaction. Foreign buyers will often pay this acceptance fee directly even if they won't allow it to be factored into a higher price for the goods.

A "documentary banker's acceptance" is a form of payment that uses the exporter's credit (supplier credit) to complete a sale. Once the products ship and the sale concludes, the exporter sells the receivable at a discount to a bank.

A "clean banker's acceptance" differs from a documentary one in that it does not have the buyer's letter of credit as collateral. Instead, the exporter must use its own credit as security. A clean BA applies to a specific transaction or shipment, just like a documentary BA. The BA is discounted with the exporter's bank. The bank then takes this readily negotiable instrument and sells it in the secondary bond market. Banks like this instrument for two reasons: It is not recorded on the bank's balance sheet, and it is always readily negotiable.

bar code A group of alternating bars and spaces representing encoded information, usually printed on product labels, but also found on parts, containers, subassemblies, or other elements of a product.

Bar codes can be read by electronic scanners and are used to input data into a computer system.

EXAMPLE: Many checkout stands at grocery stores incorporate bar code scanners to determine the price, brand, and size of an item.

barriers to entry Any factors, tangible or intangible, that prevent a competitor from entering an industry or market.

Barriers to entry are an important factor influencing a company's competitive strategy. They increase the cost or complexity of entering an industry or market, and they reduce the number of threats to a company's business. Barriers to entry can come from a number of sources: product *differentiation*, such as brand recognition and loyalty, which may be very costly or time-consuming for a new entrant to overcome; *economies of scale*, which might force entrants to incur higher costs than existing companies that produce in large quantities; high switching costs, such as retooling equipment or retraining employees; access to distribution channels (for example, new brands frequently have difficulty securing shelf space); relationships with key suppliers; proprietary technology; and government restrictions, such as licensing requirements.

Many companies work actively to create, maintain, and build strong barriers to entry. For example, soft drink companies, most conspicuously Coca-Cola and Pepsi, invest heavily in product differentiation. As a result, a potential new entrant would have to spend an inordinate amount on advertising to create a brand image that would draw customers away from Coke or Pepsi. This strong barrier has allowed Coke and Pepsi to dominate the soft drink market and discourage any possible competitors.

A company's reaction to a new entrant can also serve as a sort of barrier to entry. Competitors might be put off if an incumbent company is likely to cut prices in order to maintain market share or has plentiful resources, such as a great deal of borrowing power or excess production capacity.

Sometimes, overall industry conditions can serve as a barrier to entry. If growth is slow, the new arrival is unlikely to be easily incorporated into the industry. Frequently, when a new entrant encounters this situation, all members of the industry suffer. *See also barriers to exit.*

barriers to exit The factors that discourage a company from exiting a business product line or discontinuing a particular operation.

Many argue that barriers to exit should not influence a decision to exit a line or discontinue an operation. This approach requires that previous investments be treated as *sunk costs.* In other words, if an operation does not earn a desirable rate of return, it should be written off. Most managers, however, cannot simply walk away from many of the "perceived" barriers, such as write-offs in *book value*, past advertising spending, compensation on long-term supplier contracts, and firing or retraining employees.

Barriers to exit, real or not, have an important effect on a company's strategic position. For example, if a company is considering a large investment in a new plant that promises a large increase in market share, it is important to consider the barriers to exit that competitors will face as the plant comes on line and begins to reduce their market share. If barriers to exit are high, competitors are likely to resort to price cuts to maintain their share of the market. If competitors' plants are old and fully depreciated, they may be prepared to lower prices enough to only cover their variable costs. As long as these competitors stay in the market, prices might remain artificially low and the new plant may never become profitable.

Many barriers to exit originally served as barriers to entry, such as investments in large-capacity factories, heavy advertising to cultivate brand image, and the development of an extensive distribution system. The height of these barriers depends on whether they can be used again. For example, a factory might be redesigned to manufacture a different product. A distribution system might be reorganized to distribute the product. And brand loyalty might be transferred to the new product through a marketing campaign. *See also barriers to entry.*

Barron's Confidence Index
An index of corporate bond yields published weekly by *Barron's*.

The index comprises the yields on 10 top-grade bonds as a ratio to the Dow Jones average yield of 40 bonds. The theory behind using this ratio as a measure of investor confidence in the economy is that investors who are worried will buy high-quality bonds with lower yields; those who feel secure about the economy will buy low-grade bonds with higher yields. The spread as measured by Barron's Confidence Index indicates whether general economic optimism or pessimism predominates in the investing community.

basis points
Interest charges used to measure the market in corporate bonds.

One hundred basis points equals one percentage point of interest. The phrase "spread over Treasuries" is used by bond issuers and traders to discuss the bond market. They measure the rate earned or charged by the number of basis points over a comparable-maturity U.S. Treasury benchmark security. Companies utilizing municipal revenue bonds pay interest based on basis points plus or minus interest percentages against the prime rate.

bearer bond
Securities that are not registered to any particular holder but whose possession serves as proof of ownership.

Bearer bonds are commonly used in the U.S. financial system because it is felt that they make bonds more attractive to investors.

beginning inventory
The merchandise on hand at the beginning of an *accounting period.*

Beginning inventory is frequently used in calculating *cost of goods sold* on the *income statement. See also cost of goods sold, ending inventory.*

behavioral response
The consumer's reactions—psychological and physical—to marketing activities.

The ultimate goal of most marketing programs is met when consumers make a purchase. But marketing is also used to elicit other responses, such as generating awareness and creating or changing beliefs about a product or **brand**; altering or meeting the criteria consumers use to make a buying decision; changing or shaping attitudes; or promoting an intention to buy. Most **advertising**, for instance, focuses on creating product or **brand awareness**. Salespeople often try to help consumers learn more about a product or brand. **Image advertising** is used to bring about positive feelings or predispositions about a product or market—in other words, to shape attitudes. Many stages precede the actual overt act of buying, and strategic marketing actions are directed toward these steps as well as toward the purchase itself. *See also buying decision process.*

behavioral segmentation Subdivision of the market according to consumer behavior variables: user status, **brand** loyalty, product usage, benefits sought, usage occasion, lifestyles, and social class.

Although *descriptive* variables—age, gender, income, and geography, for example—can be and are used to divide markets into homogeneous groups, they don't give marketers much insight into consumer motivation in a particular market. Behavioral variables are a much more powerful tool for segmenting markets.

Consider benefit segmentation, which focuses on the primary benefit that the consumer seeks in a product. The marketer analyzes information about consumer desires and translates that information into marketing programs that will satisfy those desires. Of course, consumers look for as many benefits as possible from the products they buy, but the value they attach to different benefits can differ significantly. Often, they are looking for one overriding benefit. Buyers of Levi's jeans seek "durability"; buyers of Elmer's Glue-All want "adhesion"; and buyers of Lego Toys' building blocks are looking for "imaginative play." *See also market segmentation, undifferentiated marketing. Compare to demographic segmentation, preference segmentation, psychographic segmentation, volume segmentation.*

bellwether A security that the market regards as an indicator of the direction the market is moving.

Bellwether stocks are widely held by institutional investors who exercise substantial control over stock market prices and stock index movement. For years IBM was considered a bellwether stock. Current industry restructuring and recessionary impacts have caused market analysts to switch to stocks such as AT&T and General Electric as bellwether performers. In the bond market, the U.S. Treasury 20-year bond has long been considered a bellwether security. Interest rates on long-term debt are frequently tied to movements in this security.

benchmarking A process by which an organization reassesses its traditional business practices by comparing them with the best practices of other organizations.

Some people think of benchmarking as copying the practices of industry leaders. However, benchmarking is not just copying from other companies. As W. Edwards Deming stated at a lecture at Hewlett-Packard in 1986, "It is a hazard to copy. It is necessary to understand the theory of what one wishes to do." Benchmarking is more than just copying.

Westinghouse, for example, envisions benchmarking as an integrated tool within its Total Quality Improvement Process for "identifying best practices, wherever they exist, implementing and communicating those practices throughout Westinghouse to improve competitive performance and preserve our core competencies" (Paul R. Adam, senior consultant, Westinghouse Productivity and Quality Center, *Proceedings of Benchmarking Week '92*, Houston, TX: APQC, 1992; presentation notes). The Westinghouse Productivity & Quality Center's course on benchmarking uses the following definition:

> Benchmarking is a continuous search for and application of *significantly better practices* that leads to superior competitive performance. [italics added]

Westinghouse does not require teams to discover the very best practice; finding significantly better practices is sufficient to drive the improvement efforts.

Many definitions have been proposed for benchmarking, but one developed at the American Productivity and Quality Center (APQC) by the International Benchmarking Clearinghouse (IBC) Design Steering Committee represents a consensus among some 100 companies.

> Benchmarking is a systematic and continuous measurement process; a process of continuously measuring and comparing an organization's business processes against business process leaders anywhere in the world to gain information which will help the organization take action to improve its performance. (*Planning, Organizing and Managing Benchmarking: A User's Guide*, Houston, TX: APQC, 1992, p.4.)

Although benchmarking is a measurement process and results in comparative performance measures, it also describes how exceptional performance is attained. The practices that lead to exceptional performance are called enablers. Thus, the process of benchmarking results in two types of outputs: benchmarks, or measures of comparative performance, and enablers. Applying Deming's logic, the enablers represent the theory behind the process performance.

Another piece of advice from Deming also applies: "Adapt, don't adopt." Process enablers are developed to meet a specific business need within the context of a particular business environment and company culture. No two businesses are exactly alike in these areas, and practices from one business are not directly transferable to another without rigorous examination of areas that need to be translated to fit a different environment and culture. Thus, stealing shamelessly can cause trouble if the business practices of one organization don't translate to those of another.

Benchmarking follows a basic four-step approach. The four steps follow the fundamental quality method as described by the Shewhart or Deming cycle: plan, do, check, act. In the first step, planning the benchmarking study, it is necessary to select and define the process that is to be studied; identify the measures of process performance; evaluate one's own capability at this process; and determine which companies should be studied.

The first step can be reduced to answering two fundamental questions:

1. What should we benchmark?
2. Whom should we benchmark?

The second step in benchmarking is to conduct secondary and primary research. This includes an investigation of public disclosures about the particular process at target companies. It is important to learn as much as possible before making any direct contact, because many companies are completely unaware of what has been written about them in the press and trade publications. Direct communication with companies may consist of telephone surveys, written questionnaires, or site visits to make detailed observations.

The third step in benchmarking is analysis of the gathered data to determine study findings and recommendations. The analysis consists of two aspects: determining the magnitude of the performance gaps between companies, using the benchmarking metrics identified during the planning step; and identifying the process enablers that facilitated the performance improvements at the leading companies.

The final step in benchmarking involves the adaptation, improvement, and implemetation of appropriate benchmark process enablers. The objective of benchmarking is to change an organization in a way that increases its performance. Thus, benchmarking is a process with a built-in bias for action; it goes beyond just conducting a business process study or obtaining a relative measure of business performance. (*Source:* G. Watson, *Strategic Benchmarking*, Copyright © 1993 John Wiley & Sons, Inc. Reprinted by permission of John Wiley & Sons, Ltd.)

Berne Convention (for the Protection of Literary and Artistic Works of 1886)
An international agreement, originally signed in 1886 and currently signed by 80 countries, that is the oldest international treaty in the field of copyright.

The Convention established an international system of national treatment in the protection of the intellectual property of authors—creators of literary and artistic works (e.g., novels, music, works of fine art, and motion pictures). A country that is a party to the Convention must grant the same protection to the works of authors from any other country that is also a party to the Convention as it grants to its own nationals.

Under the Convention, the minimum standards include rights for the authors to permit or prohibit copying or reproduction of their works in any manner or any form. Authors' rights under the Convention are limited to a minimum term of the author's life plus 50 years (after the author's death).

The Convention is administered by the World Intellectual Property Organization (WIPO). (*Source:* L. Presner, *The International Business Dictio-*

nary and Reference, Copyright © 1991 L. Presner. Reprinted with permission of the publisher, John Wiley & Sons, Inc.)

best effort   A term relating to a specific type of arrangement with an underwriter for the marketing of a public stock issue.

A "best effort" sale means that the underwriter has the option to buy stock and the authority to sell stock, and pledges to do the best it can to sell the offering shares. Best effort sales are seldom used except for initial public offerings (IPOs) because of the risks and delays such an arrangement brings to the issuing company. The most popular form of underwriting agreement is a "firm commitment underwriting," whereby the underwriter buys all the offering shares and then resells them to the public. From an issuing company's perspective, this is clearly the best way to go.

beta   A measure of the systematic risk, or *market risk,* of a particular security or portfolio.

Systematic risk is the result of forces beyond a company's control— changes in the market, in interest rates, and in purchasing power, for example. Beta measures a security's return over time relative to the overall market. (Market return is usually measured by Standard & Poor's 500 Composite Stock Index or the Dow Jones 30 Industrials.) The higher the beta, the riskier, or the more volatile, is the stock or portfolio.

EXAMPLE: Stock X has a beta of 2.0, which means its return will be twice that of the market; in other words, if the market goes up 5 percent, stock X will climb 10 percent, and if the market falls 5 percent, stock X will drop 10 percent. If a security has a beta of 1.0, it carries the same risk as the market as a whole; if the market rises or falls 5 percent, the stock with a beta of 1.0 will also go up or go down 5 percent. If a security has a beta of 0.5, it is only half as responsive as the market; that is, if the market goes up or falls 5 percent, a security with a beta of 0.5 will climb or drop only 2.5 percent. A security with a beta of 0 carries a return that is independent of the market; an example is a risk-free security such as a Treasury bill.

Beta is frequently used to analyze the risk of equity mutual funds by showing the volatility of a fund relative to the market as a whole (as measured by the Standard & Poor's 500 Index of the most widely held stocks). A mutual fund with a beta of 1.0, for example, would have returns that match those of S&P 500. A mutual fund with a beta greater than 1.0 is more volatile, or riskier, than the market. A mutual fund with a beta less than 1.0 is not as volatile, or risky, as the market.

Beta is also used in the *capital asset pricing model* to calculate a security's expected rate of return. *See also alpha.*

better-off test   A method of evaluating the strategic impact of the acquisition of a new business unit.

The better-off test stipulates that the new unit must either (1) gain a significant *competitive advantage* through its association with the parent company or (2) offer a significant competitive advantage to the parent corporation.

When using the better-off test, it is important to determine whether the benefits offered by the acquisition of the new business unit will be accrued only once (for example, when the parent company brings in a top team of managers or consultants) or whether they will be spread over a significant time period (for example, by allowing the new unit to market its products through the parent's established *distribution channels*). In cases when the benefit comes only once, there is no reason for the parent company to hold the new unit over the long term. *See also cost-of-entry test, industry attractiveness test.*

big six A term given to the six largest CPA firms in the United States.

The relative rankings of the companies change over time, depending on the criteria used—that is, billings or number of staff. The big six are, in alphabetical order, Arthur Andersen & Co., Coopers and Lybrand, Deloitte & Touche, Ernst and Young, Peat Marwick Main & Co., and Price Waterhouse & Co.

bill of lading An official document, issued by a carrier, that details the contractual terms, such as time and place of receipt, for the delivery of goods.

When the bill is transferred to the recipient, title to the goods is also passed.

bill of material (BOM) A list of all the parts, subassemblies, raw materials, and intermediates (and the quantities of each) that go into a product.

BOMs are used along with the master production schedule to determine which items must be purchased and which production orders must be processed. In some cases, bills of material are actually used as purchasing requisitions. *See also materials requirements planning.*

blank check offering The public offering (usually an initial offering) of a shell company (i.e., a company that does not have any operating structure, that is, no assets or operations).

The prospectus gives no clue as to how the capital will be used. Investors rely entirely on the word of the shell company officers and the broker promoting the IPO that the funds will be invested in the acquisition of equity interests in solid, high-growth companies—start-ups as well as older companies. Clearly, this easily leads to scams.

Six years ago the financial world saw a great deal of publicity about unscrupulous brokers taking advantage of unwary investors by promoting "blank check" IPOs. Without question, many investors who were looking for a quick gain lost their money by relying on broker promises of potential high returns.

As a result, blank check IPOs received a bad reputation, causing many states to enact legislation that prohibits them entirely. Regulations from most other states, together with cooperative rules from the SEC and the exchanges, are now so tight that the blank check technique is virtually dead.

blanket purchase order A contract that normally covers a period of one year and may be used to buy a wide array of items carried by a distributor, such as office supplies or repair parts.

The purposes of blanket purchase orders are reducing the number of purchase orders and obtaining a better price.

bleed To reproduce an illustration or photograph so that it covers an entire page without leaving a margin.

Designed to attract attention, advertisements using this technique are called bleed ads. Most magazines charge a premium for printing bleed ads, since they require printing plates larger than those used for typical advertisements. Because bleed ads have more space available for printing, they give an artist or *art director* greater flexibility in designing or expressing a concept.

blind pool offerings Shell company stock offerings (usually initial offerings) in which, as a minimum, the prospectus identifies the industry in which capital will be invested, such as oil and gas, or commercial real estate.

In this respect, blind pools are the stock market equivalent of many private placement limited partnerships.

Like blank check shells, blind pools are normally set up to acquire equity shares, and many times controlling interest, in potentially high-return, small private companies. Also, like blank check shells, blind pools carry large risks. However, most blind pools are very legitimate. If properly constructed, they offer an excellent means for smaller companies to finance large projects or business acquisitions.

For example, a closely-held company wishes to expand into new product lines by acquiring a previously-identified going business. The acquiring company already carries a full debt load and its owners do not want to bring the company public. The solution? Form a new company without any assets, say New Corporation; initiate an exempt IPO with a private placement; and write the prospectus to show that the purpose of the IPO is to raise capital for New Corporation to make the targeted acquisition. Assuming the company or its underwriter can float the issue, the capital raised can then be used to acquire the new business in the name of New Corporation.

blue chip A *common stock* with a long history of *dividend* payments and earnings.

Because they are relatively low risk and, as a rule, provide a constant stream of income, blue-chip stocks are frequently seen as long-term investments. Companies that are considered "blue chip" vary from time to time, but current examples include AT&T, Boeing, General Electric, and IBM.

body copy The text of an advertisement other than headlines, logos, and captions.

The body copy usually contains the main thrust of an advertisement's sales message. Typically written in a conversational, one-on-one style, it explains how the advertised product will satisfy the customer's needs. The length of body copy depends on the product, the *copywriter*, and the concept of the advertisement. The only hard-and-fast rule for body copy is that it must sell the product.

BOM *See bill of material*

bond A debt obligation of a company, government body, or other organization to pay a specific amount on a stated date.

The bond matures on the stated date and the issuer pays the bondholder the bond's face value.

Interest-bearing bonds require that the issuer pay the bondholder interest on specific dates, typically semiannually. Zero-coupon bonds, such as U.S. savings bonds, are issued at a discount; that is, the bondholder buys the bond at less than face value. Though bondholders don't receive any money from zero-coupon bonds until maturity, the IRS requires that they report as taxable income the amount of interest they *would* collect each year.

Companies usually issue bonds to raise *capital.* From a corporate point of view, a bond issue has at least one advantage over a stock issue: The interest that corporations pay to bondholders is tax deductible, whereas stock dividends are not.

When a company liquidates, bondholders are entitled to collect what they are owed before common or preferred shareholders, but they rank below secured lenders. Bonds are classified as *long-term debt* on a company's *balance sheet,* and adversely affect, among other ratios, the debt/equity ratio. *See debt-to-equity ratio.*

bond buyback The purchase by a company of its own publicly traded bonds at a discount from market price.

This strategy is frequently used when market interest rates are rapidly rising, thereby causing declining bond prices.

bond valuation The process of calculating the true value of a bond by determining the *present value* of a bond's expected future cash flows and the rate of return offered by a comparable investment (that is, the rate of return required by investors).

Bond valuation requires knowledge of three key facts: (1) the amount of cash flow the investor will receive (equal to the total of the bond's periodic interest payments and its face value at maturity); (2) the date the bond matures; and (3) the investors' required rate of return.

bond yield   The return an investor receives on the original bond investment.

Yield is determined by four factors: coupon interest rate, face value, market valuation, and maturity date.

A bond issuer states that a bond will pay a set amount of interest each year, usually in two equal payments per year. The *coupon interest rate* is calculated by dividing these annual payments by the face, or par, value of the bond (usually $1,000). A bond that makes annual interest payments of $160, for example, carries a coupon rate of 16 percent ($160/$1,000 = 0.16). A bond's market value is determined by many factors: whether the bond is a new issue or already in the marketplace; the bond's coupon interest rate; current market rates; market timing; call provisions; and so on.

There are two types of bond yield: current (or simple) yield and yield to maturity. Current yield, which fluctuates according to the bond's market price, represents the interest a bond pays at a particular moment in time. The formula for current yield is as follows:

$$\frac{\text{Coupon interest payment}}{\text{Market price of bond}} = \text{Current yield}$$

If a bond is selling at $877.60, for example, and makes a coupon payment of $80 per bond, its current yield comes to

$$\frac{\$80}{\$877.60} = 0.091, \text{ or } 9.1\%$$

In other words, as long as the price of the bond remains the same, it will pay investors a return of 9.1 percent. Say, though, the price of the bond falls to $700. In that case, the current yield totals

$$\frac{\$80}{\$700} = .114, \text{ or } 11\%$$

Current yield, then, rises as bond prices fall and drops when bond prices climb.

book value (1)   The amount shown for an asset on a balance sheet.

Book value is based on historic cost—that is, the amount that was paid for the asset when it was purchased—and often differs from the market value of a given asset. The book value of a delivery truck, for instance, is the initial cost of the truck less the *accumulated depreciation.*

EXAMPLE: A company purchased a delivery truck three years ago for $5,000. The truck had an estimated useful life of five years, after which it would have no *salvage value.* Under *straight-line depreciation*, the company could write off $1,000 each year. Today, three years later, the truck is on the balance sheet as follows:

Delivery truck	$5,000
Less: accumulated depreciation	3,000
Delivery truck at book value	$2,000

book value (2)   The amount shown as *stockholders' equity* on a balance sheet.

Book value is frequently used as the starting point to negotiate the price for the purchase or sale of a *privately held company*. It is also used to calculate *book value per share.*

book value per share   The assets of a company available to common shareholders.

Book value per share indicates what each share is worth according to the historical stockholders' equity costs maintained in a company's accounting books. Book value per share is calculated as follows:

$$\frac{\text{Total stockholders' equity} - \left(\begin{array}{c}\text{Liquidation value of preferred stocks} \\ + \text{ Preferred dividends}\end{array}\right)}{\text{Common shares outstanding}}$$

In using this formula, it's important to compute an accurate value for the liquidation value of preferred stock. Some companies give holders of preferred stock liquidation premiums that exceed the par value of the preferred shares. These premiums can significantly affect the book value of common stock.

EXAMPLE: Consider the following data:

Total stockholders' equity	$10,000,000
Preferred stock, 8% dividend rate, $20 par value, $25 liquidation value, 200,000 shares outstanding	
Common stock, $40 par value, 100,000 shares outstanding	
Liquidation value of preferred stock (200,000 × $25)	$ 5,000,000
Preferred dividend:	
Par value of preferred stock (200,000 × $20)	$ 4,000,000
Preferred dividend rate	× 8%
Preferred dividend	$ 320,000

The book value of the common stock is

$$\frac{\$10,000,000 - (\$5,000,000 + \$320,000)}{100,000} = \$46.80$$

Book value can also be calculated for preferred stock with the following formula:

$$\frac{\text{Liquidation value of preferred stock} + \text{Preferred dividend}}{\text{Preferred shares outstanding}}$$

In the example above, the book value of preferred stock comes to

$$\frac{\$5,000,000 + \$320,000}{200,000} = \$26.60$$

By comparing book value per share with market price per share, financial analysts can get an indication of how the stock market views a company. Since market price per share is based on current stock prices, it is usually higher than book value per share, which is based on historical prices. If book value per share comes to *less* than the market price per share, that particular stock is probably out of favor with investors.

bookkeeping The process of recording a company's economic transactions in a set of journals and ledgers called books of account.

In the United States, the recording of a transaction *always* includes two postings, one that records the transaction itself and another that describes the transaction, hence the term "double-entry bookkeeping."

The two sides to the entry—the transaction itself and its description— must offset one another so that the net effect on the books of account is zero. That's why double-entry bookkeeping uses **debits** and **credits.** The debit side of an entry always *increases* an **asset** or expense, or *decreases* a **liability, equity** (or net worth), or revenues. For example, when cash is received, it is *debited* to the Cash account—an asset. When goods that were previously sold are returned, the entry *debits* sales.

The complementary side of an entry is a credit. When cash is received and debited to the Cash account, another account must be credited to describe the source of the cash: perhaps Bank Loan, or the payment of a receivable, or the sale of **common stock.** In these cases, the amount equal to the cash received would be *credited* to Bank Loans Payable (increasing a liability), **accounts receivable** (reducing an asset), or Common Stock Outstanding (increasing Net Worth).

Combining the debit and credit sides, the entries would be written as

Dr. (the abbreviation for debit) Cash $X
Cr. (the abbreviation for credit) Banks Loans $X

All books of account, regardless of the type of company or use of a computer, consist of three or more journals—Cash Receipts, Cash Disbursements, and General Journal are the most common—in which transactions are entered and a general ledger, where the monthly totals from the journals are posted. A company may use many subledgers and a variety of journals, but almost every company, regardless of size or accounting system, has at least cash receipts, cash disbursements, general journals, and a general ledger.

borrowing base Company assets used as collateral to secure short-term working capital loans from banks and other lenders.

In most cases, a borrowing base comprises qualified accounts receivable (normally less than 90 days old) and readily salable inventory. Most lenders will not include work-in-process inventory or special materials purchased to customer order in the borrowing base. Although the ratios vary with the nature of the business, the financial strength of the company, and the disposition of the lender, companies can borrow up to 80–85 percent of qualified receivables and 20–50 percent of shelf-item parts and raw materials as well as salable finished goods. The following example demonstrates how a borrowing base works:

	Borrowing Base	Factor	Loan
Qualified accounts receivable	$2,000	85%	$1,700
Raw material and parts inventory	1,000	20%	200
Finished goods inventory	1,500	50%	750
Total short-term loan			$2,650

bottleneck A task or machine speed that limits and therefore determines the capacity of an entire process.

A bottleneck is that task that creates excess capacity in nonbottleneck operations. In a TV assembly operation, the production line assembles 40 sets per hour. The cabinet shop cannot place more than 30 sets in cabinets per hour. Because every set must have a cabinet, the cabinet shop is the bottleneck, limiting capacity to 30 sets per hour and generating excess capacity of 10 sets per hour on the assembly line.

brand A name, term, symbol, or design, or a combination of these elements, that is intended to clearly identify and differentiate a seller's products from competitors' products.

Branding has numerous strategic benefits for marketers. It aids in product *differentiation* by offering the marketer something different to advertise and promote. A company image is often built around its brand. Consider, for example, Green Giant or L'eggs pantyhose. Promoting a particular brand also gives marketers a powerful tool for increasing their *market share.* Campbell Soup Co., for instance, which has an 80 percent share of the canned soup market, benefits from all soup advertising, because of the strong association between its brand and soup. A brand also helps its owner get repeat sales, build loyalty among consumers, and expand a product line (*see* **brand extension**). Procter & Gamble, for instance, relied heavily on its well-known Tide brand when it launched Liquid Tide.

Branding is not without its downside, though. Developing a brand identity is costly; it calls for intensive testing and huge promotional outlays. Moreover, some products—flowers, clothespins, and hamburger, for example—are difficult or impossible to brand because they lack differentiating features. Chiquita and Sunkist have succeeded in creating brands for bananas and oranges, but only through costly promotion and the creation of extensive *quality control* programs to ensure consistent products. Brands can be registered with the federal government and thereby be protected for use within a particular product category. *See also* **brand awareness, brand extension, brand mark, brand name, differentation.**

brand awareness In marketing, a measure of consumers' knowledge that a particular brand exists.

Most marketing professionals consider brand awareness the first step in making a sale. Many marketing campaigns are designed simply to create brand awareness in hope that this effort alone will sell a product.

Example: A camera company has a new type of film that is particularly effective for taking low-light photographs. After an introductory ad campaign, it conducts a follow-up study to see whether the exposure and attention have generated brand awareness. If 80 percent of the market is aware that a low-light film exists, but only 20 percent knows the *brand,* the company might want to adjust its marketing campaign to emphasize the film's *brand name.* In this case, the company created a great deal of product awareness—a high percentage of the market knows that there is a new low-light film—but failed to create a strong brand awareness. *See also* **brand, brand mark, brand name.**

brand extension A marketing strategy that takes the *brand name* of one product category and extends it to another.

Usually the new product category is similar to the old, as when Procter & Gamble extended its Folgers coffee brand to a new decaffeinated coffee or when Nabisco extended its popular Ritz crackers brand to Ritz Bits miniature crackers and Ritz Bits Sandwiches with peanut butter. Sometimes a brand is applied to a completely new product category. Coca-Cola, for example, licensed the use of its name to a clothing line and Spalding extended its brand name from sporting goods to fashionable street clothing and sunglasses in international markets.

Using brand extension has two distinct strategic advantages. The cost of introducing the new product is much lower than launching a wholly new brand, because consumers are already familiar with the name. Advertising and other promotional expenditures are more effective, because they produce greater consumer awareness and recognition for the extended brand. Moreover, because the new product's image is already established, the risk involved in introducing it is reduced. Since developmental costs are reduced, the costs of product failure are lower. Brand extension has a downside, however: A brand extension that flops makes consumers think less of the original brand.

Marketers rely on brand extension more as competition stiffens. They also use it when markets dwindle in order to ignite a new market demand.

EXAMPLE: Prince Manufacturing, the company that fueled the oversized tennis racquet craze, sought growth in a flat market by adding two more Prince racquet lines—one smaller than the standard size and another super-large racquet that has been described as "a garbage can cover."

*See also **brand, brand mark, brand name.***

brand mark The portion of a *brand* in the form of a symbol, design, or distinctive coloring or lettering; also called a logo.

Brand marks create instant recognition for a product and help to differentiate it from competitors'. Brand marks can be registered with the federal government and used on an exclusive basis.

EXAMPLE: The Ralph Lauren Polo horse; the Izod alligator; Charlie, the Star-Kist tuna; Tony the Tiger on Kellogg's Frosted Flakes; the Pillsbury Poppin' Fresh Doughboy. Other examples include the distinctive script of Coca-Cola and the easily recognizable "hot" colors used in the bull's eye that identifies Tide detergent.

*See also **brand, brand name, brand awareness.***

brand name The words, letters, or numbers of a *brand* that can be spoken aloud, such as CBS, 3M, Prell, and Budweiser.

A brand is a combination of graphics and words—the CBS eye, for instance—whereas the brand name—CBS—is just a word or words. Brand names can be registered as ***trademarks*** and protected by the federal government for exclusive use by one marketer. Brand names should be easy to pronounce (Sure deodorant, for example), have some connection with the product (Downy fabric softener), and be memorable (Odor Eaters foot deodorant pads).

It pays to steer clear of geographic terms when selecting a brand name, since, in that case, the law offers no protection against other companies in the same product category using the same name.

EXAMPLE: Three companies now produce "Smithfield Hams." The original company has been doing business in Smithfield, Virginia, since pre-

Revolutionary War days but could not legally protect its name when competitors began producing their own "Smithfield Hams."

Generic terms also make poor choices for brand names. Any word in the dictionary that can be used to describe a product is considered generic and any company can use it.

EXAMPLE: When Miller Brewing Co. introduced "Lite," which is pronounced the same as "light," it was denied exclusive rights to the term, and Anheuser-Busch and Schlitz promptly introduced their own "light" beers.

Some companies eventually find themselves in the unenviable position of having their brand name *become* a generic term. Band-Aid, Xerox, and Kleenex are all generic terms, which means that, for instance, consumers often believe that Puffs and Scotties are brands of Kleenex. When brands become generic, promotion of the brand can lead to sales of similar but competing brands.

Marketers of brands can use a manufacturer's brand alone, a distributor's brand alone, or a combination of both. They can also choose among a family brand, an individual brand, or a generic brand strategy. Marketers who sell more than one item and use the same brand name for all their products—General Electric, for instance—are using a family brand strategy. Companies relying on distributor's brands include Sears, which uses the Kenmore name for its appliances, and A&P, which brands its food products Ann Page.

Marketers use an individual brand strategy when they apply each brand name to only one product. Procter & Gamble, for instance, markets Tide detergent, Crest toothpaste, and Ivory dishwashing soap. Companies often employ this strategy when their products vary in quality and type, because it allows them to target each brand to a particular segment of the market. Sometimes a company uses family and individual brands together.

EXAMPLE: Pillsbury markets its Pillsbury's Best flour, biscuits, and cake mixes, but it also uses the Hungry Jack brand for another line of biscuits and for pancakes and waffle mixes.

Marketers use a generic brand strategy for products when consumers perceive little difference between the offerings of different companies (*see commodity*). Examples include frozen peas, chlorine, toilet tissue, and canned fruits and vegetables. Generic branding was strategically successful during the inflationary 1970s, but its impact and effectiveness has declined significantly in recent years. *See also* **brand, brand awareness, brand mark.**

brand-switching matrix A table that shows the purchasing patterns of a group of customers over two fixed time periods and highlights the switches they made between brands.

Shampoo company A, for example, might want to see how its brand fared against competitors B and C between July and August.

		Switched to (August)		
		A	**B**	**C**
Switched from	**A**	60%	20%	20%
(July)	**B**	19%	31%	50%
	C	5%	45%	50%

Brand switching matrix

Of the consumers who purchased shampoo A in July (reading horizontally on the graph), 60 percent purchased it again in August, 20 percent switched to shampoo B, and 20 percent switched to shampoo C. The diagonal line from upper left to lower right shows each brand's repeat purchase rate, which can be interpreted as brand loyalty. In this case, brand A had a repeat purchase rate of 60 percent, brand B of 31 percent, and brand C of 50 percent.

The numbers from left to right indicate the switching-in and switching-out rate for each brand. In our example, 20 percent of brand A's July sales went to both brand B and brand C in August; 50 percent of brand B's July sales went to brand C, and only 19 percent went to brand A in August; 45 percent of brand C's July sales went to brand B, with only 5 percent switching to brand A in August. So the matrix indicates that shampoo A, although it has high brand loyalty, is not taking many customers away from competitors.

breakeven analysis The calculation of the point at which sales revenue equals total production costs.

This results in neither a profit nor a loss. In order to conduct a breakeven analysis, both the *fixed costs* and *variable costs* of a product must be known. Fixed costs are those expenses, such as rent, insurance, and management salaries, that remain relatively constant regardless of the number of units produced. Variable costs are expenses, such as raw materials, utilities, and labor, that change directly with the amount of units produced.

Breakeven is calculated as

$$U = \frac{NP + FC}{SP - VC}$$

where

SP = selling price

U = number of units sold

VC = variable cost per unit

FC = fixed cost

NP = net profit (usually set at zero)

EXAMPLE: Say a company manufacturing office furniture wants to market a new filing cabinet. The cabinet will be priced at $190. The variable costs, that is, labor, energy, wood, metal, paint, and hardware, are estimated at $110 per filing cabinet. The company's annual fixed costs, that is, insurance, property taxes, administrative salaries, rent, and interest on borrowed money, total $1.6 million.

When net profit (NP) is set at zero, the breakeven point is

$$U = \frac{0 + \$1,600,00}{\$190 - \$110}$$

$$= 20,000 \text{ units}$$

In other words, the furniture manufacturer must sell 20,000 filing cabinets in order to cover its costs. If the sales forecast for the filing cabinet is 20,000 or greater, the company will probably not lose money on the venture. If sales are expected to be under 20,000 units, the company would be well advised to reconsider.

Breakeven analysis can also be used to determine the number of units that must be sold in order to meet a fixed profit goal. Say the furniture manufacturer wants a net profit of $500,000 from the new filing cabinet. By plugging this figure into the breakeven formula (NP = $500,000), management can determine that 26,250 units must be sold in order to meet the goal.

budget deficit and debt The excess in the *flow* of federal expenditure over revenue and the accumulated deficits.

The federal government has spent more than it has received in revenues in all but six years in the period since 1940 (1947–1948, 1951, 1956–1957, and 1960).

The federal budget deficit represents the shortfall in savings in the federal government sector. When the federal government runs a deficit (the usual state), other sector(s)—households, businesses, state and local governments, or foreign lenders—must make up the difference. The deficit can be exacerbated by cyclical forces. When the economy is in recession, tax receipts decline, expenditures—on unemployment insurance, welfare assistance, and other antirecession programs—increase, and so the deficit widens. The secular or structural deficit is the shortfall, exclusive of cyclical effects. The table below shows the budget position (a minus indicates a deficit) and debt levels for selected years since 1945 in billions of dollars.

Fiscal year	Budget balance	Gross debt
1945	−48.7	260.1
1950	−4.7	256.9
1955	−4.1	274.4
1960	0.5	290.5
1965	−1.6	322.3
1970	−8.7	380.9
1975	−55.3	541.9
1980	−72.7	908.5
1985	−221.7	1,817.0
1990	−278.0	3,206.3
1991	−321.7	3,599.0
1992	−340.3	4,002.7

buffer stock Any goods that are set aside in order to protect against uncertainties of supply or demand; also called safety stocks.

Buffer stock is normally carried to compensate for increases in demand over the reorder lead time or increases in the reorder lead time itself. It "buffers" the company during periods when control over inventory levels is minimal. The amount of *inventory* in excess of the average demand requirement is usually considered buffer inventory.

EXAMPLE: A shoe manufacturer might have a buffer inventory of leather. This guards against the possibility that a leather shortage or problem with a supplier will stop production. The company might also keep a buffer inventory of shoes to guard against the possibility that a sudden surge in demand will leave the company without any merchandise to sell.

Work-in-process buffer inventories (called decoupling inventories) are also frequently maintained in order to adjust for variability between the capacities of the various operations in a process.

EXAMPLE: A TV producer makes 60 units per hour. The placement of the chassis in the cabinet is limited to 20 per hour. The producer must run the cabinet operation on the three-shift basis. The daily build-up of 320 units (480 − 160 = 320) is a buffer inventory.

See also *inventory functions, work-in-process inventory*.

bundling The grouping of several products into one package.

For example, in a situation where it is expensive to identify and begin relationships with new customers, bundling might provide a way to absorb that cost over a variety of products or services. This can, however, lead to a situation where it is difficult to identify exactly which products within the bundle are actually profitable and which are not. Close analysis often shows that the elements of the bundle that are not profitable are usually subsidized by the profitable elements.

By bundling products, companies can often reduce the *buyer power* of their customers. For example, a computer company might include a software package and maintenance agreement along with a computer. This makes it difficult for the buyer to determine the true cost of each element in the bundle, so price comparisons between competitors are effectively reduced. Bundling is often appealing to buyers, despite the loss of buying power, because it offers the convenience of purchasing a group of products from a single supplier rather than going to several different sources.

Companies that bundle their products can be threatened by highly focused firms that specialize in a particular product or service within the bundle. For example, brokerage firms, which typically bundle research, market advice, and actual transactions, face a serious threat from discount brokers that simply execute transactions. Discount brokers allow investors who are not interested in research or advice to simply make their transactions without paying for any other services.

business combination The process of associating two or more different companies.

There are three forms of business combination: statutory merger, statutory consolidation, and acquisition. The differences between these three combinations is primarily a function of the legal nature of the resulting combined company.

A statutory merger occurs when two separate companies combine in such a way that one of the companies will no longer exist. This combination is best expressed by the equation

$$X + Y = X$$

A statutory consolidation occurs when two or more separate companies combine in such a way that both companies no longer exist and a new company is formed. This type of combination is best expressed by the equation

$$X + Y = XY$$

An acquisition occurs when two separate companies combine in such a way that both keep their legal identities. This type of combination is best expressed by the equation

$$X + Y = X + Y$$

business cycle The recurring pattern of macroeconomic activity and industry trends that affects the expansion or contraction of markets, a company's sales, inflation, employment, market interest rates, financial market share prices, and so on.

The U.S. economy has grown in fits and starts, particularly in the post-World War II era. Since the end of World War II, eight cycles have been identified and, on average, the overall economy has expanded for 50 months and contracted for 11 months.

A complete cycle can be measured in two ways. The first is from a peak in economic activity through a recession to its trough, through the ensuing recovery back to the "past peak" level in activity, and then through the expansion to a new peak. Alternatively, the cycle can be measured from the trough—at the end of a recession—through the recovery to the past peak, through the expansion to a new peak, and then through the new recession to a fresh trough.

Many economic activities are classified by their cyclical characteristics. For example, consumer spending for durable goods is considered *procyclical;* spending falls off more than proportionately to the decline in economic activity during recessions and outperforms the overall economy in recovery. In addition, some activities, such as housing permits, the stock market, and orders for durable goods, *lead* the economy at cyclical turning points (peaks and troughs), whereas others—the unemployment rate, inventory investment—*lag* behind the overall economy. Still others, such as industrial production, personal income, and employment, are *coincident* with overall economic activity.

An understanding of both macroeconomic and industry business cycles is essential for projecting the results of a company's operations and, hence, its internal pricing and employment policies, as well as its financing options.

business process reengineering The radical redesign of an organization's operations and management to achieve strategic breakthroughs.

It is the means by which an organization can achieve radical change in performance as measured by cost, cycle time, service, and quality, by the application of a variety of tools and techniques that focus on the business as a set of related customer-oriented core business processes rather than a set of organizational functions.

A core business process, as distinct from other processes, is a set of linked activities that both crosses functional boundaries and, when carried out in concert, addresses the needs and expectations of the marketplace and drives the organization's capabilities. Reengineering of these core business processes takes place when operational, technical, and business knowledge are used in a unified way in order to achieve sustainable competitive advantage.

Some people confuse a core business process with a core technology. For instance, if you ask an electronics company executive to describe a core process, he will likely say "board stuffing." This is, in fact, a core technology—every electronics company must stuff boards, or get a subcontractor to stuff boards, in order to build product. But board stuffing is not a core process in the way that, say, maintenance of the supply chain is for the automotive industry. There is really no ability for an electronics manufacturer to differentiate or create market advantage based on its ability to stuff boards. Board stuffing is, in fact, a price of admission.

But reengineering the supply chain process in, for example, the automotive industry could lead to staggering changes in market dynamics, and is thus a core process. The manufacturer of catalytic converters discovered an opportunity to reduce the cost of goods by 41 percent and reduce a 250-day inventory float that existed because an OEM mismanaged the supply chain.

One way to think about the differentiation between core business processes and core technologies is that a core business process combines both physical activity—the heart of core technology—with information flow, and addresses the needs and desires of the marketplace.

A limited number of core business processes—usually no more than half a dozen or so—can be identified in any company or industry, and enhancing any of those processes can lead to business improvement. (*Source:* H. Johnnsson, P. McHugh, A. Pendlebury, W. Wheeler, *Business Process Reengineering,* Copyright © 1993 John Wiley & Sons, Inc. Reprinted with permission.)

business strategy *See corporate strategy*

buyer power The ability of buyers to pressure a company to reduce its prices.

This has a direct effect on the company's profit margin. When buyer power is high, margins are reduced. Conversely, when buyer power is reduced, margins increase.

In order to develop a strategy for reducing buyer power, it is necessary to first identify its source. Buyer power is usually high in situations where (1) there are few buyers, (2) buyers are well informed about other products available on the market, (3) the costs of switching from one product to another is low, (4) buyers can pursue a strategy of *backward integration* and manufacture the product in-house, (5) the product is a substantial portion of the buyers' costs, (6) the seller competes on a cost basis, and (7) the seller is not profitable.

When companies are overly selective in terms of choosing their customers (for example, refusing to accept small orders or service customers beyond a well-defined geographic area), the buyer power of the remaining customers is increased. It is important to consider the trade-offs between the expenses involved in servicing smaller or more distant customers and the increase in buyer power (and possible decrease in profit margin) involved in servicing a small number of large customers.

Many companies reduce the buyer power of their customers by *bundling* their products into groups. For example, an equipment manufacturer might include an agreement to supply spare parts and maintenance along with the sale of a piece of machinery. This forces the customer to rely on the equipment company for services beyond the delivery of a machine and makes it difficult for the customer to threaten to switch to another equipment supplier.

Other actions that can reduce buyer power include strong product differentiation, which positions a product or service as unique in the marketplace; the establishment of multiple contacts with key customers, such as both purchasing agents and factory managers within the buying company, which makes it more difficult to switch products; financing customer purchase; and creating an inventory control system for a customer that automatically replenishes supplies. *See also five forces model, supplier power.*

buying decision process   In marketing, the method by which consumers decide to make a purchase.

The process is often divided into five stages: problem recognition, information search, evaluation of alternatives, purchase decision, and postpurchase behavior. This perspective allows marketers to focus on elements other than just the purchase decision when developing a sales campaign.

EXAMPLE: The entire cycle can easily be seen when a consumer makes a major purchase, such as a computer. In the first stage, a college freshman, John, realizes that the amount of work he has to do is no longer appropriate for a typewriter. Having recognized the problem, he visits several computer stores and gathers information about different models and capabilities (stage 2). With this information in hand, he compares different models and decides which one to buy (stage 3). Finally, John buys the computer (stage 4) and, by purchasing accessories, software, and service, indicates that his purchase was satisfactory (stage 5).

The stage or stages on which the marketer focuses determine the thrust of the sales campaign.

EXAMPLE: A computer company might encourage problem recognition by placing an advertisement in a college newspaper to highlight the amount of typing an average college student does during a semester. It may focus on the information search stage by developing brochures and pamphlets describing its computers and distributing the material on campus and at local electronics stores. If the company decides to target students who are evaluating computing alternatives, the company might focus on personal selling or run an advertising campaign comparing its computers to other models on the market. After students have made their purchase decision, the computer company can emphasize customer service and make sure its computers are widely available, perhaps even selling them through college bookstores. It can then influence postpurchase behavior by creating a mailing list and periodically sending customers new product catalogs and news on how to upgrade their computers.

buying roles The five different roles involved in the exchange process. These roles are as follows:

Initiator: The person who first recognizes an unsatisfied need or want

Influencer: The person who provides information on how to satisfy that need or want

Decider: The person who finally selects an alternative

Buyer: The purchaser of the product

Consumer: The one who uses the product

CAD *See computer-aided design*

CAE *See computer-aided engineering*

call feature An element of the agreement made between a *bond* issuer and a buyer that stipulates a time and price at which the issuer may repurchase the bond before it matures; also called a call provision.

Long-term corporate and municipal bonds usually have a 10-year call feature. When interest rates are falling, many companies and municipalities exercise the call options so they can repurchase older, higher-interest bonds and then issue new bonds at a lower interest rate. The call price of a bond—the price the issuer pays to redeem it—is usually higher than the bond's face value. The difference between the call price and the bond's face value is called the call premium—the amount the issuer pays for the privilege of repurchasing the bond early. If a bond is called in its first year, the call premium usually equals one year's interest. As bonds get closer to maturity, the call premium declines.

CAM *See computer-aided manufacturing*

camera-ready Description of an advertisement that is ready for reproduction in the printing process.

Every advertisement must be camera-ready before it goes to the printer. In an *advertising agency*, the art department puts together the camera-ready ad.

cannibalization The reduction in the sales of a product caused by the introduction of another similar product by the same company.

Cannibalization usually occurs when the market for a product is relatively static. For example, say a snack food company that has a successful line of potato chips decides to introduce a new corn chip. It is very likely that the corn chip's success might be due to potato chip customers who switch to the new chip. This strategy is effective when (1) the new chip takes market share away from competitors as well as from the established potato chip, and (2) the total sales and profitability of both the potato and the corn chips are significantly higher than the sales and profitability of the potato chips alone.

capacity A measure of the output of an organization.

Capacity measures come in several forms. An organization or plant has a technical or design capacity; a steel mill can operate on 21 turns or work shifts per week. Placing that sort of strain on the equipment will hasten a breakdown, yet technically it is possible. Capacity can also be measured by economic capacity. That same mill may operate 19 turns per week with two turns reserved for maintenance. The lost production of those turns is compensated for by reduced wear and tear on equipment and fewer shutdowns. Economic capacity can also be achieved by employing only the most efficient or lowest-cost resources.

The steel mill can raise its capacity by employing inefficient assets. Capacity is raised, but the marginal cost of the output may be high. Expansion of capacity by excessive overuse cannot be sustained over long periods.

Different industries use different measures to reflect capacity; hospitals use bed days, steel mills use tons of steel. Each organization has a set of operating conditions that define that capacity.

capital (1) The amount on the balance sheet that represents ownership in a business; also called *equity* or net worth.

Capital is the difference between *assets* and *liabilities*. In a corporation, capital equals stockholders' equity.

EXAMPLE: A small company prepared the following balance sheet:

Assets		Liabilities and owner's equity	
Cash	$5,500	Accounts payable	$3,800
Accounts receivable	900	Total current liabilities	$3,800
Inventory	2,300		
Prepaid expenses	600	Debt payable	3,000
Total current assets	$9,300	Total liabilities	$6,800
Machinery	2,500	Owners' equity	$5,600
Automobile	1,200		
Less accumulated depreciation	(600)		
	$3,100	Total liabilities and owner's	
Total assets	$12,400	equity	$12,400

In this company, capital is listed as owners' equity on the balance sheet at $5,600. It is calculated by subtracting total liabilities ($6,800) from total assets ($12,400).

capital (2) Available funds or cash, as in *working capital*, or financing, as in "raising capital."

A company can raise capital by taking on *short-term debt* and/or long-term debt as well as by issuing new *common stock* or *preferred stock*.

capital asset An asset purchased for use rather than resale.

Capital assets include (1) land, buildings, plant, and equipment; (2) patents, *goodwill,* and *trademarks;* and (3) investments in *subsidiary companies* and *affiliated companies.*

capital asset pricing model (CAPM) Part of the larger *capital market theory* that attempts to quantify investment risk.

Under CAPM, systematic risk is measured by a statistical factor labeled "beta," which is the mathematical expression of the relationship between the return on an individual security and the return on the market as a whole. The market return is measured by a market index, such as the Dow Jones Industrial Average or the Standard & Poor's 500 Composite Stock Price Index. In other words, beta measures the volatility of a given security against market averages. The CAPM theory completely ignores "unsystematic risk" as does its parent, the capital market theory.

The assumptions underlying the CAPM theory are as follows:

- All investors are risk-averse (i.e., they require a premium kicker for an investment that does not have a guaranteed return).
- Investors will hold diversified portfolios.
- All investors have identical holding periods.
- All investors have identical expectations about rates of return and capitalization rates.
- No transactions costs will be incurred.
- There is no tax impact.
- The rate received for lending money is the same as the cost of borrowing money.
- The market has perfect divisibility and liquidity.

In practice, of course, none of these assumptions is true. Pragmatically, any mathematical calculation must of necessity be based on standard, assumed-perfect conditions. However, any meaningful business valuation must include "unsystematic risk" in determining discount factors. For these reasons, neither the CAPM theory nor the broader capital market theory completely satisfies investment valuation requirements.

capital flight A term used to describe the movement of capital out of or into a given market.

Capital moved out of Mexico and other Latin American countries to the United States during the "lost decade" of the 1980s. In recent years much of the capital has returned to its original markets as democratic governments began conversions to free-market economies.

Capital is by definition very mobile, especially with instantaneous computer transfers around the world. An axiom of financial markets is that "capital will always fly to the highest-return, most-secure investments."

capital lease A lease in which the lessee acquires substantial property rights.

If any of the following conditions exists when the lease is signed, the lease must be considered a capital lease and disclosed in the *financial statements:* (1) Payments for the exclusive use of the asset approximate the asset's fair market value, (2) the lessee has sole access to the asset for all or a substantial part of its useful life, (3) the lessee can buy the asset at a discounted price at the end of the lease period, or (4) the lessee holds proof of ownership, such as legal title to the asset.

For accounting purposes, a capital lease is considered an installment purchase of an asset. So on the *balance sheet,* the asset is listed both as an *intangible asset* (that is, the rights to the leased asset) and as a *liability* (that is, the obligation to make lease payments). Similarly, both depreciation and interest expenses on the lease obligation must be disclosed on the *income statement.* Also, the disclosure of lease payments must show both the current (that is, due within one year) and the noncurrent (that is, due more than a year from the statement date) portions of the lease obligation on the balance sheet.

If none of the four conditions for a capital lease are met, the lease is considered an operating lease. That means any mention of it as an asset or obligation for future payments is disclosed in the footnotes to a company's financial statements.

capital market theory Comprises a set of complex mathematical formulas that strives to identify how investors should choose common stocks for their portfolios under a given set of assumptions.

Focused on publicly traded stocks, it has no direct bearing on valuing closely held companies; however, several intuitive segments of the theory are relevant. One of the easiest to understand is the determination of required rates of return for different levels of risk.

The capital market theory defines rate of return as the total return, including dividends, interest income, cash distributions and the appreciation of an asset's market value. The concept can be expressed in the formula

$$\text{Return} = \frac{\text{Ending price} - \text{Beginning price} + \text{Cash distributions}}{\text{Beginning price}}$$

Assume you bought an equity interest in ABC Corp. for $100,000 and held it for five years. Annual dividends of $5,000 total $25,000 over the five-year period. In year six, you sell the shares for $200,000. Your rate of return would be calculated as

$$R = \frac{\$200,000 - \$100,000 + \$25,000}{\$100,000} = 125\% = 25\% \text{ per year}$$

Although discount factors could be applied to the five-year income stream to quantify risk, the capital market theory approaches risk from a slightly different angle. It segregates risk into two components: market risk and investment risk.

"Systematic risk" is the term applied to market risk—that is, the uncertainty of future returns caused by movements in the market as a whole. "Unsystematic risk" refers to uncertainty resulting from characteristics of the individual firm, the industry, and the type of investment (e.g., minority versus controlling, equity versus debt). Total risk is the sum of systematic and unsystematic risks.

The capital market theory assumes that the required investment premium is limited to systematic risk. On the surface, this makes little sense. In closely held companies, particularly small businesses, unsystematic risk associated with management skills, product line acceptability, market position, and so on deserves far more weight than stock market movements. However, since the capital market theory was developed to value publicly traded issues, it assumes that investors have the ability to hold widely diversified portfolios, thereby eliminating or minimizing the risk attached to any specific investment.

capital markets   Markets where corporate stocks and long-term debt are traded.

The classic example of a capital market is the New York Stock Exchange, which trades the stocks and bonds of many large companies. Securities that are not sold on an organized stock exchange are said to be sold over-the-counter. Two separate categories exist within the capital market: the primary market and the secondary market. The primary market involves the sale of new issues of securities. The secondary market involves the trading of previously issued securities (which originated in the primary market). *See also* **money markets.**

capital stock (1)   In finance, the shares representing the ownership of a company.

A company's articles of incorporation establish the number and types of shares of stock that the company may issue. This information is usually called the *authorized capital stock* and is also shown in a company's **annual report.** When stock is sold, it is called *issued capital stock.* Issued capital stock that remains in the hands of stockholders (rather than being repurchased by the company as **treasury stock**) is categorized as *outstanding.*

Capital stock, as a rule, grants its owners four privileges: (1) a portion of the business profits, (2) a claim on the company's assets if it goes out of business, (3) the right to vote on management, and (4) the right to maintain proportionate ownership in the event of additional stock issues.

capital stock (2) In economics, the physical, nonhuman, but reusable, inputs to production (raw materials can be used only once).

The capital stock reflects the accumulated *investment*, net of replacement. (Replacement investment is undertaken to replace worn-out or obsolete capital and thus does not add to the stock of the capital; it merely maintains it.) Indeed, investment is undertaken in order to increase the capital stock.

The application of capital in production is the main source of productivity growth. The more capital labor has to work with, the greater the growth in output per hour worked (productivity). The capital stock grows slowly, reflecting the net increase due to investment less depreciation. The table below contrasts the level of the nonresidential (business) capital stock and nonresidential fixed investment since 1980, in billions of 1987 dollars.

Year	Capital stock	Fixed investment
1980	3,677.4	437.8
1981	3,810.6	455.0
1982	3,900.6	433.9
1983	3,970.2	420.8
1984	4,096.8	490.2
1985	4,247.8	521.8
1986	4,361.5	500.3
1987	4,457.1	497.8
1988	4,561.9	530.8
1989	4,672.9	540.0
1990	4,772.7	538.1
1991	4,824.4	500.2

capital structure The *common stock, preferred stock,* long-term debt, and *retained earnings* a company maintains in order to finance its *assets.*

Not everyone agrees that long-term debt should be included in a company's capital structure. Proponents say that it is used to finance long-term assets; opponents maintain that it is simply a liability that is due to creditors and should not be included with the other forms of *capital.*

capitalize To classify an expense as an asset because it benefits the company for more than one year.

EXAMPLE: A company, ABC Inc., is building a new warehouse. ABC will capitalize the labor costs, and they will be considered part of the value of the asset when it is listed on the *balance sheet.*

CAPM *See capital asset pricing model*

carrying costs The expenses a company incurs when it holds inventories; also called holding costs.

As *inventory* grows, carrying costs become higher. Carrying costs include storage costs, insurance, taxes, and interest on money that would have been otherwise invested if it were not tied up in inventory.

cartel   A group of sellers in a particular market that has banded together in order to influence the price by controlling the market supply.

Cartels are illegal in the United States. However, they are not illegal in world markets. The most famous cartel is the Organization of Petroleum Exporting Countries (OPEC).

By acting together to restrict the supply of a product, a cartel seeks to raise the price or at least keep the price from falling. The major assumption behind this move is that the demand for the product being sold is price inelastic. In the case of the OPEC cartel, this proved to be the case in the short run. However, over time, people began finding ways to use less oil by substituting more fuel-efficient cars and machinery, by holding their thermostats at lower levels, and by changing their general pattern of energy consumption. Thus, over the long run, the demand for oil turned out to be much more elastic than OPEC originally anticipated. This proves the point that even cartels can have a difficult time overcoming market forces.

cash basis accounting   The opposite of *accrual accounting.*

Under cash basis accounting, sales are recorded when cash is received for goods and services; expenses are recorded when they are paid. Cash basis accounting does not use *accounts receivable, accounts payable,* and accrued expenses.

Frequently, small businesses, especially small service businesses, use cash basis accounting or, more commonly, a hybrid of cash basis and accrual accounting. In a hybrid system, *inventory* is recorded on the *balance sheet* when it is paid for and written off to the *income statement* as items are sold. Tangible *assets,* such as equipment, are recorded on the balance sheet when they are paid for and depreciated. Bank loans and *long-term debt* are recorded on the balance sheet when cash is received and reduced as payments are made against the debts. Generally, all other cost and expense items are recorded directly to the income statement when they are paid for.

The *Securities and Exchange Commission (SEC)* doesn't allow public companies to use cash basis accounting or hybrid systems. Nor is cash basis accounting considered a *generally accepted accounting principle* (GAAP). The IRS, however, does permit cash basis accounting and hybrid methods for tax returns. *Compare to accrual accounting.*

cash cow   A company or product that generates cash.

The term was coined by the Boston Consulting Group as an element of its *growth/market share matrix.* Cash cows often enjoy a large market share and a strong competitive position in mature markets.

Since cash cows generally have dominant market positions, their total output is larger than that of competitors with smaller market shares. In becoming the dominant force in a market, cash cows are further along the *learning curve* than competitors, which results in lower average costs per unit. The combination of a large market share and low unit costs results in high profits and cash. In a mature market, a company with a dominant position has little need to reinvest profits and cash in projects designed to increase market share, such as aggressive marketing and advertising. Rather, the cash can be used to pay dividends, finance research and development, cover debt, and finance the development of new products or services.

It is important, however, not to simply treat a cash cow as a source of funds. Competition is often keen in a mature market, and a cash cow must be an active participant. Frequently cash cows are prematurely written off as active companies and are simply milked dry. *See also* **growth/market share matrix.**

cash dividend The money a company pays to its stockholders.

Cash dividends are usually calculated and reported on a dollar-and-cents per share basis for **common stock** and as a fixed percentage of par value (or dividend rate) for **preferred stock.**

EXAMPLE: A company has 10,000 outstanding shares of common stock and declares a $1 per share dividend for a total dividend payment of $10,000 (10,000 shares × $1). If the company also had 5,000 outstanding shares of preferred stock with a par value of $10 and a dividend rate of 7 percent, the cash dividend would total

$$
\begin{array}{rl}
5,000 & \text{shares} \\
\underline{\times \quad \$10} & \text{par value} \\
\$50,000 & \text{total par value} \\
\\
\underline{\times \quad .07} & \text{dividend rate} \\
\underline{\$3,500} & \text{cash dividend}
\end{array}
$$

cash equivalent Any asset, such as *marketable securities* held as an investment, that can easily and quickly be converted to cash.

All cash equivalents are considered current assets and are reported as such on the balance sheet.

cash flow The cash receipts less the cash disbursements from a given operation or asset for a particular period of time.

EXAMPLE: Over the period of a month, a company makes $2,000 in cash sales and pays $500 in wages, $700 for inventory, and $75 for office supplies.

Its cash flow for the period is calculated as follows:

Sales	$2,000
Less:	
Inventory	700
Wages	500
Office supplies	75
Cash flow	$ 725

cash flow statement *See statement of cash flows*

cash-to-current-liabilities ratio A ratio that measures a company's ability to pay short-term financial obligations with the cash it has on hand.

A ratio of 1 means that for every dollar a company has in short-term obligations, it has a dollar in cash on hand. A ratio much higher than 1 could indicate that a company is not actively investing its cash. The ratio is calculated by dividing the balance sheet amounts for *cash, cash equivalents,* and *marketable securities* by *current liabilities.*

$$\frac{\text{Cash + Cash equivalents + Marketable securities}}{\text{Current liabilities}}$$

See also acid-test ratio, current ratio.

causal research In *marketing research,* a project designed to help marketers understand cause-and-effect relationships.

Causal studies usually involve some type of experiment.

EXAMPLE: Information Resources BehaviorScan is a research company with facilities in several small cities. In each city, the company collects data on customer purchases for 2,500 households that also have cable television service. On the basis of their purchase behavior, certain households receive specific television commercials, whereas others do not. The company then monitors the household's subsequent buying behavior to see if the commercials influenced their future purchases.

See also marketing research. Compare to descriptive research, experimental research, exploratory research, observational research.

CD *See creative director*

cellular production A configuration of the production process based on the creation of distinct *cells* that contain all of human skills and equipment needed for groups of products or services that require similar processing steps.

Cellular production is a relatively new development that has become very popular. It offers the high variety of *outputs* available from a *job process system* and the lower costs and short response times of flow production.

When organizing a cellular production system, the range of a company's products or services is broken into groups that require similar processing steps. This is called the classification process. Groups can be created a number of different ways, such as equipment needed, size of the equipment, labor skills required, or quality requirements.

EXAMPLE: A sporting goods manufacturer might divide its output according to the type of equipment needed into three groups: racquets, such as tennis, racquetball, and squash; inflatable balls, such as footballs, soccer balls, and volleyballs; and noninflatable balls, such as golf balls and baseballs. Each group is then assigned a cell.

Usually, the classification process is not as clear-cut as in the example above. There might be a product or two that does not fit well in any of the cells (golf clubs, for example). When this is the case, the leftover outputs are assigned to a "remainder" cell, which is usually operated with a job process. In the main cells, since the products are all similar, the equipment in each cell can be set up to produce the entire group and does not have to be reconfigured for another type of output, as is necessary in a job process system. Some cells can produce an entire group of products or services with a single machine, whereas other cells may have dozens of machines and employ as many as 50 people.

Usually, different cells are managed as independent teams. In other words, the members of each cell team are responsible for conducting, scheduling, and inspecting their own work. Teamwork is a key advantage of cellular production over the more conventional job and flow production methods. In a flow shop, there is little teamwork because the equipment does most of the work, as in an automobile factory or a car wash. Individual employees are responsible for their own small part of the job without taking part in the overall process. Job shops, such as an automobile repair shop or a hospital, are organized by departments, which does create a sense of teamwork, but not in terms of specific jobs. Usually everyone is working on a different task. In cellular production, all employees are totally responsible for every aspect of a job. This creates a working environment that by encouraging communication and team building, provides challenges to meet deadlines and create quality outputs.

Converting to cellular production is usually a relatively inexpensive process. Although some cells may require special equipment, the cell form does not usually call for additional investments, only that the equipment be moved into the appropriate cell. In cases where the equipment simply cannot be moved, cellular production can still be implemented by designating the equipment as a part of a particular cell. This is called a virtual cell since the equipment is not physically a part of a cell, but it is used exclusively by one cell team.

*See also **job process system.***

Central Bank The national bank at the apex of a national banking system.

In the United States it is the Federal Reserve Bank, in Great Britain the Bank of England, in Japan the Bank of Japan, in Germany the Bundesbank, and so on. In the United States, the central bank acts independently of federal fiscal policy. The Treasury determines the division of government finance between taxation and government debt issues; the central bank determines whether the private sector will hold government-issued interest-bearing paper that cannot be used to purchase goods and services, or whether it will hold non–interest-bearing coins and currency. Central banks also have the authority to alter the amount of government securities held in the private sector by engaging in open market trading.

Central banks originate and control their respective national monetary policies. They influence the growth of money and credit and the level of interest rates on short-term securities. Central banks attempt to influence long-term economic growth through the control of the aggregate demand for money. Their principal method for achieving this is to convince the private sector that central banks view price stability as a prominent, long-range objective and that bank policies reflect that objective.

certainty equivalents In corporate finance, a method of comparing the value of two investments with difficult risk levels.

The goal is to determine the point at which an investor is indifferent to choosing between the certain return of a safe investment or the expected return of a riskier investment.

EXAMPLE: A company's financial manager can invest in junk bonds with a forecasted one-year return of $1,000 or put a portion of the company's money in U.S. Treasuries that have a certain cash flow of $800. The manager wants to know what the return must be from the riskier investment in order to equal the 6 percent rate paid by the risk-free investment.

In order to calculate the different return rates for the two investments, the manager must first calculate the *present value* of the safe (or risk-free) investment. Assume that the risk-free rate (r_f) comes to 6 percent. The formula for finding the present value of this safe investment (in other words, the point of indifference) is

$$\frac{CE_1}{1 + r_f} = \text{PV of expected \$1,000 return}$$

$$\frac{\$800}{1.06} = \text{PV of expected \$1,000 return}$$

$$\text{PV} = \$754.72$$

Once the present value of the point of indifference is known, the formula can be expanded in order to determine the rate required by the risky investment.

$$\frac{CE_1}{1 + r_f} = \frac{C_1}{1 + r_r} = \text{PV of expected \$1,000 return}$$

where

CE$_1$ = certainty of equivalent of the risky investment C$_1$

r_f = risk-free rate

PV   = present value

C$_1$ = return on the risky investment

r_r = risk-adjusted rate (the required return of the risky investment)

The required rate of return (that is, the return at which the manager will be indifferent to the two investments) for the risky investment can then be calculated:

$$\frac{\$800}{1.06} = \text{PV of expected \$1,000 return}$$

$$\text{PV} = \$754.72$$

and

$$\frac{\$1,000}{1 + r_r} = \$754.72$$

$$r_r = 0.32, \text{or } 32\%$$

In other words, the risky investment (which has a present value of $754.72) must pay a 32 percent return in order to be equivalent to the 6 percent return of the risk-free investment. The certainty equivalent method works best when the financial manager knows exactly what trade-offs he or she is willing to make (in this case, a certain $800 for a risky $1,000). Otherwise, the risk-adjusted *discount rate* would be a more appropriate method for comparing investments.

certified public accountant (CPA)   A title given to accountants who pass the Uniform CPA Examination administered by the *American Institute of Certified Public Accountants* and who satisfy the experience requirements of a given state (New York, for example, requires all CPAs to have two years of public accounting experience).

CPAs are licensed to issue an *audit opinion* on a company's financial statements.

CFO   *See chief financial officer*

change in accounting estimate   A revision of an accounting forecast or assumption.

> EXAMPLE: A company purchased factory equipment five years ago that had an estimated useful life of eight years. The company now decides that the equipment will last for another five years. That means the company must report the new, longer life of the equipment in its financial statements as a change in accounting estimate. Changes in accounting estimate are shown over current and future years. The company does not restate the years before the change.

*See also **accounting change**. Compare to **change in accounting principle**.*

change in accounting principle   A switch from one accounting principle to another.

> EXAMPLE: A company moves from **straight-line depreciation** to **sum-of-the-years'-digits method**, so it must show the effect of the change in the current year's financial statements. A change in accounting principle usually manifests itself on the income statement in an entry called **cumulative effect of a change in accounting principle**. Some changes in accounting principle, such as a new pronouncement by the **Financial Accounting Standards Board (FASB)**, require a restatement of previous year's financial statements in order to show what the effect would have been if the new principle had been applied for those years.

*See also **accounting change**. Compare to **change in accounting estimate**.*

Chapter 11   The dominant form of bankruptcy for businesses, especially for companies with a large work force and numerous **assets**.

A Chapter 11 reorganization attempts to preserve the going concern value of a business by allowing it to operate, usually without a trustee, while management negotiates a financial reorganization and a repayment plan (usually extended) with creditors. During the reorganization process, the company is freed from paying its past debts.

If the bankruptcy court decides that the company has no chance of rejoining the business community as a going concern, it will decree a **Chapter 7** proceeding, appoint a trustee, and liquidate the business's assets. *Compare to **Chapter 7**.*

Chapter 7   The conventional form of bankruptcy, especially for smaller companies, under the 1978 Bankruptcy Reform Act.

Bankruptcy attorneys usually refer to Chapter 7 proceedings as a "straight" bankruptcy.

A company in Chapter 7 must auction or sell all **assets** that are included in the bankruptcy in order to pay creditors. A court-appointed trustee gathers together and liquidates the assets of the debtor and then distributes the proceeds of the liquidation to the creditors and to him- or herself for trustee's fees. In most cases, any debts remaining after the liquidation distribution are discharged.

Rarely do liquidation proceeds cover all the company's debts. So common shareholders, who are at the bottom of the creditor ranking order, usually receive nothing. That's generally the case as well with preferred shareholders who rank immediately above common shareholders.

Chapter 7 is normally filed by a business that is beyond the point of attempting to reorganize and pay its debts. If that possibility exists, the company will use **Chapter 11.** *Compare to* **Chapter 11.**

chart of accounts   A numbered listing of the titles of all accounts used in a company's **bookkeeping** system.

They are listed in the order they appear in the **balance sheet** first and in the **income statement** second.

Every business must have a chart of accounts before setting up a bookkeeping system, since it allows the company to record transactions in the correct account. Companies without computers frequently assign identifying numbers to the accounts to make it easier to code transactions. Following is a partial chart of accounts with identifying numbers:

```
100   cash on hand
110   cash in First National Bank—regular account
111   cash in First National Bank—payroll account
120   accounts receivable
131   inventory—raw material
132   inventory—work in process
133   inventory—finished goods
200   accounts payable—trade
210   accounts payable—state of New York
220   accrued expenses
300   long-term mortgage
400   common stock
500   sales
600   cost of sales
700   selling expenses
800   administrative expenses
900   interest
```

chase demand   An *aggregate planning* strategy that maintains a minimal inventory level while changing production levels to meet expected demand for a given period.

EXAMPLE: A candy company practicing chase demand would plan on increasing production for the months of September and October in anticipation of the increased demand created by Halloween. These changes in production are typically achieved through overtime or alternately hiring and laying off employees. Since few goods are held for any significant period of time, there is very little inventory cost associated with a chase demand strategy (with the exception, perhaps, of a small **buffer stock** to insure against shortages should demand be greater than expected).

*See also **aggregate planning**. Compare to **level production**.*

cherry picking   The process of purchasing a series of products, normally sold as a bundle (*see **bundling***) by a single company, from a variety of suppliers.

EXAMPLE: A customer can either buy a complete computer package consisting of hardware, software, and a printer from one manufacturer or cherry pick and purchase each component from a different manufacturer.

Many distributors actively cherry pick products from a supplier's offerings. The selections usually reflect the distributors' evaluation of how established a product is and how well it will sell. This practice sometimes makes it difficult to establish new products that do not have the same reliable track record of more familiar offerings.

The most common response to cherry picking is to offer products in bundles that must be purchased as a group. Other responses include the establishment of incentives to distributors who purchase a full product line. By the same token, penalties, such as higher costs or reduced service, can be applied to distributors who continue to cherry pick.

Competitors can practice a form of cherry picking by selectively targeting particular products within a bundle. This can be especially effective when products are bundled. Often, a bundling strategy masks which products are making a profit and which products are actually losing money. In this situation, a competitor can determine which products are indeed profitable and focus its energy on offering single, lucrative products. For example, Virgin Atlantic Airways has targeted specific airline routes (such as London–New York and London–Boston) between the United States and London, routes traditionally dominated by British Airways.

chief financial officer (CFO)   The executive who manages all financial aspects of a company.

Chief financial officers are generally responsible for keeping accounting records, doing financial forecasting, designing accounting systems, tracking the various uses of corporate funds, raising capital, overseeing shareholder relations, and preparing SEC reports. In large companies, the CFO frequently delegates some of these responsibilities to financial vice presidents, *controllers*, and treasurers. In small companies, the CFO might perform all these activities.

Cigarette Labeling Act of 1967   An act that requires cigarette packages to carry the statement, "Warning: The Surgeon General Has Determined that Cigarette Smoking is Dangerous to Your Health."

Subsequent amendments to the act have altered the wording of the warning statement. For example: "Surgeon General's warning: quitting smoking now greatly reduces serious risks to your health."

CIM *See computer-integrated manufacturing*

CNC *See numerical control*

coaching A process by which employees are assigned a mentor, or coach, who "shows them the ropes" of a new job or task.

Coaching is frequently used—both informally and through formal mentoring programs—to help employees develop the skills required to do a particular job. Coaching requires a great deal of interpersonal skill, and it is most effective when the following tips are kept in mind.

- Coaching should be timely and should relate to a current situation or an activity that is to take place in the near future.

- Coaching sessions should focus on one or two issues rather than many.

- Coaching sessions should be frequent and concise rather than infrequent and lengthy.

- Coaches must demonstrate confidence in the abilities of employees in order to motivate employees.

- Coaching should allow employees to approach a problem in their own way instead of simply offering precise instructions. This approach increases the employees' self-confidence.

cognitive dissonance A theory on how attitudes are changed, based on the idea that people strive to maintain consistency among their opinions, knowledge, and values.

Cognitive dissonance usually arises when an attitude is directly contradicted by an experience. For example, say an employee holds the attitude that hard work will lead to advancement. If, after a year of hard work, that employee is passed over for a promotion in favor of a co-worker with a poor performance record, cognitive dissonance will be created. This leaves the employee with two options that will reduce the dissonance and create consonance between his or her attitude and experience: (1) change the attitude, acknowledging that there are other factors than hard work involved in advancement, and (2) change the experience, perhaps moving to a different company where advancement is based on performance alone.

From a management perspective, cognitive dissonance can be an important tool in changing employee attitudes. For example, if a number of employees have negative attitudes about female managers, cognitive dissonance can be created by hiring several well-qualified female managers. As employees work with the new managers, cognitive dissonance will be created between their attitudes and their experiences. In order to resolve this dissonance, the employees may change their attitudes toward female managers.

cold call   A personal selling technique in which a salesperson approaches a potential customer with little or no warning.

    The classic example of the cold-call technique is the door-to-door salesman. A more high-tech version of door-to-door cold calling is frequently used in *telemarketing*, where a salesperson telephones a number of households with a certain sales pitch. Telemarketing is cost-effective, because a single salesperson can contact a great number of potential customers over a wide territory in a short period of time. On the downside, cold calling is quite impersonal and isn't very effective in persuading people to buy expensive products. *See also personal communications channels.*

column inch   The unit by which advertising space is sold in newspapers and magazines.

    These publications are divided by width into columns (most newspapers have six per page) and measured by depth (height) in inches. A column inch measures one column width by one inch deep, about the size of an average classified ad. If an advertisement fits into a space that is three columns wide by ten inches deep, the advertiser needs to purchase 30 column inches (3 × 10 = 30). If the publication charges $25 per column inch, space for the ad will cost $750 ($25 × 30).

combination rate   A reduced rate offered to advertisers who place an advertisement in more than one publication owned by the same publisher.

    To qualify for the special rate, advertisements must be identical in copy, art, and size. Usually, too, the advertisements must run on the same day. Combination rates are frequently offered in morning and evening editions of the same newspaper or in newspapers under the same ownership.

comfort letter   A letter that expresses the opinion of the writer that certain matters have been or will be properly executed.

    The two most common uses of comfort letters are in securities registrations and in legal agreements between two parties.

    In the first instance, SEC regulations require that an independent auditor include as part of a securities registration a comfort letter stating that the information in the registration and the accompanying prospectus is correctly prepared and that no material changes have occurred since its preparation. Common usage refers to such an opinion as a "cold comfort letter," indicating that the auditors have not expressed an opinion as to the accuracy or timeliness of the information contained in the reports; they merely state that nothing has come to their attention to indicate that the information is not accurate and correctly stated.

    The second use of comfort letters arises between two parties to a legal agreement. One party issues a comfort letter to the other party stating that certain actions not clearly enunciated in the agreement will, or will not, be taken. This is often referred to as a "declaration of intent"; that is, one party *intends* to take or not take a specific action. It is not part of a legally binding contract and stands alone, outside of the referenced legal agreement.

commercial paper   Short-term securities (2 days to 270 days) issued by corporations, banks, and other borrowing organizations to raise short-term working capital.

Investors use commercial paper as a very short-term investment, perhaps awaiting other opportunities to open. Commercial paper is unsecured debt, which can be sold at a discount or bear interest. Typically, only large, quality-rated firms issue commercial paper. Issuers like commercial paper because of its maturity, its flexibility, and the absence of hard collateral. Both Moody's and Standard & Poor's rate commercial paper, making it easy for investors to verify creditworthiness.

commission   A sales incentive plan in which salespeople are paid by a fixed or sliding percentage and earn income according to the amount of sales or profit they generate.

Salespeople can work strictly for commission, or the commission can be combined with a base salary. These incentive plans are commonly found in the clothing, insurance, investment, and furniture industries.

A straight commission plan with no base salary gives managers several advantages: (1) It encourages sales representatives to work at maximum capacity; (2) it links selling costs with sales revenue; and (3) it allows management to influence the activities of the sales team by placing different commissions on different products. A straight commission plan can, however, involve large costs. Because they receive no other compensation, salespeople resist nonselling tasks, such as providing customer service or filling out sales reports, that don't generate income. Straight commission also may lead to high-pressure sales tactics that could damage customer goodwill.

Most companies pay a combination of salary and commission. Managers can then use the commission as an incentive without putting undue pressure on the sales staff. The most common arrangement is 70 percent salary and 30 percent commission. With a combination plan, managers can control the nonselling activities of the sales force and provide some measure of job stability if sales decline.

commodity   A highly standardized product or service, such as cement, wheat, steel, or eggs.

Consumers will buy a commodity from whichever manufacturer offers the lowest price. A company can move away from offering a commodity product in two ways. The first is to differentiate the product from its competitors.

EXAMPLE: Frank Perdue fed his chickens a special meal containing marigold petals to give the meat a golden hue. He went on to star in a series of memorable advertisements in which he claimed that his birds were superior to other chickens on the market. The ad campaign, combined with the golden appearance of his chickens, created the perception that Perdue chickens were of higher quality. That perception allowed for a price that is about 15 percent higher than other "commodity" chickens. (*See also* **brand**).

The second strategy is to recognize that different buyers have different needs and to tailor various marketing programs for each. For example, companies can offer longer payment terms, more reliable delivery, or a better technical assistance program in order to attract customers with something more than a low price. The key to succeeding with this strategy is to identify which customers' needs are not being met.

EXAMPLE: The manager of a brick manufacturer wants to sell his product to a construction company that does not have much warehouse space. Without the space, the company can't carry an adequate supply of bricks and is continually calling for emergency deliveries. If the brick manufacturer agrees to provide fast delivery, it can charge a premium on its materials and move away from being labeled a commodity.

common stock   Certificates that represent ownership in a corporation.

Usually, common shareholders have the right to vote for the election of corporate directors; in *privately held companies* they may also elect the corporate officers. Corporations may issue various classes of common stock—some with voting rights, some without.

Holders of common stock normally don't have any right to receive *dividends*, although if a company's earnings permit, the board of directors may elect to declare a common stock dividend, either in cash or in additional shares.

Common stock may be issued with a *par value* or with no par value. In either case, it is recorded in the *stockholders' equity* section of the *balance sheet*. *See also preferred stock, additional paid-in capital.*

common stock equivalent   A security that is not currently in common stock form but can be converted into common stock.

Examples include stock options, two-class common stocks, warrants, and contingent shares. A common stock equivalent can affect the calculation of *earnings per share* if its effect is *dilutive*. In other words, a company with 100 shares of common stock and common stock equivalents that can be converted to a total of 50 shares of common stock must calculate its earnings per share for 150 shares of common stock, whether the securities have been converted to common stock or not. *See also complex capital structure, earnings per share.*

common stock valuation   A method for determining the value of common stock.

The process uses the *present value* of a stock's expected cash flows—that is, the dividends it pays plus the expected future price when the stock is sold—and the investors' required rate of return, or the rate of return offered by a comparable investment. *See also* **equity interest valuation**.

comparison advertising An *advertising* strategy in which a company presents its product as significantly better than a competitor's, usually named (or at least implied).

EXAMPLES: Avis, in an implicit reference to Hertz, calls itself Number Two and claims it "Tries Harder." Pepsi challenges Coca-Cola on the basis of taste. Wendy's slyly suggests it offers more meat than the competitors' with its famous "Where's the Beef?" commercials. For several months, Centrum promoted itself as a more complete vitamin than Theragran-M, the market leader. As a result of its campaign, Centrum emerged as number one; Theragran then retaliated with commercials that claimed its vitamins contained twice as much A, B1, B2, and C as Centrum's.

These classic confrontations rely on undercutting the competition with direct comparisons.

competitive advantage The particular elements within a company that give it an edge over its competitors.

Competitive advantage is difficult to measure since it only appears relative to the advantages of competitors. For example, if General Motors increases production by 15 percent in a year, it may appear to be a competitive advantage. However, if Toyota increases production by 20 percent within the same period, General Motors is at a competitive disadvantage.

Securing competitive advantages is a central element of *corporate strategy*. The factors that differentiate competitors, and hence serve as competitive advantages, include price, product features and functions, time (e.g., if a product can be delivered immediately, it has a distinct advantage over its competitors that may not be able to deliver for a number of weeks), place (e.g., a local auto mechanic has an advantage over a distant service station), and perception (e.g., a product with an established positive image has a distinct advantage, all other things being equal, over a product with little or no image).

These factors can be combined in a number of different ways, but there is always the possibility that a competitor will launch a program of differentiation that will enlarge its competitive advantage over its rivals.

EXAMPLE: The athletic shoe manufacturer Nike developed its position as market leader by using cheap labor in the Far East and spending heavily on product development and marketing. Although this created a clear competitive advantage, it was short lived. Rivals, particularly Reebok (which made 95 percent of its shoes in South Korea), quickly adopted many of Nike's programs and began to pose a considerable threat.

As a result of the fleeting nature of competitive advantages, the focus of many business strategies is the development of *sustainable competitive advantages*. There are three general types of sustainable competitive advantages: (1) preferred access to customers or inputs, (2) size within the market, and (3) restrictions on rivals.

Two conditions must be met in order for preferred access to inputs or customers to work as a sustainable competitive advantage: (1) It must offer better terms than rivals will be able to get at some later date, and (2) the advantage must be enforceable, usually through binding contracts or high switching costs, which discourage customers from going to competitors.

EXAMPLE: In the viscose industry, Courtauld's has a 10 to 15 percent cost advantage over its rivals because it has pursued a strategy of *backward integration* by establishing a conveniently located subsidiary to supply dissolving pulp, which makes up about a third of the final product's cost. This substantial advantage will last as long as the supply of dissolving pulp remains constant. If more tropical forests are developed, competitors could establish their own subsidiaries and pose a threat.

Superior access to customers is similar to superior access to inputs, with the exception that it depends less on backward integration and formal contracts and more on relationships, reputation, and high switching costs. Market access is frequently dependent on consumer reactions.

EXAMPLE: ReaLemon, Borden's brand of bottled lemon juice, enjoys a competitive advantage that allows a 50 percent price premium over competing brands that offer an identical product. This advantage comes from the superior access that ReaLemon developed by being the first brand on the market. As such, it has capitalized on the consumers' aversion to risk. In other words, people buy ReaLemon because they tried it before, it is inexpensive (even though it costs more than competing brands), and other brands are untried.

Advantages of size occur because markets are limited. If a company pursues a strategy of size, rivals may be forced to remain small because of the fear that too many large companies will crowd the market and force everyone to suffer. Size, however, is only an advantage when any of the three following conditions exist: *economies of scale*, *economies of scope*, or the *learning curve*.

Economies of scale exist when a company produces, or sells, in a large enough volume to take advantage of cost reductions, such as bulk discounts on materials. This does not apply only to large manufacturing companies. Economies of scale can create a sustainable competitive advantage on a regional, or even local, level.

EXAMPLE: The discount merchandiser Wal-Mart applied economies of scale to small towns in the Sunbelt of America. Wal-Mart's strategy was to invest a great deal in establishing stores in a series of small towns. Since these towns could not provide enough business to support two discount stores, Wal-Mart easily secured a series of local monopolies. These monopolies were strengthened by the arrangement of stores in rings around regional distribution centers. This created economies of scale that cut distribution costs by 50 percent. When competitors, such as K-Mart, realized the effect of Wal-Mart's strategies, there were enough Wal-Mart stores to make it nearly impossible to compete. Although this seems to be an advantage that can be sustained indefinitely, it does have its limits. Population growth in the Sunbelt has increased dramatically in the past decade, and now many of the "small" towns that could only support a single discounter are opening up for competitors.

Economies of scope are created when a company maintains activities in related markets. When economies of scope are significant, a sustainable competitive advantage in one market can help to create a sustainable advantage in another. Economies of scope are achieved by that ability to share resources across different markets while at the same time ensuring that the cost of the resources is basically fixed.

EXAMPLE: Cincinnati Milacron, the leading machine tool manufacturer in the United States, effectively pursued economies of scope as it moved beyond the machine tool industry into robotics in the 1980s. Milacron led the U.S. machine tool industry in the 1960s and 1970s both in terms of research and development and the size of its sales and service network. With a solid customer base for computerized machine tools and R & D experience unmatched by its competitors, Milacron made the move into robotics, where is could attract many of the same customers and use its sales and service activities to create a sustainable competitive advantage.

The effects of the learning curve, combined with size, create sustainable advantages over time. The basic concept behind the advantages of the learning curve is that the longer a company is in operation, the better it does its job.

EXAMPLE: Lincoln Electric has used the learning curve to create a competitive advantage in the electric welding industry. As the first mover in the industry (John Lincoln invented the portable arc welder in 1895) Lincoln Electric parlayed what might have initially been a transient competitive advantage into an edge that allows a 7 to 15 percent cost advantage today. It accomplished this by keeping its experience within the company. The policies that allowed this include pursuing a strategy of backward integration, actively reducing worker turnover (less than 3 percent), customizing its production equipment, and passing cost reductions on to customers. This has created a situation in which competitors have trouble meeting, much less undercutting, Lincoln's prices.

Sustainable competitive advantages can also be created by limiting the options available to competitors. An important source of restraints is governmental policy, which includes patents, antitrust laws, and government subsidies.

EXAMPLE: The Heileman Brewing company gained considerable competitive advantage during the shakeout of the U.S. brewing industry in the 1970s when the government invoked antitrust laws to prevent large national brewers, such as Miller, Anheuser-Busch, and Schlitz, from acquiring small, regional brewers. As a regional brewery, Heileman was not restricted in its efforts to acquire other smaller breweries. By 1982, the strategy had tripled Heileman's market share, and the company had a *return on equity* of 29 percent. The advantages of the strategy began to fade, however, when the government blocked Heileman's proposed takeover of Schlitz and Pabst.

When competitors are forced into a defensive position, their options may be limited and there is an opportunity to create a sustainable competitive advantage.

EXAMPLE: In the 1950s, Bic introduced its Crystal pen at a price of 19 cents to compete with the industry leader Gillette. Gillette did not respond to Bic's actions because it did not want to hurt the sales of its more expensive Paper Mate line of pens. Bic's actions went unchallenged until 1970, when Gillette introduced Write Bros. pens at a more competitive price.

Competitors' options are also reduced by long response lags. In a situation where all other competitive forces are equal, a company that can get its product to market faster than its rivals has the competitive advantage.

EXAMPLE: In the 1950s, a joint venture was formed between Du Pont and Bell & Howell to enter the color film market, which was dominated by Kodak. Each time the joint venture made an improvement in their film, Kodak would improve its film almost immediately. When the competing film was finally ready for the market, Kodak totally preempted it by introducing its Kodachrome II color slide film. The Du Pont–Bell & Howell film never made it to the market.

competitive forces *See five forces model*

competitor analysis The evaluation of the intent and actions of a company's competitors.

Since *corporate strategy* is mainly a function of managing a company's strengths relative to the strengths of its competitors within the same market, competitor analysis is an important factor in gauging *competitive advantage*. Most competitor analysis focuses on the existing capabilities and strategies of competitors. Although this type of information is relatively easy to obtain, it is not always the most helpful. The information that makes competitor analysis truly useful deals with the probable future actions of competitors, such as future goals and assumptions about market trends. Many managers feel that this type of information is nearly impossible to obtain, but in many cases it is readily available—usually from a company's own sales force, suppliers, distributors, and subcontractors.

complementary products Any products, such as cameras and film or computers and software, that must be used together.

Neither product can be substituted for the other, and the sale of one increases the sale of the other.

Complementary products pose a unique set of strategic issues that can be broken into three key questions.

(1) To what extent should a manufacturer be involved in the complementary products? Consider, for example, the case of a computer manufacturer. Should it manufacture the software required by its computers, or should it rely on specialized firms and software suppliers?

(2) If the company decides to produce complementary products, should they be sold as a package (*see **bundling***) or as individual items?

(3) How should complementary products be priced in order to maximize sales and profits? In many cases, companies pursue a strategy of cross subsidization, in which one product is sold for a less profitable price, and its complement is sold at a more profitable price. This strategy is easily seen in the camera/film market. By selling cameras at very low prices, Kodak developed a base of Kodak film users. Although cameras were not a profitable item on their own, the increased profits from continuing film sales offset the loss.

complex capital structure The financing structure of a company with both *common stock* and *common stock equivalents*.

In this situation, a company must calculate two figures for *earnings per share*: (1) primary earnings per share and (2) fully diluted earnings per share. If the two figures differ by more than 2 percent, both must be disclosed in the company's financial statements. Primary earnings per share are calculated as follows:

$$\frac{\text{Net income} - \text{Preferred dividend}}{\text{Weighted average of common stock outstanding}}$$

Primary earnings per share show the amount of income attributed to each outstanding share of common stock.

Fully diluted earnings per share, however, show the amount of income attributed to each share of common stock if every *common stock equivalent* were converted into common stock.

$$\frac{\text{Net income} - \text{Preferred dividends}}{\text{Weighted average number of common shares} + \text{Common stock equivalents}}$$

See also **common stock, common stock equivalent, earnings per share, simple capital structure.**

compound interest The rate applied when interest in subsequent periods is earned not only on the original amount of a note receivable or note payable, but also on the accumulated interest from previous periods.

In other words, the interest that is earned on principal is *added* to the interest that was earned earlier.

EXAMPLE: The original amount is $100 and the annual interest rate is 10 percent. At the end of the first year, the total amount is $110 ($100 principal and $100 × .10 = $10 interest; $100 + $10 = $110). At the end of the second year, the total amount comes to $121 ($110 and $110 × .10 = $11 interest; $110 + $11 = $121).

comptroller An alternative spelling of *controller*.

The term, which like "controller" is derived from the French word *compte*, for count, describes the chief accounting executive of a company. The term is used frequently in government circles, as in Comptroller of the Currency, but today most companies use the designation *controller* instead. *See* **controller**.

computer numerical control *See* **numerical control**

computer-aided design (CAD) The use of computers in the design of products.

EXAMPLE: An architect might use a CAD system to design a large office building. The architect uses a keyboard, light pen, or mouse and pad to create an image of the building on the computer screen. As the building takes shape, the architect can instruct the CAD system to enlarge certain areas for closer examination, rotate the building to see how it will appear from different angles, determine what the building would look like if different materials were used, and so on.

The capabilities for CAD have increased rapidly in the past few years. At the same time, the prices for CAD software have fallen dramatically.

When CAD is incorporated into a design process, whether it is an architect designing a building, an engineer designing a new automobile, or a researcher designing a new medical device, *productivity* usually increases between 300 and 400 percent.

computer-aided engineering (CAE) The use of computers to generate and test the engineering specifications of a product.

EXAMPLE: In the aerospace industry, CAE is commonly used to test the structural integrity of a particular part or subassembly.

computer-aided manufacturing (CAM) The use of computers to direct manufacturing and assembly of a product.

There are two forms of CAM. Direct CAM involves the use of computers to directly control the processing equipment or material handling equipment on the production line. Material is positioned automatically, moved to the next machine, and processed. The General Electric Appliance facility at Appliance Park, Kentucky, utilizes direct computer-assisted manufacturing to a high degree in fabrication of dishwashers. Indirect CAM is the use of computers in the planning, purchasing, and inventory management involved in the manufacturing process. The computer indirectly supports the activities needed for line operation.

computer-integrated manufacturing (CIM) Integrating or linking a wide array of activities together with a computer system.

A CIM system may bring together a wide range of activities from engineering, such as computer-aided design, computer-aided engineering, and computerized drafting; business planning of scheduling, purchasing, inventory control, and MRP; and as well as the actual operations on the shop floor, including material handling, fabrication, assembly, and inspection. The idea behind CIM is elimination of overhead associated with the manufacturing process.

There are a number of excellent examples of CIM in this country, but one of the best is the Allen Bradley Company.

concurrent engineering A method of product design that incorporates input from each of the functional areas of a company.

In many cases, suppliers and customers are also included in the design process. The basic idea behind concurrent engineering is to meet the needs of all the stakeholders in the product, thus ensuring that costs are minimized, quality is maximized, and the product is brought to the market as quickly as possible.

conjoint analysis A data analysis technique in which respondents' ranking of the importance of various product attributes is seen in the preferences they show for different combinations of these attributes.

Conjoint analysis is a relatively new technique, which hinges on three key management decisions: (1) which attributes to include, (2) the level of the attributes, and (3) the combinations of the attributes.

EXAMPLE: An automobile manufacturer might perform a conjoint analysis by asking potential customers how they feel about various feature and price combinations. They may be asked, say, to compare a car with antilock brakes, air bags, air conditioning, and power windows priced at $15,000; with a car that has air bags, air conditioning, power windows, and no antilock brakes priced at $12,000; and a car that has antilock brakes, air bags, no air conditioning, and manual windows priced at $11,000, and so on. Once the data from the study have been analyzed, the manufacturer can determine the combination of features and price that is most attractive to the target market.

conservatism One of the basis accounting tenets under *generally accepted accounting principles (GAAP)*; states that a company must recognize all losses as soon as they are quantifiable (even as estimates) but cannot record gains until they are realized.

In other words, companies should anticipate losses—never gains. *See also matching principle*.

consignment A method of selling that allows the return of unsold and undamaged merchandise.

Products can be consigned from manufacturers to wholesalers and from wholesalers to retailers. Newsstands frequently sell magazines on consignment, returning unsold copies to their distributors. Payment is usually made in advance, and subsequently refunded according to the amount of returns.

consolidation The reporting of the earnings of both a parent company and its subsidiaries (*see subsidiary company*) as a single entity.

When companies are consolidated, the entire group is presented as a single company in the parent company's financial statements. A company is considered a subsidiary if another company owns more than 50 percent of its voting common stock. *See also minority interest*.

constant dollar accounting A method of measuring the items on a company's financial statements in terms of dollars with the same purchasing power—in other words, ignoring the impact of inflation or deflation.

Historic costs are converted by the following:

$$\text{Historic cost} \times \frac{\text{Average consumer price index (CPI) for the current year}}{\text{Consumer price index at the time of acquisition}}$$

Translating all accounts into constant dollars makes comparisons between years more meaningful, since all assets will be stated in dollars of equivalent purchasing power regardless of when an asset was purchased.

Consumer Credit Protection Act An act passed by Congress in 1968 requiring disclosure of all terms and conditions of finance charges in consumer credit transactions.

Consumer Goods Pricing Act of 1975 A law passed by Congress that prohibits price maintenance agreements between manufacturers and resellers in interstate commerce.

consumer market All individuals and households that purchase or acquire goods and services for personal use; also called the mass market.

The consumer market has four key characteristics: (1) a large number of buyers and sellers, (2) wide geographic distribution, (3) small individual purchases, and (4) a wide variety of different products. These characteristics lead to widespread distribution systems to link sellers and buyers. The distribution systems are designed to carry small amounts of various products across the country. With the distribution systems comes a communications system that carries information between buyers and sellers and helps to eliminate price discrepancies among geographic areas. The information flowing back and forth eventually leads to the development of more new products.

consumer motivation In marketing, the activation of the consumer toward some consumption goal.

Consumers are filled with potential needs and wants; purchase behavior results only when these needs and wants are aroused. Motivation can be biogenic or psychogenic. Biogenic motivation comes from physiological states of deprivation, such as lack of food, drink, sex, or bodily comfort. Psychogenic motivation comes from tension, which in turn comes from the need for status, recognition, security, and the like. Charles Revson, the founder of Revlon, knew the importance of psychogenic motivation when he said this about his product: "In the factory we make cosmetics: In the store we sell hope." (*See also Maslow's hierarchy of needs.*)

Some marketers take a less theoretical approach to consumer motivation, simply dividing it into three areas: store driven, brand loyal, and price driven. A store-driven consumer habitually makes his or her purchases at a particular store and will, of course, purchase only those products available at that store. A brand-loyal consumer will shop at any store as long as he or she can buy a particular brand. A price-driven consumer will shop for any brand at any store but will purchase only the product with the lowest price.

Each type of motivation requires a different marketing strategy. A company that wants to sell to store-driven consumers has to have a distribution system that gets its products into the right stores. A high-fashion clothing company might, for instance, distribute its clothes only to Bloomingdale's. A company that wants to sell to brand-loyal customers must use promotions and advertising to create strong brand awareness and image. A company that targets price-driven consumers will simply offer its products at the lowest price.

Consumer Product Safety Act of 1972 The law that established the Consumer Product Safety Commission and gave it the authority to set and enforce safety standards for consumer products.

consumer-adoption process In marketing, the description of how consumers discover, evaluate, and adopt or reject new products.

The consumer adoption process has five phases: (1) *awareness*—the potential customer realizes that the product exists but does not have any information about it; (2) *interest*—the customer is motivated to learn about the product; (3) *evaluation*—the customer decides whether to try the product; (4) *trial*—the customer buys the product to confirm his or her estimate of its utility; and (5) *adoption*—the customer becomes a regular user of the product.

continuous improvement *See kaizen*

contribution margin (CM) The amount by which sales exceed the *variable costs* (such as materials and labor) of a product or service. In other words, the amount of money that a company can use to cover *fixed costs* (such as rent and insurance) and generate a profit.

Financial managers use contribution-margin analysis to decide, among other things, whether to maintain, drop, or add to a product line; whether to manufacture or purchase a particular part or subassembly; and whether to accept special orders.

Contribution margin is calculated by subtracting variable costs from sales.

$$\text{Sales} - \text{Variable costs} = \text{Contribution margin}$$

EXAMPLE: Say a manufacturer sells 100,000 widgets at $20 per widget for total sales of 2 million. Fixed costs total $700,000 ($7 per widget), and variable costs come to $1.2 million, or $12 per widget, so the company makes a profit of $100,000. A week later, a customer offers to buy 1,000 widgets for $15 each. The company has enough idle capacity to produce the order without increasing its fixed costs. In order to decide whether it pays to sell the widgets at less than their customary price, the company must look at the contribution margin of the additional 1,000 units:

Sales, 1,000 × $15	$15,000
Less variable costs, 1,000 × $12	(12,000)
Contribution margin	$ 3,000
Less fixed costs	0
Net income	$ 3,000

The analysis shows that the company can profitably sell 1,000 widgets at $15 each, as long as it has idle capacity. The contribution margin of these widgets will add $3,000 to the company's profits with no increase in fixed costs.

control chart A tool used in quality control to monitor and control a process.

The primary objective of a control chart is to make timely decisions about whether or not a particular process is in statistical control. In any process there will be variation from one measurement or unit produced to the next. If the variation is due to purely random or chance causes, the process is said to be in "statistical control." (*Source*: L. Shirland, *Statistical Quality Control*, 1993, John Wiley & Sons, Inc.)

Theoretically, units coming off the production line should be exactly alike; they should meet the specifications exactly, and there should be no variation from unit to unit. However, this is not always the case; output may vary. Variation is either random (when we do not know the cause) or assignable (when we know the source of the variation).

To allow for variation, tolerances are set up. Tolerances represent the maximum physical variation a variable may have and still perform the function for which it was manufactured. Going beyond the tolerances results in rejected product and scrap or rework. The quality or "goodness" of the manufacturing process is measured by its output; the product is the indicator of the process. In developing control charts, a set of statistical tolerances are defined that are closer to the specifications than the physical tolerances. These limits are designed in such a way that we know the probability of a unit going beyond the statistical limits for no assignable cause. A number of observations or measurements beyond or near the statistical limits acts as a warning that *something is causing the variation* in output. The product acts as a check of the process. The fundamental idea is to spot variation *before the fact* and *prevent defects* (stop them before they start). The purpose of the control chart is to warn the operator that a process is going out of statistical control before the process produces unacceptable product. Control charts can also be used to measure attributes. In this case the control chart dislays the fraction of output not possessing the desired attribute.

A control chart can be considered as a meter or gauge. It provides a reading and perhaps a warning as well, in the same way that a tachometer measures RPM and has a red line to warn against excessive RPMs.

To appreciate the control chart, one must have some understanding of statistics and variability. With any array of homogeneous data it is possible to measure its average and its dispersion. The average is called the *mean*, and the most widely used measure of dispersion is called the *standard deviation*. If the weight of 1000 men was taken and a mean and standard deviation computed, and if one could assume a normal probability distribution, then as we moved away from the average toward the extremes of the distribution, a smaller and smaller number of observations would be at the extremes. Statistics tells us that the area between the mean $\pm$ 1 standard deviation will contain 68 percent of the sample, the mean $\pm$ 2 standard deviations will contain 95 percent of the sample, and the mean $\pm$ 3 standard deviations will encompass 99.7 percent of the sample. Thus, beyond the $\pm$ 3 standard deviation limits, one would expect to find weights of only 3 of the 1000 people sampled.

EXAMPLE: A company producing a diet product now plans to test-market a new diet product. It is seeking a community to test the product. One approach might be to seek a town where the average weight was beyond the third positive standard deviation. That difference from the first sample would probably indicate a statistically significant variation, and there would be a cause for that variation. Obesity is not a random event; it has a cause.

In the manufacturing context the control chart is a visual. Consider the diagram below:

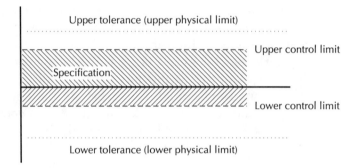

Control Chart

The middle solid line is the specification being measured. The statistical limits lie closer to the specification than the tolerances. We want to produce product that stays inside the statistical limits. Product measured outside the statistical limits cannot occur on a random basis; there must be a cause of the variation. The control chart warns us of assignable variation.

control limit The upper and lower tolerances selected by management for a *control chart.*
See *control chart.*

controller The principal accounting executive for a company.
The controller's duties include (1) financial reporting and interpretation, (2) tax administration, (3) accounting system development, (4) internal and external *audit* coordination, (5) internal controls management, and (6) cost analysis.
A controller differs from a treasurer in that the treasurer deals mainly with the financial problems of managing the company's investment portfolio, developing credit policy, and planning the company's finances.

conversion ratio A method of calculating the number of shares that the holder of a *convertible security* receives when conversion takes place.
The conversion ratio is calculated by dividing the face value of a convertible security by the conversion price that the holder pays for the common stock into which the security will be converted.

$$\frac{\text{Face value of convertible security}}{\text{Conversion price}} = \text{Conversion ratio}$$

EXAMPLE: Say a $50,000 bond is convertible into common stock at a conversion price of $25 per share. The conversion ratio is

$$\frac{\$50,000}{\$25} = 2,000 \text{ shares}$$

In other words, the holder of the convertible bond can exchange it for 2,000 shares of common stock. *See also* **convertible security.**

convertible security

Stocks and bonds, such as convertible bonds and convertible *preferred stock,* that can be converted into *capital stock* at some future date.

The number of shares a company will issue is determined by the conversion ratio.

EXAMPLE: A $10,000 convertible bond issue (10 bonds @ $1,000 each) is converted at 1 bond for 30 shares.

$$\frac{\$10,000}{\$1,000} = 10 \text{ bonds} \times 30 \text{ shares/bond} = 300 \text{ shares}$$

The bondholder will receive 300 shares. *See also* **bond, capital structure, earnings per share.**

coproduction

A type of buyback countertrade generally used for the transfer of management expertise or technology.

EXAMPLE: Say an American company wants to sell products to Jamaica. A Jamaican company is interested in buying the products but also wants to produce them in Jamaica. The American company buys an equity interest in the Jamaican operation—or it may simply provide management support. Either way, the facility is, in most cases, built by both parties. Since both the American company and the Jamaican company are involved in the operation of the new facility, the manufacture of the products is known as coproduction.

When equity interests are an element of a coproduction arrangement, both companies profit from the sale of the products. Aside from the gains made by the direct sale of the product, each partner sees several other benefits. The host partner gains new technology and management expertise, and the outside partner acquires a direct investment in a foreign country without the risk of starting a new business from scratch.

copy

The written material in an advertisement, commercial, brochure, or direct-mail piece.

Copy includes all headlines, subheadings, captions, and **body copy.** Most successful copy clearly states the benefits of a product or service. Whether that benefit is as concrete as being able to see your reflection in a clean plate or as ethereal as feeling transformed by a dab of perfume, it is always the central element of any good copy. The term "copy" originates from the time when handwritten material was received by the printer and copied into type for printing.

copyright   The exclusive right to publish and sell a literary, musical, or artistic work.

Copyright laws protect the *expression* of ideas and facts, not the facts or ideas themselves, since it is considered to be in the public interest to encourage the dissemination of the latter. In other words, Einstein's original paper describing the theory of relativity cannot be copied or published without consent, but the theory itself can be incorporated into any number of works.

The exclusive protection extended to copyright holders includes (1) the right to reproduce the copyrighted work, (2) the right to works derived from the copyrighted work, (3) the right to distribute copies of the protected work, (4) the right to perform the copyrighted work publicly, and (5) the right to display the copyrighted work publicly.

A work receives copyright protection as soon as it is created; it does not need to be registered or published.

Copyrighted works are protected for the life of the author, plus 50 years. When the copyright expires, the work enters the public domain and can be used by anyone.

Copyright Act of 1976   The law granting legal protection to original works fixed in any tangible medium of expression.

See also copyright.

copywriter   The creator of the concepts for and the text of an advertisement.

Usually a copywriter is teamed with an *art director* for a particular project. Together, the team is responsible for creating the concept, art, and design of an ad campaign. Copywriters are frequently employed by *advertising agencies* but often act as independent contractors, or freelancers (*see freelancer*).

core competence   The particular capabilities of a company that separate it from competitors and serve as the basis for growth or *diversification* into new lines of business.

These capabilities generally come from experience in producing and marketing a line of products or services and are developed by (1) assessing and developing the strengths and weaknesses of the individuals in a company, (2) applying individual capabilities to a common goal or task, and (3) coordinating individual and group efforts.

In order to identify the particular competencies of a company that might lead to a profitable opportunity, it is necessary to first consider the present line of products or services and analyze the function that they serve in their market. Nearly every consumer product has functions related to another product that might provide an opportunity.

EXAMPLE: Typewriters are capable of doing more than simply translating the written word. Although translation may have been the original intent of its designer, it is important to look at the typewriter from the perspective of the potential user. From this point of view, the typewriter does more than simply replace pen and ink; it is a word-processing machine. There are a number of attractive options that a typewriter manufacturer might have considered, including the development of the electric typewriter and the computerized word processor, both of which were introduced by IBM and not a typewriter manufacturer.

In addition to considering the present product line, it is important to identify the particular factors and skills that make up a company's present position. Although some of these factors may seem to be taken for granted, such as providing superior customer service or a rapid delivery time, they can be an important element in exploiting new opportunities in a market where products are essentially undifferentiated.

Once a company has determined its particular competencies, the next step is to match them with opportunities. It is this process that helps to solidify a company's strategic goals in relation to its *environment.* In order for a company's competence to translate into growth, it must pass three key tests: (1) It must provide access to a variety of possible markets. For example, Casio's competence in display technology allows it to consider participation in computer monitors, automobile dashboards, calculators, digital watches, and miniature televisions. (2) It should make a substantial contribution to the benefits that a customer perceives in the final product. For example, Honda's competence in the design and manufacture of engines adds significant value for its car, motorcycle, generator, and lawn mower customers. (3) It should be difficult for competitors to duplicate, as when JVC pioneered the development of videotape.

corporate advertising A form of advertising that is intended to sell the image of the corporation itself rather than just its products.

In addition, this kind of advertising may also be used to advocate a position on a particular subject of interest to the company. Unlike product advertising, which reports to *marketing,* corporate advertising typically reports to the *corporate communication* area in large corporations.

EXAMPLE: General Electric has run television commercials for several years that try to show the organization as one that is less monolithic and more down to earth. The campaign's theme is that GE brings good things to life, and the commercials include segments on the organization's development of x-ray equipment that detects breast cancer.

corporate communication An emerging functional area that combines a number of subfunctions traditionally associated with *public relations* or public affairs.

As public attitudes toward business have become increasingly negative, corporations have realized the importance of combining communications activities under one area. In the most progressive large companies, the corporate communication function typically reports directly to the president or CEO and has responsibility for creating a coherent image and identity that reflects the organization's corporate strategy or mission. In addition, the corporate communication department is responsible for *corporate advertising,* media relations, community relations, *financial communication,* employee relations, community relations and corporate philantropy, and government relations (also called public affairs).

EXAMPLE: Kmart corporation changed its strategy in the early 1990s from a low-end discount retailer to a more upscale image. The chairman and CEO wanted to reflect that change, which the company was spending millions to achieve through renovation and reconstruction of stores, through corporate communications.

The company's corporate indentity and logo were changed to reflect a more modern and upscale image. In addition, the subfunctions listed above were centralized under a vice-president of corporate communication who reports directly to the CEO. Advertising was used to reflect the change in the image, and the company's financial communications were connected more closely with the overall corporate communication effort.

corporate culture The overall style or feel of a company.

A company's culture governs how people relate to each other and their jobs. It can be summed up with the phrase "This is how we do things around here." Although it may be tempting to take the company's culture for granted, it is increasingly obvious that culture is an important factor in a comany's survival. In many cases, when a company undergoes a strategic change, its culture must also change. For example, before AT&T was forced to break up, its culture was extremely bureaucratic and oriented toward technological developments such as a touch-tone telephone, the portable telephone, and other equipment to make long-distance calling more efficient and attractive. After the break-up, however, AT&T was faced with serious competitors in both long-distance services and telephone equipment. If the firm was to survive, it had to become competitive. Chairman Robert E. Allen realigned the company by cutting 75,000 jobs, moving manufacturing out of the country where costs are substantially lower, linking executive compensation to sales performance, and delegating authority by making managers responsible for the performance of their departments. All of these changes have had a significant effect on AT&T's corporate culture. The company has begun to shift from an administrative, bureaucracy-driven culture to an independent, sales-driven culture.

Corporate culture can be developed in a variety of different ways. In most cases, it involves the development of particular norms or behaviors that are reinforced by management. For example, Sam Walton, the founder of Wal-Mart, developed a corporate culture that emphasizes hands-on management as part of an overall strategy to stay in touch with customers' needs. He accomplished this, in part, by spending three days of every week visiting different stores and talking with employees and customers. Store managers quickly imitated Walton's example and found that they were better able to understand and respond to customers' needs. In general, there are four tools that can be used to develop a particular corporate culture: (1) symbolic action, (2) participation, (3) rewards systems, and (4) information from co-workers.

Symbolic action is usually some type of management behavior, such as Sam Walton's visiting stores, that reinforces the values of a company. One of the most common forms of symbolic action is storytelling. Many companies enlist experienced managers to tell new employees about "the old days." This serves the dual function of giving new recruits a sense of the company's history and indoctrinating them into the values of the company's culture. For example, stories of the excellent customer service at Nordstrom department stores, such as the employee who bought a scarf from a competitor because she thought it would go well with an outfit that a customer was looking at, illustrate the company's culture far more vividly than an employee manual or training session.

Ceremonies frequently serve as symbolic actions as well. Mary Kay Cosmetics, for example, holds lavish sales awards dinners in which its top salespeople are presented with jewels, furs, and the legendary pink Cadillac. These dinners not only reward a select few salespeople, they motivate the entire sales force.

Allowing employees to participate in the operations of a company beyond their particular job description can frequently be an effective way to develop or change corporate culture. Advisory boards, *quality circles,* and suggestion boxes are all popular ways to encourage participation. As employees begin to get involved in the company, they develop a commitment to its culture.

Rewards systems, both monetary and nonmonetary, are frequently used to change and reinforce a company's culture. Once again, Mary Kay Cosmetics is an example. By establishing a clear system of rewards, ranging from cash to vacations to cars, the company has created a corporate culture that motivates its employees.

corporate strategy The pattern of a company's goals, purposes, and objectives and the central policies that will be used to meet them.

Corporate strategy determines the type of business the company intends to engage in; its structure as both an economic and human organization; and its intended contribution (both economic and noneconomic) to customers, employees, shareholders, and its community.

Corporate strategy is distinct from business strategy in that it refers to the competitive stance of an entire company, whereas business strategy refers to the decisions regarding individual products or services, suppliers, markets, and competitors.

	Corporate strategy	Business strategy
Competes for	• customers • suppliers • products	• finance • companies • management
Managing	• activities (usually through intervention)	• interrelationships • process (usually through reinforcement)
Value-creating activities	• fitting the business to the market	• fitting the business to the company's portfolio of *strategic business units*

Although strategy at these two levels deals with very different issues, the boundary between them is frequently indistinct. In many cases, corporate strategy directly affects the strategy of an individual business unit. At the same time, it can be argued that the business unit is little more than the means through which corporate strategy is implemented.

The pattern of decisions and goals that makes up corporate strategy generally takes effect over a long time period and serves to define the character and image of the company in terms of its customers, its owners, its employees, and its competitors. For example, the decisions that lead to a commitment to customer service (or high technology or quality) may impact the company for many years. However, some of the decisions that make up a company's strategy (particularly those involving product lines, manufacturing, and marketing) may have to change very quickly. In this situation, it is important to find a match between the long- and short-term strategic decisions.

It is the pattern of decisions and goals, and how they relate to each other, that results in consistent strategic focus. For example, short-term financial goals such as high profits or high *return on equity* may be, at one time or another, incompatible with other goals such as increased market share or sales growth over time. It is the way that individual decisions and goals are arranged within a company that give it its unique character, a character that should serve to distinguish it from competitors.

A statement of strategy should delineate (1) the products or services offered by the company; (2) the markets in which it plans to sell these products and services; (3) the *distribution channels* that will be used to reach these markets; (4) the company's profit objectives; (5) the method of financing that the company intends to use to attain its goals; (6) major policy for the main functions within the company, including manufacturing, marketing, research and development, materials procurement, personnel, and labor relations; and (7) the size, design, and culture of the company.

cost accounting   A method of accounting for the costs of operating a business by allocating these costs to the goods a company produces or the services it renders.

The main activity in cost accounting is to accumulate the actual costs of material, labor, overhead, and, in some cases, selling and administration in a format suitable for comparison to predetermined costs. When the costs are in a suitable format, they can be used to perform a variety of cost analysis techniques, including *direct costing* (which analyzes those product costs that vary directly with production or sales volume) and standard costing (which compares actual costs with preset standard costs).

cost center   A unit, whether a department, piece of equipment, process, or individual, within a company to which *direct costs* can be attributed.

In addition to direct costs, many cost centers are also assigned a portion of the company's *fixed costs*, or overhead. A factory is usually considered a cost center. Managers of cost centers are usually responsible for optimizing the difference between standard costs (that is, the direct costs and overhead assigned to the cost center by management) and actual costs. Because of this, cost centers are sometimes called responsibility centers. The key to the effective use of cost centers is an accurate assessment and assignment of direct costs and overhead. In many cases, cost allocation is a matter of tradition rather than careful analysis. This can lead to a distorted perception of the profitability of various cost centers.

EXAMPLE: In the United Kingdom's brewing industry, the three functions of brewing, property management, and retailing, mostly through pubs and public houses, were perceived as an integrated whole. Because brewers failed to consider the costs of each of these three different activities (and the rates of return provided by each) there was significant overinvestment in brewing (resulting in artificially inflated profits) and a similar underinvestment in retailing. Clearly, any strategy based on this kind of misinformation is quite dangerous.

*See also **management control systems**.*

cost leadership   A marketing strategy in which a company attempts to capture a market by offering the lowest cost product or service.

This strategy can be effective in gaining *market share*, but it has two drawbacks. First, the company may cut the price too much and lose money. Second, a cost leadership strategy creates little brand loyalty; customers will switch to another product if they can buy it at a lower price. That means competitors have an opportunity to quickly steal market share. MeisterBrau beer adopted a cost leadership strategy with the slogan, "Tastes just like Budweiser but costs less."

EXAMPLE: The McCormick Inn in Chicago used an unusual variation of cost-leadership pricing to secure publicity and entice people to stay there. Between November 16 and December 30, they offered a "Rooms by Degree" deal that pegged room rates to the outdoor temperature. If the outdoor temperature was 20 degrees, the price of a room was $20.00. If the temperature dropped to 0 degrees, the room was free.

Hotels have high *fixed costs*, largely for building, heat, and maintenance, and low *variable costs* for such items as room cleaning and laundry. So getting even a low rate for a room can help pay for some of the fixed costs. During the McCormick promotion, however, the temperature rarely dipped below 40 degrees. That meant the McCormick came out a double winner: It garnered significant publicity with its promotion as well as reasonable profits.

cost of capital The rate of return available in the marketplace on investments comparable both in terms of risk and other investment characteristics (such as marketability and other qualitative factors).

A more practical definition would be the following: the expected rate of return an investor would require to be induced to purchase the rights to future streams of income as reflected in the business interest under consideration.

Cost of capital is an integral part of the business valuation process. However, it is determined by the market and is totally out of management's control (*see capital asset pricing model*). Cost of capital represents the degree of perceived risk by potential investors: The lower is the perceived risk, the lower the cost of capital.

cost of goods sold In accounting, the cost of producing, converting, or buying an item that is sold; also called cost of sales.

Gross profit is calculated by taking the difference between sales and cost of goods sold. As a rule, cost of goods sold includes the costs of material, labor, and overhead. Cost of goods sold is listed on the *income statement* and is calculated as follows:

Sales		$10,000
Less: Cost of goods sold		
Beginning inventory	2,000	
Add: Purchases	5,000	
Cost of goods available for sale	7,000	
Less: Ending inventory	3,000	
Cost of goods sold		$4,000
Gross profit		$6,000

cost per thousand (CPM) In advertising, the cost of reaching a thousand people with an advertisement.

CPM is derived by dividing the cost to place an ad in any given medium by the size of the audience that medium reaches.

$$\frac{\text{Cost}}{\text{Audience size}} = \text{CPM}$$

EXAMPLE: A full-page newspaper advertisement costs $16,000 and the paper has a circulation of 500,000, so the CPM comes to $0.032.

$$\frac{\$16,000}{500,000} = \$0.032, \text{ or } 3.2 \text{ cents}$$

Marketers use CPM, as a rule, to compare different outlets within the same medium—two newspapers, say. This comparison is valid, however, only if the two media reach the same target audience.

EXAMPLE: A calculator manufacturer attempting to reach an audience of businesspeople could place an ad in the newspaper mentioned above and reach 500,000 people for just $0.032 per thousand. Or it could place an ad in a local business journal with a circulation of only 20,000 for $0.50 per thousand. If one compares only CPM, the newspaper is clearly a better buy. The business journal, though, could be the true better buy, since it reaches the manufacturer's *target market* more directly.

cost-benefit analysis A method of determining whether the results of a particular course of action are sufficient to justify the cost of taking it.

EXAMPLE: A regional chain of restaurants is considering expanding nationally. It conducts a cost-benefit analysis in order to compare all the expenses involved in establishing restaurants across the country with the revenue that those restaurants might generate. If the revenue outweighs the costs, the restaurant will carry out its expansion plan.

Some costs and benefits, though, are not as easily measured as expenses and revenue.

EXAMPLE: An automobile manufacturer finds that one of its cars has a defective part. If the manufacturer performs a strict analysis comparing the relative costs and benefits of a full recall versus several lawsuits, it might seem that the better course of action would be not to recall the cars and prepare to settle the lawsuits. But in this case the cost-benefit analysis ignored such intangible costs as the value of injuries to drivers or damage to the manufacturer's reputation.

cost-of-entry test A method of evaluating the strategic impact of the acquisition or start-up of a new business unit.

The cost-of-entry test states that the cost of entering a new business must not exceed the future profits generated by that business.

EXAMPLE: When Phillip Morris acquired the Seven-Up Company, it paid more than four times the company's *book value*. Had this acquisition been subjected to the cost-of-entry test, it would have shown that Seven-Up's profits needed to quadruple in order to maintain the company's preacquisition *return on investment*—a feat that was virtually impossible given the intense competition within the soft drink industry. In the end, Seven-Up's financial performance was unsatisfactory and Phillip Morris sold the company.

See also better-off test, industry attractiveness test.

cost-plus pricing In marketing, a pricing strategy in which a standard markup is added to the cost of a product. If a clothing manufacturer produces 1,000 pair of pants that cost $19,000 ($19 each) and adds a markup of $5 per pair to the cost, the price to *wholesalers* is $24 per pair, and the manufacturer collects a profit of $5,000 (21 percent). For cost-plus pricing to work, however, the seller must accurately predict the demand for its products at a given price. If the clothing manufacturer had decided to sell the pants for $35 (to generate a profit of $16,000, or 84 percent), but wholesalers balked at the high price and bought only 500 pairs of pants, the company would make only $17,500, which is $1,500 less than the $19,000 it spent to make the pants in the first place.

When implementing cost-plus pricing, it is important to consider the series of markups that can take place throughout a distribution system (*see distribution channels*). Say the clothing manufacturer sells its pants to wholesalers for $24 per pair, the wholesaler sells the pants to a *retailer* for $30 per pair (yielding a 25 percent profit), and the retailer sells the pants for $60 a pair, or a 50 percent profit. Clearly, the final price to the consumer could vary considerably, depending on which channels are used and the markup each member of the channel makes.

countertrade One of those esoteric-sounding terms that describes a very basic concept: the exchange of goods, services, and perhaps currency for other goods or services.

The most common form of countertrade—barter—has been used to transact business between two parties since caveman days. In the modern world, more convoluted countertrade techniques have evolved, but they all involve paying for merchandise or services mostly with commodities of equal value, either with or without partial payment in currency.

As an export financing tool, countertrade enables companies to sell to customers in countries that could not otherwise buy goods and services because of the absence of hard currency. Domestically, the dearth of bank credit and debt-ridden balance sheets have forced many companies—primarily small and mid-sized firms—to creatively structure barter, coproduction, or buy-back transactions to stay in business. By and large, however, countertrade is a relatively new concept in the United States.

U.S. regulatory bodies are generally opposed to countertrade, although in a free-market economy they can do little to stop it. The U.S. government recognizes that countertrade is necessary for American firms to compete in world markets, but refuses to officially sanction it. The Securities and Exchange Commission, the Internal Revenue Service, and the Justice Department have yet to figure out how to establish rules to control counterade. And the American Institute of Certified Public Accountants seems befuddled by the nonconformity of these trade practices with their generally accepted accounting principles.

Countertrade contracts vary with each deal and from customer to customer, with form and content limited only by the imagination of the parties. Some contracts are bilateral, some multilateral. They may entail part payment in goods or services and part in cash or credit. For exports, the cash portion may be in buyer or seller currency. Additional services may be performed by seller or buyer beyond mere delivery of goods. Countertrade arrangements are logically grouped under three broad headings: barter, parallel trade, and buybacks.

Barter is the oldest form of countertrade, whereby products are exchanged without invoicing or any exchange of money. "Compensation" is merely a variation on the barter theme, with the seller taking a combination of goods and currency in exchange for goods.

Parallel trade involves the execution of two separate contracts: one for the sale of goods by party A to party B and a second contract for the sale of goods by party B to party A. The two contracts are necessary for insurance coverage and possibly credit terms for each shipment. Each contract is separate from the other and individually enforceable. "Counter-purchase" is one form of parallel trade and involves actual cash transfers. Seller and buyer each pay the other for the goods received, using either a letter of credit or cash payment. If buyer and seller are from different countries, payments from both parties may be in one currency or they may be denominated in the currency used by the party originating the transaction.

Buyback countertrade agreements result from the sale of technology, a license, production lines, or even a complete factory. Full or partial payment consists of products manufactured in the production facility, or from the license or technology involved in the transaction. Buyback transactions frequently involve the importing of subassemblies, components, or other products, which a manufacturing exporter then turns into finished product. The most common use of buyback agreements relates to turnkey construction projects.

"Coproduction" is a specialized form of buyback countertrade used mainly for the transfer of technology or management expertise. For example, two companies form a joint venture to build a plant in Haiti. The U.S. company takes an equity interest in the facility. It may also furnish management support to run the facility. In either case, the facility is usually coconstructed between the U.S. and Haitian companies. Since both parties remain responsible for the operation of the facility, manufacturing the products is known as coproduction. With equity interests, both parties benefit from the sale of these products. The Haitian partner gains by generating sales within Haiti and by exporting to other nations. Most importantly, it gains new technology. The U.S. company profits through exports either to the United States or to other nations.

CPM   *See cost per thousand* or *critical path method*

creative director (CD)   The chief of the creative department at an *advertising agency*.
   The creative director is responsible for all creative aspects of the advertising the agency produces, supervises *copywriters* and *art directors*, and reports to the vice-president of creative services.

credit (1)   An entry on the right side of a T-account (abbreviated Cr.).
   In *asset* accounts, a credit signifies a *reduction* in an asset, as when cash is paid to employees. In a *liability* account, a credit indicates an *increase* in a liability, such as a loan. In an *owners' equity* account, a credit indicates an *increase* in the account, as with the issuance of common stock. In a revenue account, a credit marks an *increase* in revenue, such as a sale. In an expense account, a credit indicates a *decrease* in expenses. In the net income account, a credit indicates an *increase* in net income. *See also bookkeeping, debit*.

Account title

Left | Right

Debit | Credit

Balance sheet accounts

Assets = Liabilities + Owners' equity

Dr. | Cr.   Dr. | Cr.   Dr. | Cr.

(+) | (−)   (−) | (+)   (−) | (+)

Income statement accounts

Revenues − Expenses = Net income

Dr. | Cr.   Dr. | Cr.   Dr. | Cr.

(−) | (+)   (+) | (−)   (−) | (+)

credit (2) The ability to borrow money or purchase an item with an obligation to pay later.

critical path method (CPM) A visual project control technique for planning, scheduling, and analyzing large projects.

The critical path method allows managers to see (1) which tasks in a project have a direct effect on total project time, and (2) how best to schedule each task in order to meet the project deadline at minimum cost. The critical path method is appropriate for a wide variety of projects, from building a highway to installing a computer system to manufacturing large appliances.

For the critical path method to be appropriate, a project must have three characteristics: (1) The project must be made up of a variety of distinct tasks that, when completed, mark the end of the job; (2) the individual tasks must be independent of each other and, within the sequence of the project, may be started and stopped; and (3) the individual tasks must be performed in sequence (for example, the foundation of an office building must be in place before the roof is put on).

The heart of the critical path method is a diagram of each of the different tasks that constitute a project. First, each individual task is identified, given an identification symbol (such as A, B, C, and so on), and listed in the order in which it must be performed. The approximate time for each task is also listed. There are entries for start and finish at the beginning and end of the list. Although they do not affect the total time of the project, they are an important part of the critical path diagram.

EXAMPLE: A foundry is planning to install a particle scrubber system to meet environmental quality of air requirements. The unit must be installed as soon as possible. The process consists of the following activities.

			Times (in weeks)		
Activity	**Description**	**Predecessors**	t_0	t_l	t_p
A	Purchase components	–	1	3	5
B	Reinforce floor and modify roof	–	2	3	4
C	Fabricate collection stack	A	3	5	8
D	Build frame	B	1	2	3
E	Modify scrubber	C	1	2	8
F	Control panel	C	2	4	12
G	Install scrubber	D,E	1	2	3
H	Inspect and test	F,G	1	2	3

The first step in the process is developing the network to see the relationships among the activities.

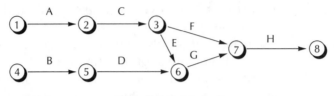

Critical Path Method

Notice that much of the work can be done concurrently. The next step is the determination of the average or mean times for each activity. This is done by using the formula for the mean:

$$\text{Mean time } t_m = (t_0 + 4t_1 + t_p)/6$$

When these are computed, the next step is calculation of the *critical path*, the longest path through the network. We identify three paths: A-C-F-H, A-C-E-G-H, and B-D-G-H. Comparing each path with the times for each activity, path A-C-F-H takes 15.17 weeks of effort and is the longest path through the network. Once this has been calculated, the variance of individual activities along the critical path is computed by using the following formula:

$$\text{Variance } \sigma^2 = [(t_p - t_0)/6]^2$$

The results are shown in the table below:

Activity	Mean time	On critical path?	Variance
A	3	yes	16/36
B	3	no	—
C	5.17	yes	25/36
D	2	no	—
E	2.83	no	—
F	5	yes	100/36
G	2	no	—
H	2	yes	4/36

Next we total the variances; they equal 145/36, or 4.03. Because the standard deviation is the square root of the variance, we take the square root of 4.03 and get a standard deviation of 2.01. Since we are dealing in weeks, this is rounded to 2.0. The project will take 15.17 weeks on average. Since there is a mean and a standard deviation, it is possible to make inference statements about completion in *n weeks*. For example, what is the probability of completing in 17.17 weeks? Since 17.17 weeks equates to the mean plus one standard deviation, using a normal distribution table, the mean-plus-one standard deviation covers 84 percent of the distribution. Thus, the chances of completion in 17.17 weeks is 84 percent. Similarly, the likelihood of completion in 19.17 weeks is 97.5 percent.

Now consider this example as a CPM problem. The distinction is that CPM uses one time estimate for each activity. Inference is not possible with CPM, and the computations are somewhat simpler. The paths are the same in the network, and two critical paths emerge. Using the middle value of the time estimates for the CPM data, the paths are

$$A\text{-}C\text{-}F\text{-}H = 14 \text{ weeks}$$
$$A\text{-}C\text{-}E\text{-}G\text{-}H = 14 \text{ weeks}$$
$$B\text{-}D\text{-}G\text{-}H = 9 \text{ weeks}$$

Since the project takes 14 weeks, any activities along the last path, B-D-G-H, can be delayed 5 weeks and all activities can be completed on time. For example, activity B can start five weeks after A has begun and the paths will still converge correctly.

critical ratio analysis   A tool used to prioritize inventories in a *flow process system*.

It highlights those stocks that are lowest relative to others. In a flow shop, goods are generally made-to-stock rather than made-to-order (*see* **make-to-order, make-to-stock**). Usually, the objective in managing a flow process is to replace stocks of finished goods before they run out. In order to accomplish this, materials *inventories* must be carefully managed. For example, a cigarette manufacturer must keep track of its inventories of tobacco, paper, and filters. In order to calculate the critical ratio for these inventories, management at the cigarette company must know (1) the remaining amount of each material in stock, (2) the rate at which that material is used (demand rate), and (3) the processing time of each type of inventory.

The critical ratio is an extension of the *runout method*, which estimates how quickly an inventory will be depleted. Runout time is calculated by dividing the remaining amount of inventory by the rate at which it is used (demand rate).

$$\frac{\text{Inventory remaining}}{\text{Demand rate}} = \text{Runout time}$$

EXAMPLE: For the cigarette company, the runout time for each inventory is calculated as follows:

Inventory	Inventory remaining (units)	Daily demand (units)	Runout time	Runout sequence
Tobacco	18	3	18/3 = 6 days	2
Paper	21	7	21/7 = 3 days	1
Filters	20	2	20/2 = 10 days	3

In other words, runout analysis shows that the cigarette company will be out of paper in 3 days, tobacco in 6 days, and filters in 10 days. This is called the runout sequence. If the inventories are ranked by runout sequence, paper would be first, tobacco would be second, and filters would be third.

The critical ratio improves on runout analysis by incorporating the processing time of each inventory into the analysis. For example, it might take 4 days to process a unit of tobacco into a batch of cigarettes, 3 days to process a unit of paper, and 15 days to process a unit of filters. The critical ratio is calculated by dividing an inventory's runout time by its processing time.

$$\frac{\text{Runout time}}{\text{Processing time}} = \text{Critical ratio}$$

In the cigarette company, the critical ratios for each inventory are as follows:

Inventory	Inventory remaining (units)	Daily demand (units)	Runout time (days)	Processing time (days)	Critical ratio	Critical sequence
Tobacco	18	3	6	4	6/4 = 1.5	3
Paper	21	7	3	3	3/3 = 1.0	2
Filters	20	2	10	15	10/15 = 0.67	1

When an inventory has a critical ratio above or near 1.0 (as with tobacco and paper) there is usually not cause for immediate concern because stock is being used more slowly than, or at about the same rate as, processing time. When a critical ratio is below 1.0 (as with filters), inventory is being used faster than the remaining processing time and a shortage is likely. The lower is the critical ratio, the greater the priority management should place on supplementing that particular inventory.

cumulative effect of a change in accounting principle In accounting, the *income statement* account showing the effect of switching from one accounting principle to another.

Cumulative effect shows the difference between the *retained earnings* reported at the beginning of the year under the old method and the retained earnings that would have been reported at the beginning of the year had the new method been used. *See also change in accounting principle, accounting change.*

current asset
In accounting, an item with a useful economic life of one year or less or the normal operating cycle of the company, whichever is greater.

Current assets are listed on the *balance sheet* and include cash and *cash equivalents, marketable securities, accounts receivable*, prepaid expenses, and inventory. Most companies list only current assets with a useful life of one year, but companies with a long operating cycle, say, a construction company working on a large project, might list current assets that have a useful life of five or six years.

current cost accounting
The measurement of assets in terms of their *replacement costs*.

For inventories, current cost is the cost of buying goods of the same type and quantity as those in inventory as of the *balance sheet* date. In determining the current cost of property, plant, and equipment, the guiding principle is service potential. In other words, the replacement cost of a factory is not the cost to duplicate the entire factory; it is the cost of duplicating the factory's capacity using present technology.

EXAMPLE: A vintner owns several small wineries, but current technology is such that only large wineries are being built. That means the replacement cost of the small wineries would be that of a single, larger operation.

In current cost accounting, only inventories and fixed assets are adjusted to reflect their replacement value. The historic costs of all other assets and liabilities are assumed to show their current costs without adjustment. *Owners' equity* under current cost accounting is determined by subtracting liabilities from the adjusted total assets.

The only changes in an *income statement* caused by current cost accounting are in cost of goods sold and depreciation expenses related to the current cost adjustments to the inventories and fixed assets on the balance sheet.

current liability
In accounting, a debt payable within one year or within the normal operating cycle of a company, whichever is longer.

Current liabilities include *accounts payable*, accrued expenses payable (such as salaries or taxes), short-term notes payable, and the correct portion of long-term debt. Current liabilities are shown on the *balance sheet* and must be paid either with a *current asset* or with the creation of another current liability.

current ratio   A measure of a company's ability to pay its short-term obligations.

The higher the current ratio, the more able a company is to satisfy its creditors. The current ratio is calculated by dividing **current assets** by **current liabilities**.

$$\frac{\text{Current assets}}{\text{Current liabilities}}$$

EXAMPLE: A company has $115,000 in current assets and $95,000 in current liabilities. Its current ratio equals

$$\frac{\$115,000}{\$95,000} = 1.21$$

In other words, the company has $1.21 in current assets for every dollar in current liabilities. A ratio greater than 1 is desirable (although a company's ratio should be compared with that of other companies within an industry to see whether it is high or low). Generally, companies with current assets containing low levels of inventory and high **accounts receivable** can operate with a lower current ratio than companies with high inventory and low accounts receivable, because inventories are not as easily converted into cash as accounts receivables. If a company's ratio is much higher than the industry's norm, it might indicate that the company is not actively investing its current assets. Although this may be attractive to creditors, it may not appeal to investors who would encourage management to invest current assets in order to achieve higher returns. *See also* **acid test ratio**.

current yield   *See bond yield*

customized marketing   A marketing strategy in which the market is segmented so completely that individual customers are identified and separate products or marketing plans are developed for each.

Customized marketing is frequently employed in the manufacture of airplanes, where producers such as Boeing, McDonnell Douglas, and Airbus customize planes to the specifications of a few major airlines. The advent of computer technology has made customized marketing possible in the **consumer market**.

EXAMPLE: In Japan, custom tailor shops measure their customers electronically, then transmit the measurements to a cutting shop where a laser cuts the cloth before it is sent to an automated sewing machine. The customer can pick up his custom-tailored suit the next day.

Customized marketing is also common in the upholstery, housing, and hairstyling businesses.

cycle In manufacturing, an event that recurs at a known frequency.
The length of various cycles are generally governed by seasonal demand.

cycle counting A method of ensuring the accuracy of a company's inventory where goods and materials are tallied on a cyclic schedule, rather than annually.
The aim of cycle counting is to find inventory items that are in error and raise a "red flag" that will trigger further research into the cause of the problem. Cycle inventory counts are generally made on a very regular basis. In many companies, counts are more frequent for fast-moving or high-value items and less frequent for slow-moving or low-value items.

cycle time The time it takes to perform each task in a process.
Frequently, the time of the longest task in the entire process is labeled as the cycle time.

EXAMPLE: A company assembles suspension systems for a major auto producer. The process is performed at five workstations in a sequence as seen below. The task times are also indicated.

Workstation	Task	Task time (minutes)	Idle time (minutes)
1	A	2.0	1.0
2	B	2.4	0.6
3	C	3.0	0.0
4	D	2.5	0.5
5	E	2.8	0.2

The cycle time for each task is the task time. This is the length of time to complete the individual task on one unit. The **bottleneck** in the operation is workstation 3, where the task takes 3.0 minutes. If all five workers are assembling units, a unit comes off the line every three minutes. The last column shows the impact of this bottleneck, with all but one station having idle time. If everyone is working, then 20 assemblies per hour are being produced (60 minutes/3 minutes per unit) and 160 per eight-hour day. This is the technological or *technical capacity* of the line. If two 10-minute breaks are allowed, and the wash-up time and start-up time consumes 10 minutes per day, then the *economic capacity* may be at 150 units per day, since 30 minutes are lost from breaks and other activities.

To measure the **efficiency** of the operation, divide the time working in the cycle by the time of the longest task. We see station 1 operating at 67 percent, or capacity, station 2 at 75 percent, 3 at 100 percent, 4 at 83 percent, and 5 at 93 percent. The overall line efficiency is then 84.7 percent.

D

days inventory In accounting, a measurement of the number of days it takes to sell the average amount of inventory on hand during a particular period of time.

As a rule, the longer it takes a company to sell its inventory, the greater the risk that it will not be sold at full value. Days inventory is extremely important to companies that carry items that are perishable or subject to rapid obsolescence, such as computers or fashion clothing. Days inventory is calculated by dividing the 365 days of a year by the *inventory turnover ratio* (inventory turnover is calculated by dividing the cost of goods sold for a specified period of time by the average amount of inventory on hand for that same time period).

$$\frac{365 \text{ days}}{\text{Inventory turnover ratio}}$$

EXAMPLE: If a company has an inventory turnover of 5.25, its days inventory ratio would be

$$\frac{365}{5.25} = 69.5$$

In other words, it took the company nearly 70 days to sell the average amount of inventory it had on hand in the past year.

See also ***inventory turnover.***

debenture An unsecured *bond,* normally in a subordinated position.

Frequently, debentures have convertible features or warrants attached that allow holders to exchange either the debenture or the warrants for common stock on a given date or when certain events occur—such as default on interest payments or bond redemption.

debit In accounting, an entry on the left side of a T-account (abbreviated Dr.). In *asset* accounts, a debit signifies an *increase* in an asset, as when cash is collected from a sale. In a *liability* account, a debit indicates a *decrease* in a liability, for example, when a loan is paid. In an *owners' equity* account, a debit indicates a *decrease* in the account, as with the payment of a *cash dividend.* In a *revenue* account, a debit marks a *decrease* in revenue. In an expense account, a debit indicates an *increase* in expenses. In the *net income* account, a debit indicates a *decrease* in net income. *See also bookkeeping, credit (1).*

debt/equity swaps The exchange of debt securities for equity interests. Several types of debt/equity swaps have become popular:

1. The swap of a Third World country's external bank debt obligations traded in secondary markets for equity interests (a) in a business being divested by the government through its "privatization" program, (b) in a privately-owned business, or (c) in a business started from scratch.

   EXAMPLE: A company purchases a Third World government debt instrument in the secondary market at a substantial discount from its face value—for example, 50 percent. It then offers to exchange this obligation with the debtor government for local currency. The rate of exchange might be, for example, equivalent to 75 percent of the debt. Soft currency is then used to build or purchase a plant or other facility in the host country for half the cost of an investment with U.S. dollars.

   Of course, companies must use their own funds to acquire the debt instrument in the first place, but most consider that a small price to pay for a bargain-basement investment.

2. The swap of a company's debt obligations with lenders for equity interests in the company.

   EXAMPLE: Assume XYZ Corp. owes $1 million to Fidelity Commerce Bank (FCB) on a term loan evidenced by a demand note. XYZ falls into arrears but has high expectations that when new product lines currently on the drawing boards are introduced in two years, the business should take off. FCB recognizes that if something isn't done with the loans, bank examiners will classify them as nonperforming, thereby requiring additional reserves and damaging the bank's capital ratio. XYZ agrees to trade a 20 percent equity share in the business to FCB in exchange for half the loan, thereby reducing debt service payments to a manageable level.

3. The swap of a company's trade obligations with a creditor for an equity interest.

EXAMPLE: A company strapped for cash owes a major supplier substantially more than it can pay. Rather than cutting off a valuable source of supply on one hand and a good customer on the other, the two parties work out a debt/equity swap: The supplier exchanges part or all of its receivable for a minority share in its customer.

4. The swap of public bonds for a minority equity interest.

EXAMPLE: Alpha Corp. has $5 million in bonds outstanding. A limited partnership, LPL, purchases $2 million of the bonds at market prices. LPL then offers to make a swap with Alpha, trading the bonds for perhaps $2.5 million worth of common shares.

Debt/equity swaps are also currently being arranged among debtors and creditors to ensure the preservation of natural habitats, for environmentally sound ventures, for college scholarships, and a variety of other purposes.

debt securities valuation A process to determine the investment value of debt securities.

Debt securities embody both the timing and the amount of income payments (interest) and return of capital (principal) within the debt instrument. This makes the risk of investing in debt securities substantially less than making equity investments.

Except for differences in the degree of risk, similar valuation methods are employed for both debt and equity securities. In both cases, the general valuation theory holds: The fair market value of a future stream of cash flows is equal to the present value of future cash flows. And in both cases, perceived risk is recognized in the capitalization rate.

Interest rates and repayment terms of any debt obligation are determined by three factors:

- Current market risk-free rates (reflected by the prime rate in banking circles and by the rate paid on U.S. Treasuries nearly everywhere else)
- Perceived risk of receiving interest and principal payments on schedule
- Collateral backing the loan (the quality of which detracting from or adding to the risk factor)

In addition to providing a base from which to negotiate with lenders for the lowest rate with the best terms, companies perform debt valuations for several other reasons:

- Excess cash may be invested in corporate or government bonds. A valuation of the debt security will ensure the right choice to maximize returns.

- A buy/sell transaction may involve the exchange of debt for equity, making it necessary to know the value of the debt security.
- Estate and gift tax laws require that debt obligations be valued at fair market value (for privately held businesses).
- When making a leveraged buyout, new classes of debt are created that must be valued along with the entire enterprise in order to allocate the purchase price among each class of participants.
- Companies may recapitalize their balance sheets to increase the amount of leverage they have to work with.
- Reorganization in bankruptcy cases involves the rearrangement of debt securities, frequently requiring the creation of new classes of debt securities or the exchange of debt for equity shares.

For a debt security traded in open markets, the market-determined present value of its future cash flows is observable from the market price of the security at any given time. The application of a security's rate of interest to its future cash flows produces a present value equal to the security's observed market price. This is called the security's "yield to maturity."

However, for privately held companies whose debt securities are not traded in open markets, security value must be calculated by using the present value formula. Three factors are needed to make the calculation.

- The amount of future cash flows generated by the security
- The timing of these cash flows
- An appropriate rate of interest or yield to maturity

The phrase "yield to maturity" is used interchangeably with the phrase "market rate of interest." When one reads or hears that the market rate of interest is 10 percent, it means the same as saying that the yield to maturity is 10 percent. *See yield to maturity.*

debt-to-assets ratio A measure of the relative obligations of a company.

Generally, the lower the debt ratio, the more financially sound a company is thought to be. The ratio is calculated by dividing a company's total debt by its total *assets.* In determining total debt, the most conservative approach is to use all *current liabilities* and *noncurrent liabilities* rather than just include those liabilities formally classified as "debt." The ratio is calculated as follows:

$$\frac{\text{Current liabilities } + \text{ Noncurrent liabilities}}{\text{Total assets}}$$

EXAMPLE: If a company has current and noncurrent liabilities totaling $780,000 and assets totaling $1,120,000, its debt ratio is

$$\frac{\$780,000}{\$1,120,000} = 0.69$$

In other words, for every dollar that the company has in assets, it has $0.69 in debt. Whether that ratio is good or bad depends on the standards of any particular industry. In general, though, companies with lower ratios are more solvent; companies with higher ratios face a greater claim on their resources by outside creditors.

debt-to-equity-ratio In accounting, a measure of the amount of debt a company has in relation to its *owners' equity.*

The ratio is calculated by dividing a company's total *liabilities* by total *stockholders' equity.*

$$\frac{\text{Total liabilities}}{\text{Total stockholders' equity}}$$

EXAMPLE: total liabilities of $3,400,000 and total stockholders' equity with a book value of $2,500,000, its debt-to-equity ratio is

$$\frac{\$3,400,000}{\$2,500,000} = 1.36$$

(For financing purposes, total stockholders' equity is adjusted for certain classes of preferred stock and convertibles.) This ratio means that for every dollar of the company owned by a stockholder, there is $1.36 owed to creditors.

Although potential creditors may be reluctant to give financing to a company with a high debt-to-equity ratio, the amount of debt often varies from industry to industry. Debt-to-equity ratios are traditionally calculated using the book values for a company's debt and stockholders' equity. However, their market values may give a more realistic measure, because they more clearly reflect current market conditions. *Key Business Ratios* and Standard & Poor's *Industry Surveys* supply data on a wide variety of *balance sheet* ratios grouped by industry and time periods.

decentralization The diffusion of authority, responsibility, and decision-making power throughout different levels of a company.

Decentralization is a departure from the classic pyramid, or functional organizational, design in which decision-making power is concentrated with top management. This design shows serious weaknesses when a company is faced with an uncertain and highly volatile *environment.* Lower-level managers often do not have the information or authority needed to make decisions, so they are pushed to upper management. Top managers quickly become overloaded with decisions, which hampers their ability to respond to environmental changes. In such a situation, many companies have found it advantageous to shift to a decentralized organizational structure. For example, since the break-up of the telephone industry, AT&T has shifted from a centralized, bureaucratic structure to a much more decentralized structure organized around different markets. This allows the company to respond more quickly to the actions of its competitors.

Companies with tasks that can easily be divided into self-contained divisions are most easily adapted to a decentralized structure.

EXAMPLE: Consider the following decentralized clothing company.

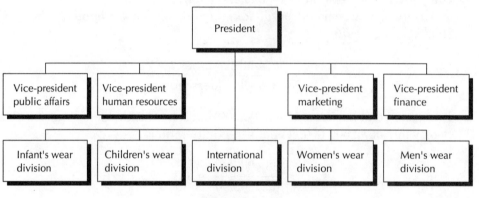

Decentralization

The clothing company is organized around both product areas (men's wear and women's wear) and markets (international). Each division has its own resources that enable it to perform its particular task; for example, infants' wear has its own production, design, testing, and marketing organizations. This enables each division to concentrate on its own set of products (or market) without getting involved in the issues facing the other divisions.

Decentralized organizations allow managers to concentrate on a specific set of products or services. Each division has the necessary resources to perform its activities, and there is no competition for shared resources. A decentralized structure is especially effective when a company's environment is complex, resulting in a variety of different factors that affect decisions regarding each product. By breaking into a series of separate divisions, a company can segment its environment and reduce the complexity faced by its managers. As a result, the managers of each division need less information than they would if they were trying to cope with a company's entire line of products and services.

*See also **functional organizational design, matrix structure, organizational environment.***

decision making   The process of choosing a course of action among alternatives.

Decision making is one of the most important, and difficult, aspects of management. The process of making choices plays a crucial role in leadership, communication, motivation, and other elements of individual, group, and organizational activities. There are a number of academic models that describe different decision-making methods, but perhaps the most practical is the following six-step problem-solving outline.

Step 1: Identify the problem. A good technique is to try to write the problem down as precisely as possible. Avoid simply listing symptoms.

Step 2: Collect data. Gather all information related to the problem. The information should cover all aspects of the problem, including who, what, where, when, why, and how. Consider the reliability of the data. Data based on rumor or opinion is not as reliable as data based on fact or truth.

Step 3: List all possible solutions. Make note of every solution that comes to mind. Ideas that may seem totally absurd might actually be helpful.

Step 4: Test possible solutions. Evaluate each of the possible solutions in terms of feasibility (What will it cost? Can it be done?), suitability (Will the problem be solved permanently or temporarily?), and acceptability (Will everyone agree to the solution?).

Step 5: Choose the best course of action. Select the solution (or combination of solutions) that works best.

Step 6: Implement the solution. If the problem is solved, the decision was correct; if the problem continues, start the process again.

decision support system   A computer system through which a user can obtain assistance in evaluating and choosing among different courses of action.

A decision support system may network to various databases, use *artificial intelligence,* or employ an *expert system* to collect and analyze the data. For example, at a small rural hospital, doctors may use a decision support system to help diagnose and treat patients. A set of symptoms would be entered into the system, which would then interact with a medical database and respond with a number of potential diagnoses and treatments.

decision tree   A type of flow chart that summarizes a potential sequence of decisions and spells out each of the possible consequences of those decisions.

EXAMPLE: Consider the following decision tree regarding a potential product launch.

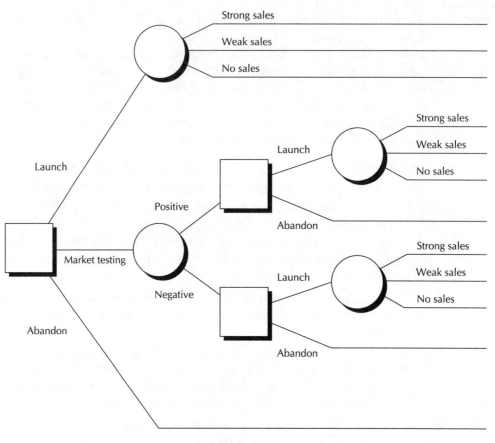

Decision Tree

Management decisions are represented by squares. Chance events are represented by circles. Lines representing the sequence of choices run between each related decision and the chance events that it creates. A probability is assigned to each of the possible consequences of a chance event. If, after receiving favorable results from market tests, the company decides to launch the product, there might be, say, a 60 percent chance of strong sales, a 30 percent chance of weak sales, and a 10 percent chance of zero sales. With these probabilities, the company can calculate its likely payoff if it pursues a particular course of action. Once all of the possible probabilities and payoffs have been calculated, the company can choose the course of action that appears to provide the most favorable outcome.

Essentially, decision trees allow management to clearly identify various options and rank them in terms of both the likelihood of their occurrence and their expected payoff. Of course, the success of decision tree analysis depends on the accurate forecasting of the probabilities of chance events. The technique has two key advantages. First, it forces managers to consider all of the ramifications of various decisions by visually showing their relation to each other. Second, it allows managers to focus on the chance events and uncertainties that will have the greatest impact on a decision.

decoupling inventory *See inventory functions*

defensiveness Reactive and protective behaviors that allow people to avoid action, change, or blame.

In organizational terms, defensiveness reduces overall effectiveness. It delays decisions, increases tensions, hampers change, inhibits risk taking, and makes evaluations unreliable.

There are three common objectives of defensive behavior: avoiding action, avoiding change, and avoiding blame. When a person seeks to avoid taking action, he or she might feign ignorance, transfer responsibility to another party, or try to stall in the hope that someone else will pick up the slack. Defensive behaviors calculated to avoid change might include a rigid adherence to corporate regulations ("The rules clearly state . . .") or a zealous attempt to protect a particular "turf" ("It's *my* job to deal with all outside vendors."). Defensive behaviors calculated to avoid blame include excessive justification and rationalization, scapegoating, or compulsive documentation of every act.

deferred charge *See deferred expense*

deferred credit *See deferred income*

deferred expense An expense incurred in one *accounting period* that will benefit future accounting periods; also called deferred charge.

A deferred expense is recorded as a *noncurrent asset* on the *balance sheet*. Examples include organization expenses to start up a business or branch, bond discount (*see bond*), plant rearrangement costs, and similar *intangible assets*. The *amortization* of these expenses to the *income statement* should be matched to the benefit the company will derive from the asset (*see matching principle*); for bond discount, the amortization is over the life of the bond. When the benefit period is indeterminable, as it is with organization expenses, moving expenses, or plant rearrangement expenses, the asset may be amortized over an arbitrary period, but no longer than 40 years.

EXAMPLE:

Dr.	Cash	$9,000	
Dr.	Deferred bond discount	1,000	
Cr.	Bonds payable		10,000

The issuance of 10-year bonds at a 10 percent discount is recorded as follows:

Year 1

Dr.	Bond discount (income statement)	$100	
Cr.	Deferred bond discount		100

For tax purposes, businesses must use the amortization stipulated by the IRS code. *Compare to deferred income.*

deferred income In accounting, an item of income that has been recorded in the books of an account as a *liability* but will not be realized until future *accounting periods;* also called a deferred credit.

EXAMPLE: Income is recorded during a construction project using the *percentage-of-completion method.* These entries record amounts due from the project:

Dr.	Unrealized receivable (noncurrent asset)	$5,000
Cr.	Deferred income (revenues) from project	5,000

In a subsequent accounting period, these entries recognize sales from the project matched with related costs:

Dr.	Deferred income (revenues) from project	$5,000
Cr.	Sales	5,000

The IRS code stipulates a different treatment for tax purposes. *Compare to deferred expense.*

deferred income tax charge In accounting, an *asset* created when taxable income is greater than reported, or income owing to a temporary difference in the recognition of revenue and expense items.

In other words, a company's tax payment is greater than the tax expense it reports in its *financial statements.* The difference is shown in financial statements as a deferred income tax charge.

EXAMPLE: Warranty expenses are deducted from a company's books in the year of a sale, but deducted on the tax return only when they are paid.

EXAMPLE: A company had sales of $10,000 and estimated and reported warranty expense as $1,000. But it actually paid only $800 on the warranties ($200 less than reported). Assuming a tax rate of 40 percent, the calculations and entries for the deferred income tax charge are as follows:

	Book income	Taxable income
Income	$10,000	$10,000
Warranty expense	1,000	800
Income before taxes	$ 9,000	$ 9,200

Tax expense ($9,000 × 40%)	$3,600
Deferred income tax charge ($200 × 40%)	80
Tax payable ($9,200 × 40%)	$3,680

*Compare to **deferred income tax liability**.*

deferred income tax liability   In accounting, an estimation of the amount of future taxes on income that has been earned and recognized for accounting purposes, but not yet recognized for tax purposes.

In other words, reported, or *book*, income will be greater than taxable income. The difference is shown in the *financial statements* as a deferred income tax liability. Eventually the two amounts will reconcile.

EXAMPLE: A company with income of $50,000 used *straight-line depreciation* for a charge of $5,000 in its financial reporting and a method of accelerated depreciation amounting to $7,500 for taxes. Assuming a tax rate of 40 percent, the calculations and entries for the deferred income tax liability are as follows:

	Book income	Taxable income
Income	$50,000	$50,000
Depreciation	5,000	7,500
Income before taxes	$45,000	$42,500

Tax expense ($45,000 × 40%)	$18,000
Tax payable ($42,500 × 40%)	17,000
Deferred income tax liability ($2,500 × 40%)	**$ 1,000**

Compare to ***deferred income tax charge.***

defined benefit pension plan   A program outlining the pension benefits that employees will receive when they retire.

The pension benefits are calculated through a formula involving years of service and compensation levels as employees near retirement. In establishing a defined benefit pension plan, a company must ensure that its *pension fund* has enough assets to pay the promised benefits. Typically, a company's reported pension expense will be different from the amount actually paid, resulting in a deferred pension *liability* or *asset. See also* ***funded pension plan.*** *Compare to* ***defined contribution pension plan.***

defined contribution pension plan   A program stipulating the annual dollar amount that an employer contributes to a pension plan.

The dollar amounts are calculated with a pension benefit formula that incorporates employee salary levels, years of service, and age. Under a defined contribution pension plan, the employer makes no guarantee of future benefits to employees, as with a *defined benefit pension plan.* Rather, there is simply a set dollar amount placed into the *pension fund* each year. *See also* ***funded pension plan.*** *Compare to* ***defined benefit pension plan.***

Delphi analysis

A forecasting technique in which a panel of experts makes predictions about the future regarding a particular issue.

Each panel member makes an individual projection or forecast, and each of the projections is assembled into a composite report, which is then reviewed by the entire group. This process is frequently restated several times until the panel reaches a consensus.

EXAMPLE: If a company is interested in a forecast of its sales in the next year, it might assemble a group of managers, consultants, and industry experts. Each individual submits his or her forecast along with an explanation of how it was developed. These individual forecasts are then summarized by management, along with a statement of the key factors that affect each report, and the summary is given to the panel for comment. In many cases, the summarized predictions lead to new individual predictions, which are again summarized and given to the panel. The process is repeated until a consensus emerges.

The Delphi technique offers two key advantages. First, panel members work individually and anonymously. This reduces contention within the group that might distort results and encourages members to express their true opinions. Second, it allows for the development of a consensus among a variety of individuals. It is important to note, however, that the success of Delphi analysis depends largely on the quality of the summary analyses, the willingness of the panel members to refine their predictions, and the manner in which information is presented to the individual forecasters.

demand

In economics, the amount of a good or service that people stand ready to buy at different prices, other factors held constant.

These other factors are (1) tastes and preferences, (2) income, (3) prices of related goods (substitutes or complements), (4) number of buyers, and (5) future expectations about market price.

The most common way to visualize demand in economic analysis is to trace the relationship between changes in a product's price and the amount that people are willing to buy. Economists assume that rational consumers will tend to buy more as price falls and vice versa. Whenever other factors change, it causes people to change the amount they are willing to buy, regardless of the price that is offered to them. These changes are often referred to as "changes in market conditions." For example, decreasing prices for personal computer software can be expected to cause people to increase the quantity demanded of this product. In addition, if the price of personal computers falls, it will cause people to buy more software, irrespective of the price of software.

demand forecasting

The estimation of expected demand for a product or service.

Demand forecasting has three main strategic applications: (1) to determine whether or not to enter a *market* (if there is not sufficient demand to justify the costs of entering the market, the company should reject the opportunity); (2) to plan short-term changes in a production schedule (such as work-force schedule and materials requirements); (3) to plan for the long-term capacity needs of a facility.

There are both formal and informal methods of forecasting demand. Informal methods include educated estimates and a "sensing" of the market. The formal methods of demand forecasting rely on either quantitative or qualitative information. Quantitative forecasting methods are broadly split into two methods: (1) those that only use historical information (such as past sales) in order to predict demand (called *autoprojection*) and (2) those that augment historical data with original information (such as *test markets* and surveys) to predict demand (called *causal*). Generally, autoprojection is the simpler, and cheaper, of the two. Autoprojection can be as straightforward as simply using an average of past sales or as complex as a multiple *regression analysis* of the different factors that influence sales. Autoprojection techniques are well suited for short-term planning and work best in relatively stable industries.

Causal methods are much more complex, usually involving a series of studies and advanced statistical techniques.

EXAMPLE: A snack food company might want to use a causal method in order to determine the demand for a new tortilla chip. A series of test markets might be conducted around the country, and their results analyzed to finally result in a forecasted demand.

Causal methods are best for medium- and long-term demand forecasts.

demand lending A form of lending that grants the lender the right to call the loan at any time, to make revolving loans only at its discretion, and to require all businesses receipts to be applied immediately to repayment.

Demand loan documents may carry a wide array of covenants that require the lender's consent for nearly any action company management may take that is not in the normal course of business—making an acquisition or purchasing a large piece of machinery or real estate, for instance.

Demand notes are the norm for smaller companies and are increasingly used in large corporations, especially those with a spotty earnings history or large debt burdens.

demand note A promisory note with no set maturity date.

The note spells out the principal amount of the loan and the interest rate; it may also identify a due date for the final liquidation of the loan. But in all cases, a demand note specifies that the entire loan must be paid back on demand by the bank. In other words, regardless of any mutually agreed-upon due date, the bank has the right to call for the entire payment at any time it wishes, unilaterally, without consent of the borrower.

Nearly all business loans to small and midsize companies are secured by demand notes in addition to other collateral. This gives a bank or other lender the right to call the loan regardless of a company's compliance with the terms of the loan agreement.

demographic segmentation In marketing, the division of the *consumer market* by age, ethnicity, sex, marital status, income, education, and geography.

Demographic segmentation is very common, since the different segments are often closely linked with preference patterns in the market. In other words, certain products will appeal to older, more educated consumers and others will appeal to younger consumers with less education. It's also relatively easy for marketers to use demographic segmentation, since the U.S. Department of Commerce, Bureau of the Census provides data in each of the demographic segments for the entire United States.

In the *industrial market,* or business-to-business market, the demographic divisions concentrate on company size, industry, and geographic location. Demographic segmentation is useful to marketers because it is easy to measure, the data are usually readily available, and it often yields productive results. *See also* *market segmentation, undifferentiated marketing. Compare to behavorial segmentation, preference segmentation, psychographic segmentation, volume segmentation.*

dependent demand *See derived demand*

depreciation An accounting method of spreading the cost of a fixed *asset,* such as plant and equipment, over its useful life.

The basic concept behind depreciation is that the value of every asset is reduced through use or obsolescence. Through depreciation, a relationship is established between the asset's ability to generate revenue and the reduction of its value. This relationship is in accordance with the *matching concept.*

EXAMPLE: A pizza restaurant buys a delivery truck for $10,000 and estimates that it will be able to make about 20,000 five-mile deliveries after which the truck will have no *salvage value.* With each delivery, the value of the delivery truck is reduced by $0.50 ($10,000 divided by 20,000 deliveries). When this reduction of value is accounted for in a company's financial statements, it is called depreciation.

When a company buys a fixed asset, it must make three management decisions with regard to depreciation: (1) which depreciation method to use (there are three that are widely used; *see* *double declining balance*

depreciation, straight-line depreciation, sum-of-the-years' digits method),
(2) how to estimate the asset's expected useful life, and (3) how to estimate
the asset's salvage value. Each of these decisions has a direct effect on
a company's income. Essentially, the higher the rate of depreciation, the
lower a company's income.

derived demand The condition where the demand for a product stems
from the demand for another product.

The demand in the *industrial market,* for example, is created by the
demand in the *consumer market.* As demand for various consumer goods
changes, the demand for the *industrial goods* that constitute them also
changes. As consumer demand for sweaters goes up in winter, for example,
so too does the demand for the wool, dye, and yarn used to make them. Demand for industrial goods is more volatile than it is in the consumer market.
In some cases, particularly when purchases are especially costly or require
a long lead time, a climb of 10 percent in consumer demand can increase
industrial demand by 100 percent. Decreases can be equally significant.

EXAMPLES: In the consumer sector, the demand for film depends on the sale
of cameras; the demand for videocassettes depends on the sale of VCRs.
Gillette markets its razors at a very low price to the consumer, knowing full
well that the sale of razors will lead to the sale of blades.

descriptive research Research that emphasizes either the frequency with
which an event occurs or some objective observation of an event or series
of events.

In other words, descriptive research explains or illuminates a particular
situation. If a company's sales suddenly start to drop, a descriptive research
project could find out why. Descriptive research is typically initiated by a
specific question or hypothesis. A restaurant, for example, might want to
develop a profile of its "average customer" with respect to age, sex, race,
geographic location, and income. *See also marketing research. Compare to
casual research, experimental research, exploratory research, observational
research.*

design capacity The *output* level at which a facility was technologically
designed to run.

EXAMPLE: A factory manufacturing toasters might have an annual design
capacity of 100,000 toasters. This goal may or may not have been met when
the factory was actually built. In many cases, when a contractor is hired to
build a new plant (or install a new piece of equipment) there is an agreed-
upon percentage (say 95%) of the design capacity that must be met before
the job is finished and payment is made.

design for manufacturability   An approach to the design of a product or service that includes both the people responsible for designing a product and the people responsible for producing a product.

Manufacturability is also known as concurrent engineering, simultaneous engineering, design for producibility, design for assembly, and a number of other names.

Manufacturability has significant advantages over traditional product design in which product engineers would design a product and pass it on to the production department without receiving the input of manufacturing engineers. A manufacturability team usually consists of designers, manufacturing engineers, marketing representatives, finance managers, R & D personnel, materials suppliers, and other interested parties. By including each of these elements, a product can quickly move from concept through production without being held up by any unexpected problems.

The manufacturability approach also has some disadvantages. Designers are limited by the practical considerations imposed by the other team members. For example, they may not be able to use certain materials or equipment that may be vetoed by other team members because of various cost, marketing, or safety concerns. Essentially, each team member sacrifices some independence and creativity in order to reduce the problems normally encountered in bringing a new product to the market.

development banks   Banks that function as coordinating and intermediary organizations to raise capital, attract investment, and provide technical assistance for the economic development of nonindustrialized countries.

Four multinational development banks are owned and funded by governments within the region, government agencies from industrialized nations, the World Bank, and large international banks. They are

- The Asian Development Bank (for Asia and the Pacific Basin)
- The African Development Bank and Fund (for Africa)
- The Inter-American Development Bank (for Latin America)
- The European Bank for Reconstruction and Development (for Eastern Europe)

In addition, regional development banks concentrate on specific, closely knit regions encompassing several countries (such as the Eastern Caribbean or Central America) and local development banks promote investment in specific countries. All development banks direct their attention to attracting new investment in infrastructure and private-sector businesses to a country or region.

differentiated marketing   A marketing strategy that segments the market and then tailors various products and offerings for each significantly different segment.

Automobile manufacturers, computer makers, and brewers all practice this strategy.

EXAMPLE: Anheuser-Busch offers Budweiser, Bud Light, Budweiser Dry, Michelob, Michelob Light, Michelob Dry, Busch, Busch Light, Busch Dry, and so on. The company's product line, then, includes regular beer, premium beer, low-calorie beer, and no-aftertaste beer. In short, it attempts to meet the vast varieties of specialized preferences in the marketplace.

As the Coca-Cola Company expanded, it began practicing differentiated marketing by introducing Diet Coke, Cherry Coke, and Coke Classic in a variety of package sizes designed to appeal to different segments of the market.

Differentiated marketing typically results in greater sales volume. It does so, however, at higher costs, since *economies of scale* are lost in producing such a wide variety of products.

differentiation   In marketing, the emphasis a competitor puts on some important product benefit, or set of benefits, that is valued by the entire market but not offered by the competition.

Differentiation is a common strategy in a *market* with many strong competitors. A company might cultivate its strength as a service leader, for example, by offering an unusually comprehensive warranty and presenting it to consumers as an advantage over its competitors. A company can also practice differentiation by associating a particular image with a product.

EXAMPLE: The selling of Marlboro cigarettes is a classic example of differentiation through image. When Marlboro was first introduced, it was positioned as a woman's cigarette, with red filters to mask lipstick stains. Sales were unimpressive, and Phillip Morris was ready to take the brand off the market. Then it contracted the Leo Burnett advertising agency and asked it to create a new way to differentiate the brand. Burnett decided to give Marlboro a masculine image. Thus was born the Marlboro Man, a cowboy who invited smokers to "come to where the flavor is. Marlboro country." The new image met with immediate success, and Marlboro became one of the best-selling cigarettes of all time.

See also differentiated marketing.

diffusion of innovation curve   A timeline of acceptance and adoption of a new product by different segments of the population.

In each product category, innovators are the first to adopt a new product. Next come early adopters, followed by early majority, late majority, and laggards. Innovators make up about 3 percent of the population and are characterized by their willingness to take risks with new products. Early adopters make up approximately 13 percent of the population; they are more cautious and act as the opinion leaders within a particular market—that is, they make reasoned, deliberate decisions about acceptance of a new product.

The early majority comprises about 34 percent of the population. They give new products careful consideration but tend to adopt them before the average person. The late majority makes up about 34 percent of the population; they are suspicious of new products and try them only after they are in wide use. Laggards are bound to tradition, dislike change, and adopt a new product only after it has been on the market long enough to take on a measure of tradition of its own. They make up about 16 percent of the population.

By identifying which segments of the market are more willing to adopt a new product, marketers can more efficiently target their efforts.

direct cost In accounting, an expense that can be attributed to a particular product or service.

Raw materials used in a product constitute a direct material cost. The salaries of plant workers constitute a direct labor cost.

direct costing A method of accounting that considers only the variable costs that can be directly linked to a product.

Fixed factory overhead is accounted for as a period cost and deducted along with the selling and administrative costs of a period. Under direct costing, the value of a company's inventory is calculated as follows:

Direct materials	$XX
Direct labor	XX
Variable factory overhead	XX
Product cost	$XX

Variable factory overhead includes those costs associated with running the factory that can be directly related to a particular product, such as the cost of electricity to run machines.

Direct costing is not allowed for either external reporting or income tax reporting; it is used for internal management only. Some of its internal uses include breakeven analysis, inventory valuation, income determination, and short-term decision making.

direct labor cost *See direct cost*

direct marketing A marketing tool designed to elicit immediate action from the consumer.

In other words, direct marketing uses various media to make sales rather than create preferences or cultivate brand images. Any direct marketing campaign has four central elements: (1) interaction with the *target market,* (2) opportunity for the customer to respond, (3) communication that can take place at any location, and (4) measurable response.

In direct marketing, interaction with the consumer is always two-way—that is, it takes the form of a conversation. The most obvious example of this interaction is a telephone call (*see telemarketing*) in which a salesperson convinces a customer to purchase a product. Two-way communication also takes place in the print media. Many mail-order sweepstakes, for example, send entries and letters that directly address the customer. "You, John Doe, may already be a winner!" By mailing in his entry, John Doe completes two-way communication with the direct marketer.

All direct marketing gives the people it targets the opportunity to respond. Whether it is via an 800 number, a coupon, or a chance to win a million dollars, the customer always has the opportunity to purchase something from the marketer. Customers who do not respond to a direct marketing effort are valuable, since they provide information, such as a profile of people who are not likely to respond, that can be used in planning subsequent marketing programs.

One of the key advantages of direct marketing is that it can take place at any location. The customer does not have to come into a store or be visited by a salesperson. Direct marketing can be performed at any time and any place where there is access to communications media.

The real value in direct marketing, however, is the marketer's ability to measure the responses its communication generates. Any response—or nonresponse—can be linked with an individual customer. The marketer can also clearly identify the specific approach that elicited that response. With these two pieces of information, the direct marketer can determine exactly which communications strategies best generate sales.

direct material cost *See direct cost*

direct method *See funds provided from operations*

direct numerical control (DNC) A manufacturing system where groups of *numerical control* machines are networked with a computer.

This allows the computer to control a given piece of equipment. *See also numerical control.*

disclosure A necessary explanation of a company's financial position and operating results.

Such information is included, either in footnotes or a supplement, in a company's *financial statements.* If a company has any information—an impending lawsuit, say—that would cause informed investors to appraise the company differently than they would without the information, it should be disclosed.

discount rate The interest rate charged by the Federal Reserve for loans to member banks.

This is a major tool of the Federal Reserve Bank in its attempt to control national monetary policy. As the Fed lowers the discount rate, banks pay less for borrowed funds and, theoretically, pass this saving along to consumer and business customers. Presumably, this increases the demand for borrowed funds and stimulates the economy with additional credit.

However, recent history has revealed the fallacy in this as a stand-alone policy. As discount rates descended, banks retained their high interest rates for loans, thereby increasing profits by the greater spread. When banks did begin to lower loan rates, consumers were so saturated with outstanding credit obligations that little new borrowing resulted. Nevertheless, the discount rate remains a favorite federal policy to influence national economy growth.

The term "discount rate" also relates to business valuations. It is the rate applied to a future stream of earnings or cash flow to calculate its present value. Discount rate and "capitalization rate" are used interchangeably to designate the premium charged by investors as compensation for the perceived risk, or uncertainty, in receiving forecasted future benefits.

discounted cash flow A method used to reduce a forecasted stream of cash flows to its present value.

Discounted cash flow is the fundamental principle underlying business valuations and is used for various purposes:

- To calculate the expected future benefits to investors in either debt obligations or equity interests
- To determine the price of a partnership interest in a buyout agreement
- To value debt obligations for debt/equity swaps
- To value minority interests
- To designate the value of partial interests in an entrepreneurial business for divorce settlements
- To assess estate taxes

Many valuation methods are used by analysts, investors, appraisers, the IRS, and others, most of which employ discounted cash flow as the primary tool. For certain types of companies, such as hotels and other real-estate–based businesses, the internal rate of return method can effectively calculate the discount rate to be used in discounted cash flow analyses.

discretionary income The amount of personal income available to a consumer after taxes and after paying for essentials such as food, housing, and utilities.

Discretionary income can be spent on nonessential items or saved. The total amount of discretionary income available is an important economic indicator, since consumers can stimulate the economy by spending this money. Marketers of merchandise other than necessities compete for discretionary dollars by targeting consumers' psychological, social, and self-esteem needs, as distinguished from their physical needs. *See also disposable income, Maslow's hierarchy of needs.*

dispatching The release of a work order from a production and planning department to the operations department.

These work orders specify the sequencing and assignment of available jobs to particular workstations. Dispatching can be either manual or computerized.

display advertisement A print advertisement in the editorial section of a publication.

Display advertising is not grouped by classification (as with classified ads), although newspapers tend to place categories of advertisers in particular sections (banks in the financial pages, restaurants in the food section, theaters and movie houses in the arts section, and so on). Display advertising further differs from classified advertising in its use of illustrations and different type sizes.

disposable income The amount of personal income available to a consumer after taxes.

Disposable income can be spent on essential or nonessential items or it can be saved. *See also **discretionary income**.*

distribution channels The various routes goods take as they travel from manufacturer to the ultimate consumer; also called marketing channels.

A channel of distribution is made up of all the intermediaries—trucking companies, railroads, storage facilities, *retail* outlets, and so on—that put products into the hands of consumers. As they move through the channel, products may stop at a series of intermediate points, the number and nature of which may vary greatly from one product to another. In some cases, the path the product takes may differ from that taken by its ownership, or title, because some intermediaries do not take title to the product but simply facilitate exchanges.

As products move from producers to ultimate consumers, various exchange transactions take place. In the process, a number of tangible and intangible items pass from one channel member to the next. First, of course, is the product or service itself. Raw materials are sold to manufacturers, which in turn produce finished products that are moved down the line to the ultimate consumer. The product is exchanged for some kind of payment, usually money.

In most cases, the title to the product, or legal ownership, also changes hands. Moreover, information is exchanged as products pass from one owner to the next. Communication backward through the channel lets manufacturers know consumers' needs. At the same time, information flows in the other direction—from manufacturer to consumer—in the form of promotion, thereby enhancing the desirability of the product and stimulating exchange. Manufacturers promote their products not only to consumer markets but also to channel members (*see **"push" strategy***).

Distribution channels typically include an independent producer that manufactures the goods; **wholesalers** that buy the goods and then distribute them to various selling locations; agent(s) who do not take title but facilitate exchanges to get goods to various selling locations; and **retailers** that finally offer the product for sale to the ultimate consumer. Each member of the channel seeks to maximize profits, sometimes at the expense of the system as a whole.

EXAMPLE: A manufacturer may increase prices to wholesalers in order to maximize profits. The wholesalers pass the higher prices, along with their own markup, to retailers, who increase the price a third time before offering the product to consumers, who may, in turn, decide to buy another product.

See also **cost-plus pricing.**

diversification
The spreading of risk between several different product lines, markets, or industries; also, for investors, the spreading of risk among various types of investments of different returns and maturities.

The concept of building a company into a "conglomerate" by the acquisition of diverse companies and product lines is an excellent example of business diversification. Maintaining a portfolio of traded stocks, corporate and government bonds, real estate, mutual funds, foreign stocks, venture capital, and precious metals represents a fully diversified investment strategy.

diversity
An increase in the heterogeneity of an organization through the inclusion of different groups.

In the past, these different groups were usually defined in terms of race, gender, and ethnicity. But the notion of diversity has come to include any person who is different from the "norm," such as gays and lesbians, the elderly, the physically and mentally handicapped, and so on.

Traditionally, diversity was managed as a "melting pot" in which managers assumed that different people would somehow assimilate and become more homogeneous. Today, most managers recognize that employees do not leave their preferences and values at home when they come to work. The challenge posed by diversity, then, is to accommodate different groups by addressing their lifestyles, values, work styles, and family needs without compromising the goals and operations of the organization.

dividend
The distribution of a company's earnings to stockholders.

Cash dividends are most common, although dividends can be issued in other forms such as stock or property.

dividend payout ratio
In accounting, a measure of the percentage of **net income** paid in **dividends.**

The ratio is calculated by dividing dividends per share by *earnings per share.*

$$\frac{\text{Dividend per share}}{\text{Earning per share}}$$

EXAMPLE: A company has a net income of $200,000, pays a dividend of $50,000, and has 50,000 common shares outstanding. Earnings per share is then $4, and dividends per share is $1. The dividend payout ratio is

$$\frac{\$1}{\$4} = 0.25, \text{ or } 25\%$$

In other words, this company distributed 25 percent of its income in dividends to its shareholders.

Some stockholders prefer companies with a high dividend payout ratio since it indicates that a high percentage of earnings is being distributed as dividends. Other shareholders are more interested in capital gains.

DNC *See direct numerical control*

double declining balance depreciation In accounting, a method of *accelerated depreciation* in which 200 percent of the *straight-line depreciation* rate is applied to the declining balance of the *asset's book value.*

An asset has no estimated *salvage value* when double declining balance depreciation is used because it is not included in the asset's book value.

EXAMPLE: An asset is worth $1,000, has a useful life of 10 years, and has a straight-line depreciation rate of 10 percent. So double declining balance would use a rate of 20 percent (10% × 200%). The annual depreciation charges would be calculated as follows:

Year	Original cost	Beginning book value		Double declining rate		Depreciation expense
1	$1,000	$1,000	×	20%	=	$200
2	1,000	800	×	20	=	160
3	1,000	640	×	20	=	128
4	1,000	512	×	20	=	102.40
5	1,000	409.60	×	20	=	81.92
6	1,000	327.68	×	20	=	65.54
7	1,000	262.14	×	20	=	52.43
8	1,000	209.71	×	20	=	41.94
9	1,000	167.77	×	20	=	33.55
10	1,000	134.22	×	20	=	26.84
11	1,000	107.38	×	20	=	21.48
12	1,000	85.90	×	20	=	17.18
13	1,000	68.72	×	20	=	13.74
14	1,000	54.98				

Under double declining balance depreciation, depreciation continues until the book value of the asset becomes inconsequential or the asset is disposed of. In order to avoid this situation, many companies switch to the straight-line method for the later years of an asset's life. Doing so allows them to depreciate the entire cost of the asset over a specified number of years. If the company had switched to the straight-line method in the example above, the calculations for the final five years of the asset's life would have been as follows:

Year	Original cost	Net book value		Straight-line rate	Depreciation expense
6	$1,000	$327.68	×	20%	$65.54
7	1,000	262.14			65.54
8	1,000	196.60			65.54
9	1,000	131.06			65.54
10	1,000	65.52*			65.54

*The final figure is $0.02 low because all of the depreciation calculations were rounded to the nearest penny.

See also *accelerated depreciation, depreciation. Compare to **straight-line depreciation, sum-of-the-years'-digits method.***

double entry bookkeeping *See bookkeeping*

Dow Jones Industrial Average (DJIA) The oldest and mostly widely quoted average used to measure and report value changes in a representative stock grouping.

It comprises a price-weighted average of 30 blue-chip industrial stocks, plus American Express and AT&T. The components of this average indicator change from time to time, but they generally represent approximately 15 to 20 percent of the market value of actively traded stocks on the New York Stock Exchange.

Casual investors continue to rely on the DJIA and other averages and indexes to judge market movement and value. However, since institutional investors carry a very large piece of the total value of each of the DJIA companies, the validity of this average for serious investors is being increasingly challenged.

The DJIA, as well as other indexes and averages, is also used for comparative purposes in certain business valuation techniques.

due diligence The process by which an investor, underwriter, lawyer, or auditor gathers and verifies the accuracy of data.

In business acquisitions, mergers, or divestitures, the gathering of data prerequisite to preparing pro forma financial statements and cash flows is called due diligence. In an initial public offering, due diligence refers to the efforts made by an underwriter to ascertain background and financial viability of the issuing company and to determine the uses to which the proceeds of the issue will be put. In the banking community, due diligence relates to the investigative efforts of the lender to determine the financial viability and collateral adequacy of the borrower.

dumping In international marketing, when a company charges less for a product than it originally cost or less than the company charges in its home market.

This technique is used to eliminate a surplus or quickly gain market share in a new country or market and is usually considered an unfair practice.

EXAMPLE: When Japanese television manufacturers entered the U.S. market with several lines of low-priced television sets, the American manufacturer Zenith accused them of dumping. Under the Antidumping Act of 1974, the U.S. Customs Bureau can institute tariffs if it sees evidence of dumping in the American market.

Dun & Bradstreet reports A source of credit information, available to subscribers, that includes data on a company's management, the nature of its business, product line, number of employees, credit history, banking relationships, legal or criminal proceedings, current debts, and record of payments to suppliers.

durable good A tangible product, such as a television or bicycle, that has a long life expectancy.

Durable products usually require personalized selling and often service, provide relatively high profit margins for the seller, and usually are sold with some sort of guarantee.

earnings per share A measure of a company's profit shown in terms of each share of common stock.

There are two types of earnings per share: primary and fully diluted. A company with a *simple capital structure* reports only primary earnings per share. The calculation for primary earnings per share is

$$\frac{\text{Net income} - \text{Preferred dividend}}{\text{Weighted-average common stock outstanding}}$$

Companies with a *complex capital structure* must report both primary and fully diluted earnings per share when the amounts differ by more than 2 percent. Fully diluted earnings per share are calculated as

$$\frac{\text{Net income} - \text{Preferred dividends}}{\begin{array}{c}\text{Weighted-average number of common shares} \\ + \text{ Common stock equivalents}\end{array}}$$

See also *common stock equivalent, complex capital structure, simple capital structure.*

ECO *See engineering change order*

economic order quantity (EOQ) A method of determining the optimum amount of materials that needs to be ordered on a regular basis.

The EOQ itself is that quantity that balances the cost of possession with the cost of acquisition. There are three assumptions that must be met in order to apply EOQ: (1) Demand is constant (say 100 units per day); (2) unit prices remain constant; and (3) all other costs remain constant.

EXAMPLE: The Richmond Company performs electrical repair work on a contract basis. It uses a significant number of light sockets annually, approximately 24,000. The accountant at Richmond has determined that it costs $50.00 to place a purchase order, and he estimates inventory carrying costs at 2% per month. This percentage is based on the value of the inventory. Richmond is presently paying $1.50 per socket. Wanting to maintain a cost balance, the accountant decides to explore the EOQ as a way of balancing costs of possession and ordering costs.

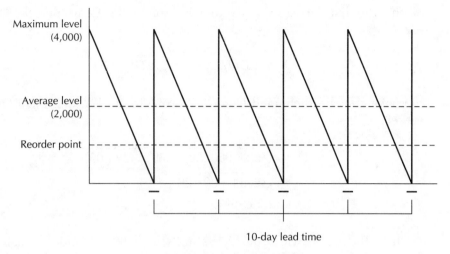

Economic Order Quantity: Exhibit 1

The EOQ is based on the following formula. The total cost of inventory is the sum of ordering costs and inventory carrying costs and the product purchased.

Let D = annual demand for the product, O = ordering cost, and C = unit cost. Let I = inventory carrying cost as a percentage of unit cost; this is done so that each unit of product bears its fair share of inventory carrying cost (a $1.00 item costs the same proportionally as the $100,000 item). Finally, let Q = the economic order quanity or the optimal-size order and TC = Cost to order + Cost of product + Cost to possess. Thus

$$TC = (D/Q)/O + CD + (Q/2)CI$$

This equation is the mathematical representation of Exhibit 2, where

D/Q = number of orders placed
CD = total cost of product purchased
$Q/2$ = average inventory as illustrated in Exhibit 1
CI = dollar value of inventory carrying cost

The total cost equation is that of a curve. We seek the minimum point on that curve and thus must use calculus to find that point. We take the first derivative of the function as seen below:

$$\frac{dTC}{dQ} = -\frac{DQ}{Q^2} + \frac{CI}{2}$$

Setting the first derivative equal to 0 and solving for Q, we find the following:

$$Q = (2DO/CI)^{.5} = \sqrt{2DO/CI}$$

Looking at the Richmond Company problem, we see that the EOQ for sockets is

$$Q = \sqrt{2(24,000)(50)/1.50 \times (12)(.02)}$$
$$= \sqrt{2,400,000/.36}$$
$$= 2,582 \text{ units}$$

Thus, Richmond will order 2,582 units, or 2,600 (rounded), each time it places an order. With that data, Richmond's accountant calculates nine orders per year (rounded), and the orders must be placed every six weeks. He establishes the lead time from the local supplier to be one week. Thus, the reorder point, that quantity of stock needed to supply Richmond during the reorder lead time, is 433 units, or one week's usage. He rounds this to 500 and advises the stock clerk to put in a requistion when the stock level reached 500 units.

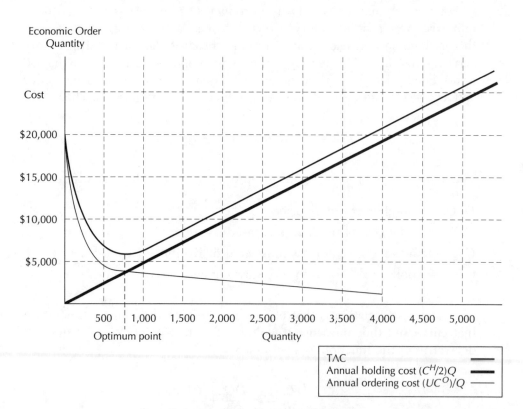

Economic Order Quantity: Exhibit 2

The total cost of that policy over and above the investment in sockets is the cost of ordering (9 orders @ $50.00 per order) and the cost of possession (1,300 units average inventory multiplied by an annual cost of 24% of $1.50, or $0.36). This equates to $450 + $468, or $918.00. Therefore, buying with the EOQ adds $0.038 to the cost of each socket for a total unit cost of $1.54.

economies of scale The lowering of costs through the production of larger volumes.

For example, say a manufacturer estimates that the setup costs for a particular product are $2,000 per setup. If the company runs one unit on the setup, it would incur a $2,000 per unit cost. If the company runs 2,000 units on the setup, the cost is $1 per unit. Basically, economies of scale arise from spreading *fixed costs,* such as administration, insurance, sales, and setup expenses, over a greater number of products.

EXAMPLE: Say a pencil factory uses $1 million in fixed costs to produce 20 million pencils per year. Management is considering adding colored pencils to the company's product line. It is estimated that 5 million colored pencils can be produced by using available slack in the company's fixed expense categories. In other words, the colored pencils would not increase fixed expenses at all. The resulting economy of scale will have the following effect:

Present fixed cost allocation: $1,000,000/20,000,000 = $0.05 per pencil
Proposed fixed cost allocation: $1,000,000/25,000,000 = $0.04 per pencil

The profitability of each pencil will increase one cent.

Economies of scale strategies are, however, limited. Because of the inherent inefficiencies of increasing facility size (such as increased bureaucracy, long lines of authority, and poor communications) the disadvantages of economies of scale can quickly outweigh their economic advantages.

Economies of scale are frequently used by managers to justify the production or expansion of a company's products or services. However, these new products can create production and marketing requirements that can cause the company to lose its competitive edge. When considering economies of scale, one must consider the source of the economies: sometimes from off-peak available capacity, sometimes from the use of common technology, other times from higher volume. If the source of the economy creates a diseconomy of scale (through either decreased efficiency or loss of competitive focus) the company should not pursue the idea. *See also economies of scope.*

economies of scope The lowering of costs through the production of a wide variety of products or services.

EXAMPLE: A toy company that aims to lower costs by using programmable robots to manufacture a variety of different board games is pursuing a strategy based on economies of scope.

The basic concept behind economies of scope is the same as for economies of scale—spreading *fixed costs* over more products or services. The only difference is that the increase in scale for economies of scope is achieved through the production of small batches of a wide variety of products rather than large batches of only a few products. *See also economies of scale.*

Edge Act

Edge Act　A federal law passed in 1919 that enables national banks to conduct foreign lending operations through federal or state-chartered subsidiaries called Edge Act corporations.

Edge Act corporations are the U.S. version of private banking. They have become a popular medium for investing in foreign securities and private businesses. These institutions are allowed to own banks in foreign countries and to invest in commercial and industrial firms, a flexibility denied to U.S. commercial banks.

Moreover, in an effort to help U.S. banks compete with foreign banks, the Edge Act permits the Federal Reserve System to set reserve requirements on foreign banks that do business in America. To put some teeth in this law, the International Banking Act was enacted in 1978. It specifically instructs the Fed to eliminate any banking regulations that put American banks (that is, Edge Act banks) at a competitive disadvantage with foreign banks operating in the United States.

Private banks (including Edge Act banks) have managed the financial affairs of wealthy individuals for many decades, offering an array of services, including but certainly not limited to investment advisory services, corporate finance, trust services, custodial services, company formations, and professional portfolio management.

Private banks have nothing to do with teller cages, money machines, home mortgages, checking accounts, and the myriad of other services offered by commercial banks. Instead, they specialize in one-on-one services, providing virtually any financial assistance investors may need for managing offshore portfolios. Private banks also sell short-term bank instruments at competitive rates to investors awaiting other long-term opportunities.

effective capacity

effective capacity　The *capacity* of an operation under normal operating conditions.

EXAMPLE: A factory with a *design capacity* to manufacture 100,000 toasters per year might have an effective capacity of only 85,000 toasters. Effective capacity can be limited by a number of factors, such as a limited supply of skilled labor, shortages of raw materials, or equipment that frequently needs repairs.

See also capacity, design capacity.

effective interest rate   The real rate of interest on a loan.

The effective interest rate is stated as an annual percentage that is applied to the entire life of the loan. Effective interest rate is calculated as

$$\frac{\text{Face value (nominal) interest on a loan}}{\text{Net proceeds of the loan}} = \text{Effective interest rate}$$

EXAMPLE: Say a company borrows $100,000 at 13 percent (the nominal interest rate) to be repaid in one year. The interest comes to $13,000 ($100,000 × 13 percent), and the effective interest rate is 13 percent ($13,000/$100,000).

Effective interest becomes more important when a loan is discounted, a common practice in which interest is deducted from the proceeds of the loan at the beginning of its term. Banks issuing discounted loans often require a compensating balance (that is, a deposit to offset the unpaid loan), which earns no interest. Compensating balances (usually expressed as a percentage of the loan) can also significantly affect the effective interest rate paid on a loan.

Let us say the $100,000 to which we just referred is discounted. The effective interest rate then becomes

$$\text{Proceeds} = \text{Principal} - \text{Interest} = \$100,000 - \$13,000 = \$87,000$$

$$\text{Effective interest rate} = \frac{\text{Interest}}{\text{Proceeds}} = \frac{\$13,000}{\$87,000} = 0.149, \text{or } 14.9\%$$

So when the loan is discounted, the effective interest rate becomes 14.9 percent, a significant increase over the original 13 percent. If a compensating balance is required, say 10 percent ($10,000), the effective interest rate becomes even higher.

$$\text{Proceeds} = \text{Principal} - \text{Interest} - \text{Compensating balance}$$
$$= \$100,000 - \$13,000 - \$10,000 = \$77,000$$

$$\text{Effective interest rate} = \frac{\text{Interest}}{\text{Proceeds}} = \frac{\$13,000}{\$77,000} = 0.169, \text{or } 16.9\%$$

So the effective interest rate on what was originally a 13 percent loan has become 16.9 percent, which is the true cost of the loan.

effective tax rate   The tax rate paid by a company.

Effective tax rate is calculated by dividing the amount of tax by taxable income.

$$\frac{\text{Tax}}{\text{Taxable income}}$$

EXAMPLE: A company with taxable income of $500,000 pays $200,000 in taxes, so its effective tax rate is 40 percent ($200,000 divided by $500,000). The effective tax rate differs from the statutory tax rate in that it shows the amount of taxes that a company actually paid as opposed to the amount mandated by the government.

efficiency A measure (expressed as a percentage) of how well a process functions.

Efficiency is calculated by dividing the total time taken to complete a job by the product of the longest *cycle time* of the entire process and the number of workstations.

$$\frac{\text{Total task time}}{\text{Cycle time} \times (n \text{ workstations})} = \text{Efficiency}$$

EXAMPLE: Say a department store is processing credit applications. It must process 600 applications per day. The job can be divided into the following seven tasks, each with its own workstation:

		Time (min)	Preceding task
1	Open applications	0.25	none
2	Read enclosed letter, noting any special requirements	0.45	1
3	Process page 1 of application	0.32	1
4	Process page 2 of application	0.30	1
5	Determine credit limit from standardized tables	0.50	3,4
6	Supervisor checks credit limit, notes applicant's address, and type of form letter to be sent	0.75	2,5
7	Assistant prepares and mails form letter	0.35	6
	Total	2.92	

The total time for the process is 2.92 minutes. The longest cycle time is 0.75 minutes for the supervisor check. With this information, the efficiency of the process can be calculated as

$$\frac{2.92}{0.75 \times 7} = 0.556, \text{or } 55.6\% \text{ efficiency}$$

Efficiency can be improved by changing the staffing of the workstations to lower the cycle time of the process. For example, if a second supervisor were hired, the work at workstation 6 could be done twice as quickly (reducing task time to 0.38 minutes). The longest task time in the process would then be 0.50 minutes for determining the applicant's credit limit. This figure then becomes the cycle time used in the efficiency calculation:

$$\frac{2.92}{0.50 \times 7} = 0.834, \text{ or } 83.4\%$$

A more theoretical approach to increasing efficiency is **line balancing.** This process calculates the minimum number of workstations needed for 100 percent efficiency and assigns them equal cycle times. Cycle time is calculated with the average daily output rate (in this case 600 applications). This approach assumes that the number of applications processed is equal to the number of applications received. If more than 600 applications come in per day, a backlog will be created. If fewer than 600 come in, there will be unnecessary idle time. Cycle time is then calculated by dividing the available work time (eight hours) by daily demand.

$$\frac{\text{Available work time}}{\text{Daily demand}} = \text{Cycle time}$$

In the example, cycle time is

$$\frac{(8 \text{ hours} \times 60 \text{ minutes})}{600 \text{ applications}} = 0.8 \text{ minutes per application}$$

In other words, in order to process 600 applications per day, an application must be completed every 0.8 minutes.

The minimum number of workstations required is calculated by dividing the total task time by the cycle time already determined.

$$\frac{\text{Total task time}}{\text{Cycle time}} = \text{Numbers of workstations}$$

In the example, at least four workstations are needed, or

$$\frac{2.92}{0.8} = 3.65$$

Although the actual number of workstations required is 3.65, it is impossible to set up 0.65 of a workstation, so the number is *always* rounded up. It may be, however, that the work cannot be divided into exactly four workstations, and five, or even six may be needed. If this is the case, each additional workstation will diminish the efficiency of the process. For example, with four workstations

$$\frac{2.92}{4 \times 0.8} = 0.912, \text{ or } 91.2\% \text{ efficiency}$$

With five workstations

$$\frac{2.92}{5 \times 0.8} = 0.730, \text{or } 73.0\% \text{ efficiency}$$

In practice, an efficiency measure anywhere between 80 and 90 percent is desirable. Any less than 80 percent means too much idle time. Any more than 90 percent indicates the process cannot adapt to a short-term increase in demand. *See also productivity.*

efficient capital markets   In finance, a theory that market prices reflect the knowledge and predictions of all investors.

In that this knowledge of financial markets is so widespread and readily available (thanks to computers and telecommunications) price changes, according to the theory, are the result of unpredictable, random events.

In other words, because so much information is available, predictions are made of the expected performance for each security, and prices are set accordingly. Price changes, then, are the result of unpredictable events (after all, if they were predictable, they would have been incorporated into security prices in the first place) that are essentially random in nature. The efficient market theory underlies the controversial proposition that a monkey selecting stocks by throwing a dart at the financial page of a newspaper has as good a chance of outperforming the market as any professional investor.

emotional appeal   An advertising message approach that tries to appeal to a consumer's psychological, social, or emotional needs, rather than practical or rational concerns.

Marketers of undifferentiated products (*see differentiation*) often use emotional appeals to gain consumer interest. Also, many marketers of products that have strong psychological components—cosmetics, travel, and clothing, for instance—use emotional appeals.

Emotional appeals fall into two categories: positive and negative. Popular negative emotional appeals include fear, guilt, and shame, which are used to motivate people to do things they should, such as using condoms and dandruff shampoo, and to stop doing things they should not, such as drinking and driving or smoking. Positive emotional appeals include love, happiness, humor, delight, and excitement. These emotional appeals can be applied to almost any product or service.

employee discharge   The firing of an employee.

Traditionally, employee-employer relations were *at-will*. In other words, either party could terminate the employment relationship for any reason and at any time without providing advance notice to the other party. Within the past few decades, however, an increasing number of employees have initiated wrongful discharge suits against their employers. Although there is no federal law that governs this practice, many states have been active in creating employee protection legislation. For example, of the 51 cases that went to court between October 1979 and January 1984 in California, 70 percent were won by employees. In these cases, the average jury award to the employee(s) was $178,184. The 19 highest awards averaged $553,318. Even when employers won a wrongful discharge suit, their legal fees were close to $100,000.

Clearly, significant costs are associated with the wrongful discharge of an employee. Because of these, it is important to clarify the legal basis for wrongful discharge suits. The three most common types of suits are based on (1) public policy violations, in which an employee is fired after refusing to break a law, such as falsifying documents; (2) breach of good faith, which generally means that the discharge was based on some arbitrary or capricious factor; and (3) breach of contract, in which an employment contract (either written or implied) is broken.

A wrongful discharge suit based on public policy violations, such as an employee's refusal to steal, lie, falsify records, or any other action that violated the law, frequently creates a tort liability for the employer in which the employee can sue for both compensatory damages (such as lost wages) and punitive damages designed to punish the employer. Additionally, public policy violations can expose individual managers to various liabilities, including criminal prosecution if he or she is responsible for giving the order to break the law.

The seminal case that guides many rulings in the area of wrongful discharge for public policy violations is *Tameny v. Atlantic Richfield Co.* (1980) in which an employee refused to take part in a price-fixing scheme. Based on the "malicious conduct" of the employer, the employee could sue for punitive damages.

Over 35 states have adopted policies limiting at-will employment in the case of a violation of public policy.

The evaluation of the second type of wrongful termination suits, those alleging violations in employer good faith, can be extremely difficult. It requires the establishment of the employer's motives and intent, which allows for a variety of different interpretations. As a result of this difficulty, relatively few states have adopted laws that limit at-will employment on the basis of breaches of good faith.

Some of the management actions that can constitute a breach of good faith are (1) distortion, falsification, or destruction of performance records, (2) the creation of heavy work loads designed to provoke resignation, (3) retaliatory discharge for employee activities such as filing a worker's compensation claim or joining a union, and (4) malicious behavior, including abusive actions, harassment, and inadequate training.

The third major type of wrongful termination suits, those involving employer breach of contract, requires the courts to examine both expressed, or written, and implied covenants made by an employer. These covenants generally create the expectation that the employee is assured of long-term employment. The most commonly used source of employer-employee contracts is the employer's written rules and policies, usually found in the employee handbook. However, statements such as "Keep up this kind of good work and you'll never have to worry about finding another job" can also be considered contracts and serve as grounds for a court action against an employer.

In some cases, length of service alone can be treated as a contract. For example, in *Pugh v. See's Candies, Inc.* (1981), an employee of 31 years was fired for an undisclosed reason. Since the employer was unable to justify the termination to the court's satisfaction, it was determined that the length of the employee's service itself created an implied contract that allowed termination only for just cause. Since the employer could not provide just cause for the termination, the employee won the case.

Over 37 states have adopted legislation that limits at-will employment with regard to explicit and implied contracts.

The most frequently used defense against wrongful discharge suits is just cause. In other words, the employer argues that the termination was motivated by a particular reason, such as violation of company policies, failure to meet performance or conduct standards, or failure to meet societal standards, such as committing a criminal offense. There is no clear legal definition of just cause. Instead, it has mainly been defined by court rulings and definitions of what is *not* just cause for termination. In most cases, the courts rely on vague terms such as arbitrary, malicious, intolerable, not in good faith, negligent, and without adequate cause. Corporate reaction to this lack of direction has generally gone in one of two ways. Some companies have attempted to develop exhaustive lists of exactly what sort of behavior is grounds for dismissal so that employees are aware of exactly which actions will cause the company to take disciplinary action, whereas others have attempted to create more universal codes for employee behavior, such as "any conduct that does not reflect well on the company. . . ." Probably the best approach is a combination of the two, where management makes it clear that certain specific behaviors will not be tolerated, but reserves the option to review specific situations.

employee stock ownership plan (ESOP) An employee benefit plan that gives employees shares in the company.

These may be voting shares but more often they are a special class of nonvoting *common stock.* The rules governing ESOPs change with revisions to the IRS code.

An ESOP is a legal entity that receives either company shares donated in the names of employees or cash that is used to purchase shares from the company. Corporations are allowed a tax deduction for part or all of their donations to ESOPs. ESOPs may borrow funds from a financial institution and use the money to acquire additional shares in the company.

Besides motivating employees by granting them shares of their company, ESOPs are used as the acquiring mechanism (through bank loans) to effect a management buyout of part or all of the company—a popular event during the 1980s.

employment The measure of the human input to the production process. There are two major measures of employment in the U.S. economy, both of which are compiled by the Bureau of Labor Statistics, U.S. Department of Labor.

The *household* survey of employment measures the employment status of the population and thus counts the number of employed persons. It counts an employed person only once, regardless of the number of jobs the person may have.

The *establishment* survey of employment measures the number of payroll jobs in the nonfarm economy (excluding farm workers and self-employed workers). Since this is a measure of jobs rather than persons there is double counting.

Employment is the primary source of personal income in the United States and so represents a key source of economic growth, because it is the source of much of the income that fuels demand. The fact that labor is a key input to the production process means that growth in employment serves as a source for output growth—the supply of goods and services.

In general, increasing employment points to an expanding economy; declining—or simply more slowly growing employment—is a sign of faltering economic growth.

empowerment A process of involving employees in their work, thus increasing their motivation.

EXAMPLE: Johnsonville Foods, a small sausage company in Wisconsin, implemented an empowerment program in which workers act as their own bosses, have the power to hire and fire one another, and purchase all company equipment. Almost every aspect of the company's operations relies on input from the workers. They designed the manufacturing line, and even wrote the manufacturing budget. As a result, in a recent six-year period, Johnsonville's return on assets doubled, sales rose 15 percent annually, and payroll increased at a rate of only half that of sales.

ending inventory The merchandise on hand at the end of an *accounting period.*

Ending inventory appears on the *balance sheet* and is an integral part of the calculation of *cost of goods sold* on the *income statement. See also beginning inventory, cost of goods sold.*

engineering change order (ECO) A revision to a design or blueprint made by an engineering department to correct or change a part.

Requests for ECOs can come from a quality control department, a manufacturing department, or a customer.

environment Any uncontrollable external factor that affects the operations of a company.

The general environment includes the political, economic, legal, social, technological, ecological, and geographic areas in which a company operates. The environmental factors relevant to a company's strategic position operate in its industry, its city, its country, the total business community, and the world.

EXAMPLE: A school's environment includes the character of its community, state, and county school boards; the tax system; national education policies; and the education policies of other nations. These environmental factors change at varying speeds. For example, technology changes very rapidly, whereas politics and policies are much slower.

By understanding the environment in which a company operates, management can identify trends, take advantage of opportunities, and counter threats to its business. Unfortunately, there is no simple way to continually track the environmental trends that affect a particular business. The theories of some environmental disciplines such as economics, psychology, and sociology are not easily translated into corporate strategy. Some techniques, however, such as detailed demographic forecasting, economic indicators, technological projections, and estimates of raw materials reserves, are readily available. In general, there is more environmental information available than is used.

In order to stay current with environmental change and plan corporate strategy accordingly, Kenneth R. Andrews, author of *The Concept of Corporate Strategy* (3rd edition, 1986, Richard D. Irwin, Inc.) suggests five questions to keep in mind:

1. What are the essential economic, technical, and structural characteristics of the industry in which the company operates?
2. What trends suggesting future change in economic and technical characteristics are apparent?
3. What is the nature of competition both within the industry and across industries?
4. What are the requirements for success in competition in the company's industry?
5. Given the technical, economic, social, and political developments that most directly apply, what is the range of strategy available to any company in this industry?

environments matrix A framework that allows managers to visualize the dynamics and structure of a particular industry.

The matrix is split on these two axes: the size of competitive advantage, and the number of potential sources of that advantage. The size of competitive advantage refers to the notion that companies competing with relatively

equal resources and capabilities will generally be only slightly ahead of their competitors. In other words, there is little chance of being able to outrun competitors by either charging a significant price premium or reducing costs. The number of potential sources of competitive advantage refers to the notion that some industries offer limited options for competition. For example, competition within a *commodity* industry, such as cement, is usually on the basis of price whereas industries with products that require complex characteristics, such as home electronics, offer multiple sources of potential competitive advantage.

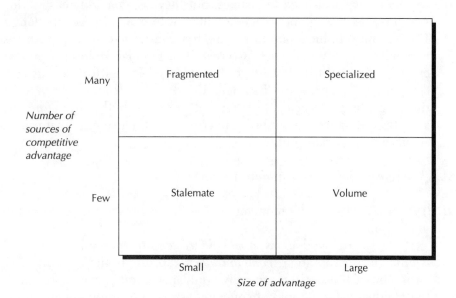

Environments Matrix

The environments matrix essentially classifies all industries into four different environments: volume, stalemate, specialized, and fragmented.

In volume industries, there are very few innovative ways to compete, but the advantages of effective competition are significant. Concentration on a limited number of competitive strategies, such as branding products, gaining a *first mover* advantage, or achieving cost superiority over competitors, frequently gives companies the lead in volume industries. An example of such a company is Boeing, which has parlayed its status as a pioneer in the aircraft industry into a commanding competitive position.

Companies in stalemate industries also have limited means of competition, but the advantages they can generate are relatively small. In many cases, however, the skills and resources needed to compete effectively are often readily available. For example, in an industry where market share can change rapidly and large-scale production is one of the only ways to establish a competitive advantage, it might be relatively simple to raise the necessary capital to build and staff that largest plant in the field. This advantage is fairly tenuous, however, because it will only last until a competitor builds a bigger plant.

Specialized industries are characterized by large competitive advantages that can come from a variety of sources. A common strategy in specialized industries is product *differentiation*, in which companies cultivate *core competencies,* such as distinctive service arrangements, proprietary product features, exclusive distribution, or unique selling approaches. When these factors can be translated into either a price premium or a cost reduction on a particular market segment, a company can enjoy a significant competitive advantage that competitors will have difficulty imitating.

Fragmented industries have the same multiple sources of competitive advantage as specialized industries, but they are generally easy to imitate, which makes any competitive edge difficult to maintain over the long term. For example, fashion boutiques are frequently able to exploit a distinct corporate competency, such as creating a popular style or trend, which creates a competitive advantage, but it only lasts until it is imitated by a competitor. Companies in fragmented industries generally have a difficult time appealing to large market segments. As a result, they frequently pursue a strategy of franchising in order to create the high volume that can lead to significant corporate profits.

EOQ *See economic order quantity*

equity In accounting, the monetary value that represents ownership interest in a business.

It is also referred to as *stockholders' equity*, net worth, and *owners' equity.* In a corporation, *common stock* represents the amount of equity owned by each party. If a company liquidates, equity owners are entitled to the residual value (if any) of company assets after creditors and preferred shareholders have been paid.

equity interest valuation The process of determining the value of a business or business interest.

Regardless of the size or type of company, or which valuation method is used, the business valuation process itself remains relatively constant. It comprises four major steps:

- Forecasting the company's cash flow for a specified number of years
- Estimating the cost of capital to be included in the valuation analysis
- Determining the continuing value of a business beyond the valuation date
- Analyzing and interpreting the results of calculations and assumptions

The most confusion usually centers on estimating the cost of capital and determining the continuing value of a business. Determining the cost of capital involves choosing a discount rate (also referred to as a capitalization rate) to discount a stream of future earnings or cash flows to present value. Theoretically a discount rate should represent the expected return on alternative investments with comparable risk. (*See* **discounted cash flow** for a description of methods for calculating the discount rate.)

Continuing value represents the stream of future benefits beyond the cash flow forecast period. Companies that have a solid position in the marketplace should continue to produce profits and cash flow to perpetuity. Only in companies whose continued success depends on the special managerial or technical skills of one or a few owner-managers may continuing value not be pertinent.

Although there are several theories for calculating continuing value, the following simplified approach works well in most cases:

Step 1. Arbitrarily choose a finite period that is long enough to make the end year insignificant for weighing investment options—such as 50 years, 75 years, or 100 years.

Step 2. Extrapolate the cash flow from the last year in your finite forecast period as typical for every year thereafter. In other words, multiply the last forecast year's cash flow times the number of years in the continuing period.

Step 3. Assume the same discount factor applies ad infinitum.

Step 4. Calculate the present value of the continuing cash stream.

Step 5. Add this present value to the sum of the annual present values derived within the forecast period.

equity kicker A stock derivative attached to a debt instrument that gives the holder the right to acquire equity interests under certain circumstances or by specific dates.

Stock warrants, rights, and options are the most common derivatives attached to bonds, debentures, and preferred stock. The convertibility feature of debentures, which permits their exchange for common shares, is another type of equity kicker.

A few examples of conditions that trigger the exercise or conversion of equity kickers include the following:

• Default on debt obligations
• A specific date in the future
• Sale or merger of the company
• Secondary public offerings
• Any action by the company that would dilute the value of the debt obligation

ERG theory A theory of motivation espoused by psychologist Clayton Alderfer.

The theory, which is similar to *Maslow's hierarchy of needs,* is based on three needs categories: (1) existence, such as the need for food, water, and shelter, (2) relatedness, such as the needs for interpersonal and social relationships, and (3) growth, such as the need to learn, be creative, or excel at a particular task. Although some theorists, including Abraham Maslow, have argued that there is a linear relationship between these needs (in other words, existence needs must be satisfied before relatedness needs, and relatedness needs must be satisfied before growth needs) Alderfer maintains that the progression (or regression) from need to need is governed by desire and frustration. This leads to three basic premises: (1) The less a need has been satisfied, the more intensely it is desired. For example, if an individual's need for a particular salary is not satisfied, he or she will be motivated to earn an increase in pay. (2) Once a lower-level need has been satisfied, there is increased desire for higher-level needs. For example, once a person has met his or her existence needs, there is an increased desire for relatedness needs. (3) When the desire for higher-level needs is frustrated, an individual will seek to satisfy lower-level needs.

ESOP *See employee stock ownership plan*

Eurobond A corporate bond denominated in U.S. dollars or other hard currencies and sold to investors outside the country whose currency is used.

Eurobonds have become an important source of debt capital for both large and small companies throughout the world. Normally, a Eurobond issue is syndicated by a consortium of international investment banks. This provides wide exposure to investors in different countries.

For example, a British company may sell a Eurobond issue through a consortium led by the merchant bank (investment bank) Morgan Grenfell to German investors who buy from an overseas affiliate of a New York bank; to Swiss investors who buy through a Swiss syndicator; and to French investors who buy from Swiss accounts. Such a wide exposure normally enables a company to pay a competitive rate while ensuring that the issue will be fully subscribed.

Eurocurrency A currency on deposit outside of its country of origin (for example, a dollar on deposit at an International Banking Facility in the United States, or a yen on deposit in the Japan Offshore Market).

Such deposits are also known as *external currencies, international currencies,* or *xenocurrencies.* The term Eurocurrency is preferred in most circles, however, and dates to one of the original banks in the market, the Banque Commerciale pour l'Europe du Nord, which carried a cable code EUROBANK. The Eurocurrency market has become a major force in international finance, reaching more than $5 trillion.

Companies with international interests find that borrowing from and making deposits in Eurobanks located in offshore banking centers results in less cost, more flexibility, and greater creativity in structuring financial instruments than domestic banks provide.

Eurodollar U.S. currency held on deposit in banks located outside the United States, mainly in Europe.

Eurodollars are commonly used for settling international transactions outside of the United States. Certain securities—debt as well as equity—are denominated in Eurodollars. This means that interest, principal repayments, or dividends are paid out of U.S. dollars deposited in foreign bank accounts.

The market for Eurodollar-denominated securities remains strong despite unfavorable U.S. dollar exchange rates and local European currency fluctuations. Many U.S. companies raise capital in European markets when U.S. market rates are unfavorable. This action can be an especially attractive avenue for companies making an initial public offering that splits into two tranches—one to be traded on U.S. exchanges, and the other, a Euro-tranche, to be traded on a European exchange.

European Community (EC) An economic alliance, formed in 1957, designed to encourage trade and economic cooperation among its members; also known as the European Economic Community and the Common Market.

Member nations include Belgium, France, Italy, Luxembourg, The Netherlands, Germany, Great Britain, Ireland, Denmark, Greece, Spain, and Portugal. Goals of the EC include the elimination of all trade barriers between member nations, the creation of a common currency, and the adoption of common regulations covering everything from banking rules to automobile emissions standards. The EC is headquartered in Brussels, Belgium.

events marketing The tying of a promotional message with an event of widespread interest to a target market.

EXAMPLES: Anheuser-Busch sponsored the Rolling Stones world concert, and AT&T sponsored a tour by jazz pianist Harry Connick, Jr.

In practicing events marketing, marketers must carefully match the event with the product.

EXAMPLE: The Timberland clothing company sponsors the Iditarod dogsled race in Alaska—a good match between product and event. Timberland's association with "the last great race" enhances the company's image as a manufacturer of rugged outdoor gear. Timberland might not have been so successful, however, if it had chosen to sponsor a golf tournament.

excess earnings business valuation method A method for determining the value of business equity interests.

The excess earnings method is used by the IRS for estate and gift tax purposes and is a popular method for determining the selling price of micro businesses and certain professional practices.

The excess earnings method (EEM) was originally defined by Internal Revenue Service Revenue Ruling 59-60 (the Ruling), and later modified by

Revenue Ruling 68-609 (still in effect in 1992). Here is a summary of the steps the Ruling calls for

1. Determine a value for all net tangible assets (excluding intangibles).
2. Establish a *normalized* earning level.
3. Estimate an appropriate capitalization rate applicable to that portion of the expected return based on or supported by net tangible assets.
4. Multiply the net tangible asset value by that rate to determine the amount of value generated by net tangible assets.
5. Subtract the amount in Step 4 from the normalized earnings from Step 2. The result is defined as *excess earnings*. Theoretically, this is the amount of earnings that could be expected above a fair return on net tangible assets.
6. Establish an appropriate capitalization rate to apply to the sum of excess earnings (presumably resulting from **goodwill**) and earnings resulting from intangible assets (patents, leases, copyrights, etc.).
7. Add this value to that derived in Step 1 to arrive at a total business valuation.

Despite the theoretical fallacies in the excess earnings approach, its simplicity and ease of calculation give it merit. For example, assume the following conditions for a small, privately owned business that keeps its books as an S corporation:

- Value of net tangible assets (equipment, vehicles, furniture and fixtures, scales, building and land, and a few pieces of machinery) totals $100,000. This value should be established by an independent appraisal using the fair market value approach.
- Normalized (meaning before extraordinary items) current year's net income (before taxes since it is an S corportion) equals $30,000.
- Using industry statistics, the return on net tangible assets should be 15 percent.
- Based on normalized net income, 30 percent will be used to capitalize excess earnings.

The value of this business would be calculated as follows:

Net tangible asset value		$100,00
Normalized earnings	$30,000	
Less: earnings attributable to net tangible assets ($100,000 × 15%)	15,000	
Excess earnings	$15,000	
Capitalized value of excess earnings ($15,000/0.30)		50,000
Total value of business		$150,000

This method has strong appeal in buying and selling small businesses, since the only items to be negotiated are the rate of return on net tangible assets (which can usually be substantiated by industry statistics) and the capitalization rate for excess earnings.

exchange rates   The prices at which one country's currency can be converted into that of another country.

Although perceptions in the currency markets of the security of a country's economic base certainly affect exchange rate movement, fluctuations are less a function of specific currency market manipulations than a fallout of a whole conglomerate of economic forces experienced on a worldwide level, such as inflation rates, interest rates, political unrest, financial market aberrations, and commodity prices. Furthermore, currency rates respond wildly to major economic shocks: local wars, oil cartel maneuvers, natural disasters, and anticipated political and economic actions of the world powers.

Within a globalized economy such as the United States, exchange rates play a critical role in virtually every aspect of financial management. Companies that import or export or that compete against companies that import or export should watch exchange rates closely and if necessary enter into futures currency contracts or trade in financial futures to maximize profit potential.

Eximbank   *See Export-Import Bank*

Eximbank's City-State Agency Cooperation Program   A cooperative program launched in 1989 between Eximbank and various city and state export finance and development agencies to help small and midsize businesses understand and use Eximbank's programs.

By working with Eximbank as the funding medium, state and local agencies offer counseling and financial assistance to help small and midsize companies create new jobs (and a higher tax base) through export markets.

Eximbank has now opened both its loan guarantee and its foreign credit insurance programs to local agency participation in the belief that this action will free up export financing for the small exporter and silence critics of Eximbank's traditional preference for large corporations and foreign buyers.

The City-State Agency Cooperation program started as an Eximbank marketing tool. City and state agencies market Eximbank guarantees and *FCIA* credit insurance through direct mail, calls to local banks and merchants, seminars, and a modest advertising campaign. They also provide technical support to smaller companies. According to Eximbank officials, this "makes exporting more accessible and creates less confusion and wasted time for local banks." Each city and state promote a slightly different program. All have the same objective, however; that of getting more small and midsize businesses and lenders involved in export trade.

See also Export-Import Bank

expectancy theory A theory that explains motivation in terms of (1) the expectation that an act will be followed by a predetermined outcome, and (2) the attractiveness of that outcome.

EXAMPLE: Say a small cutlery company promises its salespeople a monthly bonus based on a percentage of all sales over a particular quota. In this case, the expectancy theory would predict that the employees might be very motivated to exceed the quota. First, there is a clear link between sales performance and the bonus, and second, the amount of the potential bonus might be very appealing. However, if the company had promised that all salespeople who exceeded the quota would be entered in a lottery in which one of them would win a set of steak knives, expectancy theory would predict that employee motivation would be very low. First, there is no direct link between sales performance and the bonus (exceeding quota does not guarantee that a salesperson would get the knives) and second, for most employees of a cutlery manufacturer, a set of steak knives is not a very attractive bonus.

expediting Rushing a job through the production process.

As jobs fall behind schedule or are labeled as important, managers use expediters to speed them through operations. Expediters were widely used (and still are in many companies) before the advent of computerized production scheduling techniques. The use of expediters makes it very difficult to plan a good production schedule. By labeling particular jobs as "hot" and assigning them to an expediter, an entire process can be disrupted. Expediters have to gather all the necessary materials quickly, often taking them from other jobs, in order to get a particularly hot job completed. This, in turn, further delays the remaining jobs, which, in all likelihood, will have to be expedited in the future.

experience curve *See learning curve*

experimental research *Marketing research* in which the investigator controls at least one *independent variable* and observes the reaction of the *dependent variables.*

In other words, the researcher conducts an experiment. Experimental research takes two broad forms: laboratory experiments and field experiments.

EXAMPLE: A company wants to test the consumer appeal of several different product packages. If it were to conduct a laboratory experiment, it might create a movie theater environment and invite a representative group of customers to come in and watch a television show that is periodically interrupted by commercials (the independent variable). It would then record the customers' reactions (the dependent variable) to the various commercials.

If the company were to conduct a field experiment, it might show various commercials (the independent variable) to different households via cable television within a test city. Then it would measure consumer purchasing reaction (the dependent variable) by monitoring, via scanner technology, the sales from each of the commercials.

Most marketing professionals consider experimental research the most scientifically valid research method (see *research validity, external*) but there are difficulties with conducting it. Field experiments are much harder to execute than laboratory experiments, because controlling extraneous factors is more difficult. How, for instance, can a researcher testing the effect of a price reduction on sales regulate competitors' advertising? Moreover, researchers often find it difficult to gain the attention, interest, or cooperation of respondents. And it may be difficult to measure the relevant variable—such as the number of sales that actually resulted from the price reduction rather than from friends' suggestions, advertising, or just plain luck. Despite these drawbacks, however, researchers use field experiments more often than laboratory experiments.

See also *marketing research. Compare to causal research, descriptive research, exploratory research, observational research.*

expert system   A computerized system that gives users access to a particular area of expertise.

EXAMPLE: A bank might develop an expert system to evaluate loan requests. The system would be programmed with all the different rules and procedures that experienced loan officers use in evaluating loan requests. By using the system, junior loan officers can evaluate loan requests with the same skills as their superiors employ.

There are three main components to an expert system: (1) a language interface with the user, (2) an inference drive, which contains the reasoning and rules employed in any particular situation, and (3) a data base with access to further information, facts, and rules. Expert system technology is still in the development stage, but it has considerable promise for a wide range of applications.

exploratory research   Research with an emphasis on gaining broad insights and ideas surrounding a problem.

Useful for breaking down broad issues into simpler research objectives or hypotheses, exploratory research is frequently the first step in a marketing research plan.

EXAMPLE: A snack-food company is interested in developing a new jalapeño-flavored potato chip. So it assembles a group of consumers and conducts an informal interview, or *focus group interview,* to get a general idea of their reaction. The interviews tell the company that the customers are most concerned with the level of spiciness in the new chip. The company might then develop a research program to find out exactly which level of spiciness the consumer likes best.

Exploratory research has no set methodology; its main characteristic is flexibility. Researchers often change procedures as the initial issue comes into sharper focus.

EXAMPLE: Once the potato chip researchers have identified spiciness as a key concern in consumer chip preference, they can go on to devise a number of different methods to determine the most popular level of spiciness.

See also **marketing research.** *Compare to* **causal research, descriptive research, experimental research, observational research.**

Export-Import Bank (Eximbank) Federal Export-Import Bank, which came into being with passage of the Export-Import Bank Act of 1945, as amended through October 15, 1986.

Originally, its primary objective was to compensate U.S. exporters for subsidies granted competitors by foreign governments, Eximbank has reached far beyond this goal to become the primary source of export credit and guarantees for American companies.

Except in very unusual circumstances, Eximbank will not support exports to communist countries nor finance the sale of military products or services. Moreover, to qualify for Eximbank assistance, companies must provide evidence that exported goods or services have at least 50 percent U.S. content.

Upon completion of an application to Eximbank, companies may qualify for assistance under several programs, the most popular being the following:

1. The commercial bank guarantee program
2. The foreign credit insurance program
3. A cooperative financing facility with overseas banks
4. The discount loan program with U.S. banks

Applicants should be aware, however, that to get Eximbank financing or guarantees, two obstacles must be overcome:

- The inordinate amount of paperwork required for processing an application
- The subsequent extended time period before actually receiving the funds.

externality Any incidental by-products (both positive and negative) associated with a particular course of action.

Pollution is the classic example of a negative externality.

EXAMPLE: When a company discharges waste into a river, it increases the costs to the people or companies downstream that use the river and its water. Positive externalities might be gained by landscaping the grounds of a factory, and they might include increased employee morale, improved community relations, and increased property values, both for the plant and the surrounding area. Placing an accurate price on externalities is the key to their management. The company responsible for polluting the river must consider any government fines and penalties, suits by users of the river, and possibly even the cost of cleaning the river. Increasingly, companies are being held responsible for the full costs of the externalities associated with their activities.

EXAMPLE: A company operating a coal mine might be responsible for both the costs of producing coal and the costs of repairing any damage to the landscape. In some cases, these externalities form a strong *barrier to exit* because the costs of stopping an operation are greater than the costs of continuing.

Perhaps a more important issue is the management of positive externalities in such a manner that they benefit the company that created them and not its competitors. Training is a good example. Many companies invest heavily in recruiting and training employees. Occasionally, these companies are thought of as "schools" in which talented newcomers receive an education within a particular industry and then move on to other positions within different companies. One strategic response to this problem might be to stop actively recruiting recent graduates and concentrate instead on attracting trained personnel with several years' experience from competitors.

extraordinary item In accounting, an economic item that is *both* unusual and infrequent.

Extraordinary gains and losses are reported on a company's *income statement* between entries for income from discontinued operations and *the cumulative effect of a change in accounting principle*. Extraordinary items include the write-off of an intangible asset, gains on life or property insurance, restructuring charges, acts of God (such as losses from an earthquake or flood), and gain or loss from the early retirement of debt. Write-off and write-down of inventories and receivables, such as a warehouse full of unsalable merchandise or an uncollectible debt, are not considered extraordinary items because they are related to normal business activities.

401(k) plan An employee retirement plan; also called a salary reduction plan.

A 401(k) plan allows employees to set aside a certain percentage of their salary (the percentage allowed depends on the company's plan) and put it in a special retirement investment account. The amount employees can put away is adjusted for inflation each year; in 1993, it came to $8,994. The IRS does not count contributions to the plan as income. Moreover, contributions and earnings accumulate tax-free until they are withdrawn. However, employees who withdraw money without meeting certain conditions pay a 10 percent penalty on top of the tax that is due.

Most companies, through an arrangement with an investment or insurance company, provide a mix of vehicles—a guaranteed fixed-rate income fund, money market fund, and bond and stock portfolios, for example—in which employees can invest. Many employers also provide matching contributions. The total of employee contributions and employer matching funds may not exceed $30,000, or 25 percent of the employee's earnings, whichever is less.

facilitating good Any item that accompanies or adds value to a service.

For example, advertising is a service, but some might argue that advertisements are a product. In order to avoid confusion as to whether a campaign is a service or a product, advertisements are considered facilitating goods. In many service companies, such as an accounting firm, there may be no facilitating goods. These companies provide what is referred to as a pure service.

factoring A method for companies to convert *accounts receivable* into cash by transferring the collection risk to a factoring company (a "factor").

The process involves selling receivables to a factor, which then acts as principal, not agent, in collecting from the customer. Receivables are sold "without recourse," meaning that the company relinquishes all responsibility for collecting the account.

Receivables may be factored on a *notification* basis or a *nonnotification* basis. Notification means that customers are notified to remit directly to the factor; nonnotification means that customers remit to the company without knowledge that their accounts have been sold.

Factoring may involve a discount arrangement, whereby the company sells receivables for immediate cash at the face amount, less a discount (usually 15 to 25 percent), less allowances for estimated claims and returns, plus an interest rate on uncollected balances. The interest rate typically ranges from 2 to 5 percent above the prime rate.

A second option is called "maturity factoring," whereby the factor performs the entire credit and collection function and remits the collection proceeds to the company, less discounts, allowances, and commissions ranging from 0.05 to 3 percent.

Fair Package and Labeling Act of 1966 An act that regulates the packaging and labeling of consumer goods.

Manufacturers must state who made the contents of a package, what its contents are, and how much it contains.

FASB *See Financial Accounting Standards Board*

FCIA *See Foreign Credit Insurance Association*

Federal Reserve The main overseer of the banking system and the institution responsible for the conduct of *monetary policy* in the United States.

The Federal Reserve has both centralized and regional responsibilities and its organization reflects this situation. The Federal Reserve Board in Washington, DC, which consists of the Board of Governors—seven members appointed to 14-year terms by the President and approved by the Senate—plays the central role. There are also 12 Federal Reserve districts, each of which has a regional Federal Reserve Bank headed by a President. The district Banks have primary responsibility for regional banking conditions.

The main policy-making body for the system is the Federal Open Market Committee (FOMC), which consists of the seven Board Governors and five of the 12 regional Reserve Bank presidents (the President of the New York Federal Reserve Bank is an ex officio member, whereas the other four positions are filled by rotation from among the remaining 11 presidents). The FOMC conducts monetary policy by determining target levels for monetary reserves, consistent with particular levels of *interest rates* and *monetary aggregate* growth.

Federal Trade Commission Act of 1914 The act that established the Federal Trade Commission (FTC) and gave it power to enforce Section 5, which states that the FTC is responsible for promoting "free and fair competition in interstate commerce in the interest of the public through the prevention of price-fixing agreements, boycotts, combinations in restraint of trade, unfair acts of competition, and unfair and deceptive acts and practices."

feedback The extent to which the activities required by a job result in the individual getting direct information about his or her performance.

FIFO *See First-in, first-out*

finance lease A long-term rental commitment by both lessor and lessee that usually runs for the entire useful life of the asset.

The total of monthly, quarterly, or annual payments approximates the purchase price of the asset, plus finance charges. Large pieces of production equipment, heavy-duty trucks, store fixtures, and production facilities are examples of assets typically falling under a finance lease.

From the lessor's perspective, rents must be sufficient to cover the original equity investment in the asset, any debt service payments for financing the asset purchase, administrative costs, and a profit. Projected cash flow is a major factor in setting monthly rentals. Cash flow to a lessor is the sum of the (1) actual rent charged, (2) tax benefits of the lease, and (3) residual value of the asset after the lease expires. Projected tax savings and the estimated market value of the asset at the end of the lease term should increase the lessor's cash flow and reduce the rent charged.

Most finance leases are *net* leases, under which the lessee remains responsible for the maintenance of the asset, property and other taxes, and insurance premiums. The lessor's role is strictly that of a financier whose responsibility extends to financing the asset purchase but stops short of any liability arising from its use.

financial accounting An accounting method that records, interprets, and reports the historical cost transactions of a company.

A company records these transactions in *bookkeeping* journals and ledgers. To interpret the transactions, it uses, among other analytic tools, a series of ratios, such as *acid test ratio, current ratio, inventory turnover, debt-to-equity ratio,* and so on. Financial reports include *financial statements (balance sheet, income statement, statement of cash flows),* as well as special internal monetary reports that are unique to each company.

Publicly held companies must follow financial accounting principles laid down by the *Financial Accounting Standards Board (FASB)* and the *American Institute of Certified Public Accountants (AICPA).* Together, these principles are referred to as *generally accepted accounting principles (GAAP).* (The *Securities and Exchange Commission [SEC]* is ultimately responsible for establishing financial reporting standards for publicly owned companies, but it lets the FASB and AICPA set up the ground rules.)

Financial accounting methods use *accrual accounting, cash basis accounting,* or a hybrid of the two. Accounting systems are manual, computerized, or a combination of both.

Financial Accounting Standards Board (FASB) The independent institution that establishes and disseminates *generally accepted accounting principles (GAAP)* and recording practices, published as FASB Statements.

The *American Institute of Certified Public Accountants (AICPA)* and the *Securities and Exchange Commission (SEC)* both recognize the statements issued by FASB. All practicing CPAs are required to adhere to FASB guidelines in the preparation of accounting and financial reports.

financial communication A form of communication used by companies to enhance their image with Wall Street and securities analysts as well as financial reporters; also called shareholder relations or investor relations (IR).

The goal of financial communication is to increase the company's stock price and to keep analysts and shareholders aware of activities that may affect the financial performance of the company. Financial communciation professionals also take responsibility for developing the company's *annual report.* In many corporations today, the financial communication area reports to the head of *corporate communication* and has a dotted-line relationship with the chief financial officer.

financial futures A financial innovation that came into vogue during the 1980s; also called *futures contracts.*

Futures contracts include contracts on U.S. Treasury securities (bills, bonds, and notes), Eurodollars, stock indexes, and foreign currencies. The major purpose of buying or selling financial futures is to hedge against interest rate and exchange rate fluctuations.

The idea is to shift the risk of price changes from one party to a transaction to another party. The use of financial futures enables the separation of the risk of price change from risk arising from other business activities and makes possible the transfer of such risks to those who want them (speculators) from those who do not want them (hedgers).

The prices of money generated by interest rate futures (or in a more convoluted way, exchange rata or currency futures) reflect the combined views of a large number of buyers and sellers about the current status of the demand and supply of money 12 to 18 months into the future. The views are not a prediction, but merely an expression of *today's* expectations of the level of interest rates and the shape of the yield curve at some point in the future. Hedging reflects actions taken to neutralize price risk.

For example, let us assume that as a normal part of a seasonal business cycle an owner will have $100,000 in excess cash to invest in short-term securities in six months. Let us assume also that the owner expects interest rates (or exchange rates) to decline by that time. Within a small margin of error, the owner can establish the rate to be received on this future investment by buying futures contracts for six-month U.S. Treasury bills now, then buying Treasury bills in six months and selling the futures contract.

The financial futures market is an offshoot of commodity markets that have traded in futures for years. The basic principles in buying and selling foreign exchange futures are identical to those underlying forward contracts in the interbank foreign exchange market. The idea is to insure against future currency fluctuations without paying the cost of an insurance policy.

financial highlight A section of an annual report that shows selected financial data on a comparative basis.

Sales, *dividends,* and *earnings per share* are usually listed, along with any other information the company feels is of interest.

financial public relations A branch of the public relations field that specializes in corporate disclosure responsibilities, investor relations, and relations with the financial community.

Financial public relations firms are an integral part of the corporate finance team responsible for managing public issues, although their most critical role relates to smoothing the way in the investing community for companies making an initial public issue. Financial public relations specialists promote a favorable company image to attract investors and interpret SEC regulations and compliance requirements for company personnel.

financial statements A report containing financial information about a company.

There are three financial statements found in an *annual report: balance sheet, income statement,* and *statement of cash flows.*

finished goods inventory The amount of goods on hand that can be sold to customers.

Finished goods inventory is listed as a *current asset* on the *balance sheet* and is used to calculate the *cost of goods* sold on the *income statement.*

finite loading The assignment of no more jobs to a workstation than that workstation can be reasonably expected to complete in a particular time period.

In most cases, finite loading refers to a computerized operation that revises the priorities within a shop in order to level the work load for each workstation. *Compare to infinite loading.*

FIRO *See fundamental interpersonal relations orientation*

first mover The competitive advantage gained by early entry into a market.

EXAMPLE: IBM, already an established business machine manufacturer, capitalized on its status as the first mover in the computer industry with the introduction of the System 360 (a line of mainframe computers and peripheral devices) in 1964. Once the System 360 reached the market, IBM management pursued a strategy designed to reach the widest possible consumer market. The strategy included large investments in research and development and production, the expansion of its international marketing division, and a significant increase in the ranks of management. As a result, IBM became the dominant force in the computer industry.

The first mover in an industry enjoys several important advantages. First, it can set industry standards. Second, it can develop relationships with distributors, suppliers, and buyers that competitors might have a difficult time replicating. Third, it can take advantage of the benefits of the *learning curve* before its competitors. Any of these factors can be used to create a sizable and, more importantly, sustainable *competitive advantage.*

Although it may seem that the benefits of moving first are overwhelming, there are situations where they are somewhat fleeting. From the perspective of an industry follower, the first mover has made entry into a new market much easier by incurring all of the development costs and problems associated with the introduction of a new product or service; creating demand for the product; establishing distribution channels for both supplies and the finished product; and obtaining any necessary regulatory approval. Because of this, followers may be able to enter a new market at much lower costs and risk.

first-in, first-out (FIFO)

first-in, first-out (FIFO) A method of *inventory valuation* based on the concept that merchandise is sold in the order of its receipt.

In other words, if an electronics store buys 100 stereos in January and 50 in February, FIFO assumes that the units purchased in January will be sold before the units purchased in February. When inventory is valued with FIFO, *cost of goods sold* is based on the cost of older inventory.

EXAMPLE: (This illustration assumes that prices are rising. If prices were falling, the effects would be reversed.)
A company made the following purchases during a year:

January	100 units @ $70 =	$ 7,000
March	200 units @ $80 =	16,000
April	50 units @ $90 =	4,500
July	100 units @ $100 =	10,000
October	100 units @ $110 =	11,000
Total goods available for sale		$48,500

When inventory is valued under FIFO, it closely approximates the true *replacement cost* of the inventory. If *ending inventory* on December 31 is 175 units, the year-end FIFO inventory valuation is as follows:

Most recent purchase (October)	100 units @ $110 =	$11,000
Next most recent purchase (July)	75 units @ $100 =	7,500
Total inventory		$18,500

Cost of goods sold is calculated by determining the price of the inventory in the order in which it was purchased. FIFO costs of goods sold closely approximates the physical flow of goods since most companies sell their oldest merchandise first. FIFO cost of goods sold is calculated in this manner:

Total goods purchased	550 units
Ending inventory	175 units
Units sold	375 units

Cost of goods sold

Earliest purchase (January)	100 units @ $70 =	$7,000
Next earliest purchase (March)	200 units @ $80 =	16,000
Next earliest purchase (April)	50 units @ $90 =	4,500
Next earliest purchase (July)	25 units @ $100 =	2,500
Cost of goods sold	375 units	$30,000

To illustrate all the ramifications of using FIFO, it must be compared with the other common method of inventory valuation: *last-in, first-out,* or *LIFO.* The LIFO method is the opposite of FIFO. Inventory is valued on the basis of the oldest units available, and cost of goods sold is based on the most recent purchases. Continuing with the example, end-of-year LIFO inventory valuation of the same 175 units is

First purchase (January)	100 units @ $70 =	$7,000
Next purchase (March)	75 units @ $80 =	6,000
Total inventory		$13,000

Inventory under LIFO is significantly lower ($4,000) than inventory under FIFO. Since inventory valued by LIFO is stated using older costs, the inventory amount that a LIFO company reports on its **balance sheet** may have no relation to the inventory's replacement costs. When inventory is based on older costs, costs of goods sold must be based on the more current costs, resulting in a higher figure, or

Total goods purchased	550 units
Ending inventory	175 units
Units sold	375 units

Cost of goods sold

Most recent purchase (October)	100 units @ $110 =	$11,000
Next most recent purchase (July)	100 units @ $100 =	10,000
Next most recent purchase (April)	50 units @ $90 =	4,500
Next most recent purchase (March)	125 units @ $80 =	10,000
Cost of goods sold	375 units	$35,500

Cost of goods sold under LIFO is $5,500 higher than it would be if calculated under FIFO. This difference, in turn, affects net income on the *income statement*. Assume that the company had sales of $50,000:

	Income Statement LIFO	Income Statement LIFO
Sales	$50,000	$50,000
Less:		
Cost of goods sold	30,000	35,500
Net income	$20,000	$14,500

Each method has significant advantages and disadvantages. FIFO shows *current* inventory costs on the balance sheet and, by using lower historical costs for costs of goods sold (assuming inflation exists and prices have been rising), maximizes net income on the income statement. LIFO, on the other hand, shows historic inventory costs on the balance sheet and, by using higher inflation impacted current costs for cost of goods sold, reduces net income (and tax obligations). Of course, as prices decrease the exact opposite effects occur. In other words, proponents of LIFO feel that LIFO better matches current prices to current costs and FIFO proponents feel that LIFO misstates *inventories* by using their historical costs.

FIFO and LIFO are both permitted for income tax calculations, although once a company chooses a method, it cannot change it without permission from the Internal Revenue Service. However, if a company chooses LIFO for tax purposes, it must also use LIFO in its published *financial statements*. See also *last-in, first-out (LIFO)*.

fiscal policy   The Federal government's use of spending and taxation to affect the level of macroeconomic activity.

The theory is that weak economic activity requires *stimulative* fiscal policy, in the form of either tax cuts, spending increases, or a combination. Conversely, excessively robust economic activity can be suppressed by *restrictive* fiscal policy, in the form of either tax increases, spending cuts, or a combination of the two.

In practice, fiscal policy has been problematic because of institutional delays in enacting a policy response to altered economic circumstances. Fiscal policy changes are usually proposed by the President, but must be approved by Congress. Following the changes in the Federal tax code in 1986, the prospect of fiscal stimulation has been greatly limited: the swollen *budget deficit* made the possibility of further stimulus unlikely. As a result, a greater burden was placed on *monetary policy*.

fiscal year   A period of 12 consecutive months used by a company to account for and report the results of its operations.

The fiscal years of most businesses are identical to their calendar years. Many companies, however, base their fiscal years on particular business patterns.

EXAMPLE: A department store that traditionally has its highest sales in December and a great deal of returned merchandise in January might choose to operate on a fiscal year that begins on February 1.

five forces model
A framework developed by Harvard Business School professor Michael E. Porter to analyze the competitive forces within the *environment* in which a company operates.

The five forces model delineates five key structural features within an industry: threat of new entrants, threat of substitutes, *supplier power, buyer power,* and rivalry within the industry.

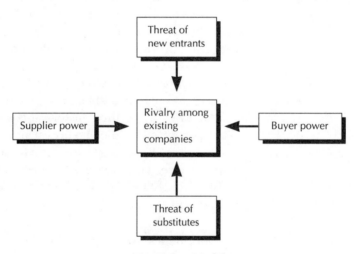

Five Forces Model

The total strength of these five forces determines the potential for profitability of an industry (where profit is measured by return on invested capital). This potential varies from industry to industry according to the collective strength exerted by the five forces. In industries like paper, tires, and steel, where the forces are strong, no individual company earns distinguished returns. However, in industries such as cosmetics, oil field equipment, and toiletries, where the forces are relatively weak, it is common for an individual company to earn a high return.

In developing a competitive strategy within a particular industry, the five forces model serves to determine the factors that affect profitability and allows a company to find a position where it can best defend itself against these factors. *See also barriers to entry, barriers to exit, buyer power, supplier power.*

fixed asset An item purchased for the operation of a business that has physical substance and a useful economic life greater than one year, and is not to be sold to customers.

Fixed assets are stated on the *balance sheet* and include buildings, machinery, equipment, and land. All fixed assets, except land, are subject to *depreciation.*

fixed cost Charges that stay constant regardless of increases or decreases in sales activity.

Rent on a factory building, for example, is a fixed cost, since it remains the same no matter how many units the factory produces. Whereas fixed costs do not change, fixed cost per unit changes as volume changes.

EXAMPLE: A company rents a factory for $10,000 per month. The total cost remains the same from month to month, but when that cost is spread over the number of units the factory produces, the amount per unit will change. If the factory produces 10,000 units, the fixed cost per unit comes to $1 ($10,000 divided by 10,000 units). If the factory then produces 100,000 units, the fixed cost per unit drops to $0.10 ($10,000 divided by 100,000 units).

Compare to variable cost.

fixed interval reorder system *See periodic inventory review system*

flexible manufacturing system (FMS) A completely automated manufacturing system.

Flexible manufacturing systems are practically unmanned. They include a computerized materials-handling system and a variety of peripheral equipment, such as robots, measuring machines, cranes, and loading and unloading stations. The equipment is programmed and controlled by a host computer, which communicates with a large database when it needs additional information.

Despite their name, most flexible manufacturing systems are machining systems that produce a somewhat limited range of products. The area of distinction that makes flexible manufacturing systems flexible is the ability to avoid a new setup when a switch is made from product to product. This requires the use of soft automation, which allows for smaller lots, smaller runs, and more responsiveness to customer needs.

Flexible manufacturing systems are extremely expensive, but they offer consistent quality, minimal labor expense, and considerable savings in time and variable costs.

flighting *See alternate weeks (A/W)*

float In finance, the amount of a corporation's outstanding stock that is available for public trading.

The less the float, the greater the volatility in share prices. For this reason, smaller companies tend to issue large numbers of shares at a very low par value to build up float.

In the banking community, float refers to the time span between the deposit of a check in the payee's bank and its clearance by the payor's bank. Traditionally, the greater the distance between the two banks (assuming they are in different states) the longer it takes to clear checks and the greater the float. For decades, banks have used float to invest customer funds during the clearing period for their own account. Many states have now passed laws limiting the amount of float to two or three days. Since modern communications technology permits instantaneous transfer of funds within the banking system, the main purpose of float is to give banks added money to invest for their own accounts.

flow process system A production system designed to produce a large number of a few products by using specialized equipment and standardized tasks.

Flow process systems usually have an uninterrupted material flow. Companies that use flow processes are called "flow shops." The flow process is used in a variety of industries that have relatively fixed *inputs,* operation time, and *outputs,* such as automobile production, steel making, a car wash, and insurance processing. There are two broad types of flow process: (1) the assembly line, such as home computer production, in which the process is designed to combine a number of components (such as disk drives and microchips) into a finished product, and (2) the production line, such as a potato chip factory, in which raw materials are manufactured into a finished product.

The main advantage of a flow process is the low per-unit cost that can be obtained by using specialized, high-volume equipment, lower labor rates, bulk materials purchasing, low in-process inventories, and efficient management.

The equipment in a flow process is generally very specialized, which reduces the level of skill (and wages) required for its operators. This type of labor force requires fewer forepersons and supervisors, which also reduces costs. Because of the high volume produced by a flow process, materials can frequently be purchased in large quantities and at significant savings. Additionally, since the process is standardized, processing times remain constant. This means that in-process inventories do not have to wait for processing, which keeps in-process inventory investment to a minimum. Flow process operations have a very precise production time, which allows management to route materials, schedule production, and meet product delivery dates efficiently.

Although the operation of a flow process is relatively simple, its design can be an enormous, and expensive, task. Not only is the equipment costly to set up, but also it frequently requires an active maintenance policy. Furthermore, specialized equipment can easily become obsolete and is difficult to dispose of or modify.

Increasing the variety of the output in a flow shop is very difficult. The equipment is usually so specialized that even a minor change in the product could result in a large investment in new machines. For example, an entirely different set of equipment may be required for a paper clip company to add a new type of clip to its product line. Even changes in the rate of production can be difficult to achieve. This drawback leads to a general reluctance to make product design changes, which can weaken a company's competitive position.

The labor force in a flow process is frequently susceptible to boredom and absenteeism. Since skilled tasks are performed by equipment, there is very little to challenge the workers. This problem is exacerbated because the work flow is generally paced by the equipment, so there is no way to offer incentive pay or other compensation based on employee productivity. Managers of flow processes usually use line balancing to pace the process according to the slowest task. This may lead to uneven work loads, which can be a point of contention among workers.

If, for any reason, such as an equipment failure or a materials shortage, a continuous flow process should stop, all work generally comes to a halt. These stoppages can be very expensive.

flow shop *See flow process system*

focus group interview A gathering of 8 to 12 people who are interviewed as a group by a facilitator, often called a moderator.

Focus groups, which are frequently used in *exploratory research,* are often videotaped and should take place in a room that allows unobtrusive observation. A soap company, for example, might send a bottle of detergent to a group of customers, then bring them together after a month to get their opinions on the product.

Results of a focus group depend heavily on the discussion within the group. With a good facilitator who poses specific questions, focus groups can help redefine a problem and suggest areas for further questioning. It can also aid researchers in learning how questions should be phrased and even what answers to expect. It is difficult to generalize the results to a larger population (*see research validity, external*). It is important to plan to conduct conclusive research to allow generalizability.

focus strategy A means of gaining *competitive advantage* by concentrating on one particular aspect of a product (such as service or durability) or a market (such as distribution or geographic area) that is important to a specific type of customer.

As markets demand increased product variety to satisfy ever-changing needs, many broad-line producers have found their competitive position threatened by focused competitors that target particular groups of users.

Although a focus strategy may be an attractive way to gain market share, it does carry three important risks. First, in that a focus strategy relies on a particular type of customer, product, *distribution channel,* or geographic region, it may lose its effectiveness as the market evolves. Second, the size of the *target market,* available to a competitor pursuing a focus strategy might limit the growth potential of the company. Third, because growth is limited, it may be difficult to take advantage of the cost reductions offered by *economies of scale* or *economies of scope.*

focused factory   A plant dedicated to producing a limited number of products as determined by a company's competitive strategy.

This strategy places clear limits on the volumes, technologies, and markets that the plant must manage.

Food and Drug Act of 1906   The act that prohibits the interstate manufacture, transport, or sale of adulterated, unsafe, or fraudulently labeled foods or drugs.

font   The name for type of one size and style.

A font includes all the letters of the alphabet, numbers from 0 to 9, punctuation marks, and frequently used symbols such as @ and &. There are thousands of different fonts, and each communicates a subtly different message. Selecting the appropriate font for an advertisement can often be a complex process. For example, the headline "A Strong, Conservative Bank" does not communicate its message well when it uses a light contemporary font such as Avante Garde. But the message is enhanced with a stronger, more classic font such as New Baskerville, boldface: "**A Strong, Conservative Bank**."

Examples of other common fonts include the following:

Avant Garde
Helvetica
New Baskerville
Courier
Palatino

forced conversion   Occurs when a convertible security is called by its issuer.

Holders of convertible securities generally have three choices: (1) accept the call price, (2) convert the securities into common shares, or (3) sell their holdings. Forced conversions normally occur when the market value of the underlying common shares has driven the selling price of the convertible security above its call price.

forecast error   The difference between forecasted demand and actual demand.

Forecast error is expressed as a percentage or an absolute value.

forecasting   The process of prediction of the sales and use of products in order to manufacture or purchase them in advance.

Foreign Credit Insurance Association (FCIA) An agent of the Export-Import Bank; provides exporters with insurance coverage against both commercial and political risk.

Eximbank lists the main goals of the FCIA as follows: 1) Protecting exporters against failure of foreign buyers to pay their credit obligations for commercial or political reasons; 2) encouraging exporters to offer foreign buyers competitive terms of payment; 3) supporting an exporter's prudent penetration of higher-risk foreign markets; and 4) giving exporters and their banks greater financial flexibility in handling overseas accounts receivable. (*Source*: Tuller, Lawrence W., *The McGraw-Hill Handbook of Global Trade and Investment Financing*, McGraw-Hill, New York, 1992.)

The FCIA offers eight separate insurance policies that help it meet these goals, ranging from new-to-export coverage (a short-term policy designed for less experienced exporters with sales of less than $750,000 over the past two years) to bank letter of credit coverage (which is only available to lending institutions).

foreign currency translation In accounting, the process of converting the *functional currency* of a foreign *subsidiary company,* branch, representative office, or other affiliated entity into U.S. dollars for *financial statement* presentation.

Subsidiaries and branches in foreign countries usually prepare financial statements in local currency. To consolidate these statements with those of the parent U.S. company, a translation to U.S. dollars must be made.

In addition, U.S. companies without foreign operations often undertake transactions, such as exports, imports, and foreign currency debt, that are denominated in foreign currencies; for financial statement purposes, they must record the monetary impact of these transactions in U.S. dollars.

Companies must address two issues when it comes to foreign currency translation:

1. What *exchange rate* should they use to translate each financial statement account?

2. What entry should they make to record the resultant gain or loss (that is, should it be taken into income, deferred to future accounting periods, or charged directly to *stockholders' equity*)?

When the *functional currency* is the currency of the foreign unit, companies must follow the *all-current* method of translation. That is, all sales (revenues) and expenses for the year are translated at the *average* exchange rate for the year. *Balance sheet* accounts are translated at the exchange rate in effect at the end of the *accounting period.*

The only translation gain or loss reported in *net income* is that occurring from transactions during the year—for example, when collections of foreign receivables are assumed to be part of the parent's equity investment and are accumulated in a separate account in the stockholders' equity section of the balance sheet. If and when the foreign unit is sold, the cumulative translation adjustment is offset against the gain or loss on the sale.

Say the foreign unit is located in a high-inflation country where the cumulative inflation rate has been more than 100 percent in the past three years. In that case, the current exchange rate is not used, since it would distort the parent's consolidated statements. Instead, historic rates in effect at the time the asset was acquired are used, as well as historic rates for *cost of sales* and *depreciation*—with average rates for other line items. A separate line item called *gain or loss on translation* effectively adjusts *retained earnings* for the difference and is used on the *income statement.*

foreign direct investment (FDI) Relates to the investment by companies from one country in businesses or projects located in a different country.

This type of investment is in contrast to investing in the traded securities of foreign companies listed on foreign stock exchanges, which is referred to as *portfolio investment.*

In modern international trade, an increasing number of companies of all sizes are finding that strategies calling for exporting from the United States together with the foreign sourcing of material or cheap labor through a foreign direct investment offers the best competitive edge in domestic as well as world markets. Many foreign direct investments in Latin America and Eastern Europe have been and continue to be made through government privatization programs. These programs represent one stage in the conversion of controlled economies to free market economies and involve the sell-off of government-owned businesses. (See *debt/equity swaps* as one method of financing this type of foreign direct investment.)

foreign exchange Conversion of foreign currency into U.S. dollars.

International trade involves commercial and financial transactions between U.S. residents and residents of foreign nations. Foreigners determine their demand and supply of goods and services on the basis of their own currencies. For exchange to occur, foreign currency must be converted to U.S. dollars.

From the end of World War II to about 1972, *foreign exchange rates*—the rate at which currencies are exchanged for one another—were fixed and allowed to fluctuate only within narrow ranges. Since the early 1970s, the U.S. dollar, along with most major currencies, has *floated* in much wider ranges. These rates have added a fresh arena of financial market uncertainty and created opportunities for speculation and trading. Understanding foreign exchange fluctuations has become important to nonfinancial managers whose business has an international dimension. In the following table exchange rates are shown between the U.S. dollar and six foreign currencies (the rates are shown in foreign currency units per dollar, except for the British pound, which is conventionally shown as dollars per pound).

	1970	1975	1980	1985	1990	1992
British pound	2.40	2.22	2.32	1.30	1.78	1.77
Canadian dollar	1.04	1.02	1.17	1.37	1.17	1.21
French franc	5.53	4.29	4.23	8.98	5.45	5.29
German mark	3.65	2.46	1.82	2.94	1.62	1.56
Italian lira	627	653	856	1,909	1,198	1,232
Japanese yen	358	297	227	238	145	127

foreign sales corporation An IRS incentive to encourage American companies to enter into export transactions.

In 1984, the Foreign Sales Corporation (FSC) replaced the old Domestic International Sales Corporation (DISC) as a means of reducing current tax liabilities on export sales. The main advantage over the old DISC is that FSCs actually reduce the tax bite: DISCs merely deferred taxes. Also, whereas the DISC was strictly a paper company, an FSC must be incorporated outside the United States, have a legitimate office, and maintain accounting records. As long as the FSC is incorporated in a qualifying country, and both the FSC and the domestic parent corporation comply with IRS accounting and documentation requirements, an FSC can save a U.S. exporter up to 15 percent of taxes on income generated through export sales.

Countries currently qualifying for FSC incorporation and operation include American Samoa, Australia, Austria, Barbados, Belgium, Canada, Cyprus, Denmark, Dominica, Egypt, Finland, France, Germany, Grenada, Guam, Iceland, Ireland, Jamaica, South Korea (Republic of Korea), Malta, Morocco, The Netherlands (but not the Netherlands Antilles), New Zealand, the Northern Mariana Islands, Norway, Pakistan, the Philippines, Sweden, Trinidad and Tobago, and the United States Virgin Islands.

Companies may set up either large FSCs—used by nearly all of the Fortune 500—or small FSCs. To be classified as a small FSC, annual export sales of the parent company must be $5 million or less. Administrative complexities and reporting requirements are significantly less for small FSCs. From a practical perspective, however, exporters with less than $50,000 in export sales find it too expensive to set up and maintain their own FSC. Recognizing this disparity, several state and trade organizations have started their own FSCs called *shared FSCs*. Shared FSCs enable any company, with any amount of export sales, to take advantage of this tax-saving device.

Many smaller exporters find it impracticable to set up a foreign office, staff it, and maintain local accounting records. FSC management companies in all qualified foreign countries handle these administrative details at a very low cost. Most large U.S. banks, law firms, and accounting firms with foreign offices provide the service, as do independent FSC management companies.

forward contract A contract to exchange an amount of one currency for another at a future date.

All foreign currency transactions involve the delivery of an amount of one currency in exchange for another. This exchange must take place at the same time, either when the contract is executed or at some agreed upon time in the future. Current foreign exchange rates are called *spot* prices. Those occurring at some time in the future are referred to as *forward* prices, and the contracts that evidence the future transaction are called *forward contracts*.

Currency deals can be made on any working day agreeable to both parties to the transaction. The transaction date may be as far into the future as both parties desire, although seldom do forward contracts extend beyond a year. Spot prices generally refer to a delivery date within the next few days, although common usage limits the time period to two working days.

Covering forward exchange rates is a form of insurance.

EXAMPLE: Assume a U.S. company contracts to ship products to a customer in Great Britain in six months. The price is $1,000. Payment is to be made against a letter of credit (L/C) denominated in U.S. dollars. The exchange rate at the date of contract is $1.00 = 0.75 pounds sterling.

The importer's treasurer believes that in six months the dollar will weaken to $1.00 = 0.50 pounds sterling, so that the shipment of goods will cost the British company 500 pounds rather than 750 pounds. The British treasurer places an order for a forward cover in the exchange market to become effective in six months. If the treasurer is right, the British company will purchase the goods for a 33 percent discount. The forward cover has no effect on the U.S. exporter, who still gets $1,000.

If the reverse situation is anticipated, that is, the treasurer believes the dollar will strengthen, then purchasing dollars at the current spot price will yield a higher return.

forward integration The expansion into activities that typically occur after a company has completed its primary or "historic" task.

EXAMPLE: If a publisher, normally concerned with the development, selection, marketing, and distribution of books, were to open a series of book stores, it would be pursuing a strategy of forward integration.

forward scheduling A method of determining the starting times for the various workstations involved in a particular job on a first-come, first-served basis.

Jobs are scheduled for various workstations as they are expected to become available. The projected completion date is then given to the customer. Forward scheduling is usually used when the delivery date for a job is set directly by a company's operations department, rather than marketing or sales. *Compare to **backward scheduling.***

four Ps Product, price, place (that is, distribution), and promotion; a common way of referring to *marketing's* four main categories of activities.

A marketing manager attempts to manipulate these four decision areas, or tools, in order to maximize consumer satisfaction and, thereby, sales.

EXAMPLE: A dairy co-op that wants to produce a new line of cheese must first develop the varieties of cheeses that appeal to a particular market, distribute the cheeses to stores where potential customers shop, promote the cheese through advertising or sales promotions, and offer it at a price that gives consumers value for their money. If the cheese does not sell well, the marketing manager at the dairy co-op must reconsider each of the four Ps. Perhaps the advertising was not effective or the price was too high. The entire process of marketing boils down to making adjustments to any or all of the four Ps. *See also **marketing mix.***

fragmented industry

Any industry with no single, dominant competitor or no market leader (*see **environments matrix***).

Fragmented industries are usually made up of small- to medium-sized companies. In many cases these companies are privately owned by people with a variety of goals and aspirations that make them willing to accept the smaller returns that are usually associated with a fragmented industry. However, in some cases these businesses can demonstrate an ability to sustain reasonably high profit levels, especially those focused on smaller geographic areas with select customer segments. Travel agencies, beauty salons, and restaurants are good examples of this phenomenon.

Most fragmented industries are distinguished by low ***barriers to entry,*** diverse customer needs, and little potential for creating ***economies of scale.*** Some industries that had previously been concentrated can become fragmented due to the emergence of a new product or technology.

EXAMPLE: In photoprocessing, the development of inexpensive, easy-to-use film-processing equipment fragmented the industry. Traditionally, the market had been controlled by a few dominant companies with large, centralized laboratories that could take advantage of the economies of scale created by the large volume of film that was processed in each lab. When the new equipment became widely available, a large number of small businesses specializing in one- to two-hour photoprocessing emerged, and the industry became fragmented. In order to combat this fragmentation and gain some control over the market, the incumbent companies aggressively bought the smaller companies. Eventually, the industry became concentrated again, and the larger companies could assert their control over the market.

freelancer

An artist, illustrator, writer, photographer, director, or producer who works on a job-by-job basis as an independent contractor.

Advertisers and advertising agencies frequently hire freelancers to service particular jobs or clients.

full cost method

A method of accounting for exploration costs by some companies in extractive industries, such as oil and gas production.

The full cost method requires that *all* exploration costs, both successful and unsuccessful, be *capitalized* and reported on the *balance sheet* as natural resource assets. *See also successful efforts accounting.*

functional currency In accounting, the currency used in the *financial statements* of an operating entity.

Financial Accounting Standards Board Statement 52 lays out specific characteristics for determining whether the U.S. dollar or the local currency of the foreign unit is the functional currency.

The U.S. dollar is the functional currency under these conditions:

1. Cash flows from foreign entities (receivables and payables) are denominated in U.S. dollars and readily available for remittance to the parent company.

2. Sales prices are influenced by worldwide competitive factors and are affected on a short-term basis by *exchange rate* changes.

3. Cost factors (material, labor, technology, supervision, and other components of the business) are obtained primarily from the United States.

4. Financing is denominated in U.S. dollars, or ongoing cash transfers are made by the parent to finance the foreign unit.

5. A high volume of intercompany transactions and extensive operational interrelations between parent and foreign units occur. For example, the foreign unit produces products in a foreign free trade zone for shipment back to the United States.

In some instances, the rules are ambiguous. In those cases, management must judge which functional currency best captures the economic effects of a foreign unit's operations and financial position. *See also foreign currency translation.*

functional organizational design An organizational design in which decision-making power is concentrated with top management.

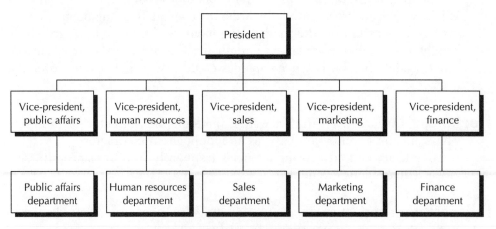

Functional Organizational Design

Functional organizations are extremely hierarchical and managers are divided into specialized functional areas.

For example, in the accompanying organizational chart, the marketing staff reports to the manager of the marketing department, who reports to the vice-president of marketing, who reports to the company's president. This structure works well when the company's *environment* is relatively stable. However, the functional structure reveals serious weaknesses when a company is faced with an uncertain and highly volatile environment. When this is the case, lower-level managers often do not have the information or authority needed to make decisions, so they are pushed to upper management. Top managers quickly become overloaded with decisions, hampering their ability to respond to environmental changes. *See also decentralization, matrix structure, organizational environment.*

fundamental interpersonal relations orientation (FIRO) A
method of studying a person's behavior in groups, based on two-person relationships.

Within the FIRO framework, two major variables provide insight into behavior: behavioral expression and interpersonal needs.

There are two types of behavioral expression: (1) wanted behavior, which is how people want others to act toward them, and (2) expressed behavior, which is how people act toward others.

Interpersonal needs	Behavioral expression	
	Expressed	Wanted
Inclusion or interaction	High: initiates actions with others.	High: needs to be included in group activities.
	Low: does not initiate actions with others.	Low: does not need to be included in group activities.
Affection or friendship	High: wants close, personal interactions with others.	High: wants others to act toward him or her in a close personal way.
	Low: does not want close, personal interactions with others.	Low: does not want others to act toward him or her in a close, personal way.
Control or influence	High: needs to control others.	High: wants to be controlled.
	Low: does not not need to control others.	Low: does not want to be controlled by others.

There are three interpersonal needs. The first is a need for inclusion or interaction. In the FIRO framework, this is measured as either high (a great need to be involved and included in group activities) or low (a desire for more privacy). The second is a need for affection or friendship. This is also measured as either high (a need for a number of close friendships) or low (a preference for more impersonal relationships). The third interpersonal need is for control or influence. Again, this is measured as either high (a strong need to control one's environment and relationships) or low (little desire to control or be controlled).

The FIRO framework gives insight into a person's behavior in a given situation. For example, a person with low inclusion needs might not do well in a job that requires a great deal of personal contact with customers or clients.

funded pension plan

A retirement plan in which an employer contributes money to a *pension fund,* which is in turn managed by a trustee who oversees the payment of benefits.

See also defined benefit pension plan, defined contribution pension plan.

funds provided from operations

In accounting, the first entry in a *statement of cash flows.*

Funds are usually defined as *working capital* or *cash.* A high level of funds provided from operations shows that a company's net income consists mostly of liquid funds, which can be easily reinvested in the company's operations or distributed to stockholders. There are two ways to determine funds provided from operations: the direct method and the indirect method. The direct method starts with the amount of cash received from operations (sales) and makes adjustments to that figure in the following categories:

1. Dividends and interest received by the company (increase)
2. Receipts of cash, such as insurance and lawsuit settlements or refunds from suppliers (increase)
3. Cash payment for wages and other goods and services (decrease)
4. Taxes paid (decrease)
5. Interest paid (decrease)
6. Other payments, such as customer refunds, lawsuit settlements, and contributions to charity (decrease)

The basic formula for the direct method is

$$\text{Cash from operations} - \text{Payments of cash for operations}$$
$$= \text{Funds provided from operations}$$

The direct method is recommended by the *Financial Accounting Standards Board (FASB),* but most companies prefer to use the indirect method.

The indirect method begins with net income and adds noncash expenses (*depreciation* and *amortization*). Next, the effects of noncash income adjustments (deferred taxes, undistributed earnings of *affiliated companies*, gains on sales of equipment, and provisions for losses) are taken out. Finally, changes in *current assets* and *current liabilities (inventory, accounts payable,* accruals, and taxes) other than cash are incorporated, resulting in the final figure for funds provided from operations.

The basic formula for the indirect method is

$$\text{Net income} \pm \frac{\text{Noncash revenue and}}{\text{expense adjustments}} \pm \frac{\text{Adjustments for}}{\text{receivables, payables,}}$$
$$\text{taxes, and inventories}$$

$$= \frac{\text{Funds provided from}}{\text{operations}}$$

future value   The value of an investment, based on the rate of interest paid at set time periods, at some point in the future.

Future values incorporate both the earned rate of interest and the amount of interest compounded on interest already earned. Interest may be compounded annually, monthly, weekly, even daily. The more frequently interest is compounded, the higher the future value of the investment.

future value of an annuity   A measurement of the value of a series of *annuity* payments at some point in the future (assuming that all payments are invested at a constant rate).

A pension fund manager, for example, might be interested in determining the future value of the annual employee payments that go into a company's pension fund.

G

GAAP See *generally accepted accounting principles*

Gantt chart A graph, developed by management scientist Henry L. Gantt around 1917, showing the sequencing of tasks and resources used in a process.

Gantt charts basically illustrate a time line with different sections blocked off to represent different tasks, workstations, projects, employees, and so on. Gantt charts can be used for a number of purposes, from tracking a particular job to planning and scheduling a series of different projects.

EXAMPLE: Consider a company with three jobs, scheduled as follows:

Job	Date due	Required processing (in order)
X	May 10	1 day at station 3, 5 days at station 2, and 2 days at station 1
Y	8	2 days at station 2, 3 days at station 3, and 1 day at station 1
Z	6	1 day at station 3, 2 days at station 1

If *backwards scheduling* were used to determine the order of each process, the following Gantt chart might be generated.

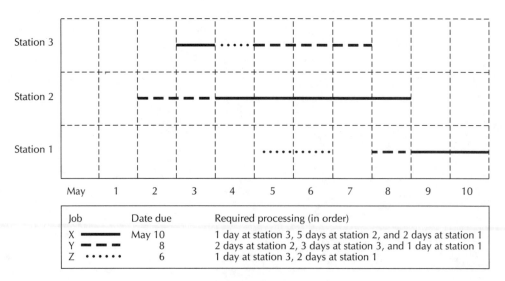

Gantt Chart

With the Gantt chart, management can quickly determine the staff and materials requirements for each station on any particular day (in the example, none of the workstations is scheduled to operate on May 1, and all three stations must run simultaneously on May 5 and 6, and must be staffed and supplied accordingly).

Although the Gantt chart is an effective means of visualizing job and facility status, it is not, in and of itself, a scheduling technique.

General Agreement on Tariffs and Trade (GATT) A multilateral treaty, the basic aims of which are (1) to liberalize and promote world trade via multilateral trade negotiations, (2) to place world trade on a secure basis, and thereby (3) to contribute to global economic growth and development.

1. *Background:* The General Agreement was negotiated in 1947. It came into force in January 1948. At the time, the 23 nations that signed the General Agreement were in the process of drawing up a charter for a specialized United Nations organization called the International Trade Organization (ITO). It was assumed that the General Agreement would be managed by the ITO.

   However, when the Charter for the ITO was not passed by the required two thirds of the U.N. General Assembly, plans for the ITO were abandoned. Thus, the General Agreement became the only international instrument that formed the foundation for international trade that was accepted by most of the world's trading nations.

2. *GATT Principles and Rules:* The General Agreement is the only multilateral, international organization that lays down specific rules for international trade. (In addition, the GATT also functions as the principal international body for negotiations about the reduction of tariff and nontariff barriers.)

   The General Agreement itself is complex, and sometimes so are its rules (embodied in the Articles of the GATT). However, all of them are based on the following fundamental Principles of International Trade:

   - **PRINCIPLE 1:** *Trade without Discrimination*—All parties that are signatories of the GATT are bound to grant to each other treatment as favorable as they grant to any other nation in the application of import and export tariffs. This is the famous "most-favored-nation (MFN) clause."

   - **PRINCIPLE 2:** *Protection through Tariffs*—Tariffs are the only internationally acceptable means for protecting domestic industry: commercial measures (i.e., nontariff barriers) are not an acceptable means for protecting domestic industry.

   - **PRINCIPLE 3:** *A Stable Basis for Trade*—A stable and predictable basis for international trade is provided by the "binding of the tariff levels" negotiated and agreed among the Contracting Parties to the GATT. (Tariff schedules in which "bound" items are listed for each country form an integral part of the GATT.) Provisions exist for the renegotiation of bound tariffs.

- **PRINCIPLE 4:** *Consultation, Conciliation, and Peaceful Settlement of Differences*—It is expected that all signatories to the GATT will consult with each other in trade matters and will aim to resolve differences in a peaceful manner, including the use of the GATT for hearings on and arbitration of disputed trade matters.

3. *GATT Headquarters:* The Secretariat of the GATT is located in Geneva, Switzerland.

4. *GATT Institutions:* The supreme GATT institution is the Session of Contracting Parties. It is held annually. Consensus is used for arriving at decisions, although voting is used on difficult issues.

Thus, when GATT members act collectively (either via consensus or vote), they are called Contracting Parties in all GATT documents and in all other documents that make reference to the status of member nations that act in accordance with their legal obligations under the GATT.

Between Sessions of the Contracting Parties, the GATT Council of Representatives is authorized to act.

5. *GATT Committee Work:* Apart from the United Nations Conference on Trade and Development (UNCTAD), the Trade Negotiations Committee (TNC) of the Group of Negotiations on Goods (GNG) oversees the work of 14 major GATT Standing Committees (or Groups) before, during, and after each round of multilateral trade negotiations. These are as follows:

a. Negotiating Group on Nontariff Measures
b. Negotiating Group on Natural Resource-Based Products
c. Negotiating Group on Textiles and Clothing
d. Negotiating Group on Agriculture
e. Negotiating Group on Tropical Products
f. Negotiating Group on Subsidies
g. Negotiating Group on GATT Articles
h. Negotiating Group on Multilateral Trade Negotiations (MTN) Agreements and Arrangements
i. Negotiating Group on Safeguards
j. Negotiating Group on Trade-Related Aspects of Intellectual Property Rights (TRIPS)
k. Negotiating Group on Trade-Related Investment Measures (TRIMS)
l. Negotiating Group on Dispute Settlement
m. Negotiating Group on the Functioning of the GATT System (FOGS)
n. Group of Negotiations on Services

In addition, Working Parties (i.e., ad hoc committees) are established (1) to investigate urgent, current issues; (2) to deal with requests for accession to the GATT; (3) to verify that agreements concluded by member nations are in conformity with the GATT; and (4) to study any issues on which member countries may later wish to make a joint decision.

Further, in accordance with Principle 4, Panels of Conciliation are established (on an ad hoc basis) to investigate disputes between member countries. (*Source:* L. Presner, *The International Business Dictionary and Reference,* Copyright © 1991 by L. Presner. Reprinted with permission of the publisher, John Wiley & Sons, Inc.)

general and administrative expenses All costs connected with the performance of general and administrative activities.

General and administrative expenses include, among others, legal and audit expenses, office expenses, office rent, office utilities, office equipment, *depreciation,* and so on, and are reported as *operating expenses* on the *income statement.*

generally accepted accounting principles (GAAP) The policies, standards, and rules followed by accountants in the preparation of *financial statements,* and in recording and summarizing transactions.

GAAP are based on (1) formal statements from an authoritative organization, such as the *Financial Accounting Standards Board (FASB)* or the *American Institute of Certified Public Accountants (AICPA),* (2) less formal industry guides, such as those issued by the AICPA, and (3) general industry practice and tradition.

generic appeal An *advertising* strategy that promotes awareness of a product category without mentioning any specific *brand names.*

EXAMPLE: The American Dairy Association sponsors commercials that promote the drinking of milk. Generic appeal advertising is usually sponsored by an industry group that represents each individual company or by the leading producer in an industry.

generic competitive strategies A popular theory in strategic management that splits business strategies into three "generic" types: *cost leadership, differentiation,* and *focus strategy.*

In other words, the theory suggests that companies should rely on either low costs, a unique product, or a product that appeals to a particular market segment.

Although the notion of simply choosing among these three options can be appealing, it often leads to an overly simplified view of strategy. When this happens, strategy is in danger of becoming a single-minded quest for a "big move" that will create a significant *competitive advantage.* A more sophisticated approach to strategy recognizes that competitive advantage is the result of many individual sets of actions that build over time. For example, in some activities, such as sales or service, it might be best to differentiate products in a way that appeals to customers, thus allowing a price premium. In other activities, however, such as standardizing product components, it might be best to pursue a strategy of cost leadership. *See also cost leadership, differentiation, focus strategy.*

generic product   An unbranded, inexpensive, plainly packaged version of a common product, such as cigarettes, cotton balls, or canned green beans.

Generics are usually of standard or lower quality than most nationally advertised brands. The drop in quality is offset by a price that can be 30 percent to 50 percent lower than branded items. The company can offer a lower price because the generic uses lower-quality ingredients, inexpensive labeling and packaging, and little advertising.

For a generic product to prove successful, consumers must perceive it as no different in quality from its branded competitors. Research has shown that generics' success has been greatest in the categories of canned fruit and vegetables, paper and plastic products, and soaps and detergents. They do not fare so well in pet products, soft drinks, and other products where consumers readily perceive differences. The other key to an effective generic product strategy: The price must be significantly below that of competing branded items. *See also brand name.*

ghost shopper   An incognito marketing specialist who goes from store to store to monitor the presentation and salesmanship accorded a company's products and those of its competitors.

Many large companies, including General Electric, Gillette, Del Monte, and J.C. Penney, employ ghost shoppers.

global marketing   The activity of a global corporation that seeks to achieve long-run, large-scale production efficiencies by producing standardized products of good value and long-term reliability for all consumers (or industrial users) in all segments of all markets; the marketing of a standardized product on a worldwide basis, with little allowance for, or acceptance of, regional or local differentiation of the marketing-mix strategies.

EXAMPLE: Coca-Cola, the quintessential global corporation, markets an identical ingredient formula and primary package worldwide. Of necessity, the labeling on the bottle, and on the secondary containers, varies (e.g., *Disfrute Coca-Cola* [Spanish] vs. *Savourez Coca-Cola* [French]). But every country's marketing program contains the same core message, the same core consumer promise, and the same core perception of benefit. (In the Coca-Cola corporate culture, it is called "One sight, one sound.")

At the physical level of corporate control of the global marketing effort is the commitment to global standardization. Every week from every plant where Coke is bottled globally, a random sampling of the product arrives in Atlanta for quality control testing, aimed at ensuring that the product is identical regardless of where it originates. (*Source:* L. Presner, *The International Business Dictionary and Reference.* Copyright © 1991 by L. Presner. Reprinted with permission of the publisher, John Wiley & Sons, Inc.)

globalization   In finance, the process of interlinking financial markets in different countries into a common, worldwide pool of funds to be accessed by both borrowers and lenders.

Globalization, a relatively new term in banking circles, has come about as a result of the growth in international trade. Money flows freely across national borders. As companies expand overseas they need to finance this expansion with local funds. Globalization provides the means to do this. The proliferation of foreign banks with branches in the United States brings globalization to the doorstep of American companies.

going private   The shift of a company's shares from public ownership to private ownership.

This shift is generally accomplished through the company's repurchase of shares or through purchases by a private investor outside the company. Usually, a company goes private when its shares are selling at a market price significantly below book value. The company can buy the assets very cheaply. Another common reason for going private, or removing its shares from the market, is to eliminate the possibility that the company might become the target of a takeover attempt. *Compare to going public.*

going public   The sale of a portion of a privately held company's common shares to the public as a means of raising equity capital.

Equity capital may be raised by selling common stock two ways: (1) to the public at large, which of course is a *public issue*, and (2) to a select group of buyers, in which case it is referred to as a *private placement.* Furthermore, both public issues and private placements may be sold nationally (interstate), or within only one state (intrastate). Public issues can also be divided into segments, or *tranches*, with one tranche sold in U.S. markets and another sold internationally.

The first time a company sells stock to the public, the issue is called an *initial public offering* or IPO. Once a company's stock begins trading in public markets, further new stock issues are called *secondary* issues. The significance of these distinctions relates to regulatory requirements, cost, stock appreciation potential, flexibility, and market acceptance. Prior to developing specific plans to sell common stock, companies must weigh each of these factors in light of capital needs, previous profitability, and management capabilities. As a start, precisely how much new capital is needed, what percentage of ownership current shareholders are willing to relinquish, and the uses to which the new capital will be applied must be determined.

goodwill   In accounting, the value of intangible *assets*, such as reputation, name recognition, and customer relations, that give a company an advantage over competitors.

Goodwill appears in a company's financial statements only if it has been paid for in a business combination using the *purchase method.* Under this method, goodwill is the difference between the purchase price of a company and the fair market value of the company's assets.

EXAMPLE: If Company ABC paid $5,000,000 for the net assets of Company 123 with a fair value of $4,000,000, the extra $1,000,000 represents goodwill. Once goodwill is recognized on the **balance sheet** as an intangible asset, it must be amortized for the period during which it provides economic benefit, not to exceed 40 years. The amortization expense is not tax deductible.

government market   All federal, state, county, and municipal offices and departments.

The government market typically makes purchases that revolve around highways, streets, parks, education, public safety, and public health. When dealing with the government, a marketer must be familiar with two major buying procedures: competitive bidding and negotiation. In competitive bidding, the government sends potential suppliers requests for proposals (RFPs) containing specifications for the product; the quantity, terms, and condition of delivery; terms of the contract; and due date of the bid. On the due date, the contract goes to the lowest bidder (unless, that is, the government agency determines that the lowest bidder cannot fulfill the order. In that case, the contract goes to the next-lowest qualified bidder). In negotiation, the government considers only a small number of companies. This purchase process usually involves very large, risky contracts that attract few competitors. *See also* **consumer market**, **industrial market.**

greenmail   The purchase and subsequent resale of a large amount of the stock of a company that has been targeted for a takeover.

The targeted company must buy back its shares at a significantly higher price, in return for which the suitor agrees to end the attempted takeover.

gross domestic product (GDP)   The main and broadest measure of U.S. economic activity.

GDP measures the output produced and income earned within the United States (exports are shown on a net basis, that is, exports minus imports).

GDP measures economic activity in two ways, although they each arrive at the same total. The *income* accounts measure the various income payments to the factors of production. The *product* accounts measure the value of the goods and services produced in a year. The two approaches must equal: The payments to the factors of production must equal the costs of production, the value of output. Totals for 1992 for the major components for the two approaches are shown in the table below. (The product account data are shown in current dollar and constant dollar terms.)

Since GDP provides a measure of overall economic activity, it is a useful benchmark to which businesses can compare their own activity. In addition, firms can gauge the cyclical nature of their own business by comparing it to the stage of GDP.

Income ($)		Product ($)	Current	Constant
Gross Domestic Product	5,951	Gross Domestic Product	5,951	4,923
Personal Income	3,933	Consumption	4,095	3,314
Corporate Profits	383	Residential Construction	218	193
Indirect Business Taxes	471	Nonresident. Fixed Invest.	548	515
Depreciation and Other		Change in inventories	5	5
Adjustments	1,164	Net Exports	−30	−42
		Government Spending	1,115	938

gross profit The excess of sales over *cost of goods sold*.

When gross profit is expressed as a percentage, calculated by dividing gross profit by sales, it is called gross profit margin.

group A gathering of individuals.

In most companies, there are three kinds of groups: functional, task, and interest or friendship. The understanding of different groups and their individual characteristics is central to the management of any large organization.

Functional groups are created by a company's structure. For example, in a marketing department, there might be a sales group. Most functional groups have a distinct superior-subordinate structure. In the sales group, for example, there might be a district sales manager with authority over the other sales representatives. Functional groups tend to exist for long periods of time. Their goals, leaders, interactions, performance requirements, and interdependencies are generally determined by the company.

Task groups are usually formed for the purpose of completing a particular job. Once the job is completed, the task group usually disbands. Therefore, the relationships between group members revolve around the attainment of a particular goal. For example, task groups are frequently used in the aerospace industry to design, build, and test a particular product, such as a missile or an airplane. There is usually an assigned leader who follows a master schedule. The leader attempts to follow the schedule and complete the project within set time, cost, and quality requirements. Task groups are often used to diagnose and resolve particular problems. For example, a university might establish a task group to develop recommendations on its curriculum.

Interest and friendship groups are formed on the basis of shared interests, beliefs, and activities. For example, within the functional group of sales representatives at a particular company, there might be a friendship group that plays tennis on weekends. These groups are usually quite informal, and can have members from a number of different functional or task groups within an organization. For example, people from different departments might be on the same softball team or work together for a charitable cause. As a result of the overlapping memberships between friendship, functional, and task groups, there is the possibility that the goals of the groups might not be in line with the goals of the company as a whole. The issue for management, then, is to be aware of these differences and to work to eliminate or reduce them so that they do not conflict with the goals and policies of the company.

group cohesion   The extent to which group members are attracted to each other and are inclined to remain in the group.

Although high group cohesion might intuitively seem to be an attractive goal, it does not always correspond with high *productivity.* Research has shown that the impact of cohesiveness is mitigated by the performance-related norms (*see group norms*) within a given group.

	Group cohesiveness	
Performance-related norms	**High**	**Low**
High	High productivity	Moderate productivity
Low	Low productivity	Low to moderate productivity

In other words, a cohesive group with high performance-related norms will be more productive than a less cohesive group with the same norms. But when performance-related norms are low, a more cohesive group will have lower productivity than a less cohesive group.

group norms   Established standards of acceptable behavior within a group.

All groups have norms. For example, golfers do not talk while putting on the green. Norms give group members direction about what to do and what not to do in various situations. When norms are widely accepted and agreed to within a group, they can be an important means of influencing group members' behavior with a minimum of outside control.

group technology   An engineering philosophy that simplifies production by organizing materials according to families that require the same design and production procedures.

Group technology is often a component of *computer-integrated manufacturing.* For example, a computer manufacturer might separate molded plastic parts, electronics, mechanical parts, and so on. This separation would allow the company to group workstations according to the different procedures demanded by each family of parts. As a result, the company would be more able to work with small batches and to provide a greater degree of differentiation between products.

growth/market share matrix A framework, developed by the Boston Consulting Group, that allows managers of diversified companies to visualize the differences in cash flow potential and growth for a number of different businesses within their portfolios.

Depending on its position on the matrix, each business is assigned a particular category that describes its standing within the company's portfolio. In other words, the growth-market share matrix shows which businesses represent investment opportunities, which should be used as sources of funds for other activities, and which are candidates for elimination from a company's portfolio.

The basic structure of the growth/market share matrix is as follows:

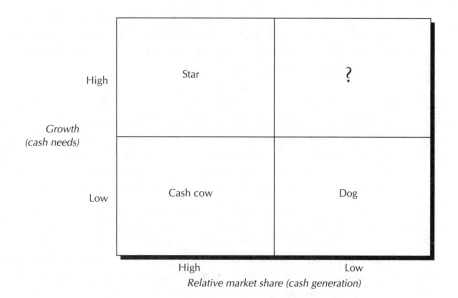

Growth/Market Share Matrix

The four categories are stars, question marks, *cash cows*, and dogs. Stars are businesses that have both market dominance and strong growth. They may or may not have the cash flow to be self-sufficient, but they promise large cash returns in the future. Question marks have high growth, low market share, and require significant amounts of cash to maintain their position in the market. Many question mark businesses are in emergent industries, and the question is whether they will ever develop a strong enough market position to earn a solid return. Cash cows typically have high market share, slow growth, and generate more cash than they use or can reasonably reinvest. These businesses are a good source of cash that can be used to increase the market position of the question mark businesses. Dogs have a poor market position and offer little chance for significant growth. They neither generate nor require substantial amounts of cash. Usually, any cash generated must be reinvested along with additional outside capital. This has earned them the title *cash traps*.

halftone A photograph that has been transformed into a pattern of dots of varying sizes.

The halftone is used to make a printing plate, which allows the photo to be reproduced. A quick glance through a newspaper will provide many examples of halftones. Look closely at any newspaper photograph and you can see the patterns of tiny dots.

hard currency Currency in which there is wide confidence in world markets, as opposed to *soft currency*, which is not accepted as legal tender outside the country of origin.

Hard currencies can be exchanged for other hard currencies as well as soft currencies throughout the world. Soft currencies cannot. Hard currency countries include, among others, the United States, Great Britain, Germany, France, Switzerland, Italy, Canada, Japan, and Australia. Soft currency countries are best exemplified by Russia, where the Russian ruble has no value outside the Commonwealth of Independent States.

When a company from a hard currency country does business in a soft currency country, some form of *countertrade* is usually required to close the deal. Exceptions occur when a soft currency country has sufficient hard currency reserves in its central bank to finance imports by national companies. This is the current status of most Latin American countries as a result of *International Monetary Fund* loans, U.S government guarantees, and improving foreign trade environments.

harvesting The maximization of short-term *cash flow* and earnings.

Maximization is generally accomplished by cutting operating costs, such as reducing the sales force; reducing new investment; reducing the product range; eliminating smaller customers; cutting back on the number of distributors; or taking advantage of any remaining strengths, such as the ability to raise prices.

Businesses that are candidates for harvesting are usually subject to some combination of the following conditions: (1) The business has a small market share that can only be increased at great cost, (2) the business does not make a contribution to a company's profits, reputation, or market position, (3) the business is in a saturated market that offers little growth potential, or (4) there are more attractive investment opportunities that require the cash currently devoted to the business that will be harvested.

The decision to harvest a particular business carries considerable risk. For example, RCA was premature in harvesting its television business, a market that had been thought to be mature with little growth potential, just when Japanese competitors were investing heavily in video tape, which revitalized the television market.

Hazardous Substances Labeling Act
An act passed in 1960 that controls the labeling of packages that contain hazardous household substances.

holding period return
The return on an investment, held over a period of time.

It is computed by dividing the investment's current income, less capital gains or losses, by the investment's purchase price, or

$$\frac{\text{Current income} - \text{Capital gains or losses}}{\text{Purchase price}} = \text{Holding period return}$$

Say stock X and stock Y were each held for one year:

	Stock X	Stock Y
Purchase price	$50	$50
Cash dividend	$8	$5
Selling price	$47	$55
Capital gain (loss)	($3)	$5

The holding period return for each stock is

$$\text{Stock X}: \quad \frac{\$8 - \$3}{\$50} = 0.10, \text{or } 10\%$$

$$\text{Stock Y}: \quad \frac{\$5 + \$5}{\$50} = 0.20, \text{or } 20\%$$

Holding period return is frequently used by financial managers (along with return records and risk measures, such as **beta**) in making investment decisions.

horizontal integration
A growth strategy in which a company buys a competitor at the same level in the distribution channel—that is, retailers buy out other retailers, say, and manufacturers buy out other manufacturers.

Horizontal strategies can help a company broaden its product line or appeal to a new segment of the market. General Motors did both when it purchased Saab in Sweden. Many major U.S. brewers have also boosted their market share by buying up smaller breweries. *See also* **vertical integration.**

horizontal marketing strategy A marketing strategy in which two or more nonrelated companies join forces to take advantage of a new marketing opportunity.

EXAMPLE: H&R Block and Hyatt Legal Services made an arrangement that allowed Hyatt's legal clinics to rent office space from H&R Block's tax preparation offices. The deal allows Hyatt to penetrate the market quickly through H&R Block's nationwide chain of offices, whereas H&R Block gets the benefit of steady rent income in an otherwise highly seasonal market.

Compare to **vertical marketing system.**

housing starts and residential construction An important economic activity in the United States, accounting for roughly 3% of total GDP in any year.

It is a highly cyclical activity for a number of reasons: (1) The expenditure involved is large. (2) As a result, building is often financed through borrowing (mortgages). (3) Because of both of these factors, the decision to build can be postponed.

Four aspects of residential construction are individually monitored by the Department of Commerce. *Housing permits* are the authorizations to build new housing units, typically required by local governments. Thus, the issuance of a housing permit is usually the first stage in construction and thus is regarded as a leading cyclical indicator. *Housing starts* represent the start of construction, when the foundation of the home or apartment building is dug. *Housing completions* measure the end of construction, whereas records of *new home sales* look at the end of the entire process.

Residential construction is incorporated into the estimates of GDP as construction progresses, using the payments that are made as construction proceeds as the main measure. This reflects the actual effect on the economy.

human resources management The actions and decisions that affect the relationships between a company and its employees.

The central issue of human resources management was perhaps best expressed by Akio Morita, the head of Sony, when he explained why he personally interviewed every new recruit by saying that "The future prosperity of Sony rests in the hands of the last person we recruited."

Traditionally, human resources management was the responsibility of a clearly defined department, such as personnel, that was responsible for hiring, training, rewarding, and discharging employees. A great deal of this work was reactive (such as responding to personal crises or labor demands) rather than proactive (such as developing an active approach to shaping the relationship between the company and its employees). In recent years, this narrow definition of human resources management has undergone a radical change.

Human resources management is now considered to be a major component of general management; in fact, human resources are now thought to be a vital corporate asset and are frequently referred to as social or intellectual capital. This development has widespread implications for corporate strategy. Just as there must be an external strategic plan for dealing with the *environment*, such as competitors, customers, and markets, there must be an internal strategic plan for dealing with employees. It is vital that these two aspects of strategy work together to further the company's overall goals.

To be an effective force within a company, human resources management must become an integral part of day-to-day activities. Implementing a strategy often requires fundamental changes in the basic beliefs that people hold about their jobs, their relations within the company, and the ways in which they can contribute to the company's success.

humorous appeal   An *advertising* strategy that relies on the power of humor to persuade consumers to purchase a product.

Humorous ads tend to attract a lot of attention and generate affection for the sponsor, but they may also obscure the message of the ad. In other words, the audience may be laughing too hard to notice the product. *See also emotional appeal.*

hygiene factors   Those factors in the workplace, such as salary, company policies, and working conditions, that, when inadequate on a job, result in employee dissatisfaction.

When hygiene factors are adequate, however, they do not bring about appreciable levels of employee satisfaction. In other words, hygiene factors are the bare minimum workplace conditions. When they are present, workers are placated. When they are absent, workers are dissatisfied.

idle time Any time spent not actively working on a process due to setup, lack of material, lack of scheduling, maintenance, and so on.

Management must be aware of idle time and, whenever possible, attempt to eliminate it.

image advertising An advertising strategy designed to promote a particular image for a company, product, or brand.

Image advertising is different from other product advertising in that it does not focus on gaining immediate sales. Instead, the advertisements build a mood, such as beauty, love, excitement, reliability, or strength. No statement is made about the product or company except those created by the images.

EXAMPLE: A natural gas company might want to create an image campaign highlighting its concern for the environment in order to promote natural gas as an environmentally sound alternative to other energy sources.

incentive plans Any rewards that motivate employees.

Incentive plans are an important tool by which top management can influence the actions of executives in order to achieve corporate goals. In establishing an incentive plan, it is important to emphasize consistency with the company's overall strategy. When considering an incentive plan in terms of its consistency with *corporate strategy*, there are four potential problem areas:

(1) *Company-divisional relationships:* Corporate management's role in multidivisional firms can vary a great deal. In some companies, management works directly with division managers. In others, management simply acts as a resource center and divisional managers are essentially independent. The incentive plans for each different structure must incorporate that structure's particular characteristics. For example, a company with a series of independent divisions might base incentives on some measure of profitability (which encourages each manager to treat his or her division as an independent company), whereas a company with less distinction between headquarters and its various divisions might base incentives on some other performance measure, such as overall sales (which encourages each division manager to coordinate his or her actions with headquarters in order to achieve corporate goals).

(2) *Interdivisional relationships:* Incentive plans affect how divisional managers work together. If there is a need for cooperation between divisions, the incentive plan will be quite different from the situation where divisions work independently.

(3) *Risk taking versus risk aversion:* Companies in emerging markets might want to encourage rapid growth by fostering a risk-taking entrepreneurial spirit in their managers. In these companies, incentive plans should be structured to reward this kind of behavior. Companies in mature markets, however, may emphasize the maintenance of market position over any significant attempts to gain market share. In these situations, incentive plans should reward behavior that avoids risk and solidifies market position, such as improving customer relations.

(4) *Short-term versus long-term:* Incentive plans have a great impact on managers' trade-off decisions. For example, if incentives are based on quarterly production figures, a factory manager might choose to skip the scheduled maintenance on a particular piece of equipment in order to produce more units of output. This decision to pursue short-term gains, possibly at the expense of a serious equipment malfunction at some point in the future, is directly motivated by the incentive plan. In this situation, it might have been preferable to have an incentive plan that emphasized long-term *productivity* rather than short-term goals.

income from continuing operations In accounting, an *income statement* entry describing after-tax revenues and expenses arising from the business's ongoing operations.

Nonrecurring gains and losses, such as the *write-off* of uncollectible accounts receivable, are included in income from continuing operations.

income statement A formal statement of the elements used in determining a company's *net income;* also called profit and loss statement.

Every company must include an income statement in its annual report. Generally the categories reported in an income statement are as follows:

Sales
Less: cost of goods sold
Gross margin
Less: operating expenses, selling expenses, and general and administrative expenses
Income from operations
Add: other income
Less: other expenses
Income before tax
Less: provision for income taxes
Income from continuing operations
Income or loss from discontinued operations (net of tax)

Income before extraordinary items or cumulative effect
Add or less: extraordinary items (net of tax)
Add or less: cumulative effect of a change in accounting principle (net of tax)

Net income

Most companies do not follow this format exactly, as one can see with Wal-Mart:

Income statement

Consolidated Statement of Income Wal-Mart Stores, Inc. and Subsidiaries
(Amounts in thousands except per share data)

	1991	1990
Revenues:		
Net sales..........................	$32,601,594	$25,810,656
Rentals from licensed departments......	22,362	16,685
Other income-net.....................	239,452	157,959
TOTAL REVENUES	32,863,408	25,985,300
Costs and expenses:		
Cost of sales.......................	25,499,834	20,070,034
Operating, selling, and general and administrative expenses...........	5,152,178	4,069,695
Interest costs:		
Debt................................	42,716	20,346
Capital leases......................	125,920	117,725
TOTAL COSTS AND EXPENSES	30,820,648	24,277,800
Income before income taxes.............	2,042,760	1,707,500
Provision for federal and state income taxes:		
Current.............................	737,020	608,912
Deferred............................	14,716	22,688
	751,736	631,600
NET INCOME	$1,291,024	$1,075,900

incremental cost The cost difference between two or more business alternatives.

EXAMPLE: If a toy company can make rubber balls in either red or blue, it might analyze the incremental costs of the two options.

	Red	Blue	Incremental costs
Materials	$10,000	$8,000	$2,000
Labor	5,000	5,000	0

In other words, there is a $2,000 incremental cost associated with the materials required to make the red balls.

independent demand   Demand for an item that is not based on demand for another item.

Independent demand is separate from derived demand, in which the demand for a product is predicated on the demand for another product.

EXAMPLE: Clothing, books, and automobiles are all subject to independent demand, whereas the fabric, paper, and metal that make them up are subject to *derived demand. See also derived demand.*

indexing   The practice of relating investments or contracts to widely known compilations or indexes.

For investors, indexing can be accomplished by weighting a portfolio in the same manner as a broad-based stock index to match the index's performance. Indexing can also mean the act of investing in a mutual fund (known as an index fund) that buys and sells stocks in the same weighting as a compiled index.

When related to business activity as opposed to investing, indexing means tying increases in selling prices to national indexes (such as inflation rates) or tying labor contract wage increases to indexes such as the cost-of-living index. As the index changes, prices and/or wage rates change in the same proportion.

indirect cost   An expense that cannot be traced back to a specific unit of production or item sold.

Management salaries, rent, and utilities, for instance, are indirect expenses.

indirect method   *See funds provided from operations*

industrial goods   All goods or services that are used in the production of other goods or services subsequently supplied to ultimate consumers.

Industrial goods fall into one of three categories: Raw materials and components, capital goods, and services and supplies. Each of these categories is involved differently in the manufacturing process.

Raw materials and components are goods that are incorporated completely into the manufacturing process. Flour that is made into bread, tires that go on a car, and leather that becomes a pair of shoes are all examples of raw materials or components. Usually, raw materials are viewed as commodities, so the marketing strategies used for them center on low price. Components, such as engine subassemblies or computer parts, however, are marketed via price and service.

Capital goods, which include factory buildings, office computers, and tools, are only partially involved with the finished product. Companies producing capital goods usually rely on marketing strategies that emphasize personal selling and service.

Supplies and services are not incorporated into the finished product at all, but rather are used to support the production of finished goods. Supplies and services, which are usually purchased on a *straight rebuy* basis, include typing paper, lubricating oil, and repair services. Since there is a great deal of standardization and little brand loyalty among these products, companies selling supplies and services must emphasize price and service in their marketing mix.

industrial market
All individuals or companies that produce or acquire goods or services that are incorporated into the production of other finished goods or services subsequently sold to consumers; also called the business or producer market.

The main difference between the industrial market and the *consumer market* is that the industrial market does not buy goods for final consumption. The industrial market has four types of buyers: manufacturers, *wholesalers,* institutional consumers, and *retailers.* Manufacturers buy goods for use in the production of their own final products. Wholesalers purchase goods from manufacturers and distributors and sell them to retail outlets. Institutional consumers are large-volume buyers and include government as well as private businesses such as restaurants, nursing homes, hospitals, hotels, and churches. Retailers offer products to the ultimate consumer for final consumption. Each of these different buyers offers the industrial marketer a different *target market. See also consumer market, government market.*

industrial policy
The course of action set by a government to influence the development of domestic industrial sectors in particular and the direction of national industrial growth in general.

A government's industrial policy may comprise such instruments as subsidies (direct and indirect), tax incentives, regional development programs, training programs for workers, and research and development (R&D) assistance.

EXAMPLE: Canadian industrial policy has come under frequent attack from various U.S. industrial sectors. Americans have claimed that, under the guise of assisting domestic industry, the Canadian government has really been subsidizing the development of competitive export industries. Such alleged activities are contrary to both the Canada–U.S. Free Trade Agreement and the General Agreement on Tariffs and Trade (GATT).

The U.S. Omnibus Trade Act of 1988 (Section 301) prohibits foreign governments engaging in export targeting. The rationale is that since export targeting uses government leverage to enhance export effectiveness, it is implicitly unfair and thus deserving of action by the U.S. Trade Representative. (*Source*: L. Presner, *The International Business Dictionary and Reference*, Copyright © 1991 by L. Presner. Reprinted by permission of the publisher, John Wiley & Sons, Inc.)

industrial production The output of U.S. factories, mines, and utilities.

This output constitutes the production of *things*—the goods portion of goods and services. (The only goods excluded are those produced in agriculture, fisheries, and forestry.) The *Federal Reserve Board* has measured industrial production since the 1920s. In fact, industrial production is an older measure of U.S. output than GDP.

Details of production are compiled for a wide array of industries, and these provide a precise benchmark for firms that operate within the covered industries. For instance, a textile firm can contrast its own recent activity with that for the industry as a whole. Production trends in a particular industry—one that is a client industry, for instance—may also point to future demand for a firm's products.

Industrial production is a coincident indicator of economic activity: It traces the behavior of the business cycle nearly exactly.

industry attractiveness test A method of evaluating the strategic impact of entering a new industry.

The attractiveness test states that the industry chosen for *diversification* must be structurally attractive or able to be made attractive. In other words, the new industry must offer returns that exceed the cost of capital required for entry. If those returns do not exist, the company must be able to restructure the industry or create a sustainable *competitive advantage* that generates returns above the industry average. The industry attractiveness test can also be used by current participants in an industry. *See also better-off test, cost-of-entry test.*

infinite loading The process of scheduling work on a work station or resource as if it has a limitless capacity to handle any and all jobs.

This process wreaks havoc on a production schedule and should be avoided. *Compare to finite loading.*

inflation An increase in the general price level.

Inflation can be regarded as either an increase in the *cost of living*, or an erosion in the value of money—a loss of purchasing power. A crucial emphasis is that inflation is a generalized rise in prices as opposed to upward pressure on the prices of particular goods because of specific supply-demand imbalances.

Increases in the rate of inflation often reflect an excess in aggregate demand relative to output, *demand pull* inflation. Moreover, expectations of increasing inflation exert an upward effect on *interest rates.* Thus, financial markets—particularly the credit and money markets—often translate signs of increased economic activity into portents of building inflationary pressures and rising interest rates.

Increases in specific costs can, by raising costs of production generally, lead to inflation that is called *cost push* inflation. This has long been noted to be a connection between wage costs and inflation. In the 1970s, however, sharp increases in oil and energy costs also led to higher inflation.

Along with the **unemployment rate**, inflation represents the other major (and usually opposite) example of poor economic performance because it also reflects a macroeconomic inefficiency.

inflation accounting
A method of financial reporting that incorporates the financial impact of changes in the price level.

Constant dollar accounting and *current cost accounting* are both inflation accounting methods.

influence
See power

informal organizational structure
The network of social relationships that develop within an organization as people work together.

The informal structure of a company is often quite different from its formal structure. Whereas many formal structures rely on strict superior-subordinate relationships, informal structures frequently circumvent this hierarchy. In many cases, the informal structure of an organization is equally as important as its formal structure. For example, in a situation where a company faces a great deal of uncertainty, say the possibility of a takeover by a competitor, employees frequently work within its informal structure to gather information and create a sense of cohesiveness and loyalty within the company that could not have been developed through any formal policies or statements.

It is important to note, however, that the informal structure of a company usually relies on rumor, innuendo, and gossip rather than facts. As a result, much of the information that flows through the informal structure is incomplete or even false.

in-house advertising agency
See advertising agency

initial public offering
See going public

innovation
A new product or service.

An innovation is distinct from an invention in that it is simply the *introduction* of something new whereas an invention is the design or *creation* of something new. An innovation may be an invention, a combination of existing elements that forms a new and unique product, or a service that has not previously been offered. *See also **product life-cycle.***

inputs The factors that are combined in the production of a product or service. At their most basic, inputs are the raw materials of a manufacturing process.

EXAMPLE: If a construction company is building a house, the inputs naturally include cement, wood, brick, wire, pipes, and glass. Inputs, however, also include other factors that are not so readily identified as the components of a finished product. For the construction company, inputs also include the facilities in which the carpenters work, the administrative system that directs their activities, the equipment and tools used to build the house, the labor and knowledge that the carpenters bring to the job, the supplies used by the carpenters and construction company, and, perhaps most important, the time to complete the project.

Managing inputs, then, is much more complicated than simply managing raw materials. It requires careful attention to the materials, equipment, facilities, labor, supplies, knowledge, and time required to complete a process.

insertion order Directions to a publisher for the exact placement and terms of a print advertisement.

An insertion order states the size of the ad, its position on the page, its position in the publication (in the sports section of a newspaper, for example), its price, and the dates on which the ad will appear. A copy of the advertisement is usually enclosed with the insertion order.

intangible asset In accounting, an item or right that has no physical substance and provides an economic benefit.

Examples include patent rights, *goodwill*, and a *copyright*. Intangible assets are shown on the balance sheet and must be *amortized* over a period not to exceed 40 years. *See also **asset**.*

intellectual property A collective term used to refer to ideas or works in the classes of industrial property or copyright.

These terms are defined as follows:

1. *Industrial property* means legal rights in the form of patents, technological inventions, trademarks, industrial designs, and "appellations of origin."

2. *Copyright* means legal rights in the form of literary works, musical works, and artistic works and in films, books, and performances of performing artists in live form and in any recorded format, including photographs, television, or other visual medium.

To qualify for inclusion in either one or both of the preceding classes, ideas and/or works must (1) be put into an appropriate formal documentary form and (2) have been filed with the appropriate national authority for the purpose of registering the material to obtain the domestic (and possibly international) legal protection for the works of the authors, owners, or inventors.

The key body that promotes and coordinates international efforts to protect intellectual property and under whose aegis a number of international agreements are administered in this regard is the World Intellectual Property Organization (WIPO). (*Source:* L. Presner, *The International Business Dictionary and Reference,* Copyright © 1991 by L. Presner. Reprinted by permission of the publisher, John Wiley & Sons, Inc.)

Inter-American Development Bank   See *development banks*

interdependence   The amount that different groups rely on each other to achieve organizational goals.

Understanding the interdependence between the different groups within an organization helps managers determine the appropriate level of intergroup coordination. There are three types of interdependence: pooled, sequential, and reciprocal.

Pooled interdependence occurs when two groups operate independently but their combined efforts contribute to the organization's overall goals. For example, in a computer software company, the shipping department and the product development team might be linked by pooled interdependence. Both groups are necessary if the company is going to develop new products and get them to customers, but they are essentially independent and distinct. In most cases, the coordination requirements between groups that are linked by pooled interdependence are lower than with either sequential or reciprocal interdependence.

Sequential interdependence occurs when one group depends on another for its inputs but the dependency flows in only one direction. For example, in a manufacturing company, the parts assembly department is linked by sequential interdependence with the purchasing department. In other words, if the purchasing department does not order an important component, the parts assembly department will be significantly affected and might even have to close down.

The most complicated type of interdependence is reciprocal. When groups are linked reciprocally, they share inputs and outputs. For example, in the computer software company, the sales department and the product development team are reciprocally interdependent. The salespeople obtain information about their customers' future needs and relay that information to the product development team. The product development team, in turn, works to develop new products to satisfy those future needs.

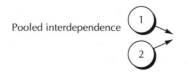

Pooled interdependence

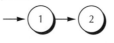

Sequential interdependence

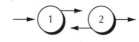

Reciprocal interdependence

Interdependence

interest expense In accounting, the *income statement* entry showing the period costs of borrowing money.

interest rates The payment borrowers make for the use of the funds that they borrow and the payment that lenders demand for the use of the funds they lend (termed *interest*), expressed as a percentage of the principal (loan amount).

This percentage is the interest rate. Interest rates typically are expressed in whole percentages and basis points. A basis point is one-hundredth of a percentage point. Thus, the U.S. Treasury 30-year bond had an interest rate of 7.09 percent in February 1993, 25 basis points less than the 7.34 percent average rate for January 1993.

There are four main components to market interest rates: (1) the risk (or default) premium, (2) the maturity premium, (3) an inflation premium, and (4) the "real" rate.

The *risk* premium is a recognition that different classes of borrowers have greater or lesser risk of default. Interest rates are higher for riskier borrowers; they are lowest for the U.S. Treasury, which is considered a "risk-free" borrower. The difference in interest rate between any other borrower and the U.S. Treasury for the same maturity is called a *quality spread*. The *maturity* premium reflects the fact that, in general, a longer loan will have a higher interest rate than a shorter loan of the same quality. The *yield curve* shows the change in interest rates as maturities are extended for a given class of loans. The *inflation* premium is a recognition that inflation may erode the purchasing power of the funds lent. Thus, interest includes compensation for the inflation *expected* over the length of the loan. The remaining portion of interest rates reflects the *real* rate of interest that must be paid to induce the lender to forego the use of the funds. (*Note:* This is not simply the interest rate less *current* inflation, but rather interest rates less the average *expected* inflation over the length of the loan. Subtracting the current inflation rate provides an *inflation-adjusted* interest rate. Often, since future interest rates are assumed to conform to an average of past rates, lenders use some such average as a proxy for expected inflation.)

The table below provides examples of these concepts for three widely different years: 1982, 1986, and 1992.

	Percentage		
	1982	**1986**	**1992**
U.S. Treasury bonds	13.00	7.68	7.01
AAA corporate bonds	13.79	9.02	8.14
Quality spread	+0.79	+1.34	+1.13
U.S. Treasury 3-year Note	12.92	7.06	5.30
U.S. Treasury 10-year Bond	13.00	7.68	7.01
Maturity spread	+0.08	+0.62	+1.71
U.S. Treasury 10-year Bond	13.00	7.68	7.01
Consumer inflation*	9.78	3.84	3.62
Inflation-adjusted rate	3.22	3.84	3.39

*Average inflation rates for previous five years used as a proxy for inflation expectations.

intermittent production   *See job process system*

internal rate of return   The *discount rate* at which the **net present value** (that is, the value of all future cash flows, in excess of the original investment, expressed in today's dollars) of an investment equals zero.

Internal rate of return is frequently used by financial managers to decide whether to commit to an investment. In most cases, an investment opportunity is accepted when the internal rate of return is greater than the **opportunity cost** (that is, the projected return on an investment of similar risk) of the capital required for the investment. Internal rate of return is expressed mathematically as

$$\text{NPV} = P_0 + \frac{P_1}{1 + \text{IRR}} + \frac{P_2}{(1 + \text{IRR})^2} + \frac{P_3}{(1 + \text{IRR})^3} + \cdots + \frac{P_4}{(1 + \text{IRR})^n} = 0$$

where

NPV $=$ Net present value of the investment

$P_0, P_1, ..., P_n =$ Cash payments in periods $0, 1, ..., n$, respectively.

IRR $=$ Internal rate of return

The actual calculation of IRR is basically a matter of trial and error. Many business calculators are programmed to perform the calculations.

EXAMPLE: Consider a project that generates the following cash flows:

P_0	P_1	P_2
−$8,000	+$4,000	+$8,000

The project's internal rate of return is expressed as

$$-\$8,000 + \frac{\$4,000}{1 + \text{IRR}} + \frac{\$8,000}{(1 + \text{IRR})^2} = 0$$

The first step in determining IRR might be to assume that it is zero. That is,

$$-\$8,000 + \frac{\$4,000}{1.0} + \frac{\$8,000}{(1.0)^2} = \$4,000$$

The net present value of the investment (with an IRR of zero) is $4,000. Since the NPV is positive, the IRR must be greater than zero. The next step might be to try 25 percent, or

$$-\$8,000 + \frac{\$4,000}{1.25} + \frac{\$8,000}{(1.25)^2} = \$320$$

The net present value of the investment (with an IRR of zero) is $320. Since the NPV is still positive, the IRR must be greater than 25 percent. The next step might be to try 26, 27, or, as luck would have it, 28 percent:

$$-\$8,000 + \frac{\$4,000}{1.28} + \frac{\$8,000}{(1.28)^2} = \$7.81$$

For practical purposes, an NPV of $7.81 is equivalent to zero (a financial calculator or a few more calculations would give a more precise IRR of about 28.0776 percent) and the IRR of the investment is 28 percent.

If the opportunity cost of the capital required for the investment is less than 28 percent, the investment has a positive net present value when discounted at the opportunity cost of capital. Say the opportunity cost of capital for the investment in the example is 20 percent; its net present value is

$$-\$8,000 + \frac{\$4,000}{1.20} + \frac{\$8,000}{(1.20)^2} = \$889$$

This is a strong indication that the investment should be pursued. If the opportunity cost of capital is greater than the investment's IRR (say 35 percent) the investment has a negative net present value, or

$$-\$8,000 + \frac{\$4,000}{1.35} + \frac{\$8,000}{(1.35)^2} = -\$647$$

This is a strong indication that the investment should not be made. *See also **net present value**.*

International Monetary Fund (IMF) A multinational organization under the aegis of the United Nations set up by the Bretton Woods Agreement in 1944.

The original purpose of the IMF was to stabilize exchange rates after World War II through the coordination and regulation of member country currency movement.

Today, the IMF no longer coordinates and regulates, although it does promote stability through surveillance and consultation with member countries. The IMF also provides minimum short-term loans to member countries for resolving balance of payment difficulties. Today the IMF is one of the most powerful and important financial institutions in the world. Its major activity in recent years has been to support the building of infrastructures in developing countries. The IMF's major thrust in this regard is to act as a police force, exercising approval authority over specific projects and investing developers prior to the awarding of financial assistance by development banks.

To obtain IMF approval, countries must reduce inflation rates, dramatically reduce budget deficits, curtail money supplies, and achieve at least a modicum of political stability. Critics cite the potential for high unemployment and social unrest that such stringent policies could bring, but so far the IMF has held its ground.

International Monetary Market (IMM) A division of the Chicago Mercantile Exchange; the premier market for foreign currency.

Other activities include trading futures in U.S. Treasury bills, certificates of deposit, and *Eurodollar* deposits.

inventory Any goods available for resale at any given time.

Inventory is recorded at the lower of cost or market value and reported on the *balance sheet*. There are three types of inventory in a manufacturing company: *raw materials*, *work-in-process*, and *finished goods*. Inventory includes both goods that are out on *consignment* and goods that are in transit. *See also beginning inventory, ending inventory.*

inventory forms The five broad categories into which inventories are classified: *raw materials inventory*; intermediaries; *work-in-process inventory*; maintenance, repair, and operating inventory; and *finished goods inventory*.

Raw materials inventories are any items to be used directly in the production of a final product. Steel, flour, paint, wood, and plastic are all commonly considered raw materials; but the definition extends to any other materials, such as spark plugs, circuitry, and engines that may have been purchased from an outside organization for use in a product.

Intermediaries include spare parts and supplies that are not necessarily incorporated into a final product, but are an integral part of its manufacture. Examples include packing material, paper, and lubricants.

Work-in-process (WIP) inventory consists of all items that have left raw materials inventory, but are not yet finished goods.

Maintenance, repair, and operating (MRO) inventories are those materials, such as tools, lubricants, or spare parts, that are held in order to keep a process flowing smoothly.

Finished goods inventory is made up of completed products. Once an item is completed, it is transferred from work-in-process inventory into finished goods inventory, after which it can be sent to distribution centers, or sold to *wholesalers, retailers,* or customers.

inventory functions The five broad operational reasons why companies retain inventories: anticipation, buffer, cycle, decoupling, and transit.

Anticipation inventories are held in anticipation of a future increase in demand. Rather than operate at peak capacity during one period and then shut down in a subsequent period, anticipation inventories can be allowed to accumulate before a period of peak demand and then sold or used during or afterward. Clothing manufacturers, for example, build up anticipation inventories in the months before Christmas, when demand for their products will be high. This strategy allows for more level production throughout the holiday season, with little idle time in the months to follow.

Buffer stock is created to protect against unexpected surges in demand. Any inventory held over and above the average demand requirement is considered buffer inventory. High buffer inventories allow companies to continue to serve customers throughout unexpected increases in demand. Excessive buffer inventories, however, can be quite expensive to maintain. Because conditions and demand vary a great deal from industry to industry, there is no rule of thumb as to what constitutes an excessive buffer inventory. However, an appropriate analysis might be to compare a company's buffer inventories with historical demand patterns within its industry.

Cycle inventories are the result of ordering materials in large batches rather than on an as-needed basis. Cycle inventories are frequently seen when the costs associated with ordering materials are greater than the costs of holding the material.

EXAMPLE: If the annual demand for a particular component is 24,000, management might decide to order a single shipment of 24,000 parts and maintain a large inventory rather than place 12 orders of 2,000 and maintain a smaller inventory.

Decoupling inventories act as cushions between two processes that operate at different speeds.

EXAMPLE: In a bakery, where a mixer can turn out cookie dough five times faster than the preceding work station can assemble ingredients, a decoupling inventory of preassembled ingredients might be maintained in order to keep the mixer operating at its desired speed.

Decoupling inventories also serve to separate the different operations in a process so that, if an element in a process breaks down, all subsequent workstations could continue to operate, at least for a short time. Without decoupling inventories, each workstation must produce at exactly the same rate; if one operation breaks down, the entire process comes to a halt.

Transit inventories, also called pipeline inventories, are, as the name suggests, in transit from one place to another and are generally unavailable for use. Transit inventories may keep a steady stream of material flowing through the production process in contrast to a single shipment. For example, in the automotive industry, Toyota uses transit inventory to keep floor stock at a bare minimum, even though its suppliers are thousands of miles away.

inventory turnover In accounting, a measure of the number of times that the average amount of inventory on hand is sold within a given period of time.

In other words, the inventory turnover ratio shows how many times a company "emptied its warehouse" over a particular period of time. This ratio is calculated by dividing the *cost of goods sold* for a specified period of time by the average amount of inventory on hand for that same time period (average inventory is calculated by adding *beginning inventory* and *ending inventory* for a given time period and dividing the sum by two), or

$$\text{Inventory turnover ratio} = \frac{\text{Cost of goods sold}}{\text{Average inventory on hand}}$$

A high inventory turnover rate might indicate that a company has low inventory levels, which may cause a loss in business. A low ratio might indicate that a company is overstocking its merchandise. This could be a reaction to a coming shortage or the result of an obsolete product line. Of course, inventory turnover ratios vary a great deal, and what may be considered high in one industry may be considered low in another industry. Occasionally, sales are used in the numerator of the ratio instead of cost of goods sold. This results in a less useful figure, but the technique may be necessary in order to make a comparative analysis. *See also days inventory.*

inventory valuation In accounting, the costs assigned to inventory.

These costs are reported on the balance sheet and used in the calculation of *cost of goods sold* on the *income statement. Generally accepted accounting principles* allow several methods of inventory valuation. *See also first-in, first-out (FIFO), last-in, first-out (LIFO),* and *average cost method.*

investment The addition businesses make to capital.

Investment consists of additions to the *fixed capital stock,* both residential (residential construction is included in investment because it is so long-lived; the useful life of a house is assumed to be at least 50 years) and nonresidential, and *changes in business inventories.* (Purchases of shares of stock are *not* investments in the economic sense unless it is newly issued stock. Otherwise, individuals are simply exchanging one form of wealth—money—for another—the shares—and no new capital is being created.)

The more conventional notion of investment is the expenditure on fixed business capital—plant and equipment. However, much of the investment in business capital is for replacement as previous capital wears out or becomes obsolete. This is the reason for the word *gross* in **gross domestic product**. Investment in net new capacity—the addition to capital—requires that businesses have positive expectations for future economic activity in general, and for the prospects for their own firms in particular. Thus investment is quite cyclical.

IPO   *See initial public offering*

job depth The amount of power that an individual has to change or influence either the job or the work environment.

For example, an assembly line worker does not have a great deal of job depth. Such a person must work at the pace of the line; the faster it moves, the more quickly the task must be performed. A company president, on the other hand, has a great deal of job depth. The president can decide what to do and when to do it. If there is a task that the individual does not want to do, it is very likely that it will be delegated to a subordinate. *See also **job range.***

job description A written statement detailing what a jobholder does, how to do it, and why it is done.

job enlargement Increasing the number of tasks that an employee performs.

Job enlargement is a popular method of combatting the boredom and fatigue created by increasingly specialized equipment that requires less and less worker skill. There are two main techniques of job enlargement: (1) Rotating workers through a variety of positions, and (2) increasing the variety of tasks for which a worker is responsible. Some *efficiency* is lost through job enlargement, but it can create a more motivated, and satisfied work force. Job enlargement is basically a *horizontal* expansion, as contrasted to ***job enrichment,*** which is essentially a *vertical* expansion. *Compare to **job enrichment.***

job enrichment A method of increasing worker satisfaction by giving employees increased roles in the production operation, such as quality control, work station scheduling, and planning.

EXAMPLE: Rather than just assembling the motor of a blender, the worker may install and inspect it. The process aims to give the worker a greater degree of autonomy and accountability by assigning him or her a *complete* task rather than a small portion of a larger job. Job enrichment is basically a *vertical* expansion, as contrasted to ***job enlargement***, which is essentially a *horizontal* expansion. *Compare to **job enlargement.***

job process system A production system designed to produce small batches of unique products; also called ***intermittent production.***

Companies using job processes are called job shops. Usually, each product in a job shop takes a different path through the organization, uses different materials and parts, requires a different amount of time, and requires different operations. Operations that use job processing include bakeries, physicians' offices, television productions companies, supermarkets, and automobile repair shops. Service companies, such as advertising agencies and tax preparation companies, that offer custom services to individual clients are frequently well suited for the job process.

The four main characteristics of a job process are (1) a large variety of *inputs*, (2) a significant amount of transport of either materials or staff, (3) grouping of equipment and staff according to function, and (4) considerable variation in the time it takes to complete a given job.

The advantage of a job shop is the ability to produce a wide variety of products at a relatively low cost.

EXAMPLE: Since most job shops perform a wide variety of tasks, general-purpose equipment can be used. General-purpose equipment is usually much less expensive and more easily available than special-purpose equipment. Because the equipment is widely used, there is a larger base of experience to draw upon in terms of operation and maintenance. Additionally, since there is a large market for used general-purpose equipment, it is easier to dispose of, which reduces the expense of obsolescence.

Because jobs come through in small batches that require different operations, workers in a job shop are likely to take more responsibility for, and pride in, their work. The pace in a job shop is not dictated by a constantly moving production line, so it is possible to establish incentives to encourage productivity. Additionally, because there is no line that is constantly moving, if one part of the operation stops, the other parts can continue working (as long as there is significant in-process inventory).

Job process systems have significant disadvantages as well. As a result of the variety in products, processes, and scheduling, it is nearly impossible for management to control a job shop when demand is high. As a result, *expediting* is frequently necessary to track down particular jobs and push them through the operation. Naturally, this can be a very expensive, and inefficient, situation.

Inventories can also be a disadvantage in a job shop. Typically, a job shop maintains significant inventories of a variety of materials and supplies. *Work-in-process inventories* also tend to build up. The total effect of all of these inventories is a significant expense and loss of space.

Because various inventories must travel between workstations, materials handling costs also tend to be high. Since jobs take different paths through the organization, it is usually impossible to invest in inexpensive materials-handling equipment, such as conveyor belts. Instead more expensive materials-handling equipment, such as forklifts or carts, is used. This equipment is typically quite large, which means that more space (beyond that needed to house the inventories) must be used, in the form of wider corridors and aisles.

job range   The variety of different tasks or operations that an individual must perform.

    The job range for an assembly line worker is quite low. For example, a worker in a paint shop described his job as "You clip on the color hose, bleed out the old color, and squirt. Clip, bleed, squirt, think; clip, bleed, squirt, yawn; clip, bleed, squirt, scratch your nose." At the other end of the spectrum, a company president has a great deal of job range. On any given day, the president might meet with employees or customers, chair a strategic planning session, address the annual stockholders meeting, or attend a conference in Hawaii.

    When job range is considered along with **job depth** (the power that an individual has to influence his or her job or working environment), one can create a graph that shows the position of every job in terms of its range and depth.

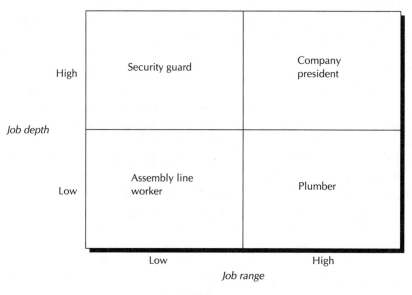

Job Range

    The assembly line worker has low depth and low range. The company president has high depth and high range. Between these two extremes is the vast majority of jobs. For example, the plumber has high job range, but low job depth. This classification reflects the fact that the plumber may be called to handle a variety of problems but is limited to a small number of fairly standard procedures in performing a particular task. Conversely, the security guard has high job depth, but low job range. The guard is responsible for a small number of tasks (such as making sure that no unauthorized personnel enter a particular building) but has a great deal of autonomy in the performance of those tasks. *See also job depth.*

job satisfaction   The set of *attitudes*, both positive and negative, that a person holds about a job.

Satisfaction is usually influenced by how well the outcomes of a particular job meet the expectations of an employee. For example, a group of employees with an average performance record who are given a 15 percent raise are more likely to have high job satisfaction than a group with a superior performance record who receive only a 7 percent raise.

Job satisfaction is the combination of several related attitudes that can be divided into three groups: (1) organizational attitudes, such as those related to salary, working conditions, promotion opportunities, and the nature of the work itself; (2) group attitudes, such as those related to morale, relations with superiors, relations with coworkers, and cohesiveness; and (3) personal attitudes, such as those related to an individual's aspirations and needs and to benefits such as training that make it possible to move to a different job.

Although high job satisfaction does not guarantee that an employee will remain with a company, in most cases, those who are satisfied will remain and those who are not will leave. Because job satisfaction can be a strong indicator of whether an employee will remain with a company, its measurement is often of great importance to management. There are many ways to measure job satisfaction, but four of the most common are these: surveys, interviews, critical incidents, and action tendencies.

Surveys frequently use ratings scales to determine the degree of an employee's job satisfaction. A typical example might include questions on salary and benefits, as shown below:

	Strongly disagree	Disagree	No opinion	Agree	Strongly agree
My salary is appropriate for the type of work I do.	1	2	3	4	5
People with the same job receive about the same pay.	1	2	3	4	5
Most of my co-workers are paid what they deserve.	1	2	3	4	5
I am able to keep up with the rising cost of living.	1	2	3	4	5
I understand the method by which my salary is determined.	1	2	3	4	5
In general, I am satisfied with my salary.	1	2	3	4	5
I am aware of the benefits available to me.	1	2	3	4	5
The benefits package provides good coverage.	1	2	3	4	5
In general, I am satisfied with the benefits package.	1	2	3	4	5

Surveys with ratings scales, such as the preceding example, offer a number of advantages in the measurement of job satisfaction. The first is that they are usually quite brief and can be filled out quickly. A second advantage is that they often use general language. This means that the same survey can be used in different areas within a company. A third advantage is that the data can be quantified (in the example, a score of 5 represents a high degree of job satisfaction and a score of 1 indicates low job satisfaction). This quantification allows for comparisons between different departments within a company. Comparisons over a period of time are also a possibility.

There are, however, some important disadvantages to survey measures of job satisfaction. The first is the assumption that all responses are completely honest. For example, if some employees feel that the survey is not entirely confidential, they may alter their responses in order to project a positive image—an image that has little relation to actual job satisfaction. A second possible disadvantage raises the question of whether the survey actually measures job satisfaction. For example, although an employee may appear to have high job satisfaction by agreeing strongly with the statement "I am happy with my job," the survey has failed to examine the various factors that actually make up job satisfaction. There may be other factors besides happiness (such as salary issues, relations with superiors, or difficult working conditions) that affect job satisfaction. If these factors are not included in the survey, measures of job satisfaction may be unreliable. A third disadvantage may be whether the survey measures job satisfaction consistently. This problem can arise in two ways. First, if there are inconsistencies within the survey (say an emphasis on salary and benefits with little consideration for working conditions, relations with co-workers, and relations with superiors), getting an accurate picture of job satisfaction is difficult. Second, inconsistencies can affect job satisfaction measures when they are measured over long periods of time. If employees fill out a different survey each month, it might be difficult to track job satisfaction from year to year.

The second common method of measuring job satisfaction is through interviews. This method allows for an in-depth exploration of the attitudes that make up job satisfaction. It is difficult to quantify the results of a series of interviews, but in many cases, this disadvantage is offset by the ability to question and probe various issues that might have been unclear if simply measured by a survey. Interviews are also prone to bias, on the part of both the interviewer and the interviewee. For example, when individuals are asked what they particularly like about a job, they often respond with internally focused comments, such as "I like being able to develop my skills"; "I appreciate the opportunity to succeed"; and "I like being able to use my creative talents." On the other hand, when asked what they dislike about a job, most individuals respond with externally focused comments, such as "I'm not making what I deserve"; "My boss doesn't give me enough direction"; and "Working conditions are terrible." In general, people are inclined to like the things over which they can exert some control (developing skills, succeeding, and using creative abilities) and dislike things over which they have no control (salary, the boss, and working conditions). As a result, responses to job satisfaction interviews are often biased.

Critical incidents are also examined through the interview method, but discussion is usually limited to a single important issue. In this process, employees are asked to discuss a particular incident or situation related to job satisfaction. A common technique is to ask individuals what they particularly like and dislike about their jobs in terms of salary, relations to co-workers, supervisors, and so on. This results in specific information that can then be analyzed in order to identify the underlying factors that are raising or lowering job satisfaction. One of the main benefits of this method is that employees can respond in any way they wish without being limited by a set of survey questions and responses. However, the method is time consuming, and there is the possibility of bias on the part of both the interviewer and the interviewee.

The fourth popular measure of job satisfaction is action tendencies. Action tendencies are the various inclinations that people have regarding their approach to, or avoidance of, work. Examples include whether someone would recommend his or her job to a friend with a similar background, how eager people are to go to work every morning, and whether they would choose the same career if they "had it all to do over again." By gathering this sort of information, job satisfaction can be measured. There are, however, some disadvantages to this approach. One is that employees might not have the self-insight to give accurate answers. A second is that the approach can be time consuming because it allows for a variety of employee responses.

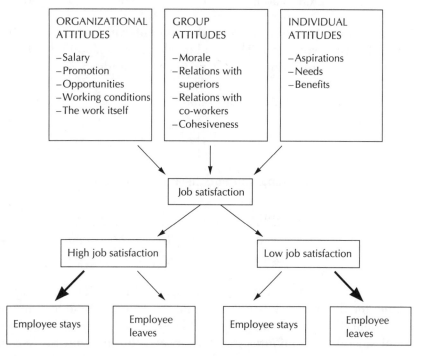

Job Satisfaction

Johnson's rule for dual workstations A method developed by scheduling researcher S.M. Johnson to determine the quickest possible time to get a number of jobs through a process with two workstations in the same order.

Johnson's rule is: If the shortest time for a job is on the first workstation, schedule it as early as possible, or first. If the shortest time for a job is on the second workstation, schedule it as late as possible, or last. Delete that job and repeat the process.

The goal of Johnson's rule is to (1) ensure maximum workstation *utilization* by methodically processing a large number of jobs and (2) avoid lengthy delays for any particular job.

EXAMPLE: Say a physician and nurse travel among rural schools conducting routine vision tests of students. An initial screening has been given to all students, and those that show a vision problem are then given a more comprehensive test by the nurse and an ophthalmological examination by the doctor. Say five students have been selected through the initial screening to receive further examination. Of course, it is desirable to conduct the comprehensive tests and examinations as quickly as possible so that the doctor and nurse can move on to another school. Based on the initial screening, the nurse estimates that the testing and examinations (beginning at 8:00 A.M.) will require the following amount of time (in minutes):

Student	1	2	3	4	5
Testing	60	15	10	20	30
Examination	10	30	60	15	30

According to Johnson's rule, the student with the shortest time in the second task is student 1. That student should be scheduled last. The student with the shortest time in the first task is student 3, so that student is scheduled first.

Thus far, the schedule is as follows:

3				1

The three remaining students have these requirements:

Student	2	4	5
Testing	15	20	30
Examination	30	15	30

The next shortest time is 15 minutes, but it appears as both the shortest time for the first task (student 2) and the shortest time for the second task (student 4). Usually this sort of situation calls for an arbitrary scheduling, but since the 15 minutes is split between the first and the second task, it is a simple matter to invoke Johnson's rule and schedule student 2 after student 3 and student 4 before student 1. Student 5 is then scheduled in the only remaining spot.

| 3 | 2 | 5 | 4 | 1 |

The entire schedule can then be illustrated on a *Gantt chart:*

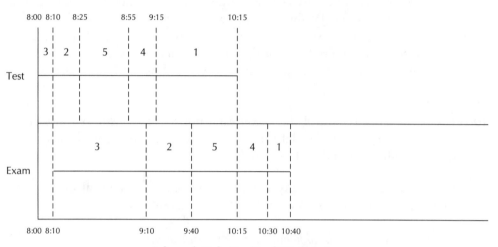

Johnson's Rule For Dual Workstations

All five students will have been screened and examined by about 11:40. Although Johnson's rule will result in an optimum schedule, it is not the only optimum schedule. It is important to note, however, that none of them will finish sooner than the one found with Johnson's rule.

joint venture (JV) A legal form of business organization between companies, whereby there is cooperation toward the achievement of common goals between entities that were, prior to the JV, separate.

There are three types of JVs: (1) contractual JVs, (2) equity JVs, and (3) hybrid JVs.

1. *Contractual JVs:* Under this type of arrangement, the JV is not created as a separate legal corporate entity. It is an enterprise in the form of an unincorporated association, created to carry out clearly defined activities and to attain specific goals over a specific period of time. There is a clear separation between the companies that agree to cooperate within this type of JV framework: each of them is responsible for its own liabilities.

2. *Equity JVs:* This arrangement is an enterprise comprising at least two partners and having the following characteristics:

    • Formation of a legal corporation with limited liability and the joint management of it by the JV partners

- Pooled equity in the corporation from which an equity ratio is determined (for example, 50–50, 49–51, 30–21–49)
- Profits and losses shared between the partners in proportion to their equity in the JV

3. *Hybrid JVs:* This commercial agreement is, as its name suggests, a cross between contractual JVs and equity JVs: (1) from the equity JV format, the hybrid JV retains the form of a separate legal entity, but one that is not necessarily a limited-liability corporation; and (2) from the contractual JV format, the hybrid type retains the specificity of time-limited activities and objectives. (*Source:* L. Presner, *The International Business Dictionary and Reference,* Copyright © L. Presner, 1991. Reprinted with permission of the publisher, John Wiley & Sons, Inc.)

journal entry   A record of the accounting impact of a business transaction.

An entry includes the date of the transaction, a short explanation, and the account(s) debited and credited.

EXAMPLE: When a company makes a cash sale, the journal entry would show the receipt of cash and the outflow of inventory.

*See also **account**, **bookkeeping**, **credit**, and **debit**.*

Journal of Marketing, The   See *American Marketing Association*

Journal of Marketing Research, The   See *American Marketing Association*

junk bonds   Debt securities rated below investment grade by credit-rating agencies.

During the 1980s, many companies large and small raised capital for business acquisitions and other expansions with junk bonds. The *below investment grade* credit rating means that the risk of receiving either interest payment or the return of principal is very high. This high risk, plus the absence of any collateral, forces junk bonds to carry very high interest rates relative to market rates.

just-in-time (JIT)   An approach to dealing with materials inventories that emphasizes the elimination of all waste and the continual improvement of the production process.

Just-in-time was originally developed in the mid-1970s by the Toyota Motor Company in Japan. The basic concept behind JIT is that materials and supplies are replenished exactly when they are needed and not before or after. More than an approach to dealing with materials, just-in-time is actually a philosophy that affects each part of a company's operations, from suppliers to interdepartmental relations to customers. The Japanese interpretation of JIT is to attempt to make products "flow like water" through a company. JIT is perhaps best suited to companies with a repetitive production process, such as automobile production, but it can be successfully adapted to companies that use *job process system* or *cellular production.*

By replenishing materials exactly when they are needed, the cost of having expensive materials sitting idle while waiting for production (and of having equipment wait for late materials) is eliminated. The savings extend to the elimination of scrap, defective products, unnecessary inventories, and wasted space.

Because of its broad nature, JIT has become a major part of many companies' competitive strategies (*see* *corporate strategy*). Toyota, for example, was able to use JIT to reduce the time it took to produce a car from fifteen days to one day. Many companies have adopted elements of JIT in their operations. IBM has a JIT system that it calls continuous flow, whereas Hewlett-Packard calls the system stockless production.

JIT has become so highly esteemed that traditional materials inventory systems are now frequently referred to as "just-in-case." In order to compare the two, almost every aspect of the production process must be considered: market priorities, suppliers, inventories, product engineering, plant capacity, process design, plant configuration, labor force, quality, maintenance, and control mechanisms.

Traditional operations generally have market priorities that dictate the acceptance of all customer orders by providing a variety of products or features from which a customer may choose. For example, most automobile companies offer customers their choice of a variety of options, such as air conditioning, power windows, and antilock brakes. These individual orders tend to complicate production, which increases both errors and costs. JIT firms, on the other hand, set strict limits on both the *target market* and variety of products. These lead to an emphasis on low cost and high quality within a well-defined market. This does not, however, mean that products produced by JIT companies do not have the features most customers want. JIT automobile manufacturers, for example, might include popular features such as air conditioning, power windows, and antilock brakes as standard equipment. Doing so simplifies production and lowers costs, which, in turn, gives the JIT company a competitive edge.

Traditionally, non-JIT companies contract with multiple materials suppliers. This strategy is intended to ensure a wide variety of materials at low prices by forcing suppliers to compete against each other. However, it also means that no single supplier gets a significant share of a company's business which provides no incentive to meet quality and delivery requirements.

JIT, with its reliance on frequent small deliveries of high-quality materials, requires an approach that integrates suppliers into the production team, often by sole sourcing to a single vendor. As a member of the team, vendors frequently help design and engineer the materials and parts being purchased. Clearly, the quantity of materials ordered must be large enough to make this involvement attractive to the vendor. By sole sourcing from a single supplier, manufacturers can frequently take advantage of quantity discounts, which can result in further cost savings.

The most significant cost savings associated with sole sourcing for JIT is the elimination of materials inspection. Quality *must* be guaranteed by the vendor. This is an element of the vendors' participation in the production team, and a distinct departure from the traditional adversarial relationship that non-JIT companies have with their suppliers.

EXAMPLE: When Harley-Davidson decided to shift to JIT for its motorcycle manufacturing, it initially faced stiff resistance from its suppliers and developed a bad reputation for ordering parts at the last minute. However, as it began to work with various vendors in order to simplify their designs and delivery systems, they began to come around. As the company began buying from fewer suppliers (most of whom were located close to manufacturing plants to reduce safety stocks held in case of transportation delays), its costs for scrap, warranty repair, and rework dropped by 60 percent. The reduction in cost and the improvement in quality allowed Harley Davidson's market share to grow from less than 4 percent to nearly 20 percent.

Sole sourcing is not, however, without considerable risks. By maintaining low inventory buffers and relying exclusively on a single supplier, a JIT company is vulnerable to expensive work stoppages and shortages if, perhaps through no fault of its own, the supplier cannot deliver as needed. Additionally, there is perhaps some loss of incentive for a supplier to continue to improve quality or costs once an exclusive contract has been granted.

Inventory management is perhaps the central element in just-in-time. In Japan, where space and materials are extremely scarce, a large inventory of any type, from raw materials to finished goods, is considered a waste of valuable resources. Traditional systems, however, view inventory as an essential component in continuing smooth operations, because inventories hide problems. If a particular task runs slower than the other tasks in a process, an expensive buffer inventory might be created to cushion its effect. Inventories also hide defective parts, which are usually not discovered until they are needed. By then, of course, it is too late, and production may have to stop. The situation may be further complicated by the use of multiple suppliers. By the time defective materials have been found, it may be too late to find out who supplied them, and a refund or termination of contract is impossible. Inventory problems can also extend to the creation of excessive finished goods inventories. For example, if a factory produces 20 percent defective goods, a traditional manager might order a 20 percent increase in production, which goes into inventory.

Just-in-time exposes all those problems. The Japanese compare inventory investments to the water in a lake with boulders, representing problems just beneath the surface. As the investment is reduced, the problems (such as defective materials or equipment) are exposed, and then solved. Inventory is reduced until all boulders have been exposed and eliminated, and inventory investment is practically nil.

JIT product engineering and design emphasizes standardization and steady improvements. The parts and materials that make up a JIT product are also standardized. Simplification is the watchword for JIT product design. Frequently, traditional product design is oriented toward meeting specialized customer requirements that change frequently, such as the different features available in an automobile from year to year. This orientation leads to a confused production process and equally confused product engineers who may have to start from scratch with each new requirement.

Plant design for non-JIT companies frequently incorporates excess capacity, such as extra equipment, partial shifts, overtime, and large *work-in-process inventories*, as a reserve for any unexpected problems. All of these result in higher costs due, for example, to the purchase and maintenance of extra equipment. Plant capacity in a JIT company, on the other hand, minimizes excess capacities (particularly work-in-process inventories) by emphasizing control and planning in order to avoid situations where extra capacity is needed.

The role of the labor force is one of the basic elements of JIT. Rather than isolating workers according to narrowly defined skills and tasks, JIT strives to develop flexible, broadly skilled workers who will seek out and solve problems as they occur. This goal is frequently accomplished by the establishment of cooperative work teams who are responsible for an entire set of tasks or products. Members of each work team must coordinate their activities in order to keep the operation flowing smoothly. This coordination is especially important since there is no inventory to cover mistakes. As a result, workers must develop a variety of skills, ranging from quality inspections to equipment maintenance. Decisions are frequently made by consensus on the production floor rather than by management edict. This type of conduct serves to enhance an attitude of cooperation.

Management plays a very different role in a JIT operation. The status symbols, such as an executive cafeteria, reserved parking places, and bonuses, that normally separate (and possibly alienate) management from workers in a traditional system are absent in a JIT company. This absence of separation encourages cooperation and reduces competition between management and workers.

The pace of a JIT system is very different from the pace of a traditional operation. Since workers can only produce when the next worker is ready, JIT workers tend to work at a constant pace. This is a marked contrast to more traditional systems in which workers produce in fits and starts as a result of time wasted looking for parts, setting up equipment, moving materials, getting instructions, and so on. In a traditional system, workers are frequently idle as they wait for the various delays. In a JIT system, an idle worker is an immediate signal to management that the process is not running smoothly and requires adjustment.

Traditional quality control involves conducting inspections at critical points in the production process to identify defective goods and correct problems. Usually, a sample of finished products is inspected before a shipment is sent to a customer. If too many defective items are found, the entire shipment is inspected item by item and the defective units are replaced. This is a time-consuming and expensive process. JIT sets perfect quality as its goal. The central element of JIT quality control is worker inspections. Each worker must check the product and its parts as they are passed on to the next worker. In this way, any defects can be spotted, and corrected, immediately.

In a JIT shop, when a piece of equipment breaks down, almost all *downstream* activity will shortly stop for lack of work, and almost all *upstream* activity will stop almost immediately because work cannot move forward. This risk of stoppages leads to a strong emphasis on preventive maintenance. Most preventive maintenance tasks are performed by equipment operators, which eliminates the need for a more traditional maintenance crew.

In a traditional company, operations planning and control are usually complicated tasks best done by computers. In many cases, however, attention is focused on planning (for inventories, material and parts shipments, maintenance schedules, and so on) rather than control. This approach leads to a series of "unexpected" problems such as equipment failures, defective materials, and products of poor quality.

The priorities are reversed in a JIT system. Control is the main focus. Rather than waste excessive time and energy planning for future events that are, at best, uncertain, a JIT company tries to respond to present conditions by developing flexible, fast operations. Of course, some planning is necessary, but it is devoted to making small improvements in operating and control systems to make a process even more flexible and responsive.

Although the advantages of JIT are very clear, many U.S. manufacturers have not adopted it. Essentially, the switch to JIT requires a large change in the overall culture of a company, rather than simply adopting a few different manufacturing procedures. It is not simply a matter of reducing inventories. Relations with suppliers, employees, and customers are all transformed. Established routines and procedures become obsolete. JIT cannot simply be established and forgotten. It requires constant improvement, in both a company's products and its processes.

kaizen   A Japanese term meaning continual improvement.

In manufacturing, kaizen refers to the elimination of all waste in labor, machinery, or production methods. Ideally, this process should involve everyone, from factory workers to upper management.

kanban   A materials management system that utilizes cards to authorize the withdrawal and production of materials.

The basic concept of a kanban system is to authorize materials for use only if there is a need for them. This *pulls* products through the production system rather than pushing them through before they are needed, which requires storage. In other words, final assembly is authorized, which triggers the authorization of subassembly production, which triggers the authorization of parts assembly, and so on. Kanban, which means *card* in Japanese, was originally developed by the Toyota Motor Company as part of its *just-in-time* manufacturing system.

Kanban relies on two types of cards: a withdrawal kanban and a production kanban. Each card usually shows only the part name and number, the work centers involved, the container capacity, and a storage location.

EXAMPLE: Assume that work flows from station A to station B in a small manufacturing company. Containers are used to carry the parts produced at station A to station B, where they are used as **inputs** in the final assembly of a product. When workers at station B see that they will be needing more parts, they take an empty container and a *withdrawal* kanban to station A, where they leave the empty container and locate a full one, which has a *production* kanban. They replace the production kanban with the withdrawal kanban, which authorizes the removal of the parts. They leave the production kanban at station A, which authorizes the production of another container of parts. The parts and the withdrawal kanban are then taken to station B.

Kanban is a very simple but effective system. Since it is entirely visual, it is very easy for management and workers to manage a smooth production flow, simple quality inspection, a minimal inventory, and clear production control.

keiretsu Corporate conglomerates whose members cooperate with each other for strategic purposes within the international business environment; a Japanese term.

There are three major types of *keiretsu* in Japan: (1) bank-centered *keiretsu*, (2) supply-centered *keiretsu*, and (3) distribution *keiretsu*.

1. Bank-centered *keiretsu* are massive industrial combines of 20 to 45 companies centered around a bank. This structure enables the companies that comprise the core of the *keiretsu* to share financial risk and to allocate investment in economically advantageous ways worldwide. There are seven major bank-centered *keiretsu* in Japan: Sumitomo, Mitsubishi, Mitsui, Dai Ichi, Kangyo, Fuyo, and Sanwa, comprising 182 companies in all.

2. Supply-centered *keiretsu* are groups of companies vertically integrated along a "supplier chain" dominated by a major manufacturer, a "channel captain." Supply-centered *keiretsu* characterize the automotive and electronics industries. They are well known for the pressure tactics used by channel captains to enforce time, cost, and delivery-schedule compliance by suppliers (and to extract price concessions from them) under strategies such as just-in-time (JIT) supply systems. Examples of important supply-centered *keiretsu* are the NEC group (electronics) and the Canon and Nikon group (semiconductor diffusion). Many of the companies in the supply-centered *keiretsu* are linked to the bank-centered *keiretsu:* the NEC group is owned 25 percent by Sumitomo *keiretsu* banks, and NEC is thus the Sumitomo group's principal electronics company; Canon is the $8-billion diversified electronics company in the Fuyo bank-centered *keiretsu*, whereas Nikon is in the Mitsubishi *keiretsu*. Canon and Nikon together hold more than 60 percent of the world market in the production of semiconductor capital equipment.

3. Distribution *keiretsu* are webs of relationships tying Japanese wholesalers and retailers to a particular manufacturer who acts as a "channel captain."

   The Japanese Fair Trade Commission (JFTC) issued guidelines on January 17, 1991, to enforce Japan's Antimonopoly Law against distribution *keiretsu* manufacturers who have engaged in systematic protectionist trading practices to restrict competition and exclude foreign companies from entering the Japanese market. Some of these protectionist trading practices are as follows:

   - Payment of rebates by manufacturers to retailers as rewards for not carrying products made by competitors
   - Payment of special rebates to wholesalers for handling the goods of a single manufacturer ("tied selling")
   - "Joint boycotts" in which rival manufacturers collude to keep out their competitors

- Cutbacks in manufacturers' shipments to punish retailers (or to punish wholesalers who, in turn, will punish retailers) who reduce prices below a level established by the manufacturers ("resale-price maintenance") (*Source:* L. Presner, *The International Business Dictionary and Reference,* Copyright © 1991 by L. Presner. Reprinted with permission of the publishers, John Wiley & Sons, Inc.)

Keogh Plan

A tax-deferred pension account designed for use by employees of unincorporated businesses or for those who are self-employed.

Under a Keogh plan (otherwise known as H.R.10), an individual may make annual contributions of the lesser of (a) 25 percent of earned income, or (b) $30,000. By IRS definition, earned income is the net income shown on Schedule C of a personal tax return (Form 1040).

Self-employed persons who use an S corporation to bill management service fees to a second wholly owned company (as many single-practitioner management consultants do) cannot use these fees as earned income. Only Schedule C income is considered earned by the IRS: income distributed from S corporations is reported on Schedule E. To use a Keogh plan, one must fit the category of a self-employed person, which means filing Schedule C.

Keynesian economics

A body of economic ideas, named after the economist John Maynard Keynes, that focuses on the core idea that government involvement in the economy is the most intelligent, reliable, and expedient way to moderate the effects of extreme fluctuations in the business cycle.

The modus used by government is called *fiscal policy*—government's authority to tax and its power to redistribute wealth by way of government expenditures.

Also termed liberal economics, demand-side economics, fiscal economics, fiscalism, or eponymously, Keynesianism. (*Source:* L. Presner, *The International Business Dictionary and Reference,* Copyright © 1991 L. Presner. Reprinted with permission of the publisher, John Wiley & Sons, Inc.)

labor force The measure of the number of persons who are either employed or unemployed.

This measure is compiled by the Bureau of Labor Statistics of the Department of Labor each month in its effort to determine the employment status of the working-age population.

The labor force is measured so that the ***unemployment rate*** can be estimated. The data are drawn from a sample of households that are statistically representative of the United States as a whole. Those who were employed in the previous four weeks are so classified. The unemployed consist of (a) those who lost a job or left employment in the past four weeks, and (b) others who actively sought employment in the past four weeks. The total of the employed and unemployed constitute the labor force, and the unemployment rate is equal to the percentage of the labor force that was unemployed. The table below presents totals, in thousands, for the labor force and its components and the unemployment rate for the 1989–1992 period.

	1989	1990	1991	1992
Population, 16 years and over	186,049	188,049	189,765	191,576
Labor force	123,869	124,787	125,303	126,982
Employment	117,342	117,914	116,877	117,598
Unemployment	6,528	6,874	8,426	9,384
Unemployment rate	5.3%	5.5%	6.7%	7.4%

last-in, first-out (LIFO) In accounting, a method of ***inventory valuation*** based on the concept that merchandise is sold in the reverse order of its receipt.

In other words, if an electronics store bought 100 stereos in January and 50 in February, LIFO will account for the sale of the February units before the sale of the January units.

In periods of inflation, LIFO results in *cost of goods sold* figures that are based on the most recent current costs, and inventory figures that are based on older, historic costs. This leads to *lower net income* than would have resulted from the *first-in, first-out (FIFO)* method because LIFO matches current costs against *revenue.* However, the inventory figure on the *balance sheet* will be *lower* under LIFO than FIFO because inventory is based on older costs.

For an in-depth discussion, *see first-in, first-out (FIFO), LIFO liquidation, LIFO reserve.*

layout   The physical grouping of centers of economic activity (that is, materials, workstations, machines, groups of people, and inventory storage areas) within a production facility.

latent market   A group of people who have a similar need or desire for a product that does not yet exist.

One example of a product with a large latent market is a painless dentist's drill. Identifying a latent market is often the first step in a successful marketing plan.

EXAMPLE: The Coca-Cola company realized a latent market existed for a low-calorie soft drink. The company quickly developed Tab and went on to capture and hold on to the majority of the new diet cola market.

leadership   The behavior and personality characteristics of people with responsibility, influence, and authority over groups.

There are two extremes of leadership behavior: authoritarian and democratic. Authoritarian leaders delegate very little authority and tend to make the bulk of the decisions affecting a group. Democratic leaders, on the other hand, delegate a great deal of authority and allow group members to make many of their own decisions. Between these two leadership extremes lies a number of different leadership styles.

Although it is widely acknowledged that effective leadership behavior is frequently the result of a particular business situation (for example, if a project must be completed within a very limited time frame, an authoritarian leadership style might be effective, whereas in a situation with little time pressure that requires extensive coordination between different individuals and departments, a more democratic style might be appropriate) there is a common misperception that democratic leaders are superior to authoritarian leaders. Most research does not support this. For example, in one study, teams of three people were presented with a series of problem-solving tasks. The teams with authoritarian leaders were instructed to simply follow orders. The teams with democratic leaders were encouraged to offer suggestions and question their orders. There was no difference in **productivity** between the groups.

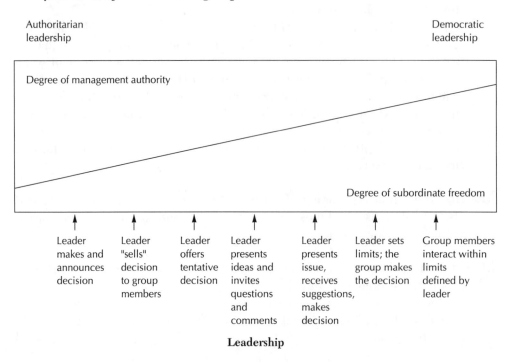

Leadership

leading, coincident, and lagging indexes (LCLg) National indicators that constitute an analytic system for assessing current and future economic trends, particularly cyclical expansions and recessions.

These indexes are grouped as leading, coincident, and lagging, according to their tendency to change direction before, during, or after the general economy turns the corner—either from recession to expansion, or from expansion to recession. The leading indexes reflect business commitments and expectations, the coincident indexes indicate the current stage of the economy, and the lagging indexes identify business cost trends.

The Bureau of Economic Analysis in the U.S. Department of Commerce releases monthly synopses of each set of indexes in press releases and in the Bureau's monthly magazines, *Business Conditions Digest* and *Survey of Current Business.*

The concept of economic indexes is that profits are the prime mover of an economy based on private enterprise and that recurring business cycles are caused by changes in the outlook for future profits. Such outlook is reflected in the leading indexes and in the ratio of the coincident index to the lagging index (which is itself a leading index).

The components of each index are as follows:

Leading Index

- Average weekly hours of manufacturing production workers (average weekly hours)

- Average weekly initial claims for unemployment compensation
- Manufacturers' new orders for consumer goods and materials industries in 1982 dollars (Manufacturers' Orders)
- Vendor performance (percent of companies receiving slower deliveries)
- Contracts and orders for plant and equipment in 1982 dollars
- New private housing building permits (Housing Starts)
- Manufacturers' unfilled orders for durable goods industries in 1982 dollars (Manufacturers' Orders for Durable Goods)
- Prices of crude and intermediate materials, monthly change (Produce Price Index)
- Stock prices of 500 common stocks (Stock Market Price Indexes and Dividends Yields)
- Money supply (M-2) in 1982 dollars (Money Supply)
- Index of consumer expectations (Consumer Confidence Index and Consumer Statement Index)

Coincident Index

- Employees on nonagricultural payrolls (Employment)
- Personal income less transfer payments in constant dollars (Personal Income)
- Industrial production index
- Manufacturing and trade sales in constant dollars

Lagging Index

- Average duration of unemployment (Unemployment)
- Inventory-to-sales ratio for manufacturing and trade in constant dollars (Inventory-Sales Ratio)
- Labor cost per unit of output in manufacturing, monthly change (Unit Labor Costs)
- Commercial installment credit outstanding to personal income ratio
- Average prime rate charged banks (Interest Rates)
- Consumer price index for services, monthly change (Consumer Price Index)

From these indexes compiled since World War II, the leading index declines for 9 months and the coincident/lagging ratio declines for 13 months before the onset of a recession. Also, the leading index predicts an expansion in the economy 4 months before it begins and the coincident/lagging index 2 months prior.

These indexes are only a rough guide to the direction of the economy; however, they can be useful in preparing pro forma forecasts and developing strategic plans.

lead time   The time from order placement to order receipt.

Components of lead time include order preparation time, supplier notification, supplier preparation time, shipping time, and receiving and inspecting time. Lead time is an important consideration in materials planning and process scheduling.

learning   Any permanent change in a person's behavior that takes place as a result of experience.

There are three broad theories that explain the process of learning: classical conditioning, operant conditioning, and social learning.

The theory of classical conditioning is based on the experiments conducted by Ivan Pavlov in which he measured the amount of saliva produced by a dog. When the dog saw a piece of meat, it increased saliva production in anticipation of a meal. When Pavlov simply rang a bell near the dog, its salivation did not increase. Over time, Pavlov linked the ringing of the bell with the presentation of meat. After repeatedly hearing the bell and getting a piece of meat, the dog was conditioned to salivate at the sound of the bell, even when no meat was offered. The dog had learned that the bell meant food.

In an organizational setting, classical conditioning can be easily observed. For example, in a manufacturing plant, when top managers from corporate headquarters were scheduled to make an inspection, the plant managers would clean their offices and wash their windows. Over time, the employees in the plant associated newly cleaned windows with an inspection and they learned to put on their best behavior whenever the windows were clean—even if there was no inspection.

Operant conditioning states that learning is based on the consequences of a person's behavior. In other words, people learn certain behaviors in order to get something they want or avoid something they don't want. This theory was best advanced by Harvard psychologist B. F. Skinner. Skinner argued that the creation of positive (or negative) reinforcements will encourage learning. For example, in the manufacturing plant, managers might want to encourage the production staff to work at a faster pace. The positive reinforcement that might bring this about could be a monthly bonus based on *productivity.*

The social learning theory builds on the basic premise of operant conditioning and argues that people learn by both experience and observation. For example, in the manufacturing plant, a new supervisor might pay close attention to the actions of the other supervisors and emulate them.

learning curve   The predictable improvements (in cost, labor hours, or machine hours) in a production process that are due to increased knowledge and experience; also called an experience curve.

Learning curves were first observed in the assembly of air frames in the 1930s where it was found that the labor hours required to assemble each plane declined as production increased. Specifically, each time output doubled, the amount of direct labor hours needed declined by a steady percentage. In other words, the fourth plane required only 80 percent as much labor time as the second, the eighth only 80 percent as much as the fourth, and the fiftieth only 80 percent as much as the twenty-fifth.

As World War II began and aircraft production increased, managers were able to incorporate the effects of the learning curve into their production plans. This allowed them to plan to manufacture more airplanes than would have been possible had production estimates been based on more conventional assumptions of level performance and constant costs.

Since the learning curve is based on increases in worker knowledge and skill, it stands to reason that operations paced by workers are more affected by the learning curve than operations paced by machines. For example, in aircraft manufacture, about 75 percent of the labor time is assembly, the rest involves workers doing machine work. In this highly worker-paced operation, an 80 percent learning rate is fairly common. When the proportion of assembly work to machine work is about 50/50, the learning rate is closer to 85 percent. If the ratio is one-fourth assembly and three-fourths machine work, the learning rate is about 90 percent. In other words, in a worker-paced operation, the direct labor on the fourth unit will take 80 percent as long as the second. In an operation where there is a balance between worker-paced and machine-paced procedures, the direct labor on the fourth unit will take 85 percent as long as the second. In a largely machine-paced operation, the direct labor on the fourth unit will take 90 percent as long as the second.

leasehold improvement
Any refurbishment made to a leased property, such as painting the interior of a rented office building.

Leasehold improvements are generally accounted for as *intangible assets* (although some companies list them under property, plant, and equipment) on the *balance sheet* and must be *amortized* over the life of the improvement or the term of the lease, whichever is shorter.

letter of credit (L/C)
A popular bank instrument stating that a bank has granted the holder an amount of credit equal to the face amount of the L/C.

In other words, a bank guarantees payment of its customer's draft up to a stated amount for a given period of time. This, in effect, transfers collection risk from the seller to the bank. In international trade, L/Cs are used extensively to guarantee payment and are called "documentary letters of credit." The holder of the L/C presents it along with other authenticating documentation to the drawer's bank and demands payment of the face amount.

Domestically, a letter of credit may serve as a guarantee that the payee will perform an act or make a payment. Used in this manner, it is called a "standby L/C." The term "standby" means that the holder cannot draw against the L/C unless the payee fails to perform or pay as agreed upon by contract. Standby L/Cs are used by the construction industry in place of surety bonds. Standby L/Cs are also frequently used as backup guarantees to a revenue bond issue or to secure loans from a large money center bank.

Letters of credit come in a variety of forms and carry a wide range of provisions. They can be revocable or irrevocable, confirmed or advised, straight or negotiated, payable at sight or over an extended period of time. A letter of credit may be transferable, assignable, or restricted.

level production
An *aggregate planning* strategy that maintains a uniform output and allows inventories to absorb increases in demand.

For example, a furniture manufacturer may maintain a stock of its most popular items in order to ensure a steady supply of its products. A level production aggregate plan increases inventory costs but offers steady employment with few overtime expenses. In a service company, where there is usually no way to stockpile inventories, a level production plan requires a constant, but poorly utilized, work force in order to meet peak demand. *See also* **aggregate plan.**

leverage
In accounting and finance, the amount of long-term debt that a company has in relation to its equity.

The higher the ratio, the greater is the leverage. Leverage is generally measured by a variation of the **debt-to-equity ratio,** which is calculated as follows:

$$\frac{\text{Long-term liabilities}}{\text{Total stockholders' equity}}$$

A company's optimal leverage depends on the stability of its earnings. A company with consistently high earnings can be more leveraged than a company with variable earnings, because it will consistently be more likely to make the required interest and principal payments.

leveraged buyout (LBO)
The purchase of controlling interest in a company using debt collateralized by the target company's assets to fund most or all of the purchase price.

This debt is subsequently repaid out of the cash flow of the acquired company. During the 1980s, LBOs were the financing mode of choice by buyers and lenders alike.

From the buyer's perspective, all or controlling interest in a company's shares could be made with very little down payment. If the value of the company's assets was equal to or greater than the purchase price, an LBO could be made with zero equity contributions. From the lender's perspective, the highly expansionist economy of the times created rapidly appreciating assets that provided more than adequate loan security. LBOs were also a very popular device used by controlling shareholders of public companies to borrow funds against the company's assets in order to buy up large blocks of its stock, thereby taking the company private.

By the 1990s, the frenetic LBO fever of the 1980s had subsided. LBOs are still a popular way to finance business acquisitions, but today lenders demand a much greater equity contribution relative to borrowed funds.

leveraging The advantage gained by using debt financing to create asset appreciation.

The theory behind leveraging is that the earnings from a company or the appreciation of an asset acquired with a very high amount of debt financing and very low amounts of equity contributions can be used to repay the debt obligation and interest. In this way, small equity interests can be "leveraging up," thereby causing an increase in the value of original investments.

Buying a house or condo with a small down payment and a high mortgage is a good example of leveraging. As the mortgage gets paid down, and the value of the dwelling appreciates, equity interests multiply geometrically.

liability An obligation payable in money, services, or goods.

Liabilities are reported on the *balance sheet* and include *accounts payable,* accrued expenses, and debt. Liabilities are classified into current (due within one year) and noncurrent (due in more than one year).

LIFO *See last-in, first-out*

LIFO liquidation A method of accounting for the sale of years-old inventory valued under LIFO.

Because this inventory is based on historic costs that can be significantly less than current inventory costs, the sale of these inventory "layers" can greatly reduce cost of goods sold and increase net income. Assume that a company made the following purchases and sales:

Year	Beginning inventory	Purchases	Sales	Cost of goods sold	Ending inventory
19X0	$ 0	100 @ $10 = $1,000	50	$ 500	50 @ $10
19X1	500	100 @ $11 = $1,100	50	550	50 @ $11
19X2	1,100	100 @ $12 = $1,200	50	600	50 @ $12
19X3	1,700	100 @ $15 = $1,500	50	750	50 @ $15
19X4	2,450	100 @ $18 = $1,800	50	900	50 @ $18
19X5	3,350	25 @ $20	200	2,725	

In 19X5, when sales suddenly increased, the company had to sell 175 units of its older inventory. Under LIFO, this inventory is valued at its historic cost, so the *cost of goods sold* is calculated as follows:

$$
\begin{aligned}
\text{Cost of goods sold} &= 25 \text{ units @ } \$20 + 50 \text{ units @ } \$18 + 50 \text{ units @ } \$15 \\
&\quad + 50 \text{ units @ } \$12 + 25 \text{ units @ } \$11 \\
&= \$200 + \$900 + \$750 + \$600 + \$275 \\
&= \$2,725
\end{aligned}
$$

By contrast, if 19X5 purchases has equaled or exceeded sales, cost of goods sold would have been

$$200 \text{ units @ } \$20 = \$4,000$$

LIFO reserve In accounting, the difference between the reported LIFO cost of inventory and its current cost, as approximated by FIFO.

Generally, companies that use LIFO will report a LIFO reserve in order to facilitate the adjustment of the inventory stated on the *balance sheet* to more current costs. *See also first-in, first-out (FIFO), last-in, first-out (LIFO), LIFO liquidation.*

limited partnership

A business structure that combines certain features of both corporations (e.g., limited liability) and standard partnerships (e.g., profit and loss pass-through).

A limited partnership consists of one or more general partners, normally the business owner(s), and one or more limited partners, usually investors. General partners manage the business of the partnership and are liable for its obligations in the same manner as in a standard partnership. Limited partners have no liability for the activities of the business, much the same as preferred shareholders in a corporation. The term "limited" designates limited legal liability in the same way that the corporate shield protects shareholders from liabilities of a corporation.

For many years, limited partnerships have been a popular medium for financing business acquisitions. Typically, the acquiring company is set up as a general partner with individual investors, and perhaps a venture capital firm, as limited partners. Limited partnerships are also used extensively to raise capital for start-up businesses, especially those involved in real estate development, oil and gas exploration, and other activities with long-term capital gain potential.

Recently, privately held companies have used limited partnerships as vehicles to raise significant amounts of equity capital for new businesses in such diverse industries as hotels, car dealerships, equipment and vehicle rental companies, resort complexes, movie theaters, booksellers, specialty farms, beer distributors, boat chartering companies, travel agencies, and technical schools.

Limited partnerships are also used in multiple corporate hierarchies for structuring offshore tax shelters and for shielding corporate real estate investments. And small business owner/managers find a limited partnership an excellent vehicle to use in various estate-planning techniques.

The income tax shelter advantages of limited partnerships were effectively eliminated in 1986. Since then, "at risk" rules and "passive activity loss" (PAL) provisions severely restrict the ability of limited partners to deduct start-up losses on their personal returns. Nevertheless, enough tax benefits still remain to encourage limited partnership investments in potentially high growth business start-ups.

line balancing A method of assigning tasks to particular workstations in order to minimize both the number of workstations and the total amount of *idle time* within the system at a given level of production.

EXAMPLE: Say a bank is processing credit applications. It is required to process 600 applications per day. The job can be divided into the following seven tasks:

		Time	Preceding task
1	Open applications	0.25	none
2	Read enclosed letter, noting of any special requirements	0.45	1
3	Process page 1 of application	0.32	1
4	Process page 2 of application	0.30	1
5	Determine credit limit from standardized tables	0.50	3,4
6	Supervisor checks credit limit, notes applicant's address, and type of form letter to be sent	0.75	2,5
7	Assistant prepares and mails form letter	0.35	6
	Total	2.92	

Line balancing determines the minimum number of workstations needed for 100 percent efficiency and assigns them equal *cycle times.* Cycle time is calculated with the average daily output rate (in this case, 600 applications). This assumes that the number of applications processed is equal to the number of applications received. If more than 600 applications come in per day, a backlog will be created. If less than 600 come in, there will be unnecessary idle time. Cycle time is then calculated by dividing the available work time (8 hours) by daily demand.

$$\frac{\text{Available work time}}{\text{Daily demand}} = \text{Cycle time}$$

In the example, cycle time is

$$\frac{(8 \text{ hours} \times 60 \text{ minutes/hour})}{600 \text{ applications}} = 0.8 \text{ minutes per application}$$

In other words, in order to process 600 applications per day, an application must be completed every 0.8 minutes.

The minimum number of workstations required is calculated by dividing the total task time by the cycle time determined above.

$$\frac{\text{Total task time}}{\text{Cycle time}} = \text{Number of workstations}$$

In the example, at least four workstations are needed:

$$\frac{2.92}{0.8} = 3.65$$

Although the actual number of workstations required is 3.65, it is impossible to set up 0.65 of a workstation, so the number is *always* rounded up. It may be, however, that because of the order in which tasks must be performed, the work cannot be divided into exactly four workstations, and five, or even six, may be needed. If this is the case, each additional workstation will diminish the efficiency of the process. Consider the bank example:

With four workstations:

$$\frac{2.92}{4 \times 0.8} = 0.912, \text{ or } 91.2\% \text{ efficiency}$$

With five workstations:

$$\frac{2.92}{5 \times 0.8} = 0.73, \text{ or } 73\% \text{ efficiency}$$

Assuming that the bank decides to use five workstations, the line can be balanced by using the LOT rule, which requires the generation of a list of all tasks whose predecessors have been completed. Each task is then considered individually, and the task with the *longest operation time* is placed in a workstation. Any other tasks that can be added to the station without exceeding the station's cycle time should be included in that workstation. The procedure for the credit application process is as follows:

Station	Tasks	Tasks available	Time assigned (min)	Idle time
1	1,2,3,4	1,2	0.70	0.10
2	3,4	3,4	0.62	0.18
3	5	5	0.50	0.30
4	6	6	0.75	0.05
5	7	7	0.35	0.45

The first tasks to assign are those that have no preceding task. Thus task 1, with a time of 0.25 minutes, is assigned to workstation 1. Tasks 2 (0.45 minutes), 3 (0.32 minutes), and 4 (0.30 minutes) are then available. According to the LOT rule, task 2 should be the first considered. Since it can be included in station 1 without exceeding the 0.80-minute cycle time, it is assigned to that station. At this point it is impossible to add any more tasks without exceeding the cycle time, so the "extra" 0.10 minutes is noted as *idle time*. Tasks 3 and 4 are the next available tasks that can be assigned to station 2. Their total time is 0.62 minutes, with an idle time of 0.18 minutes. Task 5 cannot be included in this station because its time of 0.50 minutes would exceed the cycle time of the station. Because of this, and the fact that it cannot be combined with any subsequent tasks, task 5 is the only task in workstation 3. Similarly, workstation 4 contains task 6 and workstation 5 contains task 7.

In other words, workstation 1 is responsible for opening applications, reading the enclosed letter, and making note of any special requirements. Workstation 2 is responsible for processing pages 1 and 2 of the application. Workstation 3 is responsible for determining the applicant's credit limit. Workstation 4 is responsible for checking the credit limit, noting the applicant's address, and determining the type of form letter that will be sent. Finally, workstation 5 prepares and mails the letter.

liquidity In accounting, the ability of *current assets* to meet the financial obligations of *current liabilities.*

A liquid company is less likely to default on debt and is more able to take advantage of investment opportunities than an illiquid company. *See also acid test ratio, current ratio.*

list broker An agent who arranges the sale or rental of a mailing list.

Direct-mail advertisers and market researchers use these lists in order to reach a particular target market.

EXAMPLE: A manufacturer of sporting goods equipment wants to send a catalog of its products to sports enthusiasts across the country. The list broker researches and recommends various mailing lists—subscribers to *Sports Illustrated* and *Golf Digest,* say—to which the company could direct its catalogs.

load The amount of work scheduled for a specific work center within a given time period.

A work center's load is usually expressed as standard hours of work.

load profile In manufacturing, a summary of future *capacity* requirements based on work orders (either planned or released) for a given time period.

loading The assignment of jobs to particular work centers.

Although capacity planning will determine that there is enough *capacity* to meet the master production schedule, it does not usually make any specific work center assignments. For example, some equipment might be better suited for certain jobs, or a particular team of workers might be less heavily loaded than other workers. Thus, there is usually a most efficient (or less costly) assignment of jobs.

logo *See brand mark*

London Interbank Offered Rate (LIBOR) The base lending rate that banks charge each other in the London Eurocurrency market.

LIBOR is the European equivalent of the U.S. prime rate, although it is not calculated the same way. LIBOR is an actual market rate determined by the supply and demand of Eurodollars in London's capital markets and charged by one bank to another bank. The U.S. prime rate is a fictitious rate set by money center banks based on the cost of doing business plus a profit.

With increasing frequency, the globalization of the financial system forces U.S. lenders to quote interest rates based on LIBOR rather than prime. Generally, LIBOR runs slightly less than prime. Borrowers approve of LIBOR because it represents an actual market rate, not a fictitious estimate.

long bond Thirty-year U.S. Treasury bonds or other bonds that mature beyond 10 years.

Long-bond interest rates and yields run higher than those for short-term securities because investors perceive the risk of tying up money for long time periods to be greater than for short periods. Long bond rates are frequently used as a risk-free benchmark for business valuations. They also serve as a barometer of the health of the U.S. economy, with declining long bond rates signaling a rising economic base. Rates for long-term mortgages are also tied to the rates of long bonds, which offer an alternative investment opportunity for long-term lenders.

longitudinal panel A group of participants in a market research study who are questioned at various points over a period of time.

EXAMPLE: The National Purchase Diary Panel consists of a consumer panel of 13,000 families who record their purchases of each of a number of products each month.

See also **omnibus panel**.

long-term asset In accounting, an *asset* with future economic benefits that are expected for a number of years.

Long-term assets are reported on the *balance sheet* as *noncurrent assets* and include equipment and buildings. *See also* **asset, noncurrent asset**.

long-term liability In accounting, an obligation that is due in a period of more than one year.

Long-term liabilities are reported on the *balance sheet* as *noncurrent liabilities* and include mortgages and long-term debt. *See also* **liability**.

loss leader A *retailing* strategy of putting low prices on selected items in order to attract customers or reduce inventory; also called a traffic builder.

Although this strategy does attract customers, it is not popular with manufacturers who feel that the heavy discounting of their products dilutes the image of their brands. *See also* **retailer**.

lot tolerance percentage defective (LTPD)

The actual percentage, specified by management, of defective goods in a lot of incoming materials that a company is willing to accept. *See also* **acceptable quality level, type II error.**

lower of cost or market

A rule applied to the valuation of inventories and investments.

Conservatism dictates that these accounts be stated at the lower of cost or market. Doing so could result in an unrealized loss in the financial statements.

EXAMPLE: A company has inventory with a historical cost of $1,000 and a *replacement cost* of $900. That means it must report inventories at $900 and declare an unrealized loss. When the reverse is the case (that is, inventory has a historic cost of $900 and a replacement cost of $1,000) inventory is reported at $900 and there is no recognition of any gain. The lower of cost or market rule applies to all financial reporting, regardless of the method of *inventory valuation.*

M

Magnuson-Moss Warranty / Federal Trade Commission Improvement Act An act passed in 1975 that gives the Federal Trade Commission (FTC) the power to set rules for consumer product warranties. The act also provides for consumer redress, including class action suits.

makegood A credit that a publisher or broadcaster gives to an advertiser to make up for an error or cancellation of an advertisement.

The credit generally takes the form of a rerun of the ad or commercial. Makegoods must be negotiated between the advertiser and the medium.

In print advertising, the publisher must agree on the error in the advertisement. Print makegoods are usually given when the publisher has made some mistake in printing the copy (such as misprinting an address) or the advertisement has been placed in a position in the publication other than the one specified by the advertiser.

In broadcasting, makegoods are given when the television or radio station did not deliver the audience size or composition it promised for a particular commercial or when the commercial did not run as scheduled.

make-to-order The production of goods or services made to customer-provided specifications, prints, or designs.

Make-to-order items are usually produced in small volumes with a great deal of variety between products. An advertising agency, for example, produces advertisements on a make-to-order basis for each client. *Compare to make-to-stock. See also job process system.*

make-to-stock Goods produced to the maker's specifications in anticipation of future demand, which are then stored for future sale.

Usually, make-to-stock items are produced in large batches with little variety between individual products. Once made, products are inventoried to satisfy future demand. *Compare to make-to-order.*

management by objectives (MBO) A management program that emphasizes specific, participatively set goals; a clear time period to achieve them; and performance feedback.

The goals in MBO are not simply set by managers and assigned to subordinates. Rather, they are set by a participative process that includes all affected parties, from upper management to supervisors to shop floor workers. This ensures that all concerns are heard and incorporated into the formulation of realistic objectives.

Each objective should be stated as explicitly as possible. For example, it is not enough to simply plan to improve quality or cut costs. These plans must be expressed as tangible goals that can be easily measured—to reduce returns to less than 2 percent of sales or to cut costs by 5 percent.

Each goal must have a clear time period in which it is to be accomplished— say three months, six months, or a year. This, combined with the specific nature of the goals, allows managers and employees to plan their actions realistically.

The final component of MBO is performance feedback. This feedback should occur at every level. For example, the vice-president of sales will monitor the sales of each different product. Each district manager will also monitor the sales representatives under his or her charge. On the individual level, each sales representative will monitor his or her progress toward the goal.

management control systems   The combination of penalties and rewards that shape and enforce management behavior.

Controls are required in all companies. This is due to the very nature of organizations that divide activities and responsibilities among their members. The goals and strategies of a company will be altered slightly by the needs of various individuals. For this reason, it is important to strive for consistency between corporate strategies and management control systems. For example, if a company has set a goal of increasing its output, it might establish a set of monthly production requirements for its factories. In this situation, a factory foreman might choose to put off preventative maintenance in favor of meeting the current month's production requirement. This may increase current output, but it may do so at the expense of an equipment failure at some point in the near future. It is clear that this system lacks congruence between company strategy and its management control system. Perhaps a better approach might have been to abandon short-term production requirements and focus management attention (and the management control system) on more long-term production goals.

Management control systems are almost always based on some form of financial measurement. A specific financial objective, such as increasing sales or profit, can clarify the issues and decisions faced by managers, even if it does not have the desired effect. There are four broad types of financial responsibility, each with its own set of objectives.

1. *Cost centers* are areas within a company whose *direct costs* can be measured and to which a portion of the company's overall fixed costs can be allocated. The best example of a cost center is a factory production department. In such a department, the standard costs of direct materials and labor are specified, and it is the manager's objective to minimize the differences between these standard costs and actual

costs. The manager is also responsible for a specified portion of the company's fixed costs. Again, the objective is to minimize the difference between standard costs and actual costs.

2. **Profit centers** are areas within a company that are treated as separate businesses for the purposes of management and financial control. Profit center managers are responsible for creating the best possible combination of costs and revenue, with the objective of maximizing profits. Profits can be measured in a number of different ways for the management controls of different **profit centers** and managers.

EXAMPLE: The sales manager of a product line division might be responsible for *gross profit*, whereas profit for a marketing manager in the same division might include deductions for promotions expenses and factory overhead.

3. *Revenue centers* are areas within a company that have no control over prices or costs. Sales departments are generally considered revenue centers. The financial objectives for the managers of revenue centers usually involve increasing revenue.

EXAMPLE: A sales department manager's objective is to maximize sales revenue within the constraints of his or her expense budget.

4. *Investment centers* are areas within a company where the manager is responsible for the purchase of the various assets used by the company. Investment center managers balance the need for current profits with the need to make investments that increase future profits. Their objective is generally to maximize the department's return on investment.

In establishing management control systems, two factors must be considered: fairness and goal congruence.

Fairness refers to each manager's belief that his or her financial objectives are an appropriate measure of performance. In other words, managers must believe that the management control system includes all factors that he or she can control and excludes all factors over which he or she has no control.

Goal congruence is the arrangement of the various management control systems within a company in such a way that they combine to serve the overall goals and strategies of the company. In other words, managers must not be working at cross purposes. In a management control system designed from this corporate perspective, financial objectives and measurements work to encourage management decisions that are good not only for the manager and his or her department, but for the company as well.

management information system (MIS) A centralized, usually computerized, system designed to supply managers with the necessary information to make decisions.

Traditionally, the focus of MIS was to provide managers with accurate internal information, such as sales and inventory figures. These systems were designed to speed up business processes in order to contain costs and improve administrative efficiency. In recent years, however, MIS has become externally focused, shifting the flow of information to customers, distributors, and suppliers.

EXAMPLE: The MIS system for Mrs. Fields' Cookies includes computer terminals in each of its stores. Each morning, store managers enter a sales projection based on the past year's performance and answer a series of questions posed by the computer, such as "What day of the week is it?", "Is it a: normal day, sale day, holiday, school day, or other?", and so on. Say it is a Wednesday and a school day. The computer then analyzes the store's hour-by-hour, product-by-product performance on the previous three school-day Wednesdays. Based on the information from these three Wednesdays, the MIS system creates a plan for the day that includes how many customers need to be served each hour, when to mix and bake batches of cookies, and which types of cookies to make. As the day progresses, the MIS system, through computerized cash registers, keeps track of hourly sales, revises sales projections, and makes suggestions. For example, if the number of customers is satisfactory, but the average check is too small, the system might suggest more aggressive selling or perhaps setting out a sample tray of cookies to encourage higher sales.

When used effectively, as with Mrs. Fields' Cookies, MIS can be an effective source of *competitive advantage* as well as a method to improve communication and coordination between the various departments and individuals.

management's discussion and analysis of operations A section in an *annual report,* required by the *Securities and Exchange Commission,* that summarizes the reasons for changes in operations, *liquidity, capital* resources, and *working capital* of a company.

The section is designed to help readers of *financial statements* understand the effects of changes in business activity and accounting.

manufacturing requirements planning (MRPII) A manufacturing philosophy that relies on the integration, via computer, of many of the functional areas, such as engineering, purchasing, sales, business planning, *material requirements planning,* production scheduling, *capacity* requirements planning, and accounting, within a company's operations.

There are a number of different MRPII software packages available, each of which operates in the same basic manner. Sales forecasts and basic design engineering information for each product are combined to develop a schedule for that product's materials requirements. Once this information is generated, the system goes on to develop purchase order requirements; route the product through operations; and schedule production.

marginal cost The increase or decrease in the total costs of a company that results from the output of one unit more or one unit less; also called "incremental cost."

In manufacturing firms, marginal cost typically decreases as the volume of output increases. This is a result of fixed costs being spread over a greater number of output units, thereby reducing the amount attributable to each unit. Conversely, fixed costs spread over a lesser number of output units result in a higher cost per unit. The analysis of marginal costs can be a handy tool for deciding whether to increase or decrease production.

Mathematically, economies of scale relating to labor efficiency and utilization, material purchase discounts, material scarcity, and plant utilization enable marginal cost to be graphed as a U-shape curve, with cost forming the x-axis and unit quantity the y-axis. The optimum point of the graph— namely, the lowest point—is achieved when marginal cost exactly equals average total cost.

A unit sale at a price higher than marginal unit cost will increase total company profit even though the unit sale price does not cover the total cost of producing the unit, making marginal cost the lowest possible unit sell price without detracting from total company profitability. The same analysis can be made comparing marginal cost per unit with marginal revenue per unit: To the extent marginal revenue exceeds marginal cost, the sale of additional output will result in higher profits.

marginal revenue The additional revenue a company receives resulting from the sale of one more item of *output*.

Marginal revenue is calculated by taking the difference between the total revenue both before and after the production of the extra unit. As long as the price of a product or service remains constant, marginal revenue equals price.

EXAMPLE: Say a radio manufacturer who sells car radios for $250 each would receive $250 in marginal revenue from a one-unit increase in sales. In many cases, however, additional output can only be sold at a lower price. In order to determine whether this is an advisable course of action, it is important to consider *marginal costs*. If marginal costs are greater than marginal revenue, additional units should not be produced. When marginal revenue is greater than marginal costs, the additional units should be produced.

See contribution margin.

marginal revenue = marginal cost rule In economics, a rule stating that a firm should produce up to the point where the cost of an additional unit of output (its marginal cost) is just equal to the revenue that is earned by selling the additional unit (its marginal revenue).

Furthermore, if the firm is not simply a price taker and in fact has the power to set the price of its product, it should establish the price at the level where people will demand this optimal level of output.

Following this rule enables a firm to maximize its profit or to minimize its loss. However, if the market price falls below a firm's average variable cost, then this rule will not be of help to the firm. In this situation, the best thing that a firm can do is to shut down. (*See shut-down situation.*)

market All customers who have a specific unsatisfied need or want and are *willing* and *able* to purchase a product or service to satisfy that need.

EXAMPLE: The market for automobiles consists of anyone older than the legal driving age with a need for transportation, access to roads, and enough money to purchase or make payments on a car.

To determine who might be the most likely customer, marketers look at consumer interest and income. An automobile manufacturer can look at the market with these two characteristics in mind, learn who is interested in buying a car and who can afford one, then direct its marketing effort toward those people. *See also* **available market, penetrated market, potential market, served market.**

market aggregation *See mass marketing*

market life-cycle The process by which a *market* comes into being, flourishes, and eventually disappears.

Markets have a life-cycle made up of four stages: emergence, growth, maturity, and decline. A market *emerges* as a consumer need is realized and met. For example, the need to make multiple copies of documents was imperfectly satisfied by carbon paper and mimeograph machines. Suppose an entrepreneur realized this need and envisioned a technology that could make photo-quality reproductions. With the production of the first Xerox copier, a new market emerged.

The *growth* stage of a market is marked by increasing sales and competition. Competitors will attempt to discover and fill various niches and segments of the market. In the copier market's growth stage, competitors offered portable and color copiers to satisfy different market segments. When each segment of the market has been served and the competitors begin to eat into each other's sales, the market has reached the *maturity* stage. The *decline* stage occurs when market demand for current products has waned or a new technology begins replacing the old. Eventually, the old technology will fall by the wayside and a new market will emerge.

Each stage in a market's life-cycle lends itself to a different set of marketing challenges and strategies. In the emergence stage, when there is little or no competition, a company has three options. First, it can design a product that will appeal to a small segment of the market. This strategy works well for small companies that want to avoid conflicts with larger competitors as they enter the market. The second strategy is to launch two or more products simultaneously to capture several segments of the market.

This strategy is appropriate when consumer preferences are all very different. (*See diffusion of innovation curve.*) The third strategy is to target the mass market by designing a product with the widest possible appeal. This approach works best for big companies with the resources and distribution capabilities to serve a large market.

As companies move into the market during the growth stage, they have three possible strategies as well: (1) pursue a niche strategy (*see niche marketing*) in a small segment of the market, (2) compete directly with the market pioneer, or (3) attempt to serve multiple niches in small segments of the market.

When a market enters maturity, the competitors' marketing strategies focus on finding new product innovations or price reductions in order to gain *market share.* In the decline stage, competitors must decide whether to move on to another market or continue to work for market share as other companies move on. *See also product life cycle, product maturity.*

market risk   The broad factors, such as the state of the economy or inflation, that affect all stocks; also called systematic risk.

Market risk, as opposed to nonsystematic risk, or *nonmarket risk,* which deals with the risks facing individual companies, is based on the fact that there are conditions that affect all companies. This is why stocks tend to move as a group in a particular direction. A stock's sensitivity to the factors that constitute market risk is measured by its *beta.* A stock with a beta of 2.0 is twice as sensitive to the fluctuations of the market as a stock with a beta of 1.0. For example, say stock X has a beta of 2.0 and stock Y has a beta of 1.0. If the market drops 10 percent, stock X will drop 20 percent and stock Y will drop 10 percent. *See also alpha, beta, capital asset pricing model (CAPM), nonmarket risk.*

market risk premium   The required rate of return that investors demand for a security with a given level of *market risk.*

In its broadest terms, market risk premium is the difference between the average return of the market and the going interest rate. The average market risk premium for the past 60 years has been 8.4 percent per year. The market risk premium of an individual security is calculated with the capital asset pricing model (CAPM).

market saturation   *See product maturity*

market segmentation   The breaking down of a large heterogeneous *market* into small, more homogeneous segments.

Marketers can then develop separate marketing programs, usually for different products, to meet each segment's specific needs—in other words, they can provide a *marketing mix* that suits a relatively homogeneous part of the market.

Market segmentation has both advantages and disadvantages. On the plus side, segmenting the market allows marketers to allocate promotional expenses to the most profitable segments within the total market and vary ad campaigns for each. Consumers don't have to make compromises when they purchase a product, because segmentation produces a better match between what a marketer offers and what the consumer wants.

Market segmentation also has its drawbacks: As the marketer investigates more and more market segments, research costs mount. So do production costs, because production runs are shorter and economies of scale are lost. Also, the marketer may have to sacrifice sales in one segment as it concentrates on serving another. (*See* **cannibalization.**) Coca-Cola's addition of Cherry Coke to its product offerings, for example, may have cut into its sales of Mr. Pibb.

Markets can be broken down in numerous ways, as marketers try to find distinctive groups of consumers within the total market. For some products—rubber bands, for instance—no special groups exist, so relying on **undifferentiated marketing,** or only one marketing program, makes sense. At the other extreme, for some products or services, such as furniture upholstering or tailoring, consumer demand might be highly diverse. In that case, the marketer can choose to serve all, many, or some of the market's diverse needs and desires.

In order for market segmentation to work successfully, five criteria must be met: (1) The market must be identifiable and measurable. Diet centers owners, for example, may be able to visually identify the segment to which they will appeal, but it is a lot harder to discern who in the larger market *thinks* they are overweight. (2) Market segments must be big enough to be profitable. Although only 10 percent of fur coats and jackets are sold to men, for instance, this small segment's profit potential is very high. (3) The market must be reachable; that is, marketers must be able to communicate effectively and efficiently with the segment it targets. Cable television and the proliferation of special-interest magazines have opened up more lines of communication, but reaching some segments—left-handed people, for instance—might prove more of a challenge. (4) The segment must be responsive, that is, willing and able to purchase, and (5) the segment must be stable; it shouldn't change regularly.

Markets can be segmented in two ways: descriptively (using demographic and geographic variables) and behaviorally (using attitudes, usage, and other behavioral variables). Within these two broad categories, there are many ways to segment any market. Some of the more common are age, income, gender, education, and geography.

EXAMPLES: Realizing that the number of adults aged 20 to 24 with skin problems exceeds the number of teenagers with blemishes, Richardson-Vicks introduced Clearasil Adult Care. San Francisco–based Williams-Sonoma, a 26-store cookware chain, learned that 15 percent of its cookware customers are male, so it bought mailing lists from men's magazines, such as *Gen-*

tleman Quarterly, to boost catalog sales. Coca-Cola has used behavioral as well as demographic segmentation to research a new soft drink. It discovered that children of working-class parents prefer to gulp their drinks, so it developed Mello Yello, a low-carbonated soft drink, and dubbed it "The World's Fastest Soft Drink."

Pepsi segmented the market by age and developed the "Pepsi generation" campaign to appeal specifically to a youthful segment. Virginia Slims cigarettes segmented the market according to sex and targets women.

*See also **behavioral segmentation, demographic segmentation, psychographic segmentation, volume segmentation.***

market share The total number of units of a product (or their dollar value) expressed as a percentage of the total number of units sold by all competitors in a given market.

EXAMPLE: A small commuter airline operating flights between Los Angeles and Las Vegas might carry 1,000 people a month, whereas all other airlines carry 1,500 passengers on the same route. Assuming that all the airlines charge the same fare, the commuter airline will have a market share of 40 percent for that month. The figure is calculated by dividing the number of passengers carried by the commuter airline by the total number of passengers that flew between Los Angeles and Las Vegas. (1,000 divided by $2,500 = 0.4$, or 40 percent).

Market share is a good indicator of a company's competitive standing, because it makes direct comparisons with other companies in the same market. A company may pat itself on the back for an absolute increase in sales of 10 percent, but that jump looks less impressive when the entire market's sales grew by 50 percent; clearly the company's competitors advanced more. Companies continually monitor competitors' market share to benchmark their competitive progress.

market value (1) The price at which an item can be sold.

market value (2) The *replacement cost* of an item, as used in the *lower of cost or market* rule.

marketable security In accounting, an *equity* or debt security that is easily converted into cash.

Examples include traded stocks, **commercial paper,** and Treasury bills. Marketable securities are reported at their cost as a *current asset* on the *balance sheet.*

marketing The process of planning and executing the conception, pricing, promotion, and distribution of ideas, goods, and services to create exchanges that satisfy individual and organizational objectives (this is the official definition of the **American Marketing Association**).

Nearly every part of a company's operations has something to do with marketing. A manufacturing department that designs and makes products with the consumer in mind is practicing marketing. When management decides to introduce a new product or service, that is a marketing decision. A grocery store manager who gives more shelf space to Coke than Pepsi is a marketer. A sales representative who pays special attention to a particular customer is actively involved in marketing. Even a friendly receptionist can be an effective marketer.

Marketing is, most simply, using an understanding of the consumer to meet his or her needs and the goals of the company. Marketing is not salesmanship. Salesmanship is a method of persuasion used to convince a customer to buy something. Marketing makes an effort to figure out what that customer desires then helps the company find a way to profitably meet those needs.

EXAMPLE: A sales approach for vacuum cleaners might involve company salespeople going door-to-door with a standard "all-purpose" vacuum cleaner trying to convince customers that their product can pick up everything from cat hair to cottage cheese. A marketing approach would involve finding out which features different people prefer in vacuum cleaners: Single apartment dwellers might like a vacuum cleaner that's lightweight and easy to store in a small space, for example, whereas homeowners with children might prefer a larger model that could handle a larger variety of cleaning tasks.

Armed with this knowledge, the vacuum cleaner company with a marketing orientation would make two different models to satisfy the two types of customers. In this example, the marketing strategy is focused on a company's product, but marketing can also affect pricing policy, distribution plans, advertising, and **sales promotions.** In short, everything the company does must be directed at serving and satisfying the customer's wants, needs, and preferences.

marketing channels *See distribution channels*

marketing control systems A set of monitoring mechanisms designed to keep the implementation of a marketing plan in line with the objectives of the organization.

The marketing control process consists of monitoring action programs, analyzing performance results, and, if necessary, taking corrective action.

More specifically, there are four types of marketing control systems: annual plan control, profitability control, efficiency control, and strategic control. With annual plan control, top and middle management analyze sales, market share, and sales-to-expense ratios to check continuing performance against the year's plan, so the company can take corrective action when necessary.

EXAMPLE: A manager of a software company assembles all the sales and market share information on a quarterly basis and compares it to the plan's goals, which were established at the beginning of the year. The comparison would indicate how well or how poorly the plan was performing.

The goal of profitability control, generally the responsibility of the marketing manager, is to see where a company is making or losing money. Profitability control can be applied to different markets, territories, market segments, and sales forces.

EXAMPLE: The marketing manager of the software company might be interested in conducting a profitability analysis of international sales in order to determine how well the international marketing plan is performing.

Efficiency control looks for ways to improve the impact of the various elements of the marketing mix.

EXAMPLE: The marketing manager and staff of the software company might analyze the company's advertising, sales force, distribution network, and promotions plan in order to determine if the marketing plan is cost- and time-effective.

Strategic control, usually the responsibility of top management, seeks to periodically reconcile a company's marketing strategies with the opportunities presented by the market.

EXAMPLE: In the software company, top management might meet annually in order to evaluate the company's overall performance and set new directions for the future.

A key element of all these control systems is feedback, or information that tells an organization's managers how each marketing program is doing. Then they can compare the information with action plans and budgets to determine whether the organization is achieving its goals as planned.

marketing mix The marketing tools and techniques an organization uses to achieve its marketing goals in the chosen *target market.*

The four elements of the marketing mix are (1) the product, which includes quality, assortment, service, guarantee, package, and warranty; (2) its distribution, which includes *wholesalers, retailers,* sales representatives, warehousing, inventory, and transportation; (3) its price, which includes consumer reactions, competitor reactions, and costs; and (4) its promotion, which includes advertising, publicity, and personal selling.

Each of the four elements is equally important, although some may get more emphasis than others in particular marketing situations and strategies. In the marketing of a commodity such as wheat, for example, where buyers make purchases based on price alone, pricing policy is the centerpiece of a marketing plan. Products such as perfume, on the other hand, rely heavily on promotion and advertising to attract customers. *See also four Ps.*

marketing myopia   A term coined by Theodore Levitt, professor of marketing at the Harvard Business School, to describe a company so involved with selling its product that it doesn't realize the true nature of what it is selling; eventually it finds itself overshadowed by competitors.

An often-cited example is the railroad industry, which, for the most part, has been overtaken by automobiles and airplanes. Had they not been afflicted with marketing myopia nearly a century ago, railroad company executives would have realized that they were selling transportation, not train tickets. By focusing only on the railroad business, they let other transportation companies take customers away until, finally, only a small segment of the market was served by rail. By defining their industry by product, rather than customers, railroad companies missed an enormous opportunity for growth.

Marketing News   *See American Marketing Association*

marketing orientation   A method of marketing based on an understanding of the needs and desires of the *target market.*

The goal of a company with a marketing orientation is to satisfy the needs of its customers more effectively than competitors.

EXAMPLE: A plastic garbage bag manufacturer with a marketing orientation surveys the market before developing a new product, a biodegradable bag with a drawstring handle. The survey gives the company information on the preferred size, color, price, and strength of the bag. It then incorporates this data into the product design and marketing.

marketing plan   The document that outlines a company's entire marketing strategy and tactical actions.

The marketing plan is the main tool for organizing and managing a marketing effort. Most marketing plans contain eight sections: executive summary; analysis of the current marketing situation; analysis of opportunities; objectives; marketing strategy; plan of action and tactics; financial projections and costs; and control mechanisms.

- The *executive summary* gives a short overview so that managers can easily grasp the plan.
- *Analysis of the current marketing situation* presents key background information on the product, market, competition, distribution, price, and promotion.

- *Analysis of opportunity* summarizes the issues, opportunities, threats, strengths, and weaknesses facing the product.
- *Objectives* define the plan's goals in terms of sales, market share, and profits.
- *Marketing strategy* presents the overall approach that will be used to meet the plan's goals.
- The *plan of action* details exactly how the plan will be implemented.
- *Financial projections and costs* state the anticipated financial consequences of the plan.
- *Control mechanisms* explain how the plan will be supervised and monitored.

marketing research A systematic, objective approach to developing and providing information for use in making decisions about specific marketing problems.

More than 77 percent of large companies have market research departments that consist of anywhere from one to several dozen researchers. These companies usually budget between 0.02 percent and 1 percent of sales to their research departments. Companies without marketing research departments must go to outside vendors. There are three types of marketing research companies: (1) syndicated service companies that collect and sell periodic consumer and trade information, (2) custom research companies that design and execute specific research projects, and (3) specialized marketing research firms that offer a specific service, such as facilitators for *focus group interviews,* to other research firms and departments.

Marketing research, first used in the 1920s, has become the primary information-gathering tool for marketers. In recent years, though, marketing research companies have come under fire for not using scientific methods, offering results shaded in favor of clients, and designing loaded questions. At the same time, high-tech, "single source" research has come into favor. By marrying scanner data that accurately measures in-store buying behavior with consumer characteristics, a new wave of research companies, referred to as single source firms, can now achieve much greater precision in defining target markets.

With this high-tech technique, pioneered by Information Resources, Inc., researchers put together a panel of consumers in representative towns across the country. Each panel member gets a magnetic card to present at the checkout counter of the supermarket; the card records the items that the particular consumer bought. Each panel member also fills out an extensive questionnaire on demographics, media behavior, lifestyles, and attitudes. Since the panel members also subscribe to cable television, marketers use the information they've gathered to tailor commercials to households based on the results of the questionnaires and actual purchase behavior. Clearly, scanner data with its experimental opportunities is revolutionizing the image and impact of marketing research. *See also* **causal research, descrip-**

tive research, experimental research, exploratory research, observational research.

markup The difference between the price that a *retailer* pays for a product and the price at which that product is sold.

Most retailers pursue either a high-markup, lower-volume strategy (boutiques and specialty stores, such as Giorgio of Beverly Hills and Bijan) or a low-markup, higher-volume strategy (discounters and mass merchandisers such as Wal-Mart and Kmart).

Maslow's hierarchy of needs A theory developed by psychologist Abraham Maslow to explain why people are driven by particular needs at particular times.

In order of importance, Maslow's needs are physiological, safety, social, esteem, and self-actualization. According to Maslow, a person is motivated to satisfy the most important needs first. When that need is satisfied, it is no longer a motivator, and the person will try to satisfy the next most important need.

EXAMPLE: People who are hungry are concerned only with finding food. But once they've eaten, their focus might shift to the need for safety. More than one need can be satisfied at one time by the same action. A five-course dinner party with a group of close friends serves to meet both physiological and social needs.

Marketers use Maslow's theory to understand how their products fit into the lives of potential customers.

EXAMPLE: If a consumer is interested in buying gold jewelry, the marketer can use Maslow's theory to conclude that the customer has satisfied his or her physiological, safety, and social needs and is now motivated by a need for acceptance by others.

mass marketing The mass production, distribution, and promotion of one product for all buyers; also called market aggregation.

A company that makes paper clips, for example, might practice mass marketing by offering a single standard product to the entire market. *See also **undifferentiated marketing**.*

master production schedule A schedule of what, when, and how many units of an individual product will be produced.

Covering a period at least a quarter beyond the overall procurement and production schedule, the MPS serves as the "roadmap" in defining how the production will take place.

matching concept The second of the basic *financial accounting* tenets (the first is *conservatism*).

The matching concept mandates that—except for the issues covered under the conservatism principle—expenses must be recorded in the same accounting period that the benefits, usually sales, are derived. This principle underlies the entire system of *accrual accounting.* In accrual accounting, entries made for expenses are matched with sales (or *assets* with *liabilities*), even though an item may not be paid for until future accounting periods. The matching principle also underlies the rule that expenses must be recorded in the period in which they are incurred, rather than when they are paid. Finally, the matching principle dictates that companies write off *noncurrent assets* over the accounting period during which they'll realize the assets' benefits. *Depreciation* of *fixed assets* and *amortization* of *intangible assets* are two examples.

materiality In accounting, the relative importance of an accounting error or omission in a company's financial statements.

Materiality is determined by both the amount and type of item. If an item is material, it must be disclosed in a company's *annual report.*

EXAMPLE: The omission of $1,000 in *accounts receivable* is probably not material for a company with more than a million dollars in the account. There are no hard-and-fast rules establishing the materiality of any particular item, although external auditors have their own standards.

materials requirements planning (MRP) A system of materials management designed to reduce or eliminate the need for excessive inventories by analysis of product structure and *lead times.*

By moving backward through the *master production schedule* and customer orders, MRP helps managers track the entire production process and allows purchasing, inventory, and production departments to move the right amount of materials to the right workstations at the right times.

MRP works best in companies that have mass production lines and experience uneven demand. Its effects include reduced inventories, streamlined production scheduling, and increased labor and space utilization. For example, Black & Decker, the world's largest manufacturer of power tools, with sales over $1 billion and a product line that includes nearly 20,000 items, reports that it has significantly improved materials ordering and handling, and reduced surplus materials, past-due receipts from suppliers, and engineering change orders through the implementation of MRP.

MRP is based on accurate forecasts of short-term (monthly, weekly, or even daily) demand. Once these forecasts are generated, managers can calculate the exact materials requirements for each particular product or subassembly and identify potential shortages or delays. Inventory and production staff can then schedule the production and delivery dates for each product.

MRP systems usually incorporate an extensive computer system that keeps track of the materials required, and used, in each phase of production. In order to keep the system running smoothly, every employee (from equipment operators to salespeople to purchasing agents) must continually feed accurate updates into the system. Without continuous updates, the MRP system will begin to make errors regarding the amount of stock on hand, the quantities of materials needed, and the times at which materials are needed. Everyone involved with the MRP system must use system data in each step of the production process.

The implementation of an MRP system requires a great deal of discipline and the creation of new communications channels between every participant in the production process. This leads to extra work, which can be a source of resentment from both employees and management. Managers frequently feel constrained by MRP procedures because there is no room for more informal methods of scheduling various jobs. Employees often feel saddled with an extra burden because of the extensive records and feedback that are required to keep an MRP system running smoothly. As a result, many MRP systems are prone to inaccuracies regarding the amount of materials on hand, the amount of materials required for a particular job, and the specific times at which jobs must be started and finished.

matrix structure A formal organizational structure distinguished by the establishment of dual authority.

In other words, employees have two bosses. The matrix structure was originally developed in the aerospace industry because of the need to be responsive to specific changes in technology, products, and markets. By using the matrix structure to focus on a particular product or market, it is possible to concentrate the resources needed to respond to that product or market quickly.

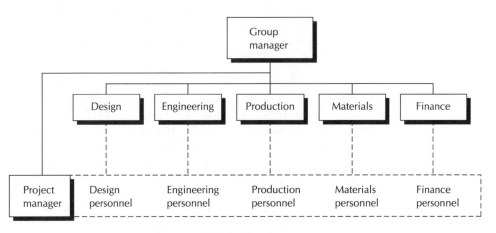

Matrix Structure

EXAMPLE: In the above diagram, authority is divided between the project manager and the managers of the design, engineering, production, materials, and finance departments. In other words, an employee in the production department for this particular project reports to both the production manager and the project manager.

Because of the dual authority of matrix structures, they can be complicated to manage. There is great potential for conflict between project managers and managers of traditional functional areas. In order to overcome these conflicts, it is important to establish clear communications links between managers and encourage the development of interpersonal skills. Despite these difficulties, in situations where it is important to maintain a full-time focus on a particular product or market, a matrix structure can offer several important advantages, including (1) the reduction of information and technological requirements, (2) concentration of specialized skills, and (3) the opportunity for management to concentrate exclusively on a particular project or market.

MBO *See management by objectives*

mechanization The mechanical replacement, or augmentation, of human skills.

An automobile factory that has installed robots to assemble each car has mechanized the process. Although mechanization significantly improves productivity, it results in both increased and decreased worker skill levels. For example, it requires a high degree of skill and expertise to set up and maintain the automobile assembly robots, but very little skill to monitor and operate them. *See also **automation.***

media buyer A person who coordinates the purchase of newspaper and magazine space or broadcast time for various companies' advertisements.

Media buyers (also called media planners) usually work in ***advertising agencies,*** but several large companies specialize in media planning and buying without offering the other services an advertising agency usually provides.

EXAMPLE: A clothing company wants to market a new style of blue jeans to a target market of urban females between 13 and 17 years old. A media buyer would determine which outlet provides the most direct access to the target audience. In this case, the best way to reach 13- to 17-year-old girls, the buyer concludes, is to place television ads during a popular situation comedy that attracts a large female teenage audience.

medium-term notes Promissory notes with a term of five to six years, usually issued by companies rather than financial institutions.

merger A combination of two or more companies.

The combination may be accomplished by the exchange of stock for stock, which results in the combining of accounts (called a tax-free pooling of interests); by forming a new company to acquire the assets of the combining companies (called a consolidation); or by a purchase, where the amount that is paid in excess of the acquired companies' book value (and that cannot be allocated to the acquired assets) is treated as goodwill on the books of the purchaser. Although consolidations and statutory consolidations are technically not mergers, the terms are commonly used interchangeably.

methods-time measurement (MTM) A system of measurement of individual motions, called micro-motions, such as reach, grab, and position.

These motions have been measured and timed using predetermined time values called *therbligs*. One therblig equals 0.0006 hour (about two seconds). In an MTM study, a repetitive job is videotaped, and the individual motions are isolated and timed, resulting in a figure for the total time required to perform the job.

micromarkets The splintering of market segments into smaller and smaller fragments based on age, sex, lifestyle preferences, geography, education, and so on; sometimes called maximarketing or regional marketing.

Marketers, then, partition the mass market into ever smaller, more homogeneous groupings so they can achieve a better fit between marketing programs and preferences in the marketplace. In the process they have stretched the limits of *market segmentation.*

Although developing special marketing plans for micromarkets is effective, it can prove costly, because marketers relinquish *economies of scale* as they focus on ever-smaller segments. *See also market segmentation, niche marketing.*

minimum lease payments The rental payments made against a *capital lease.*

The value of both the *asset* and the *liability* generated by a capital lease is determined by the discounted value of future minimum lease payments. *See also present value.*

minimum pension liability In accounting, an obligation that is recognized when the *accumulated benefit obligation* of a pension plan is greater than the fair market value of plan assets.

In other words, if a pension plan's benefit obligation, as estimated at *present* salary and service levels, is greater than the plan's assets, a minimum pension liability must be shown on the *balance sheet. See also accumulated benefit obligation, projected benefit obligation.*

minority interest An ownership interest of less than 50 percent.

In consolidated *financial statements,* minority interest is shown as a line item in the *noncurrent liability* section of the *balance sheet.*

MIS *See management information system*

mission statement A short statement of the central purposes, strategies, and values of a company.

Essentially, a company's mission statement should answer the question "What business are we in?" A good mission statement should go beyond the obvious ("This hospital is dedicated to providing health care.") and deal with a number of issues that are vital to the company. They include the company's purpose (that is, its guiding aims or *raison d'être*); strategy (that is, a short explanation of how it intends to serve its purpose); and values (that is, the basic principles that guide the actions of the company's members).

When a mission statement is considered in these broad terms, its value becomes more apparent. By understanding not only a company's goals, but its purpose, the strategies that will be used to achieve the goals, and the core values that underlie its actions, individuals are able to make better sense of their day-to-day activities. A good mission statement gives meaning to work that might otherwise have little point beyond the attainment of specific goals such as earning a specific amount of money or meeting a particular sales quota. When employees share a sense of mission, they are better able to make the trade-offs and choices that they face every day. Sharing a sense of mission creates loyalty, cooperation, commitment, and trust among employees.

modified rebuy A buying situation in the *industrial market* in which the buyer modifies the terms, such as product specifications, prices, or delivery requirements, of routinely purchased goods or services.
Compare to new task, straight rebuy.

modularity A production method, involving interchangeable subassemblies, that allows for the manufacture of a variety of slightly different products.

For example, Ford has established a modular automobile engine plant in Michigan. The equipment in the plant has been designed to build up to 12 different engine models, although only 6 are currently in production. This has been accomplished by reducing the number of parts by 25 percent. The remaining 350 engine parts are standardized (for example, the combustion chamber is the same for all 12 engines). Variations among the motors are created by assembling the parts in different ways. Because of the standardization of parts, each of the 12 engines will share about 75 percent of their parts. As a result of this modular approach, new engine variations should take only two years to develop and cost only $60 million (as opposed to the more traditional four years and $500 million).

monetarism The school of economic thought known as the "Chicago School," headed by Nobel Laureate Milton Friedman, which holds that the money supply is the chief determinant of macroeconomic activity both within a country and between countries and groups of countries; also known as *supply side economics*.

The key ideas of monetarism are as follows:

1. Change in the money supply directly affects and determines, over the long run, the levels of industrial and agricultural production, employment, and prices of goods and services.

2. Fiscal policy (that is, taxes and expenditures) has little significant effect on business-cycle events, such as inflation, deflation, recession, and depression. Therefore, monetary policy (that is, the use of the money supply and interest rates by a nation's central monetary authority) is the preferred way to control a national economy.

3. Economic stability can best be promoted by government by following a "simple money rule": Increase the money supply at a constant annual rate linked to the growth of the GNP.

4. Reduced government economic involvement equates with increased personal economic freedom, which in turn equates with increased personal political freedom.

monetary aggregates The *Federal Reserve's* three main measures of what is regarded as "money" in the U.S. economy.

These measures are sometimes popularly referred to as "money supply" measures, but this is inaccurate; the aggregates signify neither demand nor supply exclusively, but rather the equilibrium between the demand and supply of money.

The most basic, narrowest, monetary aggregate is *M1*, consisting of currency and checks (demand deposits, traveler's checks, and other checkables). A broader concept, *M2*, includes M1 plus savings and small time deposits (under $100,000), money market deposit accounts, money market mutual account balances, and some special financial deposits (overnight repurchase agreements and Eurodollar deposits). The broadest concept, *M3*, contains M2 plus term deposits (time deposits, repurchase agreements, Eurodollar deposits), and dealer-only money market mutual funds. The three concepts differ in that M1 is the closest to transactions balances that can be reused: It possesses the highest liquidity. The higher-order aggregates have less liquidity. The table below compares these aggregates (in billions of dollars) for selected years since 1960.

	M1	M2	M3
1960	140.7	312.4	315.3
1965	167.9	459.4	482.3
1970	214.5	628.1	677.4
1975	287.6	1,023.3	1,172.2
1980	408.8	1,629.5	1,987.0
1985	620.2	2,569.4	3,203.2
1990	826.1	3,339.0	4,059.8

Another difference between M1 and the higher-order monetary aggregates is that M2 and M3 each contain components that are interest rate sensitive—for instance, money market deposit accounts and time deposits. Thus, these "non-transactions" components may vary with interest rates; this is much less true of M1.

The monetary aggregates bear a relationship to the level of GDP. The level of current dollar GDP divided by the level of the monetary aggregate is equal to a concept called *velocity*, essentially the number of times a dollar turns over in a year. In recognition of this fact, the Federal Reserve has set target growth rates for the monetary aggregates as part of its conduct of *monetary policy.*

The relationship between M1 and GDP has shown a great deal of instability over the years. In the 1990s, the relationship between M2 and GDP—which previously had shown great stability—began to display an upward trend. This reflected the reaction of households to the decline in interest rates in 1990–1993, which made investors less willing to hold wealth in the form of money balances. They have sought other higher yielding forms in which to hold their wealth.

monetary policy   The *Federal Reserve's* aim to regulate the growth of the *monetary aggregates* in order to ensure sufficient credit expansion to foster economic growth, without inflation, while maintaining orderly financial markets.

The means by which the Fed attempts to achieve its monetary policy goals have changed over the years.

In the 1960s and through most of the 1970s, the Fed aimed to control monetary growth by controlling **interest rates.** Specifically, the Federal funds rate—the rate at which commercial banks lend excess reserves to banks with insufficient reserves in the overnight loan market—was the target. The Federal funds rate target was always specified in terms of its consistency with a particular rate of growth in the monetary aggregates.

In late 1979, the Fed announced a new monetary policy aimed at direct control of the amount of reserves in the banking system. This policy resulted in much greater interest rate volatility than earlier, and the consequent economic effects, particularly in the severe 1981–1982 recession, were pronounced. Ultimately, however, the policy proved effective at braking inflation. Since the mid-1980s, the exercise of monetary policy has been less severe and hybrid; a range of fluctuation in the Federal funds rate has been identified as "consistent with a particular level of reserve growth." The aim of monetary policy—economic growth, without inflation, while maintaining orderly financial markets—has remained the same.

money center banks   The private sector equivalent of the Federal Reserve Bank.

Money center banks (for example, Citibank, Chase, Chemical, BankAmerica, J.P. Morgan, Banker's Trust, Morgan Guaranty, and so on) are the primary buyers of U.S. Treasuries and the major players in the interbank market, buying and selling securities of regional and local banks. Although the United States has more than 12,000 operating banks, the Federal Reserve reports that nine money center banks control over 50 percent of all U.S. banking assets.

With banking deregulation, money center banks branched out into a variety of financial services ranging from investment banking to credit cards to foreign lending to clearinghouses for international money transfers. Most have branches scattered throughout the world. Their primary activities, however, haven't changed. They continue to act as depositories, lenders, and purchasers of government securities.

money markets   Markets for the sale of *short-term debt.*
> Examples include United States Treasury bills, certificates of deposit, and commercial paper.

morning drive time   In radio, the time segment between 6:00 A.M. and 10:00 A.M.
> Morning drive time, like *afternoon drive time,* delivers one of the largest audiences of the day. *Compare to afternoon drive time.*

MRP   *See materials requirements planning*

MRPII   *See manufacturing requirements planning*

MTM   *See methods-time measurement*

multiple sourcing   The purchase of a good or service from more than one supplier.

Myers-Briggs Type Indicator (MBTI)   A widely used personality test.
> The MBTI consists of 100 questions that ask how people act or feel in a variety of situations. The test characterizes people as introverted or extroverted (E or I), sensing or intuitive (S or N), thinking or feeling (T or F), and perceiving or judging (P or J). Once these characterizations are made, they are combined into one of 16 different personality types. For example, someone who tests as ENTP (extroverted, intuitive, thinking, perceiving) is a conceptualizer. He or she is good at many things, quick, and ingenious in solving problems—although there may be a tendency to ignore routine work.
> The MBTI is not—and should not be—used to screen or judge employees, but rather as a tool for improving employee self-awareness. Proponents of the test argue that this increased self-awareness leads to improved communication, which in turn leads to increased *productivity.* There is little concrete evidence that the MBTI actually improves productivity, but it is widely used just the same. Users include Apple Computer, AT&T, Citicorp, GE, Honeywell, 3M Co., and the United States Armed Forces.

NASDAQ *See National Association of Securities Dealers Automated Quotations System*

National Association of Securities Dealers Automated Quotation System (NASDAQ) A primary market for over-the-counter trading.

Prices of stocks traded on NASDAQ are quoted simultaneously on the NYSE and all regional exchanges, providing both buyers and sellers the best possible price at all times. The system provides a wealth of information about a stock, including its trading history, daily trading volume, dividends paid, daily high and low price, the high and low price of the last 52 weeks, daily closing price, and the price change from the previous day's close.

Minimum listing requirements for the NASDAQ are

- Publicly held shares: 100,000
- Total minimum number of shareholders: 300
- Net assets of $2 million
- Net worth of $1 million
- Two or more market makers
- Annual fee of $2,500 or $.0005 per share

In 1992, of the estimated 47,500 stocks traded on the over-the-counter market, about 4,500 were listed on the NASDAQ, the balance on "pink sheets" (*see penny stocks*).

NC *See numerical control*

net income In accounting, the result of subtracting all expenses from *revenue;* also called net profit.

Net income is reported on the *income statement.*

net present value (NPV) In corporate finance, the *present value* (that is, the value of cash to be received in the future expressed in today's dollars) of an investment in excess of the initial amount invested.

NPV is calculated as follows:

$$\text{NPV} = P_0 + \frac{P_1}{1+r} + \frac{P_2}{(1+r)^2} + \frac{P_3}{(1+r)^3} + \cdots + \frac{P_n}{(1+r)^n} = 0$$

where

NPV = net present value of the investment

$P_0, P_1, \ldots, P_n$ = cash payments in periods $0-n$

r = investors' required rate of return (the rate of return offered by a comparable investment)

Generally, P_0, the cash payment at time period zero (today), is a cash outflow and thus a negative number.

EXAMPLE: Consider an investment with the following cash flows:

P_0	P_1	P_2	P_3
$-\$100,000$	$+\$40,000$	$+\$40,000$	$+\$50,000$

The investors' required rate of return is 12 percent. The investment's net present value is

$$-\$100,000 + \frac{\$40,000}{1.12} + \frac{\$40,000}{(1.12)^2} + \frac{\$50,000}{(1.12)^3} = \$3,191$$

In other words, the investment is worth $3,191. When an investment or project has a positive NPV, it should be pursued. When an investment has a negative NPV, it should not be accepted.

new-product development The process by which a new product is brought to the market.

The new-product development process usually includes eight steps: idea generation, idea screening, concept development and testing, marketing strategy development, business analysis, product development, market testing, and commercialization. Although individual companies may skip or add steps according to their particular circumstances, each step presents an opportunity for marketers to decide whether an idea should be further developed or dropped.

EXAMPLE: A magazine publishing company interested in expanding its product line might solicit ideas for new magazines from both employees and customers in a series of brainstorming sessions with top management (step one). Once a number of ideas have emerged, the company begins to screen out some of the more improbable concepts (step two). The screening-out process might leave a single idea, say a magazine for active senior citizens, as a viable option for concept development and testing (step three). This step includes positioning the product for a potential ***target market.*** In other words, the magazine could be travel oriented and appeal to wealthier retirees, or it could concentrate on health issues and have a broader appeal.

Once the publisher has created a number of different concepts, it tests each of them with an appropriate group of target consumers. Then the company develops a marketing strategy for the most promising product concept; say it is the travel magazine (step four). The strategy describes the target market, estimates projected sales and market share, and develops future profit goals. Once the marketing strategy is in place, management conducts a business analysis in which it estimates sales, costs, and profits (step five). If all these figures look promising, the concept is developed into a physical product (step six). When prototypes of the magazine are completed and tested on a small group of consumers, full-scale ***test marketing*** begins (step seven). If market testing looks promising, management may decide to move into the last, and most expensive, step in new-product development, namely, bringing it to market (step eight).

new task   A buying situation in the ***industrial market*** where the purchaser buys a product or service, such as a new factory building or a fleet of trucks, for the first time.

New-task situations present a great opportunity to marketers, who must move as quickly and carefully as possible to make a sale. Frequently, this situation calls for a great deal of personal selling and negotiation. Some companies even assemble elite sales forces, called missionary sales forces, to approach potential new-task customers. *Compare to **modified rebuy, straight rebuy.***

New York Stock Exchange   The largest exchange in the United States.

As the following minimum listing requirements indicate, only larger companies list on this exchange.

- Publicly held shares of $1 million
- Market value of $16 million for those shares
- Annual pre-tax net income of $2.5 million
- Total minimum number of shareholders: 2,000
- Net assets of $18 million

In addition, several other requirements prohibit smaller companies from listing:

- Quarterly and annual reporting requirements are the strictest of any exchange.
- The company must engage a registrar and a transfer agent in New York City.

- Delisting is complicated and can only occur in two ways:
  1. At the request of the NYSE with approval from the SEC
  2. At the request of the company, which must be supported by a vote of two-thirds of the shareholders

     Furthermore, less than 10 percent of individual investors can vote "no."

The exchange can request delisting if the company fails to meet reporting requirements, the security trading is inactive, or if the company no longer meets initial listing requirements.

newsboy problem A generic characterization of a class of problems dealing with overstocking or understocking a perishable product.

Too much stock will satisfy all the demand but reduce profits by necessitating the disposal of unsold, now worthless, inventory. Understocking will result in no inventory but will not satisfy demand. Since the product is perishable or of no value after some period, there is no possible way to carry inventory or make up for a lost sale, hence the term newsboy problem. After one day, unsold papers are called worthless, thus perishable.

EXAMPLE: Say a newsboy, let's call him Kevin, buys copies of the morning edition of a daily paper at 7:00 A.M. and then sells them on a particular corner outside a subway station between 8:00 A.M. and 10:00 A.M. Kevin buys the papers for $0.15 and sells them for $0.25. It seems that some mornings he runs out of papers by 9:30, whereas other mornings he has several papers left at 10:00 that he cannot sell. The problem here is how to determine the optimal number of newspapers to purchase each morning in order to make the best profit.

In order to solve the problem, Kevin keeps track of the number of newspapers sold every day for 100 days (this length of time may vary from situation to situation, but it should be long enough to get an accurate measure of average demand.) On days when he sells all of his newspapers before 10:00, Kevin stays at his post and keeps track of all requests for papers.

Demand (newspapers)	Frequency (days)	Relative frequency
47	10	10%
48	25	25%
49	35	35%
50	15	15%
51	15	15%

Kevin's lowest demand for newspapers was 47 papers, and his highest demand was for 51 papers. Thus, Kevin knows that he should order between 47 and 51 newspapers, but since he can order any of the five quantities in between on any given day, he must determine which quantity will maximize profits. This requires a payoff table in which the profits for each quantity and demand level are calculated. Each entry is calculated as follows:

Number demanded × $0.25 − Number ordered × $0.15 =   Profit

If Kevin bought 50 newspapers and sold 48, his profit would be

48 × $0.25 − 50 × $0.15 = $4.50

Here is the payoff table for Kevin's newspapers:

	Demand				
Order quantity	47	48	49	50	51
47	$4.70	$4.70	$4.70	$4.70	$4.70
48	$4.55	$4.80	$4.80	$4.80	$4.80
49	$4.40	$4.65	$4.90	$4.90	$4.90
50	$4.25	$4.50	$4.75	$5.00	$5.00
51	$4.10	$4.35	$4.60	$4.85	$5.10

With this information, Kevin knows what his profit will be for any particular order quantity and demand level. Since he knows the relative frequency for each demand level, he can determine his expected daily profit for each possible order quantity. For example, if Kevin decides to order 47 papers a day, his expected daily profit will be

10%($4.70) + 25%($4.70) + 35%($4.70) + 15%($4.70) +
15%($4.70) = $4.70

If Kevin orders 51 papers per day, his expected daily profits will be

10%($4.70) + 25%($4.80) + 35%($4.90) + 15%($5.00) +
15%($5.10) = $4.90

The expected daily profit for each order quantity is as follows:

Order quantity	Expected daily profit
47	$4.70
48	$4.63
49	$4.79
50	$4.86
51	$4.90 (best)

It is clear that Kevin will maximize daily profits by ordering 51 papers per day. Although he will only sell all of his papers 15 percent of the time, his expected long-term daily return is higher than it would be if he took a more conservative approach and ordered fewer papers.

The same process used to solve the newsboy problem can be applied to any situation in which a company orders a perishable product or material and is able to establish a demand history that is an accurate reflection of future demand.

niche marketing A marketing strategy whereby companies specialize in serving a small segment of the market that is of little interest to major competitors.

Some companies specialize in specific customer groups. Oshkosh B'Gosh, for instance, found the response to its kids' denim overall so overwhelming that it now specializes in its children's line. Other niche products include the microbreweries that flourish by marketing pricey, full-bodied beers to taste-conscious consumers; Swiss-based Rolex, which produces only 450,000 watches annually and focuses on old-fashioned perfectionism and quality; L.L. Bean, the catalog marketer of camping equipment, which focuses on customer service by providing a 24-hour-a-day, 7-days-a-week phone order service; and Rent-a-Dent, the car-rental company that practices niche marketing by renting older cars in less-than-perfect condition for a much lower rate than major competitors offering new cars.

noncurrent asset In accounting, an *asset* with an expected useful life of more than one year.

Noncurrent assets are reported on the *balance sheet* and include machinery, automobiles, buildings, land, and *deferred expense. Compare to current asset.*

noncurrent liability In accounting, a financial obligation due in more than one year.

Noncurrent liabilities are reported on the *balance sheet* and include *long-term debt* and *capital lease obligations. Compare to current liability.*

nondurable good A tangible product, such as soda, fresh flowers, or a pencil, that is normally consumed in a few uses.

Since nondurable goods are purchased frequently, they are well suited to a marketing strategy that emphasizes heavy promotions, low markups, and wide availability.

nonmarket risk The factors that affect a particular company's securities; also called nonsystematic risk.

Examples of factors that contribute to nonmarket risk are poor management, an inefficient production process, an unpredicted drop in demand, and so on. The portion of a security's return that is due to nonmarket risk is measured by alpha. *See alpha. Compare to market risk.*

North American Free Trade Agreement (NAFTA) A proposed multilateral accord between the United States, Canada, and Mexico. Also referred to as the *North American Free Trade Zone (NAFTZ)*.

NAFTA would comprise both the Canada-U.S. Free Trade Agreement of 1989 (FTA) and a U.S.-Mexico Free Trade Agreement.

If successfully negotiated, NAFTA would thus extend the existing Canada-U.S. Free Trade Agreement market of 275 million people to one of almost 360 million people with the inclusion of a U.S.-Mexico Free Trade Agreement. This combined market would be larger than the 320-million-people market of the 12-member European Community (EC).

NAFTA itself would be dedicated to (1) phased, full elimination of all import tariffs; (2) elimination of all nontariff barriers; (3) establishment of binding, full, mutual protection for intellectual property rights; and (4) expeditious and equitable dispute-settlement mechanisms. (*Source:* L. Presner, *The International Business Dictionary and Reference*, Copyright © 1991 L. Presner. Reprinted with permission of the publisher, John Wiley & Sons, Inc.)

note payable A contract to pay a creditor at a future date.

A note payable may involve borrowing from a bank, making a purchase, or refinancing an *account payable.* Notes payable are reported on the *balance sheet* as either *current liabilities* or *noncurrent liabilities,* depending on whether the payment is due in one year or less. *See also note receivable.*

note receivable A contract to receive money at a future date.

Notes receivable are reported on the *balance sheet* as either *current assets* or *noncurrent assets,* depending on whether payment will be received in one year or less. *See also note payable.*

NPV *See net present value*

numerical control (NC) Any technology that allows a machine to operate automatically via coded numerical commands.

Originally, these commands were on punched paper cards or tape that would direct a machine in a manner similar to the way a player piano is controlled. In recent years, however, computers have become the main tool in numerical control—in many instances, numerical control is referred to as computer numerical control, or CNC. Numerical control is frequently a more attractive option than complete automation because it can allow for a variety of operations, speeds, materials, and so on.

Numerical control is very expensive (initial costs can run between $20,000 and $500,000) but it offers many important advantages: better equipment utilization, fewer manual operations, lower labor costs, fewer setups, consistent machining speeds and times, automatic tool selection, consistent quality, lower inspection costs, and less machining time. Numerical control also offers the potential for the development of a machining center that can easily be adapted to handle multiple processes.

observational research A data collection technique in which researchers record events in a "natural" setting.

Rather than talking to consumers, researchers using this approach merely record what they see. The researchers, of course, cannot tell with this tech- nique what people are thinking or feeling or what their motives for some action may be. Nonetheless, the observational approach is extremely effec- tive for researching certain kinds of problems.

EXAMPLE: Toy companies often use observational research in deciding what products to market. Fisher-Price, the leader in the preschool category, runs an on-site nursery school where researchers can observe children through one-way mirrors. By observation they can see whether a toy interests a child, is safe, and is easy to play with. The best test of a toy's appeal is its "play value"—that is, whether the child plays with the new toy for a few minutes, and then returns to an old favorite or whether the new toy is interesting enough to engage a child's attention for a long period.

Two Detroit-based companies, Urban Science Applications and R. L. Polk, use another observational technique. Both companies write down li- cense plate numbers at shopping center parking lots. Then researchers feed the numbers into a computer and pair them with automobile registration data in order to find out where the shopping center's customers live. A.C. Nielsen uses yet another technique to get its widely used Nielsen rating. By installing its "audimeter" in selected households, it can monitor when the television set is in use and which programs households are watching (*see* **television rating, television share**).

See also **marketing research**. *Compare to* **causal research, descriptive research, experimental research, exploratory research.**

OECD *See* **Organization for Economic Cooperation and Development**

OEM *See* **Original Equipment Manufacturer**

off-balance sheet In accounting, an item not reported in *financial state- ments* that nevertheless has an impact on the operations of a company.

For example, off-balance sheet liabilities such as pending litigation or guarantees of future performance are not reported on a company's *balance sheet* but may have a significant impact on future operations.

offshore financial center A location with banking facilities to accept deposits and make loans in currencies different from the currency's country of origin.

For example, dollars on deposit in London, yen loaned from a New York bank, or deutsch marks on deposit in Singapore. Such currencies are frequently referred to as "Eurocurrency."

Banks located in offshore financial centers (often called Eurobanks) are exempt from the bank's home country banking regulations, such as those relating to reserve requirements, legal lending limits, deposit insurance fees, interest rate ceilings, capital export controls, limits on bank asset growth, liquidity ratios, multiple taxing authorities, and capital asset ratio requirements.

All offshore financial centers, including those in the United States, offer tax preferences—usually, but not always, in the form of tax-free remittances of earnings to an offshore parent company.

Most major banking centers—New York, Chicago, San Francisco, Miami, Toronto, Tokyo, London, Paris, Zurich, Geneva, Brussels, Luxembourg, Singapore, and Amsterdam—also maintain offshore banking facilities. In the United States, the offshore banking facility is called the International Banking Facility (IBF) and is available at all money center banks. Less-endowed offshore financial centers such as the Bahamas, Cayman Islands, Panama, Channel Islands, and so on, promote their tax-haven status along with international banking facilities.

omnibus panel A group of *marketing research* participants who take part in a variety of studies over a period of time.

The Parker Pen company, for example, maintains a panel of 1,100 people that it uses to evaluate new writing instruments. *Compare to longitudinal panel.*

OPEC *See Organization of Petroleum Exporting Countries*

operating expenses In accounting, the costs of the selling and administrative activities of a business.

Operating expenses are reported on the *income statement* and are usually categorized as selling expenses and general and administrative expenses.

operating income In accounting, *revenue* less *cost of goods sold* and normal *operating expenses.*

Operating income is reported on the *income statement* and does not include items such as interest income and expense, dividend income, income taxes, and *extraordinary items.*

operating lease In accounting, a lease that does not meet any of the four requirements of a *capital lease,* namely, (1) payments for the exclusive use of the *asset* that approximate the asset's fair market value, (2) sole access to an asset for all or a substantial portion of its useful life, (3) opportunity to buy the asset at a discounted price at the end of the lease period, and (4) proof of ownership, such as legal title to the asset.

Operating leases do not have to be reported in a company's *financial statements* as a long-term *liability* and are frequently used as *off-balance sheet* sources of financing. *See also capital lease.*

operations The process of transforming raw materials, or some other form of *inputs,* into finished products, or *outputs.*

Operations is the main function of nearly every business. For example, the operations of an automobile company is the manufacture of cars. The operations of a television studio is the production of television shows. The operations of an accounting firm is the preparation of financial statements.

opinion leaders People who have expertise or influence in the eyes of consumers in the target market.

Often, marketers can quickly achieve acceptance of a product by an entire market by first targeting opinion leaders.

EXAMPLE: To gain acceptance for its Eraser Mate erasable ink pens, Gillette's Paper Mate division mailed 60,000 samples to such opinion leaders as U.S. senators, English teachers, baseball players, bankers, television personalities, and advertising executives. When Paper Mate interviewed other consumers thereafter, 40 percent had heard of the new pen and 13 percent knew the brand name—*before* Paper Mate did any advertising.

opportunity cost The amount that is sacrificed when choosing one activity over the next best alternative.

For example, if a person decides to stop working in order to attend school on a full-time basis, the opportunity cost of this decision is the amount of his or her salary that is foregone by not working. This can be contrasted with the "out-of-pocket" costs of attending school such as tuition and books. Another example of opportunity cost can be seen in the decision by a salaried person who decides to leave his or her job in order to start a business. The foregone salary is considered to be the opportunity cost of this entrepreneurial activity.

In industry, an example of opportunity cost is seen in the concept of the "hurdle rate" used by financial analysts in deciding whether to pursue a particular investment project. In financial analysis, the hurdle rate is the minimum acceptable rate of return needed to justify the investment in a capital project. If a company's managers can demonstrate that a particular project would have a rate of return that is higher than this, they are in effect saying that the benefits of this project exceed the opportunity cost of using the company's funds in this project.

option A right that is granted in exchange for an agreed-upon sum to buy or sell property.

If the right is not exercised within the specified time period, it expires and the holder forfeits the money. Options are used most frequently in securities transactions, although stock options are also used as incentive compensation for key managers.

Instead of exercising options, most investors prefer to buy and sell them in the open market before expiration, cashing in on increases in trading value. One of the interesting features of trading in options is the amount of leverage option buyers enjoy. Buyers put up a relatively small amount of money to control a large amount of common shares, potentially leveraging sizable profits.

Organization for Economic Cooperation and Development (OECD)

An international organization established in 1961 in Paris, France, to act as a global forum to stimulate world trade and economic development.

The OECD's membership consists of the world's developed countries: Australia, Austria, Belgium, Canada, Denmark, Germany, Finland, France, Greece, Iceland, Ireland, Italy, Japan, Luxembourg, the Netherlands, New Zealand, Norway, Portugal, Spain, Sweden, Switzerland, Turkey, the United Kingdom, and the United States. The development of an environment conducive to economic growth of the world's developing countries rests with the OECD.

The OECD replaced the Organization for European Economic Cooperation (OEEC), an organization formed in 1948 to guide the rebuilding of Europe after World War II. (*Source:* L. Presner, *The International Business Dictionary and Reference*, Copyright © 1991 L. Presner. Reprinted by permission of the publisher, John Wiley & Sons, Inc.)

Organization of Petroleum Exporting Countries (OPEC)

The most important international commodity group (ICG) in the world.

OPEC was officially established in Caracas, Venezuela, in 1961. Its headquarters are in Vienna, Austria. OPEC's importance derives from two facts: (1) It has a significant impact on the world price of oil and, subsequently, on the balance of payments of every country; and (2) it is the model of a successful international cartel, which OPEC has demonstrated to developing countries whose economies are primarily (if not exclusively) commodity based.

Impact on the world price of oil. Following the inability of OPEC producer countries and Western oil companies to agree upon a timetable for increasing the world price of oil (after the Tehran Conferences in 1973),

OPEC unilaterally increased the price from U.S. $2.00 per barrel to U.S. $3.40 per barrel in September 1973 and again to U.S. $11.63 per barrel in December 1973.

Further, in 1973, OPEC placed a total embargo against oil shipments to the United States and the Netherlands. The United States was targeted because of its open and (what was perceived as) "flagrantly arrogant" political and military support of Israel in the 1973 war between it and Arab states. The Netherlands was embargoed because of its strategic geographic position: Rotterdam, the world's largest port, is located in Holland at the mouth of the Rhine River. The Port of Rotterdam includes the European Community's largest oil refinery and transshipment complex. It serves not only major downstream European ports, such as The Port of Antwerp, but also is the key international transshipment facility for North America, South America, Africa, and the Middle East.

One effect of OPEC's actions in 1973 (and subsequent price increases in 1975, 1977, 1979, 1980, 1981, and, rising to the "all-time high" of U.S. $42.00 per barrel, 1982) was to drive the non-Western, nonindustrialized, non-oil producing developing countries in Africa, Asia, and Latin America into severe balance of payments deficit positions, with every prospect of them becoming increasingly indebted.

To assist these countries, OPEC created a Special Fund in 1976, which was renamed the OPEC/Fund for International Development (OPEC/FID) in 1980.

Other long-term effects of OPEC's actions were (1) the strategic drive of Western economies to better integrate their political economies and (2) innovations in the field of energy development and utilization, producing more energy-efficient products, thus reducing their dependence on imported oil and, presumably, increasing their political flexibility in their foreign policy activities.

Evidence of the first is shown by the accelerated drive toward economic, monetary, and (ultimately) political integration (and thus interdependence vis-à-vis external dependence) within the European Community. The same movement toward economic and political integration is taking place between Canada and the United States within the framework of the Canada-U.S. Free Trade Act of 1989.

Evidence of the second is found in OPEC's price reduction for oil from the "all-time high" of U.S. $42.00 per barrel in 1982 to an "all-time low" of U.S. $16.00 per barrel in 1988.

One can also adduce, from the reduction of supertanker construction by the Japanese, that Western economies use relatively less oil more efficiently than they did prior to 1973, thus driving the Japanese to reach a diminishing return in the building of very large crude carriers (VLCCs).

In an attempt to emulate the apparent success of OPEC, a number and variety of producer countries have formed international commodity groups (ICGs) with the aim (1) of controlling supply and, thus, (2) of influencing the upward movement of price for a particular commodity.

"Success" can be measured on the basis of the price inelasticity of demand for the commodity in question and, consequently, of the relative lack of substitutes for it, resulting, over time, in a relatively elastic supply response and in an increase in the producer price for it. (*Source:* L. Presner, *The International Business Dictionary and Reference,* Copyright © 1991 L. Presner. Reprinted by permission of the publisher, John Wiley & Sons, Inc.)

organizational buying The decision process that large organizations use to establish a need for *industrial goods* and services and to choose between alternative brands and suppliers.

Organizations purchase goods and services for a variety of reasons not usually seen in the *consumer market,* namely, to make profits, lower costs, and satisfy employee needs. The organizational buying decision is usually made by a group of people. Each member of the group has different responsibilities and brings a different set of criteria to the decision. In addition, each organization has its own set of formal purchasing policies and requirements.

When marketing to an organization, marketers must incorporate all these factors into their strategy.

EXAMPLE: A daily newspaper decides that it could increase profits by computerizing its printing press. Members of the editorial staff, advertising department, and print shop meet to consider several different options. The company that successfully markets its printing press to the newspaper must understand exactly what motivated the purchase decision, the process by which it was made, and the individual concerns of each member of the purchasing committee.

organizational environment The elements in a company's *environment* that affect, and sometimes dictate, its organizational design.

There are two environmental dimensions that can impact a company's organizational structure: static-dynamic and simple-complex.

The static-dynamic dimension of a company's environment describes factors that either change frequently or remain relatively constant over time. For example, a static environment might be a factory that deals with a sales team whose requests for products are fairly constant and a materials department that is routinely able to supply a steady stream of raw materials. However, if the sales team made frequent changes in its requests and the materials department had difficulty supplying raw materials, the factory would be operating in a dynamic environment.

The simple-complex dimension of a company's environment describes whether the decision-making factors in the environment are similar and few in number or different and many in number. For example, a simple environment might be a factory whose decisions are only affected by the sales department, which orders products, and the materials department, which supplies raw materials. A complex environment, on the other hand, might be a programming and planning department that must incorporate a number of different environmental factors, such as suppliers, marketing, or customers, in its decisions.

Currently, most companies operate in a dynamic-complex environment. These environments are characterized by frequent change and involve a great deal of uncertainty for managers. In this type of environment, the appropriate organizational design is vital.

EXAMPLE: When AT&T moved from a static-simple environment to a dynamic-complex environment because of the deregulation of the telephone industry, it shifted from a *functional organizational design* to a much more *decentralized* model in order to cope with the additional competition in the telephone market. This change was motivated by the need to obtain more market information and respond quickly to the actions of competitors.

See also decentralization, functional organizational structure, matrix structure.

	Static	Dynamic
Complex	Fairly low uncertainty ● many environmental factors ● environmental factors are not similar ● environmental factors remain basically the same Example: food products industry	High uncertainty ● many environmental factors ● environmental factors are not similar ● environmental factors are prone to constant change Example: commercial airline industry
Simple	Low uncertainty ● limited number of environmental factors ● environmental factors are similar ● environmental factors remain basically the same Example: soft drink industry	Fairly high uncertainty ● limited number of environmental factors ● environmental factors are similar ● environmental factors are prone to constant change Example: fast-food industry

Organizational Environment

organizational politics Actions that are not a part of a person's formal role within an organization, but that influence the allocation of advantages and disadvantages within the organization.

Political actions might include whistle blowing, spreading rumors, exchanging favors with other members of the organization, or leaking confidential information to the press.

original equipment manufacturer (OEM) The original producer of a product as differentiated from any other element in the *distribution channel.*

A product is manufactured by the OEM but may be purchased from a distributor.

outdoor advertising Any *advertising* on signs located outdoors in public places.

The term is frequently used to describe billboard advertising, but it can include everything from a placard on the side of a bus to a flier tacked to a telephone pole.

outputs A company's finished product.

There are two general types of outputs: products and services. Generally, products are tangible goods, such as a Sony Walkman, whereas services are intangible, such as a dental checkup.

outsourcing The purchase of parts from outside suppliers.

Many American small appliance manufacturers use a great deal of outsourcing. In other words, the various parts and subassemblies for a toaster or blender are manufactured by a number of different companies and are only assembled and sold by the appliance's "manufacturer." When a company is heavily outsourced, it is referred to as "hollow." In most cases, outsourcing is a good idea for relatively standard parts and components, such as nuts and bolts, that are not worth a company's time to produce. When more complex or vital parts are outsourced, there is a risk that suppliers will gain expertise in the production of critical parts, which may lead them to begin producing the finished product. This is exactly what happened in the television industry. As American television manufacturers began relying on Japanese-made components, Japanese firms began to manufacture their own brands. The Japanese television sets were inexpensive and of such high quality that they quickly captured the American market. Today, Japanese companies are the dominant force in the U.S. television market.

outstanding common stock The shares held by stockholders.

*See also **earnings per share, equity**.*

overhead The costs (such as insurance, heat, light, supervision, and maintenance) incurred by a business that cannot be directly linked to the products or services produced.

These costs are usually organized into several groups (such as factory, department, or general overhead) so they can be allocated to various areas of the company.

owners' equity The interest of the owners in the ***assets*** of a company.

Owners' equity is reported on the ***balance sheet*** and includes ***capital*** contributions and ***retained earnings***. *See also **equity**.*

paced line A production line that moves at a specific rate of output.

The classic example of a paced line is an automobile assembly line in which workers install engines, doors, windows, hoods, and so on as a conveyor moves automobiles past various workstations. A line may be operator paced so its speed depends on the proficiency of the operator, or it may be machine paced so its rate of output is determined by machine speeds. Although a paced line does create a smooth production flow, it can create a great deal of boredom and monotony for the work force.

paid-in capital in excess of par value In accounting, the excess amount over *par value* paid for a company's stock, and the value of a company's stock received from shareholders as a donation.

The amount paid by the company to buy back its *treasury stock* is treated as a reduction to paid-in capital.

par value The face value of a security.

For example, the par value of a $1,000 *bond* is $1,000. The interest, or coupon payments, paid on a bond are a percentage of the bond's par value. In other words, a 12 percent bond pays 12 percent of its par value with each coupon payment. In the same manner, the dividends paid on preferred stock are typically a percentage of the stock's par value.

With *common stock,* par value has less meaning. It is generally a set amount (such as $1 per share) used to calculate the dollar value of common shares on a company's *balance sheet.*

The par value of a security has no relation to its market price, which may be significantly higher or lower than par.

parallel trade A form of *countertrade* that involves the execution of two distinct and individually enforceable contracts: the first for the sale of goods by an exporter, the second for the purchase of the goods.

Both contracts are requirements for insurance, and sometimes credit, for each shipment. Parallel trade agreements that involve cash transfers are also known as counterpurchases. In a counterpurchase, the exporter and the buyer each pay the other (against a *letter of credit* or a wire transfer) for the goods received. These cash payments may be denominated in the same currency, or they may both be in the currency used by the party that originates the deal.

participative design *See concurrent engineering*

PBO *See projected benefit obligation*

P/E ratio *See price/earnings ratio*

penetrated market Those customers who have already purchased a product.

Knowing the penetrated market allows a marketer to gauge its position against its competitors. The penetrated market is not usually the object of a major marketing effort, but it can be an important element in a campaign to build loyalty to a particular company or product. The penetrated market might be illustrated in the following manner:

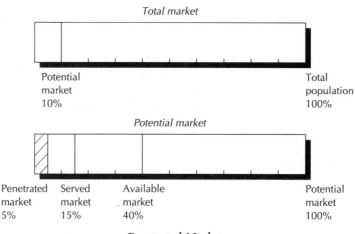

Penetrated Market

*See also **available market, potential market, served market**.*

penetration pricing In marketing, a pricing strategy in which the initial price is set at a low level in order to generate the greatest possible demand for the product.

Marketers use this strategy with the expectation that a low price will lead to such high volume that total profits will prove greater than those they could achieve with a higher initial price. The objective of penetration pricing is to reach the entire market rather than just those people willing to pay a higher price for a new product.

Marketers often use penetration pricing when the market is not divided into price segments—when, that is, there is no "elite" market willing to pay a high price. That means the strategy is appropriate for products that do not symbolize high status or when the market is not price sensitive.

EXAMPLE: Paramount Pictures released the home videocassette of *An Officer and a Gentleman* at $39.95, substantially less than the standard $59.95 to $79.95 price tag for a hit movie. The cassette took off and sold 80,000 copies at a time when 25,000 copies was the videocassette equivalent of a gold record.

Marketers also use penetration pricing in situations where competitors can enter rapidly and drive the price down. Finally, penetration pricing can prove effective when the company has large-scale production plants that can reap the benefits of *economies of scale*.

The strategy, though, has its downside. Marketers can never assume that their market position is secure—even when they offer an attractive low price. Just after Paramount came out with its $39.95 price, for instance, Warner Bros. released *Risky Business* at $39.98 and MCA offered *Jaws III* at a similar price. In fact, a low price often results in losses during a product's launch, when it is still gaining consumer acceptance. In addition, with a low-price strategy, marketers don't reach the *breakeven* point until they sell a larger quantity. For that reason, penetration is inherently more risky than high-price strategies. *Compare to perceived-value pricing, skimming, target return pricing*.

penny stocks Stocks of young public companies that are not listed on any stock exchange and typically trade at a very low price, ranging from under $1 a share to as high as $10 a share (usually a result of heavy promotions following an initial offering).

Penny stocks do not sell for pennies. Companies issuing penny stocks have not yet developed into stable businesses with established track records of sales and profits. They have not yet met what the accounting profession calls a "going-concern" standard.

Penny stocks trade in over-the-counter markets, many in Denver, Salt Lake City, or Vancouver, which have traditionally been hot penny stock markets for speculative oil, gas, and gold-mining stocks.

pension fund The money set aside by an employer to meet the obligations of a pension plan.

Pension funds are administered by trustees who actually pay the retirement benefits. *See also defined benefit pension plan, defined contribution pension plan*.

pension plan A contract in which an employer agrees to provide retirement benefits to employees.

Accounting for a pension plan involves the recognition of both the *projected benefit obligation* and the cost of funding those benefits. *See also defined benefit pension plan, defined contribution pension plan*.

perceived-value pricing A pricing approach based on the buyers' perception of value rather than the seller's costs.

The key to perceived-value pricing is to estimate accurately the consumer's understanding of the product's or service's value.

EXAMPLE: In a hair salon, the actual cost of providing a shampoo and haircut is low. Many upscale salons, however, realize that their customers perceive a good haircut as very valuable. So they commonly charge high prices that reflect the value the customer places on the haircut rather than the costs the salon incurs.

percentage-of-completion method A method of accounting for the costs and *revenues* of a long-term construction project.

Percentage-of-completion should be used when there is a reliable way to measure a project's degree of completion. Many companies involved in long-term projects prefer the percentage-of-completion method because it gives a realistic estimate of the expenses incurred and the *revenues* earned at any particular time. (*See also* **matching concept.**) Additionally, it spreads earnings over the entire span of a project, rather than declaring them all at its beginning or end. The measure of revenue to be recognized at any particular point is calculated by multiplying the percentage completed by the contract price:

$$\text{Percentage completed} \times \text{Contract price}$$

EXAMPLE: A construction company is building a bridge for $3 million over three years. The revenue recognized after the first year of construction would be calculated as follows:

$$33\% \times \$3,000,000 = \$1,000,000$$

Rather than using milestone dates to measure a project's completeness, many companies divide the costs incurred to date by the total estimated costs.

$$\frac{\text{Cost incurred to date}}{\text{Total estimated costs}}$$

Say the construction company estimates that the entire bridge will cost $2,000,000. At the end of the first year, the company has spent $900,000:

$$\frac{\$900,000}{\$2,000,000} = 0.45, \text{ or } 45\%$$

By measuring costs, the project is now 45 percent completed, so the construction company would declare revenue of

$$45\% \times \$3,000,000 = \$1,350,000$$

percentage-of-sales In marketing, a method of setting promotion expenditures based on a fixed percentage of past or predicted sales.

This technique is popular, because it directly relates expenditures to sales. For example, a company that expects to do $10 million worth of business in the next year and decides to allocate 3 percent of sales to advertising would have a $300,000 advertising budget. Many marketers, however, discount this method as a classic case of putting the cart before the horse. The reason? It is based on the premise that advertising is the direct result of sales, rather than on the more conventional wisdom, which states that sales are the direct result of advertising.

perfect competition In economics, a market that is so competitive that all its participants have virtually no control over the price.

They must act as price takers, buying and selling at the price determined by the forces of supply and demand. Such a market has the following characteristics: (1) a very large number of relatively small buyers and sellers, (2) easy entry into and exit from the market, (3) a standardized product (i.e., no product differentiation), and (4) complete information about the market price.

Good examples of perfectly competitive markets can be found in the agricultural sector of the economy. Corn, wheat, beef, pork bellies, and soybeans are all markets in which prices are determined primarily by the forces of supply and demand. The markets for foreign exchange, stocks, bonds, and certain precious metals are also perfectly competitive. However, some economists argue that certain large traders in these markets may from time to time exercise a strong influence over the price simply by trading or withholding from the market large amounts of their holdings of these financial products.

performance bond A third-party guarantee, ensuring that specific actions or payments will take place as scheduled.

A surety bond issued by a surety insurance company is the most common form of performance bond, especially for construction companies. Other guarantors include the Small Business Administration (which guarantees payment of SBA approved loans), Eximbank (which guarantees payment by foreign buyers of export orders), commercial banks (which guarantee performance against an export letter of credit or standby letters of credit against deliveries), and individuals (who guarantee payment of bank loans of small companies or other individuals).

periodic inventory review system A method of reordering inventory based on reviews conducted at equal time intervals; also called a fixed period review system.

In these systems, the reorder *point* is fixed, but the reorder *quantity* varies. Periodic review systems are most appropriate in situations where it is difficult to track inventory and the cost of *stockouts* or safety stock is not too high. Retailers frequently use periodic inventory reviews when ordering families of products. The amount to be reordered is calculated by subtracting on-hand and on-order inventory from the maximum inventory level and then adding the expected demand over the lead time for delivery.

$$\text{Reorder quantity} = \text{Maximum inventory} - \text{On-hand inventory}$$
$$- \text{On-order inventory} + \text{Demand over lead time}$$

On-hand inventory is the amount that is currently in stock. In situations where *backorders* are allowed, on-hand inventory can be negative. On-order inventory is the amount that has been purchased but has not yet been delivered. This amount is deducted to ensure that an order is not placed for the same merchandise. Demand over the lead time for the inventory is added because it is expected that a number of units will sell (and need to be replaced) between the time an order is placed and when it is actually delivered.

perpetuity *See annuity*

personal communications channels A framework for directing a sales effort to an individual.

Personal communications channels take three forms: (1) advocate channels, where company salespeople directly contact buyers in the target market, as in telemarketing; (2) expert channels, where people who have no association with a company but have knowledge and expertise about a particular product communicate with target buyers, such as a golf pro advising golfers about which clubs to buy; and (3) social channels, where family, friends, and neighbors talk with potential buyers in the target market. Identifying the personal communications channels in a *target market* and turning them into channels for marketing is important to marketers, because one-on-one communication has a greater impact than a nonpersonal advertising message.

personal consumption expenditures Estimate of total consumer spending.

Consumer spending constitutes the largest of the major components of GDP, typically equal to between 60 and 65 percent. There are three major categories within personal consumption expenditures.

Spending for *durable goods* refers to purchases of goods with a useful life of more than three years, such as motor vehicles, furniture, and appliances. Because these goods are long-lasting and generally expensive, their purchase can be postponed in times of economic uncertainty. Thus, consumption of durable goods tends to be the most cyclical portion of consumer spending.

Spending for **nondurable goods** includes purchases of food, apparel, gasoline, and heating oil. Because these goods are in the form of necessities, consumer spending for them is less cyclical than for durable goods.

The largest component of consumer spending, accounting for about half of the total, is spending on *services*. Services include housing, household operations (including utilities), transportation, and medical care. Spending on housing includes both the actual rent that renters pay and an imputed amount that homeowners implicitly make to themselves on the principle that they are *consuming* housing just as much as renters. (Note: New home purchases are treated as an investment under *residential construction*. The use a person derives from living in a house is properly classed as consumption.)

PERT   *See program evaluation and review technique*

PIMS   *See profit impact of market strategies*

pink sheets   A market for the trading of unlisted small-company common stock.

Smaller public companies that can't qualify for the NASDAQ, as well as many that do qualify but choose to avoid NASDAQ regulations, are listed on the so-called "pink sheet." Pink sheet stock trades are negotiated by phone among brokers rather than quoted electronically. A private company, the National Quotation Bureau, Inc., of Jersey City, NJ, prints a daily circular on pink paper (hence "pink sheets") that lists price quotes and brokerage firms trading in about 16,000 over-the-counter stocks (11,000 of which are not listed on NASDAQ).

Pink sheets are sold to brokers on subscription only and are not distributed to the general public. This reduces market coverage and makes it more difficult for potential investors to research these companies or obtain current price information without going through a broker. Furthermore, pink sheet prices are not market prices. They are paid advertisements by brokerage firms who want other brokers to see that they are willing to buy or sell specific securities.

Far fewer regulations govern pink sheet stocks than those listed on the NASDAQ. The National Quotation Bureau requires that listing brokers be registered with the SEC and that the traded securities be either registered or exempt from registration. Only one market-maker is needed to get a stock listed. Volume must be reported only when single-day trades total more than $10,000 or 50,000 shares. Furthermore, the Bureau does not require asset or shareholder equity minimums. Shares listed on pink sheets are generally referred to as **penny stocks.**

Shares from both new and established companies trade off pink sheets for several reasons:

- Although these companies may have been in business for a while, for one reason or another they have encountered obstacles to the development of market niches or profitability records sufficient to attract the level of investor attention necessary to drive up share prices.

- Small companies that previously were closely held might go public with a small percentage of shares, raising capital for a specific purpose with little concern for ongoing trading values.

- Shares of companies in a state of change, as in a turnaround mode, may also be listed on pink sheets while they work out their financial difficulties.

planning horizon The amount of time the *master production schedule* extends into the future.

plant within a plant (PWP) A manufacturing strategy to improve productivity and management control by establishing independent business units within a larger plant.

point-of-purchase (POP) advertising A type of *advertising* designed to trigger impulse purchases through the use of eye-catching, attractive displays at the location where customers buy the product.

Many magazines and tabloid newspapers, for example, employ point-of-purchase advertising by positioning their display racks at the checkout counters of grocery stores. Point-of-purchase advertising can include window and counter displays, free-standing end-of-aisle displays, and banners. Usually, manufacturers distribute these displays to *wholesalers* or *retailers* that sell the manufacturer's products. Manufacturers often discount their merchandise to compensate retailers for giving up valuable floor or shelf space by installing a point-of-purchase display.

pooling of interests A method of accounting for a business combination.

Under the pooling of interests method, the *assets* and *liabilities* of a newly acquired subsidiary are combined with those of the parent at their *book value.* Essentially, the pooling method assumes that the two companies combined their financial resources in order to continue operations in the same manner as before the combination. Twelve conditions must be satisfied in order to employ the pooling of interest method in a business combination. If those conditions are met, the pooling method must be used. If any of the conditions are not met, the business combination must be accounted for by the *purchase method.* The 12 conditions are as follows:

1. Each company must be autonomous and not have been a subsidiary of another company within the two years preceding the combination.

2. Each company must be independent (that is, each company may not own more than 10 percent of another combining company's *common stock*).

3. The combination must take place in a single transaction, or within one year.

4. The parent company must issue voting common stock in exchange for substantially all (90 percent or more) of the common stock of the subsidiary.

5. Neither company may change *equity* interest in voting common stock in anticipation of the combination for the two years preceding the transaction.

6. Each company may repurchase voting shares of common stock only for purposes other than the business combination.

7. The ownership interest of each individual stockholder must remain the same.

8. Stockholders' voting rights may not be restricted.

9. The combination may not be contingent on the issuance of other securities or considerations.

10. The parent company may not retire or reacquire any of the voting shares issued in the combination.

11. The parent company may not make any financial arrangements (such as a loan secured by the stock issued in the combination) for the benefit of the subsidiary's former shareholders.

12. The combined company may not dispose of a significant part of the acquired *assets* (with the exception of duplicated facilities) within two years of the combination.

Most companies prefer the pooling method for two reasons. First, the subsidiary's assets are all transferred to the parent's financial statements at their *book value*, which allows the parent to match lower *depreciation* expenses with the revenues generated by the combined companies. This allows a company to report more revenue on the income statement than when a combination is effected under the *purchase method,* which results in larger *depreciation* expenses because the subsidiary's assets must be declared at fair market value. Second, pooling of interests does not involve *goodwill*, which, when generated by the purchase method, must be *amortized* over a period not to exceed 40 years. Finally, companies prefer the pooling method because it combines the retained earnings of the two companies as if they had always been a single entity. In other words, a company with a poor earnings record can improve its financial standing by combining with a company with a good earnings record. This can result in financial statements that show consistent earnings growth and attractive *debt-to-equity* and *dividend payout* ratios. *See also purchase method.*

portfolio analysis   *See growth/market share matrix*

potential market   In marketing, those consumers who have an interest in a product.

In the case of baby formula, the *market* consists of the parents of all infants, but the potential market is limited to parents who have decided to consider alternatives to breast feeding. *See also **available market, penetrated market, served market.***

power   The ability to motivate someone to do something that they would not otherwise do.

For example, if a factory foreman sends a memo to the production manager showing that the company can save $10,000 annually by purchasing new packaging equipment, and the manager acts on the information by ordering the new equipment, the foreman has exerted power over the manager in that the manager has taken action that would not otherwise have been taken.

There are five generally accepted bases of power: legitimate, reward, coercive, expert, and referent. Different situations require the exercise of different types of power. For this reason, it is important that managers be familiar with each type of power and its potential applications.

Legitimate power, also called position power, is associated with a manager's position within a particular corporate hierarchy. For example, a company president has more legitimate power than a vice-president, who in turn has more legitimate power than a department manager. When followers respond to legitimate power, their actions are motivated by the manager's position, and not any personality-related factors such as the manager's knowledge, expertise, or past performance.

Reward power is based on the expectations of employees. For example, in many companies, employees who comply with all company rules and policies and receive positive performance appraisals receive annual salary raises. Rewards are not always financial, or even controlled by managers. In some cases, a particularly well-liked co-worker is able to exert reward power by simply maintaining friendly relations with other workers.

Coercive power is based on fear. It exists when employees believe that a manager has the ability, and the inclination, to punish them. In a corporate setting, coercive power can take the form of demotion, discipline, punishment, discharge, or pay reductions. In most cases, coercive power is used only in matters where every other type of power has failed. This is because extensive use of coercion leads to distrust and fear.

Expert power is based on competence. A manager who is widely perceived as able to analyze, implement, and guide the set of tasks assigned to a particular work group will frequently have expert power.

Referent power is based on the degree to which an employee identifies with a manager. Referent power is also called charismatic power. When a manager has referent power, employees follow requests or orders simply because this particular manager has asked them. The underlying factors that affect referent power include trust, affection, similarity, and acceptance.

PR   *See **public relations***

preference segmentation In marketing, a segmentation of the market according to consumer preference, such as levels of sweetness and spiciness in chicken wings.

Three patterns—homogeneous, diffuse, and clustered—can emerge from this type of segmentation. Homogeneous preference segments group the entire market around a particular value, such as medium spiciness and sweetness in chicken wings. Diffuse preference segments show no such grouping pattern but indicate preferences within a wide range of the product's characteristics. Clustered preference segments divide the market into several distinct groups, such as consumers who prefer mild, medium, or spicy chicken wings. By knowing the market's preference segments, the chicken wing company can tailor its product to appeal to the segments it wishes to target.

preferred stock A type of *capital stock* that gives its holders preference over common stockholders in the distribution of earnings or rights to the *assets* of a company in the event of liquidation.

Preferred stock usually pays a set *dividend.* For example, a 5 percent preferred stock pays a dividend that equals 5 percent of the total par value of outstanding shares. Preferred stocks generally do not have any voting rights.

Preferred stock may also carry a variety of features. It may be callable by the company, dividends may be cumulative, common stock warrants may be attached, or it may be convertible to common stock (*see convertible security*) under certain conditions, to mention only a few variations.

prepaid expense In accounting, an expenditure that is paid for, but not completely used or consumed at the end of an *accounting period.*

Prepaid expenses are reported as *current assets* on the *balance sheet* and could include advertising, insurance, and real-estate taxes.

present value The current value of a future payment or stream of payments.

Present value is calculated by applying a discount (capitalization) rate to the future payment(s). If $100 were invested today at 10 percent interest, compounded annually, for a period of 10 years, its present value would be approximately $38.55.

The present value method forms the cornerstone of business or equity interest valuations (*see equity interest valuation*) and is also referred to as the "discounted cash flow method" or the "discounted earnings method." It is widely used by companies and investors to determine the fair market value of a potential investment. Although it is extremely time-consuming to calculate present value manually, annuity tables, programmable calculators, and computer programs make the calculations easy and fast.

present value of an annuity A method of measuring the value of the cash flows from an *annuity* in current dollars.

Basically, the present value of an annuity is the total payment that would have to be made today in order to equal the annuity.

press release A prepared statement that is distributed to the media.

Press releases can be used for any number of situations, from the hiring of a new employee to the introduction of a new product.

pretesting The testing of the copy, design, research, marketing strategy, or any other part of an advertising campaign before its launch.

There are three broad methods of pretesting. The first is direct rating, in which a group of consumers is shown a series of ads and asked to rate them. A high rating does not guarantee an ad's success, but it does suggest that it may prove effective. In portfolio tests, consumers take as long as they want to look at a series of advertisements. Then they are asked to recall individual ads and their content. Their level of recall is an indicator of an ad's ability to stand out and communicate its message. The third method, laboratory testing, uses complicated equipment to measure consumers' physiological reactions, such as changes in blood pressure, heartbeat and perspiration, to advertisements.

price controls The use of the powers of the government to keep the price either above or below its equilibrium point.

When the government tries to keep the price of a product above equilibrium, it is said to be establishing a "price floor." Examples of a price floor can be found in the government farm subsidies programs. By either paying farmers not to use a certain amount of their land or by buying up the surplus that results from a price floor, the government helps to keep the market price above its equilibrium level.

When the government tries to keep the price of a product below its equilibrium level, it is said to establish a price ceiling. There were several situations in which the U.S. government exercised price controls in this manner during this century. During World War II, the prices of a number of essential goods were subject to price ceilings. During the second half of 1971 and part of 1972, the government established various degrees of price controls over certain goods and services. In both situations, the intent was to control or prevent inflation in the aggregate economy.

price/earnings (P/E) ratio A measure of a company's investment potential.

Literally, a P/E ratio is how much a share is worth per dollar of earnings. The price-earnings ratio is calculated as follows:

$$\frac{\text{Market price per common share}}{\text{Primary earnings per common share}}$$

A company's P/E ratio depends on investors' perceptions of a company's potential. Factors such as risk, quality of management, growth potential, earnings history, and industry conditions all come into play. *See also **common stock equivalent, complex capital structure, earnings per share, simple capital structure.***

price elasticity of demand   The effect that price changes have on sales.

Price elasticity is calculated by dividing the percent change in quantity demanded by the percent change in price. Past sales figures are usually used to estimate price elasticity.

$$\frac{\% \text{ change in quantity demanded (sales)}}{\% \text{ change in price}}$$

EXAMPLE: A watchmaker sells 100 watches a year for $1,000 each, which gives him an annual income of $100,000. If he raises the price of the watches by 4 percent to $1,040 and sells only 80 watches—that is, demand drops 20 percent—the price elasticity for the watches is −5 (−20 divided by 4) and he makes only $83,200. If demand falls by 4 percent with the same price increase—that is, 96 watches sell for $1,040 each—the price elasticity is −1 (−4 divided by 4) and the watchmaker's income is essentially unchanged. If demand falls by 2 percent with a 4 percent price hike—that is, 98 watches sell for $1,040 each—the price elasticity is $-\frac{1}{2}$ (−2 divided by 4) and the watchmaker makes $101,920. This state is called inelastic demand. The more inelastic the demand, the more the seller can make by increasing the price.

Three factors affect the price elasticity of demand for a product: (1) Other products can be substituted for it—the more alternatives there are, the more price elastic the product tends to be; (2) the product is a necessity—in that case, it tends to be price inelastic, since price doesn't matter to the buyer; and (3) the price of the product is a significant portion of the buyer's budget, which means demand for that product tends to be more price elastic. Cars and houses, then, are price elastic, whereas small, routine purchases, such as canned peaches and cereal, are less so.

primary data   In marketing, information gathered specifically for the purpose of the research project.

EXAMPLE: A bank that is researching customer satisfaction gives a questionnaire to each customer to fill out while he or she is waiting for a teller. The results of those questionnaires would be the study's primary data since it was uniquely collected for the purpose of the study. *Compare to **secondary data.***

prime rate   The interest rate established by ***money center banks*** as a measuring base against which to calculate customer interest charges.

Banks define prime rate as the rate of interest charged to their best commercial customers. Banks also claim that this rate is based on a complicated cost formula that takes into account the cost of money (interest it pays out), bank operating expenses (salaries, supplies, telephone, etc.), and housing expense (rent, depreciation, and so on).

Theoretically, the sum of these costs, plus a reasonable profit margin, equals prime rate. In practice, however, it doesn't work that way. Instead, money center banks establish a fictitious interest rate called prime, based on what the traffic will bear. All correspondent banks around the country then follow suit, regardless of what their respective cost structures may be. Obviously it doesn't cost a bank in rural Wyoming as much to operate as a bank in midtown Manhattan. Yet they both use the same prime measure to establish interest rates.

Contrary to popular opinion, the Federal Reserve Bank does *not* set the prime rate. It has nothing to do with it. Prime rate is entirely the making of money center banks.

private-label A product manufactured by a supplier and sold by a retailer under its own store or company brand.

The "Ann Page" line of products sold at A & P Food Stores, for example, are actually made by several different manufacturers. When a retailer contracts with a manufacturer for a private-label product, it usually places a large order. That fact makes private labeling attractive to most manufacturers, but it can have drawbacks. First, a manufacturer has no control over the advertising, package design, and brands under which its products will be sold. Second, when competitors lower their prices, a manufacturer may lose profits on its own products by continuing to produce at the required volume for the private label. Finally, if the manufacturer produces its own brand, it can be expensive to maintain separate inventories in both packaging materials and finished goods.

private placements and limited exempt offerings Procedures that permit a company to issue stock without filing a registration statement.

Exempt offerings generally fall into one of two categories: a private placement, or a limited offering. It should be noted that these are exemptions from the Securities Act of 1933—a federal law—and do not necessarily apply under the securities laws of all 50 states. In most cases, however, states that do require formal registrations generally have more lenient requirements than the SEC.

Private placements are used to raise a limited amount of equity capital in a relatively short period of time at the least cost. Because private placements are exempt offerings, issuing and ongoing costs are substantially less than public offerings. Although federal antifraud securities regulations must still be complied with, companies do not have to file formal registration statements.

In addition to cost savings, private placements enable a company to raise equity capital when

- The economic or market timing for an effective public offering may be way off.

- The company might not have two or three years of steadily increasing earnings (usually required to make a successful public offering).

- It is desirable to make use of the more lenient public disclosure requirements to keep company skeletons buried.

Investors in private placements may be relatives, friends, business associates, or strangers. An underwriter is usually necessary unless personal contacts with ready cash to invest can be attracted. Certain brokers specialize in keeping tabs on private investors anxious to make equity investments in closely held companies.

privately held company A company whose ownership shares—unlike *publicly held companies*—are not publicly traded.

Privately held companies come in a variety of business forms, including corporations, partnerships, proprietorships, limited partners, joint ventures, and limited liability corporations.

The accounting principles for privately held companies are identical to those for public companies with one exception: The reporting requirements from regulatory agencies such as the **Securities and Exchange Commission** and public stock exchanges do not apply to them. Privately held companies do not have to disclose full *financial statements* to the public at large, but they do make them available to lending institutions, private investors (such as venture capital funds and limited partners), and, in some instances, state regulatory agencies. *Compare to **publicly held company.***

pro forma In accounting, a *financial statement* in which the amounts stated are fully or partially estimates; from the Latin for "as a matter of form."

For example, a company making a **change in accounting principle** must prepare pro forma financial statements estimating what the previous year's earnings would have been if the new principle had been in use. Usually, companies also disclose the underlying assumptions of any pro forma statement.

process control In manufacturing, a feedback mechanism that continually monitors and corrects a process.

Process control is the activity of monitoring a process, receiving feedback on the performance of that process, and providing corrective action if a deviation becomes unacceptable. It is a feedback system that continuously monitors and corrects. The home thermostat is a process control device.

product attributes In marketing, the characteristics that describe a product.

Marketers must create a fit between a product's attributes and the needs or desires of the target market.

EXAMPLE: In shampoo marketing, attributes such as cleaning ability and fragrance might matter most to the **target market.** In order to successfully sell a shampoo in this market, it must have at least these attributes rather than an attractive package, an extra-conditioning formula, or even a low price.

Consumers vary in the attributes that matter to them and will pay more attention to a product that has the attributes that address their needs. Frequently, the market for a product can be segmented according to the product attributes that are important to different groups of consumers.

product, augmented The additional elements or attributes over and above those the consumer expects that *differentiate* a product from its competitors and make it more attractive.

EXAMPLE: Travelers purchasing a hotel room expect a comfortable bed and a clean bathroom. Effective marketing augments these elements by adding such features as fresh-cut flowers, access to computers and FAX machines, bed turndown service at night, complimentary newspapers, and express checkout in the morning. These valued additional features provide a *competitive advantage* for the hotel. Each augmentation, however, soon becomes an expectation. Strategically, the hotel must continually offer new and different product aspects if it is to maintain its differentiation.

See also *product, core; product, tangible.*

product concept The way in which a product is positioned to be perceived by consumers.
Any product can generate several product concepts.

EXAMPLE: A cosmetics company that develops a new skin cream has several options for its product concept. It might position the skin cream as (1) a soothing lotion for men to use after shaving, (2) a moisturizing night cream for women, or (3) a baby lotion that keeps an infant's skin from chafing. Each different concept results in a different *target market,* different competitors, and a different marketing strategy. By analyzing the marketing strategies of each product concept, the company can move forward and design a marketing plan for the final product.

product, core The main need or want that is fulfilled with a purchase.
The core product of a hotel is a good night's sleep; of an automotive company, transportation; and of a diet center, weight loss. See also *product, augmented; product, tangible.*

product life-cycle The process by which a product enters, grows, saturates, and leaves a market.
The product life-cycle usually consists of four stages: introduction, growth, maturity, and decline. Each phase of a product's life-cycle demands a different marketing approach.

In the introduction phase, sales are slow and profit is nonexistent, so a marketing strategy might rely on heavy advertising and promotions in order to create product awareness and stimulate sales.

EXAMPLE: When Basel Pharmaceuticals introduced Habitrol, its brand of transdermal nicotine patches that reduce the craving for cigarettes by delivering nicotine through the skin, it created a very visible advertising campaign. The ads feature photographs of determined-looking people wearing a nicotine patch and bear the headline "Portrait of a quitter." The *body copy* goes on to explain exactly what the product is and how it works. Basel's entire campaign is designed to stimulate product awareness.

During the growth phase, both sales and profits dramatically improve and the marketing focus shifts; the company may continue to advertise heavily while phasing out *sales promotions.* Advertising in the growth phase becomes increasingly focused on creating brand preference.

EXAMPLE: As the market for mountain bikes has mushroomed in recent years, brands such as Specialized, Diamond Back, and Trek have all mounted aggressive advertising campaigns to create brand demand.

The maturity stage is marked by flattening sales and stabilizing, then decreasing, profits. The marketing strategy for a mature product might concentrate on taking away market share from competitors, primarily through price reduction strategies.

EXAMPLE: As technology has improved, pocket calculator manufacturers, such as Casio, Texas Instruments, and Hewlett Packard, have all aggressively reduced their prices in order to gain market share.

A product enters decline when sales start to fall. An appropriate strategy for this stage might be to stop marketing to smaller market segments and further reduce the product's price. Alternatively, marketers can look globally to find new *target markets.*

EXAMPLE: As more and more people quit smoking (perhaps thanks to the nicotine patch) cigarette marketers must concentrate their efforts on different markets. Many companies, for example, now market their products overseas, where limits on cigarette advertising are not as great as in the United States.

*See also **market life-cycle.***

product maturity Typically, the longest phase in the *product life-cycle,* also called *market saturation.*

Many of the products on the market today are in the maturity phase. Examples include soft drinks, cigarettes, automobiles, and fast-food restaurants. So most marketing management must deal with the mature product.

Marketers divide product maturity into three phases: growth maturity, stable maturity, and decaying maturity. The growth phase is marked by sales increases, but is accompanied by a declining growth rate and a lack of new *distribution channels.* A candy company that distributes its chocolates to all the grocery stores in the country and sees a slow drop in sales increases is in this phase. In the stable phase, per-capita sales are level, and future sales are most strongly affected by population growth and replacement demand. In the decaying phase, the absolute level of sales declines as consumers move on to other products. In the case of the candy company, decaying maturity might appear years down the road when a new low-calorie chocolate product enters the market and starts to capture the company's customers.

Marketers employ two broad strategies—market modification and product modification—for a mature product: In modifying the market, a company seeks to either increase the number of users or increase the rate at which the product is used. There are three ways a company can increase the number of users of its brand:

1. It can enter new market segments.

EXAMPLE: When the market for Johnson & Johnson's No More Tears baby shampoo began to mature, the company promoted the shampoo to adult users.

2. It can challenge a competitor and attempt to take its customers.

EXAMPLE: A highly visible example of this strategy is the back-and-forth battle between Pepsi and Coke. Both companies are constantly attempting to woo away the other's customers.

3. It can try to convert nonusers.

EXAMPLE: The overnight air freight industry has grown by finding new users and proving to them that air freight has benefits that other forms of transportation don't.

There are also three ways to increase customer usage of a brand.

1. Develop new uses for a product.

EXAMPLE: Arm & Hammer successfully used this strategy by promoting its baking soda as a refrigerator deodorizer as well as a cooking ingredient.

2. Encourage more frequent use.

EXAMPLE: Cereal manufacturers might try to position their products as snack food as well as breakfast food.

3. Encourage more usage per occasion.

EXAMPLE: This strategy can be seen on the side of almost any shampoo bottle where the manufacturer encourages two applications rather than one.

A marketer can use three approaches—feature improvement, style improvement, and quality improvement—to modify a product. Feature improvement aims to expand a product's convenience, flexibility, safety, or some other product attribute.

EXAMPLE: Automobile manufacturers have developed antilock brakes, automatic transmission, and power locks in order to attract new customers. The chief drawback to this strategy, however, is that new features are easily imitated by competitors. Unless there is a clear advantage to being first on the market with a new feature, the strategy may not prove effective.

Style improvement attempts to increase sales by increasing a product's aesthetic appeal. This approach has the potential to create a strong identity for a product, but determining which customers will like a new style and which will dislike it and move to another product is difficult. Quality improvement attempts to attract customers by boosting a product's performance. As long as the company can actually improve quality (a toothpaste that cleans better has probably improved its quality more than one that has "a fresh new minty taste"), this strategy often proves effective in revitalizing a mature product. *See also* **market life-cycle, product life-cycle.**

product mix The combination of various products that a given company offers to the market.

EXAMPLE: General Foods' product mix includes coffee, desserts, cereals, household products, pet foods, and other grocery products. Within the product mix are broad groups of products, called product lines, that are similar in terms of use or characteristics. Each of General Foods' product mix members would represent a separate product line.

Product mixes differ in the number of product lines they contain. If a mix includes a large number of product lines (coffee, desserts, cereals, and so forth), it is called wide or broad. If it contains only a few product lines, it is considered narrow or limited. The width of the product mix is also known as the variety, and the depth of the mix is called the assortment.

EXAMPLE: Gaines Meal, Gaines Biscuits, Gaines Bits, and Gaines Variety constitute the assortment of dog foods that General Foods offers. A marketer can focus on changing an existing product line, on adding and deleting items from the product mix, or on changing the assortment it offers.

product positioning The competitive strategy of a company, its product, and its offer in the chosen *target market*.

EXAMPLE: A perfume manufacturer might position its product as the rarest and most exotic scent in the world. This positioning is affected by all elements of the *marketing mix.* The perfume must be made from exotic ingredients, packaged in a beautiful bottle, and given an appropriate name, say Black Orchid. In order to enhance its image of rarity, the manufacturer should then distribute it in small amounts to exclusive boutiques. All the advertising for Black Orchid would emphasize its exotic qualities and precious ingredients. Finally, it would have to carry a high price tag, as befits a scent made of the rarest ingredients on earth. This product positioning would give Black Orchid a cachet that its competitors could not easily match.

product, tangible The physical attributes (such as quality, packaging, and taste) of a product.

EXAMPLE. In the case of the Slim-Fast diet drink, the core product the company is marketing is weight loss. However, the tangible product being marketed is a drink that comes in chocolate, vanilla, and strawberry flavors and serves as a meal substitute for people who want to lose weight.

See also *product, core; product, augmented.*

production function In economics, the relationship between a firm's inputs and its output.

The "short-run" production function relates a firm's variable inputs to output while keeping at least one of its inputs fixed. As additional amounts of these variable inputs are added to the production process, the firm eventually encounters the law of diminishing returns.

In the long run, a firm is free to change all of its inputs. As it increases all of its inputs a firm may encounter increasing returns to scale, constant returns to scale, or decreasing returns to scale. In the first situation, the output increases by a greater proportion than the increase in the firm's inputs. In the second situation, the output increases by the same proportion. In the third situation, the output increases by a smaller proportion than the inputs. The reasons for these relationships are noted in the definition of economies of scale. (*See economies of scale.*)

production plan The formal statement of a company's production strategy.

A production plan is distinct from an *aggregate plan* in that it frequently deals with specific products or families of products. Production plans usually detail a company's expected resource requirements, labor requirements, changes in inventories, capacity limitations, and changes in the rate of production.

productivity A type of *efficiency* measure calculated by dividing a company's *output* by worker hours.

$$\frac{\text{Output}}{\text{Worker hours}} = \text{Productivity}$$

There are two ways to increase a company's productivity: increase outputs or decrease worker hours. Of course, productivity would be increased by doing both simultaneously.

It is also possible to use other measures of productivity, simply by using a different denominator. For example, capital productivity is calculated by dividing outputs by dollars invested. Materials productivity is calculated by dividing outputs by inventory dollars. Equipment productivity is calculated by dividing outputs by machine hours. Energy productivity is calculated by dividing outputs by kilowatt-hours. Each of these is considered a partial factor measure of productivity and serves to highlight a particular area of management concern.

When more than one factor is used, such as labor and inventory, the resulting measure is called multifactor productivity. In analyzing multifactor productivity, it is important to measure each factor in the same unit, such as dollars. When all factors (labor, capital, materials, equipment, and energy) are used, the resulting measure is called total factor productivity. This measure is frequently used in making productivity comparisons, such as those between companies or between time periods. *See also efficiency.*

profit center A separate unit or department within a company that is responsible for its own costs, revenues, and thus profit.

Profit center managers are generally free to make their own decisions regarding key issues such as price, marketing, and product positioning. *See also management control systems.*

profit impact of market strategies (PIMS) A database designed to connect the performance of different business units with the characteristics of their respective markets (such as total size or growth) and measures of their strategies (such as market share, R & D expenditures, advertising expenditures, breadth of product line, quality, and *vertical integration*).

PIMS analysis can be used in a variety of situations, including estimating the value of a company's shares in different competitive situations, the likely returns due to different strategic actions, and the impact of *vertical integration* on long-term profitability.

profit margin In accounting, the ratio of income to sales.

There are two types of profit margin: *gross profit* margin and net profit margin. Gross profit margin shows the percentage return that a company is earning over the cost of the merchandise sold. It is calculated by dividing gross profit (sales less cost of goods sold) by total sales.

$$\frac{\text{Gross profit}}{\text{Sales}}$$

The gross profit generated by a company is used to cover operating expenses such as selling and administrative expenses, taxes, and interest.

Net profit margin (also called return on sales) shows the percentage of net income generated by each sales dollar. It is calculated by dividing the income statement figure for net income after tax by total sales.

$$\frac{\text{Net income after tax}}{\text{Sales}}$$

The net profit generated by a company may be held to support future operations or distributed to stockholders.

program evaluation and review technique (PERT) A method of project scheduling and control first developed in the late 1950s by the U.S. Navy with the Lockheed Corporation and Booz-Allen Hamilton for the Polaris missile project.

PERT is very similar to the *critical path method (CPM)* in that it is a visual control tool that provides for the development of a network that shows the relationship between the activities that make up a project. Given time estimates for completion of each activity, the project manager can make inferences about the likelihood of project completion in a specified time frame. PERT is a control device that aids in the allocation and deployment of resources in complex projects. Although there were initial differences between PERT and CPM (CPM was developed at the same time by Du Pont), many current project scheduling systems use an integrated approach. *See critical path method.*

projected benefit obligation (PBO) The present value, as calculated by an actuary, of the amount owed by a company to its pension plan on the basis of *future* service and compensation levels.

See also accumulated benefit obligation, minimum pension liability.

prototype A model of a product used in testing.

Prototypes can take a number of forms, from a computer simulation to a full working model. For example, General Motors developed several prototypes of its new Impact electric car. One prototype was a clay model that was used in wind tunnel tests to determine the car's air drag. Another was a complete working model that was tested on the company's Motor Technical Center in Warren, Michigan.

PSA   *See public-service advertisement*

psychographic segmentation   The division of the *market* into segments based on how consumers live, as reflected in their values, attitudes, and interests.

In researching the lifestyle patterns of consumers, marketers focus on activities, interests, and opinions.

A recent study by the Stanford Research Institute (SRI) blended demographic and lifestyle variables (called VALS, for Values and Lifestyles) to create psychographic portraits of nine categories of American consumers. SRI first conducted a mail survey that drew responses from more than 1,600 adults. When the researchers analyzed the data, they found that Americans fell into four broad categories: need-driven, outer directed, inner directed, and combined outer and inner. They then subdivided these categories into nine lifestyle segments, each with a distinct set of values, needs, beliefs, drives, dreams, and special perspectives.

EXAMPLE: The Outer-directed Belonger segment is made up of 64 million Americans; 58 percent are female, and they have a median age of 57. The median household income is $18,000, and close to 50 percent graduated from high school. The people in this segment are aging, traditional, and conventional; they are also intensely patriotic, contented, sentimental, and psychographically stable. As consumers, they buy American cars, prefer traditional breakfast foods, and purchase canned soups. They also buy homes, freezers, and recreational equipment more frequently than other Americans.

*See also **market segmentation**. Compare to **behavioral segmentation**, demographic segmentation, volume segmentation**.*

public relations (PR)   A form of communication designed to increase public understanding and acceptance of a product, service, or company.

Public relations personnel usually take advantage of nonpaid channels of communication by issuing news releases. This technique gives public relations campaigns an air of legitimacy that paid advertising frequently lacks. Most PR campaigns deal with broad issues rather than specific products or services. To achieve their goals, they use such tools as press releases, speeches, employee training seminars, and public service activities, such as donating a percentage of sales to the American Olympic team.

Many public relations campaigns are mounted to counter negative images that result from unfavorable information or news about a company's product or *brand.* Adverse publicity has affected, among others, companies that market artificial sweeteners, tampons, and products containing asbestos.

EXAMPLE: An unknown person injected cyanide into Tylenol capsules, resulting in the deaths of seven people in the Chicago area and a public relations nightmare for the manufacturer, Johnson & Johnson (J&J). Though the Federal Drug Administration (FDA) cleared J&J of any wrongdoing, the tragic incident became front-page news.

To counter the blizzard of negative publicity, J&J launched one of the most successful public relations campaigns in history. First, it immediately recalled the product from the market. Next, J&J's CEO appeared on television shows, such as "Nightline," to explain the situation and announce what steps J&J was taking to ensure product safety. When the product did return to the shelves, it was encased in a triple-sealed, tamper-proof package. The mission of the company's public relations campaign stamped all its outward communication, including press releases, news conferences, and stories in business periodicals. The result: Tylenol recaptured the 37 percent *market share* it held before the incident.

See also *financial public relations.*

public-service advertisement (PSA) An advertisement with a message that focuses on the public good.

Most public-service advertising is sponsored by nonprofit organizations and is printed or broadcast on donated space or time. Organizations such as the United Way and the Red Cross have sponsored a number of public-service advertising campaigns.

publicly held company A company owned by the general public.

Ownership is conferred by the purchase of some form of *capital stock,* which is offered for sale on a public exchange. Publicly held companies must file their financial statements with the *Securities and Exchange Commission. Compare to privately held company.*

pull strategy A marketing approach in which the manufacturer promotes the product directly to consumers in the hope that they will request it from *distribution channel* members.

With this approach, the flow of demand for a product is backward: Consumers put pressure on the intermediaries to carry the product. Manufacturers of packaged goods often use this strategy: Heavy promotional spending by companies such as General Foods, Procter & Gamble, and General Mills draws, or pulls, their products through the distribution system. The pull strategy is most effective when the product is readily differentiated from others, appeals to the *mass market,* and carries a low price. *Compare to push strategy.*

purchase method A method of accounting for a business combination (used when any of the 12 conditions for the *pooling of interests* method are not met) that treats the *assets* of the *subsidiary company* as if the parent company had purchased them in an arm's length transaction.

Under the purchase method, the assets and *liabilities* of the newly acquired subsidiary are transferred to the parent company's books at their fair market value at the date of acquisition. If the subsidiary's purchase price is greater than the fair market value of its assets, the excess is considered *goodwill.* Goodwill must be identified as an asset on the parent company's balance sheet and amortized over a period not to exceed 40 years. *See also goodwill, pooling of interests.*

purchasing In manufacturing, those activities that relate to the acquisition of goods and services needed to support the manufacture of *output.*

purchasing, high and low involvement The degree of mental effort consumers expend in deciding to buy a product.

Recently, marketers have noticed that the way consumers learn depends on how much they care about or are interested in a given product. Automobile and home purchases, for instance, are important to consumers, but most purchases aren't. Cotton balls, facial tissues, and toothpaste, among many other products, elicit low consumer involvement.

With low-involvement products, consumers learn passively. Instead of actively seeking information so they can evaluate a product before they buy it, they pick up bits and pieces of data randomly. Television ads can effectively convey information to a passive audience: The medium is attention-grabbing, and frequent repetition of commercials helps consumers acquire random information. With high-involvement products, by contrast, consumers are already interested, so marketers can offer more rational and logical arguments to induce people to buy their products or brand. *See also buying decision process, buying roles.*

push strategy A promotional strategy in which a manufacturer uses its sales force and trade promotions to actively sell a product to *distribution channel* members, such as *wholesalers* and *retailers*, who in turn aggressively sell the product to consumers.

Manufacturers don't entirely ignore direct promotion to consumers when they employ a push strategy, but they pay more attention to promotion aimed at getting cooperation from distributors and retailers. A push strategy works particularly well for durable goods, high-priced items, and products with limited markets. *Compare to pull strategy.*

PWP *See plant within a plant*

qualified opinion An auditor's report of a company's *financial statements* when it fairly presents the company's financial position, results of operation, changes in financial position, or conformity with *generally accepted accounting principles (GAAP)* except for some particular limitation.

In other words, the auditor has been unable to obtain objective or independent evidence of a particular transaction or policy, or has doubts as to whether the enterprise can continue as a going concern. *See also adverse opinion, unqualified opinion.*

quality circle An organized activity in which workers from different segments of a production line meet regularly to discuss and solve quality problems related to their work efforts.

Quality circles were developed in Japan around 1961 and are based on the concept that workers are not usually aware of the causes of problems. Quality circles serve to educate employees about the various techniques (such as *control charts*, statistical analysis, and so on) that can be used to identify and solve problems in a production system. The overall focus of quality circles is problem solving. In recent years, quality circle problem solving has expanded beyond the production process to be applied to virtually all areas of company operations. A number of leading American companies, including Ford, American Airlines, General Electric, and 3M, have adopted quality circles.

quality of earnings In accounting, the extent to which the *net income* a company reports is sustainable in the future.

High quality of earnings often reflects conservative accounting policies. Financial ratios such as *earnings per share, current ratio,* and *inventory turnover* are all effective tools for determining a company's quality of earnings.

quality of work life (QWL) Programs designed to meet the sociotechnical problems emerging in the workplace.

Effectively combining people (socio) and machinery (technical) on the job can be a serious challenge. QWL is realized in programs such as *job enrichment* and *quality circles.*

quantity discount A price reduction to buyers based on the amount of product purchased.

EXAMPLE: A clothing manufacturer might sell shirts at $25 each for orders of fewer than 100 and for $22 each for orders of 100 or more.

Quantity discounts encourage customers to buy more from one seller rather than buying from multiple sources.

quarterly report A financial report released every three months.

Quarterly reports usually include unaudited *balance sheets, income statements,* and *statements of cash flows* along with related footnotes and an overview of the current business situation in the periods between *annual reports.*

queue time The time a job has to wait before a particular facility is available.

For example, the 15 minutes that might be spent in a bank waiting for a teller to make a transaction is that job's queue time. Queue time is a factor in almost all types of business. In a restaurant, customers might be queued up waiting for tables. In a factory, there might be a queue of partly finished products waiting to be processed on a particular machine. In an executive's office, there might be a pile of letters waiting to be answered.

There are two broad types of queueing systems: single stage and multiple stage. Single-stage systems have jobs lining up for a particular process (such as making a deposit at a bank). Multiple-stage systems have a single job waiting for a series of processes (such as in a cafeteria, in which customers line up for various types of food and then form another line to pay for their purchases).

The management (and reduction) of queue time is a central issue in many companies. A grocery store, for example, must have enough checkout counters to accomodate its customers. Queue time can be controlled by adding or reducing service facilities. Banks, grocery stores, and post offices frequently employ this technique. As the flow of customers changes throughout the day, checkout stands, tellers, and service windows are opened and closed. Queue time can also be reduced by separating customers into homogeneous groups. For example, many grocery stores have express or cash-only checkout stands.

Reducing psychological queueing time can also be an effective means of improving a queueing system. For example, most doctors' offices provide reading materials for patients in order to distract them from the time that they must wait before seeing a physician. The same purpose is served (a bit more profitably) in restaurants where waiting patrons are directed to a bar while a table is prepared.

rate card   A brochure that details the costs for *advertising* on or in a particular communications medium.

Rate cards are available from any newspaper, magazine, television station, or radio station.

rate of return   The annual percentage of income earned on an investment.

There are dozens of ways to calculate rate of return depending on the type of investment (bond, stock, real estate, operating assets), the purpose of the investment (income generation, capital gains, operating efficiency), and the maturity of the investment (short-, intermediate-, or long-term).

The rate of return on fixed-income securities is typically calculated as the current yield, that is, the annual interest or dividend payments divided by the price of the security. *Yield to maturity* is also frequently used, especially for determining the rate of return for business valuation purposes.

The rate of return on common shares is usually calculated as the annual dividend divided by the purchase price per share (called the "dividend yield"). The return may also include the appreciation gain (actual or expected) realized upon the sale of the shares (called "total return").

A variety of rates of return are utilized in the analysis of the financial performance of companies (called "ratio analysis"). The most popular include return on investment, return on equity, return on total assets, and return on sales. These ratios are all calculated by dividing the income over a period of time (usually one year) by the average investment for the period.

Internally, companies use the internal rate of return in the capital budgeting process to weight the cost/benefit of "make-versus-buy" or "buy-versus-lease" decisions for financing capital equipment additions.

raw materials inventory   The raw materials on hand at either the beginning or the end of an *accounting period.*

Raw materials inventory represents items that will be components of manufactured goods. The ending balance for a given accounting period is reported on the *balance sheet.* Raw materials inventory is also used in the calculation of *cost of goods sold* on the *income statement. See also finished goods inventory, inventory forms, work-in-process inventory.*

reach   The number of people exposed to a specific advertisement at least once during a particular time period.

If 80 percent of the *target market* will see or hear an ad, it is said to have wide reach. Advertising with a wide reach, such as a commercial on a very popular television show or an ad in a widely read magazine, can be effective in situations where (1) a company is introducing a new product, (2) a product is purchased infrequently, and (3) the *target market* is not clearly defined.

realized gain or loss In accounting, the difference between the *book value* of an *asset* and the amount received from its sale.

Realized gains and losses are reported on the income statement (usually as an element of taxable income). Occasionally, a company can report a realized loss even when there has been no sale. For example, when a long-term investment permanently declines in value, the value of the investment should be written down on the *balance sheet* and the amount of the decline in value should be reported as a realized loss on the *income statement. See also conservatism.*

reasonableness test A method of evaluating accounting information.

EXAMPLE: A company's current travel and entertainment expenses might be compared with those of previous years, the expenses reported by competitors, or industry norms. If the travel and entertainment expenses are comparatively high, they might not appear reasonable and should be investigated.

rebate A cash refund the manufacturer gives to a consumer after the purchase of a product.

Rebates are frequently used in the automobile industry to increase sales at the end of a model year and make room for new models.

recapitalization The revision to a company's capital structure.

Recapitalizations may involve the exchange of debt obligations for equity interests (an increasingly common tactic for cash-poor companies).

Recapitalizations may also involve the exchange of one type of debt security for another, such as convertible debentures to bonds. Under certain circumstances, it makes sense to recapitalize by trading preferred stock for common, or common shares for preferred.

Although bankruptcy reorganizations tend to be the major incentive for companies to recapitalize, a variety of other reasons could trigger the action. Three of the most common are:

- Reducing debt service to allow for additional borrowings
- Cleaning up a balance sheet prior to a merger or sale of the company
- Increasing tax deductions by substituting interest payments for dividends

receivables In accounting, any money due a company from customers or others.

Receivables are classified on the ***balance sheet*** as trade receivables and nontrade receivables. Trade receivables are due from customers for products or services and are either ***accounts receivable*** or ***notes receivable.*** Nontrade receivables include advances to employees, expected insurance settlements, ***dividends*** receivable, and interest receivable. All receivables are classified as either current (due within one year or the normal operating cycle of the business) or noncurrent (due within more than one year or more than one normal operating cycle).

reference group In marketing, the group that serves as a reference point when an individual evaluates his or her purchasing behavior.

Primary groups are small and intimate enough to allow all members to communicate with one another face-to-face. Examples of primary groups include one's family, a group of close social friends, and co-workers. Larger, less intimate secondary groups—trade unions, religious organizations, and professional associations, for instance—also influence consumer behavior.

The products or brands that are visible in social settings or consumed conspicuously are more heavily influenced by reference groups than other, less noticeable products. Reference groups, for example, probably don't play much of a role when a person chooses a desk lamp, but the groups' members notice, evaluate, and influence a consumer when it comes to buying a set of golf clubs. *See also **buying roles, opinion leaders.***

regional banks Large banks such as Mellon, First Chicago, Norwest, and Crocker, that function regionally in a fashion similar to ***money center banks*** at the national level.

Federal and state laws prohibiting interstate banking encouraged the growth of banks to meet the needs of large regional businesses. Within the last decade, however, legislation in several states has allowed these banks to expand statewide and to acquire banks in other states. Large regional banks have also become involved in foreign loans and many have staffed multinational personnel to handle international accounts. Regional banks serve as correspondents for smaller local banks in the same way that money center banks act as correspondents for regional banks.

regression analysis A statistical technique used to show how a dependent variable relates to one or more independent variables, or predictors.

Once the relationship is determined, it can serve as a model for making predictions.

EXAMPLE: The management of a department store is considering a move into a new location and uses regression analysis to help it select the best site. It wants to see if it can predict store sales (the dependent variable) by some of the characteristics, such as age, income, and education of the population (the independent variables) of each possible location. The data for each of the independent variables is fed into a computer, which performs the mathematical process of a regression and produces this equation:

$$SALES = \$500 + 2(AGE) + 4(INCOME) + 3(EDUCATION).$$

The regression shows that there is a positive relationship between the age, income, and education of a population and store sales. In other words, a store located in a community whose population has a high income, is older, and has a higher level of education will have more sales than a store located in an area with lower levels of these characteristics.

Regulation A filing An SEC regulation that allows small companies to make a public stock issue of up to $5 million.

Regulation A, which originated under the Securities Act of 1933, has a very complex set of rules. The major features of the regulation are as follows:

- The company files a "notification," not a "registration," statement.
- Notification is filed with a regional SEC office, not Washington.
- An offering circular, not a full prospectus, is required, with the amount of disclosure similar to that required under an S-18.
- Uncertified financial statements may be used.
- It cannot be used by a company if affiliated persons or underwriters have been convicted of securities violations or postal fraud.

Regulation D A federal securities law passed in 1982 as an attempt to establish uniform private placement requirements between the SEC and states.

Most states allow Regulation D filings; a few do not. The designation of private placement exempt offerings relates to the section of the securities regulations to which they apply. They are

- Rule 504 for offerings of up to $500,000
- Rule 505 for offerings of up to $5 million
- Rule 506 for offerings above $5 million

In addition to these three specific categories, Regulation D stipulates three other rules—501, 502, and 503—that apply to all three exemptions. The major provision states that security sales may be made only to "accredited" investors, who by definition fall into the following categories:

- An individual with an annual income of at least $200,000 in each of the two most recent years
- An individual investor (including spouse) with a net worth of at least $1 million

- An individual purchasing up to $150,000 of the security, as long as the investment does not exceed 20 percent of the investor's net worth
- Insiders of the issuing company—directors, executive officers, general partners
- Institutional investors (e.g., banks and insurance companies)
- Plans established by state government and/or their subdivisions for the benefit of their employees and that have assets in excess of $5 million, such as state employee pension funds
- Nonprofit organizations with assets exceeding $5 million
- Private business development companies defined by the Investment Advisors Act of 1940

Moreover, the issuing company must provide proof that each investor meets one of these requirements. Such proof must be in writing and attested to by the investor. Several other lesser restrictions also apply.

relationship marketing   A type of marketing in which consumers, distributors, and suppliers interact with each other personally, which lets marketers build trusting, long-term relationships with each of them.

A catering company, for instance, might be well served by relationship marketing. By establishing good relationships with suppliers, caterers can ensure that they consistently obtain the highest-quality ingredients, thus allowing them to provide good meals for clients. By consistently providing good meals made with the best ingredients, the catering company will probably be hired for future events and parties. Ideally, relationship marketing simplifies the interactions between a company, its suppliers, and its clients and creates a win-win situation where everyone involved saves time and money.

Relationship marketing recognizes the importance of building a stream of purchases over a buyer's lifetime; all contacts are made to create a perception of "we care."

remanufacturing   In manufacturing, the process of restoring worn-out products to mint condition. Remanufacturing is distinct from repairing or rebuilding a product in that a remanufactured product is considered to be brand-new.

repeat rate   The number of times a person buys a product within a particular period of time.

The repeat rate for microwave popcorn, for example, is higher than for deodorant, because the popcorn is consumed more quickly. Repeat rates are an important tool in evaluating new products and their marketing campaigns. A high repeat rate after a product launch with little advertising indicates that any additional advertising should produce much higher sales. A low repeat rate indicates that the product might need heavier promotion—or that it is a failure.

replacement cost In accounting, the current cost of replacing an existing *asset.*

EXAMPLE: If a company purchased a truck for $20,000 five years ago, its replacement cost today might be $30,000.

repurchase agreement A short-term investment, also called a "repo" or "RP," that serves as an alternative to commercial paper, certificates of deposit, or Treasury bills.

Banks sell repos under an agreement to buy back the security at a specified price. The buyback date may be fixed or open and subject to call at any time. Typically, repos are collateralized with U.S. Treasury securities, making investment risk virtually zero. This enables banks to pay interest rates below the current market rate.

research and development (R&D) costs In accounting, the cost of developing new knowledge and incorporating that knowledge into a new product.

Generally, R&D costs are considered as expenses in any given *accounting period.* However, there are two cases in which they can be *capitalized* and treated as *assets:* (1) the purchase of materials and equipment for use in development, and (2) the purchase of intangibles, such as patents and *copyrights.*

One prominent exception is the computer software industry, which has been exempted from these rules because the research and development process is its primary activity. Computer software development companies are permitted to capitalize all R&D costs as soon as they develop a marketable prototype. However, all further development costs associated with a new product must be expensed as incurred.

research validity, external A criterion by which a research project is evaluated.

External validity hinges on whether the results of a research project can be generalized to an entire population.

EXAMPLE: A detergent company conducts an experiment to test a new package design in which volunteer shoppers purchase detergents in an artificial store setting. The results, however, may fail to predict shoppers' responses to the new packaging in a real store. In other words, the study lacks external research validity.

Compare to research validity, internal.

research validity, internal A criterion by which a research project is evaluated.

Internal validity depends on the consistency of the various procedures and methods used in a research project.

EXAMPLE: If several different questionnaires were used in a citywide survey, chances are good that the results of each questionnaire will be slightly different, and the research will lack internal validity.

Compare to **research validity, external.**

reseller market   Individuals and companies that procure goods in order to rent or sell them to others at a profit.

The reseller market is a subset of the industrial market. Most *wholesalers* and *retailers* are resellers.

EXAMPLE: A supermarket operates in the reseller market when it buys food from producers across the country, places it all under one roof, and offers it for sale.

response rate   The percentage of responses generated by a *direct marketing* campaign.

If an insurance company sends 1 million fliers to potential customers and receives 30,000 phone calls about its offer, the response rate is 3 percent (30,000 divided by 1 million). Usually the response rate for any direct-mail marketing campaign does not top 5 percent. *Telemarketing* and personal selling can attain much higher response rates.

response time   The time required to produce a product or service.

A rapid response time gives an important competitive edge, both in terms of customer service and expansion into new products or markets. For example, a National Science Foundation study of the American and Japanese robotics industries showed that Japanese firms are about 25 percent faster than their American counterparts in the development of new robots. The study also found that Japanese robotics companies tend to spend about 10 percent less in the development and marketing of new robots. The main difference between the American and Japanese firms was that the Japanese spent five times more than the Americans in the development of more efficient production methods, whereas the Americans spent more money and time on marketing.

One of the most attractive benefits of a rapid response time is that, by responding more quickly to customers, managers can delay an order until they know the customers' exact requirements. This reduces the number of times that orders must be changed, which simplifies the entire production process.

retailer   Any company that sells merchandise to a final consumer.

Retail sales are highest for food stores, followed by car dealerships, department stores, gasoline stations, restaurants, and bars. Retailers vary enormously in size. The number of employees can be as few as one, as with a small shop with a single owner, or as many as 500,000, in the case of Sears Roebuck, for instance.

retained earnings The total earnings of a company, less *dividends,* since its inception.

Retained earnings is reported in the *stockholders' equity* section of the *balance sheet* and is calculated as follows: unadjusted beginning balance plus or minus prior period adjustments equals the adjusted beginning balance; then add net income and subtract dividends to obtain the ending balance.

return on assets (ROA) *See return on investment*

return on equity (ROE) *See return on investment*

return on investment (ROI) In accounting, a measure of the earning power of a company's *assets.*

A high return on investments is desirable. ROI is broadly defined as *net income* divided by investments. However, the term *investments* has three distinct interpretations in financial analysis, each of which lead to a different calculation of return on investment: return on assets, return on *owners' equity,* and return on invested *capital.*

Return on assets (ROA) is calculated by dividing net income after taxes by average total assets (average total assets is found by adding the ending balance of total assets for the previous year with the ending balance of total assets for the current year and dividing by two).

$$\frac{\text{Net income after tax}}{\text{Average total assets}}$$

ROA shows how much a company has earned on the investment of all the funds, including *current liabilities, noncurrent liabilities,* and owners' equity, committed to the company. Because ROA does not discriminate among the various sources of investment funds, it is frequently used by top management to evaluate the performances of various divisions within a company. This allows equal comparison between divisions that have control over their assets, but little say in how those assets are financed.

Return on invested capital (ROIC) shows how well a company has used the funds given to it for a relatively long period of time. Invested capital equals noncurrent liabilities plus shareholders' equity. ROIC is calculated by dividing net income after taxes by the sum of noncurrent liabilities and *stockholders' equity.*

$$\frac{\text{Net income after tax}}{\text{Noncurrent liabilities} + \text{Stockholders' equity}}$$

Some companies use ROIC to evaluate divisional performance. This is appropriate only in situations where divisional managers have significant impact on asset purchases, inventory levels, credit policies, and cash management.

Return on owners' equity (ROE) measures the return that a company has earned on the funds invested by shareholders. The ratio is calculated by dividing net income after taxes by stockholders' equity.

$$\frac{\text{Net income after tax}}{\text{Stockholders' equity}}$$

Present and prospective stockholders frequently use ROE, although it is also employed by management, which is responsible for operating the business in the best interests of its owners.

EXAMPLE:

Consolidated Balance Sheets
Wal-Mart Stores, Inc. and Subsidiaries
(Amounts in thousands)

	1991	1990
Assets		
Current assets:		
Cash and cash equivalents	$ 13,014	$ 12,790
Receivables	305,070	155,811
Recoverable costs from sale/leaseback . .	239,867	78,727
Inventories (LIFO)	5,808,416	4,428,074
Prepaid expenses	48,408	37,215
TOTAL CURRENT ASSETS	6,414,775	4,712,616
Property, plant, and equipment, at cost:		
Land	833,344	463,110
Buildings and improvements	1,764,155	1,227,519
Fixtures and equipment	2,037,476	1,441,752
Transportation equipment	63,237	57,215
	4,698,212	3,189,596
Less accumulated depreciation	−974,060	−711,763
Net property, plant, and equipment	3,724,152	2,477,833
Property under capital leases	1,298,452	1,212,169
Less accumulated amortization	−310,565	−259,943
Net property under capital leases	987,887	952,226
Other assets and deferred charges	262,101	55,809
TOTAL ASSETS	$11,388,915	$8,198,484

Consolidated Balance Sheets
Wal-Mart Stores, Inc. and Subsidiaries (cont.)

	1991	1990
Liabilities and Shareholders' Equity		
Current liabilities:		
Commercial paper......................	$ 395,179	$ 184,774
Accounts payable	2,651,315	1,826,720
Accrued liabilities:		
Salaries..............................	189,535	157,216
Other................................	539,020	473,677
Accrued federal and state income taxes...	184,512	179,049
Long-term debt due within one year	6,394	1,581
Obligations under capital leases		
due within one year	24,459	22,298
TOTAL CURRENT LIABILITIES	3,990,414	2,845,315
Long-term debt	740,254	185,152
Long-term obligations under capital leases..	1,158,621	1,087,403
Deferred income taxes....................	134,102	115,053
Shareholders' equity:		
Common stock (shares outstanding,		
1,142,282 in 1991 and		
566,153 in 1990)......................	114,228	56,614
Capital in excess of par value	415,586	180,465
Retained earnings	4,835,710	3,728,482
TOTAL SHAREHOLDERS' EQUITY.............	5,365,524	3,965,561
TOTAL LIABILITIES AND		
SHAREHOLDERS' EQUITY................	$11,388,915	$8,198,484

Consolidated Statement of Income
Wal-Mart Stores, Inc. and Subsidiaries
(Amounts in thousands except per share data)

	1991	1990
Revenues:		
Net sales........................	$32,601,594	$25,810,656
Rentals from licensed departments	22,362	16,685
Other income-net................	239,452	157,959
	32,863,408	25,985,300
Costs and expenses:		
Cost of sales	25,499,834	20,070,034
Operating, selling, and general		
and administrative expenses....	5,152,178	4,069,695
Interest costs:		
Debt	42,716	20,346
Capital leases	125,920	117,725
	30,820,648	24,277,800
Income before income taxes	2,042,760	1,707,500

Consolidated Statement of Income
Wal-Mart Stores, Inc. and Subsidiaries
(Amounts in thousands except per share data)

	1991	1990
Provision for federal and state income taxes:		
Current	737,020	608,912
Deferred	14,716	22,688
	751,736	631,600
NET INCOME	$1,291,024	$1,075,900

Income Statement Items:

Net income after tax (line 14) = $1,291,024

Balance Sheet Items:

$$\text{Average total assets (line 18)} = \frac{11,388,915 + 8,198,484}{2}$$

$$= 9,793,699$$

Noncurrent liabilities:

Long-term debt (line 27)	$ 740,254
Long-term obligations under capital leases (line 28)	1,158,621
Deferred income taxes (line 29)	134,102
Total	$2,032,977
Stockholders' equity (line 34)	5,365,524

Calculations:

Return on Assets

$$\frac{\text{Net income after tax}}{\text{Average total assets}}$$

$$\frac{1,291,024}{9,793,699} = 0.1318, \text{ or } 13.18\%$$

Return on Invested Capital

$$\frac{\text{Net income after tax}}{\text{Noncurrent liabilities } + \text{ Stockholder's equity}}$$

$$\frac{1,291,024}{2,032,977 + 5,365,524} = 0.1745, \text{ or } 17.45\%$$

Return on Owner's Equity

$$\frac{\text{Net income after tax}}{\text{Stockholders' equity}}$$

$$\frac{1,291,024}{5,365,524} = 0.2406, \text{ or } 24.06\%$$

revenue Gross income received before any deductions for expenses, discounts, returns, and so on.

Revenue is also called "sales" in most companies. A much less common usage refers to interest income, dividends, royalties, refunds, and claim settlements as revenue. Generally, however, each type of income carries its own designation—sales, income, fees, claims, and so on.

revenue recognition In accounting, the process of recording *revenue.*

Most companies recognize revenue at the time of sale, regardless of when cash will be received. When revenue is recognized, related expenses must be matched to it within that *accounting period* (*see matching principle*). Many service businesses use *cash basis accounting*, which allows them to recognize revenue only when cash is received. However, this method is not considered a *generally accepted accounting principle. See also cash basis accounting, percentage-of-completion method, successful efforts method.*

reverse split A procedure whereby corporations buy back a portion of their outstanding stock.

The effect of the reverse split is to increase the value of each remaining share outstanding while simultaneously reducing the number of shares. The main reason companies engage in such a maneuver is to raise the price of their traded shares prior to entering into mergers, business acquisitions, or joint ventures, or as a preliminary step to making a new stock issue.

reverse takeover In corporate finance, a situation in which a small company, in an effort to expand rapidly, takes over a much larger company.

Reverse takeovers are usually financed by stocks, junk bonds, and other securities designed to raise a lot of cash over a short period of time.

reward systems The types of rewards within an organization.

There are a number of different types of rewards that can be offered or received within a company, and they can be divided into two basic categories: intrinsic rewards and extrinsic rewards. Intrinsic rewards are related to the pleasure that a person feels while on the job. Examples include being able to participate in decision making, receiving more interesting work assignments, being given opportunities for personal growth, and receiving more responsibility.

Extrinsic rewards involve the environment that surrounds the work itself. The most obvious extrinsic reward is compensation, or salary. Extrinsic rewards can be further divided into direct compensation and indirect compensation. Examples of direct compensation include bonuses, profit sharing, and overtime. Examples of indirect compensation include paid vacations, health insurance, and tuition reimbursement.

The distribution of rewards can be viewed in terms of the individual, the group, or the organization. There is a great deal of latitude between the three levels, but it is generally felt that if rewards are to be directly linked to performance, they should be given on the individual level.

role conflict   A problem that occurs when a manager must perform two roles at the same time, and the performance of one role contradicts the performance of the other.

Role conflicts have been divided into five separate categories.

1. *Intrarole conflict* is created by the receiving of two conflicting messages by a manager playing a single role. For example, a factory manager might receive direction from top management that all factory personnel must wear safety equipment at all times. However, the factory workers have regularly removed some of the safety equipment because they feel it impairs their ability to do their jobs effectively. In addition, there are widespread feelings on the factory floor that many of the company's safety regulations are irrelevant. In fact, many of the workers have told the factory manager that they are grateful that the safety requirements have not been strictly enforced.

    Generally, intrarole conflicts can be reduced or resolved by evaluating the situation, prioritizing the interests of the conflicting groups, and deciding to support one of them.

2. *Interrole conflict* occurs when a manager must play a number of roles that conflict with each other. For example, many managers find that the role they play in terms of performance evaluations (that is, judge, and sometimes punisher) contradicts with their role as trainer, teacher, or developer.

    In many cases interrole conflict can be reduced by recognizing the necessity to play more than one role and relying on the advice of a trusted superior in terms of fulfilling uncomfortable roles.

3. *Role overload conflict* occurs when a manager is unable to fulfill an expected role because of an overwhelming amount of work. For example, a marketing manager might have a presentation to prepare for top management, a meeting with the company's advertising agency regarding a new campaign, an interview with a local television station regarding a recent scandal involving the company's products, and a phone message from an irate customer.

    The most effective response to role overload conflicts is to prioritize tasks, and delegate those that cannot be performed individually.

4. *Person-role conflicts* arise when the behavior required by a particular role is not consistent with a manager's personal values. For example, say a sales manager is quietly told that he can expect a 200 percent increase in orders from a particular customer if he kicks back 15 percent of his commission to the customer's purchasing agent. This creates conflicting pressures between wanting to sell more product and the reluctance to engage in any unethical practices.

In many cases, person-role conflicts can be resolved by appealing to a company's policies and code of ethics. This allows the individual to hide behind a set of values without taking a highly personal stand. However, in situations that are not covered by company policies, the dilemma becomes highly personal.

5. *Intrasender conflicts* occur when managers send out conflicting messages. For example, a purchasing manager might mandate that a particular subassembly must be purchased only from preapproved suppliers. However, none of the suppliers may have the correct subassembly. Clearly, there is a conflict between the role and its fulfillment.

Resolution of intrasender conflicts is usually accomplished by creating clear communications channels so that information flows clearly.

rollout market entry A strategy for new product introduction in which a product is launched in a number of different geographic areas over an extended period of time.

EXAMPLE: U.S. Pioneer Electronics Corp. brought its videodisc to market in 1980. It began its sales campaign by test-marketing the product in four cities: Syracuse, Dallas-Ft. Worth, Minneapolis-St. Paul, and Madison, Wisconsin. Then 60 to 90 days afterward, Pioneer introduced its product in four more cities. It continued adding four additional cities every 60 or 90 days until the rollout was completed in 1981.

Rolling out spreads the substantial costs of a new product launch over a longer period of time and provides an opportunity to fine-tune the *marketing mix* as the rollout progresses.

rough cut capacity planning A method of examining the *bottleneck* areas in a manufacturing process to determine if sufficient *capacity* is available to meet a production schedule.

The basic idea behind rough cut capacity planning is that if sufficient capacity is available in the bottleneck areas, more than sufficient capacity will be available in nonbottleneck areas.

Rule 147—Intrastate Offering A federal securities regulation that applies to stock offerings within a company's state of residence.

To qualify for an intrastate exemption, all securities must be offered and sold to persons residing within the state in which the issuing company is incorporated, and in which it does a significant portion of its business. These securities, once issued, must remain in the state. The instructions do not govern how these provisions should be monitored, however, just that issuers are held responsible.

Rule 147 does not impose any maximum amount on the offering or on the number of investors. The nonsolicitation rules of Regulation D do not apply either. It should be noted that Rule 147 is a federal regulation and relates only to federal offering requirements. This does not mean that intrastate offerings are exempt from state regulations. Nearly all states have their own set of disclosure and other requirements that must be met. Although some have adopted common regulations, most remain unique.

To meet the federal compliance requirements under Rule 147,

- The issuing company must be a resident of the state or territory in which the private placement is made.

- The issuing company must do business in the state in which all offering solicitations and sales are made. "Doing business" is defined as follows: (1) at least 80 percent of gross revenues is received from sales within the state, (2) at least 80 percent of the issuing company's assets are located within the state, and (3) at least 80 percent of the proceeds of the offering must be used within the state.

- All investors to whom securities have been solicited or sold must be residents of the state.

- Resale of securities is restricted to residents of the state; this restriction is noted on the face of the stock certificate.

- No sales of securities can be made within six months before or after the offering.

runout method A method of estimating how quickly an inventory will be depleted.

Runout time is calculated by dividing the remaining amount of inventory by the rate at which it is used (demand rate).

$$\frac{\text{Inventory remaining}}{\text{Demand rate}} = \text{Runout time}$$

See **critical ratio analysis.**

S corporation (subchapter S corporation) A tax strategy that permits certain qualifying corporations to elect to be taxed as partnerships.

Since S corporations have no legal standing, all laws, regulations, and restrictions bearing on C corporations apply here as well. The only significant difference is in the tax treatment of corporate earnings and distributions.

For tax purposes, all income and losses of a corporation pass through to its shareholders, retain the same character as they had in the corporation, and are reported on individual Form 1040 tax returns. Such a pass-through must be in the same proportion as each shareholder's stock holdings bear to the total shares outstanding. Except in the case of a C corporation converting to an S corporation, with the potential for being liable for tax under the *built-in gains* provisions, the corporation is not taxed.

To qualify for S status, a corporation and its shareholders must meet the following criteria:

1. The corporation must be a domestic corporation and not part of an affiliated group of corporations.

2. The corporation cannot own 80 percent or more of the stock of another corporation.

3. The corporation may not have more than 35 shareholders, with a husband and wife treated as a single shareholder.

4. Nonresident aliens are not permitted to be shareholders.

5. All shareholders must be individuals, estates, or certain defined trusts. They cannot be corporations or partnerships.

6. An S corporation may have no more than one class of stock issued and outstanding. All shares must bear the same rights relative to profits and assets of the corporation, except that stock may be segregated into voting and nonvoting shares for the purpose of establishing employee incentive stock option plans.

EXAMPLE: Your S corporation employs three key managers who have expressed an interest in obtaining an equity share of the business. But you, as principal shareholder, do not want to share voting powers. As an employee incentive, your company could award nonvoting shares of common stock. These shares would be subject to an agreement that if an employee leaves the company, these shares must be sold back to the company at a predetermined price, perhaps book value or book value plus a small premium. Not only do key managers get a financial stake in the business, but also knowing what the buyback price will be should motivate them to help increase the company's book value.

An election to be taxed as an S corporation must be filed on IRS Form 2553 within 75 days of the beginning of the year to which the election applies. All shareholders of the corporation must agree to the election and so affirm on the application. The S election terminates when any event occurs that would have made the corporation ineligible in the first place. The termination date is the date the event occurs.

The deduction of S corporation losses by shareholders is limited by

- The adjusted stock basis, as defined for each shareholder.
- At risk rules
- Passive activity loss (PAL) rules

S-1 registration A document filed with the *Securities and Exchange Commission (SEC)* that details the specific purpose of a proposed public offering of securities.

Although the S-1 is used by most companies, and in fact must be used by those companies not qualifying under "simplified registrations," such as the S-18 or Regulation A, it is the most complex and requires the most extensive disclosure. It also requires three years of audited financial statements.

SEC regulations identify exactly what items must be included and how financial statistics must be displayed. In addition to a variety of minor items, the following major topics must be included:

1. Name of registrant, the title and amount of securities being offered, and the date; an estimate of the minimum/maximum range of offering price and number of shares; the share price to the public; underwriting discounts and commission; proceeds to the issuer or other persons; and notices about stabilization of offering price

2. Statement of whether any securities being registered are from current stockholders; the names of these security holders; their relationship with the company; and the number of shares owned before and after the offering

3. An estimate of risk factors (those factors that make the issue speculative or of high risk), and the ratio of earnings to fixed charges

4. Use of proceeds and any dilution of shareholder interest

5. The company's dividend policy, including its dividend history, policies currently followed, restrictions on dividend payments (if any), a statement of whether future earnings are to be reinvested in the company rather than paid out in dividends, and a description of the com-

pany's debt and equity position (its capitalization) before and after the offering

6. A management discussion and analysis that provides enough information for investors to analyze the company's cash flow position

7. A business description that discloses everything an investor needs to know to make an informed judgment about investing in the shares

8. Disclosure of all pertinent information about directors, officers, and key employees

9. Company financial statements and the related auditors' opinion certificate

S-18 registration A simplified registration, specifically designed for smaller companies, that can be used by any U.S. or Canadian company not subject to continuous reporting requirements of their respective countries (except investment companies and certain insurance companies).

The total stock offering in any 12-month period cannot exceed $7.5 million. Under this simplified version, the differences from the standard S-1 registration are these:

1. An audited balance sheet for one year rather than three

2. Income statements and statements of changes in financial condition for the past two years instead of three

3. No management discussion or analyses of financial condition and no selected financial data section

safety stock *See buffer stock*

sale/leaseback A transaction whereby a company sells some or all of its hard assets to a leasing company for cash and then leases them back over a period of time.

A sale/leaseback is a popular mechanism for raising immediate capital against hard asset collateral while still maintaining control over the assets. This technique continues to be especially popular with companies that have a hard time raising new bank credit because of either overleveraged balance sheets or poor credit ratings.

Manufacturing businesses with substantial amounts of machinery and equipment and older hotels that need cash infusions for remodeling or for new appointments are the main users of this technique. Leases can be structured to include all equipment, furniture, and certain building fixtures—such as a central air conditioning system. These operating leases stay open-ended, allowing the lessee to add and delete assets at will without rewriting the lease. When an asset needs replacing, the lessor merely buys the new asset and adds its rental payment to the existing lease.

The biggest disadvantage in equipment sale/leaseback arrangements, other than losing the value of owned assets for future collateral, is the very high rental payments required by lessors. Since many companies going this route have poor bank credit ratings and a sale/leaseback presents their last chance to raise capital, lessors price the leases accordingly.

Sale/leasebacks are also popular for real property. Because real property tends to appreciate rather than depreciate over time, very often the lease value of a building far exceeds its existing mortgage.

The sale/leaseback technique for commercial and industrial buildings is not restricted to companies with poor credit ratings or those who cannot raise capital elsewhere. For example, assume a company took out a 20-year mortgage for 80 percent of a building's value. It has made mortgage payments for 10 years, and the mortgage balance has decreased 30 percent.

If the property has risen in value 3 percent per year, its market value today is 38 percent higher than when the mortgage was placed. By combining a 30 percent decrease in the mortgage loan with a 38 percent increase in the asset's market value, an equity increase of over 40 percent results. For a property originally worth $100,000, a sale/leaseback would result in a cash infusion of $82,000!

sales promotions According to the *American Marketing Association (AMA)*, those marketing activities, other than personal selling, advertising, and publicity, that stimulate consumers to buy and that boost dealer effectiveness.

Examples include displays, trade shows and expositions, demonstrations, and other selling efforts that are out of the ordinary routine. In addition to these examples, this broad definition embraces many kinds of activities, including in-store displays, sampling, coupons, contests, trading stamps, price-off deals, premiums, refund offers, sweepstakes, and rebates. Annual expenditures for these activities, which have become increasingly important in recent years, now top total spending on advertising.

Sales promotional tools fall into three broad categories: consumer promotion, trade promotion, and sales-force promotion. Consumer promotions are targeted directly to potential customers and can include coupons, contests and prizes, rebates, samples, warranties, and demonstrations. Trade promotions operate within *distribution channels* and offer programs such as cooperative advertising, display materials, and complimentary goods. Sales-force promotions target the people selling a product and include contests, bonuses, and sales rallies.

sales representative The personal link between a company and its customers.

Sales representatives, or reps, serve a variety of functions—from contacting new customers and selling products to conducting market research and servicing products.

sales response function The relationship between sales and a particular marketing tool.

Say a manager wants to see the effect of a small price change on sales volume. The manager might set up a sales response function that graphs any sales changes that are due to the price change.

salvage value In accounting, the expected price that an asset will bring when it is no longer needed by a company; also called *scrap value*.

In calculating depreciation expense, an asset's salvage value is deducted from its cost (except for declining balance methods).

EXAMPLE: A company buys a truck for $20,000. Its estimated useful life is 10 years and its estimated salvage value is $5,000. If straight-line depreciation is used, the depreciation expense would be the cost of the truck, less the salvage value, divided by its expected useful life, or

$$\$20,000 - \$5,000 = \$15,000$$

$$\frac{\$15,000}{10 \text{ years}} = \$1,500 \text{ annual depreciation expense}$$

sampling The selection of a subset of a given population as the subject for a *marketing research* study.

EXAMPLE: A newspaper interested in its customers' reaction to a new home delivery system randomly selects 200 subscribers, lets them try the new system, and measures their responses.

The key to selecting a sample is to make sure that the characteristics of the sample are representative of the population as a whole. Random sampling creates truly representative samples.

sampling frame A list of individuals or units from which a sample will be drawn.

EXAMPLE: Say an electronics company wants to survey customers who bought its high-end stereo system within the past three years. It might create a list of all those who returned warranty cards within that time period. The list will not include everyone who bought the stereo, but it should be comprehensive enough to generate a representative sample.

*See also **sampling**.*

saving Personal income that is not spent.

Personal income can be regarded on a pre-tax or after-tax basis. After-tax income is referred to as *disposable income.* Since taxes are an enforceable obligation, individuals are only free to dispose of their after-tax income. In general, there are two ways in which after-tax income can be disposed:

it can be spent (that is, *personal consumption expenditures*) or it can be saved.

The preceding description provides an important insight to the nature of saving in the U.S. economy. Saving is measured as a residual. This measurement recognizes the primary role of consumption. Individuals decide how to spend their income. Whatever is left is treated as saving. This treatment is quite different from what would happen if the various instruments people use as savings vehicles—deposits, money market mutual funds, NOW accounts, and so on—were totaled.

In the following table totals for personal income (PI), taxes, disposable personal income (DPI), personal consumption expenditure (PCE), saving, and the saving rate (as a percentage of disposable personal income) for selected years are shown.

Disposition of personal income
(Billions of dollars, except saving rate)

	1960	1965	1970	1975	1980	1985	1990
PI	409	553	831	1,307	2,265	3,380	4,664
Taxes	49	62	109	156	312	437	621
DPI	360	491	722	1,151	1,953	2,943	4,043
PCE	332	445	664	1,025	1,748	2,667	3,748
Saving*	21	35	58	100	154	189	176
Saving Rate (%)	5.7	7.0	8.0	8.7	7.9	6.4	4.3

*There is a further small residual, when PCE and Saving are subtracted from DPI, that reflects personal transfers (gifts) to foreigners and net interest payments by persons.

scientific management   A theory of management, based on the assumption that employees are rational, logical, and primarily motivated by financial rewards.

Classical management theory began in the United States after the Civil War, with the popularity of scientific management. Based on the task concept, which states that all work must be carefully planned and presented to employees (usually through detailed written instructions), scientific management viewed employees as extensions of the task they performed. *Time studies* and motion studies were frequently used in scientific management systems to break down each element of a worker's task and make it as efficient as possible. Compensation under scientific management was based on production. Workers who did not meet a particular production requirement were paid less than workers who met or exceeded the production requirement.

SEC   *See Securities and Exchange Commission*

secondary data   Information previously collected for another purpose and applied to a current problem.

A starting point for most **marketing research,** secondary data are usually found through a library search.

EXAMPLE: A mail-order clothing company wants to know which fabrics and colors have the greatest appeal to women over 40. Its researchers look for previous studies of recent trends in color or fabric preference. These studies can provide background and give direction for the current project.

*Compare to **primary data.***

secondary market The capital market where previously issued securities are traded.

The market may be (1) the New York Stock Exchange, the American Stock Exchange, or NASDAQ; (2) an informal market like over-the-counter *pink sheets;* or (3) a foreign exchange. The secondary market provides a medium within which securities can be bought and sold by investors and traders. Proceeds from the sales go to investors and dealers, not to the issuing company as is the case in a *primary market.*

secondary offering A public sale by institutional investors, large corporations, and investment bankers of previously issued securities.

Frequently, syndicates will purchase large blocks of an initial issue of securities at a fixed price and then resell them in the open market. The issuing company gains by having an assured market for its securities; the syndicate gains by the spread between purchase and sale prices.

Section 936 A section in the U.S. Internal Revenue Code that grants special privileges to branches or subsidiaries of U.S. companies doing business in Puerto Rico.

Certain U.S. corporations that derive a significant portion of their income from Puerto Rican business activities are called *936 companies* and are effectively exempt from U.S. income tax on that portion of their income derived from sources within Puerto Rico. Beginning in 1988 selected provisions applied to subsidiaries of U.S. companies in the U.S. Virgin Islands as well.

Funds repatriated to the mainland U.S. parent by 936 companies are subject to a *toll gate tax* at a maximum rate of 10 percent. As long as these funds remain in Puerto Rico they are tax-free. As a result, more than $10 billion of Section 936 funds, referred to as *qualified possession source investment income* or QPSII (quipsy) funds, have been generated, to be lent to qualifying U.S. companies for investment in projects within Puerto Rico or in qualifying projects in any Caribbean Basin Initiative (CBI) country that has executed a Tax Information Exchange Agreement with the United States. Because of the tax-free nature of these funds, loans currently carry below-market interest rates of 85 percent of London Interbank Offered Rate (LIBOR).

Investments in the following CBI countries qualify for Section 936 financing: Jamaica, Barbados, Grenada, Dominica, Trinidad and Tobago, the

Dominican Republic, and Costa Rica. Other countries are in various stages of consideration.

Caribbean Basin Partners, Ltd. (CBBP) is a good example of how 936 financing has caught on. CBBP is a partnership of Section 936 corporations that invests debt and equity in eligible small- and mid-size private sector projects with job-creating potential. It grants loans ranging from $1 million to $10 million for 10 years, up to 75 percent of the financing requirement.

Securities and Exchange Commission (SEC) The federal government agency responsible for regulating financial reporting, use of accounting principles, trading activities, and auditing practices of *publicly held companies.*

SEC requirements (issued as Accounting Series Releases and Staff Accounting Bulletins) encourage full financial disclosure in order to protect the interests of investors. Generally, the SEC defers to the opinions released by the *Financial Accounting Standards Board (FASB)* and the *Auditing Standards Board (ASB).*

securitization The use of contractual cash flows as collateral to debt issues.

When borrowing from a bank, companies execute a contractual obligation to repay the loan. Securitization creates the same type of contractual obligation to repay investors as loan documentation does to repay banks.

Whereas bank loans are collateralized with balance sheet assets (receivables, inventory, machinery and equipment, or buildings and land), securitized bonds, notes, and commercial paper are collateralized (securitized) with contractual cash flows from either balance sheet or off-balance sheet assets. Future cash flow contracts that qualify as collateral include construction contracts, credit card receivables, mortgage obligations, export orders, or any other quality future cash flow contract.

Companies sell pieces of paper (securities) to investors that represent rights to these cash flows. Examples of such securities include bond issues, commercial paper, Euronotes, short-term or medium-term notes, certificates of deposit, Eurobonds, pass-through and pay-through securities, and property income certificates. Privately held companies frequently use short-term promissory notes to evidence securitized debt obligations.

From a company's perspective, liquid secondary markets for these securities offer management the opportunity to restructure risks as economic events dictate.

For investors, securitized debt carries less risk than straight commercial paper or bonds. In most cases, it offers better returns than current market rates. And liquidity is assured by an active secondary market.

Securitization is essentially another form of transaction finance and is ideally suited to financially weak companies that need to finance specific transactions independent of other balance sheet debt or credit history.

Securitized obligations are also referred to as *asset-backed securities.*

segment reporting In accounting, the presentation of the activities and operations of various parts of a company, such as product lines, countries, divisions, and sales territories.

Segment reporting is required in the *annual report* of a company if it meets any of the following criteria: (1) revenue of the segment is 10 percent or more of total *revenue*, (2) the segment operating profit (excluding unallocable general corporate revenue and expenses, income taxes, and interest expense) is 10 percent or more of total operating profit, and (3) a segment's identifiable *assets* are 10 percent or more of total identifiable assets. Any segment that has been reported in the past should be reported again, even if it no longer meets any of the established criteria.

FASB Statement No. 14 requires that *publicly held companies* provide segment *disclosures* regarding operations in different industries, foreign operations, major customers, export sales, and government contracts. These disclosures are not required if a company derives at least 90 percent of its revenues from one industry. *Privately held companies* do not have to make these disclosures. Segments must represent at least 75 percent of a company's total revenue. Generally, no more than 10 segments are shown. Although sales or transfers between segments are not included in a company's consolidated *financial statements,* they are included in segment reports.

segmentation *See market segmentation*

self-concept The way a person sees himself or herself.

Self-concept is an important factor in management because it influences a person's perception of, and interactions with, his or her environment. A manager's self-concept may be of an intelligent, quick-witted, and enthusiastic person. In order to maintain this self-concept, he or she might undertake actions (such as bystepping company procedures in order to rush a sale through) or adopt attitudes (such as condescending to co-workers or customers) that reinforce these notions. Unfortunately, this reinforcement might come at the expense of the company.

self-liquidator A sales premium that a customer pays for rather than an advertiser.

EXAMPLE: A cat food company offers a dish monogrammed with a cat's name if customers pay $4.95 and send in a proof-of-purchase seal from a box of cat food. Since the company sells the dishes at cost, they may be inexpensive enough to motivate consumers to buy its cat food. When the customer orders a dish, the cat food company recovers its $4.95 cost.

self-managed work teams Groups that control how the goals assigned to them are to be accomplished and how to allocate their various tasks.

In most cases, self-managed work teams have collective control over the pace of work, scheduling of breaks, determination of work assignments, and inspection procedures. Totally autonomous work teams might even be able to select their members and evaluate each other's performance.

EXAMPLE: In California, General Motors (in a joint venture with Toyota) is manufacturing Chevrolet Novas and Toyota Corollas with self-managed work teams. In addition to being able to define their own jobs, the teams are given a great deal of responsibility for quality control. They conduct daily audits—a task that once fell to a separate department—and can use *stop line* cards that allow them to halt production immediately if they spot a problem.

Self-managed work teams have three key features: (1) group members must have a variety of skills that allow them to perform a number of different functions; (2) members must perform functionally interrelated tasks and be collectively responsible for the end product; and (3) there must be some kind of evaluation of the performance of the group as a whole.

senior debt
Debt securities that hold first position claims to a company's assets.

If the company were to be liquidated, senior debtholders would receive proceeds from the sale before junior debtholders, preferred shareholders, or common shareholders. The same pecking order applies in a bankruptcy proceeding; that is, interest and principal payments against senior debt will be made before any payments on other debt or equity holdings.

Because of its priority position, senior debt normally carries a lower interest rate than junior obligations. Conversely, since junior obligations such as *junk bonds* carry very few rights to the company's assets, higher interest rates must compensate.

sequencing
The order in which jobs are assigned to work centers.

These decisions can have a great impact on a company's operations in terms of being within (or exceeding) capacity requirements and completing jobs on time. To assist in the sequencing process, a number of priority rules, or heuristics, have been developed that can help one to decide which jobs should be scheduled first. Of course, priority rules vary from company to company, but some of the more common are the following:

1. *First come, first served.* The first job to arrive at a particular work center is done first. The underlying concept behind this rule is fairness. It is frequently used in service companies, such as barber shops, in which customers are included in the process itself.

2. *Shortest operation time.* Short, simple jobs are done first. This action moves them through the operations process more quickly, which can help to generate revenue quickly. Longer, more complex jobs must wait until the proper facilities are clear before they can begin.

3. *Longest operation time.* These jobs are bigger, more complex, and more profitable. As such, they should be done first.

4. *Due date.* Jobs with an earlier due date (regardless of processing time) are given priority.

5. *Static slack.* In this case, slack is calculated as a job's due date minus the time of its arrival at a given work center. Jobs with the smallest amount of static slack are scheduled first.

6. *Static slack per remaining operation.* Jobs with more operations to be completed should be scheduled before jobs with fewer remaining operations.

7. *Covert.* Jobs with the highest ratio of cost of delay d over processing time t are given priority.

8. *Random Order.*

served market The portion of the market that a company decides to pursue; also called the *target market.*

EXAMPLE: For a company that manufactures video games, the *market* consists of anyone who owns a television. The *potential market* is defined as households with children and a television. The *available market* is limited to households with children, a television, enough income to make the purchase, and a store nearby that carries the game. The *served market* consists of households with a television, access to a toy store, sufficient income to buy the product, and children within a specific age range (between 11 and 15, for example).

See also available market, market, penetrated market, potential market.

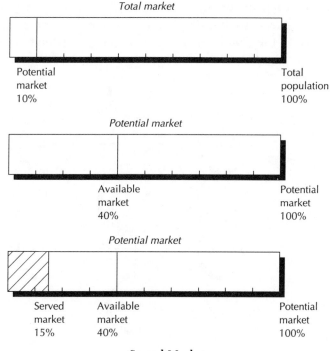

Served Market

setup costs Any costs associated with the manufacture or acquisition of parts or materials.

Setup costs include the costs of equipment downtime during a new setup, setup labor, the cost of parts used to test the new setup, and the costs of a new employee *learning curve* (that is, the cost of lower productivity in the early stages of a new process).

seven-S framework A framework developed by McKinsey & Co. consultants to assist in understanding the interrelated strategic elements that determine a company's success or failure.

Proponents of the seven-S framework, which was widely popularized in the bestselling book *In Search of Excellence* by Tom Peters and Robert Waterman, argue that the effectiveness of a company is determined by the interplay of each of the following seven factors, rather than changes in corporate structure or organization:

- Strategy—the path chosen by a company to achieve its goals
- Structure—how the company is organized
- Staff—the company's human resources
- Superordinate goals—the basic values and goals of a company
- Skills—the particular capabilities of a company
- Style—the manner in which management presents itself to employees
- Systems—the procedures, both formal and informal, that govern daily activity.

In attempting to make major changes within a company, it is important to consider each of the seven Ss. Usually, the *hard* Ss, such as strategy and structure, receive a great deal of management attention, sometimes at the expense of the *soft* Ss, such as staff and superordinate goals. Change that

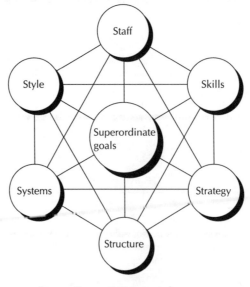

Seven-S Framework

does not consider each of the seven Ss is likely to fail. Successful change incorporates each of the Ss and attempts to find a balance that will create consistency throughout the company.

sexual harassment   Any verbal or physical abuse based solely on the sex of the victim.

Sexual harassment laws apply equally to both males and females, heterosexuals and homosexuals. Most laws are directed toward superior-subordinate relationships, but they apply to peer relationships and relationships between nonemployees and employees as well. Sexual harassment is widespread in the workplace and carries extremely high costs, both financially and personally. For example, in 1985, Cecily Coleman reached an out-of-court settlement with the American Broadcasting Corporation (ABC) for $15 million after bringing sexual harassment charges against the company resulting from unwanted sexual advances of former ABC vice-president James D. Abernathy. Also in 1985, the Equal Opportunity Employment Commission (EOEC) received a record 7,273 sexual harassment complaints. Studies have shown that up to 70 percent of female employees have experienced sexual harassment on the job. For example, one study in California showed that up to one third of all Los Angeles working women have, at one point, lost or quit their jobs because of sexual pressures in the workplace.

Many incidents of sexual harassment go unreported, for reasons such as the following:

1. Victims do not feel that they will be believed. In many cases, sexual harassment is instigated by managers or supervisors who have more interaction with and authority in dealings with higher management. These factors tend to discourage victims from reporting sexual harassment because they feel that their word will not compare favorably with the word of a trusted manager.

2. Victims cannot give a detailed account of particular incidents. Since sexual harassment often takes place in the context of casual interactions, victims frequently do not record incidents until actions become blatant.

3. Victims may be accused of inviting or encouraging harassment. A victim's reluctance to report harassment may be caused by guilt or uncertainty regarding exactly which actions "crossed the line" from casual interaction to sexual innuendo. Laughing at sexual jokes, wearing revealing clothing, and even being too friendly can often cloud the issue of the initiation of sexual harassment and discourage employees from making formal reports.

4. Victims do not trust higher management to be objective. There is a common perception, due for the most part to the fact that most sexual harassment is initiated by men and most upper management positions are held by men, that complaints of sexual harassment will not be taken seriously.

5. Victims fear punishment. Frequently, victims of sexual harassment fear reprisals, such as dismissal, denial of promotions or raises, poor performance evaluations, and so on, if they make a formal complaint.

6. Victims do not want to cause problems. In many cases, the victim of sexual harassment is hesitant to report the problem because there is a reluctance to harm the employment or reputation of the person harassing them.

Sexual harassment has only become a legal issue since the mid-1970s. The first sexual harassment suit was filed in Arizona in 1975; two female employees quit their jobs as a result of repeated sexual advances, both verbal and physical, from their supervisor. The court ruled that the company was not liable for the actions of the supervisor, that the supervisor's actions were simply his own proclivity, served no policy, and did not benefit the employer. This rationale held until 1977 when the District of Columbia Circuit Court of Appeals found that, in situations where sexual harassment affects job conditions (that is, creates economic harm such as loss of job or denial of salary increase or promotion), it is sex discrimination under Title VII of the 1964 Civil Rights Act.

In 1980, the EOEC released guidelines regarding sexual harassment. The guidelines define sexual harassment as follows:

> Unwelcome sexual advances, requests for sexual favors, and other verbal or physical conduct of a sexual nature constitute sexual harassment when (1) submission to such conduct is made either explicitly or implicitly a term or condition of an individual's employment; (2) submission to or rejection of such conduct by an individual is used as the basis for employment decisions affecting such individual; or (3) such conduct has the purpose or effect of unreasonably interfering with an individual's work performance or creating an intimidating, hostile, or offensive working environment.

The guidelines go on to state that cases of sexual harassment will be reviewed on an individual, case-by-case basis.

> In determining whether alleged conduct constitutes sexual harassment, the Commission will look at the record as a whole and at the totality of the circumstances, such as the nature of the sexual advances and the context in which the alleged incidents occurred. The determination of the legality of a particular action will be made from the facts, on a case-by-case basis.

The District of Columbia Circuit Court of Appeals again advanced the legal thinking on sexual harassment in 1981, when it ruled that sexual harassment suits did not have to hinge on economic harms. The court held that sexual propositions and insults were damaging to the emotional and psychological terms of employment whether or not they resulted in tangible economic harm.

In 1982, the Eleventh Circuit Court established the quid pro quo (that is, the giving of something for the receipt of something else) theory of sexual harassment. This theory states that sexual harassment affects not only its victims but also other employees, owing to the fact that a victim who acquiesces to sexual advances in the workplace might receive promotions and salary increases at the expense of other employees.

The result of these various rulings and policies on sexual harassment has created a system of collective law that outlines four distinct factors that constitute sexual harassment: (1) it is offensive and unwelcome; (2) it involves authority with the power to produce an intimidating work environment, (3) it is repetitive and one sided (with the exception of cases of sexual assault), and (4) it makes the victim feel powerless to stop or evade the behavior. Specific examples of clearly unacceptable behavior include the following:

- Verbal comments, compliments, and insults of a sexual nature, such as sexual jokes or pressuring for dates.

- Comments such as "You get me hot," and "I like it when you wear those tight outfits," and "You know what you have to do if you want to get ahead around here."

- Nonverbal actions such as staring luridly, leaving sexual notes around the workplace, displaying suggestive photographs, pinching, unsolicited back or neck rubs, and physical obstruction, such as rubbing against an employee in a hallway.

SFAC *See **Statements of Financial Accounting Concepts***

SFAS *See **Statements of Financial Accounting Standards***

share of voice A measure of *advertising* effectiveness based on the percentage of advertising expense that a company pays within a chosen market.

EXAMPLE: A toy company accounts for 20 percent of all the advertising expenditures in the doll market, so it can claim a 20-percent share of voice. With a 20-percent share of voice, the company should expect approximately a 20-percent *market share.* If the market share is less than 20 percent, the company is probably spending inefficiently on advertising. If the share is greater than 20 percent, the company is spending efficiently and might consider increasing its advertising budget.

shelf registration A provision in SEC regulations that permits companies to comply with the registration requirements for a public securities offering up to two years before making the actual offering.

With the registration essentially complete and *on the shelf,* corporations can make the issue when market conditions offer the highest share-price potential. Although shelf registrations must be continually updated and regular reports filed with the SEC, most companies find these a small price to pay for the ability to choose the proper timing for the issue. It is much less costly to file a shelf registration with updated reports than to refile full registrations if the first one proves untimely.

Shelf registrations are becoming increasingly popular with companies issuing *medium-term notes* where the outlook for two to five years is the crucial determinant for timing the issue.

shop floor control   In manufacturing, a system for using information from a factory shop floor to monitor the status of various workstations and product orders.

Shop floor control has five key functions: (1) assigning priorities to product orders; (2) maintaining order-by-order quantity data on *work-in-process inventories*; (3) providing *output* information used in *capacity* control; (4) informing management of the status of each product order; (5) providing data that can be used for the measurement of *efficiency, productivity,* and *utilization* of the labor force or equipment.

shortage   In economics, a condition that exists when the quantity demanded of a good or service exceeds the quantity supplied at a given price.

When this situation occurs, it indicates that the market price is below its equilibrium level. As a result, consumers may experience long lines, waiting lists, or difficulty in finding products for sale in the stores. When a shortage exists, the market price rises, thereby clearing the market of the excess demand.

short-term debt   In accounting, a debt that is due within one year.

Short-term debt is reported as a *current liability* on the *balance sheet* and includes the portion of a long-term debt due within one year.

shut-down situation   In economics, a situation in which a firm would be better off to close down its operations than to continue to produce.

It occurs when the price of the product falls below its average variable cost of production. In such a situation, the revenue earned per unit of sale (the unit price of the product) is not enough to cover a firm's unit variable cost. Therefore, there is nothing left to contribute toward a firm's fixed cost.

Expressed in another way, the shut-down situation occurs when the price is so low that a firm's operational losses exceed its total fixed cost. By shutting down, the firm minimizes its losses by having to pay only for the total fixed cost. When the price just equals a firm's average variable cost, it is referred to as the *shut-down point*.

simple capital structure   In accounting, a *capital structure* with no securities that can be converted into *common stock*.

See also capital structure, common stock equivalent, complex capital structure, earnings per share.

simple interest The interest paid on the principal of a loan when there is no compounding.

Simple interest is calculated as

$$I = P \times I_t \times n$$

where

I = simple interest rate
P = principal amount
I_t = interest rate per time period
n = number of time periods

EXAMPLE: The simple interest on $100,000 at 11 percent borrowed for eight months is

$$\$100,000 \times 11\% \times 8/12 = \$7,333$$

In other words, the interest payments on the first eight months of this loan amount to $7,333.

single sourcing The purchase of a good or service from one supplier.

Traditionally, manufacturers sought to maintain at least two suppliers for each component part. This practice served to ensure a continuous supply and, more importantly, encouraged price competition between suppliers. With the advent of *just-in-time,* manufacturers have adopted single sourcing in order to establish close relationships with a small number of suppliers. These relationships frequently lead to higher quality, shorter lead times, and a greater degree of cooperation between the manufacturer and the supplier.

sinking fund Money set aside for periodic payments in order to reduce a financial obligation.

Sinking funds are reported on the **balance sheet,** usually as *investments* or *other assets.* For example, if a company issues a sinking fund **bond,** it makes periodic payments to a trustee who then invests the money in order to be able to retire the bonds upon their maturity.

skimming In marketing, a pricing strategy in which the initial price is set high with the goal of selling the product first to people who want it and are willing to pay a premium for it. When this market is saturated, the marketer drops the price to appeal to consumers who are more price-sensitive. In this way, total *revenue* is maximized.

For skimming to prove effective, three conditions should exist: (1) The people who want the product should be largely indifferent to price, and a number of price segments should exist. (2) Consumers should know little about the costs of producing and marketing the product. In this way, they are unlikely to know they are paying a premium to acquire it. (3) The likelihood of competitors entering the market and initiating price cutting is slim.

Skimming has a number of advantages. For one, it helps the marketer recover the costs of **new-product development** more quickly. For another, the initial high price can create a prestige image for the product. Moreover, marketers recognize that it is easier to lower prices than increase them. So skimming makes sense when the marketer does not yet know how much demand there will be for the product.

The disadvantages of a skimming strategy include the following: A price that is set too high initially may hurt sales and even lead to the product's early demise. Skimming also attracts competitors who see high profits being generated and want to get in on the action. Another drawback is that the skimming strategy often makes it necessary for marketers to revise the **marketing mix** to serve new **target markets** that emerge as prices drop. Advertising, for example, is likely to become more important than personal selling, and the distribution pattern will probably shift from specialty stores to mass merchandisers. *Compare to **penetration pricing**, **target return pricing**.*

slack   The time difference between the scheduled deadline for a job and its estimated completion date.

If a job will be finished ahead of schedule, it is said to have slack time. If a job will be finished behind schedule, it is said to have negative slack time.

Slack also refers to the amount of time that a task can be delayed without delaying an entire project. *See **critical path method** (**CPM**).*

societal marketing   A marketing strategy aimed at understanding and satisfying the needs and desires of the **target market** in a way that maintains or improves both the consumer's and society's well-being.

EXAMPLE: Ben & Jerry's Ice Cream is a classic example of a company that uses societal marketing. The company has established a nonprofit foundation that is dedicated to world peace and donates a percentage of its profits to the organization. Ben & Jerry's marketing subsequently carries two messages: Enjoy our ice cream and help further world peace.

soft currency   The currency of a country that cannot be freely converted into a **hard currency**, thereby restricting its use to the country of origin.

Exporters to developing countries having soft currency frequently resort to **countertrade** arrangements as opposed to direct payments. Although some Eastern European and Latin American countries are making efforts to convert to hard currency, most continue to have insufficient dollar or other hard currency reserves to make the switch. Soft currency countries include most of Latin America, Eastern Europe, Africa, Commonwealth of Independent States, and certain Middle Eastern and South Asian countries.

span of control The number of subordinates a manager is able to direct effectively.

Traditionally, spans of control were kept small—usually under six. The trend today, however, thanks to improved training, communication, and information technology is to increase span of control up to 10 or 12.

spending multiplier A sequence of spending increases leading to income gains leading to spending gains.

Personal consumption expenditures are the largest portion of gross domestic product (GDP), but they have a vital importance quite apart from their size. Ultimately, it is consumer spending that fuels economic growth. Increases in *disposable income,* however, can be either spent or saved. On average, U.S. consumers have spent some 90 to 94 percent of disposable income in the post–World War II era. This spending, in turn, generates additional income to the factors of production used to produce the consumer goods and services purchased. This additional income, then, fuels further rounds of spending and income. Thus the *spending multiplier* is the increase in aggregate demand outside the consumption-income stream—such as increases in nonresidential investment, exports, or government spending—set off by the spending-income sequence just described.

spin-offs A form of divestiture that involves the implementation of accounting and legal steps to segregate the assets of a business unit—a division, subsidiary, branch, or product line—into a separate corporate entity.

The parent company then sells stock in the new entity, either to the public (through an *initial public offering*), management groups (as through an *ESOP*), or private investors. A spin-off to private investors or management groups usually involves the outright sale of 100 percent of the equity interest. Public offerings are normally for a minority interest.

Assets of the spin-off business unit include the product engineering drawings, name, and patents (if any), as well as its raw materials and *work-in-process* and *finished goods inventory;* its customer list, order backlog, and receivables; any machinery, test equipment, or vehicles associated with the line; and land and buildings, if the business occupies a separate facility. Not infrequently, buyers retain most of the production workers as well as the supervisory and sales personnel responsible for the product line.

Legally, a spin-off is a sale of assets. The same Bulk Sales laws that apply when all of a company's assets are sold also apply to spin-offs. The tax recognition of capital gains and ordinary income is also the same. In addition, the built-in gains provisions of the tax code may apply if the selling entity has switched from a C corporation to an S corporation.

Spinning off a business unit, especially if the products are profitable, produces several benefits:

1. The capital raised can be used to reduce outstanding debt obligations, clearing the way for future borrowings.

2. If the product line has commercial value, its selling price should exceed the cost of its supporting assets. This incremental cash premium would probably not be realized simply by continuing to sell the products in the marketplace.

3. After the spin-off has been completed, additional cost-cutting moves should be feasible, such as personnel layoffs and a sale or lease of excess production and storage space.

spoilage   Any production that does not yield salable products.

There are four types of spoilage: spoiled goods, defective goods, waste, and scrap. Spoiled goods do not meet a company's production standards and are either sold at a reduced price or discarded. Defective goods also do not meet production standards, and are either sold at a reduced price or reworked and then sold. Waste is any material that is lost during production. Scrap is a by-product of the manufacturing process that can be sold. A company's amount of spoilage should be compared with that of competitors or the industry norm to determine if the amount produced is normal or abnormal.

spot   *See advertising*

spreadsheet   A table of figures organized by rows and columns.

Spreadsheets are commonly used for accounting and financial calculations. Most spreadsheet calculations are performed by computer programs such as Lotus 1-2-3, Excel, Supercalc4, and Multiplan. These programs are frequently used for the preparation of *financial statements,* cost and performance reports, and work sheets but are especially good for making projections, such as determining what impact a different sales level will have on a company's profits.

standard cost   A predetermined cost representing the ideal or norm achievable by a company.

Standard costs form the basis of a standard cost system used extensively in manufacturing companies. At the beginning of each year, companies normally review standards for material price and usage, labor efficiency and wage rate, and overhead rates based on budgets.

In a standard cost system, all inputs to inventory are valued at standard and the variations from actual costs are written off to the *income statement* as variances. *Cost of goods sold* is always stated at standard cost. A partial income statement using a standard cost system would be as follows:

Sales		$10,000
Standard cost of sales		
Material	2,000	
Labor	1,000	
Overhead	3,000	
Total standard cost of sales		6,000
Standard gross profit		4,000
Variances		
Material price	50	
Material usage	70	
Labor efficiency	120	
Labor wage rate	50	
Overhead efficiency	100	
Overhead budget	200	
Total variance from standard		590
Total cost of sales		6,590
Gross profit		3,410

Since variances from standard are recorded when cost elements are put into inventory, they are written off in the current *accounting period.* Also, when variances from expected performance are recognized shortly after they occur, the company can take faster corrective action.

statement of cash flows A formal statement of the *cash* received and disbursed by a company.

The statement of cash flows is divided into three sections: operating activities (usually a source of cash), investing activities (usually both a source and a use of cash), and financing activities (usually a source and use of cash). When cash is received or paid for more than one activity, it is allocated to that activity that is the prime motivation for the cash flow. For example, many companies consider cash spent on new equipment to be an investment activity rather than an operating activity.

In recent years, analysts have emphasized the statement of cash flows. The information contained in a statement of cash flows is vital since most stockholder and creditor interests are settled in cash. Cash flows information can help determine a company's ability to generate future cash from operations, pay dividends, and pay maturing debts and obligations. *See also funds provided from operations.*

Consolidated Statements of Cash Flows
Wal-Mart Stores, Inc. and Subsidiaries
(Amounts in thousands)

	Fiscal year ended January 31		
	1991	1990	1989
Cash flows from operating activities:			
Net income	$1,291,024	$1,075,900	$837,221
Adjustments to reconcile net income to net cash provided by operating activities:			
Depreciation and amortization	346,614	269,406	213,629
Loss from sale of assets	3,378	5,039	1,073
Increase in accounts receivable	(58,324)	(29,173)	(30,710)
Increase in inventories	(1,087,520)	(1,076,706)	(699,607)
Decrease (increase) in prepaid expenses	11,823	(11,439)	(6,561)
Increase in accounts payable	689,435	436,990	289,769
Increase in accrued liabilities	84,739	174,112	114,954
Increase in deferred income tax	14,716	22,688	14,230
Net cash provided by operating activities	1,295,885	866,817	733,998
Cash flows from investing activities:			
Payments for property, plant, and equipment	(1,388,298)	(954,602)	(592,756)
Recoverable sale/leaseback expenditures	(235,894)	(131,464)	(204,262)
Sale/leaseback arrangements and other property sales	91,000	184,900	246,797
Decrease in other assets	7,058	7,375	9,087
Net cash used in investing activities	(1,526,134)	(893,791)	(541,134)
Cash flows from financing activities:			
Increase (decrease) in commercial paper	30,405	165,774	(85,382)
Proceeds from issuance of long-term debt	500,306	4,763	1,624
Proceeds from Walton Enterprises, Inc. stock exchange	14,000	—	—
Exercise of stock options	4,958	243	3,885
Payments for purchase of common stock	(25,826)	—	—
Dividends paid	(158,889)	(124,491)	(90,464)
Payment of long-term debt	(109,304)	(4,159)	(3,213)
Payment of capital lease obligation	(25,177)	(20,919)	(18,086)
Net cash provided by (used in) financing activities	230,473	27,211	(191,636)
Net increase in cash and cash equivalents	224	237	1,228
Cash and cash equivalents at beginning of year	12,790	12,553	11,325
Cash and cash equivalents at end of year	$ 13,014	$ 12,790	$ 12,553
Supplemental disclosure of cash flow information:			
Income tax paid	$ 721,036	$ 551,021	$473,631
Interest paid	166,134	136,762	134,048
Capital lease obligations incurred	100,972	104,122	164,845
McLane Company, Inc. liabilities at acquisition date	513,000	—	—

statement of shareholders' equity A separate element of an *annual report* detailing the individual components of *stockholders' equity* and the changes that took place within the past year.

    Stockholders' equity includes *preferred stock, common stock*, paid-in capital, *retained earnings, treasury stock*, unrealized losses on long-term investments, and *foreign currency translation* gains and losses.

Statements of Financial Accounting Concepts (SFAC) The reports published by the *Financial Accounting Standards Board (FASB)* showing the basic concepts of *financial accounting,* reporting, and *disclosure.*

    SFAC are issued in order to clarify or establish a basic accounting concept.

Statements of Financial Accounting Standards (SFAS) The rules established by the *Financial Accounting Standards Board (FASB)* regarding *financial accounting,* reporting, and *disclosure.*

    The standards deal with nearly every aspect of financial accounting, such as pensions, leases, depreciation, and presentation of *financial statements.*

stock dividend A dividend of common stock granted to shareholders rather than cash.

    Stock dividends are frequently used when companies are short of cash or when the market price of the stock is undervalued. Shareholders gain because the additional stock received is not taxed until sold, in contrast to cash dividends, which are taxed when received.

stock index An indicator used to report and measure any changes in value of representative groups of stocks.

    There are a number of different indexes, ranging from the *National Association of Securities Dealers Automated Quotations system (NASDAQ)*, which represents all over-the-counter stocks, to more narrow indexes that concentrate on stocks in a particular market sector or industry. Some of the more widely used indexes are the AMEX Major Market Index, which is a price-weighted average of 20 blue-chip stocks; the AMEX Market Value Index, which measures the performance of more than 800 issues traded on the American Stock Exchange; the *Dow Jones Industrial Average,* which tracks the performance of 30 stocks traded on the *New York Stock Exchange (NYSE);* the New York Stock Exchange Composite Index, which relates all stocks traded on the NYSE to an aggregate market value as of December 31, 1965; and Standard & Poor's Composite Index of 500 Stocks, which is a market-value-weighted index of 500 stocks, most of them traded on the NYSE but including some AMEX and over-the-counter issues.

Consolidated Statements of Shareholders' Equity
Wal-Mart Stores, Inc. and Subsidiaries
(Amounts in thousands except per share data)

	Number of shares	Common stock	Capital in excess of par value	Retained earnings	Total
Balance–January 31, 1988 ...	565,122	$ 56,511	$170,440	$2,030,316	$2,257,267
Net income..............				837,221	837,221
Cash dividends ($0.08* per share)..............				(90,464)	(90,464)
Exercise of stock options................	609	61	2,974		3,035
Tax benefit from stock options................			4,778		4,778
Other...................	(130)	(13)	(3,915)		(3,928)
Balance–January 31, 1989 ...	565,591	56,559	174,277	2,777,073	3,007,909
Net income..............				1,075,900	1,075,900
Cash dividends ($0.11* per share)..............				(124,491)	(124,491)
Exercise of stock options................	679	68	3,876		3,944
Tax benefit from stock options................			7,000		7,000
Other...................	(135)	(13)	(4,688)		(4,701)
Balance–January 31, 1990 ...	566,135	56,614	180,465	3,728,482	3,965,561
Net income..............				1,291,024	1,291,024
Cash dividends ($0.14* per share)..............				(158,889)	(158,889)
Exercise of stock options................	156	15	1,327		1,342
Other...................	(34)	(4)	(1,626)		(1,630)
Two-for-one stock split....	566,257	56,625	(56,625)		
Exercise of stock options................	506	51	2,427		2,478
Shares issued for McLane acquisition	10,366	1,037	273,659		274,696
Tax benefit from stock options................			6,075		6,075
Purchase of stock.........	(1,000)	(100)	(819)	(24,907)	(25,826)
Walton Enterprises, Inc. stock exchange.........			14,000		14,000
Other...................	(104)	(10)	(3,297)		(3,307)
Balance–January 31, 1991 ...	1,142,282	$114,228	$415,586	$4,835,710	$5,365,524

*Cash dividends per share on stock prior to July 6, 1990, have been adjusted to reflect the two-for-one stock split on that date.

366

stock split   The issuing of new shares of *common stock* by reducing *par value,* and the market price, of the stock.

Stock splits generally serve to encourage investment by lowering the price of a stock.

EXAMPLE: A company has 1,000 shares of $40 par value stock, so its total par value comes to $40,000. If the company issues a two-for-one stock split, there will now be 2,000 shares with $20 par value. The total par value remains the same ($40,000). Usually, when a company issues a two-for-one stock split, the market price will drop by half.

Compare to **reverse split.**

stockholders' equity   In accounting, the ownership interest of stockholders in a company.

See **equity.** *See also* **owner's equity.**

stockout   A situation in which a company cannot fill a customer order.

Stockouts are often the result of insufficient inventory, changes in product scheduling, or an unanticipated increase in demand. For example, a customer ordering a pair of shoes from a mail-order catalog might be told that a particular style is not in stock and that delivery of the shoes may take longer than expected. Stockouts can lead to *backorders* in which the company immediately orders the desired product from its suppliers. These are usually more expensive than regular inventory orders, and can result in significant costs, both financially and in terms of customer goodwill.

storyboard   In marketing, a visual representation of the script of a television commercial or show.

The storyboard, which resembles a comic strip, shows the key actions described in the script. Storyboards are used to present different script ideas to advertisers and can act as a guide in the actual production of a commercial.

straight rebuy   A buying situation in the *industrial market* where the purchaser reorders goods or services, such as office supplies or maintenance, on a routine basis.

Competitors find it difficult to penetrate this market, since the purchase usually involves few decision makers with little time. *See also* **modified rebuy, new task.**

straight-line depreciation   In accounting, a method of *depreciation* that generates equal depreciation expenses for each period because it assumes that the asset provides constant economic benefits.

Straight-line depreciation is simple to calculate and widely used. Straight-line depreciation charges are calculated by dividing the cost of the asset less its **salvage value** by the estimated economic life of the asset, or

$$\frac{\text{Cost} - \text{Salvage value}}{\text{Life of asset}}$$

EXAMPLE: If a company buys \$1,000,000 of new factory equipment that has a useful life of 5 years and a salvage value of \$100,000, its depreciation expense would be calculated as

$$\frac{\$1,000,000 - \$100,000}{5 \text{ years}} = \$180,000 \text{ per year}$$

*See also **accelerated depreciation**. Compare to **double declining balance depreciation, sum-of-the-years' digits method**.*

strategic business unit (SBU) A collection of product lines or product groups within a company with similar markets, competitors, or strategic problems.

In most cases, the individual units were, at one point, managed independently. The creation of SBUs, then, often cuts across established organizational structures. The key advantage of strategic business units is the ability to run a set of strategically similar businesses under the same management. This reduces the distinction between strategy formulation and strategy implementation and eliminates a great deal of otherwise redundant effort as the manager of each individual unit attempts to cope with its **environment.**

strategic planning Those actions that lead to the definition of a company's mission, the formulation of its goals, and the development of the specific strategies that will be implemented to meet those goals.

There are four basic characteristics of strategic planning:

1. It involves decisions by managers at all levels.
2. It deals with the allocation of large amounts of resources, such as capital, labor, or **capacity.**
3. It focuses on the long term, but increasingly strategic planning focuses on both the short and the long term.
4. It deals with a company's interaction with its **environment.**

subordinated debt Any debt that, in the event of a company's liquidation, is not repayable until more senior claims have been settled.

Some subordinated debt may have greater claim on the assets of the liquidated company than other subordinated debt. For example, a subordinated debenture ranks above a junior subordinated debenture. *Compare to **senior debt.***

subsidiary company A company in which a majority interest is owned by another company.

successful efforts method A method of accounting for exploration costs by companies in extractive industries, such as oil and gas.

   The costs of a successful project are *capitalized* whereas the costs of unsuccessful efforts are treated as an expense. The capitalized costs are *amortized* on the basis of the reserves produced. *See also full cost method.*

sum-of-the-years'-digits (SYD) method In accounting, a method of *accelerated depreciation.*

   Sum-of-the-years'-digits depreciation charges are calculated by assigning numbers $(1, 2, 3, 4, \ldots, n)$ where n is the estimated useful life of an asset. SYD is then calculated using the formula

$$SYD = \frac{n(n + 1)}{2}$$

The annual depreciation charges are then calculated by

$$(\text{Cost of the asset} - \text{Salvage value}) \times \frac{\text{Remaining useful life}}{\text{SYD}}$$

EXAMPLE: An asset costs \$1,000, has an estimated useful life of five years, and a salvage value of \$100. The SYD is calculated as

$$\frac{5(5 + 1)}{2} = 15$$

The annual depreciation charges are as follows:

Year	Cost − Salvage value		Remaining useful life SYD		Depreciation
1	\$900	×	$5/15$	=	\$300
2	900	×	$4/15$	=	240
3	900	×	$3/15$	=	180
4	900	×	$2/15$	=	120
5	900	×	$1/15$	=	60
			Total	=	\$900

   Sum-of-years'-digits depreciation generates higher depreciation charges in the earlier years of an asset's life than in later years. The method is appropriate in situations where an asset provides greater economic benefits at the beginning of its life than at the end. *See also accelerated depreciation. Compare to double declining balance depreciation.*

sunk costs In accounting, a cost that has already been incurred and cannot be affected by any present or future decisions.

EXAMPLE: A machine purchased five years ago for $100,000 now has a current *book value* of $30,000. The $30,000 book value is a sunk cost. It is not affected by, nor should it affect, any future decisions about the machine's replacement.

supplier credit Credit extended to a buyer from an exporter.

An exporter may choose to extend supplier credit independently, or it may obtain outside financing from government agencies, banks, or a number of other sources. Whenever an exporter records a receivable, the credit extension is considered a supplier credit.

supplier power The ability of a supplier to influence or control buyers.

As an element of the *five forces model,* which determines the profitability of an industry, supplier power is an essential part of any strategic analysis. Powerful suppliers can severely reduce the profitability of an industry, say by raising prices or reducing the quantity of their goods. For example, the chemical companies that act as suppliers to contract aerosol packagers have been able to exert their supplier power in the form of higher prices. The aerosol packagers, faced with intense competition from their own customers, many of whom created in-house packaging operations, are then limited in their ability to raise prices. As a result, profitability is reduced.

There are generally five conditions in which supplier power is high:

1. If the industry is controlled by a small number of companies and is more concentrated than the industry it sells to. When suppliers are selling to fragmented buyers, they will have considerable control over prices, terms of purchase, and quality.

2. If the suppliers are able to pursue a strategy of *forward integration,* such as developing the capacity to produce the finished product. For example, a textile company that sells to clothing manufacturers might increase its supplier power by beginning to manufacture its own line of clothing.

3. If the supplier does not face the threat of substitute products. For example, the sugar industry had a great deal of supplier power before the development of artificial sweeteners. Once substitute products entered the market, the industry's supplier power was reduced.

4. If the suppliers' products are differentiated or carry high switching costs. In many cases, if it is expensive to switch from one supplier to another, supplier power is very high. For example, supplier power might be enhanced if a company initiates a comprehensive inventory control system for its customers. Once the system is in place, buyers would face the formidable cost of developing a new inventory control system with a different supplier.

5. If the purchasing industry is not an important customer to the supplying industry. When a particular industry or company represents
a small fraction of a supplier's sales, that supplier is likely to exert a
great deal of supplier power.

supply In economics, the amount of a good or service that people stand ready
to sell at a list of possible prices, other factors being held constant.

These other factors are (1) costs, (2) technology, (3) number of sellers,
(4) future expectations about market price, and (5) weather conditions (particularly for the supply of agricultural products).

Economists expect that people are ready to sell more of their good or
service as the price rises and to sell less as the price falls, other factors
being held constant. When any one or more of these other factors change,
the entire relationship between price and quantity supplied changes. For
example, if bad weather in Florida destroys part of the orange crop, there
would be a decrease in the market supply of oranges. This means there
would be a smaller quantity of oranges supplied, regardless of what prices
are being offered for this product.

surplus In economics, a condition that exists when the quantity supplied of
a good or service exceeds the quantity demanded at a given price.

When this situation occurs, it indicates that the market price is above
its equilibrium level. As a result, sellers may experience a build up in
inventories. When a surplus exists, the market price falls, thereby clearing
the market of the excess supply.

survey A questionnaire administered through the mail, through personal interview, or on the telephone; frequently part of a *descriptive research*
project.

survey feedback *See attitudes*

SWOT analysis An acronym for Strengths, Weaknesses, Opportunities, and
Threats. SWOT analysis is a strategy analysis framework that helps managers build a corporate and business strategy that emphasizes a company's
strengths and opportunities.

Strengths are also known as *core competencies.* They include proprietary
technology, skills, resources, market position, patents, and so on. For example, a young company might properly consider the enthusiasm of its
employees, who work 12 to 14 hours per day, as a strength.

A weakness is a condition within a company that can lead to poor performance. Common weaknesses include obsolete equipment, a heavy debt
load, a poor product image, weak managerial skills, and so on.

Opportunities are current or future conditions in the *environment* that
a company might be able to turn to its advantage. For example, in the
medical industry, the increasing age of the population might be seen as an
opportunity.

Threats are current or future conditions in the environment that might harm a company. For example, if there is an increase in the gas tax, demand for recreational vehicles will probably fall.

SWOT analysis can help managers grasp their strategic situation, but it is important to assign probabilities to both opportunities and threats in order to evaluate their likelihood.

synergy The concept that the combination of two or more different businesses, activities, or processes will create an overall value that is greater than the sum of the individual parts.

Synergy is frequently discussed in **_annual reports_** and company press releases, where its value is generally limited to a rationalization for a particular action. For example, when GM purchased Hughes Aircraft, there was a great ballyhoo about the synergy between the two. Cars were going to convert to electricity and Hughes offered a great deal of expertise in that area. However, any actual synergy between the two was limited to the **_annual report._**

Essentially two types of relationships can produce real synergy. The first is the ability to transfer particular skills between the various units of each company. For example, a cosmetics business unit, which has expertise in the marketing of beauty products, might be able to transfer ideas about the packaging and promotion to a newly acquired business unit that manufactures and sells shampoo. The second is when two companies can share meaningful activities, such as a sales force or research department. For example, Proctor & Gamble uses a common sales force and distribution system for both disposable diapers and paper towels.

10-K The annual filing made by *publicly held companies* to the *Securities and Exchange Commission.*

The 10-K usually contains more financial information than an annual report, with audited *financial statements*, *disclosures* on sales, *operating income, segment reports,* and general business information.

10-Q The *quarterly reports* made by *publicly held companies* with the *Securities and Exchange Commission.*

Form 10-Q is not so comprehensive as Form 10-K. It contains interim financial reports (usually not audited), the appropriate *disclosures,* and comparative figures for the same period of the previous year.

T-groups Sensitivity training laboratories designed to encourage individual growth and personal development.

T-groups consist of 10 to 15 members and a professional facilitator. The facilitator typically starts the first session by laying the following ground rules: (1) there will be no structure, agenda, or formal procedures within the group; (2) the focus of the discussions will stay in the immediate present; and (3) the purpose of the group is to enhance each individual's understanding of individual behavior and group performance.

Once the facilitator has set the ground rules, free-flowing discussions begin. The emphasis of the discussions should be on how each member feels (as opposed to how he or she thinks) and relates to others in the group. As discussion develops, individuals are given feedback on how they are perceived by the rest of the group. This combination of discussion, reactions, and feedback allows group members to gain insights into their own behavior, and the behavior of the group.

The advantages of T-groups include the opportunity to become aware of *group norms,* gain insight into personal *blind spots,* and develop a sense of group belonging. The disadvantages of T-groups include a sense of manipulation, resentment for giving up autonomy in order to join the group, and a loss of self-confidence in the face of potentially strong group norms.

tangible asset In accounting, an *asset* with physical substance and an expected life of more than one year.

Tangible assets are usually reported as **noncurrent assets** on the **balance sheet** and include equipment, machinery, furniture and fixtures, and buildings. *See also* **asset**. *Compare to* **intangible asset**.

target market The portion of the *market* that a company decides to pursue actively.

See **served market**.

target return pricing A pricing strategy in which a marketer tries to obtain a predetermined percentage return on the **capital** it uses to produce and distribute a product.

Under this approach, the marketer determines a dollar amount for the **return on investment (ROI)** it wants to achieve. It then treats this amount as a fixed cost, that is, the amount is added to the other fixed costs—management salaries, rent, insurance, and so on—when it adds up the total cost of producing a set number of the product. When the marketer divides the total costs, including the ROI, by the quantity it will produce, the resulting number is the price. That price ensures that the marketer will recapture the costs, plus the targeted return, if it sells all the product it produces at that price.

One advantage of using this pricing strategy is its simplicity. If a company sells all the items it plans to sell, it will achieve its target return. The strategy, though, ignores the demand side of the equation—that is, consumers may not buy the amount of product the marketer planned. It also excludes the competitors' pricing strategies—thus the targeted return is not guaranteed.

Until the early 1980s, the U.S. automobile industry used target return pricing. The "Big Three" auto companies all relied on *pricing committees* that decided how many cars the automaker expected to sell, totaled up the costs, threw in a healthy profit, and simply divided these costs by expected sales. If costs rose or fell, the automakers would simply boost the price to make up the difference. Double-digit inflation in the late 1970s, though, and fierce competition from Japanese automakers combined to make a mockery of forecasted demand. That is when American auto producers turned to **sales promotions** such as **rebates**, savings certificates, contests, extended warranties, and even money-back guarantees to lure buyers into the showrooms.

tax haven A country with tax-preference laws for foreign companies and individuals.

Three classes of jurisdictions are referred to as tax havens: those that

1. Have no relevant taxes (such as, Cayman Islands, the Bahamas, Bermuda, Turks and Caicos Islands)
2. Levy taxes only on internal taxable transactions, but none at all or very low taxes on foreign source income (such as, Hong Kong and Panama)

3. Grant special tax privileges to certain types of companies or operations (e.g., the Channel Islands, Liechtenstein, and Luxembourg)

The principal functions of tax havens are to (1) avoid or postpone taxes, (2) avoid exchange controls, and (3) act as a shield against confiscation, nationalization, and other forms of expropriation. Tax avoidance does not mean tax evasion, which is strictly illegal in all civilized countries.

Tax havens are also known as *safe havens,* a concept that dates back many centuries. The most efficient and useful tax havens are also *offshore financial centers,* replete with cadres of offshore banking facilities, trust organizations, lawyers, and accountants. Many tax havens have also branched out into the rapidly expanding captive insurance business.

Modern tax haven/offshore financial centers began as safe havens for capital that might otherwise have been expropriated by politically unstable or war-torn governments in Europe and Latin America (and later in the Middle East and Africa)—not as havens to avoid taxes. Switzerland is a prime example. As private enterprise expanded, currency areas changed, and corporate taxes escalated, safe havens (tax havens) became the raison d'être for places like Bermuda, the Bahamas, and the Cayman Islands.

team building The creation of a high level of interaction between group members, and sometimes between groups, in order to foster openness and trust.

Team-building activities usually include goal setting, role analysis to delineate each member's responsibilities, and the development of relationships between team members. Of course, team-building activities vary from group to group.

technology transfer The making available of know-how (patents, industrial design, operational systems) from one trading partner to another.

Technology transfer transactions can take two basic forms: commercial and noncommercial.

- Commercially transferred technology is done via direct investment, including direct sale, the licensing of intellectual property, the contracting for consultancy services, and turnkey projects.

- Noncommercially transferred technology takes the form of technical assistance funded by official government agencies (e.g., Canadian International Development Agency). It is otherwise called *official development assistance* (ODA) and can be provided either noncontractually (i.e., free of charge) or on concessional terms.

Technology transfer also refers to a component of a type of countertrade transaction called direct offsets in which an exporter agrees either to make available technical assis tance to the importer or to conduct research and development (R&D) in the host country as a condition of winning the export contract.

EXAMPLE: A group of the Sahel nations agreed to Canadian exports of irrigation equipment provided that the companies funded local R&D in agronomy and hydrology aimed at reducing and ultimately eliminating their dependence on external agricultural inputs. (*Source:* L. Presner, *The International Business Dictionary and Reference.* Copyright© 1991 by L. Presner. Reprinted with permission of the publishers, John Wiley & Sons, Inc.)

telemarketing A major tool in *direct marketing,* in which the consumer either calls or is called by a seller, listens to a sales pitch and a description of a product, and decides whether to place an order.

Telemarketing can prove effective in both the *consumer market* and the *industrial market,* where it can reduce significantly the amount of time-consuming face-to-face personal selling between dealers and customers.

As a rule, telemarketing is considerably more expensive than other forms of direct marketing, but the higher cost is often offset by a much higher *response rate.*

television rating The percentage of households with televisions watching a given broadcast.

EXAMPLE: If 30 percent of the households with television are tuned in to "60 Minutes," the show has a rating of 30. Nationally, one ratings point equals about 921,000 homes.

Compare to *television share.*

television share The percentage of households with televisions *in use* that are tuned to a particular broadcast.

EXAMPLE: Say 50 percent of the households with televisions have the set on, and 80 percent of these are tuned to the Superbowl. In that case, the broadcast of the game has a share of 80. Television share tells the marketer the number of people watching a particular show as opposed to the number of people watching different shows at the same time.

Compare to *television rating.*

tender offer An offer to buy shares of a corporation, usually at a price in excess of market.

When a company or group of investors aims to purchase controlling interest in a corporation, it submits a tender offer to present stockholders for the purchase of their shares. Usually, but not always, the tender offer includes an offer price in excess of the current trading price of the shares in the market as an incentive for shareholders to sell.

Tender offers may be rendered in a friendly or a hostile takeover bid. In a hostile bid, the target company's board of directors may choose to block the offer with an offer of its own to purchase outstanding shares.

The **Securities and Exchange Commission** requires full disclosure from any investor or group of investors accumulating 5 percent or more of a company's outstanding shares.

test market A controlled *marketing research* experiment carried out in a carefully chosen part of the marketplace, usually a representative test city, designed to predict the sales and profit of a particular element of a marketing strategy.

Marketers can design test markets to examine nearly every aspect of the **marketing mix,** ranging from a new-product **rollout market entry** to a subtle change in an existing advertising campaign.

EXAMPLE: A soft drink company wants to introduce a new raspberry-flavored soda. It conducts a test market by introducing it for a short period in several small markets—say, Spokane, Washington; Knoxville, Tennessee; and Peoria, Illinois—all popular test markets. By analyzing sales and consumer reaction to the new soda, the company can decide whether to move forward with a full-scale introduction of the product.

Test markets have two significant drawbacks: they are expensive, and they give competitors time to react and respond to any new products or marketing strategies.

throughput time The total amount of time it takes for a product or service to move through the production process; also called *total processing time.*

For example, an insurance company training a sales staff might divide the process into the following tasks:

	Task	Time (days)
1	Prepare phase 1 of training	4
2	Select salespeople	2
3	Send salespeople to training	2
4	Train salespeople	10

The throughput time for this entire process is 18 days.

time study A process by which the amount of time required to perform a given task is computed.

The methods include direct time study, where the worker is timed with a stopwatch; **methods-time measurement (MTM),** where the job is videotaped or filmed and analyzed using predetermined time values; or historical data. A time study is distinguished from a motion study by the fact that motion studies aim to improve **productivity** whereas time studies aim to measure productivity. Time studies are usually viewed by workers with some suspicion, if not outright hostility. In fact, some unions prohibit them.

total quality management (TQM) A philosophy of total organizational involvement in improving all aspects of the quality of product or service provided by the organization; also called *total quality control*.

The basic concept behind TQM is that it is very expensive to maintain quality by inspections, and much more efficient to build quality products in the first place. As a result, responsibility for quality is placed with the workers who actually produce the products. This is called quality at the source. This is not to say that quality control departments are not an important part of TQM. Rather, they are refocused on different responsibilities, such as training employees in quality control, conducting audits of the quality of the company's parts and suppliers, making final tests of finished goods, and implementing quality control concepts throughout the company. There are many aspects to TQM, including employee empowerment in decision making, the use of teams in the organization (*see self-managed work teams, team building*), individual responsibility for products or services, and a strong customer service orientation.

Toy Safety Act An act passed by Congress in 1984 granting the government the power to recall dangerous toys quickly.

trade credit (domestic) The payment terms granted to a buyer by a supplier.

Typically, suppliers grant discounts of 1 to 2 percent to buyers willing to pay the entire invoice within 10 to 15 days, but demand payment in full within 30 days. For large orders or orders for special or scarce materials, suppliers may, under certain circumstances, grant trade credit for 60 days, 90 days, or longer.

Trade credit is normally the least expensive and easiest way to finance short-term working capital. Assuming a company's credit rating remains satisfactory, suppliers grant trade credit without any interest rate or collateral. Occasionally, however, they insist that the commodities purchased be used to secure the credit. This happens frequently when selling to a company in bankruptcy.

trade credit (international) The credit granted to buyers of exported goods and services.

Short-term trade credit may be *supplier credit* or *buyer credit*. Supplier credit is that credit extended to the buyer of exported products by the seller (the supplier-exporter). When such credit is extended directly by the seller, it is similar to domestic trade credit, except that sellers normally insist on a letter of credit as collateral. If a letter of credit is used, the buyer essentially pays for the goods immediately upon shipment, thereby eliminating the need for 30 days, 60 days, or 90 days terms.

Supplier credit may also be granted through a third party—banks, *Eximbank,* or the buyer's home country export credit agency.

Buyer credit is that credit extended directly to the buyer from a third party, that is, a grantor other than the seller. Buyer credit is frequently needed when the shipment of export orders extends over a long time period—perhaps one or two years. Such credit is usually granted by banks or export credit agencies in the buyer's home country, or by *Eximbank* or other U.S. government agencies. The credit may carry guarantees, or it may stand alone.

Another difference between supplier and buyer trade credit is that supplier credit is recorded as a receivable on the exporter's books, whereas buyer credit is not.

trade deficit An imbalance in merchandise trade that results in an excess of imports over exports.

The United States managed to keep its merchandise (goods) trade account close to balance through the first 25 years of the post–World War II era. In the 1970s trade deficits became more common, but in most years the United States managed to keep the *current account* close to balance by running a surplus on the service and investment income accounts.

In the 1980s, a rapid appreciation in the dollar's *foreign exchange* value made U.S. exports expensive in foreign markets, while foreign imports became inexpensive in dollar terms. As a result, the foreign trade deficit widened sharply. This widening only began to narrow after the dollar began to decline in foreign exchange value in 1985, but the deficit remained wide in the early 1990s. The following table shows levels for merchandise exports, imports, and the trade balance for selected years.

	Exports	Imports	Balance	
1950	10.2	9.1	1.1	
1955	14.4	11.5	2.9	
1960	19.6	14.8	4.9	
1965	26.5	21.5	5.0	
1970	42.5	39.9	2.6	
1975	107.1	98.2	8.9	
1980	224.2	249.8	− 25.5	Deficit
1985	215.9	338.1	−112.2	Deficit
1990	388.7	497.6	−108.9	Deficit
1991	416.0	489.4	− 73.4	Deficit
1992	439.3	535.5	− 96.3	Deficit

trade finance The financing of imports and exports.

Trade finance may relate to the granting of credit for the sale of goods or services, or it may refer to the financing of the production of goods to be exported. Financing may be short-term (less than 12 months), medium-term (one to seven years), or long-term (more than seven years). It may be sourced either from the exporter's country or from the importer's country. Supplier credit and buyer credit are both part of trade finance.

Commercial and political risk insurance forms an integral part of trade finance. All industrialized countries and many near-industrialized ones have government export credit insurance programs. In the United States, the **Foreign Credit Insurance Association,** an arm of **Eximbank,** insures U.S. exports against both political and commercial risk.

The following are major sources of trade finance:

- Commercial banks—in either the supplier's or buyer's home country
- Government-sponsored export credit programs
- Private export credit organizations
- Major corporations through joint venture
- Private sector, nonbank, trade finance organizations

trademark The right of a seller to exclusive use of an identifying symbol, or *brand.*

The Trademark Act of 1946 defined these marks as "names, symbols, titles, designations, slogans, character names, and distinctive features used in advertising." All trademarks are brands, but not all brands are trademarks. A trademark can include both a **brand name** and a graphic design. The word *Ford* is a brand name; but when it is printed in a certain kind of script, it becomes a trademark. When the identifying symbol is applied to a service, it is called a service mark.

transaction The exchange of something of value between two parties to the satisfaction of both.

EXAMPLE: A chef pays a fisherman $5 for a live lobster. The chef receives the lobster and the fisherman collects the $5.

Any transaction includes three key elements: (1) at least two items of value to the participants (the lobster and the $5); (2) mutually acceptable conditions (an agreed-upon price of $5 and a lobster that is, indeed, alive); and (3) a time and place of agreement (in this case, a fish market). If any of these three elements is unacceptable to either the chef or the fisherman, a system of regulations called contract laws comes into play. These are designed to protect both parties in a transaction and can be invoked by either side. *Compare to transaction, barter; transaction, monetary.*

transaction, barter A *transaction* in which the value exchanged is some item or service other than money.

Barter transactions frequently take place in the television industry. For example, a producer of a program offers a show to a television station at little or no cost, with the provision that several minutes of commercial time within that show be reserved for the producer. The show's producer then sells the reserved time to advertisers. No money changes hands in these deals, but both parties get something of value; the television station gets a show to air, and the show's producers get to sell some advertising time. *See also **transaction**. Compare to **transaction, monetary.***

transaction, monetary A *transaction* in which one of the values exchanged is money (for example, a consumer pays $300 for a stereo).
*See also **transaction**. Compare to **transaction, barter.***

transfer price The price charged when one segment of a company provides goods or services to another segment of the company.

EXAMPLE: An automobile manufacturer has one division that manufactures engines and another that manufactures spark plugs. The spark plug division will sell its products to the engine division at a set transfer price.

transformation process The process of adding value via the production process.

For example, a refinery transforms crude oil into gasoline. A bakery transforms flour and other ingredients into bread. A hospital dispenses medical care to improve the health of its patients.

The transformation process has six key characteristics that are generally of interest to management:

1. *Efficiency.* Generally measured as units of *output* per unit of *input.* An efficiency rate of 80 to 90 percent is usually desirable. When one is comparing the efficiency of two different transformation processes, it is important to choose the correct measures for inputs and outputs. For example, a department store might measure efficiency in terms of sales dollars per square foot whereas a hotel might measure efficiency in terms of room occupation.

2. *Capacity.* The maximum volume possible in a production process. New tools and equipment can increase capacity, but if their cost is too high, efficiency may be reduced.

3. *Effectiveness.* The production of the correct outputs. Effectiveness differs from efficiency in that it is known as "doing the right thing" whereas efficiency is known as "doing the thing right."

4. *Response time.* The speed at which an output can be produced. When a customer requires a custom product, or the company has decided to produce a new output, response time is the time needed to produce the first unit of the new output.

5. *Quality.* The ability of an output to satisfy a customer's requirements. If an output does not work well or does not last for a very long time, it is thought to be of poor quality.

6. *Flexibility.* The ability of the transformation process to produce different outputs.

transit advertising   Any advertisement appearing on vehicles such as buses, taxis, and subways.

Transit advertising allows advertisers to reach specific geographic *markets* with a high repetition rate. Transit advertising takes three forms: (1) car cards located inside vehicles, (2) outside posters located on the sides or back of vehicles, and (3) station posters located in terminals.

treasury stock   Shares of *common stock* that have been issued to the general public but are repurchased by the issuing company.

The shares then can either be resold at a later date or canceled. No *dividends* are paid on treasury stock, and it does not have any voting rights. Treasury stock is accounted for in two ways: the cost method and *par value.* Under the cost method, treasury stock is shown on the *balance sheet* as the cost of the reacquired shares. Under the par value method, treasury stock is reported on the balance sheet at the par value of the reacquired shares. Under either method, retained earnings are reduced by the amount of the treasury stock.

turnover ratio   A measure of the activity of a given *asset.*

There are several types of turnover ratios. Each is calculated by dividing sales or *cost of goods sold* by the particular *asset* in question. Examples include *fixed asset* turnover, which shows how well fixed assets were employed to generate sales:

$$\frac{\text{Sales}}{\text{Fixed assets}}$$

accounts receivables turnover, which indicates how well accounts receivables were managed by showing how long they were held before collection:

$$\frac{\text{Sales}}{\text{Average accounts receivable}}$$

and *inventory* turnover, which shows the number of times that the average amount of inventory on hand has sold within a given period of time. (*See also days inventory*):

$$\frac{\text{Cost of goods sold}}{\text{Average inventory on hand}}$$

two-bin system   A method of inventory control in which parts or materials are stored in two bins, one large and one small.

When the large bin is emptied, an order is placed for more materials, and the contents of the small bin are used to satisfy demand during the lead time of the new order.

The advantage of a two-bin system is that there is no need to keep detailed inventory records or constantly count inventory in order to ascertain whether to place an order. In some systems, it is the responsibility of the worker who uses the last part in a bin to place the new order. In others, a complete order form is kept in the bottom of the large bin, to be sent to a supplier in order to place the order.

type I error The rejection of a *good* lot on the basis of finding more than x defective units in a sample of n units.

A type I error is called *the producer's risk* because the producer ships an acceptable lot, only to have it rejected by the receiver. An acceptable lot is one with a percent defective that is equal to or below the *acceptable quality level*. *See also* **acceptable quality level, type II error.**

type II error The acceptance of a *bad* lot based on the inability to detect sufficient defective units within a sample to reject the entire lot.

A bad lot is one containing more than *lot tolerance percentage defective.* Type II errors are of great concern to most companies, since they want to avoid selling defective products. Of course, the level of concern varies from company to company. A pharmaceutical firm selling chemotherapy drugs would want to avoid type II errors at all costs. The consequences of selling defective drugs could be disastrous. A company making paper products, on the other hand, might not face such dire consequences if it sold a batch of defective napkins. *See also* **lot tolerance percentage defective, type I error.**

underwriting The guarantee an investment bank gives a company issuing securities that the bank will purchase the securities at a fixed price, thereby eliminating the risk of not selling the whole issue and receiving less cash than expected.

An investment bank that acts as an intermediary in the process of raising capital through public issues takes a risk by *underwriting* the issue.

Investment banks may also sell the issue on a *best efforts* basis, whereby the issuing company assumes the risk and simply takes back any securities not sold during a fixed period of time.

undifferentiated marketing A marketing strategy that looks at the entire market as a whole, with no segmentation; also called *mass* or *aggregate marketing*.

A company practicing undifferentiated marketing attempts to capture the whole market with one offer.

EXAMPLE: In its early days, the Coca-Cola Company practiced undifferentiated marketing by offering one drink in one container with one taste for the entire market.

unearned revenue In accounting, any advance payment for future goods or services.

Since the payment creates an obligation to provide the goods or service, unearned revenue is reported as a *liability* on the *balance sheet.*

unemployment rate The proportion of the workforce who have either lost employment in the past month, or who actively sought jobs unsuccessfully in that time.

The Household Survey of Employment is intended to assess the employment status of the working-age population, specifically, to distinguish between those who are employed and those who are unemployed. Unemployment represents one of the most important signs of an economy that is underperforming.

Unemployment can take four forms. (1) *Job losers* are workers who have lost their jobs either temporarily—and, so, are on layoff—or permanently.

These people represent the most widely understood notion of the unemployed. (2) *Job leavers* are those who have voluntarily left a job to relocate or to acquire new skills. An increase in the number of job leavers is regarded as a sign of confidence in the strength of the economy. Workers would be unlikely to leave employment if they thought labor markets would be weak. (3) *Reentrants* to the labor force are people who formerly were active in the labor force, but who left—most often women leaving to rear families—and are now returning. (4) *New entrants* to the labor force are people seeking employment for the first time.

The unemployment rate is equal to the number of unemployed divided by the total **labor force** (employed plus unemployed) expressed as a percent. The unemployment rate is a lagging indicator of economic activity. When a recession begins the unemployment rate may respond with a lag. More important, even after recovery starts, the unemployment rate may rise as reentrants and new entrants, believing jobs may be more readily available now that economic growth is returning, swell the labor force.

unfunded In accounting, the condition of a reserve for future contingent payments wherein the balance is insufficient to meet the obligation.

The term is used to describe an accrual for vacation pay that is not backed up with actual cash reserves. It also describes the condition of the reserve set up under an employee pension plan that is not backed by cash deposits with a trustee or otherwise. In general, any reserve that represents an allowance for future payments and that is not backed by cash deposits is referred to as an unfunded reserve. Those reserves which are partially funded with cash deposits but not in an amount sufficient to meet the full future obligation are said to be *underfunded*.

units of production method In accounting, a method of *depreciation* in which depreciation expenses are allocated by the use of the *asset* in production.

EXAMPLE: A candy company buys a packaging machine for $200,000 that it estimates will be able to put wrappers on 5,000,000 candy bars during its life. In other words, the machine will depreciate by $0.04 ($200,000 divided by 5,000,000 candy bars) every time it puts a wrapper on a candy bar. The machine's annual depreciation expense is then calculated by multiplying the depreciation per unit ($0.04) by the number of units produced during the year.

unqualified opinion The report on a company's financial statements made by an auditor who presents the company's financial position, the results of operations, and any changes in financial position, in conformity with **generally accepted accounting principles (GAAP);** also called a clean opinion. *See also adverse opinion, qualified opinion.*

utility The ability of a product to satisfy a consumer's needs.

>EXAMPLE: Interested in writing a memo, a manager makes a list of products—a crayon, a pencil, a pen, a typewriter, or a word processor—that satisfy that need. Each of these products varies in its ability to meet the manager's needs; the crayon might seem unprofessional, the pen too slow, the typewriter unable to make quick changes, and the word processor too expensive. The manager can take this list of attributes and compare it with his or her particular needs in order to arrive at a buying decision. This list is called a utility scale, and it can be applied to any type of purchase— from a simple item for a single consumer to a major purchase for a large organization.

utilization The reduction in attainable output, due to equipment failures and breakdowns, human error, materials problems, changes in demand, and so on.

>Utilization is generally less than 85 percent of an operation's *effective capacity*. For example, if a factory operating three shifts experiences a drop in demand and subsequent drop in utilization to, say, 65 percent, the factory should probably switch to using just two shifts.

value chain The collection of activities within a company that allow it to compete within an industry.

The concept of the value chain was popularized by Harvard Business School professor Michael E. Porter. According to Porter, the activities in a value chain can be grouped into two categories. The first is primary activities, which include inbound logistics, such as materials handling; operations; outbound logistics, such as distribution; marketing and sales; and after-sales service. The second is support activities, which include human resources management, company infrastructure, procurement, and technology development. Note that each of the primary activities involves its own support activities. For example, operations must be concerned with the management of the human resources in the production department, its position within the structure of the company, the procurement of equipment and maintenance services, and the development of technologies to assist in the operations function.

By considering each activity within a company in terms of the value chain, it is possible to isolate a potential source of competitive advantage. For example, the development of a clear, simple system of invoices that can easily be compared with the goods received by a customer may simplify the customer's procedures, reduce the customer's costs, and increase the attractiveness of the supplying company.

Value Line Investment Survey An investment advisory service that tracks over 1700 stocks in 91 industries.

Regular updates report the current status of each company in the survey with respect to market share price and price/earnings and other financial ratios. For each company, the Survey also presents historical financial trend data, descriptions of the company's business, major subsidiaries and locations, major institutional shareholders, names of top officers, and insider shareholdings.

Value Line has developed a unique feature whereby each stock is rated as to timeliness of purchase and safety of investment. With the aid of a complex computerized model, Value Line projects which stocks will have the best and the worst performance over the succeeding 12 months. Each stock is also assigned a risk factor that measures the volatility of the stock's price relative to market averages.

value-added tax (VAT) A tax based on the value added to a product during each stage of its manufacture and to the sale price of the finished product.

The United States does not employ value-added taxes, but they are used extensively throughout Europe and Canada. Opponents of implementing a value-added tax in the United States argue that it is merely a disguised national sales tax. Proponents point out that since the manufacturer pays a tax at each stage of production (which is deducted from the tax due on the sale of the finished product), consumers pay less than they would under a national sales tax. In fact, however, by paying a VAT at each production stage, manufacturers would certainly pass on this extra cost to consumers in the form of higher sales prices, which would also increase the base against which the final VAT would be applied.

variable cost In accounting, expenses that vary directly with changes in business activities.

For example, the cost of raw materials increases and decreases as the volume of production units changes. Total variable cost rises with the number of units produced. Per unit variable costs remain constant.

variable costing *See direct costing*

variable, dependent In a research project, a value that *changes* as a result of some separate factor.

EXAMPLE: A greeting card manufacturer wants to examine the impact an advertising campaign has had on sales of Mother's Day cards. Sales of Mother's Day cards would be the dependent variable.

Compare to variable, independent.

variable, independent In a research project, a value that *causes a change* in a separate factor.

EXAMPLE: If a snack food manufacturer wants to test the impact that a new package design has on sales, the package design would be the independent variable.

Compare to variable, dependent.

variable pricing A pricing strategy that creates a flexible price for different customers or different times.

Industries with many small, independently owned companies, such as the antique business, frequently use variable pricing. This pricing strategy can be risky since a customer may leave after discovering that another customer paid less.

variable rate bonds In corporate finance, *bonds* with an interest rate that is periodically adjusted according to changes in the prime interest rate offered by banks to their best customers.

Variable rate bonds are frequently issued when future interest rates and inflation are difficult to predict.

venture capital The main source of financing (primarily equity capital) for start-up businesses, R & D ventures, companies bringing out new product lines, and turnaround companies; also known as *risk capital.*

Since venture capital investments are, by definition, high-risk ventures, they command virtually the highest rate of return available in financial markets. Venture investors normally expect a return on investment principal of 5 to 10 times in less than seven years, in addition to dividends and/or interest during that period.

Except in rare cases, a company's cash flow during the start-up period is insufficient to pay such high returns each year. Therefore, most if not all of the cumulative gain must come from an *initial public offering (IPO)* from the company. This becomes a decisive factor in the timing and pricing of initial public shares.

Venture capital investors make the basic assumption that, as a company's products are accepted in the marketplace, sufficient investor interest will be generated to make an *IPO* feasible. The resultant trading market should then enable the original venture investors to reap substantial appreciation on their investment when they cash in their holdings. In the right situation, they may keep their holdings to see whether the market will drive the share price up, but only when the spread between the offering price and the venture fund's expected gain is fairly wide.

A company that sells equity shares directly to venture investors avoids the costly exercise of using underwriters or public stock markets and simultaneously gets cash into the company much faster than through the convoluted process of issuing public shares.

Companies use venture capital—both equity and debt—for three broad purposes:

- As *seed capital* to cover initial market research, testing equipment, facility rent, basic operating supplies, experimental materials, perhaps the payroll for a few employees, and, at least partially, the entrepreneur's living expenses. Such expenditures occur during the setting up, development, and testing stages of a new product, process, or business.

- As *working capital* during the finalization of the development stage when the product or process nears market potential. This additional financing pays for the materials, labor, overhead, and selling expenses required to produce and sell the products in quantities that meet market demand.

- As *acquisition capital* to fund the purchase of an ongoing business by an established company or group of entrepreneurial investors.

vertical integration Expansion by moving forward or backward within an industry (*see* ***backward integration*** and ***forward integration***).

EXAMPLE If a brewery were to expand its operations either to include the cultivation of barley and hops (backward integration) or to open a series of taverns (forward integration), it would be pursuing a strategy of vertical integration. Frequently, vertical integration can create an effective ***barrier to entry*** by allowing a company to achieve cost efficiencies over its competitors due to greater control over its resources or distribution.

In some cases, however, vertical integration can mask the profitability of various business segments. For example, in the brewing industry in the United Kingdom, brewers commonly pursued vertical integration by opening their own pubs. As a result, many companies consistently overstated the profits of their brewing operations and understated the profits of the pubs.

vertical marketing system (VMS) A ***distribution channel*** in which the manufacturer, ***wholesaler,*** and ***retailer*** act as a single system.

Usually owned by one member, a vertical marketing system eliminates the conflict that can occur among independent channel members.

EXAMPLE: A clothing company might buy its own warehouses and trucks and open a chain of boutiques in order to bring the manufacturing, wholesaling, and retailing of its product under the same management.

Vertical marketing systems are now the dominant method of distribution in the United States, serving between 70 and 80 percent of the market.

With a vertical marketing system, goods flow more smoothly through the channel. Since distribution members are all working together, conflicts are largely eliminated. Companies can also achieve some ***economies of scale*** with this type of system. All members of the channel, for example, can use the same ***marketing research,*** accounting programs, and advertising personnel. Nonetheless, inefficiencies get introduced in the process of restructuring the channel—and creating the new channel can require sizable financial investment. Legal restrictions may also interfere with setting up a VMS, since the government might view some vertical systems as reducing competition. Despite these drawbacks, companies in the United States and other developed countries are establishing increasing numbers of these systems.

VMS *See* ***vertical marketing system***

volume segmentation The division of the market into groups based on product usage patterns—for instance, distinguishing among light, medium, and heavy users.

Marketers that examine product usage rates often find evidence of the 80/20 principle—that is, 20 percent of the market accounts for 80 percent of the sales. This rule of thumb cannot be applied to every product, but it does suggest the importance of a small group of buyers to the health of many companies.

The beer industry, for instance, has found that the 80/20 principle is true for its market. The high-volume consumer segment is attractive to beer marketers. It is male dominated, younger, generally blue collar, less well educated than many of the peers in their age group—and its members drink copious amounts of beer.

Two studies, conducted 20 years apart, examined purchase and consumption behavior for 16 categories of products. The researchers assigned consumers to a *light half* and a *heavy half* on the basis of annual per capita purchase rates compared with the median for the category. If a household's purchasing rate was greater than zero but less than the median for the product class, it was classified in the light half. If the rate was greater than the median, it was classified in the heavy class. The researchers found that certain product categories, such as cola, frozen orange juice, and bourbon, contained segments in which one heavy-half household was equivalent to eight light-half households—clearly demonstrating the value of volume segmentation. *See also* **market segmentation.** *Compare to* **behavioral segmentation, demographic segmentation, psychographic segmentation.**

warrants A security that gives its holder the right to purchase a set number of shares of a company's *common stock* at a specified price (usually higher than the market price).

Warrants, more formally called subscription warrants, are usually issued along with a *bond* or *preferred stock*. *See equity kicker.*

wholesaler A member of a *distribution channel* that purchases or receives goods from a manufacturer, then sells them to a *retailer*.

See also retailer.

word-of-mouth advertising Any advertising communicated from a satisfied customer to another potential customer.

Word-of-mouth is not advertising in its strictest sense because the advertiser has not paid for the communication. Nonetheless, it can be a powerful marketing force.

working capital In accounting, a measure of a company's ability to service its financial obligations.

Working capital is *current assets* less *current liabilities*. Sources of working capital are (1) *net income*, (2) an increase in *noncurrent liabilities*, (3) a decrease in *noncurrent assets*, and (4) an increase in *stockholders' equity*.

work-in-process inventory Any partially completed goods on hand at the end of an *accounting period*.

EXAMPLE: A car without an engine would be classified by an automobile manufacturer as work-in-process inventory. Work-in-process inventory is classified as a *current asset* on the *balance sheet*. In an actual cost system, the beginning and ending work-in-process amounts are used in the calculation of cost of goods sold on the income statement.

Compare to finished goods inventory, raw materials inventory.

write-down In accounting, a reduction in the *book value* of an *asset*.

Assets are written down when there is strong indication that the asset's value is diminished.

EXAMPLE: If a portion of a company's *inventory* were to become obsolete, the total value of the inventory would have to be written down.

write-off In accounting, the reduction of the entire value of an *asset* as either an expense or a loss.

EXAMPLE: If a company's uninsured warehouse is destroyed in a fire, the warehouse would have to be written off as a loss or expense.

yield to maturity Rate of return used to value debt securities.

The calculation of yield to maturity results in one of three possible conditions:

- The market-determined yield to maturity is equal to the security's interest rate, in which case the security's fair market value equals its face amount.

- The yield to maturity is less than the interest rate as indicated by the market yields of similar issues, in which case the security's fair market value is greater than its face value.

- The yield to maturity is greater than the interest rate, in which case the security's fair market value is less than its face value.

Although the interest rate determines the amount of cash flows from the security, the yield to maturity indicates the fair market value of that cash flow at any point in time.

The yield to maturity calculation recognizes (1) the annual interest received, (2) the difference between the current security price and its maturity value, and (3) the number of years to maturity. The formula to calculate the yield to maturity may be expressed as

$$\text{Yield to maturity} = \frac{\text{Interest} + \dfrac{\text{Par value} - \text{Market value}}{\text{Number of periods}}}{0.6\,(\text{Market value}) + 0.4\,(\text{Par value})}$$

The 60 percent and 40 percent factors in the denominator adjust for the slight differences due to mathematical averaging over time.

Assume the following conditions:

- The coupon interest payment is $150,000.

- The par value of the security is $2,000,000.

- The market value can be estimated as the present value of principal payments, or $1,295,923.

- The number of periods is six.

The solution then becomes

$$\text{Yield to maturity} = \frac{\$150,000 + (\$2,000,000 - \$1,295,923)/6}{(0.6 \times \$1,295,923) + (0.4 \times \$2,000,000)}$$

$$= \frac{\$150,000 + \$117,346}{\$777,553 + \$800,000}$$

$$= \frac{\$267,346}{\$1,577,553}$$

$$= 16.95\%$$

Using formulas may be of interest, but it is much easier to use amortization look-up tables.

Z

zero coupon security A debt security that does not carry periodic interest payments but instead is sold at a deep discount from its face value.

At the maturity date, the holder's gain is calculated as the difference between the face value of the security and the original purchase price. This difference is treated as interest income by the IRS, and, since it is assumed to be earned over the life of the security, it is taxed annually.

Part II

Sources of Business Information

SOURCES OF BUSINESS INFORMATION

In many business situations, it's best to "go to the experts." The experts are here. "Sources of Business Information" is a listing of hundreds of books, databases, online services, periodicals, trade associations, government agencies, and research institutes that can provide the most current information available on almost any business topic, ranging from trade opportunities in Asia to competitor intelligence to environmental issues.

The listings are organized under 48 headings, starting with "General Business Information Sources." This first section, perhaps more than any other, contains sources that offer an incredible wealth of information. These listings offer a comprehensive cross section of business data that can be applied to almost any situation. The other 47 headings each relate to a specific topic. They are arranged in alphabetical order, beginning with "Accounting and Financial Reporting" and ending with "Venture Capital/Sources of Capital."

Each individual listing includes the title/name of the source, its author(s), a concise description of the information offered, date/frequency of publication, and the publisher's name. If the source is available in electronic format (computer disk, magnetic tape, CD-ROM, or through an online service such as DIALOG), the entry begins with the symbol ▮. (In most cases the source is also available in print format.)

Published sources of information—whether print or electronic—are listed within each section alphabetically by title. Many sections within "Sources of Business Information" also contain descriptions of the services provided by relevant government organizations and trade and professional associations. These descriptions, within the relevant sections, follow the listings of published sources.

"Sources of Business Information" concludes with a "Directory of Publishers, Vendors, and Database Providers" containing complete contact information—address, telephone number (toll-free when available), and FAX number (when available). Contact information for government agencies and trade and professional associations is included within the entry rather than in the "Directory of Publishers, Vendors, and Database Providers."

Essentially, "Sources of Business Information" is a "source of sources." If you need business information, you can find out where to get it (and how to get it as quickly as possible) here.

1

GENERAL BUSINESS SOURCES

ABI/INFORM®

🔑 This database is an index to 800 publications for business and related fields and also contains abstracts and full texts of articles. ABI/INFORM covers all phases of worldwide business and administration including accounting, banking, computers, economics, energy, the environment, finance, health care, human resources, insurance, international trends, law, management, marketing, public administration, real estate, taxation, telecommunications, and transportation. It also covers company news and analysis, market conditions and strategies, international trade and investment, and economic conditions and forecasts. Available online, on CD-ROM, and on magnetic tape through UMI's database licensing program. Also available online through BRS Information Technologies, BRS/AFTERDARK, Data-Star, DIALOG, ESA-IRS, HRIN (Human Resource Information Network), and OR-BIT Search Service.
Updated weekly by UMI/Data Courier.

American Statistics Index (ASI)
Statistical Reference Index (SRI)

🔑 ASI and SRI are indispensable guides to business and industry statistics. ASI is a guide to all statistics published by the federal government (about 5,000 titles). SRI is a guide to statistics published by groups and associations other than the federal government, such as universities, state governments, business organizations, and independent research centers. Both publications are available at most larger libraries (in many cases the indexed publications are also on microfiche), or they can be ordered directly from the Congressional Information Service. ASI and SRI are available on CD-ROM. ASI is also available online through DIALOG. *Published monthly, with annual compilations, by the Congressional Information Service.*

AT&T Toll Free 800 Directory

The AT&T directory is divided into two sections. The White Pages contain alphabetical listings by name of approximately 120,000 businesses, organizations, and government agencies that provide 800 service to the public. These listings also include section numbers that indicate under what product and service heading a listing may be found in the Yellow Pages, which contains listings alphabetically by subject.
Updated annually by AT&T.

The Burwell Directory of Information Brokers

Formerly the *Directory of Fee-Based Information Services*, the directory lists over 1,200 information professionals in a variety of fields, including market research, competitor intelligence, legal research, online database research, document retrieval/delivery, patent/trademark research, and library/information management consulting.
Published annually by Burwell Enterprises.

Business Dateline®

🔒 This database focuses on regional business news in the United States and Canada and covers topics such as city economics, labor markets, state regulations, and corporate news. It draws its information from more than 350 business news sources including city business journals (e.g., *Crain's New York Business*), regional business magazines (e.g., *Northern Ontario Business*), wire services (e.g., *Business Wire*), and daily newspapers. Available online, on CD-ROM, and on magnetic tape through UMI's database licensing program. Also available online through DIALOG, Dow Jones News/Retrieval, HRIN (Human Resource Information Network), MEAD Data Central's NEXIS, OCLC's EPIC Service, and VU/TEXT.
Updated weekly by UMI/Data Courier.

Business Index

🔒 A microfilm index containing a cumulative three-year index to over 800 regional business newspapers and periodicals dating back to 1979. It indexes the following national newspapers: *Christian Science Monitor, Los Angeles Times, New York Times, Wall Street Journal*, and *Washington Post*. Searches can be made according to subject, author, or company names. Many subject headings employ business slang and jargon, which makes the index more accessible to the general user. *Business Index* is available at most large libraries, or it can be ordered (along with a microfilm reader) directly from Information Access. *Business Index* is also available on CD-ROM.
Updated monthly by Information Access Company/Predicasts.

Business Information Sources

Lorna M. Daniels

Widely considered to be the most comprehensive guide available, *Business In-formation Sources* (commonly referred to as "Daniels") lists an incredible variety of business information sources. Lorna Daniels, who has acted as both Head of Reference and Business Bibliographer at Harvard Business School's Baker Library, divides the book into two sections. The first section concentrates on general business reference sources: the kinds of libraries with business reference services, indexes, government publications, abstracts, databases, handbooks, cassettes and other recordings, and looseleaf services. Chapters within this section also list sources for current information on business trends and statistics (domestic, foreign, and by industry).

The second section concentrates on specific management functions, such as finance, accounting, international management, and marketing. Entries in this section include books written for practicing managers, textbooks, periodicals, and professional associations.

Business Information Sources is available at most larger libraries.
Third edition published in 1993 by University of California Press.

The Business One Irwin Guide to Using the Wall Street Journal

Michael B. Lehmann

This book helps readers "to be their own economist." It shows how to use the information contained in the *Wall Street Journal* to analyze business trends and economic conditions.
Fourth edition published in 1993 by Business One Irwin.

Business Organizations, Agencies, and Publications Directory

Catherine M. Ehr and Kenneth Estell, editors

🔒 This directory provides information on the agencies, associations, publica-

tions, and databanks that help find business information. The directory contains 26,000 entries describing 39 types of business information arranged in five broad categories: (1) U.S. and international organizations, (2) government agencies and programs, (3) facilities and services, (4) research and educational facilities, and (5) publications and information services. The directory is available in the following alternative formats: computer diskette, online, and magnetic tape. Available online from OCLC EPIC.
Sixth edition published in 1992 by Gale Research, Inc.

Business Periodicals Index

▪ An index of about 300 business periodicals dating back to 1958, the *Business Periodicals Index* covers a number of broad subjects, such as computers, communications, marketing, and finance. In many cases, it includes publications that might not be entirely business-oriented, such as *Telecommunications, Automotive News,* and *Journal of Consumer Affairs.* Usually, the articles cited by the *Business Periodicals Index* are geared for the general reader and avoid overly technical issues. The *Business Periodicals Index* is published monthly with periodic cumulations and is available at most large libraries. The index is also available on computer disk and CD-ROM and online. Available online from BRS, OCLC EPIC and WILSONLINE.
Updated monthly, with annual cumulations, by H.W. Wilson Company.

Canadian Business and Current Affairs

▪ Business coverage includes description of companies and industry information based on English-language business periodicals and newspapers. It also contains references to filing notices with

the Ontario Securities Commission. Available online from DIALOG, Knowledge Index, and Infomart On-line.
Updated monthly by Micromedia Ltd.

Directories in Print

Charles B. Montney, editor

▪ This annual directory lists over 4,000 different directories for nearly every conceivable subject, such as education, engineering, banking, agriculture, public affairs, and health. Included are descriptions of databases, buyer's guides, membership lists, registers, handbooks, indexes, who's whos, factbooks, yearbooks, and annuals. Each entry includes the publisher's name, address, telephone number, frequency of publication, and price. *Directories in Print* is available at most large public libraries. It is also available in the following alternative formats: computer diskette, online, and magnetic tape. Available online through DIALOG as part of Gale Directories in Print.
Published annually by Gale Research, Inc.

Directory of Special Libraries and Information Centers

Janice A. Demaggio and Debra M. Kirby, editors

▪ This directory provides information on holdings, services, and personnel of special libraries, research libraries, information centers, archives, and data centers. The directory lists more than 20,000 sources of in-depth information on many general topics, as well as business and finance. Entries are arranged alphabetically and contain information on library holdings, services, personnel, addresses, FAX and telephone numbers, and electronic mail addresses. The directory is available in the following alternative formats: computer diskette and magnetic tape.

The directory is comprised of the following: Volume I Directory of Special Libraries and Information Centers (1992); Volume II Geographic and Personnel Index (1992); Volume III New Special Libraries (1993). Published by Gale Research, Inc.

Dow Jones News/Retrieval

🔒 Dow Jones, the publisher of *The Wall Street Journal* and *Barron's*, has a number of databases on financial news and general business developments, including the following:

Dow Jones Business and Finance Report; updated continuously throughout the day.

Dow Jones International News: updated daily.

Dow Jones Text Library; based on The *Wall Street Journal*, *Barron's*, *The Washington Post*, McGraw-Hill business journals, and 200 other periodicals; updated daily.

DowQuest; contains the complete text of over 400 general and specialized business publications; updated weekly.

(*Source*: Gale Directory of Databases, Volume 1: Online Databases.)

All of the above are available through Dow Jones News/Retrieval.

The Economist Atlas

The Economist Atlas shows the major political, economic, and physical aspects of the world's rapidly changing geography. It contains political and physical maps, updated to reflect such changes as the reunification of Germany; thematic maps and charts on topics such as foreign debt, balance of trade, food and hunger, the environment, and education; and 200 country and regional profiles in map, chart, and narrative format.

Published in 1992 by Henry Holt and Company (U.S. and Canada) and Economist Books (United Kingdom).

The Economist World in Figures

This text provides factual coverage of a wide variety of topics, including demography, economic strength, agriculture, industry, energy, commodities, transport, finance, trade, employment, education, and the environment. *The Economist World in Figures* provides country-by-country and regional comparisons of subjects as diverse as government debt, GDP growth, alcohol consumption, and advertising spending. *Published in 1993 by Economist Books.*

Encyclopedia of Associations: National Organizations of the U.S.

Deborah M. Burek, editor

🔒 The *Encyclopedia of Associations* is an invaluable tool for getting information on the associations connected with various businesses and industries. For example, the groups associated with the candy industry listed by the *Encyclopedia of Associations* include the National Confectioners Association of the U.S., the National Candy Wholesalers Association, and the National Candy Brokers Association. Each entry includes the association's address, telephone number, a short description of its goals and activities, number of members, budget, and any publications or conventions.

The *Encyclopedia of Associations* is available at most libraries, or it can be ordered directly from Gale (which also publishes directories of international, local, and regional associations). The encyclopedia is also available in the following alternative formats: computer diskette,

magnetic tape, and CD-ROM. Available online from DIALOG.
Published annually by Gale Research, Inc.

Encyclopedia of Business Information Sources

James Woy, editor

The *Encyclopedia of Business Information Sources* lists almanacs, directories, databases, periodicals, trade associations, and statistical sources covering a wide range of business topics and specific industries. The book is arranged alphabetically, and each entry includes a full bibliographic citation, addresses and telephone numbers of the respective publishers, and the price of various publications. The *Encyclopedia of Business Information Sources* can be found at most libraries. *The ninth edition appeared in 1992. The 1993 Supplement adds entries for 30 new subjects and expands coverage of previously listed sources. Published by Gale Research, Inc.*

Gale Directory of Databases

This directory is a guide to the electronic database industry. It contains contact and descriptive information on more than 8,100 databases, 3,100 producers, 800 online services, and 760 vendors and distributors of database products. Volume 1, *Online Databases*, profiles nearly 5,200 databases made publicly available from the producer or online service. Volume 2, *CD-ROM, Diskette, Magnetic Tape, Hand-Held, and Batch Access Database Products*, profiles more than 2,900 database products offered in "portable" form through batch processing. The directory is available in print, CD-ROM and online. Available online through DIALOG.
Published in 1993, updated and revised semiannually, by Gale Research, Inc.

Guide to Special Issues and Indexes of Periodicals

Miriam Uhlan, editor

This guide details, in alphabetical sequence, close to 1,500 U.S. and Canadian periodicals that publish special issues (e.g., directories, buyer's guides, statistical outlooks, and other features or supplementary issues appearing on a continual, annual, or other basis). Each entry lists the special issues, the subscription address and subscription price of each periodical, and the price of each special issue.
Fourth edition published in 1994 by the Special Libraries Association.

The Information Bank Abstracts

This database provides a general news source of abstracts from the *New York Times*, the *Wall Street Journal*, and other news sources. It is available online from NEXIS.
Updated daily by the New York Times Company.

Information Industry Directory

Bradley J. Morgan, editor

This publication contains nearly 4,800 entries covering producers and vendors of electronic information and related services. The directory provides details on information producers and vendors, online services and networks, CD-ROM/optical publishing products and services, information retrieval software, transactional services, library networks, information consultants, mailing list services, information-on-demand services, document delivery, consultants and service companies, professional and trade associations, and publishers. Each entry includes full address and contact information, complete descriptions of organization services, and areas of specialization. The directory is available in

the following alternative formats: computer diskette and magnetic tape.
Published in 1992 by Gale Research, Inc.

The Internet Navigator: A New User's Guide to Network Exploration

Paul Gilster

The Internet is "the network of networks" that ties together 5,000 educational, governmental, and commercial computer networks. This book shows how to access the Internet's vast resources and provides explanations of the tools for expediting electronic file transfers, searches, and network exploration.
Published in 1994 by John Wiley & Sons, Inc.

Louis Rukeyser's Business Almanac

Louis Rukeyser, Editor-in-Chief

An extensive collection of business facts and statistics, the almanac profiles 57 different industries, from advertising to video games, and covers topics such as tax fraud, mergers and reorganizations, and the labor movement.
The 1992 revised edition published by Simon and Schuster.

Management Contents

This database provides an index and abstracts of articles from more than 120 U.S. and international management journals. The four broad areas covered are banking, finance, and accounting; human resources training and benefits; sales, marketing, and advertising; and general management. It is available online through DIALOG and BRS.
Updated monthly by Information Access Company/Predicasts.

National Fax Directory

This directory lists fax contact numbers for approximately 80,000 major corporations, institutions, and agencies in the United States, including law firms, government agencies, financial institutions, and manufacturers. It is divided into two sections: the alphabetical section, where all entries are listed in a single alphabetical sequence, and the subject section, where entries are alphabetically organized.
Published and updated annually by Gale Research, Inc.

Newsletters in Print, Sixth Edition

This directory provides information on more than 10,000 newsletters. Entries are arranged in seven broad categories, including ones for business, industry, information, and communications. Also available online through DIALOG as part of Gale Directory of Publications.
Published in 1992 by Gale Research, Inc. New editions pubished biennially.

New York Times Index

This is a biweekly index, with annual cumulations, of articles published in the *New York Times*. Entries are organized according to subject and include a brief summary of each article, along with the date and page of publication. The index is available in most large libraries, or it can be ordered directly from University Microfilms International. The index is available in print, microfiche, microfilm, CD-ROM, and online. (Full text of *The New York Times* is available on CD-ROM and online through NEXIS.)
Published biweekly by University Microfilms International with three quarterly cumulations and annual index issued as the fourth quarterly.

PTS PROMPT:™ Overview of Markets and Technology

PTS PROMPT:™ *Overview of Markets and Technology* is a multi-industry database for information on companies, products, applied technologies, and markets. It contains more than 2.5 million abstracts and full-text articles and increases by over 600,000 records each year. The sources for the database include U.S. and international trade and business journals, newspapers, regional business publications, corporate news releases, highlights from corporate annual reports, U.S. and international investment analysts' reports and industry studies, and government publications. Available online from BRS, Data-Star, DIALOG, and NEXIS. *Updated every business day by the Information Access Company/Predicasts®. (Note: also available in print version published monthly with quarterly and annual cumulative indexes.)*

PTS F & S Index

This online service provides an index to 2,500 business publications. It contains more than 3.5 million citations and provides titles, sources, and dates of articles, plus a one- or two-line citation. The files cover worldwide company, product, and industry information. The *Index* is available online from DIALOG, BRS, and Data-Star. *Updated weekly by The Information Access Company/Predicasts. (Note: available in print as F & S Index United States, F & S Index Europe, and F & S Index International. These print products are published monthly with quarterly and cumulative editions.)*

PTS Newsletter Database

This online database contains the full text of more than 500 business and industry newsletters published in the United States, Europe, Latin America, the Middle East, and Asia. Available online from Data-Star, DIALOG, and Dow Jones News Retrieval. *Published and updated daily by The Information Access Company/Predicasts.*

Standard Industrial Classification Manual

Although this manual is not exactly a source of general business information, it contains the standard classification system developed by the U.S. Office of Management and Budget, and it provides two-, three-, and four-digit codes for classifying major groups, industry groups, and specific industries. It is used by both the federal government and the private sector to collect and analyze industry data. *Published in 1987 by the National Technical Information Service.*

The Standard Periodical Directory

This is an annual directory of over 85,000 periodicals published in the United States and Canada. Titles are organized by subject, and the directory includes a number of business and industry categories. Each entry includes the publication's title, the name of the editor of the publication, the publisher's name and address, frequency of publication, circulation, subscription price, and whether a periodical is available through an online database. *The Standard Periodical Directory* is available at most large public libraries. The directory is also available on computer disk. *Published annually by Oxbridge Communications, Inc.*

Statistical Abstract of the United States

Prepared by the Economics and Statistics Administration of the Bureau of the Census, the *Statistical Abstract* is the standard summary of statistics on the social, political, and economic organization of the United States. It serves as a convenient statistical reference and as a guide to other statistical publications and sources. Some of the sections in the *Statistical Abstract* of particular interest to business people include population; state and local government finances and employment; federal government finances and employment; labor force, employment, and earnings; income, expenditures, and wealth; purchasing power; cost of living; banking, finance, and insurance; manufacturing; and domestic trade and services.

Published annually by the Superintendent of Documents, U.S. Government Printing Office.

Statistics Sources

Jacqueline Wasserman O'Brien and Steven R. Wasserman, editors

This two-volume set provides guidance to over 2,000 statistics sources, including U.S., international, print and nonprint, published and nonpublished sources. For each country, *Statistics Sources* gives the name of the major statistical source as well as the national statistical office. For each subject, listings of print and electronic sources are complemented by the names and addresses of key live sources.

Published annually by Gale Research, Inc.

Ulrich's International Periodicals Directory

This directory is a listing of over 100,000 periodicals from around the world, broadly classified by subject. For example, the "Business and Economics" section includes entries for accounting, investment, small business, and general business publications. There are additional categories for particular industries

and trades, such as construction, computers, or clothing. Each entry gives the periodical's title, name and address of its publisher, circulation, language of text, subscription price, and whether it is available through an online database. *Ulrich's* can be found in most large libraries, or it can be ordered directly from R. R. Bowker. The directory is also available on computer disk, CD-ROM, and online. Online directory available through BRS and DIALOG.

Published annually by R. R. Bowker (Reed Reference Publishing).

The Wall Street Journal

The *Wall Street Journal* is the leading business and financial information newspaper in the United States. In addition to its interesting and insightful business and general news articles, it provides a treasure trove of economic and financial data on a daily, weekly, monthly, and quarterly basis. A listing of the statistical series published in the journal is as follows:

Series Description	Publication Schedule
Advance/decline (stocks)	Daily
American Stock Exchange composite transactions	Daily
Amex bonds	Daily
Auto sales	Monthly
Balance of payments	Quarterly
Balance of trade	Monthly
Banxquote index (deposit & CD interest rates)	Weekly
Banxquote money markets (deposit & CD interest rates)	Weekly
Bond market data bank	Daily
Bond yields (chart)	Weekly
Buying and borrowing (interest rates)	Weekly
Canadian markets (stocks)	Daily
Capacity utilization	Monthly
Cash prices (commodities)	Daily
Closed-end bond funds	Weekly
Commodities (article)	Daily

Series Description	Publication Schedule	Series Description	Publication Schedule
Commodity indexes	Daily	New York exchange bonds	Daily
Consumer confidence	Monthly	NYSE composite transactions	Daily
Consumer credit	Monthly	NYSE highs/lows	Daily
Consumer price index	Monthly	Odd-Lot trading	Daily
Consumer savings rates	Weekly	P/E ratios	Weekly
Corporate dividend news	Daily	Personal income	Monthly
Corporate profits (Commerce Department)	Quarterly	Producer price index	Monthly
		Productivity	Quarterly
Corporate profits (*The Wall Street Journal* survey)	Quarterly	Publicly traded funds	Weekly
		Retail sales	Monthly
Credit markets (article)	Daily	Securities offering calendar	Weekly
Credit ratings	Daily	Short interest (stocks)	Monthly
Currency trading	Daily	Short-term interest rates (chart)	Weekly
Digest of earnings report	Daily	Stock market data bank	Daily
Dow Jones Averages (six-month charts)	Daily	Treasury auction	Weekly
		Treasury bonds, notes and bills	Daily
Dow Jones commodity indexes (chart)	Weekly	Treasury yield curve	Daily
		Weekly tax-exempts (bonds)	Weekly
Dow Jones industry groups	Daily	World markets (stocks)	Daily
Durable goods orders	Monthly	World value of the dollar	Daily
Employment	Monthly	Yield comparisons	Daily
Foreign exchange rates	Daily	Yield for consumers	Daily
Foreign markets (stocks)	Daily		
Futures options prices	Daily		
Futures prices	Daily		
GDP	Quarterly		
Government agency issues	Daily		
High yield bonds	Daily		
Housing starts	Monthly		
Index trading (options)	Daily		
Industrial production	Monthly		
Insider trading spotlight	Weekly		
Inventories	Monthly		
Key currency cross rates	Daily		
Key interest rates	Weekly		
Leading indicators	Monthly		
Listed options quotations	Daily		
Long term options (stocks)	Daily		
Manufacturers' orders	Monthly		
Markets diary	Daily		
Money-fund yields	Weekly		
Money market funds assets	Weekly		
Money market mutual funds	Weekly		
Money rates	Daily		
Municipal bond index	Weekly		
Mutual fund quotations	Daily		
Mutual fund scorecard	Daily		
NASDAQ bid & asked quotations	Daily		
NASDAQ national market issues	Daily		
New securities issues	Daily		

Source: Michael Lehmann, *The Business One Irwin Guide to Using the Wall Street Journal*, 4th ed., Business One Irwin, Homewood, IL, 1993, pp. 352–354. Reprinted by permission.

The full text of the Wall Street Journal is available online through Dow Jones News/Retrieval and NEXIS.
Published Monday through Friday by Dow Jones and Company.

Wall Street Journal Index

This publication is an index to articles published in the *Wall Street Journal* from 1955 to the present and *Barron's National Business and Financial Weekly* from 1981 to the present. The index is divided into two segments: Corporate News and General News. Entries are organized by subject and company names, and each citation gives a short summary of the indexed article. Most libraries maintain back issues of the *Wall Street Journal* on microfiche or microfilm so that finding a particular article is generally a simple process. The

Wall Street Journal Index is available at most libraries.
Published monthly by University Microfilms International with quarterly updates and an annual cumulative volume.

Wilson Business Abstracts

🛈 This reference tool, available in multiple electronic formats, provides answers to business questions with abstracts from 345 business periodicals indexed in *Business Periodicals Index* (see p. 402). Searches can be done by subject, key word, company name, and SIC code. Available on Wilsondisc (CD-ROM), Wilsonline (on-line retrieval service), and Wilsontape (database licensing service).
Published and updated monthly by H. W. Wilson Company.

The World Almanac and Book of Facts

Although not solely a business publication, it does have a useful economics and business section that covers a wide variety of topics including U.S. budget receipts and outlays, national income by industry, gross domestic product, leading U.S. businesses, sales and profits of manufacturing corporations by industry group, consumer price indexes, state finance, global stock markets, personal consumption expenditures, employment statistics, and tax information.
Published annually by World Almanac.

For Further Information

See *Index to International Statistics,* p. 522

2

ACCOUNTING AND FINANCIAL REPORTING

General

Accounting and Tax Database

🔒 This database provides indexing and abstracts to articles from over 225 accounting, taxation, and financial management journals, newsletters, pamphlets, and proceedings. The *Accounting and Tax Database* also contains selected articles from an additional 850 business journals, daily newspapers, and major news magazines based on their relevance to the accounting and financial service industries. Available online through DIALOG.
Updated weekly by the UMI/Data Courier.

Encyclopedic Dictionary of Accounting & Finance

Jae K. Shim and Joel G. Siegel

This dictionary lists up-to-date technical information in over 500 major areas of accounting and finance, including financial accounting, financial statement analysis, managerial/cost accounting, investments, and financial planning.
Published in 1990 by Prentice Hall, Inc.

The Portable MBA in Finance and Accounting

John Leslie Livingstone, editor

This guide to the basics in finance and accounting covers topics like understanding

financial statements, financial forecasting and budgeting, break-even and cost-profit-volume analyses, product pricing, evaluating acquisition targets, and managing foreign exchange risk exposure.
Published in 1992 by John Wiley & Sons, Inc.

The Vest Pocket CFO

Joel G. Siegel and Jae K. Shim

This pocket-sized book offers easy-to-use solutions to many of the business problems faced by a CFO. Every major area of concern for the financial manager is covered, including financial and managerial accounting, financial analysis and planning, quantitative analysis and modeling, internal auditing and control, insurance, legal considerations, and taxation.
Published in 1992 by Prentice Hall, Inc.

Auditing

GAAS Guide 1992: A Comprehensive Treatment of Generally Accepted Auditing Standards

Martin A. Miller and Larry P. Bailey

The guide explains all Statements on Auditing Standards (SAS), Statements on Standards for Accounting and Review

Services (SSARS), and SOPs and explores the entire audit process in detail, from pre-engagement planning to writing the auditor's report. It includes sections on statistical sampling techniques and procedures, internal control structure, evidence, audit risk, and related party transactions.
Published annually by Harcourt Brace Jovanovich Miller.

Montgomery's Auditing, Eleventh Edition

Vincent M. O'Reilly, Murray B. Hirsch, Philip L. Defliese, and Henry R. Jaenicke

This is a practice-tested guide for many aspects of auditing, from standards and responsibilities, risk, and engagement strategy, through internal control, auditing specific cycles and accounts, and auditing reporting. Detailed guidelines cover the entire audit process and provide comprehensive auditing strategies and methods for 15 specific industries including high technology and emerging businesses, education, construction, government, and a range of financial services.
Published in 1990 and supplemented annually by John Wiley & Sons, Inc.

Financial Reporting and Disclosure

Governmental GAAP Guide

Larry P. Bailey

This thorough restatement and analysis of all promulgated governmental accounting standards provides reporting standards for many nonprofit organizations, including hospitals, colleges, and universities.
Published annually by Harcourt Brace Jovanovich Miller.

Accountants' Handbook

D. R. Carmichael, Steven B. Lilien, and Martin Mellman, editors

Written by 66 of the nation's leading experts in all areas of accounting, *Accountants' Handbook* offers practical guidance on the full range of standards, techniques, and procedures in financial reporting and fast, practice-oriented answers to accounting problems. Official pronouncements from SEC staff accounting bulletins, all FASB statements and interpretations, and technical bulletins are covered, along with detailed information on bankruptcy, estates and trusts, valuation of nonpublic companies, prospective financial statements, and benefits and compensation.
Published in 1991 and supplemented annually by John Wiley & Sons, Inc.

Accounting Trends and Techniques

This publication provides the latest information on corporate financial statements and auditor's reports by surveying the annual reports of 600 industrial and merchandising corporations with fiscal years ending in 1990 and 1991. It contains significant accounting presentations, citations of FASB, APB, and SEC pronouncements. Available in both print and electronic formats.
Published in 1991 by the American Institute of Certified Public Accountants.

Financial and Accounting Guide for Not-for-Profit Organizations

Malvern J. Cross, Jr., William Warshauer, Jr., and Richard F. Larkin

A guide to the financial reporting, accounting, and control problems unique to not-for-profit organizations, this text covers compliance auditing and information on state charitable solicitation accounting.
Published in 1991 and supplemented annually by John Wiley & Sons, Inc.

Financial Reporting Using Computer Graphics

Irwin M. Jarett

This publication is a collection of practical tips and techniques for making successful financial presentations with computer graphics. A practice disk is included that presents examples of computer graphics and allows users to make changes to the sample screens and observe the impact the changes have on the graphics display file.
Published in 1993 and supplemented annually by John Wiley & Sons, Inc.

GAAP: Interpretation and Application of Generally Accepted Accounting Principles

Patrick R. Delaney, James R. Adler, Barry J. Epstein, and Michael F. Foran

This guide for interpreting and applying Generally Accepted Accounting Principles (GAAP) presents real-world examples to illustrate accounting transactions and their presentation in financial statements. It is cross-referenced to the Financial Accounting Standards Board's (FASB) Current Text and covers all original FASB pronouncements. The authors explain rules, terminology, concepts, and sources of GAAP affecting accounting decisions.
Published annually by John Wiley & Sons, Inc.

Handbook of Governmental Accounting and Finance, Second Edition

Nicholas G. Apostolou and D. Larry Crumbly, editors

Divided into five parts and 41 contributed chapters, this handbook explains where FASB ends and GASB (Government Ac-

counting Standards Board) takes over, and offers the newest GAAP methods for bringing controls up to speed with demands. Topics include dealing effectively with tighter budgets and diminishing unappropriated funds, and preparing for internal and external audits.
Published in 1992 and supplemented annually by John Wiley & Sons, Inc.

Handbook of Modern Accounting, Third Edition

Sydney Davidson and Roman Weil, editors

This comprehensive resource of accounting information includes topics such as financial statements, budgeting, mergers and acquisitions, cost analysis, and cash flow.
Published in 1989 by Prentice Hall, Inc.

National Automated Accounting Research System

▮ This database contains financial statements from more than 4,200 annual reports for each year on file. It covers companies traded on the New York and American Stock Exchanges, over-the-counter, Fortune-ranked, or designated as "on-margin" by the Federal Reserve. NARS also contains the complete text of a wide variety of accounting literature. For annual reports, the current five years are always available (earlier years, from 1972, are held offline); for literature, the extent of files may vary from the inception of each publication to the current period updated. Available online through LEXIS or Total On-Line Tax and Accounting Library (TOTAL). (Source: Gale Directory of Databases, Volume 1: Online Databases).
Updated weekly by the American Institute of Certified Public Accountants (AICPA).

Financial Statement Analysis

Financial Shenanigans: How to Detect Accounting Gimmicks and Fraud in Financial Reports

Howard M. Schilit

This text provides tools for uncovering accounting gimmicks to get an accurate reading of a company's financial condition.
Published in 1993 by McGraw-Hill.

How to Read a Financial Report, Fourth Edition

John A. Tracy

This nontechnical, practical guide explains the basics of the three key financial reports—the balance sheet, the income statement, and the statement of cash flows—and the relationships between them.
Published in 1994 by John Wiley & Sons, Inc.

How To Understand Financial Statements: A Nontechnical Guide for Financial Analysts, Managers, and Executives

Kenneth R. Ferris, Kirk L. Tennant, and Scott I. Jerris

This comprehensive guide provides complete instructions on how to assess the quality of a company's reported earnings, assets, and cash flow as well as how to prepare financial statements using the most effective GAAP methods. The guide includes a ready-to-use computer disk with two programs. The first can be used to create a direct method cash-flow statement, perform ratio or cost-volume-profit analysis, and create data files. The second pro-

gram allows users to graphically evaluate up to 19 financial ratios.
Published in 1992 by Prentice Hall, Inc.

The Vest-Pocket Guide to Business Ratios

Michael R. Tyran

This guide is a collection of over 400 business and financial ratios.
Published in 1991 by Prentice Hall, Inc.

International Accounting

European Accounting Guide

David Alexander and Simon Archer, editors

In this survey of the accounting systems of 22 European countries, the financial structure of each country is researched and documented to include an extensive historical background and an expert evaluation of the legal and economic environment.
Published in 1991 by Harcourt Brace Jovanovich Miller.

Handbook for International Accounting

Frederick D. S. Choy, editor

This book addresses issues, faced by multinational companies and others, caused by diversity in accounting practices worldwide. Topics include the internationalization of the accounting function, financial analysis, harmonization, technical issues in accounting and auditing, financial reporting and disclosure, analysis, planning and control, and transfer pricing and taxation.
Published in 1991 and supplemented annually by John Wiley & Sons, Inc.

International Accounting Summaries: A Guide for Interpretation and Comparison

Coopers and Lybrand International

This single-volume reference focuses on individual countries, detailing generally accepted accounting principles of over 24 economic powers, as well as auditing requirements, financial reporting, and currency translation. It also presents the latest developments affecting the International Accounting Standards Committee and the European Community.
Published in 1991 and supplemented annually by John Wiley & Sons, Inc.

Management Accounting

The Complete Guide to Activity-Based Costing

Michael O'Guin

This step-by-step guide for implementing activity-based costing includes topics such as identifying the most and least profitable customers, calculating the real costs of buying versus manufacturing, and using pricing policies to boost profits.
Published in 1991 by Prentice Hall, Inc.

Controllership: The Work of the Managerial Accountant

James D. Wilson and James P. Colford

This comprehensive guide to the traditional functions of the controller also shows how to evaluate short-term and strategic business plans, select the preferred financial alternative choices, and maintain a financial structure to meet business objectives. Topics include the role of the controller in international operations and investor relations, the inter-

nal audit function, and recruiting, training, motivating, and managing a professional financial staff.
Published in 1990 and supplemented annually by John Wiley & Sons, Inc.

Handbook of Cost Accounting

Sydney Davidson and Roman L. Weil

The *Handbook of Cost Accounting* translates cost-accounting theory and procedures into practical examples and methods. Topics range from cost measurement to operating budgets.
Published in 1989 by Prentice Hall, Inc.

Handbook of Financial Analysis for Corporate Managers

Vincent Morrow

The *Handbook of Financial Analysis for Corporate Managers* provides scores of worksheets, checklists, and ready-to-copy spreadsheet models that make it easy to analyze, assess, and solve any financial question or problem, including identifying the most profitable product mix, discovering which cost-reduction measures will produce the greatest overall savings, and calculating break-even points.
Published in 1991 by Prentice Hall, Inc.

Management Accounting Glossary

Institute of Management Accountants (formerly, the National Association of Accountants), editor

Prepared by the 90,000-member IMA, this vest-pocket-sized guide defines 816 key terms from a variety of sources, including IMS Statements on Management Accounting, the Financial Accounting Standards Board (FASB), and Cost Accounting Standard Board (CASB).
Published in 1991 by Prentice Hall, Inc.

NAA Statements on Management Accounting

Institute of Management Accountants (formerly, the National Association of Accountants), editor

This collection of official statements provides industry-wide standards on management accounting and represents the consensus of recognized leaders in industry, public accounting, and the academic world.
Published in 1989 by Prentice Hall, Inc. A supplement was published in 1991.

Relevance Lost: The Rise and Fall of Management Accounting

H. Thomas Johnson and Robert S. Kaplan

This book explores the evolution of management accounting in American business from the early textile mills to present-day computer-automated manufacturers. The authors reveal why modern corporations must make major changes in the way they measure and manage costs.
Published in 1991 by the Harvard Business School Press.

Specialized Areas

The Accountant's Handbook of Fraud & Commercial Crime

G. Jack Bologna, Robert J. Lindquist, and Joseph T. Wells

The Accountant's Handbook of Fraud & Commercial Crime shows how to recognize and deter fraud and commercial crime. It contains techniques and methods for detecting and documenting internal and external fraud and shows how to set up monitoring and fund-control mechanisms.
Published in 1993 by John Wiley & Sons, Inc.

Accountants' Legal Liability Guide

George Spellmire, Wayne Baliga, and Debra Winiarski

The *Accountants' Legal Liability Guide* shows how to safeguard against claims in audit, tax, review, compilation, and many other professional accounting engagements. Case studies illustrate common ways in which accounting firms are exposed to legal liability. The liability insurance chapter covers topics such as self-insurance and choosing an insurance company.
Published in 1990 by Harcourt Brace Jovanovich Miller.

Accounting for Fixed Assets

Raymond Peterson

This comprehensive guide to the issues surrounding fixed asset accounting includes topics such as capitalization, amortization, depreciation, taxes, and inventory.
Published in 1993 by John Wiley & Sons, Inc.

Corporate Audit Department Procedures Manual

Michael P. Cangemi

This manual is a collection of the techniques and procedures needed to set up and run an auditing department. Matrices developed by the author detail each component of the audit function, along with the methodology necessary for managing an audit department.
Published in 1993 and supplemented annually by John Wiley & Sons, Inc.

FAS 109: Analysis and Comments on the New Accounting for Income Taxes

James O. Stepp and Lawrence N. Petzing

This guide to the changes required by FAS 109 includes topics such as implemen-

tation strategies, realization assessments, and business combinations.
Published in 1993 and supplemented annually by John Wiley & Sons, Inc.

American Accounting Association

This is an academically oriented society for educators, practitioners, and students of accounting. Members receive two quarterly journals, *The Accounting Review* and *Accounting Horizons;* a newsletter, *Accounting Education News*, published six times a year; and a semi-annual journal, *Issues in Accounting Education.* Members are eligible to serve on research and study committees and may utilize the services of the association's Clearing House on International Professor Exchange and Placement, continuing education workshops, and seminars.
American Accounting Association, 5717 Bessie Dr., Sarasota, FL 34233. Tel. (813) 921-7747.

The American Institute of Certified Public Accountants

The American Institute of Certified Public Accountants (AICPA) is a national organization of certified public accountants in the United States. It creates and grades the Uniform CPA Examination. The AICPA offers books, software, subscription services, practice aids, and CPA courses to its members. The AICPA's practice areas include the following: accounting and auditing, standards, tax information technology, the division for CPA firms, management consulting services, personal financial planning, business and industry, government, and accounting education.
American Institute of Certified Public Accountants, 1211 Avenue of the Americas, New York, NY 10036-8775. Tel. (212) 575-6200.

The National Society of Public Accountants

Dedicated to representing and supporting the professional interests of independent, local, and regional accounting and tax practitioners through education opportunities, information resources, governmental representation, and a wide range of practice assistance services, the NSPA was organized in 1945 and currently represents over 20,000 accounting and tax professionals.
National Society of Public Accountants, 1010 North Fairfax Street, Alexandria, VA 22314-1547. Tel. (703) 549-6400. Fax (703) 549-2984.

FOR FURTHER INFORMATION

*See **ABI/INFORM®**, p. 400*
***Bankruptcy and Insolvency Accounting,** p. 421*
Management Contents, p. 405

3

ADVERTISING

Advertising Media Planning, Third Edition

Jack L. Sissors and Lincoln Bumba

A comprehensive introduction to media planning, *Advertising Media Planning* includes information on (1) selecting and evaluating specific advertising media, (2) basic terms and strategies, markets, and targets, (3) audience measurement techniques, and (4) response functions, media costs, and buying functions.
Published in 1993 by NTC Publishing Group.

Advertising Media Sourcebook, Third Edition

Arnold M. Barban, Donald W. Jugenheimer, and Peter B. Turk

Advertising Media Sourcebook contains dozens of media audience measurement sources, media cost sources, media cost estimators, and media audience reach estimators. Each reference is explained in a separate entry that includes (1) an explanation of the purpose of the source, (2) a description of how to read and understand the data, and (3) a practical application of the source to a realistic advertising media situation.
Published in 1989 by NTC Publishing Group.

Broadcasting and Cable Marketplace

Formerly *Broadcasting Yearbook*, this directory is a comprehensive resource on the broadcasting and cable industries and includes the following information: listings of radio and television stations in the United States and Canada with complete contact information; information on the top 38 U.S. and Canadian MSOs and their cable systems with over 20,000 subscribers; listings for advertising and marketing services for all media; and industry yellow pages.
Published annually by R.R. Bowker (Reed Reference Publishing).

Business Publication Rates and Data

This monthly publication contains editorial profiles, advertising rates, contract and copy regulations, mechanical requirements, issue closing dates, and circulation statements on 5,500 U.S. business, technical, and trade publications and on over 500 international publications.
Published monthly by Standard Rate and Data Service (SRDS).

Business-to-Business Advertising

Charles Patti, Steven Hartley, and Susan Kennedy

Business-to-Business Advertising covers every step of the planning process before, during, and after a business-to-business advertising campaign. It shows how to understand the behavior of business buyers and segment the market to find prospects; set advertising objectives and determine a budget; and measure the results of a campaign in terms of money, message, and media.
Published in 1991 by NTC Publishing Group.

Do-It-Yourself Advertising: How to Produce Great Ads, Brochures, Catalogs, Direct Mail, and Much More

Fred Hahn

This text is a "how-to" guide for entrepreneurs and small businesses for writing, designing, and producing print ads, radio and television commercials, catalogs, flyers, brochures, and direct mail.
Published in 1993 by John Wiley & Sons, Inc.

Great Print Advertising

Tony L. Antin

Directed at the interests and needs of product managers, this text shows how to direct the creation of effective print advertising for products and includes a checklist and guide for critiquing advertisements in copy and layout form.
Published in 1992 by John Wiley & Sons, Inc.

International Advertising Handbook

Barbara Sundberg Baudot

This handbook analyzes the state of advertising in both industrialized countries and the Third World. It looks at laws and policies and their social, economic, and political impact on advertising.
Published in 1989 by Lexington Books.

Legibility of Print

Miles A. Tinker

This book, though now old, is *the* definitive study on print legibility. The author, a psychologist, conducted tests on how people read, what they can read easily, and what they cannot. This is a useful reference for product managers who are making advertising decisions, because they are often led astray by art directors who may not pay enough attention to the impact of typography in print advertisements.
Published in 1963 by the Iowa State University Press.

Media Flight Plan

Dennis G. Martin and Robert D. Coons

▐ This product teaches the basics of strategic multimedia planning, both national and spot. It consists of a workbook and diskettes for IBM (DOS) and Apple Macintosh.
Published in 1991 by Deer Creek Publishing.

National Directory of Advertising: Print Media

▐ This directory of over 27,000 media sources in the United States and Canada lists all advertising information for magazines, journals, newspapers, newsletters, directories, and catalogs. The information includes an editorial description, ad rates, contact names, circulation, frequency, and printing information. Available in print and on diskette.
Published in 1992 by Oxbridge Communications, Inc.

National Directory of Magazines

This directory provides information on over 20,000 U.S. and Canadian magazines, including staff, advertising rates, circulation size, mailing list information, and production details.
Published in 1993 by Oxbridge Communications, Inc.

Standard Directory of Advertisers

Over 137,000 marketing personnel, in nearly 26,000 advertising programs, are listed in this directory, ranging from key senior executives to marketing managers to ad directors. Entries include address, telephone number, FAX number, subsidiaries and divisions, and number of employees.

Published annually, with periodic supplements and bulletins, by National Register Publishing.

Standard Directory of Advertising Agencies

The directory of over 9,700 advertising agencies and branch offices supplies business facts on the advertising agency business. Entries include names and titles of decision makers, actual budget figures, annual billings, and much more. Available in most large libraries, the directory can also be ordered directly from National Register Publishing, where it is available in both print and magnetic tape.

Published annually by National Register Publishing.

Standard Directory of International Advertisers and Agencies

More than 2,000 companies and over 2,000 top agencies are listed in this directory covering the advertising industry in over 90 countries. Also included is a quick reference section that answers the most commonly asked questions in international business on such topics as consulates and embassies, trade commissions and chambers of commerce, and currency and exchange rates.

Published annually by National Register Publishing.

Strategic Media Planning

Kent M. Lancaster and Helen E. Katz

Strategic Media Planning is a book/software package that allows users to manage the many sources of product, media usage, and consumer behavior data for media planning. Four programs are included on IBM-compatible and Macintosh software disks: (1) ADPLAN, for media plan development and reach/frequency analysis, (2) ADCOMP, for competitive spending analysis, (3) ADGOAL, for marketing situation analysis and goal setting, and (4) ADFLOW, for budget summaries and flow chart development.

Published in 1989 by NTC Publishing Group.

Tested Advertising Methods

John Caples

This old but still valuable book was written by John Caples, one of the most successful advertising copywriters and an Advertising Hall of Famer who wrote the classic "They laughed when I sat down at the piano...." It provides real common sense, especially about getting the product benefits in the headline of the ad or in the beginning stages of the advertising copy.

Published in 1980 by Prentice Hall, Inc.

Who's Who in Advertising, 1990–91

This publication lists persons who have made conspicuous achievements that distinguish them from their contemporaries in advertising. It also lists incumbents in specified positions in the advertising industry. Vital statistics on an individual include specific occupation, family information, professional certification, awards, political affiliation, and address.

Published in 1990 by Marquis Who's Who.

Writing That Works

Kenneth Roman and Joel Raphaelson

This book is a quick read that contains many useful tips about good advertising writing; it is particularly useful for anyone who approves advertisements. The authors are leading figures in the advertising industry.

Published in 1981 by HarperCollins.

TRADE AND PROFESSIONAL ASSOCIATIONS

American Advertising Federation

The goal of the AAF is to "promote a better understanding of advertising through government relations, public relations, and advertising education in order to further an effective program of advertising self-regulation." Members receive the following publications: *AAF Annual Report to Members, AAF Washington Report,* and *American Advertising Magazine.*
American Advertising Federation, 1400 K Street NW, Suite 1000, Washington, DC 20005. Tel. (202) 898-0089.

American Association of Advertising Agencies

The AAAA is the national trade association representing the advertising business. Its membership totals approximately 750 agencies. Membership is conferred after an extensive examination of professional ability, financial integrity, and business ethics.
American Association of Advertising Agencies, 6666 Third Avenue, New York, NY. 10017 Tel. (212) 682-2500. FAX (212) 682-8391.

Association of National Advertisers, Inc.

The Association of National Advertisers serves the interests of companies that advertise regionally or nationally. Member-

ship is available only on a corporate basis. ANA provides professional programs on topics such as promotion strategy, media strategy, and television commercial production. Its publications cover the fields of advertising and marketing management, agency relations, advertising research and promotion, and merchandising and advertising issues.
Association of National Advertisers, Inc., 155 East 44th Street, New York, NY 10017. Tel. (212) 697-5950. FAX (212) 661-8057.

175 K Street NW, Washington, DC 20006. Tel. (202) 785-1525. FAX (202) 659-3711.

Magazine Publishers of America

This organization is the most important single source of information about magazines, particularly as advertising media.
Magazine Publishers of America, 575 Lexington Avenue, New York, NY 10022. Tel. (212) 752-0055.

FOR FURTHER INFORMATION

*See **The Economist World in Figures,** p. 403*
***European Advertising, Marketing, and Media Data,** p. 541*
***International Directory of Marketing Research Companies,** p. 459*
***Management Contents,** p. 405*
***PTS Marketing and Advertising Reference Service (PTS MARS),** p. 460*
***The New Marketing Research Systems,** p. 460*
***The Survey of Buying Power,** p. 462*
***The Survey of Media Markets,** p. 462*

4

BANKRUPTCY

The Bankruptcy Datasource

This subscription publication follows all public companies in bankruptcy, default, or financial distress that have assets greater than $50 million. Information is provided on each company, its creditors, committees, securities, and plans of reorganization. *Updated monthly and sold by annual subscription by New Generation Research, Inc.*

Bankruptcy and Insolvency Accounting, Fourth Edition

Grant W. Newton

This two-volume guide offers a broadbased approach to bankruptcy and insolvency. Volume 1, *Practice and Procedure*, describes the economic, legal, accounting, and tax aspects of bankruptcy proceedings. Volume 2, *Forms and Exhibits*, illustrates the concepts and practices of Volume 1 and contains specific examples of various documents used in bankruptcy cases and out-of-court settlements. *Published in 1989 by John Wiley & Sons, Inc.*

The Bankruptcy Yearbook and Annual

This text provides comprehensive coverage of bankruptcy activity during the prior year, including U.S. court data, corporate statistics, top corporate bankruptcies, trends and topics in major corporate bankruptcies, and distressed securities markets and trading. *Published annually by New Generation Research, Inc.*

Collier Bankruptcy Manual, Third Edition

L. P. King, H. P. Minkel, A. DeNatale, and H. J. Sommer

This three-volume set provides substantive analysis for handling a case under the bankruptcy code, keyed to the section numbers of the 1978 code. The *Collier Bankruptcy Manual* explains liquidation, reorganization, and debt adjustment. It also discusses applicable Rules of Bankruptcy Procedure. *Published since 1979, in looseleaf, updated with supplements and revisions by Matthew Bender and Company.*

Collier's Handbook for Trustees and Debtors in Possession

Irving Sulmeyer, M. Rush, D. M. Lynn, M. R. Rochelle, R. J. Motern, and L. P. King (editor in chief)

This handbook is a guide for trustees in Bankruptcy Code cases and for laypeople and attorneys involved in Chapter 11 cases. Part I covers the problems incurred by a trustee in cases under Chapters 7, 11, 12, and 13 and includes forms, sample letters, checklists, and worksheets. Part II, *The Debtor in Possession Handbook*,

spells out day-to-day procedures for key personnel in a Chapter 11 case.
Revised edition published in 1989 by Matthew Bender and Company.

Corporate Financial Distress and Bankruptcy: A Complete Guide to Predicting, Avoiding, and Dealing with Bankruptcy, Second Edition

Edward I. Altman

Widely regarded as one of today's leading experts on bankruptcy, Edward Altman of New York University examines the latest trends in the complex field of bankruptcy, such as debtor-in-possession, lending, and prepackaged bankruptcies. He also develops statistical classification techniques to assess the distress potential of companies and explores the applications of these models in a number of important practical areas. Two detailed case studies show how to do a thorough valuation analysis and suggest appropriate restructuring.
Published in 1993 by John Wiley & Sons, Inc.

Saving Your Business: How to Survive Chapter 11 Bankruptcy and Successfully Reorganize Your Company

Suzanne Caplan

This book shows how to recognize the signs of a failing business and how to file for Chapter 11 bankruptcy (reorganiza-tion) rather than Chapter 7 (liquidation). It shows how to manage a company through the bankruptcy process; communicate with all parties in a bankruptcy, including secured and unsecured creditors, customers, and employees; continue to do business with creditors; and rebuild a business after bankruptcy.
Published in 1992 by Prentice Hall, Inc.

The Small Business Bankruptcy Kit

Robert L. Davidson III

This book is directed at the interests and needs of owners of small businesses, whether sole proprietorships, partnerships, or corporations. It provides guidance to work alongside legal and tax professionals by explaining what bankruptcy is, who is eligible to file for it, and how to choose the best types of bankruptcy— Chapter 7, liquidation; Chapter 11, reorganization; Chapter 12, family farmer; and Chapter 13, wage earner. The book helps small business owners understand the role of trustees in the bankruptcy law; how statutes, priorities, and creditor demands affect financial rights; protection against damaging actions by creditors; and discharging debts while retaining full control of the business. Includes forms and record-keeping worksheets.
Published in 1992 by John Wiley & Sons, Inc.

For Further Information
*See **Predicasts' F & S Index of Corporate Change**, p. 451*

5

BENCHMARKING

Benchmarking: A Tool for Continuous Improvement

Kathleen H.J. Leibfried and C.J. McNair

The text, a guide to the process of benchmarking, includes several interesting case studies: Avon, Janssen Pharmaceutica, and Exxon Chemical.
Published in 1992 by HarperCollins.

The Benchmarking Book

Michael J. Spendolini

This basic guide to benchmarking by a retired Xerox employee focuses on developing, launching, and managing a benchmarking study.
Published in 1992 by AMACOM.

The Benchmarking Management Guide

Gregory H. Watson, et al.

This study of benchmarking by the American Productivity & Quality Center was originally published as a user's guide to benchmarking for the 130 member companies of the International Benchmarking Clearinghouse. It contains a wealth of information from surveys of the member companies (including DEC, Hewlett-Packard, IBM, Unisys, Westinghouse, and Xerox).
Published in 1993 by Productivity Press.

Benchmarking: A Practitioner's Guide for Becoming and Staying the Best of the Best

Gerald J. Balm

This book is by the quality consultant at IBM Rochester who facilitated their benchmarking efforts that led to the Baldrige Award. It contains a unique manufacturing case study.
Published in 1992 by the Quality & Productivity Management Association (QPMA).

Benchmarking: The Search for the Best Practices That Lead to Superior Performance

Robert C. Camp

The first book on benchmarking, Camp's reference describes in detail the historic approach that was developed at Xerox during the 1980s and the L. L. Bean benchmarking study.
Published in 1989 by Quality Press/American Society for Quality Control (ASQC).

The Benchmarking Workbook: Adapting Best Practices for Performance Improvement

Gregory H. Watson

This workbook is targeted to support teams in conducting benchmarking studies. It

presents a simplified process and walks the team through a case study. The book contains helpful forms and is rich in reference material.
Published in 1992 by Productivity Press.

INCITE

■ A software tool available from Quest Management Systems, INCITE offers reports on various competitive factors, which are referred to by the system as Essential Elements of Information (EEIs). EEIs can be created and maintained for a number of different market, industry, or business situations and can be accessed either through standard report formats, such as set benchmarks or competitive profiles, or through a series of specific inquiries.

Features include a reference library, which allows managers to integrate information on competitors into a single database; a search mode, which allows managers to locate specific information within the reference library through a series of key words or phrases; and an audit card, which notes the source, date of entry, and any comments for any information entered into the reference library database.
Updated as needed, approximately every 12 months, by Quest Management Systems.

Strategic Benchmarking: How to Rate Your Company's Performance Against the World's Best

Gregory H. Watson

Watson's third book on benchmarking fills a notable gap: It is aimed at the executive audience and focuses on the linkage of benchmarking to the strategic planning process. This book uses detailed case studies to illustrate how Hewlett-Packard, Ford, General Motors, and Xerox applied benchmarking concepts during the 1980s.
Published in 1993 by John Wiley & Sons, Inc.

6

BUSINESS PLANS

Business Plan Workbook

Gary A. Cooper

This looseleaf manual is a comprehensive guide to the creation of a business plan. The workbook covers plans to attract investors to a new venture and plans to convince top management to support a particular project, product, or profit center.
Published in 1989 by Prentice Hall, Inc.

Creating a Winning Business Plan

Gregory I. Kravitt

Workbook format guides the reader in the development of a customized business plan to help determine and positively present the viability of a business start-up, business expansion, or business turnaround. Shows how to assess present information about management, ownership, employees, investment criteria, competitive analysis, production and operations, and government regulations.
Published in 1992 by Probus Publishing Co.

The Entrepreneur's Guide to Building A Better Business Plan: A Step-By-Step Approach

Harold J. McLaughlin

The guide combines the fundamentals of business planning with a step-by-step approach to developing a business plan. It details the necessary components for an effective business plan including the charter and goals for both products and ser-

vices; market and market share data; detailed departmental plans; and financial data. A number of sample business plans are included.
Published in 1992 by John Wiley & Sons, Inc.

The Ernst & Young Business Plan Guide

Eric S. Siegel

This comprehensive guide to planning, writing, and implementing a business plan provides a focus on the three roles of a business plan: As a tool for raising money, an aid to mapping out the future, and a measure for evaluating a company's performance. Features include the following: a model business plan interspersed throughout the text, with segment-by-segment critique; current examples of successful S corporations & C corporations; and sections on funding and financial methods, provisions for restructuring and bankruptcy, and the most recent laws and regulations.
Published in 1993 by John Wiley & Sons, Inc.

How to Really Create a Successful Business Plan Software

This software program takes users step-by-step through the process of creating a business plan. The program asks users the questions they need to create a plan; also users plug in numbers to create cash flow statements, income statements, and balance sheets. The program is MS-DOS-based and requires 60K of memory. *Published in 1992 by Inc. Business Resources.*

How to Really Create a Successful Business Plan Video

This video uses examples and interviews with people at companies like Ben & Jerry's and Pizza Hut for an overview of how to put together a successful business plan. *Released in 1992 by Inc. Business Resources.*

The Inc. Guide to Creating a Successful Business Plan

The guide takes readers step-by-step through the planning process, using excerpts from the actual business plans of companies like Celestial Seasonings, Software Publishing, Ben & Jerry's, and Pizza Hut. Topics covered include understanding the type of business plan that is right for different individuals and how to price a product or service. *Published in 1990 by Inc. Business Resources.*

The Total Business Plan: How to Write, Rewrite, and Revise

Patrick D. O'Hara

Text provides a complete description of the business planning process, from concept, market planning, strategy development, research sources, and pricing concepts to writing the plan and revising it when presenting it to different target audiences. *The Total Business Plan* shows how to tailor the business plan using spreadsheet analysis, a word processor, and computer graphics. *Published in 1992 by John Wiley & Sons, Inc.*

COMPETITOR INTELLIGENCE

Business Researcher's Handbook: The Comprehensive Guide for Research Professionals

This handbook shows readers how to fine-tune information requirements, organize research projects efficiently, manage investigations to get top value for time and money, and present information to management.
Published in 1983 by Washington Researchers, Ltd.

Competitor Intelligence Manual and Guide

Kirk M. Tyson

This collection presents hundreds of techniques and strategies for getting information on competitors—new product plans, sales, costs, profits, and distribution networks.
Published in 1990 by Prentice Hall, Inc.

Competitor Intelligence: How to Get It, How to Use It

Leonard M. Fuld

This book shows how to obtain information legally and ethically about important aspects of the operations of competitors including income statements and balance sheets; marketing strategy; sales force deployment; product features; and plant capacity. The author provides a methodology for intelligence gathering and pro-

vides specific advice for obtaining competitor intelligence in 50 major industries.
Published in 1986 by John Wiley & Sons, Inc.

How Competitors Learn Your Company's Secrets

Text presents the step-by-step process of preparing an entire company to resist incursions by outside information-gatherers.
Published in 1984 by Washington Researchers, Ltd.

How to Find Information about Companies

This three-volume work covers both intelligence sources and methodologies for researching specific types of businesses. Volume 1 provides more than 9,000 sources of intelligence including published and electronic sources; federal, state, and local regulators; and company experts. Volume 2 shows how to research specific aspects of a company including products and services, personnel, distribution, and market share. Volume 3 shows how to research various types of companies: privately held, divisions and subsidiaries, foreign firms, service industry companies, and acquisition candidates.
Volume 1 published in 1978, updated in 1992; Volume 2 published in 1991; Volume 3 published in 1992 by Washington Researchers, Ltd.

Investext®

🔒 This database provides financial and market intelligence information. It provides the full text of over 300,000 reports from investment banks, research firms, consulting firms, and brokerage houses. Covers companies from the United States, Canada, Europe, and Japan. Also available in CD-ROM. Available online from CompuServe, Data Star, DIALOG, Dow Jones News/Retrieval, and NEXIS.
Updated daily by Thompson Financial Networks.

Understanding the Competition: A Practical Guide to Competitive Analysis

The guide leads readers through practical, action-oriented, and time-saving techniques for industry-, corporate-, and business-level analyses.
Published in 1984 by Washington Researchers, Ltd.

Who Knows about Industries and Markets

Publication is a listing of 2,200 U.S. government experts who are willing to answer questions (usually for free) about particular markets or industries. Each entry includes complete contact information.
Published annually by Washington Researchers, Ltd.

TRADE AND PROFESSIONAL ASSOCIATIONS

The Society of Competitor Intelligence Professionals

The SCIP assists members in assessing the behavior and strategies of their competitors. Membership carries with it a subscription to *Competitive Intelligence Review*. SCIP has local chapters in many cities as well as affiliates in Europe and Japan.
The Society of Competitor Intelligence Professionals, 1818 18th Street NW, #225, Washington, DC. 20006. Tel. (202) 223-5885. FAX (202) 223-5884.

FOR FURTHER INFORMATION

See ***The Burwell Directory of Information Brokers**, p. 400*
***Company Intelligence**™, p. 448*
***Hoover's Handbook of American Business**, p. 450*
***Hoover's Handbook of World Business**, p. 522*
***INCITE**, p. 424*
***Nelson's Directory of Investment Research**, p. 445*
***PTS Prompt:**™ **Overview of Markets and Technology**, p. 406*
***Strategic Benchmarking: How to Rate Your Company's Performance Against the World's Best**, p. 424*

8

COMPUTERS AND INFORMATION TECHNOLOGY

Business Software Companion

Tom Badgett and Corey Sandler

This guide provides project-by-project guidance on how to use popular business software including WordPerfect, 1-2-3, Word, DOS, DBase, Paradox, FoxPro, Quattro Pro, and Smartcom. It shows how to set up the printer, copy DOS files, format disks, set up a 1-2-3 spreadsheet, and format letters in WordPerfect.
Published in 1993 by John Wiley & Sons, Inc.

Buyer's Guide to Micro Software

This online database is a directory of microcomputer software available for business and professionals in the United States. It provides directory, product, technical, and bibliographic information on leading software packages. Each disk includes directory information; technical specifications, including required hardware and operating systems; and an abstracted product description. Available through BRS and DIALOG.
Published and updated monthly by On-line, Inc.

Computer Database ASAP

Database provides full text abstracting and indexing from over 150 journals covering every aspect of the computer, telecom-munications, and electronic industries. *Computer Database ASAP* helps user find answers to questions regarding hardware, software, peripherals, robotics, neural networks, satellite communications, and videotext. It also includes product evaluations; comparisons and best buys; and profiles, complete with financial information, on computer, telecommunication, and electronic firms. Available through CompuServe and DIALOG.
Published and updated weekly by Information Access Company /Predicasts.

Computer Industry Almanac

Egil Juliussen and Karen Juliussen

The *Computer Industry Almanac* is a compilation of facts, figures, and rankings covering every aspect of the computer business. It profiles over 2,000 companies, provides a wide variety of rankings of computer companies, and looks at technology trends and industry forecasts.
Published annually by Computer Industry Almanac.

Datapro Reports

Datapro publishes a wide variety of specialized information services that analyze information technology products and services in communications, information systems, microcomputer/work group

computing, office technologies, banking, retail, and manufacturing automation. These publications analyze products; provide managers with guidance in planning, designing, and managing communications, computers, and software environments; and profile vendors of information technology. Most publications are updated monthly; and international reports are available in communications, microcomputers, office technologies, and information systems.
Published by Datapro Information Services Group.

Datapro Software Directory

This three-volume directory provides profiles of over 11,000 midrange and mainframe software products. It includes information on features, price, compatibility, date of introduction, and installed base of each software product. It is also available on CD-ROM (as Datapro Software Finder™) and online from DIALOG.
Published and updated monthly by Datapro.

Datapro Directory of Microcomputer Software

This three-volume directory provides profiles of over 18,000 applications and software systems packages. It is also available on CD-ROM (as Datapro Software Finder™) and online from DIALOG (as Datapro Software Directory).
Published and updated monthly by Datapro.

Encyclopedia of Computer Science

Anthony Ralston, editor

This single-volume reference of over 600 articles covers the entire field of computer science: Hardware, computer systems, information and data, software, mathematics of computing, theory of computing,

methodologies, applications, and computing milieus.
Published in 1992 by Van Nostrand Reinhold.

How to Computerize Your Small Business

Patrick O'Hara

For the absolute beginner, this book is a comprehensive reference for setting up a computer system. It covers word processing, spreadsheet analysis, databases, software and hardware selection, and peripherals.
Published in 1992 by John Wiley & Sons, Inc.

ICP Software Information Database

This database, available both in print and on CD-ROM, profiles over 16,000 software products. The print version, *ICP Software Directories,* is in four volumes. *The Systems and Utilities Directory* includes profiles of products important to Management Information Systems and data processing management, such as resource management, data management, networking applications development, and programming. *The Cross Industry Applications Directory* is a directory of business software that includes products targeted to all industries, for example, office automation, spreadsheets, word processing, desktop publishing, accounting, and human resources. *The Industry Specific Applications Directory* of specialized software includes products targeted to markets such as insurance, banking, and manufacturing. *The Master Index* contains five separate indexes and is a road map to the foregoing three volumes. All of the information in these four volumes is available on a single CD-ROM disk.
Published three times yearly, in January, May, and September, by ICP.

Information Security: Dictionary of Concepts, Standards and Terms

Dennis Longley, Michael Shain, and William Caelli

This dictionary contains 3,500 entries on all aspects of information security.
Published in 1993 by Stockton Press.

Information Sources in Information Technology

David Haynes, editor

This comprehensive guide to sources of data on information technology includes topics such as input and output technologies, data processing, magnetic media, networks, artificial intelligence, electronic mail, word processing, human-computer interactions, legislation, and copyright.
Published in 1990 by R. R. Bowker (Reed Reference Publishing).

PC Magazine

Each issue contains many useful articles, surveys, products testing, and advice on personal computer hardware, software, and related equipment and services.
Published monthly by Ziff-Davis Press.

Que's Computer Buyer's Guide: The Best Source for Choosing a System That's Right for You

Guide provides information on IBM, Apple, and IBM-compatible PCs. It also explains software programs, printers, and modems.
Published annually by Que.

The Software Encyclopedia 1992

The encyclopedia offers thousands of fully annotated listings for new and established software programs. Entries are indexed two ways: by title and by compatible system and application.
Published in 1992 by R.R. Bowker (Reed Reference Publishing).

The Software Reviews on File Subscription Service

This subscription service offers summaries of more than 600 software programs per year. Each month *Software Reviews on File* provides condensations and abstracts of the actual reviews of more than 45 programs. It also includes software news briefs providing updates on the computer program industry, new software releases and upgrades, and bestseller lists of the most popular software sold in the various categories (e.g., database management, finance, word processing). Each monthly edition includes an A-to-Z cumulative index by subject (accounting, finance, management, computer graphics, education, personal finance, investments, and desktop publishing).
Available in looseleaf as annual subscription; updated monthly with a cumulative index by Facts on File.

Telecommunications Directory, Fifth Edition

John Krol, editor

Directory provides detailed descriptions of more than 2,300 national and international communications systems and services, voice and data communications services, local area networks, and electronic mail services. The *Telecommunications Directory* also includes information on consultants, associations, research institutes, publishers, information services, and regulatory bodies.
Published in 1991 by Gale Research, Inc.

TRADE AND PROFESSIONAL ASSOCIATIONS

Data Processing Management Association

Organization is for managerial personnel, staff, educators, and individuals interested in the management of information resources. Professional education programs include EDP-oriented business and management principles self-study courses and a series of videotaped management development seminars. Association conducts research projects and seminars.
Data Processing Management Association, 505 Busse Highway, Park Ridge, IL 60068. Tel. (709) 825-8124.

Information Technology Association of America

The ITAA is an organization composed of companies in the information technology business. ITAA has several divisions: American Software Association; Entrepreneurs Division; Information Technology Services; Processing and Network Services; and Systems Integration. ITAA serves as an industry advocate and offers members a range of services including assistance on computer law and a comprehensive publications program (e.g., Membership Directory, Software and Services State Tax Report and New Products and Services Guide).
ITAA, 1616 N. Ft. Myer Drive, Suite 1300, Arlington, VA 22209-3106. Tel. (703) 522-3106. FAX (703) 522- 2279.

FOR FURTHER INFORMATION

See ABI/INFORM®, p. 400
Information Industry Directory, p. 404
The Internet Navigator: A New
   User's Guide to Network Exploration,
   p. 405

9

CONSULTING SERVICES AND CONSULTANTS

Consultants and Consulting Organizations Directory

Janice McLean, editor

🔒 *Consultants and Consulting Organizations Directory* lists over 17,000 consultants and consulting companies in the United States and Canada. Entries are arranged according to 14 broad fields, such as agriculture or marketing, and include each company's name, address, telephone number, FAX number, principals, date founded, description of services, description of clients, geographic area of operation, any recent publications, and special services. The directory also includes an index that lists each consulting company by name, location, area of specialization, and personal name. The directory is also available in the following alternative formats: computer diskette, online, and magnetic tape. Available online from HRIN.
Published in 1992 by Gale Research, Inc.

The Consultant's Proposal, Fee, and Contract Problem-Solver

Ron Tepper

This manual on conducting a consulting practice covers topics like generating leads, writing proposals, setting fees, and structuring contracts.
Published in 1993 by John Wiley & Sons, Inc.

The Contract and Fee-Setting Guide for Professional Consultants

Howard L. Shenson

The step-by-step guide for conducting a consulting practice covers each stage of the consulting process, from fee-setting and proposal-writing to drawing up the contract and issuing the report.
Published in 1990 by John Wiley & Sons, Inc.

The Directory of Management Consultants

The directory profiles 1,534 firms with 3,040 offices in the United States, Canada, and Mexico. Entries are indexed by services offered, industry, geography, and key principals. A description of each firm and key data on revenues and number of professionals are also included.
Published in 1993, and biennially, by Kennedy Publications.

Dun's Consultants Directory

The directory identifies, locates, and classifies the top 25,000 consulting firms in nearly 200 major specialties, including agriculture, data processing, finance

and accounting, health and medicine, and telecommunications. Entries are organized alphabetically, geographically, and by specialty.
Published annually by Dun & Bradstreet Information Services.

Experts Contact Directory

Nora Paul

The directory is a selective compilation of contact information on 25,000 academic and government workers in the United States who have expertise in their fields. Arranged by hundreds of subject areas, the directory covers business, physical science, technology, government and public affairs, law, and many other topics.
Published in 1993 by Gale Research, Inc.

How to Succeed as an Independent Consultant

Herman Holtz

This guide to conducting a consulting practice includes topics such as government procurement rules, consulting as a second career, and getting the best value from the latest technology, including laptops, desktop publishing, and voice mail.
Third edition published in 1993 by John Wiley & Sons, Inc.

FOR FURTHER INFORMATION
See **The Burwell Directory of Information Brokers, p. 400**
Direct Marketing Consultants, p. 465
European Consultants Directory, p. 542
Information Industry Directory, p. 404
Nelson's Guide to Pension Fund Consultants, p. 491

10

COPYRIGHTS, PATENTS, AND TRADEMARKS

General

BNA's Patent, Trademark and Copyright Journal

This 20- to 40-page newsletter contains summaries covering current case law and legislative developments in the area of patent, trademark, and copyright law.
Published weekly by Bureau of National Affairs, Inc.

Daphne Hammond & Associates, Ltd.

This Washington, DC–area business can obtain, in many instances on a one-day basis, copies of patents, trademark application files and registrations, and copyright deposit material.
Daphne Hammond & Associates, Ltd., 2518 Ft. Scott Drive, Arlington, VA 22202. Tel. (703) 683-6295. FAX (703) 415-0618.

International Treaties on Intellectual Property

Marshall A. Leaffer, editor

Text is a collection of the full texts of the world's major agreements in all disciplines of intellectual property law—patent, trademark, copyright, and industrial design.
Published in 1990 by Bureau of National Affairs, Inc.

Intellectual Property: Financial Strategies for Licensing and Joint Ventures

Gordon V. Smith and Russell L. Parr

Text analyzes the business economics of licensing and joint venture strategies involving intellectual property. Topics include deriving royalty rates that are appropriate for licensing agreements and deriving profit splits and equity ownership splits for joint ventures.
Published in 1993 by Bureau of National Affairs, Inc.

McCarthy's Desk Encyclopedia on Intellectual Property

J. Thomas McCarthy

Comprehensive encyclopedia defines words and phrases in patent, trademark, copyright, trade secret, entertainment, and computer law. Each entry features the following: identification of the area of intellectual property law; its meaning and significance, fully annotated with cases, statutes, regulations, treaties, and

bibliographic citations; and cross references to other entries. Decisions of the U.S. Court of Appeals for the Federal Circuit that radically changed traditional rules and definitions are highlighted.
Published in 1991 by Bureau of National Affairs, Inc.

Official Gazette of the U.S. Patent and Trademark Office

This two-part journal covers the registration of patents and trademarks. The patent part contains all patents issued by the U.S. Patent and Trademark Office each week. The trademark part contains all applications that the Patent and Trademark Office accepts for registrations each week as well as all registrations, registration renewals, and use affidavits it accepts each week.
Published weekly on Tuesday by the U.S. Government Printing Office.

Patent, Trademark, and Copyright Laws

Jeffrey M. Samuels, editor

Guide considers the most recent changes in the laws pertaining to trademarks, patents, and copyrights.
Published in 1991 by Bureau of National Affairs, Inc.

Protecting Trade Secrets, Patents, Copyrights, and Trademarks

Robert C. Dorr and Christopher H. Munch

This comprehensive guide to the laws, options, and issues affecting the protection of intellectual property includes topics like federal and state laws governing patents, copyrights, and trademarks, and providing integrated protection for products or services.
Published in 1990 by John Wiley & Sons, Inc.

United States Patents Quarterly, Second Series

Published weekly since 1929, this case law reference offers the full text of decisions involving patents, trademarks, copyrights, and unfair competition issues. Weekly advance sheets give fast notification and full text of pertinent decisions from the U.S. Supreme Court, U.S. Court of Appeals for the Federal Circuit, U.S. Claims Court, U.S. District Courts, Patent and Trademark Office Board of Patent Appeals and Interferences, Patent and Trademark Office Trademark Trial and Appeals Board, U.S. Tax Court, U.S. International Trade Commission, and state courts.
Published weekly by Bureau of National Affairs, Inc.

World Intellectual Property Guide Books

Four-volume set covers patent, trade secret, copyright, trademark, and unfair competition law in the United States, United Kingdom, Canada, and Germany.
Published annually and updated periodically by Matthew Bender and Company.

Copyrights

The Copyright Book: A Practical Guide, Fourth Edition

William S. Strong

The Copyright Book is a comprehensive guide to the most recent changes in U.S. copyright law, including case law on databases and compilations; copyrighting architectural designs; distributing software; *look and feel* cases; the moral rights of creators implied in the Berne convention; the implications of the Kinko's case;

and new guidelines for off-air videotaping for educational use.
Published in 1992 and updated biennially by Massachusetts Institute of Technology Press.

The Copyright Handbook: How to Protect and Use Written Works

Stephen Fishman

The handbook provides forms and step-by-step instructions for protecting all types of written expression under U.S. and international copyright law. It contains detailed reference chapters on such major copyright-related topics as copyright infringement, fair use, works for hire, and transfers of copyright ownership.
Published in 1992 by NoLo Press.

How to Copyright Software

M.J. Salone

Written expressly for software developers, this book explains copyright laws and how to enforce them; how to enforce development rights; and how to register a copyright for maximum protection. It also discusses who owns a copyright on software developed by more than one person.
Published in 1990 by NoLo Press.

How to Protect Your Creative Work: All You Need to Know about Copyright

David A. Weinstein

This book contains information about copyright subject matter, how copyright is acquired, the extent of copyright protection, and how to register a copyright with the U.S. Copyright Office. It contains sample agreements and registration forms.
Published in 1987 by John Wiley & Sons, Inc.

Patents

Attorney's and Agents Registered to Practice Before the United States Patent and Trademark Office

This source is a listing with contact information.
Published and updated periodically by Superintendent of Documents, U.S. Government Printing Office.

CLAIMS™/U.S. Patent Abstracts

This database contains patents listed in the general, electrical, and mechanical sections of the Official Gazette of the U.S. Patent Office and U.S. design patents. *CLAIMS™/U.S. Patent Abstract* covers the period 1950 to the present and is available through DIALOG.
Updated weekly by IFI/Plenum Data Corporation.

Inventing and Patenting Sourcebook

Richard C. Levy

The sourcebook is a combination *how-to* guide and directory that takes readers step-by-step from the point of inspiration to the point of sale. The introductory essay offers advice on how to patent and trademark a product and how to select a company to approach for licensing. Book contains 35 usable forms; sample agreements; and applications for patents, trademarks and copyrights. Each directory section provides information sources and contacts, including patent attorneys and agents, university innovation research centers, venture capital firms, and national and regional inventor organizations.
Published in 1992 by Gale Research, Inc.

The Inventor's Notebook

Fred Grissom and David Pressman

The Inventor's Notebook is a guide to the documentation of the activities that are normally a part of successful independent inventing. Topics include conceiving, building, testing, legally protecting, marketing, and financing an invention. Forms, instructions, references to relevant areas of patent law, and space for notes, drawings, calculations, and photographs are included.
Published in 1992 by NoLo Press.

PATDATA

🔒 Database includes detailed information and abstracts for all utility patents issued by the U.S. Patent and Trademark Office since 1971 and all reissued patents since July 1, 1975. The historical development of a particular patent can be traced back to 1836. Available online through BRS Information Technologies.
Updated weekly by BRS Information Technologies.

Patents, Copyrights and Trademarks

Frank H. Foster and Robert L. Shook

This book is a guide to protecting the rights to an invention, product, or trademark. Its coverage includes patent licensing, foreign patents, protecting computer technology, and selecting a trademark.
Second edition published in 1993 by John Wiley & Sons, Inc.

Patent It Yourself

David Pressman

A guide for inventors interested in obtaining a patent, *Patent It Yourself* explains the entire process from patent search to the actual application.
Published in 1992 by NoLo Press.

Trademarks

Brands and Their Companies

🔒 This is a two-volume set of current information on more than 240,000 trade names, trademarks, and brand names of consumer-oriented products and their 43,000 manufacturers, importers, marketers, and/or distributors. It is available in print and in the following alternative formats: computer diskette, online, and magnetic tape. Available online through DIALOG as TRADE NAMES DATABASE.
Published annually by Gale Research, Inc.

Companies and Their Brands

🔒 *Companies and Their Brands* lists 43,000 alphabetically arranged companies that manufacture, distribute, market, and import consumer-oriented products and the trade names, brands, and trademarks they hold. Each entry includes complete contact information. Text is available in print and in the following alternative formats: computer diskette, online, and magnetic tape. Available online through DIALOG as TRADE NAMES DATABASE.
Published annually by Gale Research, Inc.

Compu-Mark U.S.

This national trademark-searching organization provides information about registered and unregistered names and marks in the United States and elsewhere by searching the U.S. Patent and Trademark Office records, state registration files, and information sources about unregistered marks.
Compu-Mark U.S., 1333 F Street NW, Washington, DC 20004. Tel. (800) 421-7881.

Directory of Canadian Trademarks

This directory lists all active pending and registered trademarks filed with Consumer and Cooperative Affairs Canada since 1867. The information includes owner name, trademark, registration, and serial number.
Published annually by Thomson & Thomson.

Directory of U.S. Trademarks

This directory is a comprehensive index of active trademarks filed, registered, and renewed at the U.S. Patent and Trademark Office. It includes both pending and registered trademarks and has over one million new and updated transactions. The information contained on each transaction includes the trademark, design indicator, last reported owner, registration, and serial number.
Published annually with three cumulative updates each year by Thomson & Thomson.

Euro Trademark Journal

This journal provides a source of trademark information for European Community countries, Madrid Agreement countries, Switzerland, Austria, Liechtenstein, Eastern Europe, Scandinavian countries, Finland, and Turkey. It lists compilations of new filings and applications in products and classes selected by the user.
Published weekly by Thomson & Thomson.

How to Protect Your Business, Professional, and Brand Names

David A. Weinstein

This book for the businessperson provides information on how to select and protect a business name and trademark. Usable forms and sample agreements are included.
Published in 1990 by John Wiley & Sons, Inc.

International Brands and Their Companies

Susan L. Stetler, editor

🔒 *International Brands and Their Companies* contains listings of 80,000 consumer-oriented products in countries other than the United States and of the approximately 20,000 companies that make, market, or distribute them. Lists are available in print and in the following alternative formats: computer diskette, online, and magnetic tape. Available online through DIALOG as TRADE NAMES DATABASE.
Published in 1992 by Gale Research, Inc.

International Companies and Their Brands

Susan L. Stetler, editor

🔒 *International Companies and Their Brands* contains listings of 20,000 international manufacturers, exporters, and distributors of 80,000 consumer products. Available in print and on computer diskette, online, and on magnetic tape. Available online through DIALOG as TRADE NAMES DATABASE.
Published in 1992 by Gale Research, Inc.

State Trademark and Unfair Competition Law

State Trademark and Unfair Competition Law is a state-by-state guide to the laws concerning trademark registration, corporate and trade name registration, unfair business practices, false advertising,

and franchising or business opportunity statutes.
Published in 1987 by Clark Boardman Callaghan.

Thomson & Thomson

This trademark-searching organization provides information about registered and unregistered names and marks in the United States and elsewhere by searching the U.S. Patent and Trademark Office records, state registration files, and information sources about unregistered marks.
Thomson & Thomson, 500 Victory Road, North Quincy, MA 02171-2126. Tel. 1-800-692-8833.

Trademark: How to Name Your Business & Product

Kate McGrath and Stephen Elias

Comprehensive do-it-yourself trademark guide designed for small businesses includes topics like conducting a trademark search, registering a trademark, and protecting and maintaining a trademark.
Published in 1992 by NoLo Press.

Trademark Alert

This weekly publication contains information on all new trademark applications filed with the U.S. Patent and Trademark Office. Also available are industry-specific editions of Trademark Alert that allow users to zero in on product categories of most interest to them.
Published weekly by Thomson & Thomson.

Trademarkscan®-Federal

This database on trademarks and servicemarks covers the period from 1884 to the present. It provides information on all active registered trademarks and service marks and applications for registration filed at the U.S. Patent and Trademark Office. Pending applications include both actual use and intent to use applications. Database is available in both online and CD-ROM formats through DIALOG.
Published and updated twice weekly by Thomson & Thomson.

Trademarkscan®-State

This database contains information on trademarks and service marks registered with the secretaries of state in the 50 states and Puerto Rico and is available in both online and CD-ROM formats through DIALOG.
Published and updated weekly by Thomson & Thomson.

Trademarkscan®-UK

This database contains information on all actively registered trademarks and service marks recorded at The Trademarks Branch of the Patent Office of the United Kingdom and is available through DIALOG.
Published and updated weekly by Thomson & Thomson.

Trademark Service Corporation

This trademark-searching organization provides information about registered and unregistered names and marks in the United States and elsewhere by searching the U.S. Patent and Trademark Office records, state registration files, and information sources about unregistered marks.
Trademark Service Corporation, 747 Third Avenue, New York, NY 10017. Tel. (212) 421-5730.

World Trademark Journal

This journal provides trademark information for over 200 countries. It lists compilations of new filings and applications in products and classes selected by the user. *Published weekly by Thomson & Thomson.*

Public Libraries

Copies of patents can be obtained from U.S. Patent and Trademark Office depository libraries, located in most large cities. Many libraries keep copies of patents in a microfiche format. Many libraries provide trademark-searching services through a computer database for a small fee.

U.S. Copyright Office

The U.S. Copyright Office provides information about and registers copyrights. *United States Copyright Office, Register of Copyrights, Library of Congress, Washington, DC 20559. Tel. (202) 707-3000.*

U.S. Patent and Trademark Office

The U.S. Patent Office grants and registers patents and trademarks. The office will also provide an index of patents, from which printed copies of patents can be ordered. Copies of patents can also be found at depository libraries located in larger cities. [In many cases, it can be very frustrating to try to get information on patents over the phone. Often it helps to contact the Patent and Trademark Office's Scientific Library at (703) 557-2955. The library carries both U.S. and foreign patents and provides limited search services.] *U.S. Patent and Trademark Office, Office of Public Affairs, Washington, DC 20231. Tel. (703) 305-8341.*

United States Trademark Association

This nonprofit organization promotes trademarks as essential to commerce throughout the world. Its activities include educating business, the press, and the public to the proper use and the importance of trademarks. More than 2,100 businesses belong to the USTA. *United States Trademark Association, 6 East 45th Street, New York, NY 10017-1487. Tel. (212) 986-5880. FAX (212) 687-8267.*

CORPORATE AND INDUSTRIAL FINANCIAL DATA

Almanac of Business and Industrial Financial Ratios

Leo Troy

This annual volume provides comparative financial data on more than 180 fields of business and industry. It ranks small, medium, and large companies by 22 financial factors.
Published annually by Prentice Hall.

The Business One Irwin Business and Investment Almanac

Sumner N. Levine and Caroline Levine, editors

This resource provides a comprehensive overview of U.S. and international business. Its coverage includes industry surveys; a review of general business and economic indicators; the U.S. Government budget, receipts, and deficits; capital sources for start-up companies and small businesses; coverage of the U.S. and international stock market situation; bonds and money market instruments; options and futures; and taxes.
Published annually by Business One Irwin.

The Business One Irwin Investor's Almanac

Phyllis S. Pierce, editor

This annual publication includes, through the previous calendar year, complete Dow

Jones averages with earnings, dividends, and price-earnings ratio; and records of common and preferred stocks and bonds listed on the New York Stock Exchange and the American Stock Exchange showing the year's high and low prices, net change, volume, and dividend, and the year's most active stocks.
Published annually by Business One Irwin.

BusinessWeek Corporate Scoreboard

Each quarter *BusinessWeek* presents the profit results for 900 companies in 24 industries. The results included in the "Scoreboard" include sales, profits, return on invested capital, return on common equity, price-earnings ratio, growth in common equity, growth in earnings per share, market value, and earnings per share. First-quarter results appear in a May issue; second-quarter in August; third-quarter in November; and fourth-quarter in February.
Published quarterly by BusinessWeek.

The BusinessWeek Global 1000

This annual July feature in a *Business-Week* issue provides a country-by-country ranking of the 1,000 largest companies ranked by market value (share price multiplied by latest available number of shares outstanding translated into U.S. dollars). It also includes share price; price/book

value ratio; price/earning ratio; sales; profits; and return on equity.
Published annually in a July issue of BusinessWeek.

The BusinessWeek 1000: America's Most Valuable Companies

This annual special issue measures the value that the stock market places on 1,000 corporations and provides insight into the long-term outlook for these companies and the industries that they are a part of. The data presented include market value, sales, profits, margins, return on invested capital, return on common equity, assets, recent share price, high/low price, book value per share, price-earnings ratio, dividends, shares, outstanding earnings per share, and analysts' consensus estimates for earnings in the current year.
Published annually in an April issue of BusinessWeek.

COMPUSTAT

The Compustat Database comprises financial (income statement, balance sheet, statement of changes in financial position), business segment, and market data on over 7,600 U.S. and Canadian public companies. Twenty years of annual, 12 years of quarterly, 7 years of business segment, and 360 months of stock prices and dividend data are available for companies and over 270 industry groups as well as selected data for more than 6,000 companies that no longer file with the SEC. Available online through ADP Network Services, Compuserve, Interactive Data, FactSet Data Systems, Warner Information Technologies, and Standard & Poor's Compustat Services.
Updated weekly by Standard & Poor's.

Disclosure® Database

This database provides in-depth financial information on over 12,500 companies.

The information comes from reports filed with the U.S. Securities and Exchange Commission by publicly owned companies. Excerpts of 10-K and 10-Q financial reports are included as well as 20-F financial reports and registration reports for new registrants. Available online through BRS, DIALOG, CompuServe, Dow Jones News/Retrieval, and NEXIS.
Updated weekly by Disclosure®, Inc.

Disclosure Worldscope™ Global

This database provides information on over 9,000 companies from 40 countries. It includes general corporate information; financial statements; ratios (annual and five-year averages); and market data. Available in CD-ROM, magnetic tape, and online. Specific industry studies are available in a printed reference catolog. Available online through Dow Jones News/Retrieval.
Updated monthly by Disclosure®, Inc.

Dow Jones News/Retrieval

Dow Jones, the publisher of the *Wall Street Journal* and *Barron's*, has a number of databases that provide current information on market activities. They include the following:

Dow Jones Enhanced Current Quotes. Gives current quotes for common and preferred stocks and NASDAQ prices. Updated continuously throughout the day. Available online through Dow Jones News/Retrieval.

Dow Jones Futures and Index Quotes. Provides current and historical quotes for contracts traded on North American Stock Exchanges. Updated continuously throughout the day. Available online through Dow Jones News/Retrieval.

Dow Jones Real-Time Quotes. Provides real-time stock quotes from North American exchanges. Updated continuously throughout the day. Available online through Dow Jones News/Retrieval.

(*Source:* Gale Directory of Databases, Volume 1: Online Databases.)
All of the above published and updated by Dow Jones.

Dun's Financial Record Plus

🔋 This resource provides financial data on 750,000 U.S. businesses, both public and private. The information available includes balance sheet, income statement, and 14 widely used business ratios. Coverage is for up to three years and includes company name, address, SIC code, number of employees, and D-U-N-S number. Available online through DIALOG and the Dow Jones News/Retrieval.
Updated quarterly by Dun & Bradstreet Credit Services.

Forbes Annual Report on American Industry

This annual report (in a January issue) from *Forbes Magazine* analyzes 21 industries and looks at the results of companies within the industry according to the following criteria: profitability; growth in sales and earnings per share; sales; net income; and profit margin. Forbes identifies and profiles one standout performer in each industry by sorting out those with the highest profits per employee, the highest sales per employee, the best return on equity, and the lowest debt levels. Subjective criteria are also applied in selecting its standout company.
Published annually by Forbes Magazine.

Industry Norms and Key Business Ratios

Contains financial norms and business ratios for over 800 lines of business developed from over one million financial state-ments in the Dun & Bradstreet financial profiles of both public and private corporations. The businesses are arranged according to broad industry categories.
Published annually by Dun & Bradstreet Information Services.

Media General Financial Services Database

🔋 This database is gathered primarily from company reports and SEC filings. It provides stock information and information from company annual and quarterly reports. Included in the database is information on more than 7,000 publicly held companies (companies listed on the New York Stock Exchange, the American Stock Exchange, and the NASDAQ over-the-counter market), 3,000 bonds, 2,300 mutual funds, and 175 industry groups and the financial markets. Available online through DIALOG and Dow Jones News/Retrieval.
Updated weekly by Media General Financial Services.

Moody's Handbook of Common Stocks and Moody's Handbook of OTC Stocks

These two handbooks offer information on over 2,000 companies representing 85 percent of total U.S. dollars traded. Company profiles include operating and stock performance summaries as well as a complete business overview.
Published quarterly by Moody's Investor Services.

Moody's Manuals

The Moody's Manuals are a valuable source of financial and other business information on both corporations and government institutions. There are eight manuals in this service: *Bank and Finance Manual, Industrial Manual, In-*

ternational *Manual, Municipal and Government Manual, OTC Industrial Manual, OTC Unlisted Manual, Public Utilities Manual*, and *Transportation Manual*. The coverage of companies in the manuals includes financial data, description of business lines, corporate structure, corporate history, and corporate executives. The *Municipal and Government Manual* provides information on federal, state, and local government financing. The manuals are published annually and updated weekly or semi-weekly through the New Report Service for each manual. The manuals are also available online through DIALOG as *Moody's Corporate News—U.S.* (corresponds to the News Reports of the following manuals: *Bank and Finance, Industrial, OTC Industrial, OTC Unlisted, Public Utility*, and *Transportation*) and Moody's Corporate News International, which corresponds to the News Reports of the *International Manual.*
Published annually by Moody's Investor's Service and updated weekly or semi-weekly through the News Report Service for each manual.

Nelson's Directory of Investment Research

This two-volume work shows how to find research that's been done on 10,500 public companies in both the U.S. and throughout the world. The Nelson's Directory provides in-depth profiles of over 400 investment research firms, including a listing of key research executives and descriptions of research services offered. There are also profiles of 10,500 publicly owned companies. The profiles include information on key executives, a five-year operations summary, and the names and phone numbers of security analysts for each company profiled.
Published annually by Nelson's Publications.

RMA Annual Statement Studies

This annual volume contains composite financial data on manufacturing, wholesaling, retailing, service, and contract businesses. It includes average balance sheet and income data for 392 different industries as well as five-year trend data for almost all of these industries. The data in the book can be used to compare an individual business's performance with the performance of the industry as a whole.
Published annually by Robert Morris Associates (The Association of Bank Loan and Credit Officers).

SEC ON-LINE™

This is a full-text database of reports filed by companies with the U.S. Securities and Exchange Commission. It includes 10-Ks, 10-Qs, 20-Fs, annual reports, and proxy statements. Available online through DIALOG and LEXIS.
Updated weekly by SEC On-line, Inc.

Standard & Poor's Corporation Records

This resource provides financial data and corporate descriptive information including contact information, business summary, products and services, sales, and corporate structure on approximately 12,000 publicly held U.S. and Canadian corporations. Also available online as Standard & Poor's Corporation Records Plus News through DIALOG and Knowledge Index. Also available on CD-ROM.
Updated biweekly by Standard & Poor's Corporation.

Standard & Poor's Industry Surveys

This resource provides a financial and business picture of 21 industries and more than 1,300 companies within these industries. Surveys are produced for the following industry groups: aerospace and air

travel; autos, auto parts, and rubber; banks and financial services; chemicals; computers and office equipment; electric utilities; electronics; food and beverages; gas utilities; health care, drugs and cosmetics; insurance and investment; leisure time; media; metals; oil and oilfield services; railroads and trucking; steel and heavy machinery; telecommunications; textiles, apparel and home furnishings. An annual *Basic Survey* is prepared for each industry group analyzing the operating environment of the industry and key issues faced by the industry and providing financial data on key companies within the industry. The annual *Basic Survey* is supplemented by a monthly *Trends and Projections* newsletter; a monthly *Earnings Supplements;* and a periodic *Current Survey* providing an up-to-date analysis of issues facing the industry.
Each survey is published annually by Standard & Poor's and updated as indicated above.

Standard & Poor's Stock Reports

This looseleaf service provides two-page reports, each of which offers a succinct profile of the activities and financial position of one of over 4,000 companies. Reports are issued on all companies listed on the New York Stock Exchange, the American Stock Exchange, and more than 1,500 of the most active and widely held companies whose securities are traded over the counter and on regional exchanges, including Canada.
Looseleaf service updated weekly; paper edition published quarterly by Standard & Poor's.

The Value Line Investment Survey

This weekly service reports on and evaluates approximately 1,700 stocks in 91 industries. Each stock's most recent price is reported as well as its current rankings for timeliness and safety (future price sta-

bility and the company current financial strength). Approximately every 13 weeks each stock is given a full-page report. The report analyzes the company's business and looks at how the stock stands in relation to other stocks in terms of safety and probable performance over the next 12 months and how the stock's future prospects are assessed. Also available online through CompuServe as Value Line Annual Reports; Value Line DataFile; Value Line Estimates and Projection File; and Value Line Quarterly Reports.
Updated weekly by Value Line Publishing.

CORPORATE LISTINGS, OWNERSHIP AND RANKINGS

America's Corporate Families

A collection of detailed information on 11,000 U.S. ultimate parent companies and their 67,000 U.S. subsidiaries, divisions, and major branches. Listed companies have a net worth of at least $500,000, or net sales of $25 million, or 250 + employees, and a controlling interest in one or more subsidiary companies.
Published annually by Dun & Bradstreet Information Services.

America's Corporate Families and International Affiliates

America's Corporate Families and International Affiliates lists information on a total of 32,000 companies. It contains more than 1,500 U.S. ultimate parents with over 15,000 foreign subsidiaries, and nearly 3,000 foreign ultimate parents with more than 12,000 U.S. subsidiaries. To be included, a corporate family must have a U.S. family member or one or more family members elsewhere.
Published annually by Dun & Bradstreet Information Services.

Business Rankings Annual

This resource is compiled by the Brooklyn Public Library Business Library. It is a guide to published rankings and lists taken from leading business publications. The annual is arranged by subject and includes nearly 4,500 rankings, including profit, market share, sales, ex-ecutive salaries, best-selling products, and advertising budgets. Each entry names a "top ten" along with the ranking criteria; the number of listings in the original source; and the name, date, and page of the original source. Entries are indexed according to each item ranked. Also available on diskette and magnetic tape.
Published annually by Gale Research, Inc.

Canadian Dun's Business Identification Service

This is a directory listing more than 650,000 Canadian businesses from major corporations to rural merchants. Entries include complete contact information.
Published annually by Dun & Bradstreet Information Services.

Canadian Key Business Directory

This is a directory offering detailed information on more than 20,000 major businesses in Canada that generate $20 million in sales, employ 75 individuals, have a net worth of $3.5 million, or have branches with more than 500 total employees. (All dollar figures reflect Canadian currency.) Entries are indexed alphabetically, geographically by province and city, and by line of business. Information on the executives, officers, and managers of these companies is also included.
Published annually by Dun & Bradstreet Information Services.

Company Intelligence™

🔒 This database combines company news with company directory information. Over 140,000 U.S. and 30,000 international companies are included in the directory. Data includes current address, ownership, and financial and marketing information. The U.S. company information is derived from Ward's Business Directory (see below, this chapter) and news articles are indexed by the Information Access Company. International Directories come from print directories published by Graham and Trotman of London. Also available online through DIALOG.

Directory information updated annually and news information updated daily by Information Access Company/Predicasts.

The Corporate Directory of U.S. Public Companies

The directory lists over 9,500 publicly traded firms having at least $5 million in assets. Entries are arranged alphabetically by parent company name and provide general background, stock data, and business description information.

Published annually by Gale Research, Inc.

Directory of Corporate Affiliations

🔒 This is a two-volume reference listing nearly 6,000 parent companies with $10 million or more in annual sales, and over 50,000 subsidiaries, divisions, and affiliates. It provides company statistics, information on key personnel, chain of command, and financial data. Also available on magnetic tape. Available online through DIALOG as CORPORATE AFFILIATIONS.

Published annually with bimonthly updates by National Register Publishing (Reed Reference Publishing).

Directory of Leading Private Companies

🔒 This directory lists more than 22,000 privately owned businesses with more than $10 million in annual sales. Entries include information on key operating department managers, pension fund management, accounting, major professional service suppliers, and computer systems. Available online through DIALOG as CORPORATE AFFILIATIONS.

Published annually by National Register Publishing (Reed Reference Publishing).

Directory of Multinationals

John Stopford

🔒 This two-volume directory deals exclusively with companies that control important foreign investments. It includes information on about 450 companies that account for the bulk of the world's direct foreign investment. All companies have at least $500 million in foreign sales. The Directory lists the value of exports and foreign production of these companies.

Fourth edition published in 1993 by Stockton Press.

The Dun & Bradstreet Reference Book of American Business

This book is a collection of business and credit information on over 3 million large and small companies across the United States. Entries include the demography of a firm's location, how long a company has been in business, and its financial strength and overall credit appraisal. Regional and state guides are available in addition to the national edition.

Published annually by Dun & Bradstreet Information Services.

Dun's Business Identification Service

This is a collection of microfiche cards that lists nearly 10.2 million U.S. businesses.

Entries cover large companies as well as companies that are either privately held or too small or too localized to be profiled elsewhere. The service is available in alphabetical or geographical sequence and can also be purchased in Canadian and international editions. The service includes the D-U-N-S® Numbers to aid in further research.

Published twice yearly by Dun & Bradstreet Information Services.

Dun's Business Rankings

This is a ranked list of 25,000 public and private companies within 67 industries in the United States. Companies are ranked by both sales volume and number of employees. Entries include each company's sales volume and rank, number of employees and rank, name, address, telephone number, SIC code, and the company's stock ticker symbol (where possible).

Published annually by Dun & Bradstreet Information Services.

Dun's Directory of Service Companies

This directory offers detailed information on 50,000 of the largest service enterprises with 50 or more employees in the following lines of business: accounting; auditing and bookkeeping; advertising and public relations; amusement and recreation; architecture and engineering; consumer services; executive search; health; hospitality; management consulting; motion pictures; repair; research; social services; and law firms.

Published annually by Dun & Bradstreet Information Services.

Dun's Electronic Business Directory

This online directory provides information on approximately 9 million public

and private businesses and professionals located in the United States. Entries include the following information: name, address, phone number, SIC code, and number of employees. Available online through DIALOG.

Updated quarterly by Dun & Bradstreet Information Services.

Dun's Regional Business Directory

This three-volume set offers information on 20,000 public and private leading regional businesses. Each edition of *Dun's Regional Business Directory* covers a single Economic Area Indicator. EAIs combine Standard Metropolitan Statistical Areas (SMSAs) with additional surrounding counties that have related economic impact. Regional coverage is currently available for 52 EAIs throughout the country.

Published annually by Dun & Bradstreet Information Services.

The Forbes 500 Annual Directory

This annual directory by Forbes magazine (in an April issue) ranks the 500 largest publicly traded U.S. companies by four different criteria: sales, profits, assets, and market value. The total number of companies ranked in the 1993 directory was 774, reflecting the fact that some companies made the list by some but not all of Forbes' criteria.

Published annually by Forbes magazine.

The Fortune Directory

This directory includes the results and rankings of Fortune's four annual "500" listings: the Industrial, Service, Global Industrial, and Global 500.

Published annually by Fortune Magazine.

Fortune 500 Largest U.S. Industrial Corporations

This is an annual listing of the top 500 industrial companies (ranked by sales volume and categorized by industry) in the United States. Each issue also includes a "Who Did Best and Worst Among the 500" section, which evaluates the list according to total return to investors, return on sales, return on assets, return on stockholders' equity, profits, change in sales, money lost, sales per employee, and sales per dollar of stockholders' equity.
Published annually in an April issue of Fortune Magazine.

Fortune 500 Service Companies

This is a listing of the 500 largest nonindustrial companies in the United States. The rankings of companies are within service areas. There is no overall 1–500 ranking as in the Fortune 500 Largest U.S. Industrial Companies. The issue is widely available and can be found in nearly all libraries.
Published annually in a June issue of Fortune Magazine.

Guide to Canadian Manufacturers

This is a collection of information on the top 15,000 manufacturing locations in Canada that employ 20 or more individuals or generate $5 million or more in sales (in Canadian currency). Each entry shows company name, address, telephone number, and four-digit SIC codes.
Published annually by Dun & Bradstreet Information Services.

Hoover's Handbook of American Business

This is an interesting and readable profile of 500 American organizations. It includes public and private companies and some nonprofit and government organizations. The criteria for selection include sales and number of employees, growth potential, and public visibility. Each organization gets a one-page profile that includes company description and history, ten years of financial and stock data, a description of where the company does business and which parts make money, executive names and titles, and complete contact information. Each organization is rated on a scale from A to F. The rankings are based on Hoover's analysis of the company's financial performance (sales and earnings growth and return on equity), financial strength (relative indebtedness), innovation within the industry, and dominance and market share within the industry.
Published annually by The Reference Press, Inc.

International Directory of Corporate Affiliations

This is a directory offering information on over 57,000 companies around the world. It provides an in-depth view of the non-U.S. parent companies and U.S. and worldwide holdings of international companies. The directory provides company statistics, information on key personnel, chain of command, and financial data. Available in print and on disk. The directory is also available through DIALOG as CORPORATE AFFILIATIONS.
Updated semiannually by National Register Publishing (Reed Reference Publishing).

Manufacturing USA

Arsen J. Darnay, editor

Manufacturing USA provides company profiles and rankings for about 460 top manufacturers. Organized by industry according to four-digit SIC codes, entries provide facts and tables on a number

of subjects, ranging from general industry statistics to shipments and employment trends for each industry. Within each industry, profiles provide general industry statistics, indices of change, selected ratios, product share, statistical analyses by state and regions, occupations employed by various industries, up to 75 leading companies ranked by sales, and other valuable data. Entries are indexed by product, company name, occupations employed, and SIC code.
Second edition published in 1992 by Gale Research, Inc.

Million Dollar Directory Series

🔒 This six-volume directory profiles more than 160,000 U.S. companies, 90 percent of them privately owned, with a net worth of $750,000 or more, 250 or more employees, or $25 million in annual sales. Entries include information on headquarters location, SIC number, and company officers. Also available online through DIALOG.
Published annually by Dun & Bradstreet Information Services.

Minority Organizations: A National Directory

This is a comprehensive source of information on approximately 9,700 minority organizations. Minority groups in the directory are defined to include black, Hispanic, Asian, and Native American. Each entry provides contact and background information.
Fourth edition published in 1991 by Garrett Park Press.

National Directory of Minority-Owned Business Firms

This directory lists information on more than 40,000 minority business enterprises, arranged according to SIC business de-

scription. Entries include company address, contact name, FAX number, date founded, business description, trading areas, number of employees, and sales volume.
Published annually by Business Research Services. Distributed in the United States and Canada by Gale Research, Inc.

National Directory of Women-Owned Business Firms

This directory lists 25,000 women-owned business enterprises, arranged according to SIC business description. Entries include company address, contact name, FAX number, date founded, business description, trading areas, number of employees, and sales volume.
Published annually by Business Research Services. Distributed in the United States and Canada by Gale Research, Inc.

Predicasts' F & S Index of Corporate Change

🔒 This index covers changes in ownership of U.S.-based companies, both public and private. The *Index of Corporate Change* provides information on company formations, mergers and acquisitions, joint ventures, bankruptcies, liquidations, reorganizations, foreign operations, and name and subsidiary changes. Index entries identify the companies involved and the nature of the change, and each entry includes a complete source citation. Also available online through BRS and DIALOG as part of PTS F & S Indexes.
Published quarterly with annual cumulative edition by Information Access/Predicasts.

Regional Directories of Minority & Women-Owned Business Firms

This three-volume reference lists thousands of minority- and women-owned business enterprises, organized by state and SIC business description. Entries include company address, contact name, FAX number, date founded, business description, trading areas, number of employees, and sales volume.

Published annually by Business Research Services. Distributed in the United States and Canada by Gale Research, Inc.

Service Industries USA

Arsen J. Darnay, editor

Service Industries USA provides figures on more than 150 service industries and more than 4,000 leading public and private corporations and nonprofit institutions. The book is divided in two parts. Part 1 provides industry data for the United States and individual states, using various federal statistics for service industries. Each entry contains a description, general statistics, indices of change, selected ratios, statistical analyses by state and region, occupations employed, and more. Part 2 offers Metro Area Statistics, arranged alphabetically by metro area and SIC code, for more than 600 metropolitan areas in the United States. Entries are indexed according to SIC code, services, metro area, company/nonprofit organization, and occupation.

Published in 1992 by Gale Research, Inc.

Ward's Business Directory of U.S. Private and Public Companies

⯐ This five-volume set contains information on over 130,000 U.S. public and private companies with sales of at least $500,000. Ward's emphasizes private companies (about 90 percent of the listings). Volumes 1–3 contain an alphabetial listing of the firms, including addresses, telephone numbers, sales, number of employees, and the names of up to five corporate officers. Volume 4 is a geographic state-by-state guide to the entries. Volume 5 organizes the entries according to four-digit SIC codes and ranks each company within a given code according to its sales. Avail-

able on diskette and magnetic tape.

Published annually by Gale Research, Inc.

Who Owns Whom—North America

This one-volume reference lists North American parent companies, subsidiaries, and associates. The directory's one volume is divided into four sections: The first lists subsidiaries and associates of parent companies registered in the United States that conduct business in other parts of the world; the second lists subsidiaries and associates of parent companies registered in Canada; the third lists foreign parent companies with subsidiaries and associates in the United States and Canada; and the fourth is an alphabetical index that links any family member to its ultimate parent.

Published annually by Dun & Bradstreet Information Services.

FOR FURTHER INFORMATION

See *The BusinessWeek Global 1000,*
   p. 442
The BusinessWeek 1000: America's Most
   Valuable Companies, p. 443
Disclosure® Database, p. 443
Disclosure Worldscope™ Global, p. 443
European Business Rankings, p. 541
International Directory of Company
   Histories, p. 522
Moody's International Manual and News
   Reports, p. 523
Moody's Manuals, p. 444
PTS PROMPT:™ Overview of Markets
   and Technology, p. 406
PTS F & S Index, p. 406
COMPUSTAT, p. 443
SEC ON-LINE™, p. 445
Standard & Poor's Register of
   Corporations, Directors, and
   Executives, p. 454
Thomas Register of American
   Manufacturers, p. 559
World Trade Centers Association World
   Business Directory, p. 524
Worldwide Branch Locations of
   Multinational Companies, p. 524

13

CORPORATE OFFICERS AND DIRECTORS

The Corporate Director

Leo Herzel and James B. Carlson

The Corporate Director supplies simple, accurate descriptions of the main legal problems directors face in the context of important strategic and business problems, such as proxy fights, mergers, acquisitions, takeovers, and bankruptcy.
Published in 1993 by McGraw-Hill, Inc.

The Corporate Finance Bluebook

The Corporate Finance Bluebook lists leading financial executives in over 5,200 companies and 20,000 subsidiaries. Entries include sales/earnings/assets/liabilities, contact information, major suppliers, and wholly owned U.S. subsidiaries.
Published annually by National Register Publishing.

Corporate Yellow Book

The *Corporate Yellow Book* lists the names and titles of over 39,000 U.S. corporate executives. Included within this list are more than 10,000 corporate board members. Entries include officers' names, titles, addresses, telephone numbers, and a short description of each company's business, including product lines and annual revenues. The *Corporate Yellow Book* includes four indexes that allow users to access the entries according to company or subsidiary, industry, state, or an individual's name.
Published quarterly by Monitor Publishing Company.

International Corporate Yellow Book

This is a directory of key executives and officers within leading non-U.S. companies. Entries include the names, addresses, telephone, FAX, and telex numbers of over 30,000 executives; names, titles, and affiliations of corporate board members; descriptions of each company's business and production lines; an estimate of each company's annual revenue; and each company's main subsidiaries and affiliates. Entries are indexed by company name, industry, individual names, and U.S. subsidiaries.
Published annually by Monitor Publishing Company.

NASDAQ Yellow Book

This is a directory of the executives running the younger high-growth companies in the United States. The *NASDAQ Yellow Book* lists the names, titles, and telephone numbers of over 20,000 key executives in these smaller companies. Entries also include the names, titles, and affiliations of corporate board members; descriptions of each company's business and product lines; an estimate of each company's annual revenue; and addresses, telephone numbers, and FAX numbers for each company as well as its main subsidiaries and affiliates (both domestic and foreign). Entries are indexed by company name, executive name, state, and industry.
Published annually by Monitor Publishing Company.

Owners and Officers of Private Companies

🔒 This is a directory of over 100,000 executives in over 44,000 leading private companies with more than $5 million in sales in the United States. Each entry includes company name, address, and telephone number; key executives' names and titles; SIC codes; annual sales figures; and number of employees. Entries are indexed by company name, geographic area, and SIC code. Also available on diskette and magnetic tape.

Published annually by the Taft Group. Distributed by Gale Research, Inc.

Reference Book of Corporate Managements

This is a four-volume set profiling the officers within 12,000 U.S. companies. Entries include condensed resumes listing each officer's business background and work history, along with name, title, year of birth, marital status, military service, and college(s) attended with the dates of degrees earned.

Published biennially by Dun & Bradstreet Information Services.

Standard & Poor's Register of Corporations, Directors, and Executives

🔒 A three-volume set, the *S & P Register* is a leading directory of company information. Volume 1, called *Corporations*, is an alphabetical listing of over 55,000 North American (mostly U.S.) companies, including their addresses, telephone and FAX numbers, subsidiaries, names and titles of key corporate officers, number of employees, and a bit of financial information such as gross sales. Volume 2, called

Directors and Executives, contains listings for about 70,000 corporate officers, partners, directors, trustees, and so on. The listings include the place and date of birth, place of residence, schools attended, and professional affiliations. Volume 3 is a series of indexes. The *S & P Register* is available in both print and online versions. Customized excerpts are available on computer disk. Online versions are available from DIALOG and Mead Data Central's LEXIS and NEXIS services.

Published biennially by Standard & Poor's.

Who's Who in Finance and Industry, 27th Edition, 1992–93

This book provides substantive biographies of approximately 25,000 North American and international professionals in the following fields: accounting, advertising, banking and finance, communications, construction and engineering, industrial and commercial firms, insurance, investment companies, retail trade, transportation, and utilities.

Published biennially by Marquis Who's Who.

FOR FURTHER INFORMATION

See *Canadian Key Business Directory,*
  p. 447
The Corporate Directory of U.S. Public
  Companies, p. 448
Directory of Corporate Affiliations, p. 448
Hoover's Handbook of American
  Business, p. 450
Moody's Manuals, p. 444
Nelson's Directory of Investment
  Research, p. 445
Ward's Business Directory of U.S. Private and Public Companies, p. 452
World Trade Centers Association World
  Business Directory, p. 524

DEMOGRAPHICS, MARKETING DATA, AND MARKETING RESEARCH

American Demographics

This monthly business magazine is written for marketers, advertisers, and business planners. Articles generally deal with demographic trends and their implications for business.
Published monthly by American Demographics, Inc.

Asian Americans Information Directory

Karen Backus and Julia C. Furtaw, editors

Directory of more than 5,200 organizations, agencies, institutions, programs, services, and publications concerned with Asian-American life and culture has separate sections that cover 19 Asian groups represented in the United States including Chinese, Filipino, Indonesian, Japanese, Laotian, Pacific Islander, and Thai. Each entry within a nationality section provides pertinent data such as name, address, telephone number, and contact person. The directory is available in print, on computer diskette, and on magnetic tape.
Published in 1992 by Gale Research, Inc.

Atlas Software™

This software package helps businesspeople to take geographical considerations (e.g., market potential by sales territory or distribution coverage by product or customer locations by zip code or street address) into decision making in order to optimize sales territories, target customers, and select site locations.
Published by Strategic Mapping, Inc.

Black Americans Information Directory 1992–93

Julia C. Furtaw, editor

Collection of more than 4,800 entries provides contact information on a wide range of nonprofit, private, public, educational, and governmental organizations and agencies concerned with African-Americans. There are also descriptions of important sources of information, educational programs, publications, and media. The directory is available in print, on computer diskette, and on magnetic tape.
Second edition published in 1991 by Gale Research, Inc.

The Boomer Report

This newsletter monitors the approximately 77 million members of the Baby Boom Generation. It tracks the news stories, market studies, surveys, books, and journals that report on boomers.
Published monthly by FIND/SVP.

Brand Advantage

This publication is a two-volume collection of key consumer marketing information about men and women 18 years and older. It provides usage and brand user information on nearly 3,600 consumer products in over 300 brand categories. Volume I covers food and consumables. Volume II covers products and services. The data is organized demographically—for example, household income, employment status, or geographic region.
Published annually by Standard Rate and Data Service (SRDS).

Business Lists-on-Disc™

Database helps user find demographic information on business by providing data on 10 million businesses on a single CD-ROM disk. Business Lists-on-Disc helps users research and analyze markets by SIC code, geography, employment size, and annual sales volume.
Published in 1993 with annual updates by American Business Information.

CEDDS: The Complete Economic and Demographic Data Source

This three-volume set contains economic and demographic forecasts to 2015 and historical data from 1970 for every county, state, and metropolitan area in the United States. More than 70 different ranking tables are included, such as projected growth in new jobs and forecast of population increase. It also includes an analysis of regions of the United States that identifies trends and looks at the strengths and weaknesses of the economy. Available in print, disk, and CD-ROM.
Published annually by Woods & Poole Economics, Inc.

CENDATA

This online database, compiled by the U.S. Bureau of the Census, Data Access and Use Staff, contains current and projected data on U.S. business (business establishments, employees, payroll figures) and demographic and population data (from the 1990 census). It also includes demographic data from 200 other countries. Available online from DIALOG and CompuServe.
Updated daily by the U.S. Bureau of the Census.

Census Catalog and Guide

This publication of the U.S. Bureau of the Census is a catalog and guide to the programs and services of the Census Bureau. It describes or lists recent products and provides a useful product overview chart. There are also separate chapters for products dealing with the following topics: agriculture; business (trade and services); construction and housing; foreign trade; geography; governments; international; manufacturing and mineral industries; population; transportation; and the 1990 Census of Population and Housing. A "Sources of Assistance" section includes the following information: a listing of the organizations (and contact information) involved in the state Data Center Program (see. p. 463) and the Business/Industry Data Center Program; organizations, contact information, and services/data holdings of organizations involved in the National Clearinghouse program; participants and contact information for participants in the Federal-State Cooperative Program for Population Estimates; a listing of Federal Depository Libraries; Bureau of the Census Regional Information Offices; and staff and programs of the Census Bureau in Washington, D.C.
Published annually by the Superintendent of Documents, U.S.

Government Printing Office. (The catalog
is updated monthly through a free
publication, the Monthly Product
Announcement.)

Consumer Market Developments, 1991

This publication offers select market statistics along with eight-year projections of consumer spending and key economic indicators such as the Consumer Price Index, Housing Starts and Permits, Unemployment, and Department Store Sales.
Published in 1992 by Fairchild Books.

Consumer Power: How Americans Spend Their Money

Margaret Ambry

Text is a comprehensive collection of statistics on consumer spending and income over nine product and service categories.
Published in 1992 by New Strategist Publications.

Consumer USA

Collection profiles major consumer goods manufacturers, with complete contact information. Other features include a directory of major retailers in the United States and a guide to official and nonofficial business information sources.
Second edition published in 1992 by Gale Research, Inc.

County and City Data Book: A Statistical Abstract Supplement

This extensive collection of county and city data includes entries on demographics, wages, unemployment, and workers' compensation.
Published annually by the U.S. Government Printing Office.

Data Pamphlets (for an Individual County, State, or Metropolitan Statistical Area)

These pamphlets are 90-page reports containing demographic and economic data for specific geographical areas. Each pamphlet provides a forecast to 2015 and historical data from 1970. It also includes an economic analysis of the area that identifies trends and looks at strengths and weaknesses of the economy. The pamphlets are available in print and on disk.
Updated annually by Woods & Poole Economics, Inc.

Databased Marketing: The Manager's Guide to the Super Marketing Tool of the 21st Century

Herman Holtz

Comprehensive guide to the techniques involved in setting up and managing a database marketing program includes topics like developing consumer databases, pursuing niche market groups, and selecting consultants to build marketing databases.
Published in 1992 by John Wiley & Sons, Inc.

Demographic Yearbook

Comprehensive collection of international demographic statistics covering 220 countries or areas includes information on population, birth rates, infant mortality, marriage, and divorce.
Published annually by United Nations Publications.

Directory of Marketing Information Companies

This directory, published by American Demographics Magazine, lists companies

providing products and services that help decision makers analyze and reach their customers.
Published annually by American Demographics, Inc.

Dun's Census of American Business

This directory of company statistics categorizes entries according to SIC codes and groups them according to sales volume and number of employees. The information in the *Census* can be used to establish the size of a market; identify competitors; project sales potential; determine distributor locations; and determine locations for branches, retail outlets, and service centers.
Published annually by Dun & Bradstreet Information Services.

Findex: The Directory of Market Research Reports, Studies, and Surveys

▯ Annual listing of more than 500 research companies and publishers that produce over 12,000 market research reports is organized alphabetically and includes title of report, description of contents, date of publication, number of pages, purchase price, name of publisher, and complete contact information. *Findex* is also available online through DIALOG.
Published annually with a midyear supplement by Cambridge Information Group.

FIND/SVP Industry and Market Research Reports

FIND/SVP publishes industry and market research reports in many specific areas including beverages, biotechnology, business and financial services, chemicals, computers, consumer and leisure products, demographics, drugs, electronics, energy, health care, high-technology materials, household products, metals and mining, office supplies and equipment, packaging, paper and forest products, personal care, plastics, retailing, the service industry, software, telecommunications, transportation, waste management, and water management.
Published by FIND/SVP.

The Focus Group Directory

Directory lists companies that provide focus group facilities, focus group research, and focus group moderators. The directory is organized geographically.
Published annually by the New York Chapter of the American Marketing Association.

The Hispanic-American Almanac

Nicolas Kanellos, editor

Reference offers information on Hispanic-American history, life, and culture. The almanac covers all aspects of culture and civilization of Hispanic-Americans in the United States including explorers, racial diversity, education, labor and employment, and religion. The narrative text is supplemented with photographs, maps, and charts and includes bibliographic information for further research.
Published in 1992 by Gale Research, Inc.

Hispanic Americans Information Directory 1992–93

Julia C. Furtaw, editor

This directory of more than 4,800 Hispanic organizations, agencies, programs, and publications is in 16 separate chapters and covers a wide range of topical data relating to Hispanic culture, includ-

ing national, state, and local Hispanic associations; print and broadcast media, including Hispanic publishers; bilingual education programs; and federal, state, and local government agencies.
Published in 1992 by Gale Research, Inc.

The Information Catalog

The free catalog lists recent market research studies and offers dozens of market, industry, and company studies. The prices for these studies range from 15 to several thousand dollars.
Published every two months by FIND/SVP.

The Insider's Guide to Demographic Know-How

Diane Crispell

This book shows how to use demographic analyses to obtain useful information about the customers of a business: their age, marital status, earnings, and the products they want. Topics include performing demographic analyses, how to avoid paying for useless information, rules of thumb to ensure the accuracy of the data, and names and telephone numbers of data specialists in the federal government.
Published in 1993 by Probus Publishing.

International Directory of Market Research Organizations

Directory provides an alphabetical listing by country of companies doing marketing research. The information includes data, location facilities; research facilities; product expertise; expertise of international research; and contact information.
Eleventh edition published in 1993 by The Market Research Society. Available in the United States through MacFarlane and Company Inc.

International Directory of Marketing Research Companies

Known as the "Green Book," this directory provides information on companies that provide marketing research and advertising services. It includes listings of 1,500 companies in the United States and 65 other countries. The companies listed provide such services as audience research and measurement and certification of newspaper and magazine circulation.
Published annually by the New York Chapter of the American Marketing Association.

The Lifestyle Market Analyst

This marketing sourcebook provides demographic and lifestyle data for the top 210 areas of dominant influence (ADIs) in the United States. It is organized by geographic location, lifestyle preferences, and consumer segments.
Published annually by Standard Rate and Data Service (SRDS).

The Lifestyle Zip Code Analyst

This marketing sourcebook looks at the demographics, economics, and lifestyles of over 11,000 U.S. zip codes.
Published annually by Standard Rate and Data Service (SRDS).

Market Research Handbook (Canada)

This reference work provides information for analyzing Canadian markets at the provincial, regional, and national levels. Information is provided on international trade; merchandising and services; popu-

lation and labor force; income and spending; housing, motor vehicles, and household facilities and equipment; and census data.
Published annually by Statistics Canada.

Market Share Reporter

🔒 Collection of more than 2,000 market share entries is organized by four-digit SIC codes and indexed alphabetically. Entries are compiled from a wide variety of sources and include descriptive title of the report; data and market description; remarks on the history, scope, and other characteristics of the study; list of producers/products along with their assigned market share; source citation (title, date, and page number of published sources). *Market Share Reporter* is available in print, on line, on computer diskette, and on magnetic tape. Available online through NEXIS.
Published annually by Gale Research, Inc.

PTS Marketing and Advertising Reference Service (PTS MARS)

🔒 This database provides users with abstracts of literature on the marketing and advertising of consumer goods and services. It provides information on market size and share, marketing strategies, consumer research, and advertising campaigns and budgets. Available online through DIALOG.
Updated every business day by Information Access/Predicasts.

Markets of the U.S. for Business Planners

Thomas F. Conroy, editor

This two-volume reference provides historical and current profiles of 183 urban market areas and provides the following information: business and economic profiles; projections for 1995 and 2000; market area maps; and analytical commentary.
Published in 1992 by Omnigraphics, Inc.

Marketsearch: International Directory of Published Market Research

Publication is a directory of industrial market research from companies that have produced more than 20,000 published studies. Entries are arranged by subject area, such as agriculture, cosmetics, electrical engineering, cable television, and medical electronics. Each entry includes the country where the study was produced; the date of the study; complete contact information; and the price of the study (in the local currency).
Published annually by MacFarlane and Co., Inc.

The New Marketing Research Systems: How to Use Strategic Database Information for Better Marketing Decisions

David J. Curry

Reference book for packaged goods marketers and retailers, direct marketers, advertising agency professionals, and market researchers describes and analyzes marketing research systems based on technology that permits the collection, storage, and use of disaggregate data. Single-source, geodemographic, and micromerchandising systems are forging market data from scanners and other electronic sources into tools that solve marketing problems. The author develops critical evaluations of existing systems of new technology from the United States and Europe as well as a wide variety of databases and reports from commercial vendors including A. C. Nielsen, Information Resources, Inc., and CACI Federal.
Published in 1992 by John Wiley & Sons.

The Numbers News: The Newsletter for Serious Trendwatchers

This monthly newsletter analyzes trends—such as working mothers, men's and women's incomes, and consumer spending—that impact marketing and business decisions.
Published monthly by The Numbers News.

The Seasons of Business: The Marketers Guide to Consumer Behavior

Judith Waldrop

This book, written by the research editor of *American Demographics Magazine*, analyzes how events such as weather patterns, agricultural cycles, and hours of daylight affect consumer behavior.
Published in 1992 by American Demographics, Inc.

SMARTdisk™ Strategic Market Analysis: Resources and Techniques

▮ This interactive program is designed to help users understand and predict consumer behavior. It offers an overview of trends that affect the demands for goods and services (e.g., ethnic diversity, household structure) and helps users find the data they need for decision making. It shows how to combine data from the Bureau of Labor Statistics Consumers Expenditure Survey with demographic information to make consumer demand projections.
Published in 1992 by American Demographics, Inc.

Sourcebook of Zip Code Demographics, Census Edition

The *Sourcebook of Zip Code Demographics* profiles residential zip codes regarding population, housing, household income, education, labor force, and other data taken from the 1990 Census Summary Tape File for 1990 Zip Codes.
Published in 1992 by CACI Marketing Systems and distributed by Gale Research, Inc.

State and Metropolitan Databook 1991, Fourth Edition

▮ This reference work, prepared by the Bureau of the Census of the U.S. Department of Commerce, provides a wide variety of information on the states and metropolitan areas of the United States. It includes the latest statistics from the 1990 population count and the 1987 economic census data. Available in print and on diskette suitable for input for leading spreadsheets, database, and mapping programs.
Published in 1991 by the Superintendent of Documents, U.S. Government Printing Office. (Note: For diskette information contact the Bureau of the Census at (301) 763-4100.)

Statistical Record of Black America

One-volume resource provides hundreds of current statistical facts on African-Americans. Data come from a wide variety of published and unpublished statistics from private, commercial, and governmental sources. Entries are arranged in 19 broad subject chapters and cover population, business and economics, vital statistics, family, labor and employment, education, spending, crime, politics, and religion.
Second edition published in 1992 by Gale Research, Inc.

Statistical Record of Women Worldwide

Linda Schmittroth, editor

One-volume resource provides hundreds of current statistical facts on women world-

wide. Data are culled from hundreds of published sources, including periodicals, government documents, association and corporate reports, and research centers. Entries are arranged by subject area and present statistical information in the form of charts, tables, and lists, along with complete bibliographic citations.
Published in 1991 by Gale Research, Inc.

The Survey of Buying Power

This volume contains statistics based on the 1990 census. It provides at least 20 pieces of demographic and socioeconomic data for every metropolitan area, county, and major city in the United States. It also contains 26 individual metromarket ranking tables covering population, income, retail sales, household data and a buying power index. *The Survey of Buying Power* can be used to gauge market potential, set and measure sales quotas and performance, and allocate a media and advertising budget.
Published annually by Sales and Marketing Management magazine.

The Survey of Media Markets

This volume lists 13 pieces of demographic and socioeconomic data for each of the 210 Areas of Dominant Influence (ADIs) in the United States, as well as detailed breakouts showing metropolitan and nonmetropolitan coverage. It also contains five-year projections for population, income, and retail sales for metromarkets and their component counties.
Published annually by Sales and Marketing Management magazine.

United Nations World Population Report

The *World Population Report* contains worldwide demographic data with forecasts to the years 2000 and 2025.
Published annually by the United Nations.

Ward's Sales Prospector: A Directory of Leads by State and Industry

❗ Five-volume reference contains regional guides to nearly 134,000 privately and publicly held U.S. companies. Entries are arranged geographically. Within each volume, 17,000 to 34,000 companies are listed, first by state and zip code, then ranked by SIC code. Rankings typically include names of up to five key officers for each company, company type, fiscal year-end data, year established, annual sales, and number of employees. The directory is available in print, on computer diskette, and on magnetic tape.
Published annually by Gale Research, Inc.

Women's Information Directory

Shawn Brennan, editor

Directory is a guide to approximately 6,000 organizations, agencies, institutions, programs, and publications concerned with women in the United States. Information is arranged under 20 chapters, such as national associations, women's centers, research centers, publications, and electronic databases.
Published in 1992 by Gale Research, Inc.

The Zip Code Mapbook of Metropolitan Areas, Second Edition

The Zip Code Mapbook includes 320 U.S. metropolitan areas, each on an 11-by-17-inch map. Each map shows 1990 zip code boundaries, county boundaries, major highways, and location of city centers. It includes Metropolitan Statistical Areas codes and Metropolitan Area Summary Data from the 1990 census.
Published in 1992 by CACI Marketing Systems.

Bureau of the Census

🛈 Part of the U.S. Department of Commerce, the Bureau collects, tabulates, and publishes a wide variety of statistical data about the people and the economy of the United States. It makes available the statistical results of its censuses, surveys, and other programs through reports, computer tape, CD-ROM, and microfiche. It also prepares special tabulations sponsored and paid for by data users. The Bureau has 12 regional offices.

The Bureau of the Census has an online data system, CENDATA (see p. 456 for a description), available through CompuServe and DIALOG. For content information about CENDATA you may contact the Data Access and Use Staff of the Data User Services Division of the Bureau of the Census at (301) 763-2074.

Additional sources of Census Products and Services include the following:

Data Centers. The Census Bureau has a State Data Center Program available in all states and the District of Columbia, Puerto Rico, Guam, and the Virgin Islands. The Census Bureau furnishes data products, training in data access, and technical assistance to the data centers, which in turn make it available to the public. Some states also participate in the Census Bureau's Business/Industry Data Center Program, receiving economic data, assistance, and training to further economic development and assist businesses and other users in the use of economic data. For more information contact the National Service Program at the Bureau of the Census at (301) 763-1384.

National Clearinghouse for Census Data Services. This is a referral service of outside organizations for users needing special assistance in obtaining and using statistical data and related products prepared by the Census Bureau. The names of organizations and contact information can be obtained from the *Census Catalog and Guide* (see p. 456).

Census Bureau Training Activities. The Census Bureau conducts seminars and workshops in Washington D.C. and other cities. Contact the Training Branch, Data User Services Division, Bureau of the Census at (301) 763-1510.

Census Bureau Customer Service. This service provides general information about products and services at (301) 763-1510. The *Census Catalog and Guide* also lists Bureau subject matter specialists who may be consulted by telephone.

Telephone Contacts for Data Users. This is a free pamphlet provided by the Census Bureau. It lists the names and telephone numbers of experts in various areas, such as construction, foreign trade, transportation, and so on.

American Marketing Association

🛈 The AMA is a professional society for marketing and market research executives, sales and promotion managers, academics, and others interested in the field of marketing. It fosters research, sponsors seminars, and conducts more than 30 annual conferences and symposia.

American Marketing Association, 250 S. Wacker Drive, Suite 200, Chicago, IL 60606. Tel. (312) 648-0536.

See **American Business Climate and Economic Profiles, p. 473**
ABI/INFORM®, p. 400
American Statistics Index, p. 400
Area Wage Survey, p. 485
Bureau of Economic Analysis, p. 477
Bureau of Labor Statistics, p. 478
The Burwell Directory of Information Brokers, p. 400
Dun's Regional Business Directory, p. 449
The Economist World in Figures, p. 403

15

DIRECT MARKETING

Business-to-Business Direct Marketing Resource Guide

This text reveals the many resources available to help build almost any business-to-business marketing plan. It includes information on database strategies, tips on business-to-business lead generation and customer retention, and uses of state-of-the-art technology, along with a sampling of a recent ECHO award-winning business-to-business case study; guidelines for improving business-to-business mail delivery; and supplier indexes.
Published in 1992 by Direct Marketing Association, Inc.

The Complete Direct Mail List Handbook: Everything You Need to Know About Lists and How to Use Them for Greater Profit

Ed Burnett

Information provided includes the 35 major types of mailing lists, the rules for direct mail testing, the five factors that influence response, how to interpret test results and what to do about them, what it costs to "buy" a customer, and updated information on databanks, merge/purge, and computers.
Published in 1988 by Prentice Hall.

Database Marketing: The Ultimate Marketing Tool

Edward L. Nash

Database Marketing is a guide for developing and implementing database mar-keting strategies. Topics include building an in-house database; using database marketing in the packaged goods, financial services, and business-to-business areas; and tailoring strategic and creative approaches to the target market.
Published in 1993 by McGraw-Hill, Inc.

Desktop Direct Marketing: How to Use Up-to-the-Minute Technologies to Find and Research New Customers

Sunny Baker and Kim Baker

Showing how to use the latest technologies to create and disseminate direct marketing material, this book includes information on software, online services, databases, and electronic advertising.
Published in 1993 by McGraw-Hill, Inc.

Direct Mail List Rates and Data

This directory provides information on over 10,000 mailing lists that reach business, consumer, and farm markets. It contains list descriptions, selections and sources, rental rates, usage restrictions, and test arrangement.
Available on subscription, with new directory available bimonthly, from Standard Rate and Data Service (SRDS).

Direct Marketing Consultants

This directory provides the names of specialists who meet the diversified needs of the direct marketing business. Specialties include mergers and acquisitions,

strategic planning and development, catalogs, fulfillment, database marketing, and fundraising.
Published in 1993 by Direct Marketing Association, Inc.

The Direct Marketing Handbook, Second Edition

Edward L. Nash, editor in chief

This handbook is an authoritative encyclopedia of direct-mail information by one of the industry's best-known practitioners.
Published in 1991 by McGraw-Hill, Inc.

Direct Marketing Magazine

This publication is for companies using direct mail along with other forms of media to communicate with and reach their customers.
Published monthly by Hoke Publications, Inc.

The Directory of Business-to-Business Catalogs, Second Edition

⚑ This directory lists close to 6,000 companies in 35 different product areas, from automotive to telecommunications, that sell to businesses. Available in print and on CD-ROM.
Published in 1993 by Grey House Publishing.

Direct Marketing Marketplace: The Directory of the Direct Mail Industry

This directory contains entries for 19,000 direct-marketing companies, executives, suppliers, prominent individuals, agencies, consultants, and media buyers involved in the direct-marketing industry. The listings include company names, addresses, phone numbers, products, services, chief executives, and sales and advertising volume.
Published annually by National Register Publishing Co (Reed Reference Publishing).

Directory of Mail Order Catalogs

⚑ In this comprehensive directory containing over 7,300 entries for mail-order companies selling consumer products throughout the United States, entries include company contact information, mailing list size, and availability. Available in print and on CD-ROM.
Published annually by Grey House Publishing.

DMA 1992–1993 Statistical Fact Book

This text gives direct marketers the most recent and relevant statistical support required for putting together a strategic plan and a client proposal. Information provided includes response rates, conversion rates, return on investment, allowable acquisition, costs per piece in the mail, test quantities, and roll-out numbers. Includes more than 325 charts taken from over 100 studies and sources.
Published in 1993 by Direct Marketing Association, Inc.

The Handbook of International Direct Marketing

Adam Baines, editor

This review of the world's top 40 markets for international direct mail covers key export markets in Asia, Australasia, Europe, Latin America, and the Middle East. It supplies the latest analysis of each country as a receiver and supplier of direct mail. Country-by-country guides specify DM facilities and free services; database and list services; trends in DM volumes;

national consumer protection legislation; postal rates and services; and other vital information.
Published in 1992 by The European Direct Marketing Association.

The Fifth Annual Guide to Telemarketing: 1991/1992

Eugene B. Kordahl and Arnold L. Fishman

This text reports on all aspects of telemarketing for all levels of the telemarketing industry. It provides information on sales, costs, growth rates, supplier and user segmentation, salaries, organization, production, and finance and presents profiles of 26 inbound markets, 19 telemarketing service bureaus, and 14 foreign telemarketing national profiles.
Updated in 1991 by National Telemarketing, Inc.

Lead Generation Handbook

Bernard Goldberg

A comprehensive manual on designing and implementing lead programs to generate quality sales opportunities to motivate sales people, this text includes 16 chapters detailing the planning, creation, execution, and management and analysis of all facets of lead generation for direct-mail and telemarketing sales, seminars, trade shows, and customer programs.
Published in 1992 by Direct Marketing Publishers.

NTC's Dictionary of Direct Mail and Mailing List Terminology and Techniques

Nat G. Bodian

NTC's Dictionary of Direct Mail and Mailing List Terminology and Techniques

defines 1,500 key terms and concepts within the mailing list industry.
Published in 1991 by NTC Publishing Group.

National Directory of Mailing Lists

Containing information on over 20,000 mailing lists, this directory includes quantity, pricing, and contact information. Available both in print and on diskette.
Published annually by Oxbridge Communications.

National Directory of Catalogs

This publication contains more than 7,000 entries on U.S. and Canadian catalogs, including contact information, products carried, and list rental data. Available in print and on diskette.
Published annually by Oxbridge Communications.

The New Direct Marketing: How to Implement a Profit Driven Database Marketing Strategy, Second Edition

David Shepard Associates

This book shows how to target customers, expand the use of database marketing, and develop large database systems without dependence on mainframes.
Published in 1993 by Business One Irwin.

Successful Direct Marketing Methods

Bob Stone

This collection of practical how-to direct marketing tips includes topics like the scope and application of direct marketing, choosing the right media, creating and

producing an effective direct-marketing offer, and building and managing a direct-marketing operation.
Published in 1993 by NTC Publishing Group.

Successful Telemarketing

Bob Stone and John Wyman

Successful Telemarketing is a step-by-step guide to setting up and managing a telemarketing operation. A number of case studies are included, from companies such as AT&T, General Electric, B.F. Goodrich, and Quaker Oats.
Published in 1992 by NTC Publishing Group.

Telemarketer's Guide to State Laws

Julie Crocker, editor

This compilation of all state laws affecting direct marketing today comprises a review of major telemarketing legislation, including ADMRP (automatic dialing and recorded message player), monitoring, and registration bills. A state-by-state list of the relevant telemarketing state statutes is included.
Published annually by Direct Marketing Association, Inc.

TRADE AND PROFESSIONAL ASSOCIATIONS

Direct Marketing Association

■ Founded in 1917, this organization is for those involved in direct marketing and those who want to know more about it. Services include Direct LINK, a direct-marketing database; the DMA Library, featuring over 500 reference books and approximately 120 trade publications; and conference and seminar presentations.
Direct Marketing Association, Inc., 11 West 42nd Street, New York, NY 10036-8096. Tel. (212) 768-7277.

FOR FURTHER INFORMATION

*See **Information Industry Directory**, p. 404*
***The New Marketing Research Systems**, p. 460*

16

DISTRIBUTORS AND DISTRIBUTION MANAGEMENT

American Wholesalers & Distributors Directory

Deborah M. Burek, editor

🔒 The *American Wholesalers & Distributors Directory* gives descriptive listings of more than 20,000 American wholesalers and distributors and their products. Listings cover all types of consumer products, including computers, agricultural machinery, ammunition, jewelry, camping equipment, hand tools, and grocery items. Each entry includes the company's name, address, telephone number, FAX number, principal product lines, number of employees, estimated annual sales volume, principal officers, and SIC code. In addition to entries for each individual company, the directory ranks the top 50 companies (by sales) for each four-digit SIC code. The *American Wholesalers & Distributors Directory* is also available in the following alternative formats: computer diskette and magnetic tape.
Published annually by Gale Research, Inc.

The Distribution Management Handbook

James A. Tompkins and Dale Harmelink, editors

The handbook features the contributions of 30 experts in the field. Topics include distribution planning and design, warehousing methods, and quality turnarounds.
Published in 1992 by McGraw-Hill, Inc.

European Wholesalers & Distributors Directory

Linda Irvin, editor

🔒 The *European Wholesalers & Distributors Directory* contains descriptive listings of about 5,000 wholesalers and distributors of finished consumer goods and industrial products in Western and Eastern Europe. Product lines covered include automobiles, electronic parts and equipment, construction materials, furniture, TV and radio, hardware, footwear, books, newspapers, and so on. Entries are arranged alphabetically by product line and then by country and provide (when available): company name; address; telephone, telex, cable, and FAX numbers; contact name; year established; territory of distribution; annual revenue (expressed in local currency); officer names; number of employees; and products. Entries are indexed by company names, products, geographic listings, and territories served. The *European Wholesalers & Distributors Directory* is also available in the following alternative formats: computer diskette and magnetic tape.
Published in 1992 by Gale Research, Inc.

Guide to Distributorship Agreements

Text is a detailed guide to the process of negotiating and drafting a distributorship agreement.
Published in 1988 by ICC Publishing Corporation.

Reinventing the Warehouse: World Class Distribution Logistics

Roy L. Harmon

This book looks at the latest developments in warehouse management and presents warehouse designs for high-quality, low-cost customer service. The author analyzes superior operations in many area including retail warehousing, logistics, and service parts warehousing.

Published in 1993 by the Free Press.

FOR FURTHER INFORMATION

*See **The Japanese Distribution System**, p. 534*

17

DIVERSITY

Affirmative Action Handbook

George W. Johnston, Peter S. Saucier, and Dawn S. Hyde, editors

The handbook is a guide to understanding and managing affirmative action. Chapters include the following: The Office of Federal Contract; Affirmative Action and the Supreme Court; Reverse Discrimination as an Issue; and Affirmative Action Plans for Individuals with Handicaps and Veterans.
Published in 1992 by Government Institutes, Inc.

America's Work Force Is Coming of Age: What Every Business Needs to Know to Recruit, Train, Manage, and Retain an Aging Work Force

Catherine Fyock

Book is a guide to addressing the key issues involved in analyzing and addressing the increasingly important role of the older employee in the workplace.
Published in 1991 by Lexington Books.

Beyond Race and Gender: Unleashing the Power of Your Total Work Force by Managing Diversity

R. Roosevelt Thomas, Jr.

Beyond Race and Gender offers an action plan for dealing with the specific issues that arise in an ever more diverse workplace. It enables readers to examine the culture of their organization carefully and analyze the cultural roots that can sabotage a diversity program.
Published in 1992 by AMACOM.

Managing a Diverse Workforce: Regaining the Competitive Edge

John P. Fernandez

This guide to many diversity-related issues and problems includes topics such as accommodating diversity, upgrading skills, resolving conflicts, and reducing turnover.
Published in 1991 by Lexington Books.

Managing Diversity: A Complete Desk Reference and Planning Guide

Lee Gardenswartz and Anita Rowe

Guide to managing diversity in the workplace includes these topics: recruiting, training, mentoring, and promoting diverse employees to eliminate high turnover rates; building cohesive, productive, cross-cultural work teams; and using assessment tools built around a number of diversity-related issues.
Published in 1992 by Business One Irwin.

Sexual Harassment on the Job: What It Is and How to Stop It

William Petrocelli and Barbara Kate Repa

Sexual Harassment on the Job covers all aspects of the problem—from annoying behavior to physical abuse. It describes what harassment is and gives specific strategies to end it, including confronting the harasser, using a company complaint procedure, filing a state or federal sexual harassment claim, and bringing a lawsuit. This book also offers guidance to employers who want to create a policy against sexual harassment and a procedure for handling complaints.

Published in 1992 by NoLo Press.

TRADE AND PROFESSIONAL ASSOCIATIONS

The American Institute for Managing Diversity, Inc.

Affiliated with Morehouse College, The Institute holds public seminars and develops in-house programs on the issue of developing and managing a diverse work force.

The American Institute for Managing Diversity, Inc., P.O. Box 38, 830 Westview Drive SW, Atlanta, GA 30314. Tel. (404) 524-7316. FAX (404) 524-0649.

FOR FURTHER INFORMATION

See Asian Americans Information Directory, p. 455

Black Americans Information Directory, p. 455

Building the Competitive Workforce: Investing in Human Capital for Corporate Success, p. 516

The Hispanic-American Almanac, p. 458

Hispanic Americans Information Directory, p. 458

National Directory of Minority-Owned Business Firms, p. 451

National Directory of Women-Owned Business Firms, p. 451

Managing Workforce 2000: Gaining the Diversity Advantage, p. 518

Minority Organizations: A National Directory, p. 451

Regional Directories of Minority & Women-Owned Business Firms, p. 451

Statistical Record of Black America, p. 461

Statistical Record of Women Worldwide, p. 461

Women's Information Directory, p. 462

18

ECONOMIC DATA, TRENDS, AND PROJECTIONS: UNITED STATES

American Business Climate and Economic Profiles

Priscilla Cheng Geahgian, editor

This text provides facts and figures for the larger cities in the United States, arranged by 300 Metropolitan Statistical Areas (MSAs) and 50 states. The information provided includes gross state product figures, income data, labor force statistics, and state tax rates and incentives. A separate section ranks each MSA and state by 22 criteria, including education, personal and per capita income, labor, land area, population, quality of life, and sales.
Published in 1992 by Gale Research, Inc.

BLS Electronic News Release Service

This database contains the full text of the Bureau of Labor Statistics' monthly release on consumer and producer prices, earnings, and employment, and quarterly releases on productivity, employment costs, collective bargaining, and import and export price indices. Available online from the Bureau of Labor Statistics.
Updated monthly and quarterly from the U.S. Bureau of Labor Statistics.

Business Statistics 1963–91

This research tool, prepared by the Bureau of Economic Analysis of the Department of Commerce, enables users to track business trends from 1963 through 1991. It covers production, manufacturing and labor costs, consumption of goods, and employment levels in the United States. It also covers export and import statistics classified by country and continent as well as by type of commodity and dollar amount. Data are provided monthly for the last four years, and annual totals for prior periods. An historical appendix includes monthly data for some entries to 1963.
Published in 1992, and biennially, by the Superintendent of Documents, U.S. Government Printing Office.

BusinessWeek Index

This weekly feature of BusinessWeek provides a quick review of production indicators, foreign exchange, prices, leading indicators, monthly economic indicators, monetary indicators, and money market rates.
Published weekly by McGraw-Hill.

DRI Forecasts

DRI/McGraw-Hill produces and makes available online a number of time series databases on the U.S. economy, including the following.

DRI Fixed Investment Forecast. Covers expenditures for durable equipment and construction. Updated monthly.

DRI Consumer Markets Forecast. Covers national consumer spending and discretionary income. Short-term forecasts updated monthly; long-term forecasts updated semiannually.

DRI County Forecast. Covers employment, income, and demographics for all U.S. counties. Updated semiannually.

DRI Current Economic Indicators. Provides key economic indicators for the United States, other industrialized countries, and developing countries. Updated periodically.

DRI Metropolitan Area Forecast. Contains quarterly and annual economic demographic forecasts for metropolitan statistical areas. Updated twice a year.

DRI U.S. Annual Model Forecast. Provides macroeconomic and microeconomic forecasts of the U.S. economy. Updated monthly.

(*Source*: Gale Directory of Databases, Volume 1: Online Databases.)

Available online from DRI/McGraw-Hill.

Early Economic Outlook

FAX-based information delivery system tracks key economic indexes. Each daily one-page report covers a particular topic, such as industrial production, employment, and unemployment. Every Monday the report offers an inflation outlook, and on Friday the report covers economic issues dealing with Germany, Japan, the United Kingdom, or France.
Published daily by the Center for International Business Cycle Research.

ECONBASE:Time Series and Forecasts

🔍 This time series database of macroeconomic and microeconomic data contains economic data arranged by month, quarter, and year. Available online from DIALOG.
Updated monthly by WEFA Group.

Economic Bulletin Board

🔍 This online system has access to news releases and other information from the Department of Commerce, Department of Labor, Federal Reserve, and other economic agencies in the U.S. government. Data are usually available within an hour of their release. The *Economic Bulletin Board* is available by subscription from the Economics and Statistics Administration of the U.S. Department of Commerce. A $35.00 registration fee covers two hours of connect time on the system (exclusive of telephone charges); additional time is paid by the minute ($0.20 between 8:00 AM and noon, $0.15 between noon and 6:00 PM, and $0.05 from 6:00 PM through 8:00 AM). *Updated daily by the U.S. Department of Commerce.*

Economic Indicators

Joseph Plocek

Economic Indicators discusses in detail the 20 leading economic indicators, including the Consumer Price Index, the Purchasing Managers Report, the Merchandise Trade Balance, Housing Starts and Permits, Civilian Unemployment Report, and Department Store Sales.
Published in 1991 by Prentice Hall, Inc.

Economic Report of the President

This report is an invaluable source of information on economic conditions in the United States. In addition to the usually short report of the president, there is an extended (200+ pages) discussion of particular topics from the past year's economy by the Council of Economic Advisors. The most useful part of the report, however, is the roughly 130-page compendium of economic data organized into 10 categories: (1) national income or expenditure, (2) population, employment, wages, and productivity, (3) production and business activity, (4) prices, (5) money stock, credit, and finance, (6) government finance, (7) corporate profits and finance, (8) agriculture, (9) international statistics, and (10) national wealth.

The data are presented annually, in most cases from 1946 through the most recent year. The breadth, historical range, and topical nature (for instance, the GDP data for the fourth quarter of the year that just ended) are features that make this an invaluable reference source.
Published annually by the U.S. Government Printing Office.

Employment and Earnings

This monthly publication prepared by the Bureau of Labor Statistics provides data on (1) the Household Survey, the source for the breakdown of the labor force into its employed and unemployed components and for the unemployment rate, and (2) the Establishment Survey, the source of data on employment, and hours worked by industry in the nonfarm payroll sector.
Published monthly by the U.S. Government Printing Office.

The Federal Reserve Bulletin

This monthly publication of the board of governors of the Federal Reserve System is the main source of data on money and credit in the United States. There are usually one to three articles on aspects of monetary policy and the monetary economy. In addition, the latest minutes of the Federal Open Market Committee and any regulatory changes are reported. The back of the report is given over to extensive data on money and credit conditions.
Published monthly by the Board of Governors of the Federal Reserve System.

Historical Statistics of the United States, Colonial Times to 1970, Parts I and II

These three volumes are supplements to the *Statistical Abstract of the United States* and contain many of the same series constructed back through history. It is a specialized reference source that may be useful under certain circumstances. In many cases, the reconstructed data reflect the work of noted economic historians.
Published in 1975 by the U.S. Government Printing Office.

The McGraw-Hill Encyclopedia of Economics, Second Edition

Douglas Greenwald, editor in chief

Text is a comprehensive reference on more than 300 topics in economics.
Published in 1993 by McGraw-Hill, Inc.

The New Palgrave Dictionary of Money and Finance

Peter Newman, Murray Milgate, and John Eatwell, editors

This three-volume authoritative reference contains over 1,000 essays on U.S. and international aspects of money, banking, and finance. It has overviews of the world's financial institutions and markets, analysis of the latest innovations in financial instruments, and explanations of economic and monetary theories. Several of the contributors are Nobel laureates in economics. The articles cover topics such as the savings and loan crisis and German monetary unification.
Published in 1993 by Stockton Press, The Macmillan Publishing Company.

OECD Economic Surveys: United States

Publication is an annual report on the U.S. economy. The 1992 issue reviewed the nature of the U.S. economic recovery and the short-term outlook for the economy. It documents medium-term trends in incomes, productivity, investment and saving; and examines the federal budget deficit problem.

Published annually by the Organization for Economic Cooperation and Development (OECD).

Predicasts' Basebook

The *Predicasts' Basebook* provides historical data on U.S. business and economic activities. It contains over 26,000 statistical time series and is based on over 300 statistical publications from the federal government, national trade associations, and agencies providing data on subjects ranging from demographics and economic indicators to specific industries. The data cover production, consumption, imports, exports, expenditures, shipments, and employment statistics. The data in Predicasts' Basebook cover a 14-year period. (Online equivalent is PTS U.S. Time Series™.)

Published annually by Information Access/Predicasts.

Predicasts' Forecasts

This quarterly publication provides nearly 50,000 short- and long-range projections for products, markets, industries, and the economy of the U.S. marketplace. *Predicasts' Forecasts* is based on projections reported by experts in over 500 worldwide business, trade, and economic sources. (Online equivalent is PTS U.S. Forecasts™.)

Published quarterly, with an annual cumulative volume, by Information Access/Predicasts.

PTS U.S. Forecasts™

 This is the online equivalent of Predicasts' Forecasts. Available online through

Data-Star and DIALOG.

Published and updated quarterly by Information Access/Predicasts.

PTS U.S. Time Series™

 This is the online equivalent of the Predicasts' Basebook. Available online through Data-Star and DIALOG.

Published and updated quarterly by Information Access/Predicasts.

Survey of Current Business

Published monthly by the U.S. Department of Commerce, Economics and Statistics Administration, Bureau of Economic Analysis, the *Survey* is the most important and comprehensive source of U.S. government-compiled economic data. There are three main sections to the *Survey*, which are conveniently color-coded.

The *white* pages contain three types of material. First is the "Business Situation" section, which summarizes in an objective manner the recent economic situation as characterized in the latest economic data. Second is the presentation of the detailed *National Income and Product Account* tables, presenting the GDP data in all its forms, components, and related measures. Third are special articles and tables on regularly compiled measures such as international trade and capital flows, capital stock, and state personal income.

The *yellow* pages present economic data classified by cyclical characteristics. This section classifies some 250 economic indicators by whether they lead, coincide with, or lag behind overall economic activity.

The *blue* pages present monthly data on some 1,900 economic indicators, including personal income, industrial production, employment, manufacturing, consumer prices, and so on.

Published monthly by the U.S. Government Printing Office

The United States Industrial Outlook

This business report prepared by the International Trade Administration of the U.S. Department of Commerce provides overviews, economic analysis and projections (including production, employment, import competition, and prices) for over 350 manufacturing, service, and high-tech industries, ranging from supercomputers to valve and pipe fittings. Industry forecasts are given for the year of publication and five years thereafter. The *U.S. Industrial Outlook* also provides profiles of international competition and international trade forecasts.
Published annually by the Superintendent of Documents, U.S. Government Printing Office.

Using Economic Indicators to Improve Investment Analysis

Evelina Tainer

The book shows how economic indicators relate specifically to the investment strategies of individual investors, traders, and long-term institutional investors.
Published in 1993 by John Wiley & Sons, Inc.

GOVERNMENT AGENCIES

Bureau of Economic Analysis

Part of the Department of Commerce, the role of the Bureau of Economic Analysis is to provide statistics on economic growth, inflation, regional development, and the United States' role in the world economy. BEA's current regional, national, and international estimates first appear as news releases, available by phone, online through the Economic Bulletin Board (see p. 474), and in printed reports. Phone information is available as follows: leading indicators, (202) 898-2450; Gross Domestic Product, (202) 898-2451; Personal Income and Outlays, (202) 898-2452; Merchandise Trade, Balance of Payments, U.S. International Transactions, (202) 898-2453.

BEA written reports are as follows:

BEA Reports: Gross Domestic Product. Contain a summary of National Income and Product Account Estimates and feature GDP and corporate profits. Published monthly, available by subscription.

BEA Reports: Personal Income and Outlays. Contain a summary of National Income and Product Account estimates and feature personal income and outlays. Published monthly, available by subscription.

BEA Reports: Regional Reports. Provide summary estimates of state personal income (quarterly and annual) and of county and metropolitan personal income (annual). Published six times a year, available by subscription.

BEA Reports: International Reports. Provide summary estimates of merchandise, trade, balance of payments basis (quarterly), summary of international transactions (quarterly), capital spending of majority-owned affiliates (semiannual), and direct investment (annual). Published 13 times a year; available by subscription.

BEA Reports: Composite Index of Leading, Coincident, and Lagging Indicators. Provide summary estimates of the composite indices. Published monthly, available by subscription.

Survey of Current Business. See p. 476.

Business Statistics 1963–91. See p. 473.

All BEA Reports available from the Superintendent of Documents, U.S. Government Printing Office.
For further information, contact the Public Information Office, Bureau of

Economic Analysis, Department of Commerce, Washington, DC 20230. Tel. (202) 523-0771.

Bureau of Labor Statistics (BLS)

The BLS collects, analyzes, and publishes data on employment, unemployment, prices and consumer expenditures, wages, productivity, economic growth, and employment projections. BLS data are issued in monthly, quarterly, and annual news releases and bulletins, reports, special publications, and periodicals. Data is available in both print and through an electronic news service, magnetic tape, diskettes, and microfiche.

BLS publications include the following:

Consumer Expenditure Survey. Published annually.

Consumer Price Index. Published monthly, available by subscription.

CPI Detailed Report. Provides comprehensive reports on consumer price movements and statistical tables, charts, and technical notes. Published monthly, available by subscription.

Producer Price Indexes. Published monthly, available by subscription.

Employment and Earnings. Covers employment and unemployment developments and statistical tables on national, state, and area unemployment, hours, and earnings. Published monthly, available by subscription. (See description on p. 475.)

Compensation and Working Conditions. Reports on employee compensation, including wages, salaries, benefits, and safety and health. Published monthly, available by subscription.

All BLS reports are available through the Superintendent of Documents, U.S. Government Printing Office.
Office of publications, Bureau of Labor Statistics, Department of

Labor, Room 2822, 441 G Street NW, Washington, DC 20212. Tel. (202) 606-5886.

The American Economics Association

Organization is a forum for educators, business executives, government administrators, journalists, lawyers, and others interested in economics and its application to present-day problems. It encourages historical and statistical research into actual conditions of industrial life and provides a nonpartisan forum for economic discussion. It sponsors the National Registry for Economists, a placement service. *American Economics Association, 204 Broadway, Suite 305, Nashville, TN 37203-2418. Tel. (615) 322-2595.*

The Conference Board

The Conference Board is an organization that serves senior corporate executives. It provides a professionally managed research program in several areas, including economics. Its staff includes specialists in economic forecasting, consumer markets, public economic policy, and regional and global economic analysis. The Conference Board produces proprietary economic indicators including the "Help Wanted Index" and the "Consumer Confidence Survey."
The Conference Board, 845 Third Avenue, New York, NY 10022. Tel. (212) 759-0900. FAX (212) 980-7014.

FOR FURTHER INFORMATION
*See **ABI/INFORM®**, p. 400*
American Statistics Index, p. 400
The Business One Irwin Business and Investment Almanac, p. 442

19

ECONOMIC DATA, TRENDS, AND PROJECTIONS: WORLDWIDE

Balance of Payments Statistics Yearbook

This two-part yearbook contains balance of payments statistics for most of the world. Part I includes aggregate and detailed presentations. Part II provides tables of data illustrating area and world balance of payments components and aggregates. Available in print and on magnetic tape.

Published annually by the International Monetary Fund.

Direction of Trade Statistics

Publication provides data on exports and imports for over 135 countries. Available in print and on magnetic tape.

Published quarterly, with an annual cumulative volume, by the International Monetary Fund.

DRI Databases

DRI produces and makes available online a number of time series databases on various countries and regions of the world economy, including the following.

DRI Asian Forecast. Provides economic forecasts for Australia, Hong Kong, India, Indonesia, Korea, Malaysia, People's Republic of China, Philippines, Singapore, Taiwan, and Thailand. Updated quarterly.

DRI Current Economic Indicators. Provide key economic indicators to Argentina, Australia, Austria, Belgium, Brazil, Canada, Chile, Columbia, Denmark, Finland, France, Germany, Greece, Hong Kong, Indonesia, Ireland, Israel, Italy, Japan, Korea, Mexico, Netherlands, Norway, Singapore, South Africa, Spain, Sweden, Switzerland, Taiwan, Thailand, United Kingdom, United States, and Venezuela. Updated as new data are available.

DRI Europe. Covers the macroeconomic, microeconomic, and financial indicators for Austria, Belgium, Denmark, Finland, France, Germany, Greece, Ireland, Italy, Netherlands, Norway, Portugal, Spain, Sweden, Switzerland, and UK. Updated weekly/monthly or quarterly/annually depending on data.

DRI European Forecast. Provides economic forecasts for Austria, Belgium, Denmark, Finland, France, Germany, Greece, Ireland, Italy, Netherlands, Norway, Portugal, Spain, Sweden, Switzerland, Turkey, and the UK. Updating varies by country and forecast.

DRI Japanese Forecast. Provides economic forecasts for the Japanese economy. Updated semiannually.

DRI Latin American Forecast. Provides economic forecasts for Argentina, Brazil, Chile, Colombia, Ecuador, Mexico, Peru, and Venezuela. Updated quarterly.

DRI World Forecast. Provides macroeconomic and microeconomic forecasts for 49 countries as well as regional forecasts. Updated from monthly to quarterly, depending on country.

(*Source:* Gale Directory of Databases, Volume 1: Online Databases.)

Available online from DRI/McGraw-Hill.

Economic and Energy Indicators

The Central Intelligence Agency compiles this semimonthly resource. Coverage includes economic and energy information on the major developed countries that before the end of the Cold War were known as "non-Communist."
Published semimonthly by the National Technical Information Services.

Economic Literature Index

◨ Offered by the American Economics Association, the *Economic Literature Index* is an index of worldwide economic literature taken from nearly 300 journals. Also available on CD-ROM and online. Available online through DIALOG.
Published and updated quarterly by the American Economics Association.

The Economist: Economic and Financial Indicators

A weekly feature of the magazine *The Economist,* this valuable source of international business information provides data and commentary on output, demand, and jobs, prices, and wages, commodity prices, currency, exchange rates, money and interest rates, and world stock markets.
Published weekly by The Economist.

The Economist Guide to Global Economic Indicators: Making Sense of Economics

The guide discusses and interprets all of the major economic indicators that relate to GDP and GNP; growth, trends, and cycles; population, employment, and unemployment; government revenues and expenditures; money and financial markets; and industry and commerce.
Published in 1993 by John Wiley & Sons.

Foreign Economic Trends and Their Implications for the United States

These reports on various countries of the world are prepared by the International Trade Administration of the U.S. Department of Commerce. They include key economic indicators, a brief summary of the state of the economy of the country, the current situation and economic trends, an industrial report, agricultural report, foreign trade situation, living costs, monetary situation, and implications for the United States.
Published by subscription by the Superintendent of Documents, U.S. Government Printing Office.

Government Finance Statistics Yearbook

◨ Yearbook provides information on International Monetary Fund member countries on the various units of government, government accounts, the enterprises and financial institutions that governments own and control, and the national sources of data on government operations. It provides data on central government revenues, grants, expenditures, lending finance, and debt. Available in both print and magnetic tape.
Published annually by the International Monetary Fund.

Industrial Policy in OECD Countries

This annual review analyzes recent government initiatives to promote industrial development and adjustment in OECD countries. It also reviews trends in industry on the bases of industrial production, inputs, and performance, thus enabling users to make international comparisons. *Published annually by the OECD.*

IntEc CD-ROM: The Index to International Economics, Development and Finance

This bibliographic database covers articles and research papers on economic development, international trade and monetary policy from 1981 to the present. *Published quarterly by Chadwyck Healey, Inc., each issue cumulating the file and replacing the previous disk.*

International Financial Statistics

Publication provides a source of international statistics on all aspects of international and domestic finance. It provides, for most countries of the world, data on exchange rates, international liquidity, international banking, money and banking, interest rates, prices, production, international transactions, government accounts, and national accounts. Available in print, on CD-ROM, and on magnetic tape. *Published monthly by the International Monetary Fund. An annual Yearbook Issue is published in September and contains data for over 35 years for countries covered in monthly issues.*

Labour Force Statistics

Publication is an annual statistical report on the population and labor force of the 24 member countries of the OECD. *Published annually by the OECD.*

Long Term Prospects for the World Economy

Text reviews the prospects of the world's major regions, assesses the factors likely to affect the world economy, and looks at issues like the North American Free Trade Agreement, European integration, and global environmental issues. *Published in 1992 by the OECD.*

Main Economic Indicators

Publication provides monthly statistics on OECD countries including recent changes in each economy and statistics and/or indicators for GNP, industrial production, deliveries, stocks and orders, construction, wholesale and retail sales, employment, wages, prices, finance, foreign trade, and balance of payments. Also available in single copy or by subscription in either print or diskette. Also available online from DRI/McGraw-Hill. *Published monthly by the OECD.*

Market Movers: Understanding and Using Economic Indicators from the Big Five Economies

Mark Jones and Ken Ferris

Market Movers covers almost 100 of the leading economic indicators from the world's five most important economies: the United States, United Kingdom, France, Germany, and Japan. *Published in 1992 by McGraw-Hill, Inc.*

Monthly Statistics on Foreign Trade (Series A)

Publication provides an overall picture of trade of OECD countries. Available by subscription in print or on diskette. *Published monthly by OECD.*

OECD Economic Outlook

This is a twice-yearly survey of economic trends and prospects in OECD countries (Australia, Austria, Belgium, Canada, Denmark, Finland, France, Germany, Greece, Ireland, Italy, Japan, Luxembourg, the Netherlands, New Zealand, Norway, Portugal, Spain, Sweden, Switzerland, Turkey, the United Kingdom, and the United States). Available in print and on diskette, as a single copy and by subscription. Diskette contains background economic data and projection, but no analysis.
Published semiannually by the OECD.

OECD Economic Surveys

Economic surveys are done almost every year for each OECD country. Each survey analyzes the country's economy, provides statistical information, and makes short-term projections. A set of surveys is available by subscription.
Published annually by OECD.

The OECD STAN Database for Industrial Analysis

The Structural Analysis Industrial Database covers 46 manufacturing sectors in 12 OECD countries from 1980 to 1990.
Published in 1992 by the OECD.

One Hundred Years of Economic Statistics

Thelma Liesner

This volume brings together 100 years of principal economic indicators for nine industrial nations: the United States, Canada, Italy, the United Kingdom, France, Japan, Australia, Germany, and Sweden.
Published in 1990 by Facts on File.

Overseas Business Reports

Prepared by the U.S. Department of Commerce, each report offers a wide range of economic and business statistics and background information on a particular country.
Published periodically by the U.S. Government Printing Office.

PTS International Forecasts™

This is the online equivalent of Worldcasts (see below). Available online through DIALOG and Data-Star.
Updated monthly by Information Access/Predicasts.

UN Statistical Yearbook

The *UN Statistical Yearbook* contains economic and social information on 220 countries and territories. Topics include imports and exports, demographics, GDP, employment, and inflation.
Published annually by United Nations Publications.

Worldcasts

Publication provides short- and long-range business and economic forecasts for products and markets outside of the United States. *Worldcasts* consists of eight volumes, four of which deal with products and four with distinct regions of the world. Available online as PTS International Forecasts™(see above).
Published annually by Information Access/Predicasts.

World Economic and Business Review

World Economic and Business Review offers analysis of the business and economic

environment in over 200 countries around the world.
Published annually by Blackwell Publishers.

World Economic Outlook: A Survey of the Staff of the International Monetary Fund

World Economic Outlook offers economic statistics and forecasts for the international community. Forecasts are made based on considerations such as inflation, interest, debt, capital flows, and policy options available to the major economic groups on the planet.
Published semiannually by the International Monetary Fund.

World Economic Survey

This assessment of the world economy provides an overview of important developments of the previous year and the outlook for the future. It analyzes the growth in the world economy, policy positions, international trade and payments, and international capital flows to developing countries.
Published annually by United Nations Publications.

World Tables

■ *World Tables* contains a variety of business and economic statistics on 146 different countries. Topics include interest and debt, private consumption, GDP, and much more. *World Tables* is available in print and on computer diskette.
Published annually by Johns Hopkins University Press.

GOVERNMENT AGENCIES

International Trade Administration (ITA)

The ITA maintains a staff of over 350 analysts who provide free information on a wide variety of industries, such as automobiles, aerospace, confectionary products, construction, electronics, and textiles. Analysts will provide information on U.S. and international markets, current statistics, projections, trend analysis, and more. See Appendices of this text for a complete listing.
Address: U.S. Department of Commerce, International Trade Administration, Herbert C. Hoover Building, 14th and Constitution NW, Washington, DC 20230. Tel. (202) 482-2000.

FOR FURTHER INFORMATION

See **Bureau of Economic Analysis, p. 477**
The Conference Board, p. 478
Demographic Yearbook, p. 457
Economic Literature Index, p. 481
The Economist World in Figures, p. 403
F & S Index International, p. 521
Index to International Statistics, p. 522
Statistical Reference Index, p. 400
The Wall Street Journal, p. 407
Western European Economic Organizations, p. 545
World Factbook, p. 524

20

EMPLOYEE AND EXECUTIVE COMPENSATION

American Salaries and Wages Survey

🔹 *American Salaries and Wages Survey* contains over 33,000 salary statistics taken from more than 300 government, business, and news sources. Entries are arranged alphabetically by profession, and then location, and contain the following: occupation, specialization, and industry; location; frequency of salary cited; the low-, mid-, and/or high-salary ranges; source of information; and survey or publication date. *American Salaries and Wages Survey* is also available in the following alternative formats: computer disk and magnetic tape.
Published annually by Gale Research, Inc.

AMS Office Salaries Report

The *AMS Office Salaries Report* contains salary information for 20 administrative and clerical office jobs.
Published annually by Administrative Management Society.

Area Wage Survey

Produced by the Bureau of Labor Statistics, U.S. Department of Labor, the *Area Wage Survey* covers 70 metropolitan areas and contains information on earnings and benefits in professional, technical, clerical, office, and other occupations.
Published annually by the U.S. Government Printing Office.

Available Pay Survey Reports: An Annotated Bibliography

Available Pay Survey Reports is a comprehensive bibliography of compensation surveys that covers many types of jobs and organizations. Available as either a U.S. volume or an international volume.
Published in 1987 by Abbott, Langer, and Associates.

Compensation, Fifth Edition

Robert E. Sibson

Compensation covers the planning, implementation, and management of employee compensation.
Published in 1990 by AMACOM.

Compensation and Benefits Review

This publication provides an in-depth look at crucial issues in the fields of compensation and benefits. Articles are written by leading academic and consulting experts.
Published bimonthly by the American Management Association.

The Compensation Handbook

Milton L. Rock and Lance A. Berger

The Compensation Handbook is a guide to the administration of compensation

from clerical pay through top executive compensation.
Published in 1991 by McGraw-Hill, Inc.

CompFlash

This publication provides a monthly update of current developments in compensation and benefits, for example, tax proposals, new government regulations, innovative retirement plans, health care benefits, union demands, and executive perks.
Published monthly by the American Management Association.

Employee Compensation and Benefits Alert

This reference service provides information on current developments in pay (wages, salaries, commissions, and cash bonuses), benefits (retirement plans, health care, insurance, family care, and tuition assistance), and special executive compensation plans.
Published biweekly by Warren, Gorham & Lamont.

Executive Compensation

A three-volume looseleaf service (which includes a monthly newsletter), *Executive Compensation* reports on the latest compensation developments and issues.
Published in 1991 by McGraw-Hill, Inc.

Executive Compensation Answer Book

V. P. Kuraitis, Janet Ambrosi Wertman, and Bruce Overton

The *Executive Compensation Answer Book* offers concise answers to 700 essential compensation questions, including: how to attract and retain top talent, how

to create incentives for peak performance, and how to boost profitability.
Published in 1993 by Panel Publishers.

Executive Compensation Service Reports: Reports on International Compensation

The reports cover 17 West European countries and Turkey. Individual reports list compensation for 10 top management, 17 middle management, and 22 employee-level positions and make projections regarding salary, cost of living, and merit increases.
Published annually by Wyatt Data Services.

Forbes: Chief Executive Compensation Survey Issue

This annual report on executive compensation, published in a May issue of *Forbes* magazine, reports on the annual compensation of 800 chief executives. It includes information on salary and bonuses; "other" compensation, which includes payments under long-term compensation plans, thrift plan contributions, company paid health and insurance plans, and restricted stock awards; stock gains realized from the exercise of stock options; and stock owned, which includes the value of the chief executive's stock holdings as a percentage of the firm's total market value. The report also includes information on the company's performance in terms of sales and profits.
Published annually in a May issue of Forbes magazine.

Journal of Compensation & Benefits

The *Journal of Compensation & Benefits* covers new developments in, and of-

fers in-depth analysis of, compensation and benefit issues.
Published monthly by Warren, Gorham & Lamont.

National Survey of Professional, Administrative, Technical, and Clerical Pay

Annual survey is compiled by the Bureau of Labor Statistics.
Published by the U.S. Government Printing Office.

The New Pay

Jay R. Schuster and Patricia K. Zingheim

The New Pay describes, discusses, and pleads for incentive pay for the mass of employees.
Published in 1992 by Lexington Books.

Software for Compensation Executives: A Directory of Resources

This directory provides information about 90 compensation software programs and more than 100 spreadsheets and statistical compensation programs. Published in looseleaf.

Updated quarterly by the American Compensation Association.

Top Executive Compensation

Top Executive Compensation reports the results of an annual survey of the compensation of the five highest paid executives in various industry and size categories.
Published annually by Conference Board, Inc.

TRADE AND PROFESSIONAL ASSOCIATIONS

American Compensation Association (ACA)

The ACA is a nonprofit organization engaged in the design, implementation, and management of employee compensation and benefits programs. It offers courses in salary administration, direct compensation, benefits design and administration, executive compensation, and variable pay programs. Its publications include the *ACA Journal*, a quarterly publication, and *ACA News*, a monthly newsletter.
American Compensation Association, P.O. Box 29312, Phoenix, AZ 85038-9312. Tel (602) 951-9191. FAX (602) 483-8352.

FOR FURTHER INFORMATION

*See **The Conference Board**, p. 478*

21

EMPLOYEE BENEFITS

401(k) Plans: A Comprehensive Guide

Bruce J. McNeil and Michael E. Lloyd

401(k) Plans: A Comprehensive Guide uses a question-and-answer format to give a complete step-by-step analysis of 401(k) plans. It discusses the benefits for both the employer and the employee, the qualification requirements, the ERISA requirements, the tax consequences to all parties, and the variations of 401(k) plans.
Published in 1993 by John Wiley & Sons, Inc.

The 401(k) Plan Management Handbook

Jeffrey M. Miller and Larry Chambers

The 401(k) Plan Management Handbook is a comprehensive guide to setting up and managing a 401(k) plan from design and compliance issues to hiring a consultant. Topics include plan sponsor issues, investment management, participant record keeping and communications, legal compliance issues, and fiduciary responsibility under ERISA.
Published in 1991 by Probus Publishing, Inc.

Benefits Coordinator

This reference service provides a complete analysis of the tax and legal issues affecting the full range of employer-provided benefits other than pensions. Published as a seven-volume loose-leaf service with updates and *Employee Benefits Alert Newsletter* issued every other week.
Published biweekly by Warren, Gorham & Lamont.

BNA Pension Reporter

Published since 1974, the *BNA Pension Reporter* focuses on both private and public sector pension and employee benefits programs. Each issue reports on the latest pension developments in Washington, DC and the states.
Published weekly by Bureau of National Affairs, Inc.

The Complete Guide to Cost-Effective Employee Benefit Programs

Joseph G. Kozlowski and Walter Oleksy

The guide delivers a complete set of strategies and cost-control programs designed to reduce the cost of benefits while still attracting and motivating employees.
Published in 1987 by Prentice Hall, Inc.

Employee Benefits Cases

Published since 1981, *Employee Benefits Cases* provides the full text of precedent-

setting federal and state employee benefits cases. Cases are organized three ways: topically, by point of law, and by title of case. Back volumes are available.
Published weekly by Bureau of National Affairs, Inc.

Employee Benefits Dictionary

Virginia L. Briggs, Michael G. Kushner, and Michael J. Schinabeck

The dictionary defines more than 1,000 terms relating to tax-qualified and non-qualified retirement and deferred compensation arrangements; welfare benefit plans; and insurance, securities, and trust law.
Published in 1992 by Bureau of National Affairs, Inc.

Employee Benefits Handbook

Jeffrey Mamorsky, editor

This handbook looks at the complete spectrum of benefits packages and analyzes their advantages and disadvantages, tax and legal considerations, actuarial problems and employer cost.
Published in one volume with annual update by Warren, Gorham & Lamont.

Employee Benefits Infosource™

█ This database covers literature dealing with a wide variety of topics in the computer industry field, including compensation, disability, stock option plans, stock ownership plans, flexible benefits, medical and dental insurance, pension plans, unemployment, and workers' compensation. Available online through DIALOG.
Updated monthly by the International Foundation of Employee Benefits Plans.

Employee Benefits Infosource™ User's Guide and Thesaurus

This publication is a practical guide to using the Employee Benefits Infosource™ database (see preceding). It helps users save on-line time by targeting searches. It provides explanations of database mechanics and terminology and listings of journal sources, journal codes, and sources included in the database.
Published in 1990 by the International Foundation of Employee Benefits Plans.

Employee Benefits Management

This subscription service explains and reports on the tax and nontax aspects of employee benefits for employers, plan administrators, and benefits specialists. Special emphasis is placed on cost containment and data analysis.
Published twice monthly by Commerce Clearing House.

Employee Benefits Software Directory

This directory contains descriptions of approximately 400 benefits-related software packages in administration of 401(k) plans, claims filing, flexible benefits programs, COBRA compliance, benefits administration, and workers' compensation programs.
Published in looseleaf with quarterly updates by the American Compensation Association.

Employee Benefits: Valuation, Analysis, and Strategies

Steven G. Vernon

Employee Benefits: Valuation, Analysis, and Strategies provides detailed coverage

of strategies and insights into understanding and communicating the value of benefits, from both employer and employee perspectives.
Published in 1993 by John Wiley & Sons, Inc.

Employee Benefits Report

Employee Benefits Report covers new developments in, and offers in-depth analysis of, employee benefits.
Published monthly by Warren, Gorham & Lamont, Inc.

Employee Benefits Resource Guide, Second Edition

This publication is a bibliography of source materials relating to employee benefits including abstracts of books and descriptions of journals, services, and databases.
Published in 1990 by the International Foundation of Employee Benefits Plans.

ERISA: A Comprehensive Guide

Martin Wald and David E. Kenty

This one-volume guide covers the Employee Retirement Income Security Act of 1974 (ERISA). Topics include health and welfare plans, severance, employee benefit plans, and pension plans.
Published in 1991 by John Wiley & Sons, Inc.

ERISA: The Law and the Code

This guide to the Employee Retirement Income Security Act of 1974 (ERISA) covers such topics as the new code section on retiree health accounts, premium changes in Pension Benefit Guarantee Corporation benefit plans and excise tax changes.
Published in 1991 by Bureau of National Affairs, Inc.

The Executive's Guide to Controlling Health Care and Disability Costs: Strategy-Based Solutions

Bruce N. Barge and John G. Carlson

This book is for senior executives who are involved in making decisions about an organization's health care, workers' compensation, and disability costs. The authors show that by making health concerns a part of an overall organizational strategy, executives can promote employee well-being, provide needed health benefits, contain costs, and ensure the organization's long-term financial stability.
Published in 1993 by John Wiley & Sons, Inc.

Flexible Benefits: A How-To Guide, Third Edition

Richard E. Johnson

This guide is designed to help evaluate, develop, and implement a flexible benefits plan that will serve the interests of both employer and employees. It includes information on pricing of multiple-option health plans.
Published in 1989 by the International Foundation of Employee Benefits Plans.

Fundamentals of Flexible Compensation, Second Edition

Karen L. Frost, Dale L. Gifford, Christine A. Seltz, and Kenneth L. Sperling

This resource offers comprehensive coverage of flexible compensation programs: their origins and objectives, rules and regulations, current trends, designing specific program options, and structure and financing.
Published in 1992 and supplemented annually by John Wiley & Sons, Inc.

The Handbook of Employee Benefits: Design, Funding and Administration

Jerry S. Rosenbloom

This two-volume work is a comprehensive look at medical benefits, flexible benefits plans, and employee benefits communication.
Published in 1993 by Business One Irwin.

Health Care Handbook

Jeffrey D. Mamorsky

This text provides analysis and guidance on a broad range of issues affecting employer-provided health care, including plan design, funding and delivery, cost management, employer initiatives, legal compliance, communication, and administration.
Published in one volume with annual updates by Warren, Gorham & Lamont.

Nelson's Guide to Pension Fund Consultants

This guide provides profiles of over 350 consulting firms covering 1,800 consultants at 750 offices. Contact on formation is included.
Published annually by Nelson's Publications.

Pension Claims: Rights and Obligations

Stephen R. Bruce

Pension Claims: Rights and Obligations analyzes claims involving contribution and benefits programs, accruals, vesting, fiduciary duties, discrimination, and plan termination. Leading court decisions and helpful examples are frequently incorporated into the text.
Published in 1988 by Bureau of National Affairs, Inc.

Pensions and Other Employee Benefits: A Financial Reporting and ERISA Guide

Richard M. Steinberg, Ronald J. Murray, and Harold M. Dankner

This guide covers accounting, filing, reporting, and auditing for pensions and Other Postretirement Employee Benefits (OPEBs), health and welfare plans, employee stock option plans, and more.
Published in 1993 by John Wiley & Sons, Inc.

Retiree Health Benefits: Employer Obligations, Retiree Rights

William J. Danish

Retiree Health Benefits: Employer Obligations, Retiree Rights explores the history of benefit offerings, the "real" cost issues confronting corporations, accounting strategies for dealing with promises of lifetime benefits, legal implications, and strategies for addressing these issues from both a short- and a long-term perspective.
Published in 1993 by John Wiley & Sons, Inc.

Retirement Savings Plans: Design, Regulation and Administration of Cash or Deferred Arrangements

David A. Littel, Donald C. Cardamone, and Wilhelm L. Gruszecki

Retirement Savings Plans offers clear consultant-like advice and step-by-step explanations of 401(k) plans, simplified employee pensions (SEPs), 403(b) tax-deferred annuities, and nonqualified plans.
Published in 1992 by John Wiley & Sons, Inc.

Trends in Pensions 1992

This reference, prepared by the Pension and Welfare Benefits Administration of the U.S. Department of Labor, provides federal government statistics on private pensions. The data come from more than 50 government publications and a wealth of previously unpublished statistics. Trends in private pensions are also described and analyzed.

Published in 1992 by the Superintendent of Documents, U.S. Government Printing Office.

Worker's Compensation Report

Worker's Compensation Report covers initiatives, trends, and controversies involving injuries and disabilities, state actions, judicial issues, legal strategies and settlements, retaliation, loss prevention, rehabilitation strategies, and medical cost containment.

Published biweekly by Bureau of National Affairs, Inc.

TRADE AND PROFESSIONAL ASSOCIATIONS

Employee Benefits Research Institute

This organization develops public policy on employee benefits through research publications and educational programs. Its publications include *EBRI's Benefits Outlook* (monthly), *EBRI Issue Briefs* (monthly), *EBRI Quarterly Pension Investment Report*, and *Employment Benefits Notes*.

Employee Benefits Research Institute, 2121 K Street NW, Washington, DC 20037. Tel. (202) 659-0760. FAX (202) 775-6312.

International Foundation of Employee Benefits Plans

This organization conducts research on employee benefits plan management and cosponsors the Certified Employee Benefit Specialist Program in the United States and Canada. Publishes *Employee Benefits Quarterly, Employee Benefits Basics,* and *International Foundation of Employee Benefits Plans Digest* (monthly).

International Foundation of Employee Benefits Plans, 18700 West Bluemound Road, Box 69, Brookfield, WI 53008. Tel. (414) 786-6700.

FOR FURTHER INFORMATION

See **American Compensation Association,** p. 487
Compensation and Benefits Review, p. 485
CompFlash, p. 486
The Conference Board, p. 478
Employee Compensation and Benefits Alert, p. 486
Management Contents, p. 405

22

ENVIRONMENTAL ISSUES

Canadian Environmental Directory

This national directory draws together the whole network of individuals, agencies, firms, and associates active in environment-related activities in Canada. Main alphabetical listings are organized by government, organization, and education/research establishments. The government section is further broken down by federal, provincial, and municipal levels and the ministries, departments, agencies, and so on operating within these divisions.
Published annually by Gale Research, Inc.

Costing the Earth: The Challenge for Governments, the Opportunities for Business

Francis Cairncross

Costing the Earth chronicles how industries worldwide are changing the way they produce goods to meet the growing demands of a "green" economy.
Published in 1992 by Harvard Business School Press.

Directory of Environmental Information Sources

This directory lists federal and state government resources; professional, scientific, and trade organizations; newsletters, magazines, and periodicals; and online databases.
Published in 1992 and biennially by Government Institutes, Inc.

Encyclopedia of Environmental Information Sources

The encyclopedia is a "source of sources," providing a convenient method to compile subject-specific lists for further research. Each entry offers a number of ways to locate information, such as abstracting and indexing services; bibliographies; directories, dictionaries, and encyclopedias; online databases; periodicals and newsletters; research centers and institutes; statistical sources; trade associations and professional societies; government organizations; and more.
Published in 1993 by Gale Research, Inc.

Enviroline® On-line

This online service provides complete bibliographic citations and custom-edited abstracts of over 170,000 articles and reports on environmental issues. Available online through DIALOG and Orbit Search Service. Also available on magnetic tape and CD-ROM.
Published and updated monthly by R. R. Bowker (Reed Reference Publishing).

Environmental Abstracts

This monthly publication provides abstracts of literature dealing with environmental issues including air, water, and noise pollution; control technologies; and resource management.
Published monthly, with a cumulative volume published annually as Environmental Abstracts Annual, by R. R. Bowker (Reed Reference Publishing).

The Environmental Law Handbook

The handbook offers current compliance information on environmental law fundamentals, enforcement and liabilities, the 1990 Clean Air Act amendments, the 1990 Oil Pollution Act, and OSHA penalties.
Published in 1991 by Government Institutes, Inc.

Environmental Industries Marketplace

Environmental Industries Marketplace contains 10,000 entries arranged alphabetically by company name. Companies listed include engineering firms, land surveyors, manufacturers, distributors, research facilities, retailers, wholesalers, transportation companies, disposal firms, and others.
Published biennially by Gale Research, Inc.

Environmental Regulatory Glossary, Fifth Edition

The glossary records and standardizes over 4,000 terms, abbreviations, and acronyms.
Published in 1990 by Government Institutes, Inc.

Environmental Reporter

This weekly subscription service reports on and provides texts of EPA regulations and enforcement activities, congressional hearings, and state government actions. Subscribers receive reference binders providing the full text of federal laws and regulations and selected state laws and regulations and court decisions.
Published and updated weekly by Bureau of National Affairs, Inc.

Environmental Statutes

Environmental Statutes contains the complete text of all major environmental laws. Contents include the Occupational Safety and Health Act; Resource Conservation and Recovery Act including the Hazardous and Solid Waste Amendments of 1984; Safe Drinking Water Act; Toxic Substances Control Act; CERCLA/Superfund (SARA); Clean Water Act; National Environmental Policy Act; Pollution Prevention Act of 1990; FIFRA; and more.
Published in 1992 by Government Institutes, Inc.

Environmental Telephone Directory, 1993–1994

The directory contains extensive EPA information; complete addresses and telephone numbers for all U.S. senators and U.S. representatives with their environmental aides; full information on Senate and House committees and subcommittees and federal and executive agencies dealing with environmental issues; and detailed information on state environmental agencies.
Published in 1993 by Government Institutes, Inc.

Environmental Trends

This text presents the dramatic changes of land use in the United States, including human settlements, recreation sites, industry, and energy exploration. Maps, charts, and graphs are presented in full color. Various environmental topics covered include minerals and energy, water, climate and air quality, land resources, wetlands and wildlife, protected areas, population, transportation, and environmental risks and hazards. Statistical tables and graphs are also included.
Published in 1990 by the Superintendent of Documents, U.S. Government Printing Office.

EPA Headquarters Telephone Directory

This directory contains names and telephone numbers for EPA headquarters personnel in Washington, DC as well as all 10 EPA regions. A table is included for converting the Washington Interagency Telecommunications System (WITS) telephone numbers to outside commercial numbers.
Published in 1990 by the United States Government Printing Office.

Gale Environmental Sourcebook: A Guide to Organizations, Agencies, and Publications

Karen Hill and Annette Piccirelli, editors

The sourcebook provides descriptive information on over 8,000 environmental organizations, information services, products, and a number of other sources. Each entry contains full contact information.
Published in 1992 by Gale Research, Inc.

The Green Consumer, Second Edition

This study analyzes how different businesses have responded to environmental concerns and looks at why many companies have not offered products consumers see as "green."
Published in 1993 by FIND/SVP.

International Environmental Law Special Report

The report is a collection of essays by noted authorities on international environmental law. Topics include international clean air issues, developments in environmental law in Eastern Europe, regulation of imports and exports, envi-

ronmental regulation in Japan, environmental regulation in Mexico, and more.
Published in 1992 by Government Institutes, Inc.

Recycling Sourcebook

The sourcebook provides more than 40 in-depth essays and case studies on the present state of recycling. Covering a wide range of topics including materials technology, reduction and reuse, and programs, the essays illustrate how the challenges in the industry are being addressed by various institutions.
Published in 1992 by Gale Research, Inc.

Resource Guide to State Environmental Management, Second Edition

▐ This guide lists facts on state environmental, health, and resource departments, as well as special commissions and boards. Also included are listings of state environmental/natural resources budgets and a detailed directory of more than 75 state environmental programs. Also available in electronic format as the *Directory of State and Environmental Officials*.
Published in 1990 by The Council on State Governments.

State Environmental Law Annual Report, 1992 Edition

Written by highly regarded law firms in 41 states, the report provides a nationwide perspective on environmental law trends in each state. Report covers AL, AK, AZ, AR, CA, CO, CT, FL, GA, HI, ID, IL, IN, KS, KY, ME, MD, MA, MI, MN, MO, MT, NV, NH, NJ, NM, NY, NC, OH, OK, OR, PA, PR, RI, TX, UT, VA, WA, WV, WI, and WY.
Published in 1992 by Government Institutes, Inc.

State Environmental Law Handbooks

Each handbook gives complete coverage of a state's organizational structure; required permits and reports; hazardous and solid waste disposal; air, water, and natural resources regulation; and the relationship between federal and state regulations.
Published annually, and updated as needed, by Government Institutes, Inc.

Statistical Record of the Environment

Statistical Record of the Environment offers the results of more than 850 environmental studies. Topics include consumer issues, regulatory trends, financial incentives, control and management issues, production and consumption trends, and government and industry information. Each presentation provides the following: name of chart and listing organization; full text of most charts, graphs, and tables; annotations explaining foreign terms, symbols, and so on; and complete bibliographic citations.
Published in 1992 by Gale Research, Inc.

World Energy and Nuclear Directory

The directory lists energy-oriented organizations throughout the world. Alphabetically arranged within country sections, entries describe organizations involved in a wide range of energy-related scientific research, including electricity, direct energy conversion, biological energy sources, natural gas, coal technology, and other research on renewable forms of power.
Published in 1991 by Gale Research, Inc.

World Guide to Environmental Issues and Organizations

The guide provides information on major environmental issues—from acid rain to "green politics" in leading countries. Directory information includes contact data on over 250 environmental monitoring and pressure groups throughout the world.
Published in 1991 by Gale Research, Inc.

GOVERNMENT AGENCIES

U.S. Environmental Protection Agency (U.S. EPA)

The mission of the agency is to abate pollution in the areas of air, water, solid waste, pesticides, radiation, and toxic substances. The agency was created to permit coordinated and effective governmental action on behalf of the environment. Some of the key offices of the agency are the following:

Main Administration	(202) 260-4700
Office of International Activities	(202) 260-4870
Administration and Resources Management	(202) 260-4600
Enforcement	(202) 260-4134
Office of General Counsel	(202) 260-8067
Office of Policy, Planning, and Evaluation	(202) 260-4332
Office of the Inspector General	(202) 260-4610
Solid Waste and Emergency Response	(202) 260-4610
Prevention, Pesticides, and Toxic Substances	(202) 260-2902

EPA, 401 M Street SW, Washington, DC 20460. Tel. (202) 260-2090.

National Technical Information Service (NTIS)

NTIS has a large collection of environmental information including handbooks

and guides, regulations and updates, economic studies and applied technology. (NTIS free catalog PR-868).
National Technical Information Service, 5285 Port Royal Road, Springfield, VA 22161.

Coalition for Environmentally Responsible Economics (CERES)

This project, initiated by the Social Investment Forum, establishes standards for evaluating corporate environmental performance. Signatory companies to the CERES Principles adopt basic codes of environmental performance and commit to conducting an annual self-evaluation of their progress in implementing the Principles.
Coalition for Environmentally Responsible Economics, 711 Atlantic Avenue, Boston, MA 02111. Tel. (617) 451-0927. FAX (617) 482-6179.

Council on Economic Priorities (CEP)

Established to provide ratings on and information about corporate social performance, the Council publishes *Shopping for a Better World,* a shoppers' guide to corporations. CEP's Corporate Environmental Data Clearinghouse tracks and reports on environmental performance of the Standard & Poor's 500 companies. Information on other aspects of corporate

performance is available from CEP's Institutional Investor Research Service.
Council on Economic Priorities, 30 Irving Place, New York, NY 10003, Tel. (212) 420-1133.

Environmental Law Institute

This center for research and education on environmental law and policy sponsors program in areas like education and training, publications, and policy research and technical assistance.
Environmental Law Institute, 1616 P Street NW, Suite 200, Washington, DC 20036. Tel. (202) 328-5150

Global Environmental Management Initiative

This organization was formed by a coalition of corporations to foster environmental excellence by businesses worldwide. Efforts include work groups, publications, and symposia focusing on issues such as total quality environmental management, stakeholder communications, and the International Chamber of Commerce Business Charter of Sustainable Development.
Global Environmental Management Initiative, 1828 L Street NW, Suite 711, Washington, DC 20036. Tel. (202) 296-7449, FAX (202) 296-7442.

FOR FURTHER INFORMATION

See ABI/INFORM®, p. 400
The Economist World in Figures, p. 403
National Technical Information Service/
   Federal Government Electronic
   Bulletin Boards, p. 511

23

EXPORTING AND IMPORTING

A Basic Guide to Exporting

This guide, prepared by the U.S. Department of Commerce, is a comprehensive how-to guide for exporting products and services. Its coverage includes a description of what must be done before the sale (developing an export strategy, doing market research, preparing products for export), making the sale (pricing, export regulations), and what must be done after the sale (documentation, methods of payment, financing transactions).
Published in 1992 by the Superintendent of Documents, U.S. Government Printing Office.

American Export Register

Publication provides a way to find the full range of U.S. products and services available to serve the export market. Its coverage includes over 200,000 products and service listings; an alphabetical listing of nearly 43,000 U.S. firms; product listings in 10 languages (Arabic, Chinese, French, German, Italian, Japanese, Portuguese, Russian, Spanish, and English); and a directory of import/export services (e.g., banks, cargo carriers, customs house brokers, U.S. embassies and consulates, and chambers of commerce).
Published annually by Thomas International Publishing Company.

U.S. Department of State Background Notes

These notes are a collection of short, authoritative pamphlets about various countries, territories, and international organizations published by the Office of Public Communication, Bureau of Public Affairs, Department of State. Each *Background Notes* provides economic and trade information, features information about a country's people, land, history, government, political conditions, and foreign relations.
Published by the U.S. Government Printing Office. Available as a set or by subscription.

Bureau of the Census Foreign Trade Report: Annual U.S. Exports, Harmonized Schedule B Commodity by Country

Prepared by the Foreign Trade Division of the Bureau of the Census and available in print and on CD-ROM, the report details all U.S. exports.
Published annually by the U.S. Government Printing Office.

Bureau of the Census Foreign Trade Report: Monthly Exports and Imports—SITC Commodity by Country

A comprehensive listing of U.S. exports and imports, the report is available in print and on CD-ROM.
Published monthly by the U.S. Government Printing Office and available by subscription.

Business America

This publication of the U.S. Department of Commerce is designed to help

U.S. companies sell their products and services overseas.
Published biweekly by the U.S. Government Printing Office.

Commerce Department's "Flash Facts" Service

If one has a touch-tone telephone and a fax machine, the Commerce Department can provide a user with instant information on exporting to a particular region or country. Simply call the numbers listed here and follow the instructions, and the requested information will be faxed free of charge. "Flash Facts" are available from the following Commerce Department offices:

Eastern European
  Business Informa-
  tion Center
  (EEBIC)   (202) 482-5745
Office of Mexico   (202) 482-4464
Office of the Pacific
  Basin   (202) 482-3875
      or (202) 482-3646
Business Information
  Service for the
  Newly Independent
  States (BISNIS)   (202) 482-3145
Offices of Africa,
  Near East and
  South Asia   (202) 482-1064

For further information call the International Trade Administration of the Department of Commerce at (202) 377-3808.

Country Marketing Plans

These plans cover 67 countries and are prepared annually by the commercial sections of the American embassies for the U.S. Foreign and Commercial Service of the Department of Commerce. The plans are available in both print and electronic formats from either the Commercial Information Management System or the National Trade Databank (see p. 502).
Published annually by the U.S. Government Printing Office.

The Diplomat

This "Newsletter of International Business and Social Etiquette" also provides a brief background on each covered country. Available by single copy or subscription.
Published by The Diplomat.

Directory of U.S. Exporters
Directory of U.S. Importers

These guides contain business profiles of more than 23,000 active exporters and 22,000 active importers. They also contain a product index listing traded products with their harmonized commodity code numbers, customs information, listings of foreign consulates and embassies, and international banks providing foreign service.
Published annually by the Journal of Commerce.

Export Administration Regulations

A complete listing of all Export Administration regulations is available. A new complete version of the regulations is issued every December. Regulations are amended on an irregular schedule, and updated information is sent only to subscribers.
Published annually by the U.S. Government Printing Office.

The Exporter

Published monthly, *The Exporter* covers the latest developments in trade and finance issues, rules, and regulations.
Published monthly by The Exporter.

Exporter's Encyclopaedia

The *Encyclopaedia* covers more than 170 world markets and offers information on everything from import licensing and ex-

change regulations to documentation requirements to listings of 150 U.S.-based foreign trade zones. There is also a section with information on international risk and payment conditions for more than 100 countries.
Published annually by Dun & Bradstreet Information Services.

Exporter's Encyclopaedia Country Profile Series

A supplement to Dun & Bradstreet's *Exporter's Encyclopaedia*, the Country Profile Series consists of 20 individual reports—one dedicated to each of the top U.S. trading partners. Among the topics covered in each Country Profile are import licensing regulations, customs tariff information, import taxes, preshipment procedures, documentation requirements, key contacts with addresses and telephone numbers, product standards information, and business travel notes. Country profiles are available for Austria, Belgium, Brazil, Canada, China, France, Germany, Hong Kong, Israel, Italy, Japan, South Korea, Mexico, The Netherlands, Saudi Arabia, Singapore, Spain, Switzerland, Taiwan, and the United Kingdom.
Published annually, by Dun & Bradstreet Information Services.

Exporting: From Start to Finance

L. Fargo Wells and Karin B. Dulat

Exporting From Start to Finance is a comprehensive guide to the intricacies of establishing an exporting operation.
Published in 1991 by Liberty Hall Press/McGraw-Hill, Inc.

Export Reference Manual

Subscription service provides the import requirements of 200 countries.
Updated weekly by Bureau of National Affairs, Inc.

Export Sales and Marketing Manual

John R. Jagoe

The manual shows how to secure foreign markets and buyers, price and budget for export, write export contracts, ship overseas, and receive payment.
Published annually by Export USA Publications.

The Export Yellow Pages

This directory lists U.S. companies that have registered in the U.S. Department of Commerce Office of Export Trading Company Affairs Contact Facilitation Database. To register or obtain a single copy, contact the Department of Commerce local offices.
Published by the U.S. Government Printing Office.

Fast-Track Exporting

Sandra L. Renner and W. Gary Winget

Fast-Track Exporting is a step-by-step guide for small to midsized companies interested in quickly setting up an exporting operation.
Published in 1991 by AMACOM.

Going Global: How Europe Helps Small Firms Export

William E. Nothdurft

Going Global explores how European countries help their small- and medium-size firms successfully export their products. The Europeans have created well-integrated public- and private-sector export assistance programs, and this book brings together the lessons learned to help other countries develop high-yield export assistance programs. Some of the issues addressed include who should be helped

with exporting, the forms of assistance most effective for reaching and serving targeted firms, where assistance should be delivered, and how export assistance should be financed.
Published in 1992 by the Brookings Institution.

The Handbook of International Trade Finance

Campbell Dunford, editor

The handbook, written by 15 industry experts, delivers authoritative guidance on how to achieve and maintain business relationships in other countries in a rapidly changing global scene. It covers the fundamentals of international trade, financial and legal concerns, long-term financing, countertrade, and key contact points for establishing businesses abroad.
Published in 1992 by Prentice Hall, Inc.

"Importing From" Guides

Each member of this series of country-specific guides covers the following areas: finding suppliers; exporting industries and products; shipping and freight transport policies; background to import/export policies; banking, finance, and foreign investments; setting up a business; travel and custom tips; and labor relations. The guides and their year of publication follow:

Importing from Brazil (1992)
Importing from China (1992)
Importing from Czechoslovakia (1992)
Importing from Hong Kong (1991)
Importing from India (1991)
Importing from Korea (1991)
Importing from Malaysia (1991)
Importing from Mauritius (1992)
Importing from Mexico (1992)
Importing from Philippines (1991)
Importing from Poland (1992)
Importing from Singapore (1992)

Importing from Taiwan (1991)
Importing from Thailand (1991)
Importing from Vietnam (1991)

Published by Probus Publishing, Inc.

Import Reference Manual

Subscription service analyzes all import laws and indexed texts of import statutes, regulations, and Executive Orders.
Updated six times a year by Bureau of National Affairs, Inc.

The International Trade Reporter

Published since 1974, the *International Trade Reporter* offers timely and thorough coverage of U.S. trade policy. Regular articles cover topics such as pending legislation; congressional hearings; and proposed regulations and actions by the International Trade Commission, Commerce Department, Office of the U.S. Trade Representative, and Export-Import Bank. Available online through NEXIS.
Published weekly by Bureau of National Affairs, Inc.

Journal of Commerce

This daily newspaper covers the latest domestic and foreign economic developments and provides specific in-depth coverage of export and import opportunities. Features include a daily page of export trade leads from the U.S. Departments of Agriculture and Commerce; a weekly series on conducting business in foreign countries, highlighting such information as the country's current and potential imports and exports, documentation and entry requirements, tariffs, quotas, and currency restrictions; detailed guides to ocean shipping liner services and sailing schedules; and advice for new or small exporters that examines critical aspects of successful importing including government regula-

tions, labeling rules, and freight and shipping insurance. Available online through DIALOG.
Published daily by the Journal of Commerce.

Key Officers of Foreign Service Posts

Directory lists the name, title, address, and telephone number of key overseas personnel.
Published three times per year by the U.S. Government Printing Office.

National Negotiating Styles

Hans Binnedijk, editor

National Negotiating Styles is a study of the negotiating styles of the major trading partners of the United States, written by academics and others knowledgeable in the field.
Published in 1987 by the Center for the Study of Foreign Affairs; available through the U.S. Government Printing Office.

The National Trade Databank

▪ This CD-ROM database of international trade information was developed by the U.S. Department of Commerce. The National Trade Databank can be used on any IBM-compatible personal computer with a CD-ROM reader. It provides profiles of screened businesses throughout the world that are interested in importing U.S. products. It provides information about specific industries and companies worldwide and is compiled from the following government sources:

Board of Governors of the Federal Reserve
Central Intelligence Agency
Export-Import Bank of the United States
Office of the U.S. Trade Representatives
Overseas Private Investment Corporation

Department of State
International Trade Commission
Small Business Administration
University of Massachusetts
Department of Agriculture, Foreign Agriculture Service
Department of Commerce/Economics and Statistics Administration (ESA), Bureau of Economic Analysis
Department of Commerce/Bureau of Export Administration (BXA)
Department of Commerce/ESA, Bureau of the Census
Department of Commerce/International Trade Administration
Department of Commerce/National Institute of Standards and Technology
Department of Commerce/ESA, Office of Business Analysis
Department of Energy/Energy Information Administration
Department of Labor/Bureau of Labor Statistics
Updated monthly by the U.S. Department of Commerce/Economics and Statistics Administration.
[For more information, call the Department of Commerce at (202) 482-2164.]

The OEL Insider

This monthly newsletter of the Office of Export Licensing covers items of current or topical interest to exporters. Available by subscription.
Published monthly by the U.S. Government Printing Office.

Official Export Guide

This comprehensive annual contains an abbreviated Schedule B directory of U.S. goods and services, Bureau of Export Administration Regulations, market profiles, and port information.
Published annually by North America Publishing Co.

Profitable Exporting: A Complete Guide to Marketing Your Products Abroad, Second Edition

John E. Gordon

Excellent, useful guide to the opportunity and intricacies of exporting covers a wide variety of topics including export readiness, identification of the most opportune markets, and organizing export functions as well as marketing, financial, and pricing analysis. It contains an extremely helpful guide to the resources offered by the U.S. Department of Commerce.

Published in 1993 by John Wiley & Sons, Inc.

The United States-European Community Trade Directory

John S. Gordon and Timothy Harper

This directory of international business and trade resources in the United States and the European Community provides a wide range of contacts (agencies, services, institutions, and private companies) useful to importers, exporters, investors, professionals, and corporate managers who want to do business in Europe. The first part covers resources available in the United States. The second section covers resources available, on a country-by-country basis, in Europe.

Published in 1993 by John Wiley & Sons, Inc.

U.S. Customs House Guide

Comprehensive reference contains an abbreviated Harmonized Tariff Schedule of the United States (known as HS or HTS), U.S. Customs regulations, port profiles, and directories.

Published annually by North America Publishing Co.

U.S. Exports of Merchandise on CD-ROM

Compiled by the U.S. Bureau of the Census, the database gives detailed export data on a variety of products, including their value, quantity, destination, shipping weight, and country of origin.

Updated monthly by the Foreign Trade Division, U.S. Bureau of the Census.

U.S. Imports of Merchandise on CD-ROM

Compiled by the U.S. Bureau of the Census, the database gives detailed import data on a variety of products, including their value, quantity, destination, shipping weight, and country of origin.

Updated monthly by the Foreign Trade Division, U.S. Bureau of the Census, Washington, DC 20023. Tel. (301) 763-7662.

World Trade

World Trade is a magazine that covers issues of general interest in international trade.

Published monthly by Taipan Press, Inc.

GOVERNMENT AGENCIES

United States Department of Commerce

The International Trade Administration of the U.S. Department of Commerce provides a wide-ranging array of services to help companies do business overseas. The U.S. and Foreign Commercial Service has 47 district and 21 branch offices in the United States and 132 Overseas Commercial Sections in 68 countries outside of the United States. (A list of district overseas offices is in Appendices.) The U.S. and F.C.S.

provides services geared to the marketing and information needs of the U.S. exporting and international business communities. The U.S. and F.C.S. will do the following:

A. Help pinpoint export prospects by

1. preparing research reports performed on location in overseas markets. Contact number is (202) 482-5037.
2. developing a customized sales survey that offers a quick assessment of how a product will sell in an overseas market. Contact number is (202) 482-3334.
3. providing online trade leads through its Economic Bulletin Board. To subscribe call (202) 482-3190.
4. providing a one-stop source of international trade data, the National Trade Databank (see p. 502 for more information). Contact number is (202) 482-3190.
5. checking the reputation, reliability, and financial status of prospective trading partners through World Traders Data Reports. Contact number is (202) 482-1171.

B. Help make overseas contacts

1. through its agent/distribution service, a customized overseas search for qualified agents, distributors, and representatives of U.S. firms. Contact number is (202) 482-1171.
2. by providing sales leads from international firms seeking to buy or represent U.S. products and services through the Trade Opportunities program. Contact number is (202) 482-2504.
3. by providing mailing labels and lists of prospective customers through the Export Contact List Service. Contact number is (202) 482-2504.

C. Promote products and services through

1. *Commercial News USA,* an international marketing magazine promoting U.S. products and services in 170 countries. Contact number is (202) 482-4918.

2. Gold Key Service, offered by Foreign Commercial Service in 47 countries. This custom-tailored service for U.S. firms planning to visit a country provides orientation briefings, market research, introductions to potential partners, and assistance in developing a sound marketing strategy. Contact number is (202) 482-0115.
3. Matchmaker Trade Delegations, an organization that matches U.S. firms with prospective agents, distributors, and other kinds of business contact overseas. Contact number is (202) 482-3119.
4. Foreign Buyer Program, which supports leading U.S. trade shows in industries with high export potential. Contact number is (202) 482-0481.

The International Trade Administration also has industry specialists with expertise and knowledge of export opportunities in a wide range of industries—from abrasives to yeast. A listing of these industry specialists will be found in Appendices on p. 648.

The International Trade Administration's country specialists will provide you with export information and opportunities from Afghanistan to Zimbabwe. A listing of country specialists will be found in Appendices on p. 644.

Trade and Professional Associations

American Association of Exporters and Importers (AAEI)

The AAEI represents both exporters and importers before the executive and legislative branches of the U.S. government, as well as government regulatory agencies. It works against "self-defeating restrictions on trade no matter which industry sector is threatened." The AAEI publishes *The International Trade Alert,* special information bulletins on new or fast-breaking issues, and *International Trade Monthly.* *American Association of Exporters and Importers, 11 West 42nd Street, New York, NY 10036. Tel. (212) 944-2230. FAX (212) 382-2606.*

American Countertrade Association

The purpose of the American Countertrade Association is to promote trade and commerce among U.S. companies and their international competitors through the use of countertrade.

American Countertrade Association, 121 S. Meramec Avenue, #1102, St. Louis, MO 63105-1725. Tel. (314) 727-5522. FAX (314) 727-8171.

For Further Information

See **Business Statistics 1963–91,** p. 473
Census Catalog and Guide, p. 456
Direction of Trade Statistics, p. 480
Economic Bulletin Board, p. 474
The Handbook of International Direct Marketing, p. 466
Monthly Statistics on Foreign Trade (Series A), p. 482
National Technical Information Service/ Federal Government Electronic Bulletin Boards, p. 511
PTS International Forecasts™, p. 483
The United States Industrial Outlook, p. 477
Worldcasts, p. 483
World Factbook, p. 524

FEDERAL GOVERNMENT (U.S.)

Catalog of Federal Domestic Assistance

This comprehensive listing of all grant, loan, insurance, and other programs of government aid is available in print and through the Federal Assistance Programs Retrieval System, a nationally accessible computer system. Call (202) 708-5126 for further information.

Published annually with periodic supplements by the U.S. Government Printing Office.

CIS/INDEX to Publications of the United States Congress

This monthly publication indexes abstracts and analyzes the publications of 300 active House, Senate, and Joint Committees and Subcommittees. These publications include committee hearings, reports, documents, and special publications. Information in the Index helps the user find out who supports and opposes proposals and programs; tap authoritative sources of statistics, projections, and analyses; develop proposals that conform to the plans of federal agencies; and find competitive business information. Available in print, online, and on CD-ROM (the latter under the product name of *Congressional Masterfile 2*). Available online through DIALOG.

Published monthly, with annual cumulative volume, by Congressional Information Service.

Commerce Business Daily

Commerce Business Daily announces products and services wanted or offered by the federal government and lists bids and proposals requested by the government as well as contract awards and surplus sales. The full text equivalent is also available online from DIALOG.

Published daily by the U.S. Government Printing Office.

Committees in the U.S. Congress

Garrison Nelson

This two-volume work presents a comprehensive history of congressional committee membership dating back to 1947. Data include committee membership in Congress, the length of membership for each member, and leadership positions held by each member. Volume 1 is organized by committee, showing all members for each Congress, as well as the members' seniority. Volume 2 details each member's committee assignments throughout his or her career and offers brief descriptions of committee jurisdictions.

Published in 1993 by Congressional Quarterly Books.

Congressional Quarterly Weekly Report

The *Weekly Report* offers comprehensive coverage of the activities of Congress with in-depth articles, listings of House and Senate roll call votes, the status of various appropriations, and a complete index. *Published weekly by Congressional Quarterly, Inc.*

Contracting with the Federal Government

Frank M. Alston, Margaret M. Worthington, and Louis P. Goldsman

Contracting with the Federal Government provides timely and practical information regarding the rules and regulations that define the federal procurement process. *Published in 1992 by John Wiley & Sons, Inc.*

The Federal Database Finder

This publication identifies thousands of government data sources that can be accessed by computer. Sources of interest to businesspeople include, for example, news about the latest economic indicators. *Published in 1993 by Information USA, Inc.*

Federal Information Center Program

Established by the government, Federal Information Centers are clearinghouses for people who want information on the U.S. federal government. Frequently, the staff of a local information center can answer a question or find an expert who can. Residents of over 70 cities have direct access to the centers via local or toll-free numbers. Callers in four states — Iowa, Kansas, Missouri, and Nebraska — have statewide toll-free service. A list of toll-free numbers is found in Appendices. Written inquiries may be directed to the address below. *Federal Information Center, P.O. Box 600, Cumberland, MD 21501-0600.*

Federal Procurement Report

Report lists all of the procurement actions of all government agencies. *Published annually by the General Services Administration, Federal Procurement Data Center.*

Federal Regional Yellow Book: Who's Who in the Federal Government's Departments, Agencies, Courts, Military Installations and Service Academies Outside of Washington, DC

Publication provides addresses, titles, and telephone numbers of over 18,000 key federal decision makers based in about 4,000 regional offices outside of Washington, DC, and includes three indexes organized by key words, locations, and names. *New editions are published semiannually by Monitor Publishing Company.*

Federal Staff Directory

The directory contains timely information on the executive branch of the U.S. government and its 32,000 key executives. Complete contact information is provided as well as 2,600 detailed biographies. *Published annually by Staff Directories, Ltd.*

Federal Yellow Book: Who's Who in Federal Departments and Agencies

Directory provides up-to-date listings of all changes in federal leadership and department and agency reorganizations. Complete listings include names, titles, office locations, and telephone numbers of administrators and top staff aides in the Executive Offices of the President and Vice President; the 14 cabinet-level federal departments; more than 70 indepen-

dent federal agencies; and federal information centers in 72 cities.
New editions published quarterly by Monitor Publishing Company.

Government Contracting Manual

Timothy J. Healy

Guide shows small and medium-sized businesses how to land a government contract. Topics include bidding strategies, checklists covering every step of the bidding cycle, and government agencies that bid out work.
Published in 1990 by Prentice Hall, Inc.

Government Printing Office (GPO)

This organization is the primary source for printing, distribution, and sales of government documents. The GPO is responsible for the tens of thousands of magazines, pamphlets, and books published by the government each year. In most cases, the information in these publications is geared toward general readers and is written with a minimum of technical jargon. The Government Printing Office offers several guides to its publications, some of which are noted later in this section. Generally, the GPO only carries current titles. Obtaining a document older than a year or two might be impossible. If this is the case, the GPO will be able to recommend a library that carries the necessary document.

Government Printing Office Bookstores

The GPO maintains a number of bookstores throughout the country that stock popular government publications. A complete list of bookstores will be found in Appendices on p. 643.

Guide to Congress

A single-volume reference, the *Guide to Congress* is a comprehensive guide to the history and intricacies of the legislative branch. Topics include the recent trend toward leadership weakness, the growth of subcommittee power, the budget process, and controversies surrounding pay and honoraria.
Published in 1991 by Congressional Quarterly, Inc.

How to Find Business Intelligence in Washington

A directory of business information collected by the U.S. government, *How to Find Business Intelligence in Washington* lists thousands of sources that can provide free industry reports, marketing data, publications, and databases.
Published in 1992 by Washington Researchers, Ltd.

The Insider's Guide to Winning Government Contracts

Richard L. Porterfield

The *Insider's Guide* is directed at small business owners and provides step-by-step instructions on selling to the government. Features include an appendix listing the products and services purchased by the government, contact information on over 1,200 government buying offices, and interpretations of laws, regulations, and requirements involved in procuring federal contracts.
Published in 1992 by John Wiley & Sons, Inc.

Internal Telephone Directories

The internal telephone directories of various federal departments are an excellent way to locate a particular person or expert within the government. These directories include the name, title, and telephone number of the people that work in specific offices and divisions. The Departments of Defense, Energy, Health and Human Services, Labor, State, and Transportation all make their directories available to the public. Directories can be ordered through the Government Printing Office.

If, for some reason, the Government Printing Office is unable to provide a particular internal telephone directory, it might be a good idea to turn to the Freedom of Information Clearinghouse. Acting on the Freedom of Information Act of 1966, which requires federal agencies to make public any identifiable records when requested (with certain exceptions, such as internal personnel information or classified defense secrets), the clearinghouse may be of assistance in obtaining a particular telephone directory. The Freedom of Information Clearinghouse can be reached at the address that follows.
Freedom of Information Clearinghouse, P.O. Box 19367, Washington, DC 20036. Tel. (202) 833-3000.

Legislation Information and Status Office (LEGIS)

In order to find a congressional transcript pertaining to a particular subject, contact LEGIS. The staff there will be able to find out if there is a specific hearing regarding any current bills in Congress. Additionally, LEGIS will perform a free keyword search on their database (printouts are 20¢ per page and there is a $5.00 minimum) to determine which bills and committees have dealt with the topic at hand.

Once LEGIS has provided the information on the committees and legislation pertaining to a particular topic, obtaining a transcript is a matter of contacting the committee or congressperson and finding out where transcripts are available.

Legislative Information and Status, H2 Room 968, Ford House Office Building, Washington, DC 20515. Tel. (202) 225-1772.

Lesko's Infopower

Matthew Lesko

Infopower is a sourcebook that contains the names of over 30,000 sources and experts—mostly from the federal, as well as state, government(s)—from whom users can obtain free or low-cost advice. Sections of particular interest to businesspeople include careers and the workplace; information on people, companies, and mailing lists; economics, demographics, and statistics; patents, copyrights, and trademarks; energy; the Freedom of Information Act; and government databases and bulletin boards. Available in print or online. Available online through CompuServe.
Published in 1990 by Information USA, Inc.

Monthly Catalog of United States Government Publications

The *Monthly Catalog* provides a record and index of all publications received by the Government Printing Office (GPO). The bulk of the catalog is a listing of documents according to their issuing agencies. For example, all Department of Labor publications, regardless of subject, are grouped together. In addition to this grouping, the *Monthly Catalog* provides seven indexes that allow users to find a particular publication quickly. The indexes are these: author, title, subject, title keyword, stock number (a numerical listing of GPO sales stock numbers), contract number (an alphabetical list of contract, project, and grant numbers related to technical reports), and series/report (an alphabetical list of report numbers and series statements). Indexes are compiled semiannually and annually. Although a publication or document might be included in the *Monthly Catalog*, this does not mean that it is available from the Government Printing Office (however, order forms are included in each issue). It may have to be ordered from the issuing agency. The *Monthly Catalog* is available at most larger libraries and is accessible through online databases, including DIALOG and BRS.

Published monthly by the U.S. Government Printing Office.

National Technical Information Service (NTIS)

▐ The National Technical Information Service is the main source for the public sale of research, development, and engineering reports sponsored by the government. The NTIS also offers a selection of technical reports prepared by foreign and local governments. There are well over a million reports available covering a wide range of topics. Of particular interest to the business community are the reports under the heading "Behavioral and Social Science," which includes topics such as administration and management, economics, human factors engineering, and personnel selection.

There are several different ways to find a specific report. Some of the more effective include the following:

(1) *NTIS Products and Services Catalog*. A free catalog describes all of the print sources and computer databases of NTIS. The catalog can be ordered directly from the NTIS (Tel. (703) 487-4650; FAX (703) 321-8547).

(2) *Government Reports Announcements & Index (GRA & I); Government Reports Annual Index (GRAI)*. A comprehensive bibliography of NTIS documents, published biweekly, each issue abstracts about 2,500 new titles, arranged by subject categories and subcategories. An index is included that allows access to the reports by keyword, personal author, corporate author, contract or grant number, and NTIS order or report number. Each year, the 26 issues of GRA & I are compiled to form the *Government Reports Annual Index* (GRAI). Both can be found at most large libraries, are accessible through online database vendors, and can be ordered directly from the NTIS.

(3) *Abstract Newsletters*. Published weekly, *Abstract Newsletters* contains summaries of new technical reports. There are 26 different weekly newsletters, each devoted to a different topic, such as *Administration & Management, Business & Economics*, and *Manufacturing Technology*. All of the titles summarized in the *Abstract Newsletters* are also included in the GRA & I. The newsletters can be found at many libraries, although some libraries with narrow research interests might only subscribe to select titles. The newsletters can also be ordered from the NTIS, either through its *NTIS Products and Services Catalog* or by contacting the NTIS order department.

(4) *NTIS Online Bibliographic Databases*. NTIS sells bibliographies that result from online database searches. Well over 3,000 bibliographies are available. In most cases, the bibliographies have 100 to 200 entries. Published searches can be ordered directly from the NTIS. The NTIS Online Bibliographic Database is available on CD-ROM or online through commercial vendors, including BRS and DIALOG, listed in the free NTIS catalog PR-287. The database is also available on direct lease to research and development organizations and agencies. Call (703) 487-4929 for more information.

National Technical Information Service/Federal Government Electronic Bulletin Boards

The U.S. Government has a wide variety of government bulletin boards that contain a great store of useful information, including many files that can be downloaded to the caller's own computer. Much of the information is available without charge, as is access to the system, and others are available for a fee. The NTIS number, which can be reached by a computer and modem, is (703) 321-8020.

Bulletin Board #: Name	Comment
3:ALIX (Lib. of Congress)	:Automated Library Information Exchange
6:CIC-BBS (GSA)	:Consumer Information Center
7:CLU-IN (EPA)	:Superfund Data and Information
9:CRS-BBS (Dept. of Justice)	:Americans with Disabilities Act Information
10:Computer Security (NIST)	:National Computer System Lab. Computer Security BBS
13:EBB (Dept. of Commerce)	:Economic data and information
14:ELISA System (DoD)	:Department of Defense export license tracking system
16:EPUB (Dept. of Energy)	:Energy information and data
19:FERC-CIPS BBS (Dept. of Energy)	:Federal Energy Regulatory Commission
22:Federal BBS (GPO)	:Government Printing Office and government data (fee-based)
26:Labor News (Dept. of Labor)	:Dept. of Labor Information and Files
27:Magawatt 1 (Dept. of Energy)	:Information on Energy and the Department of Energy
40:SBA On Line (SBA)	:Small Business Administration Information and Data
47:USCS-BBS (Customs)	:Customs and Exchange Rate Data and Information
60:LC News Service (LOC)	:Library of Congress News Service
61:STIS (NSF)	:Science & Technology Information System
67:Offshore-BBS (Interior)	:Offshore Oil & Gas Data
68:TQM-BBS (T. Glenn)	:Total quality management
78:SWITCH BBS (EPA&SWANA)	:Solid waste management
82:CABB (Dept. of State)	:Passport Information Travel Alerts

Official Congressional Directory

This resource for identifying the components of the three branches of the federal government contains an alphabetical list of the members of Congress with their addresses, rooms, and telephone numbers; biographical sketches of members, including descriptions of congressional districts and ZIP codes; boards, commissions, and advisory organizations; Capitol officers and officials; committees, committee assignments, and more. Text covers all federal departments from Agriculture to Veterans' Affairs. It also lists the foreign representatives of the diplomatic service and consular offices in the United States.

Published annually by the Superintendent of Documents, U.S. Government Printing Office.

Subject Bibliography Index

This index is a listing of over 250 major subjects with specific bibliographies for each, representing over 15,000 periodicals, guides, pamphlets, and booklets. Bibliographies of interest to business researchers include accounting and auditing; banks and banking; business and business management; employment and occupations; foreign trade and tariff; government specifications and standards; insurance; labor-management relations; marketing research; occupational safety and health; personnel management, guidance, and counseling; prices, wages, and the cost of living; small business; taxes and taxation. The Bibliography Index is updated periodically; it is available at most larger libraries and can be ordered from the Government Printing Office.
Published by Superintendent of Documents, U.S. Government Printing Office.

United States Government Manual

An all-inclusive guide to the offices and agencies within the federal government, the *Government Manual* also includes information on organizations affiliated with the government, such as the PanAmerican Health Organization and the Smithsonian Institution. Each department within the government is broken down into its individual bureaus and offices. Key individuals within those offices are identified along with Federal Information Centers and regional offices. The *Government Manual* can be found in most large libraries, or it can be ordered from the Government Printing Office.
Published annually by Superintendent of Documents, U.S. Government Printing Office.

U.S. House of Representatives Telephone Directory, 1992

Directory lists Washington and home district telephone numbers and office addresses of each member of the U.S. House of Representatives. It also provides contact information for each Representative's staff, House committee members and staff, Joint Committee members and staff, House offices and staff, and general support offices as well as telephone numbers of U.S. Senators and U.S. government agencies.
Published in 1992 by the Superintendent of Documents, U.S. Government Printing Office.

Using Government Publications, Revised Edition

Text shows how to access the wealth of print and electronic information available in government publications.
Published in 1993 by Oryx Press.

Who Knows: A Guide to Washington Experts

Publication lists 14,000 experts in the federal government within 13,000 areas of expertise. Each entry contains complete contact information.
Published in 1992 by Washington Researchers, Ltd.

FOR FURTHER INFORMATION

See American Statistics Index, p. 400
Statistical Abstract of the United States, p. 406
Statistical Reference Index, p. 400
Who Knows about Industries and Markets, p. 428

25

FRANCHISING

Directory of Franchising Organizations

The directory lists the top franchises in the United States. Each entry includes a description of the franchise, contact information, and the cost of investment.
Published annually by Pilot Books.

The Encyclopedia of Franchises and Franchising

Dennis L. Foster

The encyclopedia covers every aspect of the franchise industry in an A-to-Z format.
Published in 1990 by Facts on File.

Franchise Annual: Complete Handbook and Directory

The directory lists approximately 5,000 franchisors in the United States, Canada, and other countries along with discussions of the pros and cons of franchising and detailed descriptions of relevant state and federal regulations.
Published annually by Info Press.

Franchise Bible: A Comprehensive Guide

The *Franchise Bible* covers both sides of the franchising business: the franchisor's and the franchisee's. It shows how to expand a business by franchising, and how to go into business for yourself by buying a franchise. It includes an offering circular; sample franchise agreements; a list of laws affecting franchise transfers, renewals and terminations; state franchise registration and business opportunity statutes; and filing fees of franchise registration states. Available in three-ring binder or in paperback.
Published in 1991 by Oasis Press.

Franchise Fraud: How to Protect Yourself Before and After You Invest

Robert L. Purvin, Jr.

This book helps potential franchisees protect themselves before entering into a contractual relationship with a franchisor. It shows how to avoid being the victim of what the author calls fraudulent practices of franchisors, such as overstating the market and promises of training and promotional support that are never fulfilled. The author shows in specific detail what to look for in a franchise and the questions to ask when entering a franchise agreement.
Published in 1994 by John Wiley & Sons, Inc.

Franchise Opportunities Handbook

The *Franchise Opportunities Handbook* is prepared by the U.S. Department of Commerce and includes descriptions of U.S. franchises as well as various government assistance programs.
Published annually by the Superintendent of Documents, U.S. Government Printing Office.

The Franchise Option: How to Expand Your Business through Franchising

The Franchise Option covers such topics as test marketing, managing franchise infrastructure relationships, and nurturing and terminating franchise relationships. *Published in 1987 by the International Franchise Association.*

Franchising

Gladys Glickman

Franchising is organized into four looseleaf volumes and covers all areas of franchising, including franchise agreements; legal, business, and tax considerations; antitrust considerations; and franchise alternatives, such as distributorships, leases, branch operations, and limited partnerships.
Periodically updated by Matthew Bender & Co., Inc.

Franchising and Licensing: Two Ways to Build Your Business

Andrew Sherman

Franchising and Licensing is a step-by-step guide to the intricacies of franchising a business. Topics include raising capital, the development of operations manuals, the creation of a prototype, franchise agreements, franchise marketing, franchisee relationships, and so on.
Published in 1991 by AMACOM.

The Franchising Handbook

Andrew Sherman, editor

The handbook analyzes the management, operations, marketing, financial, and legal issues that are particular to the franchising industry. Contributors to the book include many franchising professionals, and it carries the endorsement of the International Franchise Association.
Published in 1993 by AMACOM.

The Rating Guide to Franchises

Dennis L. Foster

This guide profiles franchise opportunities in the United States and Canada. It gives a rating (from one to five stars) to each franchisor based on six performance areas: industry experience, franchising experience, financial strength, training and services, fees and royalties, and satisfaction of franchisees. The profile also includes an overview of the franchise, franchisor services, initial investment, and fees and royalties. Contact information is also included.
Published in 1990 by Facts on File.

Running a Successful Franchise

Kirk Shivell and Kent Banning

Running a Successful Franchise offers detailed, practical information on running a franchise within the constraints of a franchise agreement. Topics include *transitioning* from corporate life to franchise ownership, setting up and implementing management and reporting procedures, creating purchasing and inventory control policies, developing sales and marketing programs, and resolving the most common areas of conflict between franchisors and franchisees.
Published in 1992 by McGraw-Hill, Inc.

Source Book of Franchise Opportunities

The source book is a listing of leading franchisors. Entries, which include complete contact information, are classified by product or service and are indexed by company name.
Published annually by Business One Irwin.

Worldwide Franchise Directory

In this listing of nearly 1,600 American, Canadian, and overseas franchisers, entries are arranged alphabetically under approximately 80 primary categories such as computer sales and service, real estate services, and tax preparation. Also included are profiles of nonfranchised chain operations with company-owned outlets. Each entry provides highlights, a general description, background sketch on the franchise, start-up and agreement information, foreign outlet contacts, training provided, financing available, number of outlets and expansion plans, equipment needed, and profile sources. The directory is available in print and in these alternative formats: computer disk and magnetic tape.
Published annually by Gale Research, Inc.

The American Association of Franchisees and Dealers

Formed in 1992, the AAFD represents the interests of franchisees and dealers. Its purpose is to help bring "fairness to franchising," and it proposes and supports federal and state legislation to develop and maintain equality in the relationship between franchisor and franchisee.
The American Association of Franchisees and Dealers, P.O. Box 81887, San Diego, CA 92138-1887. Tel. (toll free) 1-800-733-9858.

International Franchise Association

This association is for firms in utilizing the franchise method of distribution in all industries. It holds symposia, workshops, and trade shows. Publications include *Franchise Legal Digest*, a bimonthly publication, and *Franchise Opportunities Magazine*.
International Franchise Association, 1350 New York Avenue NW, Suite 900, Washington, DC 20005. Tel. (202) 628-8000.

26

HUMAN RESOURCE MANAGEMENT, TRAINING, AND RETRAINING

The AMA Handbook for Employee Recruitment and Retention

Mary F. Cook, editor

This comprehensive book combines the contributions of 14 experts to create a guide to every aspect of recruiting highly qualified employees and keeping them on the job. Topics include planning, recruitment and selection programs, performance management, training, compensation, benefits, and family issues.
Published in 1992 by AMACOM.

American with Disabilities Act Handbook

This is a basic resource on the Americans with Disabilities Act for people with disabilities and for businesses. It contains annotated regulations for all three titles of the Act, resources for obtaining further assistance, and an appendix containing supplementary information concerning implementation.
Published in loose-leaf format in 1992 by the Superintendent of Documents, U.S. Government Printing Office.

Building the Competitive Workforce: Investing in Human Capital for Corporate Success

Philip Mirvis, editor

This book, based on the Louis Harris and Associates "Laborforce 2000" survey, assesses the competitive strengths and weaknesses of the work force of North American companies. Academic and corporate experts analyze a wide range of issues that affect work force quality including company policies on education and training, the aging work force, work and family issues, and employee health benefits.
Published in 1993 by John Wiley & Sons, Inc.

The Complete Do-It-Yourself Personnel Department

Mary F. Cook

This complete guide to managing a personnel department has these features: over 150 reproducible personnel forms, checklists and reports, model policies and programs, and ready-to-use manuals and handbooks.
Published in 1991 by Prentice Hall, Inc.

The Corporate Reference Guide to Work-Family Programs

Ellen Galinsky, Dana E. Friedman, and Carol A. Hernandez

This highly useful reference book on work-family issues as they relate to corporate operations looks at work-family programs in a wide variety of industries, shows how much they cost, and indicates the ones likely to yield the greatest return on investment.
Published in 1991 by Families and Work Institute.

Disability Management: A Complete System to Reduce Costs, Increase Productivity, Meet Employee Needs, and Ensure Legal Compliance

Sheila H. Akabas, Lauren B. Gates, and Donald E. Galvin

Disability Management is an examination of how to manage disability in the workplace, save money and careers, and help companies comply with the Americans with Disabilities Act.
Published in 1992 by AMACOM.

Employee Involvement and Total Quality Management: Practices and Results in Fortune 1000 Companies

Edward E. Lawler III, Susan Albers Mohrman, and Gerald E. Ledford, Jr.

This study presents the first systematic data to show that companies are more competitive and productive and create higher-quality services when employees are involved in decisions about their jobs and work environment.
Published in 1992 by Jossey-Bass.

Globalizing Management: Creating and Leading the Competitive Organization

Carole Barnett, Vladimir Pucik, and Noel Tichy, editors

This book analyzes the human talent that global businesses will need to compete in the 1990s. It looks at issues like building a globally competitive workforce, making cultural diversity a competitive advantage, building a top leadership team, and successfully implementing strategic alliances.
Published in 1992 by John Wiley & Sons, Inc.

Guide to Employee Handbooks

Robert J. Nobile

This guide shows how to update, upgrade, or create an employee handbook. It provides a model handbook, handbook development guidelines, warnings about overlooked laws governing employment policies, and handbook statements.
Published annually by Warren, Gorham & Lamont.

HR Alert

Biweekly news service reports on the latest developments impacting human resources management.
Published biweekly by Warren, Gorham & Lamont.

HRIN Daily Developments Database

This is a full-text database of print and electronic sources of information covering a broad range of issues of interest to human resource professionals. Coverage includes topics such as benefits and training, legislation and regulation, and employee rights. Available online from HRIN: The Human Resource Information Network.
Published and updated daily by the Human Resource Information Network.

Human Resource Director's Portfolio of Personnel Forms, Records, and Reports

Axel R. Granholm

This book is a collection of 249 tested personnel forms, records, checklists, policy statements, sample letters, and reports.
Published in 1988 by Prentice Hall, Inc.

The Human Resource Directory

This directory contains information on 15,000 people in the human resource/

personnel field.
Published in 1993 by Hunt Scanlon Publishing.

The Human Resources Yearbook

Mary F. Cook, editor

The yearbook is a comprehensive directory of human resources facts, trends, laws, issues, programs, and information. Topics include statistics on labor productivity; wages and benefits; and costs of recruiting, training, and relocating.
Published in 1991 by Prentice Hall, Inc.

Managing Workforce 2000: Gaining the Diversity Advantage

David Jamieson and Julie O'Mara

This book shows how to attract, make the best use of, and retain employees of different skills and perspectives.
Published in 1991 by Jossey-Bass.

Manual of Personnel Policies, Procedures, and Operations

Joseph D. Levesque

This manual delivers a complete blueprint for creating or improving a human resource policy manual. It provides forms and letters, model job descriptions, interviewing techniques, legal requirements, and pay plans.
Published in 1986 by Prentice Hall, Inc.

Organizational Capability: Competing from the Inside Out

David Ulrich and Dale Lake

This text shows the correlation between successful people management and the bottom line. It explains the benefits to the organization of involving employees in the planning and implementation process and allowing them to see the fruits of their labor. The aim is to show how focusing on organizational capability will not only meet short-term financial requirements but also build a solid foundation for the future.
Published in 1990 by John Wiley & Sons, Inc.

Personnel Director's Legal Guide

Steven C. Kahn, Barbara Berish Brown, Brent E. Zepke, and Michael Lanzarone

This publication provides practical legal guidance on recruiting, hiring, and initial placement; compensation, training, promotion, and transfer; discipline, termination, and layoff; affirmative action; retirement plans; performance appraisal; and occupational health and safety.
Published in one volume with annual updated supplements by Warren, Gorham & Lamont.

Personnel Selection in Organizations

Neal Schmitt, Walter C. Borman, and Associates

This book analyzes personnel selection procedures and identifies areas in which ongoing research is needed. Coverage includes fairness in selection, computerized psychological testing, firings, layoffs, and replacement.
Published in 1992 by Jossey-Bass.

Work, Families and Organizations

Sheldon Zedeck, editor

This book brings together theories and research dealing with the interrelationships between work and family. It looks at job stress, dual-career families, and working at home.
Published in 1992 by Jossey-Bass.

The Work of Nations: Preparing Ourselves for the 21st Century

Robert B. Reich

This text provides an insightful look at the skills individuals will need to compete in the twenty-first century. The author's view is that each nation's primary assets will be composed of the insights and skills of its citizens.
Published in 1991 by Alfred A. Knopf.

TRADE AND PROFESSIONAL ASSOCIATIONS

American Society for Training and Development

This professional association is for persons involved in the training and development of business, industry, education, and government employees. Publications include *National Report on Human Resources*, a monthly newsletter; *Training and Development Magazine*, published monthly; *Models for HR Practices*, a four-volume series; and other books and publications.
American Society for Training and Development, 1640 King Street, Alexandria, VA 22313. Tel. (703) 683-8100.

The Conference Board

The Conference Board is an organization that serves senior corporate executives. It provides a professionally managed research program in several areas, including the changing nature of the work force. The Conference Board's Work and Family Group looks at how employers are responding to the challenge of diversity in

the work force and provides reports on employer initiatives.
The Conference Board, 845 Third Avenue, New York, NY 10022. Tel. (212) 759-0900 or (toll-free) 1-800-872-6273. FAX (212) 980-7014.

Institute for International Human Resources

This association for executives responsible for international personnel administration acts as a clearinghouse for information on issues and concerns in international human resource management and provides a forum for networking.
Institute for International Human Resources, 606 N. Washington Street, Alexandria, VA 22314. Tel. (703) 548-3440.

GOVERNMENT AGENCY

Equal Employment Opportunity Commission (EEOC)

The EEOC conducts investigations of job discrimination under Title VII of the Civil Rights Act of 1964, the Americans with Disabilities Act of 1992, the Equal Pay Act of 1963, and the Age Discrimination in Employment Act of 1967.
Equal Employment Opportunity Commission, 1800 L Street NW, Washington, DC 20507. Tel. (202) 663-4900 or 1-800-USA-EEOC.

FOR FURTHER INFORMATION

See ABI/INFORM®, p. 400
Complying with ADA: A Small Business Guide to Hiring and Employing the Disabled, p. 550
EEOC Compliance Manual, p. 550
Employer's Guide to the Americans with Disabilities Act, p. 551
Management Contents, p. 405

27

INTERNATIONAL BUSINESS (GENERAL)

Business International

This weekly newsletter covers developments in international management, marketing, finance, law, licensing, exporting, taxation, accounting, personnel, and planning.
Published weekly by The Economist Intelligence Unit.

Cities of the World, Fourth Edition

Publication is a four-volume collection of up-to-date facts on over 1,500 cities located in 140 countries. Entries include maps of capital cities and photographs depicting city life. Volumes cover (1) Africa, (2) Western Hemisphere (excluding the United States), (3) Europe and the Mediterranean Middle East, and (4) Asia, the Pacific and the Asiatic Middle East (plus a comprehensive index).
Published in 1993 by Gale Research, Inc.

Countries of the World and Their Leaders Yearbook

Countries of the World is compiled from information gathered by the U.S. Department of State and the Central Intelligence Agency. It provides information on 170 countries. Reports range from 4 to 20 pages and typically cover everything from politicians to geography to defense to agriculture and trade.
Published annually by Gale Research, Inc.

Directory of Multinationals

John M. Stopford

This two-volume directory deals exclusively with companies that control important foreign investments. It includes information on about 450 companies that account for the bulk of the world's direct foreign investment. All companies included in the directory have at least $500 million in foreign sales. The Directory lists the value of exports and foreign production of these companies.
Fourth edition published in 1993 by Stockton Press.

Doing Business in Canada

The law firm of Stikeman and Elliot

Coverage includes full treatment of individual and corporate taxation, accounting procedures, contracts and agreements; the Investment Canada Act, export/import regulations, intellectual property law; banking and employment law; securities law regulation; and language legislation.
First published in 1984 by Matthew Bender, it is issued in looseleaf and is updated periodically with revisions.

The Economist Intelligence Unit

The Economist Intelligence Unit is part of the Economist Group, which also publishes the weekly magazine, *The Economist*. The EIU provides a wide range of subscription services that analyze and forecast change in the political, economic, regulatory, and business environments for 180 countries. These include the following:

Country reports. Each report analyzes the political and economic status of a country, including the political structure, economic structure, and the 12- to 18-month outlook. Published quarterly.

Country Profiles. Each report provides an annual perspective on the long-term political and social issues affecting each country covered. Published annually.

World Outlook. A one-volume overview that forecasts the political and economic trends in more than 180 countries. Information about each country includes a comprehensive six-year series of macroeconomic indicators. Published annually.

Country Forecasts. Each report provides the political, economic, and business trends in 55 countries for the next five years. Published quarterly.

Country Risk Service. Each report assesses the solvency of 82 developing and highly indebted countries. Reports analyze growth, budget deficits, trade and current accounts, foreign financing requirements and sources, and debt service. Published quarterly.

Published by the Economist Intelligence Unit.

Encyclopedia of Associations: International Organizations

🔒 The encyclopedia lists more than 11,000 international organizations, including over 5,000 national organizations of countries other than the United States. Entries are arranged in 15 general subject areas and are indexed geographically, by executive name, and by keyword. The encyclopedia is also available in the following alternative formats: computer diskette, online, magnetic tape, and CD-ROM. Available online through DIALOG. *Published annually by Gale Research, Inc.*

Europa World Yearbook

A comprehensive listing of facts and figures on more than 200 countries, the yearbook also provides key contact information. Every country survey provides economic and demographic statistics; constitutional policies and viewpoints of prominent political parties; national press organizations, including names of principal officers and locations of foreign bureaus; and trade and industry contacts and information.
Published annually by Europa Publications, Ltd. Distributed in the United States and Canada by Gale Research, Inc.

F & S Index International

🔒 This text provides one- or two-line summaries and an index of business and trade journal articles covering business activities in Canada, Latin America, Africa, the Middle East, Asia, and Oceania. Entries are arranged by product and industry using a SIC coding system and alphabetically by company. Also available online through BRS, DIALOG, and Data-Star as part of PTS F&S Index.
Published monthly with quarterly and annual cumulative updates by Information Access/Predicasts.

Financial Times

This daily newspaper, edited in the UK, is an important source of international business, financial, and economic news. Also available online through DIALOG as the Financial Times Company Abstracts (containing abstracts of articles referring to specific companies) and Financial Times Fulltext.
Published daily by The Financial Times Business Information, Ltd.

The G. T. Guide to World Equity Markets, Seventh Edition

This guide provides information and analysis on the performance, structure, operation, and character of the world's equity markets. It covers 50 countries with a wide range of information including market capitalization, market performance, investment climate, rights and restrictions concerning investors, taxation, and investment controls.
Published in 1992 by Euromoney Books.

Hoover's Handbook of World Business

Alan Chai, Alta Campbell, and Patrick J. Spain, editors

A resource for information on the world's largest and most influential companies, the handbook provides nearly 200 in-depth corporate profiles including 100 European companies and 40 Japanese companies, along with companies from Australia, Brazil, Chile, Hong Kong, Singapore, Turkey, Venezuela, and other countries. The handbook also provides business and economic profiles of 67 countries and 5 regions. These profiles include overview and economic history; trade and business contacts, including embassies and chambers of commerce; and economic and demographic data.
Published annually by The Reference Press Inc.

Index to International Statistics (IIS)

This index is a guide to the coverage of statistical publications from the major intergovernmental organizations, including the Organization for Economic Cooperation and Development (Main Economic Indicators), International Labor Organization (Yearbook of Labor Statistics), and International Monetary Fund (International Financial Statistics). The IIS covers approximately 1,700 titles from about 100 issuing sources. Available by subscription only.
Published monthly, with annual cumulative volume, by Congressional Information Service.

International Directory of Company Histories

Six-volume reference contains historical information on 1,250 companies with sales of $2 billion or more. Entries provide information on founders, expansions, losses, labor/management actions, and other significant milestones. Corporate profiles also include company name, address, telephone/FAX numbers, number of employees, sales, market value, and principal subsidiaries.
Published in 1992 by Gale Research, Inc.

International Dun's Market Identifiers

▪ This database contains sales, financial, marketing, and ownership information on over 2 million Asian, African, and European companies. Information provided includes name, address, sales volume, SIC code, and number of employees. Available online through DIALOG and Dow Jones News/Retrieval.
Updated quarterly by Dun & Bradstreet Information Services.

International Marketing Data & Statistics

A comprehensive guide to international marketing data, the text covers more than 150 countries. Twenty-six data sections present comparative statistics and demographics for economic indicators, energy resources, consumer expenditures, and consumer prices.
Fifteenth edition published in 1992 by

Euromonitor. Distributed in the United States and Canada by Gale Research, Inc.

Kompass International Guides

🔲 *Kompass Guides* provide company and product information and are available for the following 45 countries: Australia, Austria, Bahrain, Belgium, Brunei, Bulgaria, Canada, Czechoslovakia, Denmark, Egypt, Finland, France, Germany, Greece, Holland, Hong Kong, Hungary, Iceland, India, Indonesia, Ireland, Israel, Italy, Japan, Korea, Luxembourg, Malaysia, Malta, Mexico, Morocco, New Zealand, Norway, Philippines, Poland, Portugal, Saudi Arabia, Singapore, Spain, Sweden, Switzerland, Taiwan, Tunisia, Turkey, United Arab Emirates, and United Kingdom. The Kompass Guides for Canada, the UK, the countries of Europe, and the countries of the Asia/Pacific region are available online through DIALOG.
Each guide is published annually by Kompass.

Moody's International Manual and News Reports

🔲 The two-volume manual is a source of financial and business information on over 5,000 companies and institutions in 100 countries. Entries include the history and business of each company, financial information, and capital structure. The weekly news reports that accompany the manual provide ongoing coverage of the latest development in each firm, such as mergers and acquisitions, joint ventures, interim earnings, and new stock and bond offerings. The International News Reports are also available online through DIALOG.
The Manual is published annually and the News Reports are published biweekly by Dun & Bradstreet Information Services.

Principal International Businesses

This source provides facts and figures on 50,000 of the world's leading companies in 145 countries, including data on senior management, line of business, and contact information.
Published annually by Dun & Bradstreet Information Services.

Thomson Bank Directory International

This volume lists, by country, bank offices involved in international trade. The listings include head offices, branches, agencies, and representative offices located in countries other than the United States; financial figures in national currency and U.S. dollars; and complete contact information.
Revised and updated every six months by Thomson Financial Publishing.

Who's Who in International Banking

Who's Who profiles nearly 4,000 bankers from 1,000 banks around the world. Entries include education, career, civic interests, professional memberships, honors, and publications. A country-by-country banking directory is also provided.
Published in 1992 by R. R. Bowker (Reed Reference Publishing).

Who's Who in International Organizations

Three-volume collection provides biographical and contact information for 12,000 individuals prominent in 7,000 organizations worldwide.
Published in 1992 by R. R. Bowker (Reed Reference Publishing).

World Directory of Stock Exchanges

Maurice Garneau

This two-volume directory provides information on the performance of all stock exchanges of the world.
Published annually by W.I.S.E.R. Research.

World Factbook

Compiled by the U.S. Central Intelligence Agency staff, this valuable reference provides demographic, economic, and geographic data on every country in the world.
Published annually by the Superintendent of Documents, U.S. Government Printing Office.

World Markets Desk Book: A Region-by-Region Survey of Global Trade Opportunities

Lawrence W. Tuller

The desk book is a region-by-region survey of 50 of the world's principal markets. Each profile covers what products and services are needed in which countries; each country's political and economic stability; internal competition and regional strategy; resource cost and availability; formal and informal trade barriers; and factors influencing market entry, such as government regulations and incentives, cultural hurdles, and infrastructure development.
Published in 1992 by McGraw-Hill, Inc.

World Retail Directory and Sourcebook

This book lists 3,500 addresses of retailers, information sources, libraries, conferences, and trade fairs in Western and Eastern Europe, North America, Central and South America, Africa and the Middle East, and the Far East and Oceania.

Published in 1992 by Euromonitor. Distributed in the United States and Canada by Gale Research, Inc.

World Trade Centers Association World Business Directory

Four-volume publication lists more than 100,000 businesses in 190 countries interested in international trade opportunities. Companies listed include both WTCA member and nonmember companies. Typical entries include company name; address, phone, FAX, and telex numbers; business activities and products; import/export designations; revenue figures; number of employees; key officers; and corporate message. Entries are indexed alphabetically, by business activities, and by product. The directory is also available in the following alternative formats: computer diskette and magnetic tape.
Published in 1992 by Gale Research, Inc.

The World Trade System

Robert Fraser, editor

Trade profiles are presented for every country in the world. Each profile covers principal imports, principal exports, principal trading partners, membership of regional trading associations, and political information.
Published in 1992 by Gale Research, Inc.

Worldwide Branch Locations of Multinational Companies

Worldwide Branch Locations of Multinational Companies provides contact, financial, and other information on nearly 20,000 branches, plants, and subsidiaries belonging to more than 500 multinational companies headquartered around the world.
Published in 1992 by Gale Research, Inc.

Yearbook of International Organizations

Union of International Associations, Brussels, editor.

Three-volume reference contains information on over 28,000 organizations active in over 200 countries around the world. The yearbook is available in print and CD-ROM.
Published annually by R. R. Bowker (Reed Reference Publishing).

FOR FURTHER INFORMATION
See ABI/INFORM®, p. 400
America's Corporate Families and International Affiliates, p. 447
Business Publication Rates and Data, p. 417
The BusinessWeek Global 1000, p. 442
Canadian Dun's Business Identification Service, p. 447
Canadian Key Business Directory, p. 447
Collaborating to Compete: Using Strategic Alliances and Acquisitions in the Global Marketplace, p. 580
Company Intelligence™, p. 448
Disclosure Worldscope™ Global, p. 443
Dow Jones News/Retrieval, p. 403
Dun's Business Identification Service, p. 448
The Economist Atlas, p. 403
The Economist World in Figures, p. 403
Globalizing Management: Creating and Leading the Competitive Organization, p. 517
Guide to Canadian Manufacturers, p. 450
The Handbook of International Direct Marketing, p. 466
Handbook for International Accounting, p. 413
International Accounting Summaries: A Guide for Interpretation and Comparison, p. 414
International Advertising Handbook, p. 418
International Brands and Their Companies, p. 439
International Companies and Their Brands, p. 439
International Corporate Yellow Book, p. 453
International Directory of Corporate Affiliations, p. 450
International Directory of Market Research Organizations, p. 459
International Directory of Marketing Research Companies, p. 459
International Environmental Law Special Report, p. 495
International Research Centers Directory, p. 568
International Tax Summaries: A Guide for Planning and Decisions, p. 583
International Treaties on Intellectual Property, p. 435
Mangagement Contents, p. 405
Market Research Handbook (Canada), p. 459
NASDAQ Yellow Book, p. 453
Nelson's Directory of Investment Research, p. 445
One Hundred Years of Economic Statistics, p. 483
Overseas Business Reports, p. 483
PTS F&S Index, p. 406
PTS Newsletter Database, p. 406
PTS PROMPT:™ Overview of Markets and Technology, p. 406
Standard Directory of International Advertisers and Agencies, p. 419
Statistics Sources, p. 407
Ulrich's International Periodicals Directory, p. 407
United Nations World Population Report, p. 462
The United States Industrial Outlook, p. 477
The World Almanac and Book of Facts, p. 409
World Intellectual Property Guide Books, p. 436
World Trademark Journal, p. 441
Worldcasts, p. 483
Worldwide Franchise Directory, p. 515

28

INTERNATIONAL BUSINESS (ASIA AND AUSTRALIA)

1992 Korea Directory

General traders, importers, exporters, manufacturers, agents, and banks operating in Korea are listed.
Published in 1992 by The Korea Directory Company.

1992 3W Register of Chinese Business

This directory provides information on over 30,000 Chinese companies, including information on ownership, assets, number of employees, sales, and products. It also contains an SIC code index, general information on Chinese provinces, international ports, and telephone city codes. Available in print, CD-ROM, and floppy disk.
Published in 1991 by 3W International Publishing.

Asia: A Directory and Sourcebook

This sourcebook provides major sources of marketing information inside and outside Asia. It identifies all major independent and government organizations as well as detailed profiles of all of the major companies.
Published in 1992 by Euromonitor. Distributed in the United States and Canada by Gale Research, Inc.

Asia 1991/92: Measures and Magnitude

This "Top 500" company directory for all Asian nations, excluding the People's Republic of China, contains "region at a glance" sections complete with charts and graphs.
Published in 1991 by Asian Finance Publications, Ltd.

Asia and Pacific Review: The Business and Economic Report, 1991/92

Collection of reports on all countries of Asia includes key indicators, historical overviews, and recent political and economic trends.
Published in 1991 by World of Information.

Asian Company Handbook

This reference provides the latest financial information on over 1,000 companies on the stock exchanges of Hong Kong, the Republic of Korea, Taiwan, Thailand, Malaysia, and Singapore. The information includes overseas offices, export destinations, sales, stock ownership, a share price chart, and business results.
Published in 1992 by Toyo Keizai Shinposha.

Asian Markets: A Guide to Company and Industry Information Sources, Second Edition

Collection of information sources on Asian markets can be used to track foreign competitors, obtain market studies, track trade leads, and contact a number of experts. Entries include complete contact information.
Published in 1992 by Washington Researchers, Ltd.

Asia-Pacific Dun's Market Identifiers

🔒 This resource provides information on businesses in countries located within Asia as well as Australia and New Zealand. The information provided includes sales volume, marketing data, address, phone number, and key executives. Available online from DIALOG.
Published and updated monthly by Dun & Bradstreet Information Services.

Asia's 75,000 Largest Companies

The top 75,000 companies in 10 countries in the Asia/Pacific region, including Hong Kong, Japan, Malaysia, Philippines, Taiwan, Indonesia, South Korea, Singapore, and Thailand, are ranked.
Published annually by Dun & Bradstreet Information Services.

Business Asia

This biweekly newsletter provides short-term economic forecasts, examines business and economic trends, and analyzes major regulatory and policy developments.
Published biweekly by the Economist Intelligence Unit.

China Statistical Yearbook 1990

Data issued by the Chinese government cover a number of business and economic topics including population, trade, economic indicators, and production.
Published in 1991 by State Statistical Bureau of the People's Republic of China.

Consumer Asia

These statistical and analytical surveys of Asian consumer markets concentrate on Hong Kong, Taiwan, Singapore, South Korea, Indonesia, and Malaysia and contain assessments and overviews of the region as a whole. Individual chapters concentrate on specific subjects, including energy issues, labor costs, population factors, financial markets, and demography.
Published in 1992 by Euromonitor. Distributed in the United States and Canada by Gale Research, Inc.

Doing Business in China

William P. Streng and Allen D. Wilcox, editors

A guide to all areas of business law in the People's Republic of China, the book closely examines key issues and potential pitfalls involved in import/export transactions, technology transfers, banking and financial transactions, tax matters, and joint ventures.
First published in 1989 by Matthew Bender and Company, this book is issued in looseleaf and is updated periodically with supplements and revisions.

Dun's Asia/Pacific Key Business Enterprises (Expanded)

Two-volume directory lists 30,000 companies in 14 Pacific Rim countries that have annual sales of at least $10 million U.S. and/or employ 500 or more individuals. Profiles include company name, contact

information, trading address, lines of business, import/export status, parent company name, annual sales in local currency, and number of employees.
Published annually by Dun & Bradstreet Information Services.

Far East and Australasia

Far East and Australasia offers essays on topics of concern to the region as a whole, details on international and regional organizations active there, and surveys and directories for each nation and territory.
Published in 1992 by Gale Research, Inc.

International Business/China

This newsletter tracks issues and trends in the People's Republic of China and provides in-depth corporate case studies.
Published biweekly by the Economist Intelligence Unit.

Jobson's Yearbook of Public Companies in Australia and New Zealand

This directory provides full company listings, including corporate structure, five-year financial tables, and operating results, on more than 2,000 public companies in Australia and New Zealand that are listed on either (or both) of those country's stock exchanges.
Published annually by Dun & Bradstreet Information Services.

Key Business Directory of Australia

Two-volume set lists more than 20,000 prominent public and private businesses engaged in commercial and industrial activities in Australia. Volume I provides details on leading business enterprises, including information on marketing, sales,

purchasing, and financial operations. Volume II provides information on businesses operating in the middle company size sector of Australian commerce and industry. All information is arranged alphabetically, geographically, and by line of business.
Published annually by Dun & Bradstreet Information Services.

Key Business Directory of Indonesia/Thailand

Companies listed in this directory were selected on the basis of their annual turnover in excess of Rupiah 10 billion in Indonesia and 150 Baht in Thailand and/or at least 50 employees. Three sections offer alphabetical listings of 1,500 public and private companies, a breakdown of the businesses into major industries (SIC codes), and a geographical list of companies by state.
Published annually by Dun & Bradstreet Information Services.

Key Business Directory of Malaysia

Directory lists companies with annual turnovers in excess of $18 million and/or at least 50 employees. Three sections offer alphabetical listings of 1,500 private and public companies, a breakdown of the businesses into major industries (SIC codes), and a geographical list of companies by state.
Published annually by Dun & Bradstreet Information Services

Key Business Directory of Singapore

A comprehensive listing of leading businesses in Singapore, the directory is divided into three sections—alphabetical, product classification, and a "Directory of Directors," which lists the names and titles of over 6,900 directors and key executives. Entries cover company name, ad-

dress, telephone and FAX numbers, line of business, names of chief executives, number of employees, annual sales, import/export status, and SIC codes.
Published annually by Dun & Bradstreet Information Services.

Key Indicators of Developing Asian and Pacific Countries

Collection of statistics regarding key production output, trade, and finance of all Asia/Pacific countries includes charts and tables.
Published in 1991 by Economics and Resource Development Center, Asian Development Bank.

Kompass International Guides for the Asia Pacific Region

Kompass Guides provide company and product information and are available in individual editions for the following countries in the Asia/Pacific region: Australia, Brunei, Hong Kong, India, Japan, Korea, Malaysia, the Philippines, Singapore, and Taiwan. Also available online through DIALOG as Kompass Asia/Pacific.
Published and updated annually by Kompass International.

Kothari's Industrial Directory of India, Thirty-seventh Edition

Directory provides facts and figures on almost 2,500 joint stock companies of India and also includes general economic and business information and a statistical profile of the Indian economy.
Published in 1991 by Kothari Enterprises.

Major Companies of the Far East and Australasia, 1992–93

This source provides information and data on 4,500 companies of the Far East and Australasia. Volume 1 covers Southeast Asia; volume 2 East Asia; and volume 3 Australia and New Zealand. The coverage of each company includes its financial performance, products and services, organizational structure, and key executives.
Published in 1992 by Graham and Trotman. Distributed in the United States and Canada by Gale Research, Inc.

Marketing to China: One Billion New Customers

Xu Bai Yi

This comprehensive guide to China's rapidly changing consumer market has appendices that include Chinese rules and regulations governing trademarks, advertising, foreign investment, and import/export corporations.
Published in 1991 by NTC Publishing Group.

Philippine Yearbook

Government-issued body of statistical data covers all aspects of Philippine demographics, economy, and trade.
Published annually by Republic of the Philippines, National Statistics Office.

Republic of China, 1987: A Reference Book

Well-organized reference book covers Taiwan's demographics, economy, and government organization.
Published in 1987 by Hilit Publishing Company, Ltd.

Statistical Yearbook of the Republic of China

Collection of data, produced by the Taiwanese government, covers a number of business and economic issues, including population, the economy, trade, and production.

Published annually by Directorate-General of Budget, Accounting, and Statistics of the Republic of China.

Who Owns Whom — Australasia and the Far East

One-volume directory is divided into three sections: Section 1 lists subsidiaries and associates of parent companies registered in Australia, Hong Kong, Indonesia, Japan, Malaysia, New Zealand, Papua New Guinea, the Philippines, Singapore, South Korea, Taiwan, and Thailand; Section 2 lists foreign parent companies with subsidiaries and associates in the Far East and Australasia; Section 3 is an alphabetical index that links any family member to the ultimate parent.

Published annually by Dun & Bradstreet Information Services

FOR FURTHER INFORMATION

*See **DRI Databases (DRI Asian Forecast)**, p. 480*
***The Economist Intelligence Unit**, p. 520*
***The Handbook of International Direct Marketing**, p. 466*
***International Dun's Market Identifiers**, p. 522*
***PTS Newsletter Database**, p. 406*

29

INTERNATIONAL BUSINESS (EASTERN EUROPE AND THE COMMONWEALTH OF INDEPENDENT STATES)

Consumer Eastern Europe

Information and essays on the market for consumer goods and services in Eastern European countries include chapters on demography, economic indicators, standard of living, household characteristics, advertising and media access, regional distribution, consumer expenditure, market demand, and service industries.
Published in 1992 by Euromonitor.
Distributed in the United States and Canada by Gale Research, Inc.

Eastern European Business Directory

Frank X. Didik

This publication is a directory of companies—and the products and services they produce and offer—in Poland, Czechoslovakia, Hungary, Bulgaria, Romania, the former East Germany, and the former Soviet Union. The information also includes company name and full contact information.
Published in 1993 by Gale Research, Inc.

Eastern Europe and the Commonwealth of Independent States 1992

Eastern Europe and the Commonwealth of Independent States 1992 examines the social, political, and economic background of the region in specially commissioned introductory essays by leading experts. Separate chapters then examine different countries and include a geographical profile, a chronology, essays on recent history and the economy, statistical surveys, and various directory material.
Published in 1992 by Gale Research, Inc.

The East European Opportunity: The Complete Business Guide and Sourcebook

Marvin Zonis and Dwight Semler

The East European Opportunity covers economic, political, cultural, and historical issues in Czechoslovakia, Romania, Hungary, Poland, Bulgaria, and Yugoslavia. Each country is covered in a separate section that offers detailed information on the labor force, demographics, education, agriculture, geography, and industry.
Published in 1992 by John Wiley & Sons, Inc.

Handbook of Reconstruction in Eastern Europe & The Soviet Union

Stephen White, editor

The handbook provides a closeup look at political and economic changes in the eastern European countries of Germany,

Bulgaria, Hungary, Czechoslovakia, Yugoslavia, Albania, Romania, Poland, and the former Soviet Union. Features include a detailed chronology for each country; a summary of political and economic relations; and brief biographies of key personalities.
Published in 1991 by Longman Group. Distributed in the United States and Canada by Gale Research, Inc.

International Business/East Europe

This newsletter provides commercial intelligence on business in central and Eastern Europe and the Commonwealth of Independent States. Its coverage includes key macroeconomic indicators, legal and tax updates, OECD trade analysis, and company case studies.
Published weekly by the Economist Intelligence Unit.

Major Business Organizations of Eastern Europe and the Commonwealth of Independent States

This collection of information on more than 2,000 business organizations in Albania, the Baltic republics, Bulgaria, the Commonwealth of Independent States, Czechoslovakia, Hungary, Poland, Romania, and Yugoslavia provides contact information, key officials, full descriptions, and import/export data. Ministries and Chambers of Commerce entries provide infor-

mation on the scope of their activity and names of key officials.
Second edition published in 1992 by Graham & Trotman. Distributed in the United States and Canada by Gale Research, Inc.

GOVERNMENT AGENCIES

National Technical Information Service (NTIS)

The NTIS in cooperation with the office of the General Counsel of the U.S. Commerce Department has established the Central and Eastern Europe Texts Service, which provides lists of legal and regulatory information on the countries of Eastern Europe (NTIS free catalog PR-883). NTIS also works with the Commerce Department's Eastern European Business Information Center to provide documents on doing business in Eastern Europe (NTIS free catalog PR-882).
National Technical Information Service, 5285 Port Royal Road, Springfield, VA 22161. Tel. (703) 487-4600.

FOR FURTHER INFORMATION

See **Commerce Department's "Flash Facts" Service (Eastern European Business Information Center)**, p. 499
The Economist Intelligence Unit, p. 520
Encyclopedia of Business Information Sources: Europe, p. 541
Euro Trademark Journal, p. 439
European Wholesalers & Distributors Directory, p. 469
F & S Index Europe, p. 542
Kompass International Guides, p. 523

30

INTERNATIONAL BUSINESS (JAPAN)

Consumer Japan

Extensive collection of information on the Japanese consumer includes a market overview, a statistical fact file, major consumer markets, listings of major Japanese companies and retailers, and sources of more information.
Published in 1990 by Euromonitor. Distributed in the United States and Canada by Gale Research, Inc.

Destination Japan: A Business Guide for the 90s

Publication provides information for American businesses interested in exporting products to Japan, export financing assistance programs, customs clearance documentation, foreign trade barriers, market information trade leads, and more. It also focuses on property protection rights, including patents, trademarks, copyrights, trade secrets, and other intellectual property rights in Japan.
Published in 1991 by the Superintendent of Documents, U.S. Government Printing Office.

Doing Business in Japan

Zentaro Kitagawa, editor.

Guide for Japanese business dealings focuses on all substantive areas, including contracts, business organizations, and regulation; employment law; securities; intellectual property; competition law; and taxation.
First published in 1980 by Matthew Bender, this book is issued in looseleaf and is updated periodically with supplements and revisions.

Industrial Groupings in Japan

This essential listing of Japanese corporations and their associated conglomerates, or Zaibatsu, includes an analysis of the financial interrelationships between the two.
Published biennially by Dodwell Marketing Consultants.

Japan Company Datafile

Well-organized listing of Japanese companies includes data on company background, senior personnel, sales, stockholders, and subsidiaries. Information is limited to one page per company.
Published in 1992 by Toyo Keizai Shinposha.

Japan Company Handbook

This two-volume reference is published quarterly. The first volume, or *first section*, provides financial information on all Japanese corporations listed in the First Section of the Tokyo, Osaka, and Nagoya Stock Exchanges. The second volume does the same for the second section of the exchanges. Information on each company includes corporate names and order of listing, industry of company and its position in the industry, future prospects, income data, sales breakdown, stock prices, stock price chart, company financial data, facility investment, R & D expenditure, number of employees, and principal office.
Updated quarterly by Toyo Keizai Shinposha.

Japan Economic Newswire™Plus

This full-text database is a source for a wide variety of English-language news articles covering business, financial, economic, and political developments in Japan, as reported by Kyodo News Service of Tokyo. Available online through DIALOG and NEXIS.
Updated daily by Kyodo News International.

Japan Trade Directory 1992–93

Directory contains information on 2,900 Japanese companies that export or import products and services. Information on specific companies is organized by products or services, geographic location in Japan, and company name. Company profiles provide financial data, corporate structure, full information on trade contacts, and the company's interest in importing or exporting.
Published in 1992 by JETRO (Japan External Trade Organization).
Distributed in the United States and Canada by Gale Research, Inc.

Japanese Affiliated Companies in the U.S. and Canada, 1991–92

Data on 9,569 Japanese affiliates operating in the U.S. and Canada as of October 1990 are presented. Geographically arranged entries provide company name; parent company name and the location of its headquarters in Japan; North American address; year of establishment; telephone, telex, and FAX numbers; executive officers' names; type of business and product; and operating status.
Published in 1991 by JETRO (Japan External Trade Organization).
Distributed in the United States and Canada by Gale Research, Inc.

The Japanese Distribution System: Opportunities and Obstacles—Structure and Practices

Michael R. Czinkota and Masaaki Kotabe, editors

The Japanese Distribution System offers up-to-date information on Japan's often difficult-to-penetrate distribution network. Topics include retail, wholesale, and just-in-time distribution; successes of firms operating in Japan; trade practices; industry-specific practices; and case studies of major companies.
Published in 1992 by Probus Publishing Company, Inc.

Japanese Overseas Investing

This listing of the overseas subsidiaries of over 3,000 Japanese companies includes information on annual sales or production, partner firms, business results, capital, and investment ratios. Entries are arranged alphabetically by company.
Published in 1992 by Toyo Keizai Shinposha.

JapanSite™: Desktop Target Marketing for Japan

The purpose of JapanSite is the evaluation of site and trade areas in Japan, primarily Tokyo. It is a desktop PC application with databases, mapping files, and software. It provides access to reporting, mapping, and bar charts for over 4,000 geographic areas in the Tokyo market. Data items in JapanSite include households, labor force, population, and business establishments.
Published by Demosphere International, Inc.

Keiretsu: Inside the Hidden Japanese Conglomerates

Kenichi Miyashita and David Russell

Text looks at the inner workings of Keiretsu, the Japanese corporate alliances, specifically Mitsubishi, Mitsui, Sumitomo, Sanwa, Fuyo, and Dai-Ichi Kangyo. It reports on how they do business and what it is like for foreign companies to compete with them.
Published in 1993 by McGraw-Hill, Inc.

Kompass Japan

🔒 This five-volume directory contains business information compiled from the database of Tokyo Shoko Research, the Japanese data and credit rating service. The information about companies includes a description of products and services, capital, number of employees, CEO, and full contact information. Company listings are divided into sections that correspond with the 10 major geographic sections of Japan. Also available online through DIALOG as part of Kompass Asia/Pacific.
Published annually by Kompass.

Tokyo Business Today

Monthly magazine publishes articles on business, industry, and finance in Japan.
Published monthly by Toyo Keizai Shinposha.

White Papers of Japan

Extensive collection of various data on Japan includes economic indicators, labor force, technology, and transportation systems.

Published annually by The Japan Institute of International Affairs.

Who's Who in Japan 1991–92

Biographies of prominent business leaders and a listing of Japanese public and private institutions are presented.
Published in 1991 by Asia Press Co., Ltd.

GOVERNMENT AGENCIES

National Technical Information Service (NTIS)

NTIS makes available major Japanese on-line information systems through agreement with the Japan Information Center of Science and Technology. Call NTIS at (703) 487-4819 for more information.
National Technical Information Service, 5285 Port Royal Road, Springfield, VA 22161.

FOR FURTHER INFORMATION

See **DRI Databases (DRI Japanese Forecast), p. 480**
The Economist Intelligence Unit, p. 520
The Handbook of International Direct Marketing, p. 466
Japan's High Technology: An Annotated Guide to English Language Information Sources, p. 568
Market Movers: Understanding and Using Economic Indicators from the Big Five Economies, p. 482
OECD Economic Outlook, p. 483
OECD Economic Surveys, p. 483
The OECD STAN Database for Industrial Analysis, p. 483
PTS Newsletter Database, p. 406

31

INTERNATIONAL BUSINESS (LATIN AMERICA)

Business International's Guide to Doing Business in Mexico

Gary Newman and Anna Szterenfeld

A collection of information on Mexican markets and opportunities, the guide discusses a number of different topics, including the Free Trade Agreement, field intelligence, unwritten rules for business success, and analyses of key Mexican industries.
Published in 1993 by McGraw-Hill, Inc.

Consumer South America

Detailed data on trends in the changing markets of South American countries are assembled. Market factors for the region are divided into four chapters: 1) general market profile of the region, 2) comparative statistical profiles of the markets of each country, 3) market sizes for specific consumer products, and 4) country-by-country surveys.
Published in 1992 by Euromonitor. Distributed in the United States and Canada by Gale Research, Inc.

Doing Business in Brazil

J. M. Pinheiro Neto

Overview of Brazilian business laws includes banking and investment law, commercial law, contract law, import/export regulations, patent and trademark law, and corporate law.
First published in 1979 by Matthew Bender, this book is issued in looseleaf and is updated with revisions and monthly newsletters.

Doing Business in Mexico

Joseph J. Norton

This publication covers legal aspects of trade with Mexico, including export incentives, the *Maquiladora* program, and legal aspects of importing goods into Mexico. It includes texts of U.S. and Mexican laws, treaties, and forms.
First published in 1980 by Matthew Bender, this book is issued in looseleaf and is updated with supplements and revisions periodically.

International Business—Latin America

This newsletter analyzes the economic, political, and regulatory trends in South and Central America, Mexico, and the Caribbean. Coverage includes market forecasts, key economic and business indicators, in-depth looks at corporate strategies, exchange controls, and licensing regulations.
Published weekly by the Economist Intelligence Unit.

Latin American Markets: A Guide to Company and Industry Information Sources

Information sources are listed for both the United States and the featured countries of Mexico, Brazil, Venezuela, Columbia, Chile, Argentina, Dominican Republic, Costa Rica, Jamaica, Panama, Bolivia, Ecuador, El Salvador, and Peru. Sources

include country and regional experts, market and business research, databases and publications, government regulators, and trade promotion programs.
Published in 1992 by Washington Researchers, Ltd.

Latin America's Top 25,000

This one-volume directory offers information on approximately 25,000 enterprises in more than 30 Latin American countries, including Brazil, Argentina, Venezuela, Peru, Chile, and Mexico. Business listings are arranged alphabetically, geographically, and by line of business.
Published annually by Dun & Bradstreet Information Services.

South America, Central America, and the Caribbean 1991

This text is a comprehensive sourcebook on the region as a whole, with detailed statistics and directories for the major countries in the Latin American and Caribbean region, including the Bahamas, Barbados, Belize, French Guiana, Guadeloupe, Martinique, Puerto Rico, and 39 others. Topics include the debt crisis, trade, drugs, and deforestation and its effect on the environment.
Published in 1991 by Europa.
Distributed in the United States and Canada by Gale Research, Inc.

Statistical Abstract of Latin America

This two-volume reference provides the latest figures for the 20 countries of Latin America. Coverage includes the following areas: geography, land use, land tenure, transportation, communication, population, health, education, welfare, politics, religion, military, labor, income, and industrial production.
Published in 1991 by University of California, Latin American Center.

For Further Information

See *Commerce Department's "Flash Facts" Service (Office of Mexico)*, p. 499
The Directory of Management Consultants, p. 433
DRI Databases (DRI Latin American Forecast), p. 480
The Economist Intelligence Unit, p. 520
The Handbook of International Direct Marketing, p. 466
Kompass International Guides, p. 523
PTS Newsletter Database, p. 406

INTERNATIONAL BUSINESS (MIDDLE EAST)

Dun's Guide to Israel

Collection profiles more than 10,000 leading companies in Israel. Information includes company names, addresses, telephone and FAX numbers, name of chief executives, SIC codes, number of employees, annual sales, and products exported. Text is in both English and Hebrew. Also available online through Data-Star.
Published annually by Dun & Bradstreet Information Services.

Major Companies of the Arab World 1992–93

Text is a collection of information on more than 6,500 major companies in 19 Arab countries, including Algeria, Egypt, Iraq, Libya, Saudi Arabia, and Syria. Company profiles are arranged by country and include complete contact information, names of directors and management staff, principal activities, number of branch offices, principal bank, financial details, principal shareholders, date of establishment, and number of employees.

Profiles are indexed by name, country, and business activity within each country.
Published in 1992 by Graham & Trotman. Distributed in the United States and Canada by Gale Research, Inc.

Middle East and North Africa 1992

Comprehensive guide to the Middle East and North Africa offers a collection of expert, informed essays on topics of concern to the region, details on international and regional organizations, and surveys and directories for each nation and territory. For each country, signed articles cover its physical and social geography, recent history, and economy.
Published in 1992 by Europa. Distributed in United States and Canada by Gale Research, Inc.

FOR FURTHER INFORMATION

See *The Economist Intelligence Unit, p. 520*
The Handbook of International Direct Marketing, p. 466
PTS Newsletter Database, p. 406

INTERNATIONAL BUSINESS (WESTERN EUROPE)

1992 The Single Market Handbook

Comprehensive handbook on "Europe 1992" is divided into four sections and offers information and contacts for more information on subjects such as how the removal of trade barriers and new legislation will affect business; trade controls; foreign trade; transport and distribution; and media developments.
Published in 1990 by Euromonitor.
Distributed in the United States and Canada by Gale Research, Inc.

British Business Rankings

Britain's 5,000 largest employers are first listed in an alphabetical section showing number of employees, headquarters locations, and main SIC codes. They are then listed in rank order within counties, by employee numbers, by sales, and within SIC groupings. Entries contain full addresses and telephone numbers.
Published annually by Dun & Bradstreet Information Services.

Consumer Europe 1992

Consumers in 24 Western European countries, such as Austria, Belgium, Denmark, Finland, France, Germany, Great Britain, the Netherlands, Norway, Poland, Spain, Sweden, and Switzerland are considered in depth. Entries include statistics on the production, sales, distribution, consumption, and other aspects of more than 250 consumer product categories.
Published in 1990 by Gale Research, Inc.

Dun's Europa

This four-volume reference work provides information on over 60,000 companies in the European Community and most of the countries from the European Free Trade Association (Austria, Switzerland, Sweden, Norway, Finland, and Turkey). Information includes executives, principal business, percent of sales that are exported, annual sales, bankers used by the company, nominal capital, issued capital, net profit or loss, and contact information.
Published in 1993 by Dun & Bradstreet International.

Directory of EC Industry Information Sources

This reference lists European Community contacts and organizations according to their industrial specialization. Coverage includes finding European partners, online business databases, and business and trade statistics.
Published in 1992 by Stockton Press.

Directory of European Banking and Financial Associations

Collection of information on European banking and insurance institutions covers Austria, Belgium, Cyprus, Denmark, Finland, France, Germany, Greece, Ireland, Italy, Luxembourg, Malta, the Netherlands, Norway, Portugal, Spain, Sweden, Switzerland, Turkey, and United Kingdom. The text identifies

the main banking association that represents the relevant domestic banking industry, and offers details relating to the central bank, as well as details relating to the main associations dealing in life and other types of insurance.
Published in 1990 by St. James Press. Distributed in the United States and Canada by Gale Research, Inc.

Directory of European Business

World of Information, editor

The directory delivers details on the top companies, organizations, government agencies, main business services, and sources of business information in 31 countries, including Eastern Europe and the former Soviet Union. Structured by country and subdivided under profession, entries offer full company name and contact information, number of employees within the country and worldwide, activities and specialties, and parent company and/or subsidiaries.
Published in 1992 by R. R. Bowker, Inc. (Reed Reference Publishing).

Directory of European Industrial and Trade Associations

Richard Leigh, editor

Formerly called the *Directory of European Associations, Part One*, the directory describes 6,000 industrial and trade associations. It includes national associations for all European countries (except the United Kingdom and Ireland) and regional associations of national significance. Entries contain full contact information, membership data, activities, and publications.
Published in 1991 by CBD Research, Ltd. Distributed in the United States and Canada by Gale Research, Inc.

Doing Business in France

Moquet Borde

A practice-oriented reference provides all the basic concepts of French business law and practice. It includes in-depth analysis of the French tax system; banking, securities, and bankruptcy procedures; practical treatment of accounting and auditing; and commerce regulations.
First published in 1983 by Matthew Bender and Company, it is issued in looseleaf and is updated periodically with supplements and revisions.

Doing Business in Ireland

Patrick Ussher and Brian O'Connor, editors

Text covers matters pertinent to the Irish business and legal situation, with emphasis on investment incentives, taxation, employment law, export/import restrictions, and product liability.
First published in 1987 by Matthew Bender and Company, it is issued in looseleaf and is updated periodically with supplements and revisions.

Doing Business in Spain

Fernando Pombo

This guide to the business and legal environment in the newest member of the EEC includes information on foreign investment incentives, exchange controls, taxation, labor relations, and more.
First published in 1987 by Matthew Bender and Company, it is issued in looseleaf and is updated periodically with supplements and revisions.

Doing Business in the United Kingdom

Clifford Chance

Publication provides all the necessary legal background for planning business transactions and dealing with problems arising from trade and investments in the U.K., including the business, private, commercial, and regulatory laws of England, Scotland, and Northern Ireland.

First published in 1985 by Matthew Bender and Company, text is issued in looseleaf and is updated periodically with supplements and revisions.

The Economist Atlas of the New Europe

One-volume reference is organized in nine sections: (1) Communications and Infrastructure, (2) Industry and Commerce, (3) Finance, (4) Politics, (5) International Relations, (6) War and Defense, (7) Nature and the Environment, (8) Peoples and Culture, and (9) Europe 2000. In each category, the atlas examines every country in terms of the effects of European political and economic unity and the nature of regionalism across the continent.

Published in 1992 by Henry Holt & Co.

The Economist Guide to the European Community

Dick Leonard

Comprehensive text on the origins and operations of the European Community is divided into four main parts: (1) The Background, (2) The Institutions, (3) the EC's Competences, and (4) Special Problems.

Published in 1992 by Economist Books.

Encyclopedia of Business Information Sources: Europe

M. Balachandran, editor

🔧 Business information sources are listed under approximately 1,000 alphabetically arranged business subjects. Within each topic category, entries are divided geographically and then by type of resource. The sources cited include a wide variety of both print and electronic sources. Available in print, on disk, and magnetic tape.

Published in 1992 by Gale Research, Inc.

European Advertising, Marketing, and Media Data

Comprehensive collection of marketing statistics of 16 major Western European markets considers topics like demographics, media options, and budgetary considerations.

Second edition published in 1992 by Euromonitor. Distributed in the United States and Canada by Gale Research, Inc.

European Business Rankings

Lesley Ripley Greenfield, editor

🔧 More than 2,250 business statistics and rankings throughout Europe are collected. Ranking entries cover products, institutions, industries, companies, services, demographics, and economic trends for both individual countries and Europe-wide data. Each entry contains the top 10 names in each list; and the ranking criteria, the total number of items listed in the original rankings, and the name, date, and page of the source also are given. Available in print and on disk and magnetic tape.

Published in 1992 by Gale Research, Inc.

European Communities Encyclopedia and Directory

A comprehensive guide to the European Community (EC), the text is arranged in three sections. The encyclopedia section holds in-depth descriptions of the people, events, and groups making up the EC. The directory section offers complete contact information for all major EC organizations. The essays and statistics section contains six essays covering the political, legal, economic, and social frame-

works of the Community, as well as statistical surveys covering all areas of the EC.
Published in 1991 by Europa.
Distributed in the United States and Canada by Gale Research, Inc.

European Consultants Directory

Karin Koek, editor

🔒 The directory lists more than 7,500 consultants who are experts in areas such as marketing, politics, health, and computer technology in 27 countries across Western and Eastern Europe. Entries are grouped by country, by broad subject terms, and then alphabetically by consulting organization. Each listing contains the name of the organization; address; telephone, telex, and FAX numbers; principal executive; annual consulting revenues; and geographic areas served. The directory is available in print, on computer diskette, and on magnetic tape.
First edition published in 1992 by Gale Research, Inc.

European Dun's Market Identifiers

Provides information on 2 million businesses in 26 European countries, including sales volume, marketing data, address, phone number, and key executives. Available online from DIALOG.
Updated quarterly by Dun & Bradstreet.

European Marketing Data and Statistics 1992

Collection of more than 100,000 statistics covers the broad marketing parameters of European business. Statistical data are presented on population, employment, production, trade, economy, living standards, consumption, market size, retailing, consumer expenditures, housing and households, health and education, culture

and mass media, communications, and travel and tourism.
Published in 1992 by Euromonitor.
Distributed in the United States and Canada by Gale Research, Inc.

European Markets: A Guide to Company and Industry Information Sources, Fourth Edition

Each entry in this guide to more than 5,000 information sources on European business and industry offers complete contact information, including address; telephone, telex, and FAX numbers; and names of specific contact people.
Published in 1992 by Washington Researchers, Ltd.

European Trends

This quarterly publication reviews issues and developments that affect the European Community. Coverage includes topics such as progress toward the integrated market and policies affecting different sectors, progress on the General Agreement on Trade and Tariffs (GATT) negotiations, environmental, policies and legislation, and recent cases before the EC Court of Justice.
Published quarterly (by subscription) with an annual supplement by the Economist Intelligence Unit.

F & S Index Europe

🔒 This publication is an index of business and trade journal articles covering business activities in the European Economic Community, Western European countries outside the EEC, Eastern Europe, and the commonwealth of Independent States. Each entry contains a two-line summary of the article cited. Entries are arranged alphabetically and by SIC code.

Available in print and online. Available online through DIALOG as part of the PTS F & S Indexes.

Published monthly, with quarterly and annual compilations, by Information Access/Predicasts.

ICC International Business Research

This is a source of business intelligence on UK and European companies. It contains over 15,000 stockbroker research reports that provide analysis and opinion on companies and industries. Available online from DIALOG.

Updated weekly by ICC information Group Ltd.

Industrial Research in the United Kingdom

This authoritative guide to more than 3,500 research and technology laboratories, centers, and associations in the United Kingdom is arranged in six chapters: (1) industrial firms, (2) research associations and their consultants, (3) government departments and their laboratories, (4) universities and polytechnics, (5) trade and development associations, and (6) learned and professional societies.

Fourteenth edition published in 1992 by Longman Group. Distributed in the United States and Canada by Gale Research, Inc.

Kompass International Guides

Kompass guides provide product and company information for organizations in the following countries: Austria, Belgium, Denmark, Finland, France, Germany, Greece, Holland, Ireland, Italy, Luxembourg, Norway, Portugal, Spain, Sweden, Switzerland, and the United Kingdom. Also available online through DIALOG as Kompass Europe.

Each guide is updated annually by Kompass.

Major and Medium Companies of Europe 1992–93

Six-volume collection is arranged into three two-volume sets: Volume I covers the continental European Economic Community. Volume II deals with the United Kingdom. Volume III covers Western Europe outside the European Economic Community. Each company entry includes (where available) contact data, principal activities, principal banks, number of employees, brand names, and trademarks.

Third edition published in 1992 by Graham & Trotman, London. Distributed in the United States and Canada by Gale Research, Inc.

Major Companies of Europe 1992–93

Three-volume collection lists more than 8,000 of Europe's leading corporations with sales in excess of $130 million. Each company entry includes (where available) contact data, principal activities, principal banks, number of employees, brand names, and trademarks. Three indexes are included—alphabetical, alphabetical by country, and alphabetical by business activity.

Twelfth edition published in 1992 by Graham & Trotman, London. Distributed in the United States and Canada by Gale Research, Inc.

Major Financial Institutions of Continental Europe 1992

More than 1,100 profiles of Europe's leading financial institutions are arranged within country chapters. Entries provide name of firm; address; telephone, telex, and FAX numbers; name of chairman; names of board members; principal business activities; and number of employees.

Fourth edition published in 1992 by Graham & Trotman, London. Distributed in the United States and Canada by Gale Research, Inc.

Medium Companies of Europe 1992–93

Publication is a three-volume directory of 7,000 of Europe's privately owned and fast-growing medium-sized firms. Volume I covers the continental European Economic Community. Volume II deals with the United Kingdom. Volume III covers Western Europe outside the European Economic Community. Each company entry includes (where available) contact data, principal activities, principal banks, number of employees, brand names, and trademarks.

Third edition published in 1992 by Graham & Trotman, London. Distributed in the United States and Canada by Gale Research, Inc.

Pan-European Associations

Alphabetical guide to more than 5,000 multinational, nongovernmental associations in Europe has entries that include full contact information, subjects of interest, activities, affiliations, membership statistics, and publications.

Second edition published in 1991 by Graham & Trotman. Distributed in the United States and Canada by Gale Research, Inc.

The Price Waterhouse European Companies Handbook

Handbook is published in three volumes: Northern Europe; Central and Southern Europe; and Eastern Europe. The information is compiled from the *Financial Times Analysis* database. Entries include company address, directors, major shareholders, and financial performance.

Published annually by Euromoney Publications PLC.

Trade Associations and Professional Bodies of the United Kingdom

Patricia Millard, editor

Directory contains information on nearly 4,000 British associations. Each entry includes a complete organizational description and full contact information. Entries are indexed geographically and by subject. *Eleventh edition published in 1993 and biennially by Gale Research, Inc.*

United Kingdom Business Finance Directory 1990

Each entry in this directory of more than 1,500 British financial institutions includes a complete organizational profile and full contact information. Entries are indexed by institution, subject area, and category of service.

Published in 1990 by Graham & Trotman. Distributed in the United States and Canada by Gale Research, Inc.

The United States–European Community Trade Directory

John S. Gordon and Timothy Harper

Directory of international business and trade resources in the United States and the European Community provides a wide range of contacts (agencies, services, institutions, and private companies) useful to importers, exporters, investors, business professionals, and corporate managers who want to do business in Europe. The first part covers resources available in the United States. The second section covers resources available on a country-by-country basis in Europe.

Published in 1993 by John Wiley & Sons, Inc.

Western European Economic Organizations

Robert Fraser, editor

Publication is a comprehensive guide to information about economic organizations in Western Europe, such as central banks, government agencies, regulatory bodies, stock exchanges, and a wide range of political, industrial, labor, academic, and campaigning organizations. Entries include full contact information, principal officers, organizational structure, funding, aims and objectives, role in national and economic policy making, history, affiliations, and publications.

Published in 1992 by Longman Group. Distributed in the United States and Canada by Gale Research, Inc.

Who Owns Whom—Continental Europe

Two-volume guide traces the structure and ownership of multinational corporate groups operating in Europe. Volume I lists parent companies in alphabetical order by company name as well as by parent companies registered outside Europe that have continental subsidiaries and/or associates. Volume II offers an alphabetical listing of subsidiaries and associates and shows their parent companies.

Published annually by Dun & Bradstreet Information Services.

Who Owns Whom—United Kingdom and Republic of Ireland

Two-volume guide traces the structure and ownership of multinational corporate groups operating in Britain and Ireland. Volume I is divided into four sections. The first and second sections list parent companies in alphabetical order by com-

pany name. The third section lists parent companies registered outside the United Kingdom and Republic of Ireland that have subsidiaries and associates operating within those countries. The final section offers details of each listing. Volume II offers an alphabetical listing of subsidiaries and associates, while also showing their parent companies.

Published annually by Dun & Bradstreet Information Services.

Who's Who in European Business

Over 3,000 biographies from nearly 30 countries, covering the chief executives and other leading executives of Europe's top companies, are presented. Profiles include career information, education, languages spoken, honors, and interests.

Published in 1992 by R. R. Bowker (Reed Reference Publishing).

FOR FURTHER INFORMATION

See *The Economist Intelligence Unit,*
   p. 520
Euro Trademark Journal, p. 439
European Accounting Guide, p. 413
*European Venture Capital Association
   (EVCA), p. 590*
*European Venture Capital Association
   (EVCA) Yearbook, p. 588*
*European Wholesalers & Distributors
   Directory, p. 469*
F & S Index Europe, p. 542
*The Handbook of International Direct
   Marketing, p. 466*
International Dun's Market Identifiers,
   p. 522
OECD Economic Outlook, p. 483
OECD Economic Surveys, p. 483
*The OECD STAN Database for
   Industrial Analysis, p. 483*
Trademarkscan®-UK, p. 440

34

THE JOB MARKET

Best Resumes for $75,000+ Executives

William Montag

Collection of techniques designed to get high-paying jobs includes 75 real-life resumes and cover letters for 50 mainstream positions, a listing of high-impact words and phrases from motivating résumés and cover letters; and examples of special skills, knowledge, and expertise.
Published in 1992 by John Wiley & Sons, Inc.

Beyond the Uniform: A Career Transition Guide for Veterans and Federal Employees

W. Dean Lee

Comprehensive job-hunting and career transition guide is especially designed for the military veteran entering civilian life. Topics include résumés, cover letters, interviews, networking, salary, and advice for family members.
Published in 1991 by John Wiley & Sons, Inc.

The Canadian Guide to Working and Living Overseas

This guide is for both entry-level job seekers and experienced professionals. It focuses on international development work, profiling over 700 government, private-sector, nongovernmental, and international organizations.
Published in 1992 by Intercultural Systems (ISSI).

Career Advisor Series

Each volume of this series offers an insider's perspective on a particular field, plus listings for hundreds of opportunities for finding entry-level positions and internships. Material in each book is divided into four parts: (1) advice from the pros, (2) job search information, (3) company listings, and (4) additional job-hunting resources. Titles include *Book Publishing Career Directory, Advertising Career Directory, Business and Finance Career Directory, Marketing and Sales Career Directory, Travel and Hospitality Career Directory, Radio and Television Career Directory, Newspapers Career Directory, Public Relations Career Directory, Magazines Career Directory,* and *Health Care Career Directory.*
Each directory published and updated periodically by Gale Research, Inc.

Career Guide to Industries

This companion to the *Occupational Outlook Handbook* (see p. 549) is prepared by the U.S. Bureau of Labor Statistics of the Department of Labor. From an industry perspective it provides information on careers in 40 diverse industries, accounting for approximately 75% of wage and salary jobs in the United States. It provides information on the nature of the industry, employment, working conditions, training, advancement, and industry outlook.
Published in 1992 by Superintendent of Documents, U.S. Government Printing Office.

CPC Annual: Who's Who in Career Planning, Placement, and Recruitment

Formerly the *College Placement Annual*, this publication lists 2,000 companies that actively recruit college graduates as well as 2,000 college placement offices. Entries include complete contact information.
Published annually by the College Placement Council.

CPC National Directory

National directory lists placement officers at corporations and university career services.
Published annually by the College Placement Council.

Directory of Executive Recruiters

Directory has listings of 3,700 offices for over 2,000 search firms in the United States, Canada, and Mexico. Each entry includes full contact information. Entries are indexed by management functions, industries, geography, and 5,800 individuals.
Twenty-second edition published in 1993 by Kennedy Publications.

The Directory of Outplacement Firms

Full-page profiles of about 250 firms are presented. Each entry includes full contact information, staff size, annual revenues, fee schedules, and names of 1,100 key principals. A 100-page overview of the outplacement industry is also included.
Seventh edition published in 1993 by Kennedy Publications.

Electronic Job Search Revolution: Win with the New Technology That's Reshaping Today's Job Market

Joyce Lain Kennedy and Thomas J. Morrow

This book provides an overview on how to use electronic technology to conduct a job search. It provides information on computer résumé databases by showing how they work, what they cost, and where they're located. It also looks at applicant tracking software, electronic recruitment ads, and computer-assisted interviewing. A companion volume is *Electronic Resume Revolution* by the same authors. It shows how to prepare a résumé that will be scannable by computers.
Both books published in 1994 by John Wiley & Sons.

Executive Employment Guide

Annual listing of approximately 100 employment agencies and executive search firms has entries that include complete contact information.
Published annually by the American Management Association.

Executive Recruiters of North America

Christopher W. Hunt and Scott A. Scanlon, editors

The directory contains information about approximately 350 executive recruiters in North America and Mexico. It covers both generalist recruiters as well as specialists in a wide variety of industries. Each listing contains contact information and a profile of the firm.
Published in 1993 by Hunt Scanlon Publishing.

The Hidden Job Market: A Job Seeker's Guide to America's 2,000 Little Known but Fastest-Growing High Tech Companies

This book is a guide to jobs with small, but fast-growing, high-tech companies. Many industries are covered, including environmental, consulting, genetic engineering, energy, telecommunications, online services, and educational and training software.
Published annually by Peterson's.

The Job Bank Series

Each book in this series of 18 books covers a major United States job market. Each book covers a city or business region and provides company listings by industry, an assessment of the economic outlook for the area, and contact information for professional associations, chambers of commerce, and executive search and job placement agencies. Current titles in the series cover the following cities/regions: Atlanta, Boston, Chicago, Dallas/Fort Worth, Denver, Detroit, Florida, Houston, Los Angeles, Minneapolis/St. Paul, New York, Ohio, Philadelphia, Phoenix, San Francisco Bay area, Seattle, St. Louis, and Metro Washington, DC.
Each title is published and updated periodically by Bob Adams, Inc.

Job Hunter's Sourcebook: Where to Find Employment Leads and Other Job Search Resources

Michelle LeCompte, editor

🔲 Each listing within these 155 professional and occupational profiles includes full contact information and descriptions of employment leads, including sources of help-wanted ads, such as journals, newsletters, and online services; placement and job referral services of professional associations; employer directories and networking lists; handbooks and manuals; employment agencies, search firms, and job hotlines; internships; and salary surveys. The *Job Hunter's Sourcebook* is available in print, on computer disk, and on magnetic tape.
Published in 1991 by Gale Research, Inc.

Job Seeker's Guide to Private and Public Companies

Charity Anne Dorgan and Jennifer Mast, editors

🔲 Four-volume set describes the employment opportunities available in a variety of public and private companies. Information includes company benefits, corporate affiliations, and human resources contacts. The guide is available in print, on computer diskette, and on magnetic tape.
Published in 1992 by Gale Research, Inc.

Launching a Business Career: Tips and Secrets on Finding the Ideal First Job

Richard Fein

Comprehensive guide outlines proven job-hunting strategies. Topics include step-by-step advice on structuring a persuasive resume, mistakes to avoid, and salary negotiation.
Published in 1992 by John Wiley & Sons, Inc.

National Business Employment Weekly

Publication is a weekly compilation of all recruitment advertising from the regional editions of the *Wall Street Journal* plus editorial information and articles on job search strategies and career guidance.
Published weekly by Dow Jones & Co.

Occupational Outlook Handbook 1992–1993

This reference book is produced by the U.S. Bureau of Labor Statistics of the Department of Labor. It describes about 250 occupations in detail, covering 107 million jobs. Each occupation includes the following information: the nature of the work; working conditions; how many jobs the occupation provided in 1990; training, qualifications needed and opportunities for advancement; job outlook; factors that will affect employment through the year 2005; how much people in this occupation generally earn; and sources of additional information.
Published in 1992 by the U.S. Government Printing Office

Peterson's Job Opportunities for Engineering, Science, and Computer Graduates

Each guide profiles companies hiring both entry-level people and experienced professionals. Complete contact information for each company is provided.
Published annually by Peterson's.

Professional Careers Sourcebook, Second Edition

Sourcebook includes profiles of 110 professional careers. Each profile has information on general career guides, professional associations, standards and certification agencies, directories of educational programs, handbooks related to the profession, and professional periodicals.
Published in 1991 by Gale Research, Inc.

Researching Your Way to a Good Job

Karmen Crowther

This comprehensive guide to doing research as an integral part of the job hunt includes topics like investigating a company's background, products and services, current financial situation, and management style; incorporating advance knowledge into a persuasive resume and cover letter; and the various types of informational material available.
Published in 1993 by John Wiley & Sons, Inc.

What Color is Your Parachute?

Richard N. Bolles

A career self-help guide, this book provides a systematic approach on finding a job or a career that is right for each person, as well as advice on how to handle the process psychologically.
First published in 1970 and updated annually by Ten Speed Press.

Worldwide Guide: The Only Guide to Global Job Opportunities

This guide profiles approximately 250 international companies hiring people at all levels, from entry-level to experienced professionals. Profiles contain background information about the company and provide complete contact information.
Published annually by Peterson's.

35

LABOR AND EMPLOYMENT LAW

Affirmative Action Compliance Manual for Federal Contractors

Monthly loose-leaf service provides summaries of the latest court rulings, regulatory activity, and congressional actions dealing with affirmative action. The service also provides a comprehensive reference manual containing actual internal policy instructions used by the Office of Federal Contract Compliance Programs.
Updated monthly by Bureau of National Affairs, Inc.

BNA Employee Relations Weekly

Weekly service offers complete coverage and broad perspective on every aspect of employee relations. Topics covered include substance abuse testing, employee privacy rights, child care and elder care benefits, early retirement, health care cost containment, and pay equity.
Published weekly by Bureau of National Affairs, Inc.

Complying with the ADA: A Small Business Guide to Hiring and Employing the Disabled

Jeffrey G. Allen

This text is a comprehensive guide for owners and managers of small businesses to the Americans with Disabilities Act. It covers recruitment, interviewing, testing, compensation, training, and other issues involved in hiring the disabled and offers guidelines for accessibility under the concept of *reasonable accommodation*.
Published in 1993 by John Wiley & Sons, Inc.

Drafting and Revising Employment Contracts

Kurt H. Decker and H. Thomas Felix

Employer's guide to the legal aspects of employment contracts covers all of the general legal principles for forming, drafting, and implementing employment contracts. Employment contracts clauses are examined in both general and specialized terms. The book contains actual sample clauses involving compensation, restrictive covenants, alternate dispute resolution mechanisms, and legal issues that arise over employee termination as well as complete contract examples involving various occupations, professions, and employers.
Published in 1991, with a 1992 supplement, by John Wiley & Sons, Inc.

EEOC Compliance Manual

Loose-leaf service offers advance notice of possible regulatory changes, key EEOC activities, and new employment testing guidelines. EEOC notices are distributed as soon as they are issued, covering such topics as age discrimination, equal pay processing procedures, and issuing notices of right to sue.
Updated periodically by Bureau of National Affairs, Inc.

The Employee Handbook: A Complete Ready-to-Use Model with Sample Policies and Procedures

Richard T. Egbert

This comprehensive guide to the creation or revision of an employee handbook

comes with ready-to-use policies and procedures that can be tailored to specific needs or situations.
Published in 1990 by Prentice Hall, Inc.

Employer's Guide to the Americans with Disabilities Act

James G. Frierson

A comprehensive guide to the ADA, the book clarifies the changes needed to comply with the act, defines controversial terms such as *disabled* and *qualified,* and outlines policies that both accommodate employees and avoid liability.
Published in 1992 by John Wiley & Sons, Inc.

Employment Guide

Loose-leaf service covers a wide range of company policy issues, including hiring, retirement, safety and health, wages and salaries, dealing with unions, employee benefits, rules and discipline, and employment laws and regulations. Model forms and checklists and ready-to-use policies are included.
Updated regularly, with a biweekly news service, by Bureau of National Affairs, Inc.

Employment Law Deskbook

The law firm of Shawe and Rosenthal

Comprehensive loose-leaf reference covers every stage of the employer/employee relationship, from the initial employment application through termination. Features include practical charts, checklists, tables, and sample forms. A state-by-state summary of key employment-related statutes is included.
Published in 1989, and updated with annual revisions, by Matthew Bender and Company.

Fair Employment Practices

Loose-leaf guide, issued weekly since 1969, to equal employment opportunity laws, policies, programs, and rules covers federal and state laws and regulations (full text), regulated actions, court decisions (full text), EEOC rulings (full text), recordkeeping and reporting, and company and union practices.
Published weekly by Bureau of National Affairs, Inc.

A Handbook for Grievance Arbitration

Arnold M. Zack

This comprehensive guide prepares arbitrators and representatives of unions and management for arbitration. The text is arranged chronologically, beginning with advice on avoiding arbitration, progressing to arrangements for the hearing, then covering the hearing itself, and concluding with the decision.
Published in 1992 by Lexington Books.

Individual Employment Rights

Loose-leaf service offers the full text of major decisions from around the country involving employment rights issues outside the traditional labor-management relations context, such as invasion of privacy; wrongful discharge; lie detector testing; defamation; AIDS, drug, and alcohol testing; employment at will; and performance appraisal.
Published biweekly by Bureau of National Affairs, Inc.

Labor Arbitration Reports

Loose-leaf service covers the latest awards and settlements in every type of labor dispute, including rulings by arbitrators, boards, and fact-finding bodies; arbitrator's interpretations of contract terms; and

practices and procedures. Issues covered include drug and alcohol testing, absenteeism, sexual harassment, discipline and discharge, seniority, pay, benefits, and overtime.
Published weekly by Bureau of National Affairs, Inc.

Labor Law

Theodore W. Kheel

This 11-volume publication is a loose-leaf guide to all aspects of management relations. Topics include Taft-Hartley Act, Labor-Management Reporting and Disclosure Act, rights of individual employees, union representation of employees, economic coercion by management and labor, federal wage and hour laws, discrimination, sexual harassment, Railway Labor Act, and ERISA. *Labor Law* also includes the monthly *Labor and Employment Law Newsletter,* prepared by the New York law firm of Kaye, Scholer, Fierman, Hays & Handler.
Published in 1973, and updated with supplements and replacement pages four times yearly, by Matthew Bender and Company.

Labor Law Developments

Carol Holgren, editor

Papers presented at the Southwestern Legal Foundation Labor Law Institute by outstanding practitioners, labor law professors, and NLRB members appear annually.
Published annually since 1967 by Matthew Bender and Company.

Labor Law Reports

This 16 volume loose-leaf reference set covers the latest legal developments in management/labor relations. Topics addressed include labor relations, employ-

ment practices, wages and hours, and state labor laws.
Updated weekly by Commerce Clearing House, Inc.

The Law of the Workplace: Rights of Employers and Employees

James Hunt

Text is a basic resource on state and federal labor statutes, rules, and regulations, and the agencies that administer and enforce them. The book explains laws governing work eligibility, plant closings, bankruptcy, medical insurance, maternity leave, and affirmative action programs. Main chapters also address hiring and firing, workplace privacy, collective bargaining, and pensions.
Second edition published in 1988 by Bureau of National Affairs, Inc.

Managing ADA: The Complete Compliance Guide

Robert A. Naeve and Art Cowan

A how-to-comply guide to the 1990 Americans with Disabilities Act, *Managing ADA* includes the full text of the Act, lists of resources, checklists, flowcharts, analysis, and interpretation of the legislation. It discusses types of employers and facilities affected; employment, accommodation, and public service requirements; and how to adjust employment policies and procedures to comply.
Published in 1992 and supplemented annually by John Wiley & Sons, Inc.

Primer on Equal Employment Opportunity, Fifth Edition

Nancy Sedmak and Michael D. Levin-Epstein

An introduction to federal fair-employment practices, the primer covers sexual harass-

ment; affirmative action; and discrimination based on age, sex, national origin, and religion. Materials on the Immigration Reform and Control Act, the Americans with Disabilities Act, legislation enacted in response to the Supreme Court decision on pensions, and the Age Discrimination in Employment Act are also included.
Fifth edition published in 1991 by Bureau of National Affairs, Inc.

Primer on Individual Employee Rights

Alfred G. Feliu

A comprehensive guide to the expanding field of employee rights, the primer covers relevant employee rights legislation, contract rights, hiring procedures, employees' rights to information, employee testing, lifestyle and privacy issues, negligence claims, and public policy issues.
Published in 1992 by Bureau of National Affairs, Inc.

Primer of Labor Relations, Twenty-fourth Edition

John J. Kenny and Linda G. Kahn

A survey of federal labor regulation and policy, this volume explains the three major statutes—the Wagner Act (National Labor Relations Act), Taft-Hartley Act (Labor-Management Relations Act), and Landrum-Griffin Act—as well as other important laws, as they have been interpreted by courts and the national Labor Relations Board.
Twenty-fourth edition published in 1989 by Bureau of National Affairs, Inc.

Primer on Occupational Safety and Health

Fred Blosser

Comprehensive, nontechnical introduction to occupational safety and health laws includes topics such as federal and state requirements of OSHA, performance and specification standards, the standard-setting process, standards enforcement, the rights and responsibilities of employees and employers under OSHA, recordkeeping requirements, and antidiscrimination provisions.
Published in 1992 by Bureau of National Affairs, Inc.

Primer on Wage and Hour Laws, Second Edition

Joseph E. Kalet

This collection of concise, expert discussions of basic federal wage and hour requirements highlights the 1989 amendments to the Fair Labor Standards Act and reviews such issues as compensatory time eligibility, retaliations, "regular" versus collectively bargained rates of pay, "willful" violations, statutes of limitations, recordkeeping, enforcement, damages, and penalties.
Second edition published in 1990 by Bureau of National Affairs, Inc.

Primer on Workers' Compensation, Second Edition

Jeffrey V. Nackley

Comprehensive outline of the laws governing job-related injuries, accidents, and diseases addresses topics like work-related stress, partial disability, federal preemption, settlements, and rehabilitation. Also included is a state-by-state summary of laws, scheduled injuries, and workers' compensation agencies.
Second edition published in 1989 by Bureau of National Affairs, Inc.

Sexual Harassment in Employment Law

Barbara Lindemann and David D. Kadue

Text is an in-depth study of the law surrounding sexual harassment. Topics in-

clude specific details from recent cases, plus theories on harassment including *quid pro quo*, hostile environment, and harassment by supervisors, co-workers, and nonemployees.
Published in 1992 by Bureau of National Affairs, Inc.

Stay Out of Court: The Manager's Guide to Preventing Employee Lawsuits

Rita Risser

Comprehensive guide to employment law is designed to give managers the tools to prevent employee lawsuits. The text addresses every potential trouble area in employee relations, including discrimination, harassment, wrongful termination, drug testing, and references. Specific coverage is given to dismissing employees without being sued, preventing sexual harassment, illegal questions to avoid in interviews, writing disciplinary warnings, and counseling troubled employees.
Published in 1993 by Prentice Hall, Inc.

U.S. Labor and Employment Laws, 1991 Edition

Ruth Clarke West, editor

This one-volume reference contains all of the constitutional provisions and major federal laws governing employment in both the private and public sector. Topics include federal sector labor relations, constitutional provisions, antitrust, labor-management relations, fair employment practices, veterans' employment and training, wage-hour laws, and alien employment.
Published in 1991 by Bureau of National Affairs, Inc.

Your Rights at Work, Second Edition

Darien A. McWhirter

A comprehensive guide to employment law, *Your Rights at Work* covers recent de-

velopments, such as the 1991 Civil Rights Bill, the new definition of sexual harassment, new laws on age and handicap discrimination, and numerous changes in the law on privacy in the workplace, including the Polygraph Protection Act. Also included are state-by-state checklists showing how different states interpret employee rights and obligations.
Published in 1992 by John Wiley & Sons, Inc.

Your Rights in the Workplace

Dan Lacey

Comprehensive guide to employee workplace rights includes topics like illegal firing and layoffs; wages and overtime; maternity and parental leave; unemployment and disability insurance; workers' compensation; job safety; and sex, race, and age discrimination.
Published in 1991 by NoLo Press.

GOVERNMENT AGENCIES

Equal Employment Opportunity Commission (EEOC)

The EEOC acts on charges of job discrimination under: Title VII of the Civil Rights Act of 1964 prohibiting discrimination by employers based on race, color, religion, sex, or national origin; the Americans with Disabilities Act of 1990; the Equal Pay Act of 1963; and the Age Discrimination in Employment Act of 1967.
Equal Employment Opportunity Commission, 1800 G Street NW, Washington, DC 20506. Tel. 1-800-USA-EEOC

National Labor Relations Board (NLRB)

The NLRB is charged with preventing and remedying unfair labor practices by employers and labor organizations and conducting secret ballot elections in union representation elections.

National Labor Relations Board, 1717 Pennsylvania Avenue NW, Washington, DC 20570. Tel. (202) 254-8064.

U.S. Department of Labor

The Department of Labor is a rich source of information on the latest developments in labor law and relations. Key offices within the department include the Employment and Training Administration; Bureau of Labor-Management Relations and Cooperative Programs; Pension and Welfare Benefits Administration; Bureau of Labor Statistics (which publishes a helpful telephone directory that lists the bureau's experts and their areas of expertise); Office of Productivity and Technology; Occupational Safety and Health Administration; Assistant Secretary for Veterans' Employment Training; and the Women's Bureau.

Department of Labor, 200 Constitution Avenue NW, Washington DC 20210. Tel. (main number) (202) 523-6666; (public affairs) (202) 523-7316.

Note: In addition to these federal agencies, most states have a State Labor Department and a State Human Rights Commission that also enforce labor and employment laws and provide a wealth of free information.

For Further Information

See *Guide to Employee Handbooks,*
 p. 517
Personnel Director's Legal Guide, p. 518

36

MANAGING A COMPANY

Bass and Stogdhill's Handbook of Leadership: Theory, Research, and Managerial Application

Bernard M. Bass. and Ralph M. Stogdhill

Text is a comprehensive and authoritative presentation of the theories and models of leadership in organizations.
Second edition published in 1990 by The Free Press.

The Change Masters: Innovation and Entrepreneurship in the American Corporation

Rosabeth Moss Kanter

Publication is an influential and extremely interesting analysis on how individuals can gauge change in their organizations.
Second edition published in 1983 by Simon and Schuster.

Corporate Culture and Performance

John P. Kotter and James L. Heskett

Authors analyze how the culture of an organization influences its economic performance, using extensive case studies from companies like Hewlett-Packard, Xerox, and Nissan in their analysis.
Published in 1992 by The Free Press.

Influence without Authority

Allan R. Cohen and David L. Bradford

The authors employ many interesting and useful case studies to show how to influ-
ence people at work over whom you have no authority. Highly useful book at a time when many companies are trying to do away with rigid hierarchical structures.
Published in 1989 by John Wiley & Sons, Inc.

Intelligent Enterprise: A Knowledge and Service Based Paradigm for Industry

James Brian Quinn

This book is an analysis of how technology revolutionizes a company's strategy and services. The author shows that companies will derive competitive advantage from knowledge of a few highly developed core service skills.
Published in 1992 by The Free Press.

Managing across Borders: The Transnational Solution

Christopher Bartlett and Sumantra Ghoshal

This book shows how to manage companies in today's global business environment, including how to develop organizational structures, administrative processes, and management perspectives.
Published in 1989 by Harvard Business School Press.

Managing for Excellence: The Guide to Developing High Performance in Contemporary Organizations

David L. Bradford and Allan R. Cohen

This book, directed at middle managers, provides the useful concept of the *man-*

ager as developer. The authors show how managers can foster the growth and development of their subordinates.
Published in 1984 by John Wiley & Sons, Inc.

Managing with Power: Politics and Influence in Organizations

Jeffrey Pfeffer

Pfeffer, a professor at the Stanford Business School, shows that effective use of power is an important aspect of effective leadership. He presents an effective analysis of power and politics at the organizational level.
Published in 1992 by Harvard Business School Press.

The Portable MBA in Management

Allan R. Cohen, editor

This book covers a broad array of important management topics, including building a vision, creating teams, power and influence, organizational change, strategic negotiating, and managing diversity. Each chapter is written by a leading person in the field.
Published in 1993 by John Wiley & Sons, Inc.

TRADE AND PROFESSIONAL ASSOCIATIONS

America Management Association

Association membership includes managers in industry, commerce, government, and nonprofit organizations, as well as university teachers of management. Its purpose is to increase knowledge and skills in management areas. The association maintains an extensive library and conducts the Management Information Service, which provides films, cassettes, tapes, and records covering all areas of management studies and expertise. Publications include *Management Review,* a monthly magazine specializing in management trends and techniques, and *Compensation and Benefits Review,* a bimonthly journal.
American Management Association, 135 West 50th Street, New York, NY 10020-1201. Tel. (212) 586-8100.

The Conference Board

The Conference Board is an organization that strives to help senior executives explore and exchange ideas that have an impact on business and society. It has a professionally managed research program that reports on a variety of issues including corporate governance, compensation, quality and productivity, the work force, global leadership, economics, and business and education.
The Conference Board, 845 Third Avenue, New York, NY 10022. Tel. (212) 759-0900 or (toll-free) 1-800-872-6273. FAX. (212) 980-7014.

FOR FURTHER INFORMATION

See **Building the Competitive Workforce: Investing in Human Capital for Corporate Success,** p. 516
Globalizing Management: Creating and Leading the Competitive Organization, p. 517
Managing Workforce 2000: Gaining the Diversity Advantage, p. 518
Organizational Capability: Competing from the Inside Out, p. 518
Strategic Benchmarking: How to Rate Your Company's Performance Against the World's Best, p. 424

37

MANUFACTURING AND QUALITY

The Baldrige Quality System: The Do-It-Yourself Way to Transform Your Business

Stephen George

Explains how to use the Malcolm Baldrige National Quality Award to manage quality in an organization by using the Baldrige criteria to measure and evaluate quality.
Published in 1992 by John Wiley & Sons, Inc.

Corporate Quality Universities: Lessons Learned from Programs That Produce Results

Jeanne C. Meister

Detailed study assesses quality training programs, such as Motorola University, that return employees to the corporate classroom for lessons in quality and continuous improvement.
Published in 1993 by Business One Irwin.

Delivering Quality Service: Balancing Customer Perceptions and Expectations

Valarie A. Zeithaml, A. Parasuraman, and Leonard L. Barry

This book provides a model on service quality that shows how to balance a customer's perception of the value of a service with the customer's need for that service.
Published in 1990 by The Free Press.

The Deming Management Method

Mary Walton

This book explains and applies the principles of W. Edwards Deming. The author analyzes Deming's "14 Points for Managers" and "Deadly Diseases of Management."
Published in 1986 by the Putnam Publishing Group.

Juran on Quality by Design

J. M. Juran

This comprehensive guide to planning, setting, and reaching quality goals employs three case examples that encompass the three major sectors of the economy—service, manufacturing, and support. The text offers a practical plan for companies to achieve strategic, market-driven goals by following a structured approach to planning quality.
Published in 1992 by The Free Press.

Out of the Crisis

W. Edwards Deming

W. Edwards Deming is America's quality guru, and this book presents his philosophy on how the style of American management has to be transformed.
Published in 1986 by Massachusetts Institute of Technology, Center for Advanced Engineering Study.

Reinventing the Factory: Productivity Breakthroughs in Manufacturing Today

Roy L. Harmon and Leroy D. Peterson

Providing the latest thinking on the concepts that are reinventing manufacturing, this text looks at the focused factory—the organization of existing plants into multiple, smaller "factories within a factory." *Published in 1990 by The Free Press.*

Thomas Register of American Manufacturers

🔲 This comprehensive (26-volume) guide to the products, services, catalogs, trademarks, and shipping services of American manufacturing companies enables users to locate the companies supplying products and services; shows how to get catalogs, capabilities brochures, and detailed shipping information; provides profiles of over 150,000 U.S. companies, provides trademarks, brand names, and names and addresses of owners. Also available online through DIALOG as *Thomas Register Online.*
Published annually by Thomas International Publishing Company, Inc.

Total Quality Control, Third Edition, Revised

Armand V. Feigenbaum

Text is a comprehensive, authoritative handbook on using quality to manage an organization.
Published in 1991 by McGraw-Hill, Inc.

GOVERNMENT AGENCY

National Technical Information Service (NTIS)

NTIS and the Federal Quality Institute have established a central clearinghouse for total quality management and have available both a free brochure (Publication number PR–894) and a free bibliography (Publication number PR–868).
National Technical Information Service, 5285 Port Royal Road, Springfield, VA 22161. Tel. (703) 487-4650.

TRADE AND PROFESSIONAL ASSOCIATIONS

American Society for Quality Control (ASQC)

ASQC is a large and diverse professional organization, with more than 200 local chapters, 19 divisions, and 7 technical committees. Membership includes subscription to *Quality in Progress*, a monthly magazine, and *On Q*, a newsletter.
American Society for Quality Control, P.O. Box 3066, Milwaukee, WI 53201-3066. Tel. 1-800-248-1946 or (414) 272-8575. FAX (414) 272-1734.

National Association of Manufacturers (NAM)

Association channels the views of manufacturers on public policy to the White House, federal agencies, and congress. NAM provides telephone assistance for members with questions about specific issues and concerns relating to their field. Publications include *America's Workforce in the 1990's: Trends Affecting Manufacturers; 1992 Association Council Directory,* which lists more than 160 manufacturing trade associations; and others.
National Association of Manufacturers (Washington Headquarters), 1331 Pennsylvania Avenue NW, Suite 1500 North Lobby, Washington, DC 20004-1703. Tel. (202) 637-3000.

FOR FURTHER INFORMATION
*See **Guide to Canadian Manufacturers**, p. 450*
Manufacturing USA, p. 450
National Technical Information Service/ Federal Government Electronic Bulletin Boards, p. 511
Statistical Abstract of the United States, p. 406

38

MERGERS AND ACQUISITIONS

Acquisitions, Mergers, Sales, Buyouts, and Takeovers

Charles A. Scharf, Edward E. Shea, and George C. Beck

Comprehensive guide provides detailed and practical information on leveraged buyouts, financial valuation methods, technology licensing, government rules, and joint ventures.
Fourth edition published in 1991 by Prentice Hall, Inc.

The Acquisitions Yearbook

Edward E. Shea

Comprehensive yearbook reviews the past year's developments in the field of mergers and acquisitions. Topics include financial valuation methods, government regulations, and joint ventures.
Published annually by Prentice Hall, Inc.

The Art of M & A: A Merger/Acquisition/Buyout Guide

Stanley Foster Reed

Comprehensive guide covers issues and developments in the field of mergers and acquisitions, such as strategic alliances; international issues involving opportunities in (the former) Eastern Bloc countries; and turnarounds, bankruptcies, and restructuring
Second edition published in 1993 by Business One Irwin.

Business Organizations: Corporate Acquisitions and Mergers

Byron E. Fox and Eleanor M. Fox

Text is a four-volume guide to the antitrust, corporate securities, and financial aspects of mergers and acquisitions. *Published in looseleaf and updated periodically with supplements and revisions by Matthew Bender and Company.*

Buyouts Newsletter

Newsletter reports on current developments in the field of mergers and acquisitions. Coverage includes developments in fund formations, leveraged acquisitions, and all types of special situations.
Published biweekly by Securities Data Company Publishing.

Directory of Buyout Financing Sources

Information is presented on hundreds of sources of equity, mezzanine and debt financing for leveraged buyouts, leveraged acquisitions, recapitalizations, restructuring, and other transactions. Entries for each firm cover its investment or lending criteria, key contacts, preferred deal sizes and types, and services offered.
Published annually by Securities Data Company Publishing.

Directory of M & A Intermediaries

Each entry in this collection of in-depth profiles of over 500 investment banks, business brokers, and other dealmakers includes information on services offered, fees charged, geographic/industry focus, and preferred transaction size.
Published annually by Securities Data Company Publishing.

M & A Filings Database

■ Database contains detailed abstracts of every original and amended mergers and acquisitions document released by the Securities and Exchange Commission since early 1985. Users are provided with an array of M & A transaction information on publicly traded companies, including company name, SIC code, ticker symbol, CUSIP number, and other vital information. Available online through WESTLAW and DIALOG.
Updated daily by Charles E. Simon & Co.

Managing Acquisitions: Creating Value through Corporate Renewal

Philippe C. Haspeslagh and David B. Jemison

This book provides managers with a different perspective on the mergers and acquisitions process. In the authors' opinion, the traditional view of corporate acquisitions, which looks only at pre-acquisition strategic fit, addresses only the potential for creation. The authors maintain that real value is created after the acquisition through managerial actions, not financial engineering.
Published in 1991 by The Free Press.

Mergers & Acquisitions

Ernst & Young

Text is a complete back-to-the-basics guide to structuring, financing, and integrating a merger or acquisition. Topics include restructuring financially troubled companies, niche acquisitions, international mergers and cross-border alliances; and partial buy-ins.
Second edition published in 1992 by John Wiley & Sons, Inc.

Mergers and Acquisitions Manual

Simon Partner

Step-by-step guide to mergers and acquisitions incorporates ready-to-use forms, contracts, letters, and documents that can be used when buying, selling, or defending a company.
Published in 1991 by Prentice Hall, Inc.

Mergers and Acquisitions Sourcebook

Text is an annual guide to M & A activity of the previous year.
Published annually by Quality Services Company.

Mergers & Corporate Policy

Newsletter reports on the most recent developments in the field of mergers and acquisitions. Coverage includes developing deals and acquisition strategies; conditions in the junk bond and distressed credit markets; trends in commercial bank lending; legal and legislative developments; and full details on proposed, completed, and withdrawn mergers, acquisitions, and divestitures.
Published weekly by Securities Data Company Publishing.

The Merger Yearbook

Text covers deals that were announced, completed, or withdrawn in the previous year, including corporate acquisitions, mergers, divestitures, and leveraged buyouts. Complete information on every transaction in every major industry sector is given, including facts on parent companies, prior owners, prices, and types of payment. The yearbook is organized by Standard Industry Classification (SIC). *Published annually by SDC Publishing.*

FOR FURTHER INFORMATION

See ***Corporate Finance Sourcebook 1992,*** *p. 588*

Predicasts' F & S Index of Corporate Change, *p. 451*

39

NEW PRODUCT DEVELOPMENT

Compressing the Product Development Cycle

Bernard N. Slade

This guide to developing and implementing a faster new product development process analyzes the principal reasons for America's long development cycles, explores the factors that drive the product cycle, and proposes practical steps to shorten the product's path to market.
Published in 1992 by AMACOM.

How to Bring a Product to Market for Less Than $5,000

Don Debelak

Step-by-step guide to getting a product to market for the smallest possible investment includes topics like setting up a product flow chart, predetermining manufacturing costs, and reducing expenses.
Published in 1991 by John Wiley & Sons, Inc.

New Product Development Checklists

George Gruenwald

Collection of proven, ready-to-use checklists for developing new products from

mission to market allows managers to assign responsibilities, review and evaluate progress, and make go/no go decisions.
Published in 1991 by NTC Publishing Group.

New Product Development: Managing and Forecasting for Strategic Success

Robert J. Thomas

This book analyzes the strategic nature of new product development and shows both how to manage the process and use forecasting tools to achieve company targets. It provides in-depth material on forecasting market opportunity, estimating sales and profits, entering markets, and tracking a new product's launch. Spreadsheet models are also provided.
Published in 1993 by John Wiley & Sons, Inc.

New Product Development Planner

Jeannemarie Caris-McManus

Publication is a loose-leaf guide to the development, testing, and commercialization of new products.
Published in 1991 by AMACOM.

Profiting from Innovation

William G. Howard, Jr. and Bruce R. Guile

Nuts-and-bolts handbook demonstrates how managing technical resources and innovations is key to business success. Topics include using project teams for commercialization, managing quality, integrating systems, and knowing when to quit.
Published in 1991 by The Free Press.

PTS New Product Announcements Plus®

▪ This online database provides the full text of news releases by organizations in both manufacturing and service industries. The news releases provide information on new product introduction, new technologies, licenses, and joint ventures. Available online from Datastar and DIALOG.
Updated weekly by Information Access Company/Predicasts.

Revolutionizing New Product Development

Steven C. Wheelright and Kim B. Clark

This book on product development shows how leading companies use cutting-edge principles to bring high-quality products to market faster than the competition. The companies used as examples include Honda, Compaq, Applied Materials, Sony, and The Limited. The authors show how these companies used innovative practices such as design for manufacturability, quality function deployment, computer-aided design, and computer-aided manufacturability.
Published in 1992 by The Free Press.

For Further Information

See ***A Directory of Strategic Management Software Tools, p. 581***
PTS PROMPT: ™ ***Overview of Markets and Technology, p. 406***

40

REAL ESTATE

The Arnold Encyclopedia of Real Estate, Second Edition

Alvin L. Arnold

This authoritative work provides definitions and explanations of terms and expressions used in the practice of real estate, including legal and banking terms as they relate to real estate.
Published in 1993 by John Wiley & Sons, Inc.

Commercial Real Estate Leases: Preparation and Negotiation

Mark A. Senn

This two-volume set is for real estate professionals needing information and guidance on how to structure sound, workable leases for commercial office space, shipping centers, or single-tenant properties. The first volume is a legal analysis of the lease, and the second volume consists of forms that have been used successfully in thousands of leases.
Published in 1990, and supplemented in 1992, by John Wiley & Sons, Inc.

Directory of Foreign Investment in the U.S.: Real Estate and Businesses

Nancy Garman, editor

This directory lists more than 11,000 real estate properties and businesses that are wholly or partly owned (at least 10 percent) by foreign investors. Entries are arranged in two sections. Section I—Real Estate—is arranged alphabetically by city within each of the United States and provides details on foreign real es-

tate investments. Each entry includes foreign owner's name and country; property name, address, and telephone number; property description; purchase date and price; and seller. Section II—Businesses—lists foreign-owned manufacturing, service, retail, wholesale, and import/export firms in the United States.
First edition published in 1991 by Gale Research, Inc.

Finance, Insurance & Real Estate USA

Arsen J. Darnay, editor

This publication is a collection of statistical profiles and listings of leading companies involved in the finance, insurance, and real estate industries, including mortgage bankers and brokers; foreign trade and international banks; savings and loan institutions; securities and commodities brokers and services; insurance carriers, agents, and brokers; and real estate firms. Each entry offers detailed profiles that include statistics on selected assets and liabilities, inputs/outputs, revenues, occupations, employment, and state and regional data.
Published in 1992 by Gale Research, Inc.

Foreign Investment in United States Real Estate

Jeremy D. Smith

This comprehensive guide to real estate investment in the United States includes the legal, financial, and tax aspects of acquiring property. Topics include protecting against U.S. tax liability, exchanging risk losses, and the impact of U.S. immigration law on real estate transactions. *Published in 1992 by John Wiley & Sons, Inc.*

Limited Partnerships: How to Profit in the Secondary Market

Richard Wallack and Brent R. Donaldson

The secondary trading of real estate limited partnership interests is an underdeveloped market that is growing. This book provides one of the best explanations available on how this market works and how to make money in it. *Published in 1992 by Dearborn Trade.*

Managing and Leasing Residential Properties

Paul Lapides

This book presents the basic tools necessary for successful residential management. It includes guidance for setting policies, procedures for implementing policies, and forms. *Published in 1992, and supplemented annually, by John Wiley & Sons, Inc.*

The McGraw-Hill Real Estate Handbook, Second Edition

Robert Irwin, Editor in Chief

This encyclopedia of real estate covers residential, commercial, office, and industrial properties and row land. It looks at current finance, investment, and tax issues; the best financing methods; property management; and computerized investment analysis. *Published in 1993 by McGraw-Hill, Inc.*

Modern Real Estate Practice Series

Each volume of this series of books covers real estate practices in specific states.

Coverage includes topics such as real estate law, financing, and fair housing. Books in the series include the following: Arizona, Alabama, Connecticut, Idaho, Illinois, Maryland, Massachusetts, Minnesota, New Hampshire, New York, Pennsylvania, Ohio, Virginia, and Wisconsin. *Each book is updated periodically by Dearborn Trade.*

Negotiating Real Estate Transactions

Mark A. Senn, editor

Hands-on guide to all kinds of real estate contracts, financial arrangements, letters, agreements, and leases includes comprehensive material on contracts for purchase and sale, construction, real estate finance, opinion letters, and environmental issues in real estate transactions. *Published in 1988, and supplemented annually, by John Wiley & Sons, Inc.*

The Real Estate Directory of Major Investors, Developers, and Brokers 1992

Comprehensive guide to major real estate companies (portfolios of $1 million and over) profiles more than 4,100 firms and 7,600 executives. *Published in 1992 by National Register Publishing (Reed Reference Publishing).*

Real Estate Limited Partnerships

Theodore S. Lynn, Harry F. Goldberg, and Michael Hirshfeld

Overview of the organization, structure, and ongoing operating consequences of private real estate limited partnerships addresses topics like passive loss limitation, at-risk rules, and bankrupt partnerships. *Published in 1991 by John Wiley & Sons, Inc.*

Structuring Real Estate Joint Ventures

Robert Bell

Guide to structuring and managing real estate joint ventures includes topics like The Uniform Partnership Act; financial instruments such as participating mortgages and leases; and international investment. *Published in 1991 by John Wiley & Sons, Inc.*

Uniform Standards of Professional Appraisal Practice: Applying the Standards

Dennis S. Tosh and William B. Ragburn

This book provides coverage of The Appraisal Foundation's standards including appraising, reporting, and reviewing personal property and business valuation. *Published in 1992 by Dearborn Trade.*

TRADE AND PROFESSIONAL ASSOCIATION

National Association of Realtors (NAR)

The NAR is a federation of 50 state associations and 1,848 local real estate boards. It promotes education, high professional standards, and modern techniques in specialized real estate work such as brokerage, appraisal, property management, and land development. It also conducts research programs and maintains a library on subjects relating to real estate areas. *National Association of Realtors, 430 N. Michigan Avenue, Chicago, IL 60611-4087. Tel. (312) 329-8200.*

FOR FURTHER INFORMATION

*See **ABI/INFORM®**, p. 400*

41

RESEARCH AND DEVELOPMENT

Directory of American Research and Technology

This annual directory lists over 11,000 U.S. and Canadian corporate facilities active in commercially-applicable basic or applied research and includes key personnel, complete contact information, staff size, and research activities. The directory is available in print, online, on CD-ROM, and on magnetic tape. Available online through ORBIT Search Service.
Published annually by R. R. Bowker (Reed Reference Publishing).

Government Research Directory

Thomas J. Cichonski, editor

This directory of more than 3,700 research facilities and programs of the U.S. government lists research facilities operated by the federal government, contractor-operated facilities, user-operated facilities supported by the federal government, government-supported cooperative research programs, government agencies and bureaus that are research organizations, and administrative offices and similar units. Each entry includes the following contact information: name, address, telephone, and FAX number; description of the center's history and current status; information on research activities and programs; and details on publications, seminars, and libraries. The directory is available in print, on computer diskette, online, and on magnetic tape. Available

through DIALOG as part of Research Centers and Services Directory.
Seventh edition published in 1992 by Gale Research, Inc. New editions published biennially.

International Research Centers Directory 1992–93

Thomas J. Cichonski, editor

This directory of 7,200 government, university, independent, nonprofit, and commercial research centers in more than 145 countries includes in each entry full contact information, research activities, and publications. The directory is available in print, online, and on magnetic tape. Available online through DIALOG as part of Research Centers and Services Directory.
Seventh edition published in 1993 by Gale Research, Inc. New editions published biennially.

Japan's High Technology: An Annotated Guide to English Language Information Sources

Dawn E. Talbot, editor

Text identifies over 500 directories, online databases, abstracting and indexing tools, newsletters, and translation guides that provide information on Japanese high technology.
Published in 1991 by Oryx Press.

NTIS Online Bibliographic Database (National Technical Information Service)

🔥 This online database provides information on government-sponsored research and development. Available from DIA-LOG as online database and in compact disk format. It is a multidisciplinary database whose coverage includes administration and management, business and economics, energy, health planning, library and informational science, and transportation.

Updated biweekly by the National Technical Information Service, U.S. Department of Commerce.

R&D Ratios and Budgets

This research service is designed for professional managers seeking information on the R&D budgeting practices of major corporations.

Published annually by Schonfeld & Associates. Available through FIND/SVP.

Research Centers Directory 1992

Annette Piccirelli, editor

🔥 Directory lists 12,548 nonprofit research and development companies in the United States and Canada. Entries are grouped into 17 chapters covering 5 broad categories. Each entry includes the name of the parent institution, full contact information, year established, number of staff, research activities, and publications. The directory is available in print, online, and on magnetic tape. Available online through DIALOG as part of Research Centers and Services Directory.

Seventeenth edition published in 1992 by Gale Research, Inc.

Research Services Directory

Annette Piccirelli, editor

🔥 Directory includes more than 4,000 for-profit research and development com-

panies in the United States and Canada. Entries include complete contact information, company description, principal clients, rates, memberships, description of services, equipment, databases, patents, licenses, and publications. The directory is available in print, online, and on magnetic tape. Available online through DIALOG as part of Research Centers and Services Directory.

Fifth edition published in 1992 by Gale Research, Inc. New editions published every three years.

Third Generation R&D

Philip A. Roussel, Kamal N. Saad, and Tamara J. Erickson

Third Generation R&D outlines a pragmatic method for linking R&D to long-term business planning. Topics include integrating technology and research capabilities with overall management strategy, breaking organizational barriers that isolate R&D, fostering a spirit of partnership between R&D and other units, and creating managed portfolios of R&D projects that match corporate goals.

Published in 1991 by Harvard Business School Press.

The U.S. Sourcebook of R&D Spenders

Text gives information on publicly owned corporations that spend on R&D. The directory includes corporate name, address, telephone number, projected R&D budget for calendar year, annual R&D growth, projected sales for calendar year, sales growth rate, and R&D to sales ratio.

Published annually by Schonfeld and Associates. Available through FIND/SVP.

FOR FURTHER INFORMATION

See *Industrial Research in the United Kingdom, p. 543*

National Technical Information Service/ Federal Government Electronic Bulletin Boards, p. 511
PTS PROMPT:™ *Overview of Markets and Technology, p. 406*

42

SMALL BUSINESS AND ENTREPRENEURSHIP

Allen Fishman's Business Financing Kit

Allen Fishman

This collection of tools and techniques for obtaining financing for expanding an established business, funding an acquisition, or starting a new business includes ready-to-use applications, letters, checklists, and business plans.
Published in 1990 by Prentice Hall, Inc.

Business Plans to Manage Day-to-Day Operations: Real Life Results for Small Business Owners and Operators

Christopher R. Malburg

Guide shows step-by-step how to develop a business plan, then use it as a blueprint for conducting the day-to-day operations of a small business. Topics include setting goals, building teams, delegating responsibilities, and motivation. A computer disk that offers the latest tools for business charting and forecasting is included.
Published in 1993 by John Wiley & Sons, Inc.

Choosing a Business Form: To Incorporate or Not to Incorporate

Richard P. Mandell

This easy-to-understand overview of a complex topic is a chapter in the book *The Portable MBA in Finance and Account-*ing (edited by John Leslie Livingstone). It examines whether a business should be organized as a sole proprietorship, partnership, corporation, or some other legal form. The pluses and minuses of each form, the exposure of the owners of the business to personal liability, and the impact of the business form on income taxes paid are examined.
Published in 1992 by John Wiley & Sons, Inc.

The Complete Guide to Money and Your Business

Robert E. Butler and Donald Rappaport

Comprehensive guide to small business finance and financial management considers topics like getting, using, managing, and keeping money; preparing and using balance sheets and income statements; and minimizing tax liabilities.
Published in 1987 by Prentice Hall, Inc.

The Complete Handbook for the Entrepreneur

Gary Brenner, Joel Ewan, and Henry Custer

A comprehensive handbook addresses the 120 topics most entrepreneurs will need to consider while starting or operating a business. Topics include sales forecasting, using a corporation as a tax shelter, and conducting market research.
Published in 1989 by Prentice Hall, Inc.

The Entrepreneur and Small Business Problem Solver: An Encyclopedic Reference and Guide, Second Edition

William A. Cohen

This comprehensive reference covers all aspects of starting and managing a business—legal aspects, sources of capital, developing a business plan, buying a business, protecting ideas, leasing and buying equipment, record keeping, financial management, and marketing and advertising.
Published in 1990 by John Wiley & Sons, Inc.

External Assistance for Start-Ups and Small Businesses

Elizabeth J. Gatewood and Keiron E. Hylton

This chapter of *The Portable MBA in Entrepreneurship* (see p. 574) is an informative and useful overview of the wealth of information and resources available from nonprofit organizations and federal, state, and local government. It contains a guide to the myriad Small Business Administration programs, such as Small Business Development Centers, Service Corps of Retired Executives, Small Business Institutes, Financial Assistance Programs, Procurement Assistance, and Export Assistance.
Published in 1994 by John Wiley & Sons, Inc.

Free Help from Uncle Sam to Start Your Own Business (or Expand the One You Have), Third Edition

William Alarid and Gustav Berle

This highly practical book covers a wide variety of topics useful to people in small business, such as, selling to the federal government; obtaining government financial assistance; getting government help for international trade; and help for women, minorities, and the disadvantaged.
Published in 1992 by Puma Press.

Going Public

Paul Joubert

This chapter in *The Portable MBA in Finance and Accounting* (edited by John Leslie Livingstone) is a practical guide to the pluses and minuses of taking a company public. It looks at the factors involved in managing an initial public offering (IPO) of stock.
Published in 1992 by John Wiley & Sons, Inc.

Guerrilla Financing: Alternative Techniques to Finance Any Small Business

Bruce Brechman and Jay Conrad-Levinson

This book looks at nontraditional ways to get money to finance a small business. Some of the funding sources include receivable financing, equipment financing, real estate financing, government financing, and bank financing. The authors also cover traditional venture capital and informal venture capital.
Published in 1991 by Houghton Mifflin.

How to Buy a Business: Entrepreneurship through Acquisition

Richard A. Joseph, Anna M. Nekoranel, and Carl H. Steffans

This book shows how the active small business marketplace works and covers a wide range of topics, including finding and evaluating acquisition candidates; financing, negotiating, and structuring the deal;

legal and tax implications; and determining current and future value.
Published in 1992 by Dearborn Trade.

How to Buy or Sell the Closely Held Corporation

Lawrence C. Silton

Strategies and practical working aids to help buy or sell a closely held company are considered, including valuing a business, negotiating price and terms, guaranteeing payment, and minimizing taxes.
Published in 1987 by Prentice Hall, Inc.

How to Form Your Own Nonprofit Corporation

Anthony Mancuso

Written for arts groups, educators, social service agencies, medical programs, environmentalists, and anyone who wants to start a nonprofit organization, this book explains all the legal formalities involved in forming and operating a tax-exempt nonprofit corporation. Features include detailed information on differences between all 50 states; ready-to-use forms for articles, bylaws, and minutes; and complete instructions for obtaining federal 501(c)(3) tax exemption and for qualifying for public charity status with the Internal Revenue Service.
Published in 1990 by NoLo Press.

How to Form Your Own Corporation without a Lawyer for Under $75

Ted Nicholas

This book shows how to save legal fees by using a simple set of instructions to incorporate without using a lawyer. It includes forms like a certificate of incorporation and other useful material.
Published in 1992 by Dearborn Trade.

Inc: The Magazine for Growing Companies

This general-interest business magazine is geared toward entrepreneurs and small business owners. Coverage includes tips and advice on starting and running a small business, profiles of leading entrepreneurs, and rankings of successful entrepreneurial companies.
Published monthly by the Goldhirsh Group, Inc.

The Legal Guide for Starting & Running a Small Business

Fred S. Steingold

Comprehensive guide to the legal issues involved in establishing and running a small business includes topics like, whether to form a sole proprietorship, partnership, or corporation; buying a franchise or existing business; negotiating a lease; hiring and firing employees; working with independent contractors; and resolving business disputes.
Published in 1992 by NoLo Press.

Money Sources for Small Business: How You Can Find Private, State, Federal, and Corporate Financing

William Alarid

This book shows how to obtain cash from federal and state governments, venture capital clubs, small business investment companies, and computerized matching services.
Published in 1991 by Puma Press.

The New Venture Handbook

Ronald E. Merrill and Henry D. Sedgwick

Complete guide to setting up and running an entrepreneurial business covers

topics like developing a business concept, conducting market surveys, team building, buying an existing business or franchise, and day-to-day managing.
Published in 1992 by AMACOM.

The Partnership Book: How to Write a Partnership Agreement

Dennis Clifford and Ralph Warner

Step-by-step guide to drafting and writing a partnership agreement has sample clauses covering all key issues—from partners' initial contribution to what happens if one leaves.
Published in 1991 by NoLo Press.

The Portable MBA in Entrepreneurship

William Bygrave, editor

This book presents an overview of the most important topics and issues involved in starting, managing, and growing a business. The topic coverage includes entry strategies for starting a business, marketing for start-up businesses, developing a business plan, equity financing, debt and other forms of financing, external assistance for start-ups, legal and tax issues, protecting intellectual property, harvesting a business, and the economics of entrepreneurship.
Published in 1994 by John Wiley & Sons, Inc.

Purchase and Sale of Small Businesses: Tax and Legal Aspects, Second Edition

Marc J. Lane

Publication contains more than 100 complete forms commonly used in the purchase or sale of a business.
Published in 1991 by John Wiley & Sons, Inc.

The Small Business Incorporation Kit

Robert L. Davidson, III

Comprehensive reference deals with everything from what incorporation means to the pros and cons of do-it-yourself incorporation to the actual running of the corporation.
Published in 1992 by John Wiley & Sons, Inc.

Small Business Sourcebook

Carol A. Schwartz, editor

Volume One of this two-volume directory provides a small business profile for each of 224 different small businesses including a variety of retail, service, and manufacturing operations. Volume Two includes general small business information. These resources cover federal and state government agencies, venture capital firms, incubators, and other sources of information and assistance.
Fifth edition published in 1992 by Gale Research, Inc.

Starting and Operating a Small Business in [Name of State]

Looseleaf packets are available under this title for each of the 50 states and the District of Columbia. Each packet is divided into eleven chapters. Chapters 1 through 10 cover federal laws, regulations, and tax codes that affect small businesses. These chapters are the same in each of the 51 packets. Chapter 11 in each packet deals with the particular conditions of an individual state and includes forms, checklists, and a directory of state information sources and assistance offices.
Published annually by Oasis Press/PSI Research.

The States and Small Business: A Directory of Programs and Activities, 1989

This directory is designed to help potential and existing business owners who are seeking management, financial, or procurement information and assistance at the state level. It contains a complete list of small business development centers and subcenters and a directory of names, addresses, and telephone numbers of the SBA's 10 regional advocates.

Published in 1989 by the Superintendent of Documents, U.S. Government Printing Office.

Taking Money Out of Your Corporation: Perfectly Legal Ways to Maximize Your Income

M. John Storey

This book discusses 30 techniques, ranging from compensating family members to barter to retirement planning, that are designed to maximize the personal assets of business owners.

Published in 1993 by John Wiley & Sons, Inc.

GOVERNMENT AGENCIES

Small Business Administration (SBA)

The SBA has a wide variety of programs and activities to help entrepreneurs and small businesses (usually defined as organizations with $5 million or less in yearly sales). The SBA is headquartered in Washington, DC and has 108 field offices (see Appendices, pp. 639 to 642 for addresses and phone numbers). SBA headquarters has a toll-free (1-800-827-5722) "answer desk" that provides an automated guide to information and services available through the SBA. One can speak with an operator by calling the SBA field offices. Although many have automated answering machines to guide you through available services, you can eventually reach people to field your questions.

Some SBA activities and their headquarters telephone number (at which it is also possible to speak with individuals) follow:

Financial assistance	(202) 205-6490
Disaster assistance	(202) 205-6734
Surety bonds	(202) 205-6540
Minority Small Business Development	(202) 205-6540
Women's Business Ownership	(202) 205-6673
Innovation, Research and Technology	(202) 205-6450
International Trade	(202) 205-6720
Small Business Development Centers	(202) 205-6766

Address: Small Business Administration, 409 Third Street NW, Washington, DC 20416. Tel. (800) 827-5722.

TRADE AND PROFESSIONAL ASSOCIATIONS

American Women's Economic Development Corporation

AWED offers programs designed specifically for women business owners and women contemplating business ownership, including expert individual counseling, training programs conducted by experienced business people, networking sessions, and peer group support for any stage of business development. Services include counseling, offered at the New York office or by telephone, and the AWED hotline to answer urgent questions. AWED also offers membership in American Women in Enterprise, which includes a subscription to *Women in Enterprise* newsletter, access to a business advice hotline, and discounts on many executive services.

American Women's Economic Development Corporation and American Women in Enterprise, 641 Lexington Avenue, Ninth Floor, New York, NY 10022. Tel. (toll-free) 1-800-222-AWED (1-800-222-2933) or (212) 692-9100 in New York City.

The MIT Enterprise Forum®

Organization provides advice, support, and educational services to innovative and technology-based companies. Case presentations that address the needs of start-up as well as more established companies

are conducted at meetings held twice a month.

MIT Enterprise Forum of Cambridge, Inc., Massachusetts Institute of Technology, Room W59-220, 201 Vassar Street, Cambridge, MA 02139. Tel. (617) 253-8240. FAX (617) 258-7264.

FOR FURTHER INFORMATION

See **National Technical Information Service/Federal Government Electronic Bulletin Boards, p. 511**
The Small Business Bankruptcy Kit, p. 422

43

STATE AND LOCAL GOVERNMENT

The Book of the States

Publication provides comparative data on issues such as state constitutions, elections and federal-state relations, as well as reports on problems and major issues in state finances; government reorganization, management, productivity, and efficiency; and state offices.
Published in 1992 by The Council of State Governments.

Economic Development in the States (three-volume series)

Volume 1: State Business Incentives and Economic Growth: Are They Effective? A Review of the Literature. Text looks at the effect of business incentives on state economic growth. A comprehensive bibliography on state business incentives is included.

    Volume 2: The Changing Arena: State Strategic Economic Development. New approaches to economic development in a changing economic environment are featured. Comments from corporate executives are included.

    Volume 3: The States and Business Incentives: An Inventory of Tax and Financial Incentive Programs. Book describes what states have done by means of tax and financial programs to create, expand, and recruit business and industry.
All three volumes published in 1989 by The Council of State Governments.

Key Indicators of County Growth 1970–2010 (1992 Edition)

▪ This directory provides an overview of economic data and demographic trends of the economies in counties of the United States. It provides historical and projected data for key indicators including population, personal income, total employment, and earnings per job. Available in print and on PC data disks.
Published in 1992 by NPA Data Services.

Moody's Municipal and Government Manual and News Reports

Comprehensive loose-leaf resource offers information on 15,000 municipalities and over 1,100 federal, state, and local government and regulatory agencies. Entries cover states, counties, cities, towns, villages, taxing districts, and school districts, and contain complete bond descriptions, Moody's ratings, and key statistics and financials. Twice weekly news reports provide ongoing coverage of important changes and developments with regard to the states, municipalities, or government agencies.
Published annually by Moody's Investors Service (Dun & Bradstreet); news reports are published twice weekly.

Municipal Yellow Book: Who's Who in the Leading City and County Governments and Local Authorities

Sourcebook provides complete listings of names, titles, addresses, and telephone numbers of people involved in the shaping and administration of policy and the writing and enforcement of regulations. Also listings of all departments, agencies, subdivisions, and branches of municipal governments are included.
New editions published semiannually by Monitor Publishing Company.

National Survey of State Laws

Richard A. Leiter, editor

Current state laws—how they differ, and how they are similar—are considered for a range of relevant business topics in all 50 states and the District of Columbia. Each law listed is treated as a separate chapter, beginning with a general description of the law, followed by state-by-state summaries that compare specific differences between these laws.
Published in 1992 by Gale Research, Inc.

State Administrative Officials Classified by Function 1993–94

High-ranking administrators are grouped by function rather than title. Names, addresses, and telephone numbers of state officials are provided in 147 areas, including such categories as Child Support Enforcement, Geographic Information Systems, and Recycling.
Published in 1993 (and biennially) by The Council of State Governments.

State and Local Statistics Sources

*M. Balachandran and
S. Balachandran, editors*

This collection of 40,000 citations to state and local statistics, arranged in 54 state and territorial chapters, covers more than 50 subjects, including agriculture, banks and banking, communications, foreign trade, insurance, salaries and wages, and so on.
Second edition published in 1993 by Gale Research, Inc.

State and Metropolitan Databook 1991 (Fourth Edition)

This reference work, prepared by the Bureau of the Census of the U.S. Department of Commerce, provides a wide variety of information on the states and metropolitan areas of the United States. It includes the latest statistics from the 1990 population count and the 1987 economic census data. Available in print and on diskette suitable for input for leading spreadsheet, database, and mapping programs.
Published in 1991 by Superintendent of Documents, U.S. Government Printing Office. (Note: For diskette information contact the Bureau of the Census at (301) 763-4100.)

State Elective Officials and the Legislatures 1993–1994

Arranged alphabetically by state, this directory lists key executive branch officials and supreme court justices and offers the names, addresses, party affiliations, and districts of state legislators.
Published in 1993 (and biennially) by the Council of State Governments.

State Legislative Leadership, Committees and Staff 1993–1994

This directory is divided into two sections: Legislative Organization, which offers legislative leadership committee and research agency contacts state-by-state, and Legislative Directory, which lists leadership contacts by function for all states. The volume also provides names, addresses, and telephone numbers.
Published in 1993 (and biennially) by The Council of State Governments.

State Statistical Abstracts

Most of the states publish statistical abstracts containing data of a nature similar to *The Statistical Abstract of the United States*. See Appendices, pp. 665–669, Guide to State Statistical Abstracts.

State Yellow Book: Who's Who in the Executive Branches of the 50 State Governments

Organized by branch of government, this directory provides information on over 35,000 state leaders in the executive branch and the legislative branch. Also, it profiles all 50 states, the District of Columbia, and the insular U.S. territories, including demographics, history, state maps, and geographical information; fiscal, economic, and educational data; military installations; and sources for obtaining public records. County information is also provided, including county name and seat and ZIP codes.
New editions published quarterly by Monitor Publishing Company.

FOR FURTHER INFORMATION

See American Business Climate and Economic Profiles, p. 473
Business Dateline®, p. 401

County and City Data Book: A Statistical Abstract Supplement, p. 457
Data Pamphlets (for an Individual County, State, or Metropolitan Statistical Area), p. 457
The Dun & Bradstreet Reference Book of American Business, p. 448
Lesko's Infopower, p. 509
Resource Guide to State Environmental Management, p. 495
State Environmental Law Annual Report, p. 495
State Environmental Law Handbooks, p. 496
State Tax Reports, p. 584
State Trademark and Unfair Competition Law, p. 439
The States and Small Business: A Directory of Programs and Activities, p. 575
Statistical Abstract of the United States, p. 406
Telemarketer's Guide to State Laws, p. 468
Trademarkscan®-State, p. 440
The Zip Code Mapbook of Metropolitan Areas, p. 462

44

STRATEGIC PLANNING AND JOINT VENTURES

The Art of the Long View: Planning for the Future in an Uncertain World

Peter Schwartz

Interesting and gracefully written book describes how to use the "scenarios" approach to chart a company's future. Scenarios are stories that help one to visualize and chart different kinds of futures in an uncertain world.
Published in 1991 by Doubleday.

Business Alliances Guide: The Hidden Competitive Weapon

Robert Porter Lynch

Comprehensive guide to planning, negotiating, and managing strategic partnerships includes topics like deciding among various types of alliances, finding the best partner, the six most costly mistakes involved in alliances, and measuring risks and rewards.
Published in 1993 by John Wiley & Sons, Inc.

Collaborating to Compete: Using Strategic Alliances and Acquisitions in the Global Marketplace

Joel Bleeke and David Ernst, editors

Text explores the increasingly effective expansion methods of cross-border alliances and acquisitions. Topics include the following: whether cross-border alliances and acquisitions will work for the reader's own firm; difficulties breaking into the Japanese market and the European Economic Community; and decision-making techniques for structuring and managing global collaborations.
Published in 1993 by John Wiley & Sons, Inc.

Competitive Advantage: Creating and Sustaining Superior Performance

Michael E. Porter

A sequel to *Competitive Strategy* (see next entry), this book shows managers how to evaluate the competitive position of the individual firm. The author provides a framework of value chain analysis to look at the underlying activities of an organization.
Published in 1985 by The Free Press.

Competitive Strategy: Techniques for Analyzing Industries and Competitors

Michael E. Porter

Many consider this book, by Harvard Business School's Professor Porter, to be the most influential book on strategy in recent years. It focuses on the need to understand industry structure and the behavior of competitors within that structure.
Published in 1980 by The Free Press.

A Directory of Strategic Management Software Tools

Planning Review magazine publishes an annual guide to software products of interest to managers and stategic planning professionals. The directory provides the name of the product, describes its functions, notes its compatibility with DOS, Windows, UNIX, ASCII, and so on, and provides supplier information. Software tools for the following areas are covered: realational spreadsheets, specialty planning tools, proprietary shareholder value models, decision support models, data analysis, project management, competitive intelligence tools, new product introduction tools, tools for developing visual representations and models of a business, and spreadsheet add-in products.
Published annually in the July/August issue of Planning Review.

Growing Your Business Internationally: How to Form Profitable Overseas Partnerships, Alliances, and Joint Ventures

Marvin V. Bedward and Mark V. Anderson

Step-by-step guide to business expansion in international markets covers topics like finding the right partner, negotiating the partnership, managing the relationship, and forming partnerships and alliances in Asia and Europe.
Published in 1992 by Probus Publishing, Inc.

PIMS™ Competitive Stategy Database

▌ This source provides financial and marketing data on stategic business units of 2,700 companies in several hundred worldwide industries. Information includes income statements, balance sheets, market share, and degree of product differentiation and quality. Available online through the Stategic Planning Institute.
Updated periodically by The Stategic Planning Institute.

Real-Time Strategy: Improvising Team-Based Planning for a Fast Changing World

Lee Tom Perry, Randall G. Scott, and W. Norman Smallwood

Text is an in-depth look at how self-directed teams formulate and implement operational level strategies in real time. Book can be very useful for managers wanting to keep up to date with the evolution from top-down strategic planning to involving a much wider array of managers and business professionals in strategy development and implementation.
Published in 1993 by John Wiley & Sons, Inc.

Strategic Planning for the Entrepreneurial Business

Self-study course offered by the American Management Association (AMA) covers a wide variety of subjects, including identifying business opportunities, expanding market share, entering new markets, and strengthening competitive position.
Published by American Management Association.

Strategic Planning: What Every Manager Must Know

George A. Steiner

Comprehensive guide to strategic planning includes topics like organizing a planning system, acquiring and using information, identifying opportunities, developing

objectives, and translating strategic plans into current decisions.
Published in 1979 by The Free Press.

Strategic Planning Workbook, Second Edition

Joseph C. Krallinger and Karsten C. Hellebust

This book unites theory and practice and provides a system for strategic planning. It shows how to evaluate the performance of a business critically and looks at the most current methods for using debt financing, cash flow, and working capital in budgeting and developing a strategic plan.
Published in 1993 by John Wiley & Sons, Inc.

Strategy: Seeking and Securing Competitive Advantage

Cynthia A. Montgomery and Michael E. Porter, editors

Seminal articles from the *Harvard Business Review* are presented.
Twelfth edition published in 1991 by Harvard Business School Press.

TRADE AND PROFESSIONAL ASSOCIATIONS

The Planning Forum

This international business organization is dedicated to advancing the understanding and practice of strategic management as the integrating force for improving organizational performance and achieving global competitiveness. This mission is accomplished through a variety of knowledge-based services: the annual International Strategic Management Conference; the Research & Education Foundation; *Planning Review*, a bi-monthly peer-reviewed business journal; and *Network*, a monthly executive briefing.
The Planning Forum, 5500 College Corner Pike, P.O. Box 70, Oxford, OH 45056-0070. Tel. (513) 523-4185. FAX (513) 523-7599.

FOR FURTHER INFORMATION

See ***CEDDS: The Complete Economic and Demographic Data Source, p. 456***
Markets of the U.S. for Business Planners, p. 460
Predicasts' F & S Index of Corporate Change, p. 451

45

TAXES

Bender's Federal Tax Service

🔒 This service organizes tax information into different topical areas. Coverage includes individuals, corporations, partnerships, estate and gift taxes, business expenses, tax accounting, compensation, procedures, and administration. Available in print and CD-ROM.
Publication initiated in 1989 in looseleaf. Updated monthly with revisions and a weekly newsletter by Matthew Bender and Company.

Bender's Master Federal Tax Handbook

This publication is an abridgment of *Bender's Federal Tax Service* (see preceding entry).
Published annually by Matthew Bender and Company.

Daily Tax Report

This subscription service provides reports each business day on tax information, policy, and court decisions.
Reports published every business day by Bureau of National Affairs, Inc.

The Ernst & Young Tax Guide

Text presents information that taxpayers need each year to comply with income tax filing requirements. The guide includes *IRS Publication 17, Your Federal Income Tax,* along with comprehensive commentary, usable tax return forms, and hundreds of tips and explanations.
Published annually by John Wiley & Sons, Inc.

The Federal Tax Directory

🔒 *The Federal Tax Directory* is an online service containing a comprehensive list of names, addresses, and telephone numbers for 17,000 tax officials in Congress, the courts, executive agencies, and states. The same information is also provided for tax-related organizations, corporate tax managers, international tax specialists, and tax journalists. Available online through LEXIS.
Updated monthly by Tax Analysts.

Federal Tax Guidebook, Second Edition

Alan Prigal

Guidebook explains the basic rules of income, estate, and gift taxes. Its coverage includes income and deductions, business transactions, corporate distributions, fiduciary income tax, and pension and profit-sharing plans.
Published since 1986 in looseleaf and updated twice annually with supplements and revisions by Matthew Bender and Company.

International Tax Summaries: A Guide for Planning and Decisions

Guide to the tax systems of over 100 countries in North America, South America, Europe, Asia, Africa, and the South Pacific includes topics such as corporate and individual taxes; nonresident tax liabilities; capital gains; available grants and incentives; controls; restrictions; and fines.
Published annually by John Wiley & Sons, Inc.

S Corporation Tax Guide

Robert Jamison

Guide to the complex rules of S corporation taxation devotes special attention to tax-planning and tax-saving strategies. Topics include eligibility requirements, filing a subchapter S election, selecting the S corporation's tax year, income measurement and reporting, distributions to shareholders, passive activity rules and limits, and changing from a C corporation to an S corporation.
Published annually by Harcourt Brace Jovanovich Miller.

Small Business Tax Planner

Two-volume reference contains dozens of how-to tax-planning articles that are organized by subject and tailored for the small-business tax planner. A detailed topic index lists specific areas of interest, such as how to choose whether to use a C corporation, an S corporation, or a partnership; reduce the cost of maintaining a qualified plan; deduct the legal expenses of a small business; plan buy-sell agreements; and more.
Published in loose-leaf format with monthly updates by Research Institute of America Tax Publishing Division.

State Tax Reports

This subscription service provides specialized issues covering the state and local tax levies of each state.
Monthly reporting (twice monthly for California and New York) by Commerce Clearing House, Inc.

The Tax Adviser

Publication reports on tax developments and presents suggestions that show how to save money in tax planning and tax compliance. *The Tax Adviser* reports and comments on IRS rulings and proposed regulations, court decisions, and legislation.
Published monthly by The American Institute of Certified Public Accountants.

Tax Notes Today (TNT)

Comprehensive daily tax information service contains both current news and full-text tax documents. The file is updated each business day of the year. In addition to standard tax documents from Congress, the IRS, and the courts, *TNT* includes U.S. Treasury tax correspondence, congressional testimony, and government reports. Tax documents generally appear online in full text within 24 hours of their release. Most documents are prefaced by detailed analytical summaries and are classified by Code section. *TNT* is also available online through LEXIS and DIALOG.
Updated daily by Tax Analysts.

Tax Practice Series

This tax subscription service covers a wide variety of tax issues including alternative minimum tax, C corporations, compensation planning, compliance computation of tax liability, deductions, estate and gift taxation, exempt organizations, foreign taxation, gross income, IRS practice and procedure, partnerships, private foundations, S corporations, tax accounting, tax credits, and taxation of trusts.
Subscription service with weekly supplements published by the Bureau of National Affairs, Inc.

Your Federal Tax Advisor

Authoritative guide to newly enacted tax law changes features complete A-to-Z explanations of newly enacted tax laws; an in-depth look at new tax changes, including tax breaks, revenue codes, rulings, regulations, and court decisions; solutions to

the most common practical tax questions; and tax reduction strategies.
Published annually by Prentice Hall, Inc.

National Tax Association (NTA)

NTA membership consists of government and corporate tax officials, accountants, consultants, economists, attorneys, educators, and others interested in the field of taxation. Its purposes are to promote scientific, nonpolitical study of taxation and encourage better understanding of the common interests of national, state, and local governments in matters of taxation and public finance.
National Tax Association–Tax Institute of America, 5310 E. Main Street, Suite 104, Columbus, OH 43213. Tel. (614) 864-1221.

For Further Information

See Accounting and Tax Database,
  p. 410
The Business One Irwin Business and
  Investment Almanac, p. 442
FAS 109: Analysis and Comments on the
  New Accounting for Income Taxes,
  p. 415

TRAVEL AND RELOCATION

Craighead's International Business, Travel, and Relocation Guide to 71 Countries, 1992–93

Formerly *International Business Travel and Relocation,* the guide offers information about the economies, customs, communications, tours, attractions, and other aspects of 71 countries around the world. Individual country profiles are divided into five sections and include maps, statistics, restrictions, currency, culture, transportation, and health.
Sixth edition published in 1992 by Gale Research, Inc.

The Ernst & Young Almanac of U.S. Business Cities: A Guide to America's 66 Leading Business Centers

Ernst & Young

This almanac provides detailed information about the business environment of 66 major American cities, including industry trends, business incentives, labor costs and availability, real estate costs, workforce educational levels, and socioeconomic data.
Published in 1994 by John Wiley & Sons.

International Herald-Tribune Guide to Business Travel: Asia

Robert K. McCabe

Detailed information is presented on transportation, business practices, currency, hotels, restaurants, and nightlife in 16 cities in Asia including Tokyo, Hong Kong, Beijing, and Singapore.
Published in 1988 by NTC Publishing Group.

International Herald-Tribune Guide to Business Travel: Europe

Allan Tillier and Roger Beardwood

For each of 27 cities in Europe, this guide offers advice on hotels, restaurants, transportation, nightlife, how to conduct business, and attractions. Detailed maps that highlight hotel locations are included.
Published in 1992 by NTC Publishing Group.

Worldwide Travel Information Contact Book 1991–92

Burkhard Herbote, editor

Country-by-country guide offers more than 25,000 business information sources. Entries contain full contact information for national and international ministries, departments, and boards of tourism; hotel, travel, and transportation associations; travel agencies/tour operators; mapping agencies; national railways, park authorities, and departments of wildlife; mountain and ski clubs; tourist newspapers and magazines; chambers of commerce; and embassies.
Second edition published in 1992 by Gale Research, Inc.

FOR FURTHER INFORMATION

See *Cities of the World*, p. 520
National Technical Information Service/ Federal Government Electronic Bulletin Boards, p. 511

VALUING A BUSINESS

Handbook of Business Valuation

Thomas L. West and Jeffrey D. Jones, editors

Comprehensive guide to business valuation approaches and methods examines subjects such as business and real estate appraisals, valuation methods, special purpose methods, financial statements, appraisal reports, and the use and abuse of expert witnesses. A series of worksheets helps users record asset values, calculate cash flow, and compute value.
Published in 1992 by John Wiley & Sons, Inc.

Valuation: Measuring and Managing the Value of a Company

Tom Copeland, Tim Koller, and Jack Murrin

The authors of this book are associated with the management consulting firm of McKinsey and Company. The book enables readers to estimate the value of alternative corporate and business strategies and the value of specific programs within these strategies; assess major transactions such as mergers, acquisitions, divestitures, recapitalization, and share repurchases; and review and target the performance of business operations.
Published in 1990 by John Wiley & Sons, Inc.

Valuing Small Business and Professional Practices

Shannon Pratt

Authoritative step-by-step guide to business valuation includes cash value analysis, valuing minority interests, and court decisions affecting the valuation of specific types of professional practices.
Second edition published in 1993 by Business One Irwin.

VENTURE CAPITAL/SOURCES OF CAPITAL

Buyouts Directory of LBO Financing Sources

Over 600 companies and organizations that provide acquisition financing are listed, including complete contact information.
Published biennially by Securities Data Company Publishing.

Corporate Finance Sourcebook 1992

Entries in this directory of more than 20,000 key financial experts in 3,645 organizations providing corporate growth capital contain complete contact information. A mergers and acquisition section, covering public offerings of the past three years and mergers and acquisitions over $100 million, is also included.
Published in 1992 by National Register Publishing (Reed Reference Publishing).

The Ernst & Young Guide to Raising Capital

Ernst & Young

This is a guide to raising capital to foster business growth, develop new products, and expand into new markets; it provides information on a wide variety of strategies to help business owners and entrepreneurs meet their goals, including joint ventures, public issues, management buyouts, franchising, Employee Stock Ownership Plans, and cross-border alliances.
Second edition published in 1994 by John Wiley & Sons.

European Venture Capital Association (EVCA) Yearbook

This annual volume presents the results of the annual European venture capital survey of the following countries: Austria, Belgium, Denmark, Finland, France, Germany, Greece, Hungary, Iceland, Republic of Ireland, Italy, The Netherlands, Norway, Portugal, Spain, Sweden, Switzerland, and the United Kingdom. It also includes a directory of all EVCA members that lists full addresses, details, contact names, and an outline of each member's investments criteria.
Published annually by European Venture Capital Association.

IVCI Directory of Domestic and International Venture Groups

Over 145 venture groups in the United States and overseas are listed, including complete contact information.
Published annually by International Venture Capital Institute, Inc.

Pratt's Guide to Venture Capital Sources

Comprehensive worldwide guide to the entire venture capital industry provides investment, operating, and management data on nearly 800 venture capital firms. The guide offers current information on competitors, industry sectors, and leading venture capital firms in the United States, Canada, and around the world. Firm listings include name,

address, telephone number, FAX number, geographic/industry investment preferences, management roster, capital under management, recent investments, compensation method, project preferences, and type of financing provided.
Published in 1992 by Securities Data Company Publishing.

SBA Loans: A Step-by-Step Guide

Patrick D. O'Hara

Guide provides clarification of the Small Business Administration guaranteed loan program, how to apply, and how to improve one's chances of qualifying.
Published in 1989 by John Wiley & Sons, Inc.

Technology Capital Network, Inc.

This not-for-profit confidential network provides high-net-worth individuals with a mechanism for examining opportunities to invest in entrepreneurial ventures. TCN also serves professional venture capital funds and corporate investors. TCN provides entrepreneurs with a cost-effective process for reaching wealthy individuals and others interested in investing in early-stage or high-growth private companies.
MIT Enterprise Forum of Cambridge, Technology Capital Network, Inc.

Venture Capital at the Crossroads

William D. Bygrave and Jeffry A. Timmons

Text examines the venture capital industry and its role in the creation of new businesses. It provides original research on the dimensions of the industry and how risk taking and the time perspectives of its practitioners are changing.
Published in 1992 by Harvard Business School Press.

Venture Capital Directory

Over 400 companies that offer funding for small and minority-owned businesses are listed, including complete contact information.
Published annually by Forum Publishing Co.

Venture Capital Journal

Newsletter covers the full spectrum of activities that involve or interest venture capitalists, their limited partners, and growing businesses. Features include accurate, timely data on disbursements, fundraising totals, capital commitments, and venture-backed initial public offerings (IPOs); the "Venture Capital 100" index of aftermarket performance of leading venture-backed companies; and new techniques to improve or expand in the venture capital and private equity marketplace.
Published monthly by Securities Data Company Publishing.

The Venture Capital Review

Magazine reports on issues of special relevance to the European venture capital industry.
Published quarterly by the European Venture Capital Association.

Venture Capital: Where to Find It

Directory of the members of the National Association of Small Business Investment Companies includes complete contact information.
Published annually by the National Association of Small Business Investment Companies.

European Venture Capital Association (EVCA)

The EVCA has 290 members from 22 countries. It promotes the development of venture capital in Europe through lobbying activities with the European Commission and through networking among EVCA members. The organization encourages the transnational syndication of venture capital investments within Europe. The EVCA also runs a number of training programs. The monthly *Newsline* is published for members.

European Venture Capital Association, Kieberpark-Minervastraat 6, Box 6, B-1930, Zavertem, Belgium. 32 2 720 60 10. FAX: 32 2 725 30 36.

National Venture Capital Association (NVCA)

The NVCA comprises over 200 professional venture capital organizations. The association fosters a broader understanding of the importance of venture capital to the vitality of the U.S. economy and is interested in stimulating the free flow of capital to young companies.

National Venture Capital Association, 1655 North Fort Meyer Drive, Suite 700, Arlington, VA 22209. Tel. (202) 528-4370. FAX (703) 525-8841.

FOR FURTHER INFORMATION

See ***The Business One Irwin Business and Investment Almanac, p. 442***

DIRECTORY OF PUBLISHERS, VENDORS, AND DATABASE PROVIDERS

3W International Publishing
3000 Atrium Way, Suite 252
Mt. Laurel, NJ 08054
Tel. (609) 273-9588
FAX (609) 271-0518

Abbott, Langer, and Associates
548 First Street
Crete, IL 60417
Tel. (708) 672-4200

ABILL Communications
355 Park Avenue South
New York, NY 10017
Tel. (212) 592-6200
(toll-free) 1-800-253-6708

Bob Adams, Inc.
260 Center Street
Holbrook, MA 02343
Tel. (617) 767-8100
FAX (617) 767-0994

Administrative Management Society
1101 14th Street NW, No. 1100
Washington, DC 20005
Tel. (202) 371-8299

AMACOM
See: American Management Association

American Business Information
5711 S. 86th Circle
P.O. Box 27347
Omaha, NE 68127
Tel. (402) 593-4565
FAX (402) 331-6681

American Compensation Association
14040 N. Northsight Boulevard
Scottsdale, AZ 85260-3601
Tel. (602) 951-9191
FAX (602) 483-8352

American Demographies, Inc.
P.O. Box 68
Ithaca, NY 14851
Tel. (607) 723-6343
(toll-free) 1-800-828-1133

American Economics Association
2014 Broadway, No. 305
Nashville, TN 37203
Tel. (615) 322-2595

American Institute of Certified Public
  Accountants (AICPA)
1211 Avenue of the Americas
New York, NY 10036-8775
Tel. (212) 575-6200

American Management Association
135 W. 50th Street
New York, NY 10020-1201
Tel. (212) 586-8100

American Management Association
Extension Division
P.O. Box 1026
Saranac Lake, NY 12983-9986
Tel. (518) 891-5510

American Marketing Association
25 S. Wacker Drive, Suite 200
Chicago, IL 60606
Tel. (312) 648-0563

Asia Press Co., Ltd.
Dowa Building 4F
2122 Ginza 7-Chome
Chiyoda-ku
Tokyo 104, Japan

Asian Finance Publications, Ltd.
3/F Hollywood Center
233 Hollywood Road
Hong Kong

ASQC Quality Press (American Society
   for Quality Control)
611 E. Wisconsin Avenue
Milwaukee, WI 53202
Tel. (414) 272-8575

AT&T Toll Free 800 Directories
55 Corporate Drive
Room 24C36
Bridgewater, NJ 08807

Matthew Bender and Company
11 Penn Plaza
New York, NY 10001
Tel. (212) 967-7707

Blackwell Publishers
238 Main Street
Cambridge, MA 02142
Tel. (617) 225-0430

R. R. Bowker (Reed Reference
   Publishing)
121 Chanlon Road
New Providence, NJ 07974
Tel. (toll-free) 1-800-521-8110

Brookings Institution
1775 Massachusetts Avenue NW
Washington, DC
Tel. (202) 797-6258
FAX (202) 797-6004

BRS Information Technologies
BRS Search Service
8000 Westpark Drive
McLean, VA 22102
Tel. (toll-free) 1-800-289-4BRS
FAX (703) 893-4632

Bureau of National Affairs, Inc.
9435 Key West Avenue
Rockville, MD 20850
Tel. (toll-free) 1-800-372-1033

Bureau of the Census
Foreign Trade Division
Room 2005, Building 3
Washington, DC 20233
Tel. (301) 763-7682

Burwell Enterprises
3724 FM 1960 West, Suite 214
Houston, TX 77068
Tel. (713) 537-9051
FAX (713) 537-8332

Business America
Superintendent of Documents
Pittsburgh, PA 15250-7954
FAX orders (202) 512-2250

Business One Irwin
1818 Ridge Road
Homewood, IL 60430
Tel. (708) 798-6000
(toll-free) 1-800-634-3961

BusinessWeek
1221 Avenue of the Americas
39th Floor
New York, NY 10020
Tel. (212) 512-2511

CACI Marketing Systems
1100 N. Glebe Road
Arlington, VA 22201
Tel. (toll-free) 1-800-292-2224
FAX (703) 243-6272

Cambridge Information Group
7200 Wisconsin Avenue
Bethesda, MD 20814
Tel. (301) 961-6744
(toll-free) 1-800-843-7751

Center for International Business
   Cycle Research
Uris Hall, Columbia University
New York, NY 10027
Tel. (212) 280-2916

Center for the Study of Foreign Affairs
Foreign Service Institute
U.S. Department of State
2201 C Street NW
Washington, DC 20520
Tel. (202) 647-4000

Chadwyck Healy, Inc.
1101 King Street
Alexandria, VA 22314
Tel. (703) 683-4890
FAX (703) 683-7589

and

Cambridge Place
Cambridge CB2 1NR
England
Tel. 0223 311 479

Clark Boardman Callaghan
375 Hudson Street
New York, NY 10014
Tel. (212) 929-7500
FAX (212) 924-0460

College Placement Council
62 Highland Avenue
Bethlehem, PA 18017
Tel. (215) 863-1421
(toll-free) 1-800-544-5272

Commerce Clearing House, Inc.
4025 W. Peterson Avenue
Chicago, IL 60646
Tel. (312) 583-8500
(toll-free) 1-800-248-3248

CompuServe Incorporated
P.O. Box 20212
Columbus, OH 43220
Tel. (614) 457-8600
(toll-free) 1-800-848-8990

Computer Industry Almanac
225 Allen Way
Incline Village, NV 89451-9608
Tel. (702) 831-2288
FAX (702) 831-8610

Conference Board, Inc.
845 Third Avenue
New York, NY 10022
Tel. (212) 759-0900
(toll-free) 1-800-872-6273
FAX (212) 980-7014

Congressional Information Service
4520 East-West Highway, Suite 800
Bethesda, MD 20814-3389
Tel (301) 654-1550
(toll-free) 1-800-638-8380
FAX (301) 654-4033

Congressional Quarterly, Inc.
1414 22nd Street NW
Washington, DC 20037
Tel. (202) 887-6279
(toll-free) 1-800-432-2250

Council of State Governments
Iron Works Pike
Box 11910
Lexington, KY 40578-1910
Tel. (606) 231-1939

Data Processing Management Association
505 Busse Highway
Park Ridge, IL 60068
Tel. (708) 825-8124

Datapro Information Services Group
600 Delran Parkway
Delran, NJ 08075
Tel. (toll-free) 1-800-328-2776
FAX (609) 764-8953

Data-Star
485 Devon Park Drive
Wayne, PA 19087
Tel. (toll-free) 1-800-221-7754

and

114 Jermyn St
London SW1Y 6HJ
England
Tel. 071 930 5503

Dearborn Trade
520 North Dearborn Street
Chicago, IL 60610-4354
Tel. (312) 863-4400
(toll-free) 1-800-245-2665
FAX (312) 836-1021

Deer Creek Publishing
3990 North 480 East
Provo, UT 84604
Tel. (801) 225-0702

Demosphere International, Inc.
4300 Fair Lakes Court
Fairfax, VA 22033
Tel. (703) 802-0100
FAX (703) 802-0102

Department of Labor/Bureau of
   Labor Statistics
U.S. Department of Commerce
Economics and Statistics Administration
Washington, DC 20230
Tel. (202) 482-1986
FAX (202) 482-2164

DIALOG Information Services, Inc.
33460 Hillview Avenue
Palo Alto, CA 94304
Tel. (415) 858-7069
(toll-free) 1-800-334-2564

Diamond, Inc.
1-4-2 Kasumingaseki
Chiyoda-ku, Tokyo 100
JAPAN
Tel. (03) 35046381
FAX (03) 35046397

Direct Marketing Publishers
c/o Direct Marketing Association, Inc.
11 West 42nd Street
New York, NY 10036-8096
Tel. (212) 768-7277
FAX (212) 599-1268

Disclosure®, Inc
5161 River Road
Bethesda, MD 20816
Tel. (301) 951-1300

Dodwell Marketing Consultants
C.P.O. Box 297
Tokyo, Japan 100-91

Doubleday
1540 Broadway
New York, NY 10036
Tel. (212) 354-6500
FAX (212) 302-6985

Dow Jones and Company, Inc.
P.O. Box 300
Princeton, NU 08543-0300
Tel. (609) 520-4000

Dow Jones & Co.
National Business Employments Weekly
P.O. Box 435
Chicopee, MA 01021
Tel. (toll-free) 1-800-562-4868

DRI/McGraw-Hill
Data Products Division
24 Hartwell Avenue
Lexington, MA 02173
Tel. (617) 863-5100

Dun & Bradstreet Information Services
3 Sylvan Way

Parsippany, NJ 07054
Tel. (201) 605-6000
(toll-free) 1-800-526-0651
FAX (201) 605-6911
Moody's Investor Services
(toll-free) 1-800-342-5647

Dun & Bradstreet United Kingdom
Holmers Farm Way
High Wycombe
Bucks HP 12 4 UL
United Kingdom
Tel. 0494-422 000
FAX 0494-422 260

Economics and Resource Development
   Center
Asian Development Bank
P.O. Box 789
1099 Manila, Philippines

The Economist Books
Axe and Bottle Court
70 Newcomen Court
London SE1 1YT
England

The Economist Intelligence Unit
Subscriptions Department

   P.O. Box 154
   Dartford, Kent
   DA1 1QB England
   Tel. 0322-289 194
   FAX 0322-223 803

   215 Park Avenue South
   New York, NY 10003
   Tel. (212) 460-0600
   FAX (212) 995-8837

   10th Floor
   Luk Kwok Centre
   72 Gloucester Road
   Wanchai, Hong Kong
   Tel. (852) 529-0833
   FAX (852) 865-1554

Entrepreneur Group, Inc.
2392 Morse Avenue
Irvine, CA 92714
Tel. (714) 261-2325
FAX (714) 755-4211

Euromoney Books
Plymouth Distributors Limited
Estover Plymouth PL6 7PZ
United Kingdom
FAX 44 752 695 668

Euromoney Publications PLC
Nestor House, Playhouse Yard
London EC4V 5EX
United Kingdom

Euromonitor PLC
87-88 Turnmill Street
London EC1M 5QU
Tel. (071) 2518024
FAX (071) 6083149

Europa Publications Inc.
18 Bedford Sq.
London WCI 3JN
Tel. (071) 5808236

European Direct Marketing Association
34 rue de Gouvernement
Provisoire
13-1000 Brussels
Belgium
Tel. 2 2176309

European Venture Capital Association
Kieberpark-Minervastraat 6
Box 6, B-1930
Zavertem, Belgium
Tel. 32 2 720 60 10
FAX 32 2 725 30 66

Export USA Publications
4141 Parklawn Avenue South
Minneapolis, MN 55435

The Exporter
34 West 37th Street
New York, NY 10018
Tel. (212) 563-2772

Facts on File
460 Park Avenue South
New York, NY 10016
Tel. (toll-free) 1-800-443-8323
FAX (212) 213-4578

Fairchild Publications
Seven West 34th Street
New York, NY 10001

Tel. (212) 630-3880
(toll-free) 1-800-247-6622

Families & Work Institute
330 Seventh Avenue
New York, NY 10001
Tel. (212) 465-2044
FAX (212) 465-8637

The Federal Reserve Bulletin
Publications Services
Board of Governors of the Federal
   Reserve System
Washington, DC 20551

The Financial Times Business
   Information, Ltd.
50-64 Broadway
London SW1 0DB
Tel. (071) 7992002
Fax (071) 7992259

FIND/SVP
625 Avenue of the Americas
New York, NY 10011
Tel. (212) 645-4500
(toll-free) 1-800-346-3787

Forbes, Inc.
60 Fifth Avenue
New York, NY 10011
Tel. (212) 620-2200
FAX (212) 620-2417

Foreign Trade Division
U.S. Bureau of the Census
Washington, DC 20023
Tel. (301) 763-7662

Fortune Magazine
229 West 28th Street
New York, NY 10001
Tel. (toll-free) 1-800-541-1000

Forum Publishing Co.
383 East Main Street
Centerport, NY 11721
Tel. (516) 754-5000

The Foundation Center
79 Fifth Avenue
New York, NY 10003
Tel. (212) 620-4230
(toll free) 1-800-424-9836

The Free Press
A Division of Macmillan Inc.
866 Third Avenue
New York, NY 10022
Tel. (toll-free) 1-800-323-7441

Gale Research, Inc.
835 Penobscot Building
Detroit, MI 48226
Tel. (313) 961-2242
(toll-free) 1-800-877-4253
FAX (313) 961-6083

Garrett Park Press
P.O. Box 190 B
Garrett Park, MD 20896
Tel. (301) 946-2553

General Services Administration
Federal Procurement Data Center
7th & D Streets SW, Room 56552
Washington, DC 20407

Goldhirsh Group, Inc.
488 Madison Avenue
New York, NY 10022
Tel. (212) 326-2600

Government Institutes Inc.
Four Research Place
Suite 200
Rockville, MD 20850
Tel. (301) 921-2300
FAX (301) 921-0373

Government Printing Office
Superintendent of Documents
U.S. Government Printing Office
Washington, DC 20402
Tel. (202) 783-3238

Graham & Trotman, Sterling House
66 Wilton Road
London SW1V 1DE
United Kingdom
Tel. (071) 8211123
FAX (071) 6305229

Grey Castle Press
Pocket Knife Square
Lakeville, CT 06039
Tel. (203) 435-2518
FAX (203) 435-8093

Harcourt Brace Jovanovich Miller
6277 Sea Harbor Drive
Orlando, FL 32877
Tel. (toll-free) 1-800-831-7799

HarperCollins Publishers
10 East 53rd Street
New York, NY 10022
Tel. (212) 207-7000
(toll-free) 1-800-242-7737

Harvard Business School Press
Harvard Business School Publishing
   Division
Boston, MA 02163
Tel. (617) 495-6192

Hilit Publishing Company, Ltd.
3rd Floor, No. 1 Hsin-yi Road, Sec. 4
Taipei, Taiwan, R.O.C

Hoke Publications, Inc.
224 Seventh Street
Garden City, NY 11530-9823
Tel. (516) 746-6700

Henry Holt & Co., Inc.
115 West 18th Street
New York, NY 10011
Tel. (212) 886-9200
FAX (212) 633-0748

Houghton Mifflin Co.
One Beacon Street
Boston, MA 02108
Tel. (617) 725-5000
(toll-free) 1-800-225-3362
FAX (617) 227-5409

Human Resource Information Network
College Park North
9585 Valparaiso Court
Indianapolis, IN 46268
Tel. (317) 872-2045

Hunt Scanlon Publishing
Two Pickwick Plaza
Greenwich, CT 06830
Tel. (203) 629-3629

ICC Information Group Ltd.
ICC Online Services Division
Field House
72 Oldfield Road
Hampton, Middlesex TW12 2HQ
England

ICC Publishing Corporation
156 Fifth Avenue, Suite 820
New York, NY 10010
Tel. (212) 206-1150

ICP
823 East Westfield Blvd.
Indianapolis, IN 46620
(toll-free) 1-800-428-6179
Tel. (317) 251-7727
FAX (317) 251-7813

IFI/Plenum Data Corporation
3202 Kirkwood Highway
Wilmington, NC 19808
Tel. (919) 392-0068

Inc. Business Resources
Department 4413
P.O. Box 1365
Wilkes-Barre, PA 18703-1365
Tel. (toll-free) 1-800-524-1013

Info Press
728 Center Street
P.O. Box 550
Lewiston, NY 14092-0550

Information Access
   Company/Predicasts
11001 Cedar Avenue
Cleveland, OH 44016
Tel. (216) 795-3000
(toll-free) 1-800-321-6388

Information USA, Inc.
3720 Farragut Avenue
P.O. Box E
Kensington, MD 20895
Tel. (301) 942-6303
(toll-free) 1-800-955-7693
FAX (301) 929-8907

Intercultural Systems (ISSI)
P.O. Box 588, Station B
Ottawa, Ontario K1P 5P7
Tel. (613) 238-6169
FAX (613) 238-5274

International Foundation of Employee
   Benefits Plans
18700 West Bluemound Road
Box 69
Brookfield, WI 53008
Tel. (414) 786-6700

International Franchise Association
1350 New York Avenue NW,
   Suite 900
Washington, DC 20005
Tel. (202) 628-8000

International Monetary Fund,
   Publications Services
700 19th Street NW, Suite C-100
Washington, DC 20431
Tel. (202) 623-7000

International Venture Capital
   Institute, Inc.
P.O. Box 1333
Stamford, CT 06904
Tel. (203) 323-3143

Iowa State University Press
2121 State Avenue
Ames, IA 50010
Tel. (515) 292-1040
FAX (515) 292-3348

Richard D. Irwin, Inc.
1818 Ridge Road
Homewood, IL 60430
Tel. (708) 798-6000
(toll-free) 1-800-634-3961

Peter Isaacson Publications Pty. Ltd.
46-50 Porter Street
Prahan Victoria 3181 Australia
Tel. 61 3 520 5555
FAX 61 3 521 2990

The Japan Institute of International
   Affairs
19th Mori Building
1-20 Toranmon 1-Chome
Minato-ku
Tokyo, Japan

Japan Special Libraries Association
Kinokuniya Bookstore Co., Ltd.
17-1 Shinjuku-ku
Tokyo, Japan 160-91

The Johns Hopkins University Press
701 West 40 Street
Suite 275
Baltimore, MD 21211-2190
Tel. (301) 338-6900
FAX (301) 338-6998

Jossey-Bass Inc. Publishers
350 Sansome Street
San Francisco, CA 94104
(415) 433-1767

Journal of Commerce
2 World Trade Center
New York, NY 10048
Tel (212) 837-7000

Kennedy Publications
Templeton Road
Fitzwilliam, NH 03447
Tel. (603) 585-6544
(toll-free) 1-800-531-0007
FAX (603) 585-9555

Alfred A. Knopf, Inc.
201 East 50th Street
New York, NY 10022
Tel. (212) 751-2600
(toll-free) 1-800-638-6460
FAX (212) 572-2593

Kompass Japan
Shinjuku Hikari Building
5-6-11
Shinjuku
Tokyo 160 Japan
Tel. 81 3 3226-8877
FAX 81 3 3226-9922

Kompass U.K.
Reed Information Services
Windsor Court
East Grinstead House
East Grinstead, West Sussex RH19 1XA
England
Tel. 0342 326972

Kompass USA
c/o Globetech Publishing
30 Cannon Road
Wilton, CT 06897
Tel. (203) 762-3432

The Korea Directory Company
C.P.O. Box 3955
Seoul, Korea

Kothari Enterprises
Kothari Buildings
Utthamar Gandhi Road

Madras 600 034
India

Kuala Lumpur Stock Exchange
3rd, 4th, and 5th floor, Exchange
   Square Off Jalan Semantan,
   Damansara Heights
50490 Kuala Lumpur
Malaysia

Kyodo News International
50 Reckefeller Plaza
New York, NY 10020
Tel. (212) 586-0152

Lexington Books
c/o Macmillan Publishing
100 Flint Street
P.O. Box 500
Riverside, NJ 08075-7500
Tel. (toll-free) 1-800-323-7445

LEXIS
(see Mead Data Central)

Liberty Hall Press/McGraw-Hill
Blue Ridge Summit, PA 17214
Tel. (toll-free) 1-800-822-8158

Longman Group UK Ltd.
Longman House
Burnt Mill, Harlow Essex
CM20 2EJ
Tel. (0279) 426721
FAX (0279) 431059

MacFarlane and Co., Inc.
One Park Place
1900 Emery Street NW
Atlanta, GA 30318
Tel. (404) 352-2290
FAX (404) 352-2299

The Market Research Society
15 Northburg Street
London, EC1 0AH
England

Marquis Who's Who
Macmillan Directory Division
3002 Glenview Road
Wilmette, IL 60091
Tel. (708) 256-6067

Massachusetts Institute of Technology
Center for Advanced Engineering
Studies
MIT
77 Massachussets Avenue E52-473
Cambridge, MA 02139
Tel. (617) 253-1000

McGraw-Hill, Inc.
1221 Avenue of the Americas
New York, NY 10020
Tel. (212) 512-2000

Mead Data Central
9443 Springboro Pike
P.O. Box 933
Dayton, OH 45401
Tel. (513) 865-6800
(toll-free) 1-800-227-4908

Media General Financial Services
P.O. Box 85333
Richmond, VA 23293
Tel. (804) 649-6549
(toll-free) 1-800-446-3922
FAX (804) 649-6097

MIT Enterprise Forum of Cambridge
Technology Capital Network, Inc.
201 Vassar Street
Cambridge, MA 02139
Tel. (617) 253-7163

The MIT Press
55 Hayward Street
Cambridge, MA 02142
Tel. (617) 253-5646
(toll-free) 1-800-356-0343
FAX (617) 258-6779

Monitor Publishing Company
104 Fifth Avenue, 2nd Floor
New York, NY 10011
Tel. (212) 627-4140
FAX (212) 645-0931

Moody's Investor Services
Dun & Bradstreet Corporation
99 Church Street
New York, NY 10007
Tel. (212) 553-0300

Robert Morris Associates
(The Association of Bank Loan and
Credit Officers)
One Liberty Place
Philadelphia, PA 19103-7398
Tel. (215) 851-0585

National Association of Small Business
Investment Companies
1199 North Fairfax Street, No. 200
Alexandria, VA 22314
Tel. (703) 683-1601

National Register Publishing
121 Chanlon Road
P.O. Box 31
New Providence, NJ 07974
Tel. (toll-free) 1-800-521-8110
FAX (908) 665-6688

National Technical Information
Service
5285 Port Royal Road
Springfield, VA 22161
Tel. (703) 487-4600
(toll-free) 1-800-336-4700

Nelson Publications
One Gateway Plaza
Portchester, NY 10573
Tel. (914) 937-8400
FAX (914) 937-8908

New Generations Research, Inc.
225 Friend Street
Boston, MA 02114
Tel. (617) 573-9550

New Strategist Publications
P.O. Box 242
Ithaca, NY 14851
Tel. (607) 273-0913

New York Chapter of the American
Marketing Association
310 Madison Avenue
New York, NY 10017
Tel. (212) 687-3280

New York Law Publishing Company
111 Eighth Avenue
New York, NY 10011
Tel. (212) 741-8300
(toll-free) 1-800-888-8300

The New York Times
229 West 43rd Street
New York, NY 10036
Tel. (212) 556-1573
FAX (212) 556-6862

NEXIS
(see Mead Data Central)

NoLo Press
950 Parker Street
Berkeley, CA 94710
Tel. (toll-free) 1-800-992-6656
FAX (510) 548-5902

North America Publishing Co.
401 North Broad Street
Philadelphia, PA 19108
Tel. (215) 238-5300

NPA Data Services
1424 16th Street NW
Suite 700
Washington, DC 20036
Tel. (202) 265-7685

NTC Publishing Group
4255 West Touhy Avenue
Lincolnwood, IL 60646
Tel. (toll-free) 1-800-323-4900

Oasis Press/PSI Research
300 North Valley Drive
Grant's Pass, OR 97526
Tel. (503) 479-9464
(toll-free) 1-800-228-2275

Omnigraphics, Inc.
Penobscot Bldg.
Detroit, MI 48226
Tel. (313) 961-1340

Online, Inc.
11 Tannery Lane
Weston, CT 06883
Tel. (203) 227-8466

ORBIT Search Service
8000 Westpark Dr.
McLean, VA 22102
Tel. (toll-free) 1-800 456-7248

Organization for Economic Cooperation
and Development
OECD Publications and Information
Center

2001 L Street, Suite 700
Washington, DC 20036-4910
Tel. (202) 785-6323
(toll-free) 1-800-456-OECD or
1-800-456-6323
FAX (202) 785-0350

Oryx Press
4041 North Central Avenue
Phoenix, AZ 85012
Tel. (602) 265-2651
(toll-free) 1-800-279-6799

Oxbridge Communications, Inc.
150 Fifth Avenue
New York, NY 10011
Tel. (212) 741-0231
(toll-free) 1-800-955-0231
FAX (212) 633-2938

Panel Publishers, Inc.
36 West 44th Street
New York, NY 10036
Tel. (212) 790-2000
FAX (212) 302-5119

Peterson's
Department 2326 Carnegie Center
P.O. Box 2123
Princeton, NJ 08543-2123
Tel. (toll-free) 1-800-338-3282
FAX (609) 243-9150

Pilot Books
103 Cooper Street
Babylon, NY 11702
Tel. (516) 422-2225

Planning Review
P.O. Box 70
Oxford, OH 45056-0070
Tel. (513) 523-4185

Predicasts
11001 Cedar Avenue
Cleveland, OH 44106
Tel. (216) 795-3000
(toll-free) 1-800-321-6388

Prentice Hall, Inc.
44 Sylvan Avenue
Engelwood Cliffs, NJ 07632
Tel. (201) 592-2000

Probus Publishing Company, Inc.
1925 N. Clybourn Avenue
Chicago, IL 60614
Tel. (toll-free) 1-800-776-2871
Fax (312) 686-6250

Productivity Press, Inc.
Box 3007
Cambridge, MA 02140
Tel. (617) 497-5146
(toll-free) 1-800-274-9911
FAX (617) 864-6286

Puma Press
1670 Coral Drive
Santa Monica, CA 03454
Tel. (toll-free) 1-800-255-5730, ext. 10

The Putnam Berkley Group
200 Madison Avenue
New York, NY 10016
Tel. (212) 951-8400
(toll-free) 1-800-631-8571
FAX (212) 213-6707

Quality Press/American Society for
   Quality Control (ASQC)
611 E. Wisconsin Avenue
Milwaukee, WI 53202
Tel. (414) 272-8575
FAX (414) 272-1734

Quality and Productivity Management
   Association
300 N. Martingale Road
Suite 230
Schaumburg, IL 60173
Tel. (708) 619-2909

Quality Services Co.
5920 Overpass Road
Santa Barbara, CA 93111-2048

Que Corporation
(A Division of Macmillan Publishing
   Company)
11711 N. College Avenue
Suite 140
Carmel, IN 46032
Tel. (317) 573-2500
FAX (317) 573-2583

Quest Management Systems
580 Kirts Boulevard, Suite 315

Troy, MI 48084
Tel. (313) 362-3770
FAX (313) 362-4686

or

Four Commerce Park Square
23200 Chagrin Boulevard
Beachwood, OH 44122
Tel. (216) 292-8288
FAX (216) 464-7609

Reed Information Services, Ltd.
Windsor Court
East Grinstead
West Sussex RH 19 1XD
United Kingdom
Tel. 0342 326 972
FAX 0342 317 241

Reed Reference Publishing
121 Chanlon Road
Princeton, N.J.
Tel. (908) 665-2867
(toll-free) 1-800-521-8110

The Reference Press, Inc.
6448 Highway 290 East, Suite E104
Austin, TX 78723
Tel. (512) 454-7778
FAX (512) 454-9401

Republic of the Philippines
National Statistics Office
Manila, Philippines

RIA Tax Publishing Division, Research
   Institute of America Inc.
910 Sylvan Avenue
Englewood Cliffs, NJ 07632-3301
Tel. (toll-free) 1-800-431-9025

St. James Press
233 Ontario Street
Chicago, IL 60611
Tel. (312) 787-5800
(toll-free) 1-800-345-0392
FAX (312) 787-6448

Sales and Marketing Magazine
355 Park Avenue South
New York, NY 10017
Tel. (212) 592-6200
(toll-free) 1-800-253-6708

Schonfeld & Associates, Inc.
One Sherwood Drive
Lincolnshire, IL 60069
Tel. (708) 948-8080
FAX (708) 948-8096

SEC On-line, Inc.
201 Moreland Road
Hauppage, NY 11788
Tel. (516) 864-7200

Securities Data Company Publishing
  (SDC Publishing)
40 West 57th Street
New York, NY 10019
Tel. (212) 765-5311
FAX (212) 765-6123

Sibson and Co., Inc.
212 Carnegie Center, CN
Princeton, NJ 08543
Tel. (609) 520-2700

Charles E. Simon & Co.
1333 H Street NW
Suite 500
Washington, DC 20005
Tel. (toll-free) 1-800-543-4502
(202) 289-5300 in Washington, DC

Simon and Schuster
1230 Avenue of the Americas
New York, NY 10020
Tel. (212) 698-7000
Customer Service tel. (515) 284-6751
FAX (212) 698-7007

Special Libraries Association
1700 18th Street NW
Washington, DC 20009
Tel. (202) 234-4700
FAX (202) 265-9317

SRDS (Standard Rate and Data Service)
3004 Glenview Road
Wilmette, IL 60091
Tel. (708) 256-8333
(toll-free) 1-800-323-4588
FAX (708) 441-2252

Staff Directories, Ltd.
Mt. Vernon, VA 22121-0062
Tel. (703) 739-0900

Standard & Poor's
25 Broadway
New York, NY 10004
Tel. (212) 208-8000
(toll-free) 1-800-221-5277 (sales)
1-800-852-1641 (customer service)
FAX (212) 412-0543 (sales)
FAX (212) 412-0241 (customer service)

Statistics Canada
Statistical Reference Center
R. H. Coats Bldg., Lobby
Holland Avenue
Ottawa, Ontario
K1A 0T6
Tel. (613) 951-8116

Stock Exchange of Singapore, Ltd.
1 Raffles Place
24-00 OUB Centre
Singapore 0104

Stockton Press (The Macmillan
  Publishing Company)
257 Park Avenue South
New York, NY 10010
Tel. (212) 637-4400
(toll-free) 1-800-221-2123
FAX (212) 673-9842

Strategic Mapping, Inc.
3135 Kifer Road
Santa Clara, CA 95051
Tel. (408) 970-9600
FAX (408) 970-9999

The Strategic Planning Institute
1030 Massachusetts Avenue
Cambridge, MA 02138
Tel. (617) 491-9200
FAX (617) 491-1634

Sutton Place Publications
221 S.W. 64th Street
Pembroke Pines, FL 33023
Tel. (305) 996-1530

Tax Analysts
6830 N. Fairfax Avenue
Arlington, VA 22213
Tel. (toll-free) 1-800-955-2444
FAX (703) 533-4444

Ten Speed Press
P.O. Box 7123
Berkeley, CA 94707
Tel. (415) 845-8414
(toll-free) 1-800-841-2665

Thomas Publishing Co., Inc.
One Penn Plaza
New York, NY 10119
Tel. (212) 695-0500

Thompson Financial Networks
11 Farnsworth Street
Boston, MA 02210
Tel. (617) 345-2000
(toll-free) 1-800-662-7878

Thomson Financial Publishing
4709 West Golf Road
Skokie, IL 60076-1253
Tel. (toll-free) 1-800-443-2824

Thomson & Thomson
500 Victory Road
North Quincy, MA 02171-2126
Tel. (toll-free) 1-800-692-8833

Toyo Keizai Shinposha Ltd.
1-2-1 Nihonbashi Hongokucho
Chuo-ku
Tokyo 103, Japan
Tel. (03) 32465469

Trademark Service Corporation
747 Third Avenue
New York, NY 10017
Tel. (212) 421-5730

UMI/Data Courier
620 S. Third Street
Louisville, KY 40202-2475
Tel. (502) 583-4111
(toll-free) 1-800-626-2823
FAX (502) 589-5572

United Nations Publications
United Nations
New York, NY 10017
Tel. (212) 963-7680
(toll-free) 1-800-553-3210

United States Bureau of the Census
Washington, DC 20233

  Census Customer Services
  Tel. (301) 763-4100

Census Public Information Office
Tel. (301) 763-4040

Census CD-Rom
Tel. (301) 763-4677

CENDATA
Tel. (301) 763-2074

United States Copyright Office
Register of Copyrights
Library of Congress
Washington, DC 20559
Tel. (202) 707-3000

United States Government Printing
  Office
Superintendent of Documents
Washington, DC 20402
Tel. (202) 783-3238

University Microfilms International
300 North Zeeb Road
Ann Arbor, MI 48105
Tel. (313) 761-4700
(toll-free) 1-800-521-0600
FAX (313) 665-5022

University of California, Latin
  American Center
2334 Bowditch Street
Berkeley, CA 94720
Tel. (510) 642-2088
FAX (510) 642-3460

University of California Press
California Princeton Fulfillment
  Service
1445 Lower Ferry Road
Ewing, NJ 08618
Tel. (609) 883-1759
(toll-free) 1-800-822-6657
FAX (toll-free) 1-800-999-1958

or

2120 Berkeley Way
Berkeley, CA 94720
Tel. (510) 642-4247

Value Line Publishing
711 Third Avenue
New York, NY 10017
Tel. (212) 687-3965
FAX (212) 986-3243

Van Nostrand Reinhold
115 Fifth Avenue
New York, NY 10003
Tel. (toll-free) 1-800-842-3636

Warren, Gorham & Lamont, Inc.
One Penn Plaza
New York, NY 10119
Tel. (212) 971-5000
(toll-free) 1-800-922-0606

Washington Researchers, Ltd.
2612 P Street NW
Washington, DC 20007
Tel. (202) 333-3533

WEFA Group
401 City Line Avenue
Suite 300
Bala Cynwyd, PA 19004
Tel. (215) 660-6300
FAX (215) 660-6477

John Wiley & Sons, Inc.
605 Third Avenue
New York, NY 10158
Tel. (212) 850-6000
(toll-free) 1-800-225-5945

H. W. Wilson Company
950 University Avenue
Bronx, NY 10452
Tel. (212) 588-8400
(toll-free) 1-800-367-6770
FAX (212) 590-1617

W.I.S.E.R. Research
8955 13th Avenue, Suite 5

Montreal, Quebec H1Z 3L1
Canada

Woods & Poole Economics, Inc.
1794 Columbus Road NW
Suite 4
Washington, DC 20009-2805
Tel. (toll-free) 1-800-786-1915

World Almanac
Scripps Howard
200 Park Avenue
New York, NY 10166

The World Bank, Publications
    Department
1818 H Street, NW
Washington, DC 20006
Tel. (202) 477-1234

World of Information
21 Gold Street
Saffron Walden
Essex, CB10 1EJ
United Kingdom

Wyatt Data Services
218 Route 17 North
Rochelle Park, NJ 07662
Tel. (201) 843-1177

Ziff-Davis Press
5903 Christie Avenue
Emeryville, CA 94608
Tel. (415) 601-2000
(toll-free) 1-800-688-0448
FAX (415) 601-2099

Appendices

APPENDIX 1

INTERNATIONAL TIME ZONES
Standard Time in 100 Major Cities around the World When It Is 12:00 Noon in New York

City	Time	City	Time
Alexandria, Egypt	7:00 P.M.	London, England	5:00 P.M.
[1]Amsterdam, Netherlands	6:00 P.M.	Los Angeles, California	9:00 A.M.
Anchorage, Alaska	7:00 A.M.	[1]Madrid, Spain	6:00 P.M.
Asuncion, Paraguay	1:00 P.M.	Manila, Philippines	1:00 A.M. (next day)
Athens, Greece	7:00 P.M.	Melbourne, Australia	3:00 A.M. (next day)
Auckland, New Zealand	5:00 A.M. (next day)	Mexico City, Mexico	11:00 A.M.
Baghdad, Iraq	8:00 P.M.	Miami, Florida	12:00 Noon
Bangkok, Thailand	12:00 Midnight	Montevideo, Uruguay	2:00 P.M.
Beijing, China	1:00 A.M. (next day)	Montreal, Quebec	12:00 Noon
Belgrade, Yugoslavia	6:00 P.M.	[1]Moscow, Russia	8:00 P.M.
Berlin, Germany	6:00 P.M.	Nairobi, Kenya	8:00 P.M.
Bogota, Colombia	12:00 Noon	Nome, Alaska	6:00 A.M.
Bombay, India	10:30 P.M.	Oslo, Norway	6:00 P.M.
Boston, Massachusetts	12:00 Noon	Ottawa, Ontario	12:00 Noon
[1]Brussels, Belgium	6:00 P.M.	Panama City, Panama	12:00 Noon
Bucharest, Romania	7:00 P.M.	[1]Paris, France	6:00 P.M.
Budapest, Hungary	6:00 P.M.	Perth, Australia	1:00 A.M. (next day)
[1]Buenos Aires, Argentina	2:00 P.M.	Philadelphia, Pennsylvania	12:00 Noon
Cairo, Egypt	7:00 P.M.	Prague, Czechoslovakia	6:00 P.M.
Calcutta, India	10:30 P.M.	Quito, Ecuador	12:00 Noon
Cape Town, Republic of		Rangoon, Burma	11:30 P.M.
So. Africa	7:00 P.M.	Regina, Saskatchewan	10:00 A.M.
Caracas, Venezuela	1:00 P.M.	Reykjavik, Iceland	4:00 P.M.
[1]Casablanca, Morocco	6:00 P.M.	Rio de Janeiro, Brazil	2:00 P.M.
Chicago, Illinois	11:00 A.M.	Rome, Italy	6:00 P.M.
Colombo, Sri Lanka (Ceylon)	10:30 P.M.	Saigon, Vietnam	1:00 A.M. (next day)
Copenhagen, Denmark	6:00 P.M.	Saint John's, Newfoundland	1:30 P.M.
Delhi, India	10:30 P.M.	Saint Louis, Missouri	11:00 A.M.
Denver, Colorado	10:00 A.M.	Salt Lake City, Utah	10:00 A.M.
Detroit, Michigan	12:00 Noon	San Francisco, California	9:00 A.M.
Djakarta, Indonesia	12:00 Midnight	San Juan, Puerto Rico	1:00 P.M.
Dublin, Ireland	5:00 P.M.	Santiago, Chile	1:00 P.M.
Geneva, Switzerland	6:00 P.M.	Sao Paulo, Brazil	2:00 P.M.
Glasgow, Scotland	5:00 P.M.	Seattle, Washington	9:00 A.M.
Halifax, Nova Scotia	1:00 P.M.	Shanghai, China	1:00 A.M. (next day)
Havana, Cuba	12:00 Noon	Singapore	12:30 A.M. (next day)
Helsinki, Finland	7:00 P.M.	Sofia, Bulgaria	7:00 P.M.
Hong Kong	1:00 A.M. (next day)	Stockholm, Sweden	6:00 P.M.
Honolulu, Hawaii	7:00 A.M.	Sydney, Australia	3:00 A.M. (next day)
Houston, Texas	11:00 A.M.	Tehran, Iran	8:30 P.M.
Istanbul, Turkey	7:00 P.M.	Tel Aviv, Israel	7:00 P.M.
Jerusalem, Israel	7:00 P.M.	Tokyo, Japan	2:00 A.M. (next day)
Johannesburg, Republic of		Toronto, Ontario	12:00 Noon
So. Africa	7:00 P.M.	Vancouver, British Columbia	9:00 A.M.
Juneau, Alaska	9:00 A.M.	Vienna, Austria	6:00 P.M.
Karachi, Pakistan	10:00 P.M.	[1]Vladivostok, Russia	3:00 A.M. (next day)
Kuala Lumpur, Malaysia	12:30 A.M. (next day)	Warsaw, Poland	6:00 P.M.
La Paz, Bolivia	1:00 P.M.	Washington, D.C.	12:00 Noon
Leningrad, Russia	8:00 P.M.	Wellington, New Zealand	5:00 A.M. (next day)
Lima, Peru	12:00 Noon	Winnipeg, Manitoba	11:00 A.M.
[1]Lisbon, Portugal	6:00 P.M.	Zurich, Switzerland	6:00 P.M.

[1]Time is one hour in advance of the standard meridian.

607

APPENDIX 2

WEIGHTS AND MEASUREMENTS CONVERSIONS
Approximate Conversion Measures
Source: Statistical Abstract of the United States

Symbol	When you know conventional	Multiply by	To find metric	Symbol
in	inch	2.54	centimeter	cm
ft	foot	30.48	centimeter	cm
yd	yard	0.91	meter	m
mi	mile	1.61	kilometer	km
in^2	square inch	6.45	square centimeter	cm^2
ft^2	square foot	0.09	square meter	m^2
yd^2	square yard	0.84	square meter	m^2
mi^2	square mile	2.59	square kilometer	km^2
	acre	0.41	hectare	ha
oz	ounce*	28.35	gram	g
lb	pound*	.45	kilograms	kg
oz (troy)	ounce**	31.10	gram	g
	short ton (2,000 lbs)	0.91	metric ton	t
	long ton (2,240 lbs)	1.12	metric ton	t
fl oz	fluid ounce	29.57	mililiter	mL
c	cup	0.24	liter	L
pt	pint	0.47	liter	L
qt	quart	0.95	liter	L
gal	gallon	3.78	liter	L
ft^3	cubic foot	0.03	cubic meter	m^3
yd^3	cubic yard	0.76	cubic meter	m^3
F	degrees Fahrenheit (subtract 32)	0.55	degrees Celsius	C

Symbol	When you know metric	Multiply by	To find conventional	Symbol
cm	centimeter	0.39	inch	in
cm	centimeter	0.33	foot	ft
m	meter	1.09	yard	yd
km	kilometer	0.62	mile	mi
cm^2	square centimeter	0.15	square inch	in^2
m^2	square meter	10.76	square foot	ft^2
m^2	square meter	1.20	square yard	yd^2
km^2	square kilometer	0.39	square mile	mi^2
ha	hectare	2.47	acre	
g	gram	.035	ounce*	oz
kg	kilogram	2.21	pounds	lb*
g	gram	.032	ounce**	oz (troy)
t	metric ton	1.10	short ton (2,000 lbs)	
t	metric ton	0.98	long ton (2,240 lbs)	
mL	mililiter	0.03	fluid ounce	fl oz
L	liter	4.24	cup	c
L	liter	2.13	pint (liquid)	pt
L	liter	1.05	quart (liquid)	qt
L	liter	0.26	gallon	gal
m^3	cubic meter	35.32	cubic foot	ft^3
m^3	cubic meter	1.32	cubic yard	yd^3
C	degrees Celsius	1.80	degrees Fahrenheit (after subtracting 32)	F

*For weighing ordinary commodities.
**For weighing precious metals, jewels, etc.

APPENDIX 3

THE 100 BEST COMPANIES TO WORK FOR IN AMERICA

From *The 100 Best Companies to Work for in America* by Robert Levering and Milton Moskowitz. Copyright © 1993 by Robert Levering and Milton Moskowitz. Used by permisson of Doubleday, a division of Bantam Doubleday Dell Publishing Group, Inc.

Acipco
Advanced Micro Devices
Alagasco
Anheuser-Busch
Apogee Enterprises
Armstrong
Avis
Baptist Hospital of Miami
BE&K
Ben & Jerry's Homemade
Beth Israel Hospital Boston
Leo Burnett
Chaparral Steel
Compaq Computer
Cooper Tire
Corning
Cray Research
Cummins Engine
Dayton Hudson
John Deere
Delta Air Lines
Donnelly
Du Pont
A.G. Edwards
Erie Insurance
Federal Express
Fel-Pro
First Federal Bank
  of California
H.B. Fuller
General Mills
Goldman Sachs
W.L. Gore & Associates
Great Plains Software
Hallmark Cards

Haworth
Hershey Foods
Hewitt Associates
Hewlett-Packard
Honda of America
  Manufacturing
IBM
Inland Steel
Intel
Johnson & Johnson
SC Johnson Wax
Kellogg
Knight-Ridder
Lands' End
Lincoln Electric
Los Angeles Dodgers
Lotus Development
Lowe's
Lyondell Petrochemical
Marquette Electronics
Mary Kay Cosmetics
McCormick
Merck
Methodist Hospital
Microsoft
Herman Miller
3M
Moog
J.P. Morgan
Morrison & Foerster
Motorola
Nissan Motor Manufacturing
Nordstrom
Northwestern Mutual Life
Odetics

Patagonia
J.C. Penney
Physio-Control
Pitney Bowes
Polaroid
Preston Trucking
Procter & Gamble
Publix Super Markets
Quad/Graphics
Reader's Digest
REI
Rosenbluth
  International
SAS Insititute
J.M. Smucker
Southwest Airlines
Springfield
  ReManufacturing
Springs
Steelcase
Syntex
Tandem
TDIndustries
Tennant
UNUM
USAA
U S WEST
Valassis
  Communications
Viking Freight System
Wal-Mart
Wegmans
Weyerhauser
Worthington Industries
Xerox

APPENDIX 4

THE FORTUNE 100
The Largest U.S. Industrial Corporations

Source: Fortune Magazine, April 19, 1993. Reprinted by permission. *Fortune*, Copyright © 1993. Time, Inc. All rights reserved.

Rank 1992	Rank 1991	Company	Location	Sales $ millions	Sales % change from 1991
1	1	General Motors	Detroit	132,774.9	7.3
2	2	Exxon	Irving, Texas	103,547.0	0.3
3	3	Ford Motor	Dearborn, Mich.	100,785.6	13.3
4	4	Intl. Business Machines	Armonk, N.Y.	65,096.0	(0.5)
5	5	General Electric	Fairfield, Conn.	62,202.0	3.3
6	6	Mobil	Fairfax, Va.	57,389.0	0.8
7	7	Philip Morris	New York	50,157.0	4.3
8	8	E.I. Du Pont De Nemours	Wilmington, Del.	37,643.0	(3.1)
9	10	Chevron	San Francisco	37,464.0	1.8
10	9	Texaco	White Plains, N.Y.	37,130.0	(1.1)
11	11	Chrysler	Highland Park, Mich.	36,897.0	25.6
12	12	Boeing	Seattle	30,184.0	3.0
13	13	Procter & Gamble	Cincinnati	29,890.0	9.1
14	14	Amoco	Chicago	25,543.0	(0.2)
15	17	Pepsico	Purchase, N.Y.	22,083.7	11.7
16	16	United Technologies	Hartford	22,032.0	3.6
17	15	Shell Oil	Houston	21,702.0	(2.2)
18	19	Conagra	Omaha	21,219.0	8.8
19	18	Eastman Kodak	Rochester, N.Y.	20,577.0	4.7
20	20	Dow Chemical	Midland, Mich.	19,177.0	(0.7)
21	22	Xerox	Stamford, Conn.	18,261.0	2.4
22	23	Atlantic Richfield	Los Angeles	18,061.0	2.1
23	21	McDonnell Douglas	St. Louis	17,513.0	(6.4)
24	26	Hewlett-Packard	Palo Alto, Calif.	16,427.0	13.0
25	24	USX	Pittsburgh	16,186.0	(5.7)
26	25	RJR Nabisco Holdings	New York	15,734.0	5.0
27	28	Digital Equipment	Maynard, Mass.	14,027.0	0.0
28	29	Minnesota Mining & Mfg.	St. Paul	13,833.0	4.1
29	34	Johnson & Johnson	New Brunswick, N.J.	13,846.0	10.5
30	27	Tenneco	Houston	13,606.0	(3.1)
31	32	International Paper	Purchase, N.Y.	13,600.0	7.1
32	39	Motorola	Schaumburg, Ill.	13,341.0	17.2
33	33	Sara Lee	Chicago	13,321.0	6.9
34	37	Coca-Cola	Atlanta	13,238.0	12.7
35	31	Westinghouse Electric	Pittsburgh	12,100.0	(5.4)
36	36	Allied-Signal	Morris Township, N.J.	12,089.0	1.7
37	30	Phillips Petroleum	Bartlesville, Okla.	11,933.0	(9.7)
38	41	Goodyear Tire & Rubber	Akron	11,923.6	7.9
39	38	Georgia Pacific	Atlanta	11,847.0	2.8
40	40	Bristol-Myers Squibb	New York	11,805.0	4.5
41	42	Anheuser-Busch	St. Louis	11,400.8	3.6
42	•	IBP	Dakota City, Neb.	11,129.7	0.9
45	35	Rockwell International	Seal Beach, Calif.	10,995.1	(8.6)
44	45	Caterpillar	Peoria, Ill.	10,194.0	0.1
45	47	Lockheed	Calabasas, Calif.	10,138.0	3.4

Rank				Sales	
1992	**1991**	**Company**	**Location**	**$ millions**	**% change from 1991**
46	49	Coastal	Houston	10,062.9	4.8
47	57	Merck	Whitehouse Station, N.J.	9,800.8	11.8
48	52	Ashland Oil	Ashland, Ky.	9,595.8	2.9
49	46	Aluminum Co. of America	Pittsburgh	9,588.4	(3.9)
50	60	Archer Daniels Midland	Decatur, Ill.	9,344.1	9.1
51	58	Weyerhauser	Tacoma	9,259.9	6.1
52	56	Unilever U.S.	New York	9,216.8	4.1
53	54	Citgo Petroleum	Tulsa	9,166.7	2.7
54	51	Raytheon	Lexington, Mass.	9,118.9	(2.5)
55	48	Unocal	Los Angeles	8,948.0	(8.5)
56	43	Occidental Petroleum	Los Angeles	8,940.0	(13.2)
57	61	American Brands	Old Greenwich, Conn.	8,840.3	5.5
58	50	General Dynamics	Falls Church, Va.	8,731.0	(8.8)
59	44	Sun	Philadelphia	8,626.0	(15.8)
60	53	Monsanto	St. Louis	8,485.0	(5.0)
61	55	Baxter International	Deerfield, Ill.	8,471.0	(5.0)
62	59	Unisys	Blue Bell, Pa.	8,421.9	(3.2)
63	63	Textron	Providence	8,347.5	6.5
64	62	TRW	Cleveland	8,311.0	5.0
65	70	Hanson Industries NA	Iselin, N.J.	8,288.3	16.7
66	74	Abbott Laboratories	Abbott Park, Ill.	7,894.2	14.0
67	71	American Home Products	New York	7,873.7	10.9
68	68	General Mills	Minneapolis	7,795.5	8.6
69	65	Ralston Purina	St. Louis	7,768.0	5.1
70	64	Emerson Electric	St. Louis	7,706.0	3.8
71	77	Texas Instruments	Dallas	7,470.0	9.7
72	69	Pfizer	New York	7,414.8	3.8
73	78	Whirlpool	Benton Harbor, Mich.	7,309.4	8.0
74	67	Borden	New York	7,142.6	(1.3)
75	76	Kimberly-Clark	Dallas	7,091.1	3.8
76	81	Apple Computer	Cupertino, Calif.	7,086.5	12.3
77	75	Hoechst Celanese	Somerville, N.J.	7,044.0	3.7
78	90	Colgate-Palmolive	New York	7,035.4	15.5
79	72	Deere	Moline, Ill.	6,960.7	(1.3)
80	79	H.J. Heinz	Pittsburgh	6,628.5	(0.8)
81	84	CPC International	Englewood Cliffs, N.J.	6,599.0	6.4
82	85	Miles	Pittsburgh	6,499.0	4.9
83	73	W.R. Grace	Boca Raton, Fla.	6,329.6	(8.9)
84	95	Eli Lilly	Indianapolis	6,282.3	7.3
85	82	Campbell Soup	Camden, N.J.	6,278.5	0.8
86	83	Honeywell	Minneapolis	6,254.0	0.5
87	92	Kellogg	Battle Creek, Mich.	6,190.6	7.0
88	66	Union Carbide	Danbury, Conn.	6,167.0	(16.0)
89	86	Cooper Industries	Houston	6,158.5	(0.1)
90	91	North American Philips	New York	6,138.0	1.2
91	80	Amerada Hess	New York	5,970.4	(7.0)
92	88	Martin Marietta	Bethesda, Md.	5,970.1	(2.1)
93	106	Intel	Santa Clara, Calif.	5,922.5	21.0
94	96	PPG Industries	Pittsburgh	5,857.7	2.3
95	99	Litton Industries	Beverly Hills	5,741.4	8.1
96	93	Reynolds Metals	Richmond	5,620.3	(2.8)
97	100	Warner-Lambert	Morris Plains, N.J.	5,597.6	8.3
98	89	Quaker Oats	Chicago	5,586.0	(8.4)
99	104	Levi Strauss Associates	San Francisco	5,570.3	13.6
100	97	Northrop	Los Angeles	5,550.0	(2.7)

APPENDIX 5

THE WORLD'S 100 LARGEST INDUSTRIAL CORPORATIONS

Source: *Fortune* Magazine, July 26, 1993. Reprinted by permission. *Fortune*, Copyright © 1993. Time, Inc. All rights reserved.

Rank				Sales	
1992	1991	Company	Location	$ millions	% change from 1991
1	1	General Motors	United States	132,774.9	7.3
2	3	Exxon	United States	103,547.0	0.3
3	4	Ford Motor	United States	100,785.6	13.3
4	2	Royal Dutch/Shell Group	Britain/Netherlands	98,935.3	(4.7)
5	5	Toyota Motor	Japan	79,114.2	1.3
6	7	IRI	Italy	67,547.4	5.4
7	6	International Business Machines	United States	65,096.0	(0.5)
8	11	Daimler-Benz	Germany	63,339.5	10.5
9	8	General Electric	United States	62,202.0	3.3
10	9	Hitachi	Japan	61,465.5	3.1
11	10	British Petroleum	Britain	59,215.7	1.5
12	12	Matsushita Electric Industrial	Japan	57,480.8	0.5
13	13	Mobil	United States	57,389.0	0.8
14	17	Volkswagen	Germany	56,734.1	23.2
15	18	Siemens	Germany	51,401.9	14.6
16	14	Nissan Motor	Japan	50,247.5	2.8
17	15	Philip Morris	United States	50,157.0	4.3
18	19	Samsung	South Korea	49,559.6	11.5
19	16	Fiat	Italy	47,928.7	2.4
20	20	Unilever	Britain/Netherlands	43,962.6	6.5
21	21	ENI	Italy	40,365.5	(1.7)
22	24	ELF Aquitaine	France	39,717.8	7.0
23	26	Nestlé	Switzerland	39,057.9	9.8
24	25	Chevron	United States	38,523.0	4.7
25	27	Toshiba	Japan	37,471.6	5.7
26	22	E.I. Du Pont De Nemours	United States	37,386.0	(2.5)
27	23	Texaco	United States	37,103.0	(1.1)
28	33	Chrysler	United States	36,897.0	25.6
29	32	Renault	France	33,884.9	15.1
30	28	Honda Motor	Japan	33,369.6	0.9
31	29	Philips Electronics	Netherlands	33,269.7	10.1
32	34	Sony	Japan	31,451.9	7.9
33	30	ABB Asea Brown Boveri	Switzerland	30,536.0	2.8
34	38	Alcatel Alsthom	France	30,529.1	7.5
35	31	Boeing	United States	30,414.0	2.8
36	40	Proctor & Gamble	United States	29,890.0	9.1
37	35	Hoechst	Germany	29,570.6	3.0
38	37	Peugeot	France	29,387.4	3.5
39	39	BASF	Germany	28,494.3	1.3
40	36	NEC	Japan	28,376.5	(0.8)
41	46	Daewoo	South Korea	28,333.9	11.7
42	41	Fujitsu	Japan	27,910.7	7.1
43	42	Bayer	Germany	26,625.3	2.9
44	45	Mitsubishi Electric	Japan	26,502.3	3.7
45	43	Total	France	26,141.5	1.5

Rank				Sales	
1992	1991	Company	Location	$ millions	% change from 1991
46	44	Amoco	United States	25,543.0	(0.2)
47	49	Mitsubishi Motors	Japan	25,482.2	8.2
48	47	Nippon Steel	Japan	23,990.8	(2.5)
49	52	Mitsubishi Heavy Industries	Japan	23,011.3	7.1
50	50	Thyssen	Germany	22,731.5	0.6
51	56	Pepsico	United States	22,083.7	11.7
52	55	Robert Bosch	Germany	22,036.5	8.7
53	53	United Technologies	United States	22,032.0	3.6
54	62	INI	Spain	21,654.2	14.2
55	51	Imperial Chemical Industries	United States	21,548.9	(3.5)
56	48	PDVSA	Venezuela	21,375.0	(10.9)
57	60	PEMEX (Petróleos Méxicanos)	Mexico	21,292.8	10.3
58	58	Conagra	United States	21,219.0	8.8
59	54	Mazda Motor	Japan	20,867.4	1.5
60	64	BMW (Bayerische Motoren Werke)	Germany	20,611.2	11.2
61	57	Eastman Kodak	United States	20,577.0	4.7
62	65	Nippon Oil	Japan	19,863.8	7.2
63	59	Dow Chemical	United States	19,080.0	(1.2)
64	71	Repsol	Spain	18,618.3	14.8
65	76	Mannesmann	Germany	18,234.8	21.6
66	66	Xerox	United States	18,089.0	1.5
67	67	Atlantic Richfield	United States	18,061.0	2.1
68	61	British Aerospace	Britain	17,838.9	(6.0)
69	63	McDonnell Douglas	United States	17,513.0	(6.4)
70	68	Petrofina	Belgium	17,468.8	(1.0)
71	81	Hewlett-Packard	United States	16,427.0	13.0
72	69	Usinor-Sacilor	France	16,418.6	(4.7)
73	92	Metallgesellschaft	Germany	16,390.5	23.0
74	70	United StatesX	United States	16,186.0	(5.7)
75	83	Ferruzzi Finanziaria	Italy	16,136.8	12.4
76	78	Ciba-Geigy	Switzerland	16,119.4	7.7
77	74	Rhône-Poulenc	France	15,886.5	4.1
78	82	Viag	Germany	15,784.7	9.5
79	77	RJR Nabisco Holdings	United States	15,734.0	5.0
80	110	BTR	Britain	15,726.1	30.6
81	79	Ruhrkohle	Germany	15,712.0	5.4
82	72	Preussag	Germany	15,697.8	(0.9)
83	75	Idemitsu Kosan	Japan	15,662.9	4.3
84	84	Canon	Japan	15,348.9	7.7
85	88	Volvo	Sweden	14,920.7	11.5
86	154	Fried. Krupp	Germany	14,820.5	62.3
87	101	Ssangyong	South Korea	14,609.7	14.3
88	87	NKK	Japan	14,605.5	5.4
89	98	Petrobrás	Brazil	14,599.8	12.7
90	96	Sunkyong	South Korea	14,530.3	11.2
91	93	Saint-Gobain	France	14,296.9	7.4
92	91	Electrolux	Sweden	14,048.7	5.4
93	86	Digital Equipment	United States	14,027.0	–
94	73	Grand Metropolitan	Britain	13,964.6	(10.1)
95	90	Minnesota Mining & Mfg.	United States	13,883.0	4.1
96	94	Bridgestone	Japan	13,859.8	4.8
97	104	Johnson & Johnson	United States	13,846.0	10.5
98	97	Sumitomo Metal Industries	Japan	13,803.0	6.0
99	85	Tenneco	United States	13,606.0	(3.1)
100	102	International Paper	United States	13,600.0	7.1

APPENDIX 6

AMERICA'S 100 MOST ADMIRED COMPANIES*

Source: Fortune magazine, February 8, 1993. Reprinted by permission. *Fortune*, Copyright © 1993.
Time Inc. All rights reserved.

1. Merck 8.74	35. Abbott Laboratories 7.26	68. Ameritech 6.95
2. Rubbermaid 8.58	36. Apple Computer 7.25	69. Legget & Platt 6.95
3. Wal-Mart Stores 8.42	37. Reader's Digest 7.25	70. Martin Marietta 6.94
4. 3M 8.41	38. Illinois Tool Works 7.24	71. Pacific Telesis Group 6.94
5. Coca-Cola 8.19	39. AT&T 7.22	72. Shell Oil 6.94
6. Procter & Gamble 8.09	40. Northwestern Mutual 7.21	73. H.F. Ahmanson 6.92
7. Levi Strauss 7.96	41. Springs Industries 7.21	74. Atlantic Richfield 6.91
8. Liz Claiborne 7.95	42. Colgate-Palmolive 7.17	75. Knight-Ridder 6.91
9. J.P. Morgan 7.93	43. Eli Lilly 7.17	76. Schering-Plough 6.91
10. Boeing 7.88	44. Alcoa 7.16	77. Deere 6.90
11. Kimberly-Clark 7.87	45. American Intl. Group 7.16	78. Phelps Dodge 6.90
12. Corning 7.86	46. Great Western Finan. 7.16	79. ConAgra 6.89
13. Johnson & Johnson 7.83	47. Bankers Trust N.Y. 7.15	80. Federal Express 6.88
14. PepsiCo 7.77	48. Berkshire Hathaway 7.15	81. Ingersoll-Rand 6.88
15. Pfizer 7.76	49. Southwestern Bell 7.15	82. Huffy 6.87
16. General Mills 7.71	50. Philip Morris 7.13	83. MCI Communications 6.87
17. United Parcel Service 7.70	51. Xerox 7.11	84. Dayton Hudson 6.86
18. Motorola 7.69	52. Amoco 7.09	85. Eaton 6.86
19. Golden West Financial 7.58	53. Bell Atlantic 7.09	86. NationsBank 6.86
20. American Brands 7.56	54. Unilever U.S. 7.07	87. New York Life 6.83
21. Cooper Tire & Rubber 7.56	55. Bristol-Myers Squibb 7.06	88. Dow Jones 6.81
22. Du Pont 7.46	56. VF 7.05	89. Mobil 6.81
23. BellSouth 7.44	57. Bandag 7.04	90. Bausch & Lomb 6.79
24. Hewlett-Packard 7.44	58. PPG Industries 7.04	91. BankAmerica 6.78
25. Sara Lee 7.42	59. Exxon 7.03	92. Ford Motor 6.78
26. Shaw Industries 7.38	60. R.R. Donnelley 7.03	93. New York Times 6.77
27. General Electric 7.37	61. Pacific Gas & Electric 7.00	94. Campbell Soup 6.76
28. Harley-Davidson 7.36	62. A. Schulman 7.00	95. GTE 6.76
29. Herman Miller 7.36	63. Burlington Resources 6.98	96. Stanley Works 6.76
30. Intl. Flavors & Frag. 7.36	64. Emerson Electric 6.98	97. UST 6.76
31. Dow Chemical 7.33	65. International Paper 6.97	98. Crown Cork & Seal 6.75
32. Morgan Stanley Group 7.30	66. Reynolds Metals 6.97	99. Goodyear 6.75
33. Anheuser-Busch 7.28	67. Standard Fed. Bank 6.96	100. Union Pacific 6.75
34. Gillette 7.28		

*The Fortune Magazine Corporate Reputations Survey includes a total of 311 companies in 32 industries that appeared in the 1992 Fortune 500 and Fortune Service 500 directories. Over 8,000 senior executives, outside directors, and financial analysts were asked to rate the 10 largest companies in their own industry (or sometimes a shorter list) on eight attributes of reputation using a scale of 0 (poor) to 10 (excellent). Fortune 500 companies are assigned to a group based on the activity that contributed most to their 1991 industrial sales; Service 500 companies to a group based on the activity contributing most to their service sales.

In addition, the survey firm of Clark Martire & Bartolomeo examined the relationship between poll data and the financial performance of the companies, as published in the Fortune 500 and Service 500 directories. Twelve measures of performance were combined with the data into a spreadsheet. (Insurance companies were excluded because their data were incompatible.) A multiple regression was run to analyze the relationship between financial performance and the reputation score. The resulting equation was used to predict a reputation score based solely on financial performance.

614

APPENDIX 7

THE *INC.* 500 AMERICA'S FASTEST-GROWING PRIVATE COMPANIES*

Source: *Inc.* magazine, October 1992. Reprinted with permission, *Inc.* magazine. (October, 1992). Copyright 1992 by Goldhirsh Group, Inc., 38 Commerical Wharf, Boston, MA 02110.

Rank (1991)	Company/Location	Business Description	Sales Growth 1987–91 (% increase)	'91 sales ($000)	'87 sales ($000)	Profit range**		No. of employees		Date founded
						'91	'87	'91	'87	
1.	Kingston Technology Fountain Valley, CA	Mfrs. periph. for PCs	117,122%	$140,666	$120	A	A	110	2	1987
2.	Gateway 2000 (1) N. Sioux City, SD	Mfrs. & sells PCs	41,355	626,798	1,512	C	D	1,193	11	1985
3.	M.D. Enterprises of Connecticut N. Haven, CT	Provides HMO coverage to employers	35,767	83,212	232	D	F	163	20	1987
4.	Veragon Houston, TX	Mfrs. & sells diapers	33,687	34,125	101	F	F	110	30	1987
5.	Insight Distribution Network Tempe, AZ	Mkts. computers & computer prods.	25,545	61,548	240	D	D	250	10	1986
6.	Sterling Healthcare Group Coral Gables, FL	Provides health-care-mgmt. svcs.	21,705	28,128	129	C	F	40	0	1987
7.	Indeck Energy Services (38) Buffalo Grove, IL	Develops & operates cogeneration power plants	18,828	77,793	411	F	F	126	16	1985
8.	Communique Telecommunications Ontario, CA	Provides telecommunications svcs.	14,395	18,844	130	E	F	60	20	1983
9.	Technology Works (4) Austin, TX	Designs, mfrs., & mkts. computer-memory add-on prods.	12,747	28,264	220	D	F	100	20	1983
10.	Transitional Technology Anaheim, CA	Mfrs. helical scan tape subsysts. for computer market	9,823	11,511	116	D	A	46	4	1987
11.	Parsons Technology Hiawatha, IA	Develops software	9,771	28,033	284	D	D	235	2	1984
12.	MacTemps Cambridge, MA	Provides Macintosh temporary-personnel svcs.	9,437	13,447	141	D	B	72	3	1986
13.	Telephone Express Colorado Springs, CO	Provides long-distance telecommunications svcs.	8,771	18,451	208	C	A	80	24	1987
14.	Worthington Voice Services Worthington, OH	Provides 900-phone-number info. svcs.	8,599	9,134	105	A	A	9	2	1987
15.	Alliance Employee Leasing Dallas, TX	Provides employee-leasing svcs.	8,029	174,618	2,148	E	F	37	7	1986
16.	Administaff Kingwood, TX	Provides staff-leasing svcs.	7,316	298,360	4,023	D	E	11,380	430	1986
17.	Active Voice Seattle, WA	Develops voice-processing equip. & software	7,152	11,531	159	B	B	90	8	1983
18.	Dunsirn Industries Neenah, WI	Converts & sells IBM prods.	7,125	9,754	135	C	F	62	12	1987

*The *Inc.* 500 were selected from more than 21,000 candidates. To be eligible, a company must be independent and privately held; must show at least $100,000 in sales, but no more than $25 million in sales, for 1987; and must show a sales increase between 1990 and 1991. Sales figures for agencies (such as travel agencies, collection agencies, advertising agencies, and so on) are net sales to the company. Regulated banks and utilities are not eligible. Information was verified using tax forms and confirmation letters from certified public accountants, and through telephone interviews with company officials. The final ranking is a percentage of sales growth over the five year period.

**Profit range: A. 16% or more; B. 11% to 15%; C. 6% to 10%; D. 1% to 5%; E. Break-even; F. Loss

Rank (1991) Company/Location	Business Description	Sales Growth 1987–91 (% increase)	'91 sales ($000)	'87 sales ($000)	Profit range** '91	'87	No. of employees '91	'87	Date founded
19. **Salepoint Systems** San Diego, CA	Develops & sells IBM prods.	7,000%	$7,810	$110	A	F	30	7	1986
20. **Mega-Sys** Greenwood, IN	Provides logistics & transportation svcs.	6,967	7,703	109	D	F	13	2	1986
21. **Jelyn & Co.** Fort Washington, PA	Mfrs. & distr. sweaters	6,915	8,769	125	B	C	15	2	1987
22. **Powerfood** Berkeley, CA	Mfrs., mkts., & distr. a sports energy bar	6,714	10,970	161	D	F	56	0	1985
23. **MapInfo** Troy, NY	Mfrs. computer software	6,671	7,042	104	C	F	80	8	1986
24. **Metrica** San Antonio, TX	Provides data-processing, systs.-integration, & research svcs.	6,269	8,152	128	D	F	145	9	1984
25. **Shiva** (18) Cambridge, MA	Designs & mfrs. internetworking prods.	5,957	28,044	463	F	F	130	7	1985
26. **Parexel International** (11) Waltham, MA	Provides pharmaceutical R&D svcs.	5,922	25,652	426	D	F	550	16	1983
27. **Corporate Express** (10) Boulder, CO	Distr. office prods.	5,909	36,413	606	F	C	167	35	1985
28. **McArthur/Glen Group** McLean, VA	Develops retail real estate	5,754	24,000	410	F	F	124	9	1986
29. **MVM** (244) Falls Church, VA	Provides security & investigative svcs.	5,685	24,181	418	D	F	798	30	1979
30. **B&V Technology** (122) Idaho Falls, ID	Mfrs. pharmaceutical, home, & personal-care prods.	5,647	18,275	318	A	A	231	18	1981
31. **Mastech Systems** Pittsburgh, PA	Provides custom programming & systs.-integration svcs.	5,438	13,513	244	B	D	247	4	1986
32. **Maximum Strategy** San Jose, CA	Develops & mkts. storage solutions for computing systs.	5,331	7,820	144	A	D	25	6	1986
33. **AAMP of America** Clearwater, FL	Wholesales auto stereo parts	5,089	6,694	129	B	F	29	4	1987
34. **Florida Infusion** Palm Harbor, FL	Distr. pharmaceuticals & medical supplies	5,060	21,931	425	B	B	16	2	1987
35. **Global Mail** Sterling, VA	Provides intl. mail svcs.	5,018	8,803	172	C	C	45	4	1987
36. **Federal Investment** E. Providence, RI	Develops real estate & provides property-brokerage svcs.	4,972	12,629	249	B	C	20	3	1987
37. **Contract Manufacturer** Madill, OK	Mfrs. horse, stock, flatbed, & cargo trailers	4,962	5,619	111	D	E	68	12	1976
38. **Glitterwrap** Westwood, NJ	Sells metallic & iridescent gift wrap & tote bags	4,926	10,404	207	D	D	75	2	1987
39. **StarPak** (23) Denver, CO	Provides software & fulfillment svcs.	4,779	12,930	265	D	F	125	14	1978
40. **Trigen Energy** (70) White Plains, NY	Provides heating & cooling to buildings	4,595	44,900	957	D	F	105	0	1986
41. **Focus Healthcare Management** Brentwood, TN	Provides workers' comp medical-cost-mgmt. svcs.	4,564	11,521	247	D	F	200	40	1986

Rank (1991) Company/Location	Business Description	Sales Growth 1987–91 (% increase)	'91 sales ($000)	'87 sales ($000)	Profit range** '91	'87	No. of employees '91	'87	Date founded
42. **Mustang Engineering** Houston, TX	Provides engineering svcs. for oil & gas industry	4,546%	$15,286	$329	C	C	230	10	1987
43. **Corporate Child Care Management** Nashville, TN	Develops & manages employer-sponsored child-development centers	4,306	6,344	144	F	F	400	5	1987
44. **Staff Relief** Houston, TX	Provides contract nursing svcs. to hospitals	4,276	13,521	309	D	D	600	0	1987
45. **American Megatrends** (2) Norcross, GA	Designs & mfrs. computer motherboards	4,165	70,210	1,646	A	D	114	10	1985
46. **Panoramic** Fort Wayne, IN	Mfrs. & mkts. panoramic-X-ray equip. for dental profession	4,143	5,855	138	A	F	20	5	1986
47. **Melaleuca** (105) Idaho Falls, ID	Mkts. pharmaceuticals	4,143	100,765	2,375	A	B	728	28	1985
48. **Adtran** Huntsville, AL	Designs, mfrs., develops, & sells electronic equip.	4,038	42,621	1,030	A	F	225	23	1986
49. **User Techonology Associates** Arlington, VA	Provides computer svcs.; designs & develops systs.	3,934	12,424	308	B	F	250	3	1985
50. **Micro-Frame Technologies** Ontario, CA	Develops cost-mgmt. software for PCs	3,881	5,454	137	B	F	46	8	1985
51. **Tycom Limited Partnership** Santa Ana, CA	Mfrs. precision cutting tools	3,848	11,450	290	F	F	210	15	1986
52. **Conmec** Bethlehem, PA	Rebuilds, repairs, & supplies rotating equip.	3,819	19,401	495	D	C	110	7	1987
53. **Registry** Wellesley, MA	Provides contract computer-personnel svcs.	3,809	16,927	433	D	F	54	10	1986
54. **Presidio** Suitland, MD	Provides computer-systs. integration, prods., & svcs.	3,792	4,087	105	E	F	15	3	1986
55. **Abacus** (43) San Francisco, CA	Sells & svcs. PC systs.	3,615	30,276	815	D	D	103	31	1979
56. **Softrub** Pacoima, CA	Mfrs. & mkts. soft-sided portable spas	3,555	6,359	174	D	F	70	3	1986
57. **Select Ticketing Systems** Syracuse, NY	Produces & installs computerized box-office & outlet ticketing systs.	3,547	8,024	220	D	F	69	7	1986
58. **Kofax Image Products** Irvine, CA	Develops image-processing hardware & software	3,503	10,342	287	F	F	96	7	1975
59. **CMG Health** Owings Mills, MD	Manages health-treatment centers	3,381	10,442	300	F	D	95	3	1985
60. **Leasing Solutions** (12) San Jose, CA	Leases computer equip.	3,286	23,295	688	D	F	48	12	1986
61. **Word Petroleum** (125) Enid, OK	Explores for, produces, & mkts. natural gas & related prods.	3.258	146,886	4,374	D	B	79	70	1971
62. **Auto Kontrols** Houston, TX	Designs, mfrs., & installs electrical systs.	3,128	7,941	246	D	F	40	8	1987

Rank (1991) Company/Location	Business Description	Sales Growth 1987–91 (% increase)	'91 sales ($000)	'87 sales ($000)	Profit range** '91	Profit range** '87	No. of employees '91	No. of employees '87	Date founded
63. **Compurex Systems** Easton, MA	Buys, sells, & leases digital computer equip.	3,064%	$15,123	$478	D	F	16	2	1987
64. **Premiere Merchandising** Inglewood, CA	Provides promotional marketing svcs.	3,043	3,489	111	E	F	12	2	1987
65. **National Safety Associates** (24) Memphis, TN	Mfrs. water- & air-filtration systs.	2,946	284,891	9,353	A	D	650	150	1970
66. **Fortitech** Schenectady, NY	Mfrs. vitamin & mineral premixes	2,902	5,223	174	C	F	18	4	1986
67. **Calais Home** Houston, TX	Builds single-family houses	2,894	9,491	317	D	F	20	5	1986
68. **Abacus Technology** Chevy Chase, MD	Provides info.-systs. consulting svcs.	2,890	12,407	415	C	F	104	9	1983
69. **Wind River Systems** Alameda, CA	Develops & distr. computer operating systs. & development tools	2,871	17,085	575	C	E	125	12	1983
70. **EduCare Community Living** (15) Austin, TX	Provides long-term health care for the disabled	2,862	13,685	462	C	F	320	18	1986
71. **Coldwater Creek** Sand Point, ID	Sells nature-related gifts through a catalog	2,814	10,869	373	A	A	54	4	1984
72. **Cadapult Graphic Systems** Paramus, NJ	Sells, svcs., & supports computer graphics systs.	2,785	4,125	143	D	F	8	1	1987
73. **Pacific Trading Overseas** Miami, FL	Exports chemicals & plastic resins	2,769	5,423	189	B	E	3	2	1982
74. **Cardboard Gold** (208) Santa Ana, CA	Distr. sports-collectible supplies & accessories	2,760	11,154	390	C	E	16	2	1985
75. **Atlantic Coast Textiles** Atlanta, GA	Wholesales textiles & linens	2,739	3,322	117	D	E	8	2	1987
76. **Intl. Computers & Telecommunications** Rockville, MD	Supports high-tech systs.	2,682	11,269	405	E	F	205	9	1981
77. **Grand Aire Express** Monroe, MI	Flies on-demand passenger & cargo air charters	2,640	3,808	139	A	A	41	3	1985
78. **Montgomery Development** Syracuse, NY	Provides general-contracting svcs.	2,625	6,349	233	D	D	25	5	1986
79. **BitWise Designs** Schenectady, NY	Mfrs. computers & workstations for imaging marketplace	2,611	2,928	108	D	F	10	6	1985
80. **Vermont Teddy Bear** Shelburne, VT	Mfrs. & sells teddy bears	2,562	5,245	197	E	F	130	30	1982
81. **Item Products** Houston, TX	Creates modular building systs.	2,552	3,845	145	A	A	31	3	1982
82. **Tampa Bay Vending** Tampa, FL	Operates full-line vending co.	2,541	2,747	104	A	C	35	5	1987
83. **Collegiate Sports Design** New Strawn, KS	Mkts. collegiate-sports-championship souvenirs	2,534	4,294	163	F	D	6	1	1986
84. **Deneba Systems** (84) Miami, FL	Develops & mkts. microcomputer software	2,532	8,421	320	A	A	60	10	1986
85. **Complete Health Services** (494) Birmingham, AL	Provides managed-care svcs.	2,483	159,651	6,182	D	F	410	40	1985

Rank (1991) Company/Location	Business Description	Sales Growth 1987–91 (% increase)	'91 sales ($000)	'87 sales ($000)	Profit range** '91	'87	No. of employees '91	'87	Date founded
86. Fiber Optic Technologies Englewood, CO	Designs & installs voice & data network systs.	2,453%	$5,949	$233	D	C	73	4	1985
87. PAI (77) Oak Ridge, TN	Provides engineering & environmental-consulting svcs.	2,453	7,454	292	C	C	65	5	1983
88. Summit Marketing Group Rochester, NY	Publishes information dictionaries; mkts. catalog memberships	2,451	4,516	177	D	D	159	6	1987
89. Payroll 1 MidAtlantic McLean, VA	Prepares payroll taxes	2,424	2,549	101	B	F	52	4	1986
90. Nationwide Remittance Centers McLean, VA	Provides national wholesale & retail lockbox svcs.	2,412	9,899	394	F	F	175	12	1985
91. MediServe Information Services Tempe, AZ	Provides software svcs. to hospitals	2,404	2,704	108	B	F	20	4	1985
92. Cap Toys Bedford Heights, OH	Mfrs. toys	2,392	18,264	733	C	F	30	5	1987
93. Tramex Travel Austin, TX	Operates travel-mgmt. co.	2,365	14,764	599	D	B	37	18	1984
94. Ma Laboratories San Jose, CA	Mfrs. computer prods.	2,355	52,470	2,137	D	D	70	5	1983
95. All Green Marietta, GA	Provides lawn, tree, & shrub care & indoor pest control	2,330	9,476	390	D	F	240	73	1987
96. Goodman Music Los Angeles, CA	Sells musical instruments & recording equip.	2,305	10,968	456	D	D	40	5	1977
97. Sonic Solutions San Rafael, CA	Mfrs. software & hardware for digital audio systs.	2,301	5,787	241	A	F	30	6	1986
98. Payroll 1 (140) Royal Oak, MI	Provides computerized payroll & payroll-tax svcs.	2,296	3,737	156	C	F	100	12	1986
99. Center for Applied Psychology King of Prussia, PA	Distr. psychologically oriented children's toys, games, & books	2,290	4,373	183	D	F	18	3	1985
100. SMTEK (141) Newbury Part, CA	Mfrs. electronics for space, defense, & medical mkts.	2,284	9,204	386	D	F	85	13	1986
101. Business Computer Training Institute Mill Creek, WA	Runs computer-training schools	2,266	8,801	372	D	F	162	36	1986
102. Ethix (135) Beaverton, OR	Provides health-care-mgmt. svcs.	2,236	19,412	831	A	F	341	30	1982
103. Red Rose Collection Burlingame, CA	Operates national mail-order co.	2,233	6,345	272	C	F	54	4	1987
104. JTS Enterprises Houston, TX	Distr. & trades chemicals & provides consulting svcs.	2,209	18,864	817	D	A	3	1	1986
105. Eastern Computers Virginia Beach, VA	Provides systs.- & electronic-engineering prods. & svcs.	2,195	49,834	2,171	C	F	400	75	1980
106. Allstar Builders Miami, FL	Provides commercial & industrial general-contracting svcs.	2,182	4,860	213	B	B	18	5	1987

Rank (1991) Company/Location	Business Description	Sales Growth 1987–91 (% increase)	'91 sales ($000)	'87 sales ($000)	Profit range** '91	Profit range** '87	No. of employees '91	No. of employees '87	Date founded
107. **MediCenter** (178) Lawton, OK	Operates company-sponsored medical centers	2,172%	$12,516	$551	B	A	92	17	1984
108. **Advanced Systems Technology** (195) Atlanta, GA	Provides technical & engineering svcs.	2,166	11,669	515	D	F	155	8	1981
109. **Marathon Systems** San Francisco, CA	Develops & integrates business-systs. software	2,138	4,744	212	D	D	47	10	1987
110. **DSS** Carmel, CA	Provides contract food & industrial-engineering svcs.	2,135	4,380	196	D	E	180	5	1985
111. **Data Storage Marketing** Boulder, CO	Distr. microcomputer components & periph.; mfrs. microcomputers	2,109	68,944	3,121	E	D	145	7	1987
112. **Vercon Contruction** Greenville, SC	Provides general-contracting svcs.	2,107	32,006	1,450	D	E	55	5	1987
113. **ProServe** (42) Denver, CO	Manages institutional food-svcs. programs	2,107	8,255	374	D	C	325	3	1984
114. **Earth Care Paper** (39) Madison, WI	Retails & wholesales prods. made from recycled paper	2,099	5,102	232	F	C	45	4	1983
115. **Symmetrix** (30) Lexington, MA	Provides engineering svcs.	2,098	18,884	859	C	F	115	12	1986
116. **Atlantic Network Systems** Cary, NC	Distr. data & voice-communications prods.	2,081	2,814	129	D	F	8	1	1987
117. **Ribbon Outlet** Somerville, NJ	Retails ribbon, lace, & trim	2,068	14,354	662	E	F	450	14	1985
118. **Corporate Staffing Resources** Elkhart, IN	Provides temporary, contract technical, & executive-search svcs.	2,011	12,938	613	D	F	60	5	1987
119. **Genpack USA** Bridgewater, MI	Provides contract packaging svcs.	1,985	3,440	165	C	F	20	4	1987
120. **Copifax** Berlin, NJ	Distr. & svcs. copiers, faxes, & digital duplicators	1,944	4,292	210	D	F	42	5	1987
121. **Intuit** (47) Menlo Park, CA	Develops finan. software	1,926	44,539	2,198	C	B	242	13	1984
122. **Certified Abatement Systems** Houston, TX	Removes asbestos & lead paint	1,915	4,010	199	A	C	25	10	1987
123. **D. J. King Trucking & Excavating** E. Windsor, CT	Provides site contracting	1,911	2,614	130	E	F	28	6	1987
124. **Microtest** (126) Phoenix, AZ	Develops & mkts. LAN diagnostic & connectivity prods.	1,894	17,209	863	B	D	108	13	1984
125. **SalesTalk** Mountain View, CA	Provides product demonstrators for mfrs.	1,889	7,359	370	D	D	40	2	1986
126. **Gensym** Cambridge, MA	Supplies real-time expert systs.	1,885	10,499	529	C	F	90	16	1986
127. **Technical Management Services** Arlington, VA	Provides computer-systs.-development consulting svcs.	1,877	6,109	309	C	F	90	15	1981
128. **Automated Systems Design** Roswell, GA	Designs & installs networks	1,861	2,883	147	D	F	32	1	1986
129. **Gym Masters** (104) Albany, CA	Owns & manages fitness centers	1,855	6,237	319	D	F	60	4	1985

Rank (1991)	Company/Location	Business Description	Sales Growth 1987–91 (% increase)	'91 sales ($000)	'87 sales ($000)	Profit range** '91	Profit range** '87	No. of employees '91	No. of employees '87	Date founded
130.	Digital Network Associates New York, NY	Sells equip. & svcs. for interconnecting computer systs.	1,842%	$5,633	$290	B	A	20	2	1985
131.	MediSense Cambridge, MA	Mfrs. & sells medical equip.	1,840	89,782	4,629	F	F	786	193	1981
132.	Digidesign (204) Menlo Park, CA	Designs, mfrs., & sells digital audio recording systs.	1,833	13,881	718	B	C	84	13	1984
133.	Walklett Burns Malvern, PA	Provides systs.-integration svcs.	1,794	2,140	113	D	D	30	3	1985
134.	Automation Partners International San Francisco, CA	Provides technology prods. & svcs. to law firms	1,774	21,795	1,168	F	D	120	10	1986
135.	JRL Systems Austin, TX	Designs & mfrs. market controllers & printers	1,758	2,935	158	B	C	18	3	1985
136.	Advanced Computer Systems (250) Fairfax, VA	Develops computer systs.	1,752	11,410	616	D	C	250	25	1982
137.	D&K Enterprises Carollton, TX	Mfrs. personalized books & child IDs, & analyzes signatures	1,750	1,924	104	A	A	18	1	1987
138.	Bruce Co. Washington, DC	Provides environmental-consulting svcs. to federal govt.	1,740	2,134	116	D	B	66	10	1985
139.	Thomas-Conrad (22) Austin, TX	Mfrs. LAN prods.	1,724	30,614	1,678	D	D	225	13	1985
140.	Joe Koch Construction Youngstown, OH	Builds single-family homes	1,714	5,532	305	B	D	21	6	1986
141.	Spray Systems Environmental Tempe, AZ	Provides contract environmental svcs.	1,697	8,626	480	C	C	125	6	1985
142.	Coastal Environmental Services Linthicum, MD	Provides environmental-consulting services	1,692	2,760	154	D	B	33	4	1987
143.	Design Automation Systems Houston, TX	Integrates computer systs.	1,687	5,360	300	B	B	14	4	1985
144.	Johnson & Co. Wilderness Products Bangor, ME	Mfrs. & distr. wilderness prods.	1,686	1,822	102	D	F	13	1	1987
145.	Pelton & Associates Redondo Beach, CA	Provides marketing-communications svcs.	1,673	8,902	502	D	D	22	8	1987
146.	Advanced Cellular Systems Graynaro, PR	Provides cellular-telephone svcs.	1,673	8,066	455	D	F	39	4	1986
147.	ROW Sciences (139) Rockville, MD	Provides health & biomedical-research & computer svcs.	1,641	19,798	1,137	D	D	300	6	1983
148.	Cutchall Management (99) Omaha, NE	Owns & operates restaurants	1,631	3,324	192	C	D	60	1	1986
149.	Atkinson-Baker & Associates Burbank, CA	Provides court-reporting svcs.	1,631	3,860	223	D	C	30	3	1987
150.	Digital Instruments Santa Barbara, CA	Mfrs. high-resolution scanning probe microscopes	1,628	16,591	960	A	A	52	3	1987

Rank (1991) Company/Location	Business Description	Sales Growth 1987–91 (% increase)	'91 sales ($000)	'87 sales ($000)	Profit range** '91	Profit range** '87	No. of employees '91	No. of employees '87	Date founded
151. **Northwest Pine Products** (327) Bend, OR	Produces wood chips for pulp & paper industry	1,628%	$12,819	$742	C	D	34	9	1984
152. **Waste Reduction Systems** Houston, TX	Provides waste-disposal, materials-recovery, & garbage-collection svcs.	1,625	6,643	385	D	F	85	4	1986
153. **Command Medical Products** Ormond Beach, FL	Mrfs. disposable medical prods.	1,613	3,118	182	F	E	130	5	1983
154. **H. J. Ford Associates** (138) Arlington, VA	Provides info.-systs. & engineering svcs.	1,603	8,275	486	C	F	76	5	1981
155. **Computer One** Albuquerque, NM	Sells, svcs., & supports Macintosh & related third-party prods.	1,587	7,507	445	D	F	16	12	1987
156. **Recom Technologies** (165) San Jose, CA	Provides engineering, info.-systs., & technical-support svcs.	1,583	9,172	545	D	D	209	12	1980
157. **Fanamation** (86) Compton, CA	Develops, mfrs., & sells coordinate measuring machines & software	1,578	5,620	335	F	F	48	9	1985
158. **Taylor Medical** Beaumont, TX	Wholesales medical prods.	1,574	81,061	1,841	F	F	500	35	1987
159. **Dickens Data Systems** (90) Norcross, GA	Mrfs. computer periph., publishes software, & integrates systs.	1,565	35,800	2,150	C	B	85	23	1981
160. **Travelpro Luggage** Deerfield Beach, FL	Mfrs. & distr. luggage	1,556	4,090	247	A	F	15	2	1984
161. **David Mitchell & Associates** (150) St. Paul, MN	Provides computer consulting svcs.	1,555	6,671	403	C	C	100	6	1984
162. **Glenn-Runnion** Charlotte, NC	Provides computer-training svcs.	1,552	1,652	100	B	F	25	4	1986
163. **McGinnis Farms** Alpharetta, GA	Sells nursery stock, landscaping supplies, & irrigation prods.	1,538	7,109	434	D	F	44	12	1987
164. **Am-Pro Protective Agency** (257) Columbia, SC	Provides security-guard svcs.	1,533	34,122	2,089	E	E	1,193	78	1982
165. **Laflin Environmental Services** Houston, TX	Provides industrial hygiene consulting svcs.	1,521	1,767	109	B	A	14	3	1986
166. **SWFTE International** (216) Hockessin, DE	Develops, mkts., & publishes software	1,520	2,025	125	A	E	11	3	1983
167. **Palm Tree Packaging** Apopka, FL	Mfrs., imports, & exports floral packaging	1,517	2,150	133	D	D	17	2	1987
168. **Keypoint Technology** Walnut, CA	Mfrs. & distr. computer periph.	1,511	60,253	3,740	C	D	54	10	1987
169. **World-Wide Refinishing Systems** Waco, TX	Refinishes bathtubs & tiles	1,499	2,974	186	A	F	20	3	1968
170. **Ithaca Software** Alameda, CA	Develops portable 3-D-graphics software systs.	1,491	2,801	176	B	C	29	5	1985
171. **MAR Oil & Gas** Santa Fe, NM	Produces & sells natural gas & oil	1,490	2,449	154	D	F	4	2	1981

Rank (1991) Company/Location	Business Description	Sales Growth 1987–91 (% increase)	'91 sales ($000)	'87 sales ($000)	Profit range** '91	'87	No. of employees '91	'87	Date founded
172. **J. L. Honigberg & Associates** Chicago, IL	Imports & distr. specialty fruits & vegetables	1,478%	$6,547	$415	D	D	14	4	1986
173. **Regency Coffee** New Prague, MN	Mfrs. & retails gourmet coffee	1,461	2,810	180	F	F	55	3	1986
174. **Custom Applications** Billerica, MA	Develops & mkts. desktop-publishing software	1,441	5,209	338	B	D	38	3	1986
175. **American Fashion Jewels** (119) S. San Francisco, CA	Retails fashion jewelry	1,429	23,900	1,563	E	D	145	8	1985
176. **Creative Product** Fairburn, GA	Provides contract packaging svcs.	1,420	4,711	310	D	D	109	11	1984
177. **Allied Holdings** Torrance, CA	Operates auto-parts distr., golf-club mfr., & employment & ad agcys.	1,419	30,485	2,007	F	F	200	4	1984
178. **Groundwater Protection** Orlando, FL	Provides environmental drilling & remedial construction svcs.	1,416	6,927	457	D	F	85	8	1986
179. **Three Springs** (130) Huntsville, FL	Provides residential treatment for troubled adolescents	1,415	5,029	332	A	C	89	11	1985
180. **PBR Consulting Group** Philadelphia, PA	Provides PC & tech consulting svcs.	1,412	5,019	332	D	A	52	12	1987
181. **Biosym Technologies** San Diego, CA	Develops, sells, & supports software	1,406	22,869	1,519	D	F	160	50	1984
182. **Gardner/Fox Associates** Bryn Mawr, PA	Provides general-contracting svcs.	1,404	5,100	339	D	D	45	2	1987
183. **Maier Group** (72) New York, NY	Supplies home videos	1,396	6,012	402	C	F	18	7	1986
184. **Action Temporary Services** Evansville, IN	Provides temporary-personnel svcs.	1,393	1,896	127	D	D	7	1	1986
185. **S&W Foundation Contractors** (294) Richardson, TX	Provides foundation, drainage, & structural repair svcs.	1,392	2,014	135	D	E	45	5	1986
186. **Tova Industries** Louisville, KY	Mfrs. dehydrated food prods.	1,383	2,936	198	C	C	30	9	1985
187. **Hub City Florida Terminals** Orange Park, FL	Provides freight-transportation svcs.	1,375	21,738	1,474	D	D	14	3	1986
188. **U.S. Computer Maintenance** (113) Farmington, NY	Provides on-site maintenance of DEC & Sun computers	1,371	4,678	318	B	B	40	8	1986
189. **American Fastsigns** Dallas, TX	Franchises computer-generated vinyl-sign covers	1,365	3,457	236	D	C	28	3	1986
190. **MRI Manufacturing & Research** (242) Tucson, AZ	Mfrs. & develops silicone catheters	1,363	2,707	185	C	F	84	16	1985
191. **Combined Resource Technology** Baton Rouge, LA	Mkts. business-cost-reductions svcs.	1,360	1,489	102	A	F	13	4	1986
192. **Iconics** (31) Foxborough, MA	Develops data-acquisition software	1,347	7,250	501	A	F	50	11	1986

Rank (1991) Company/Location	Business Description	Sales Growth 1987–91 (% increase)	'91 sales ($000)	'87 sales ($000)	Profit range** '91	Profit range** '87	No. of employees '91	No. of employees '87	Date founded
193. **Software Technical Services** Atlanta, GA	Provides software consulting svcs.	1,337%	$2,846	$198	A	C	15	3	1983
194. **EMC Engineers** Denver, CO	Provides utilities, facilities, & environmental-engineering svcs.	1,335	3,687	257	D	F	43	4	1976
195. **R&R Recreation Products** Englewood Cliffs, NJ	Provides marketing & product-development svcs.	1,325	3,377	237	C	F	4	2	1979
196. **Noble Oil Services** Sanford, NC	Provides petroleum-waste-recycling svcs.	1,323	2,647	186	D	A	36	5	1984
197. **Micro Information Services** (94) Mequon, WI	Provides computer-networking svcs.	1,318	3,376	238	D	F	25	3	1983
198. **Shepard-Patterson** Conshohocken, PA	Provides info.-technology svcs.	1,318	1,432	101	D	D	32	4	1986
199. **Gupta Technologies** (156) Menlo Park, CA	Develops & distr. database-mgmt.-systs. software prods.	1,318	21,295	1,502	D	C	141	19	1984
200. **Computer Service Supply** Londonderry, NH	Supplies, repairs, & refurbishes computer parts	1,306	2,418	172	C	F	14	4	1987
201. **Fostec** Auburn, NY	Mfrs. fiber optics for illumination	1,305	2,009	143	D	F	28	11	1987
202. **DAZSER & DAZSER/MD** (82) Tampa, FL	Subfranchises Jani-King commercial cleaning operations	1,301	5,171	369	F	A	16	5	1986
203. **Comprehensive Technologies Intl.** (169) Chantilly, VA	Develops software; provides systs.-integration & networking svcs.	1,298	33,298	2,382	D	D	547	60	1980
204. **Stamina Products** Springfield, MO	Wholesales home exercise equip.	1,290	13,942	1,003	D	F	14	5	1987
205. **Union Pointe Construction** Salt Lake City, UT	Provides general-contracting svcs.	1,289	7,934	571	D	F	18	5	1986
206. **Dominant Systems** Ann Arbor, MI	Integrates computer systs.	1,289	1,625	117	D	D	10	3	1987
207. **Country Originals** (424) Jackson, MS	Designs & wholesales gifts & decorative prods.	1,275	2,517	183	D	D	22	2	1986
208. **Audio Partners** Auburn, CA	Publishes books on cassette	1,273	1,579	115	D	D	9	1	1987
209. **American Packaging & Assembly** Albertson, NY	Provides contract packaging svcs.	1,267	1,764	129	A	F	200	20	1980
210. **Peripheral Land** (80) Fremont, CA	Integrates mass-storage prods. for microcomputers	1,264	25,140	1,843	D	D	106	25	1985
211. **Taggart** Cody, WY	Manages restaurants, trucking co., mining facility, & gas distributors	1,263	15,669	1,150	F	F	230	36	1986
212. **Metrographics Printing & Computer Svcs.** Fairfield, NJ	Provides printing & computer svcs.	1,261	2,015	148	C	D	10	2	1987
213. **Securities Service Network** (478) Knoxville, TN	Provides investment-brokerage svcs.	1,260	4,636	341	D	C	70	5	1983
214. **St. Supery Vineyards & Winery** Rutherford, CA	Produces & sells wine	1,249	3,453	256	F	F	60	6	1982

Rank (1991) Company/Location	Business Description	Sales Growth 1987–91 (% increase)	'91 sales ($000)	'87 sales ($000)	Profit range**		No. of employees		Date founded
					'91	'87	'91	'87	
215. U.S. Hospitality Nashville, TN	Publishes hotel-guest-svcs. directories	1,245%	$1,385	$103	A	D	18	3	1986
216. Research Information Systems Carlsbad, CA	Provides computer software & info. svcs.	1,243	3,868	288	A	A	45	5	1982
217. Camelot Systems Haveville, MA	Mfrs. automated liquid-dispensing systs.	1,237	4,654	348	D	E	35	10	1987
218. Piedmont Group Oakland, CA	Provides photo-copying & desk-top-publishing svcs.	1,235	2,029	152	F	F	25	5	1987
219. Fulton Computer Products Rockville Centre, NY	Resells computer hardware, soft-ware, & periph.	1,229	13,276	999	C	C	20	7	1982
220. Pet Venture Arlington, VA	Operates retail pet-food & pet-supplies stores	1,228	5,829	439	F	C	70	12	1986
221. IQ Software Norcross, GA	Develops & mkts. software programs	1,226	7,795	588	A	D	70	10	1984
222. HazWaste Industries Richmond, VA	Provides environ-mental-consulting svcs.	1,219	11,453	868	D	F	159	30	1987
223. Small Systems Management (461) Wilmington, DE	Sells, svcs., & installs PSs & LANs	1,218	2,294	174	D	F	7	3	1985
224. Carlson Co. Newport Beach, CA	Manages commer-cial property	1,215	2,209	168	A	B	57	13	1986
225. International Computer Graphics Fremont, CA	Distr. computer-aided design periph.	1,209	23,576	1,801	D	D	28	6	1984
226. Personnel Management (35) Shelbyville, IN	Provides temporary-help svcs.	1,207	9,488	726	D	D	45	7	1986
227. System Connection (40) Provo, UT	Mfrs. & distr. computer cable & accessories	1,204	6,468	496	C	C	50	4	1985
228. Telamon (368) Indianapolis, IN	Distr. & svcs. telecommunica-tions equip.	1,204	9,490	728	D	E	40	8	1984
229. Data Sciences (455) Roseville, MN	Mfrs. instruments for biological research	1,202	2,005	154	D	F	33	10	1983
230. Fisher Industrial Services Glencoe, AL	Runs hazardous-waste-mgmt. facility	1,200	6,528	502	C	B	78	17	1985
231. Neumann Developments Janesville, WI	Builds homes & commercial projects & devel-ops real estate	1,200	17,446	1,342	C	C	40	3	1980
232. Van G. Miller Waterloo, IA	Operates buying group for home-medical-equip. cos.	1,197	3,060	236	A	F	13	5	1986
233. Jackson Hewitt Tax Service Virginia Beach, VA	Provides income-tax-preparations svcs.	1,197	4,447	343	A	F	72	6	1985
234. Sonetics (222) Portland, OR	Mfrs. commu-nication equip. for high-noise environments	1,194	3,390	262	C	B	28	4	1983
235. Diversified Pacific Construction Irvine, CA	Provides general-contracting & construction-mgmt. svcs.	1,189	11,616	901	D	E	16	6	1979

Rank (1991) Company/Location	Business Description	Sales Growth 1987–91 (% increase)	'91 sales ($000)	'87 sales ($000)	Profit range** '91	'87	No. of employees '91	'87	Date founded
236. **Impact Printhead Services** (87) Austin, TX	Refurbishes print-head components in dot-matrix printers	1,180%	$6,683	$522	B	A	104	10	1984
237. **Associated Family Photographers** Phoenix, AZ	Provides family-portrait photography	1,173	24,658	1,937	D	D	700	200	1984
238. **J.B. Dollar Stretcher Magazine** (303) Richfield, OH	Publishes advertising-coupon magazine	1,162	1,565	124	C	F	7	3	1985
239. **Inside Communications** Boulder, CO	Publishes cycling books & magazines	1,156	2,863	228	F	F	19	6	1987
240. **LBS Capital Management** Safety Harbor, FL	Provides invest-ment advice & money-mgmt. svcs.	1,154	2,031	162	A	B	10	3	1986
241. **IVT Limited** Huntington Station, NY	Provides con-sulting & finan.-research svcs.	1,151	2,665	213	C	D	4	2	1986
242. **Compusense** Bedford, NH	Develops & integrates computer soft-ware & hardware	1,148	1,597	128	A	A	18	2	1983
243. **Ergodyne** St. Paul, MN	Designs, mkts., & sells ergonomic safety equip.	1,147	12,385	993	B	A	27	5	1983
244. **Electronic Ballast Technology** Torrance, CA	Designs, develops, & mfrs. ballasts for flourescent lamps	1,146	42,218	3,389	C	E	450	55	1982
245. **United Staffing** (3) Troy, NY	Provides employee-leasing svcs.	1,141	33,761	2,720	F	F	42	17	1986
246. **Restek** Bellefonte, PA	Mfrs. gas chromo-tography prods.	1,137	6,445	521	A	C	61	10	1985
247. **Systems & Programming Solutions** Milwaukee, WI	Provides computer consulting svcs. & custom software	1,135	1,519	123	B	A	25	2	1987
248. **Spray-Tech** (332) Longwood, FL	Provides exterior home improvements	1,131	17,070	1,387	D	D	110	17	1982
249. **Directed Electronics** (241) Vista, CA	Mfrs. electronic automotive-security prods.	1,127	35,222	2,871	D	D	95	38	1986
250. **Coverall North America** (274) San Diego, CA	Franchises com-merical cleaning svcs.	1,127	18,302	1,492	D	C	125	18	1985
251. **Compterized Diagnostic Imaging Center** Riverside, CA	Operates radiology imaging centers	1,127	10,413	849	B	B	60	20	1987
252. **DataLOK** (305) Los Angeles, CA	Provides document storage, retrieval, & delivery svcs.	1,125	3,174	259	B	F	41	12	1984
253. **Charter Oak Consulting Group** Hartford, CT	Provides mgmt.-consulting svcs.	1,121	3,652	299	F	C	10	4	1987
254. **Delta Environmental Consultants** (19) St. Paul, MN	Provides environ-mental-consulting svcs.	1,116	44,528	3,661	D	C	509	88	1986
255. **Southern Audio Services** (132) Baton Rouge, LA	Mfrs. audio equip. for trucks	1,116	8,951	736	C	D	61	11	1983
256. **Computer Equity** Chantilly, VA	Integrates telecommunica-tions & computer systs.	1,115	11,922	981	D	F	49	5	1987
257. **Applied Computer Technology** Fort Collins, CO	Mfrs. & sells com-puter prods. & svcs.	1,113	5,384	444	D	F	25	2	1986

Rank (1991) Company/Location	Business Description	Sales Growth 1987–91 (% increase)	'91 sales ($000)	'87 sales ($000)	Profit range**		No. of employees		Date founded
					'91	'87	'91	'87	
258. **Envoy Global** Portland, OR	Provides business telecommunications svcs.	1,110%	$3,969	$328	D	F	30	8	1986
259. **Key Construction** (367) Wichita, KS	Provides general-contracting svcs.	1,097	12,489	1,043	C	D	50	10	1978
260. **Advantage Construction & Remodeling** Arlington, TX	Provides residential remodeling svcs.	1,096	1,974	165	C	B	21	5	1985
261. **European Toy Collection** Portage, IN	Designs, mfrs., & imports children's gifts & toys	1,095	2,342	196	D	C	9	1	1985
262. **National Catastrophe Adjusters** (500) Indianapolis, IN	Provides catastrophic-insurance-adjusting svcs.	1,092	1,574	132	D	F	32	6	1984
263. **National Contract Staffing** (112) Las Vegas, NV	Operates employee-leasing co.	1,088	24,952	2,100	D	F	20	3	1985
264. **Sentinel Systems** Hampton, VA	Distr. AT&T security prods.	1,086	4,601	388	D	F	15	6	1985
265. **Hospitality Network** Henderson, NE	Provides pay movies & cable TV to hotels	1,081	14,885	1,260	F	F	65	12	1983
266. **Barclays Law Publishers** (234) S. San Francisco, CA	Provides info. svcs. for legal profession	1,079	8,243	699	A	A	65	9	1984
267. **First Benefits** (255) Anderson, IN	Provides health-care mgmt. for employee-benefits plans	1,073	5,253	448	D	A	98	9	1985
268. **JMR Electronics** (430) Northridge, CA	Mfrs. computer periph.	1,070	11,627	994	C	D	141	21	1982
269. **InfoSource** (268) Winter Park, FL	Develops PC training software	1,067	1,506	129	E	F	42	3	1983
270. **Maritime Services** Hood River, OR	Provides ship-construction svcs.	1,065	3,904	335	E	E	30	4	1986
271. **American Cargo Systems** Overland Park, KS	Provides transportation-brokerage svcs.	1,064	5,784	497	D	F	14	3	1986
272. **GS Industries** Padadena, TX	Sells & svcs. communication & navigation electronics for ships	1,063	2,001	172	D	A	10	2	1987
273. **Scientech** (247) Idaho Falls, ID	Provides nuclear-safety, environmental, & security svcs.	1,062	21,489	1,849	D	C	198	26	1983
274. **A.M. Express** (188) Escanaba, MI	Provides trucking & heavy-hauling svcs.	1,062	1,754	151	D	B	24	3	1985
275. **Sahara** Bountiful, UT	Provides construction svcs.	1,056	15,143	1,310	C	C	27	7	1985
276. **Broadcast Plus Productions** Universal City, CA	Provides prod. equip. & svcs. to TV industry	1,050	1,564	136	C	F	2	1	1982
277. **Vector Engineering** Grass Valley, CA	Provides solid-waste-mgmt. consulting svcs.	1,048	2,135	186	D	C	32	10	1986
278. **World Travel Partners** Atlanta, GA	Provdes travel-mgmt. svcs.	1,043	176,781	15,463	D	D	425	120	1987
279. **Lai, Venuti, & Lai** (454) Santa Clara, CA	Provides advertising svcs.	1,041	1,745	153	C	A	12	4	1985
280. **Van Mar** (219) East Brunswick, NJ	Mfrs. & sells women's intimate apparel	1,035	26,718	2,355	D	D	125	14	1980

Rank (1991) Company/Location	Business Description	Sales Growth 1987–91 (% increase)	'91 sales ($000)	'87 sales ($000)	Profit range** '91	'87	No. of employees '91	'87	Date founded
281. **Vanguard Automation** Tucson, AZ	Mfrs. custom automated-assembly systs.	1,034%	$6,748	$595	D	C	96	1	1984
282. **AST/The Data Group** Chalfont, PA	Provides software applications & svcs.	1,032	8,571	757	A	A	65	6	1979
283. **S. Cohen & Associates** McLean, VA	Provides energy- & environmental-consulting svcs.	1,027	9,058	804	D	C	45	8	1981
284. **Achen-Gardner** Chandler, AZ	Provides general-contracting svcs.	1,025	8,529	758	D	D	55	5	1986
285. **DataServ** Farmington Hills, MI	Provides techno-logical integration svcs.	1,022	4,172	372	B	C	25	6	1986
286. **GET Travel** (243) Walnut Creek, CA	Provides group travel arrangements	1,021	4,025	359	D	D	20	2	1985
287. **Groundwater & Environmental Svcs.** (167) Wall, NJ	Provides environ-mental-consulting svcs.	1,019	15,563	1,391	A	C	145	12	1985
288. **Huckwell/Weinman Associates** Kirkland, WA	Provides economics & environmental-planning consulting svcs.	1,012	1,245	112	C	E	9	2	1986
289. **DCT Systems** (275) St. Paul, MN	Sells & svcs. microcomputers	1,006	103,696	9,372	D	D	189	27	1984
290. **Auto-Soft** (229) Bountiful, UT	Develops & mfrs. inventory-control software	1,001	5,537	503	B	D	45	5	1985
291. **Computer Communication** Waterbury, CT	Provides sales & support of critical care computer components	999	9,796	891	B	B	16	4	1984
292. **Hernandez Engineering** (145) Houston, TX	Provides engineering & technical svcs.	998	16,977	1,546	D	D	345	24	1983
293. **Design Fabricators** Boulder, CO	Mfrs. custom com-mercial fixtures & furniture	998	3,260	297	B	D	53	10	1987
294. **Label Technology** Merced, CA	Mfrs. & prints labels	997	3,137	286	D	F	30	5	1986
295. **Eastern Group** (217) Alexandria, VA	Explores for & pro-duces gas & oil, & provides related svcs.	990	52,794	4,844	D	B	90	32	1981
296. **Papa John's International** (380) Louisville, KY	Sells take-out pizza	980	19,254	1,782	C	F	220	15	1985
297. **Communications, Marketing & Distr. Svcs.** Atlanta, GA	Warehouses, distr., designs, & prints corporate literature	980	2,085	193	C	E	43	3	1987
298. **Sonny Hill Motors** Platte City, MO	Sells & svcs. automobiles	978	138,808	12,972	D	D	350	40	1987
299. **Binary Arts** (474) Alexandria, VA	Mfrs. & imports puzzles, mazes, maps, & games	970	2,001	187	B	F	5	2	1985
300. **Electronic Label Technology** (98) Tulsa, OK	Mkts. systs. for creating bar-coded labels & tags	964	15,340	1,442	D	D	63	6	1985
301. **Artistic Impressions** (458) Lombard, IL	Sells paintings & lithographs through home parties	962	7,519	708	C	F	38	7	1985
302. **ESW** Dyer, IN	Provides custom industrial training	961	1,411	133	C	F	30	4	1987
303. **MC Strategies** Atlanta, GA	Provides consulting svcs. to health-care organizations	959	4,046	382	C	B	110	17	1986

Rank (1991)	Company/Location	Business Description	Sales Growth 1987–91 (% increase)	'91 sales ($000)	'87 sales ($000)	Profit range**		No. of employees		Date founded
						'91	'87	'91	'87	
304.	Engineering Management & Economics Rockville, MD	Provides computer systs.-engineering, prods., & consulting svcs.	955%	$1,203	$114	C	F	15	3	1987
305.	Govind & Associates Corpus Christi, TX	Provides engineering consulting svcs.	955	7,545	715	D	D	170	25	1984
306.	USA Direct (293) Manchester, PA	Provides direct-mail svcs.	954	18,164	1,723	C	F	331	17	1985
307.	Sterling Environmental Services Amherst, NY	Provides hazardous-waste-mgmt. svcs.	951	4,121	392	C	D	8	3	1985
308.	Evergreen Environmental Group (73) Crestwood, KY	Provides environmental-engineering svcs.	950	4,230	403	A	A	29	5	1986
309.	Chico's (198) Fort Meyers, FL	Sells women's apparel & accessories	945	23,177	2,217	C	B	240	45	1983
310.	Fitec International Memphis, TN	Imports & exports commercial fishing prods.	944	34,397	3,296	D	C	480	5	1984
311.	TL Care (271) San Francisco, CA	Mfrs. & sells infant clothing & accessories	941	3,404	327	D	D	6	2	1985
312.	ABA Personnel Services San Francisco, CA	Provides employment-search svcs.	937	4,408	425	D	F	12	4	1986
313.	United International Engineering Albuquerque, NM	Provides engineering svcs.	937	13,710	1,322	B	D	175	14	1982
314.	Aztech Controls (85) Mesa, AZ	Distr. valves & fittings	935	6,252	604	C	D	20	7	1986
315.	Koch International Westbury, NY	Records, distr., & mkts. music	931	14,014	1,359	D	D	60	8	1987
316.	American Playworld Ogden, UT	Mfrs. playground equip.	931	13,903	1,349	B	A	157	29	1978
317.	Z-Barten Productions Culver City, CA	Mfrs. confetti, gifts, & craft items	928	1,449	141	B	F	25	4	1984
318.	Siciliano (411) Springfield, IL	Provides construc-tion svcs.	927	7,588	739	D	C	50	8	1968
319.	Main Street Muffins Akron, OH	Mfrs. frozen bakery products	924	1,106	108	C	F	17	6	1986
320.	McCool's Carpet Outlet Kokomo, IN	Sells flooring prods.	924	2,007	196	B	B	7	1	1967
321.	Barclays Oxygen Homecare Englewood, CO	Provides in-house oxygen svcs.	920	3,643	357	A	B	32	6	1985
322.	ESE Marshfield, WI	Provides process control & data-acquisition engineering svcs.	916	2,540	250	D	C	25	3	1981
323.	Athletic Fitters (256) Eden Prairie, MN	Retails athletic shoes & apparel	916	8,115	799	B	B	41	4	1983
324.	Roux Associates (233) Huntington, NY	Provides environmental-consulting & mgmt. svcs.	909	11,895	1,179	D	D	108	20	1981
325.	McNerney Heintz (66) Barrington, IL	Provides admin-istrative mgmt. svcs. for medical organizations	904	9,357	932	C	C	171	47	1985
326.	Precision Response (285) Miami, FL	Provides integrated-direct-marketing svcs.	904	16,182	1,612	B	D	250	63	1981
327.	Canvasback (495) Milwaukee, WI	Designs & mfrs. women's sportswear	904	6,744	672	B	C	50	13	1978
328.	Fenders & More Nashville, TN	Distr. auto parts & accessories	903	9,742	971	D	F	55	6	1986

Rank (1991) Company/Location	Business Description	Sales Growth 1987–91 (% increase)	'91 sales ($000)	'87 sales ($000)	Profit range** '91	'87	No. of employees '91	'87	Date founded
329. **Creative Producers Group** St. Louis, MO	Produces videos, plans events, & provides training svcs.	902%	$1,403	$140	B	D	10	3	1985
330. **Deckers** Carpinteria, CA	Mfrs., distr., & mkts. sandals	899	11,617	1,163	B	F	200	37	1973
331. **Medical Equipment Repair Services** Sarasota, FL	Sells & svcs. respiratory equip.	898	1,058	106	D	F	14	4	1984
332. **MWW/Strategic Communications** (158) River Edge, NJ	Provides PR svcs.	893	3,138	316	C	D	24	5	1986
333. **Leopardo Construction** Glendale Heights, IL	Provides general-contracting & consulting svcs.	890	55,248	5,583	D	F	105	27	1979
334. **Wasser Industries** Seattle, WA	Provides technical & marketing-communications svcs.	887	3,722	377	D	D	7	2	1980
335. **Spec-line Laminated Products** Doraville, GA	Mfrs. furniture, cabinets, millwork, & specialty wood prods.	884	1,457	148	B	D	31	5	1986
336. **Geerlings & Wade** Canton, MA	Retails mail-order premium wines	880	3,077	314	C	F	13	2	1986
337. **Nature's Recipe Pet Foods** (170) Corona, CA	Mfrs. specialty pet food	880	21,182	2,162	A	A	40	4	1981
338. **Safesite Records Management** Billerica, MA	Provides business-records-mgmt. svcs.	875	6,366	653	F	F	152	25	1986
339. **Tri-Services** Chesapeake, VA	Provides contract general svcs. to the military	873	1,401	144	D	E	50	15	1987
340. **MMI of Mississippi** (223) Crystal Springs, MS	Mfrs. health-care furniture & laboratories	871	2,698	278	A	F	14	9	1986
341. **Travel Store** Los Angeles, CA	Provides travel svcs.	868	23,670	2,445	D	D	40	16	1975
342. **Oreman Sales** (162) Kenner, LA	Distr. computers & accessories	868	61,987	6,405	C	D	72	12	1980
343. **Flexible Personnel** Fort Wayne, IN	Runs temporary-employment service	868	7,964	823	F	F	29	10	1980
344. **Commonwealth** (236) Cincinnati, OH	Provides contract warehousing svcs.	866	4,184	433	D	A	30	3	1985
345. **Staff Leasing** Bradenton, FL	Leases perma-nent employees to businesses	864	154,447	16,027	D	D	11,310	1,001	1984
346. **North American Processing** Niles, IL	Imports & distr. meat prods.	863	137,164	14,237	D	D	13	7	1987
347. **Touchstone Research Laboratory** Triadelphia, WV	Provides R&D svcs.	859	2,291	239	D	F	23	11	1980
348. **Remote Control International** (79) Carlsbad, CA	Provides software-publishing svcs.	858	4,263	445	D	D	50	10	1985
349. **Southwest Royalties** Midland, TX	Produces oil & gas	856	17,589	1,840	D	B	70	17	1983
350. **ERM-Rocky Mountain** Englewood, CO	Provides environmental-consulting svcs.	856	4,750	497	B	B	56	6	1986
351. **Applied Utility Systems** Santa Ana, CA	Provides engineering consulting svcs.	852	6,813	716	D	D	27	7	1985

Rank (1991) Company/Location	Business Description	Sales Growth 1987–91 (% increase)	'91 sales ($000)	'87 sales ($000)	Profit range**		No. of employees		Date founded
					'91	'87	'91	'87	
352. **EDECO** Tulsa, OK	Provides engineering consulting svcs. to petroleum & gas industry	843%	$7,140	$757	C	F	170	19	1972
353. **SoMat** Urbana, IL	Provides data-acquisition-&-analysis-systs. svcs.	841	1,750	186	D	F	10	4	1982
354. **Litle & Co.** (16) Salem, NH	Provides credit-card processing svcs.	841	45,954	4,885	D	F	101	25	1986
355. **Saturn Electronics & Engineering** (307) Rochester Hills, MI	Provides electronic-& electromechanical-engineering svcs.	841	14,975	1,592	C	D	325	20	1985
356. **R&M Business Systems** Elk Grove Village, IL	Sells & svcs. office equip.	840	3,534	376	C	F	38	6	1987
357. **System Resources** (264) Burlington, MA	Provides high-tech engineering svcs.	836	12,682	1,355	C	C	139	36	1985
358. **Metters Industries** (463) McLean, VA	Provides systs.-engineering svcs.	836	29,406	3,142	D	F	350	54	1981
359. **MDM Engineering** (398) San Clemente, CA	Provides engineering & technical svcs.	836	10,135	1,083	C	C	125	23	1984
360. **Enecotech Group** Denver, CO	Provides environmental-consulting svcs.	830	14,990	1,611	C	C	200	18	1984
361. **Griffis/Blessing** Colorado Springs, CO	Manages, invests in, & develops real estate	830	1,116	120	A	F	25	4	1985
362. **Shields Health Care** Brockton, MA	Provides medical diagnostic-imaging svcs.	829	28,372	3,054	A	A	120	9	1986
363. **Allsup** (333) Belleville, IL	Provides claims svcs. to health-care industry	827	6,036	651	A	C	89	9	1984
364. **Teubner & Associates** Stillwater, OK	Researches & develops communications software	825	2,247	243	C	F	16	1	1983
365. **American International Construction** Houston, TX	Builds metal structures & mini-warehouses	821	20.245	2,199	D	B	200	7	1985
366. **Stretcho Fabrics** Hawthorne, NJ	Mfrs. stretch-knit fabrics	820	10,015	1,088	D	D	7	3	1987
367. **Routing Technology Software** (232) Vienna, VA	Develops & supports Roadshow software	820	6,736	732	A	F	65	8	1983
368. **MBS Communications** Cheshire, CT	Provides telephone-answering svcs.	817	1,220	133	B	F	33	3	1986
369. **Team Spirit** (365) Omaha, NE	Retails team apparel	817	13,470	1,469	B	B	90	25	1985
370. **Gravity Graphics** Brooklyn, NY	Silk-screens activewear	816	2,556	279	D	C	42	5	1984
371. **Hofgard Benefit Plan Administrators** Boulder, CO	Administers employee-benefits plans	813	1,370	150	F	F	28	3	1986
372. **S&S Management & Consulting** Somerset, MA	Provides mgmt.-consulting svcs. to small & midsize cos.	810	2,166	238	B	F	7	5	1986
373. **Saloom Furniture** (272) Gardner, MA	Mfrs. tables & chairs	807	5,740	633	C	C	65	17	1981
374. **Option Technologies** Mendota Heights, MN	Develops & distr. software & hardware	805	995	110	C	F	7	1	1986

Rank (1991) Company/Location	Business Description	Sales Growth 1987–91 (% increase)	'91 sales ($000)	'87 sales ($000)	Profit range** '91	Profit range** '87	No. of employees '91	No. of employees '87	Date founded
375. **Micro Dynamics** (245) Silver Spring, MD	Develops & mkts. document-imaging & text-retrieval prods.	803%	$6,585	$729	D	E	55	14	1985
376. **Datastorm Technologies** Columbia, MO	Develops & publishes software	803	17,821	1,974	A	D	93	11	1985
377. **Genesis Automation** Shelton, CT	Develops & mfrs. robotic equip. for fast-food industry	800	2,088	232	F	A	13	5	1986
378. **Refco Investments** Melrose Park, IL	Leases packaging & processing equip.	799	1,178	131	A	A	4	2	1984
379. **Environmental Operations** St. Louis, MO	Provides environmental-consulting svcs.	799	1,824	203	D	D	29	4	1986
380. **ABL Electronics** Hunt Valley, MD	Mfrs. & distr. computer & networking cabling & accessories	792	3,204	359	D	C	39	18	1981
381. **Barry T. Chouinard** Northfield, VT	Dyes textiles & distr. T-shirts	791	3,672	412	C	B	20	6	1975
382. **American Insurance Management Group** Atlanta, GA	Provides insurance-brokerage svcs.	791	15,709	1,764	D	F	100	12	1986
383. **Commercial Benefits** Woodland Hills, CA	Sells life & health insurance; provides employee-benefits svcs.	790	2,563	288	A	D	20	7	1987
384. **Compu-Call** N. Attleboro, MA	Purchases & sells computer hardware in the IBM marketplace	789	5,202	585	D	D	9	3	1987
385. **Terra Vac** (284) San Juan, PR	Provides environmental-cleanup svcs.	789	14,244	1,602	C	B	32	15	1985
386. **Integratrak** Seattle, WA	Develops telemanagement software	789	2,186	246	B	F	27	8	1986
387. **Allen Systems Group** Naples, FL	Sells computer software	788	8,198	923	C	B	120	10	1986
388. **Wek Enterprises** Buena Park, CA	Mfrs. cotton clothing	783	7,358	833	D	D	35	4	1987
389. **EnviroSearch International** Salt Lake City, UT	Provides environmental-consulting & engineering svcs.	783	2,111	239	D	B	39	5	1984
390. **Landex Construction** San Diego, CA	Provides commercial & light industrial construction svcs.	782	7,024	796	D	F	21	4	1983
391. **Traco Manufacturing** Orem, UT	Mfrs. & resells portable shrink-wrap machines & other prods.	778	2,827	322	B	B	14	5	1986
392. **Modern Technologies** (172) Dayton, OH	Provides technical & engineering svcs.	777	32,936	3,756	C	B	477	81	1985
393. **Todisco Jewelry** New York, NY	Mfrs. jewelry	772	4,003	459	D	F	100	3	1986
394. **Integrity Industries** Kingsville, TX	Mfrs. specialty chemicals	772	6,253	717	C	D	16	4	1986
395. **Penn Property & Casualty** (443) Lemoyne, PA	Provides insurance & surety-bond brokerage svcs.	770	3,690	424	D	E	10	2	1985

Rank (1991) Company/Location	Business Description	Sales Growth 1987–91 (% increase)	'91 sales ($000)	'87 sales ($000)	Profit range** '91	'87	No. of employees '91	'87	Date founded
396. **Concord Holding** New York, NY	Administers & distr. mutual funds	770%	$13,959	$1,605	A	F	56	7	1987
397. **Knowledge Systems** (214) Cary, NC	Provides object-technology software & svcs.	768	2,040	235	F	F	29	2	1986
398. **Heritage Asset Management Group** (407) Dallas, TX	Provides real-estate svcs.	767	1,752	202	D	A	72	14	1985
399. **Asia Source** Fremont, CA	Wholesales computer parts & systs.	765	67,021	7,750	D	E	50	1	1987
400. **Logos Systems** Houston, TX	Develops health-care software & svcs.	765	908	105	F	F	10	3	1987
401. **Sun Coast Resources** Houston, TX	Wholesales gasoline & diesel fuel	764	86,154	9,972	D	D	14	7	1985
402. **Zeiders Enterprises** (330) Woodbridge, VA	Provides profes-sional mgmt. svcs.	764	3,515	407	D	C	90	10	1984
403. **Carretas** Albuquerque, NM	Designs & fabricates kiosks, pushcarts, & store fixtures	761	1,868	217	D	F	30	4	1987
404. **Marketing Profiles** (190) Maitland, FL	Develops & mkts. database software for finan. institutions	760	8,379	974	C	B	53	5	1984
405. **Summit Builders** Phoenix, AZ	Provides general-contracting svcs.	760	27,216	3,164	D	D	49	21	1986
406. **Microserv** (321) Kirkland, WA	Provides technical svcs.	754	5,485	642	D	B	98	14	1986
407. **Optimation Technology** Rush, NY	Provides industrial-engineering & systs.-integration svcs.	753	1,441	169	C	F	25	5	1985
408. **Turbine Consultants** Milwaukee, WI	Provides svcs. & repairs to electric-utility cos.	750	5,294	623	A	A	11	4	1984
409. **Oakville Forest Products** (152) Oakville, WA	Produces wood chips & pulp for paper industry; dries lumber	750	6,883	810	D	A	17	7	1986
410. **Strifler Group** Dallas, TX	Provides info.-systs. consulting svcs.	749	2,200	259	A	A	30	5	1984
411. **Gulf Coast Hair Care** (185) Panama City, FL	Operates hair-salon franchise	749	2,597	306	D	F	140	30	1985
412. **Kenley** Mason, OH	Mfrs. & distr. holiday prods.	747	2,583	305	A	F	6	1	1985
413. **Plastronics Plus** E. Troy, WI	Provides custom plastic injection molding	744	4,982	590	D	D	80	15	1985
414. **Nutech Laundry & Textiles** (457) Hyattsville, MD	Manages laundry-plant & hotel-laundry systs.	744	3,901	462	C	F	130	20	1984
415. **Western Fiberglass** Windsor, CA	Mfrs. fiberglass secondary containment	740	2,074	247	F	D	30	5	1983
416. **Boston Preparatory** New York, NY	Mfrs. sportswear	737	1,172	140	A	C	4	1	1986
417. **Field Brothers Construction** (131) Marion, OH	Provides general-contracting svcs.	736	12,115	1,450	C	B	155	25	1975
418. **HMA Behavioral Health** (339) Worcester, MA	Provides medical & mental-health screening svcs.	731	2,268	273	D	B	22	6	1982

Rank (1991) Company/Location	Business Description	Sales Growth 1987–91 (% increase)	'91 sales ($000)	'87 sales ($000)	Profit range** '91	'87	No. of employees '91	'87	Date founded
419. **SVL Analytical** Kellogg, ID	Provides environmental-monitoring, cleanup, & analysis svcs.	727%	$3,068	$371	D	F	75	7	1972
420. **OCS Group** Pittsford, NY	Provides info.-mgmt., engineering, & technical-writing svcs.	726	5,661	685	B	D	119	18	1982
421. **MIC Industries** Reston, VA	Mfrs. mobile auto-building machines	724	20,696	2,513	A	D	98	7	1981
422. **TME** (410) Houston, TX	Develops, finances, & manages outpatient diagnostic-imaging centers	722	12,237	1,489	F	F	171	60	1983
423. **Design Basics** Omaha, NE	Design, catalogs, & mkts. home plans; publishes home-plans magazine	721	2,111	257	A	F	28	9	1983
424. **Arbor Systems** Carrollton, TX	Mfrs. & mkts. aftermarket computer & communications equip.	721	2,611	318	C	D	16	3	1987
425. **Proteus** (342) Albuquerque, NM	Provides computer-systs.-integration prods.	715	4,883	599	D	C	79	10	1980
426. **Lifetime Products** (337) Clearfield, UT	Mfrs. basketball equip.	715	27,133	3,330	C	D	218	64	1986
427. **Gale Group** (230) Winter Park, FL	Designs, mfrs., & mkts. retail lawn & garden prods.	715	58,086	7,131	F	D	400	80	1981
428. **Bulk International** (421) Troy, MI	Sells candy, nuts, & gifts in bulk	714	16,251	1,997	D	F	138	22	1983
429. **Stone Computer & Copier Supply** Tulsa, OK	Distr. computer & copier supplies	711	2,936	362	D	E	18	5	1986
430. **ATV** (296) Cleveland, OH	Wholesales & distr. computers	710	21,404	2,641	D	F	52	20	1980
431. **Pioneer Software** Raleigh, NC	Develops software	709	2,329	288	B	B	27	4	1986
432. **Florida Marketing International** Ormond Beach, FL	Provides Macintosh training seminars & tutorials	707	7,649	948	A	A	23	8	1987
433. **Bendco/Bending & Coiling** (418) Pasadena, TX	Mfrs. pipes & pressure vessels	704	4,360	542	D	A	53	23	1984
434. **Globaltech** Titusville, NJ	Sells electronic digital balances	702	2,495	311	D	D	16	2	1986
435. **Bike Pro USA** (488) Phoenix, AZ	Mfrs. bicycle packs & bags	700	1,024	128	D	E	26	8	1985
436. **Horizon Data** (108) Reston, VA	Integrates computer & knowledge-based systs.	700	10,382	1,298	C	C	50	12	1983
437. **Partnership Group** (202) Lansdale, PA	Provides child care, elder care, & referral svcs.	699	7,413	928	D	F	100	20	1982
438. **Complete Property Services** Oldsmar, FL	Provides general-contracting & insurance svcs.	698	2,435	305	B	C	25	4	1984
439. **Mattern Construction** Preston, CT	Provides general-contracting svcs.	698	2,865	359	C	A	9	1	1987

Rank (1991) Company/Location	Business Description	Sales Growth 1987–91 (% increase)	'91 sales ($000)	'87 sales ($000)	Profit range** '91	'87	No. of employees '91	'87	Date founded
440. **Quintiles Transnational** (402) Morrisville, NC	Provides health-care consulting & mgmt. svcs.	697%	$30,461	$3,821	C	C	320	45	1982
441. **Sunrise Terrace** Fairfax, VA	Develops & manages housing for the elderly	697	12,157	1,525	C	C	378	100	1981
442. **Sherikon** Chantilly, VA	Provides engineering & other svcs.	696	14,128	1,774	D	E	193	16	1985
443. **Music Tech of Minneapolis** Minneapolis, MN	Runs private music school specializing in popular music	694	1,406	177	D	D	50	12	1985
444. **Northwest Micro** Beaverton, OR	Integrates micro-computer systs. & distr. microcomputer components	694	7,395	931	D	D	19	4	1987
445. **U.S. Xpress** (338) Tunnel Hill, GA	Provides interstate motor-carrier svcs.	691	141,928	17,932	D	D	2,104	270	1985
446. **Magnet** (334) Washington, MO	Mfrs. advertising refrigerator magnets	688	12,679	1,609	C	D	192	25	1983
447. **Loan Pricing** (161) New York, NY	Provides database svcs. to finan. institutions	688	3,717	472	D	F	41	11	1985
448. **Energy Dynamics** (203) New Berlin, WI	Mfrs. diesel electric-generator sets	687	10,088	1,282	D	C	26	7	1984
449. **U.S. Structures** Richmond, VA	Builds wooden patio decks	686	11,000	1,400	F	C	25	4	1980
450. **Univest Financial Group** Marietta, GA	Audits & analyzes mortgages & loan portfolios	686	16,500	2,100	A	F	78	26	1985
451. **Source Technologies** (356) Charlotte, NC	Sells computer printers	683	5,436	694	D	D	16	3	1986
452. **Pleasant Co.** (69) Middleton, WI	Mkts. children's merchandise	683	64,263	8,210	B	F	228	23	1986
453. **Skender Construction** Palos Hills, IL	Provides construction-mgmt. svcs.	682	4,272	546	F	C	28	6	1979
454. **GreenLine** Bowling Green, OH	Grows & processes fresh green beans	682	2,228	285	D	F	32	11	1986
455. **Zia Cosmetics** (426) San Francisco, CA	Mfrs. natural skin-care prods.	679	1,247	160	D	E	16	3	1985
456. **Cadmus Group** Waltham, MA	Provides environmental-consulting svcs.	676	6,453	832	D	D	90	20	1983
457. **Buschman** Cleveland, OH	Mfrs. paper prods.	675	1,310	169	A	D	11	3	1976
458. **Megasource** (235) Bloomfield Hills, MI	Provides health-care consulting svcs. & software	673	7,162	926	A	F	63	13	1983
459. **Hazco Services** Dayton, OH	Distr. safety equip. to hazardous-waste industry	671	11,090	1,438	C	B	65	15	1986
460. **Schweitzer Engineering Laboratories** (273) Pullman, WA	Designs & mfrs. protective relays for electric-utility cos.	670	15,634	2,030	A	A	84	17	1982
461. **Humanix Temporary Services** Spokane, WA	Provides temporary svcs.	670	2,663	346	D	D	9	2	1986
462. **PPOM** (154) Southfield, MI	Provides PPO health-care svcs.	669	12,394	1,612	D	D	115	22	1982

Rank (1991) Company/Location	Business Description	Sales Growth 1987–91 (% increase)	'91 sales ($000)	'87 sales ($000)	Profit range**		No. of employees		Date founded
					'91	'87	'91	'87	
463. **Executive Software** (76) Glendale, CA	Develops & mkts. software for VAX/VMS computers	667%	$15,210	$1,982	B	C	95	12	1981
464. **Schnaubelt Shorts** (399) Coraopolis, PA	Mfrs. & sells designer bicycle apparel	666	1,387	181	C	F	47	32	1983
465. **FourGen Software** (146) Edmonds, WA	Develops & sells accounting software & CASE tools	665	5,051	660	C	C	84	15	1982
466. **Forcum/Mackey Construction** Ivanhoe, CA	Performs commercial & industrial construction work	663	7,963	1,043	D	D	18	14	1983
467. **Home Care Affiliates** (128) Louisville, KY	Provides home health-care svcs.	662	31,157	4,091	D	F	436	133	1986
468. **Harmony Schools** (480) Princeton, NJ	Provides child-care svcs.	661	2,663	350	D	F	104	60	1980
469. **Roelynn Business Products** Hazlet, NJ	Contracts out business-form & commercial printing projects	660	1,041	137	D	F	6	1	1985
470. **Posi-Clean** Wheeling, WV	Rebuilds & mfrs. engine oil coolers & heat exchangers	659	2,019	266	B	D	28	8	1985
471. **Mendez Excavation** Breckenridge, CO	Provides general-contracting svcs.	659	2,906	383	B	A	35	5	1982
472. **Loop Restaurant** Jacksonville, FL	Operates restaurants	658	4,788	632	B	A	75	10	1981
473. **Creative Staffing** Miami, FL	Provides temporary & permanent job-placement svcs.	658	7,144	943	D	D	24	4	1985
474. **Cucci International** Torrance, CA	Mfrs. screen-printed & embroidered apparel	657	2,930	387	C	C	34	3	1981
475. **Metalize Texas** Bastrop, TX	Provides electro-chemical metallizing svcs.	656	885	117	E	F	25	5	1985
476. **Diplomatic Language Services** Arlington, VA	Provides language training & translation	655	2,750	364	D	A	122	36	1985
477. **SNL Securities** Charlottesville, VA	Publishes newsletters & databases for finan.-svcs. industry	654	2,337	310	C	F	27	8	1987
478. **NationaLease Purchasing** Oakbrook Terrace, IL	Operates truck-leasing cos.	654	23,664	3,140	D	D	12	6	1965
479. **CMS Communications** (45) Bridgeton, MO	Sells, maintains, & repairs telecommunications equip.	649	18,283	2,440	C	B	152	12	1985
480. **Authorized Cellular/Security One** Roseville, MI	Sells & svcs. cellular phones	646	1,828	245	B	F	20	2	1983
481. **Thomure Medsearch** St. Louis, MO	Provides physician recruiting & placement svcs.	644	1,599	215	B	A	50	4	1987
482. **DCS Software & Consulting** (388) Dallas, TX	Provides IBM-computer consulting svcs.	644	4,439	597	D	D	90	17	1981
483. **Supplemental Health Care Services** Tonawanda, NY	Provides medical-staff placement svcs.	641	6,515	879	F	C	1,100	40	1984

Rank (1991) Company/Location	Business Description	Sales Growth 1987–91 (% increase)	'91 sales ($000)	'87 sales ($000)	Profit range** '91	'87	No. of employees '91	'87	Date founded
484. **AccSys Technology** (206) Pleasanton, CA	Designs & mfrs. linear accelerator systs. & related components	640%	$3,256	$440	D	F	22	7	1985
485. **Visual Concepts Media** Bloomfield, CT	Produces corporate videos	638	826	112	D	A	6	2	1987
486. **De-Mar** Clovis, CA	Provides plumbing, heating, & air-conditioning svcs.	632	3,109	425	B	C	35	5	1976
487. **J and M Laboratories** Dawsonville, GA	Develops, mfrs., & researches hot melt equip.	628	2,861	393	A	B	50	8	1985
488. **Monterey Homes** Scottsdale, AZ	Builds luxury communities	627	20,528	2,822	D	F	30	5	1986
489. **American Teleconferencing Svcs.** (157) Overland Park, KS	Provides conference-call svcs.	627	3,462	476	D	A	43	8	1984
490. **Asosa Personnel** Tucson, AZ	Provides personnel recruiting & temporary-help svcs.	627	4,087	562	D	F	22	15	1964
491. **National Business Group** Atlanta, GA	Distr. computer connectivity hardware & software	626	8,652	1,192	D	D	13	4	1987
492. **CareFlorida** Miami, FL	Provides HMO svcs.	624	75,677	10,454	D	F	189	50	1985
493. **Dan Flickinger Inc.** Seattle, WA	Owns contemporary-home-furnishings stores	624	1,802	249	F	F	9	3	1987
494. **Reunion Time** Tinton Falls, NJ	Provides class-reunion-planning svcs.	622	2,511	348	C	F	11	4	1985
495. **Tracer Research** Tucson, AZ	Detects contaminants in soil, water, tanks, & pipelines	620	8,943	1,242	C	F	93	23	1984
496. **Phoenix Controls** (101) Newton, MA	Mfrs. laboratory airflow-control systs.	618	7,662	1,067	D	F	74	8	1985
497. **Apogee Research** (163) Bethesda, MD	Provides finan.-consulting svcs.	614	3,065	429	D	D	35	6	1986
498. **Mastersoft** (269) Scottsdale, AZ	Develops & publishes software	614	2,043	286	A	F	16	5	1986
499. **Copyco** Deerfield Beach, FL	Distr. copiers, faxes, & digital duplicators	614	6,706	939	D	F	89	16	1986
500. **Falcon Microsystems** Landover, MD	Distr. & integrates Macintosh LANs & software	606	138,938	19,679	D	F	249	82	1983

APPENDIX 8

WHO PAYS THE MOST? AVERAGE ANNUAL PAY BY INDUSTRY AND STATE

Source: Bureau of Labor Statistics. Reprinted by permission from *The Numbers News*, December 1992, © 1992 American Demographics, Inc.

State	Private Total	Private Manufacturing	Private Finance	Private Services	Government
United States	$24,177	$30,082	$31,008	$23,048	$26,561
Alabama	$20,738	$23,423	$23,999	$20,539	$23,538
Alaska	**29,088***	28,434	27,647	23,480	**35,140**
Arizona	21,687	30,677	26,069	20,838	24,592
Arkansas	18,602	20,933	22,871	17,237	21,028
California	26,847	33,646	33,170	**26,826**	30,942
Colorado	23,609	31,365	27,434	22,360	25,701
Connecticut	**30,560**	**37,768**	**39,605**	**27,511**	**31,535**
Delaware	25,681	**39,808**	25,961	21,431	25,443
District of Columbia	**32,693**	**41,748**	**38,688**	**33,663**	**39,446**
Florida	21,366	27,134	26,835	21,906	25,278
Georgia	23,106	24,600	29,584	22,802	23,427
Hawaii	23,176	25,886	27,891	22,497	28,082
Idaho	19,396	25,573	21,871	19,193	20,859
Illinois	26,181	31,668	33,817	24,047	27,079
Indiana	22,331	30,295	23,812	19,138	23,669
Iowa	19,289	26,655	24,253	16,529	22,351
Kansas	20,883	27,225	23,966	18,820	21,506
Kentucky	20,334	26,289	23,394	18,221	22,610
Louisiana	21,691	29,307	23,245	19,921	20,753
Maine	20,221	25,656	27,106	19,116	23,788
Maryland	24,672	31,874	29,432	24,941	31,358
Massachusetts	27,854	34,738	**35,238**	**27,208**	29,256
Michigan	25,880	**37,105**	26,818	22,613	27,492
Minnesota	23,499	31,096	29,919	20,491	26,623
Mississippi	18,130	20,032	21,629	17,469	19,490
Missouri	22,535	28,436	26,390	20,302	23,721
Montana	17,745	24,259	21,217	16,180	21,864
Nebraska	18,734	23,590	23,955	17,685	22,058
Nevada	22,293	26,900	25,165	21,504	28,396
New Hampshire	23,403	30,550	27,630	22,037	24,801
New Jersey	**29,634**	**36,224**	35,470	**28,041**	**31,923**
New Mexico	19,368	23,938	21,160	20,563	23,220
New York	**29,780**	34,536	**47,176**	26,784	**31,077**
North Carolina	20,702	23,434	25,801	19,786	23,122
North Dakota	17,599	21,799	21,290	16,705	20,189
Ohio	23,347	31,868	25,884	20,672	25,131
Oklahoma	20,794	26,563	22,810	18,385	21,579
Oregon	21,724	28,141	25,294	19,555	25,415
Pennsylvania	23,892	29,615	28,779	22,923	27,575
Rhode Island	22,243	25,856	28,733	20,952	28,277
South Carolina	19,889	24,609	22,678	18,095	22,940
South Dakota	16,450	19,883	21,179	15,706	19,926
Tennessee	21,239	24,783	25,725	20,500	23,155
Texas	23,898	29,809	28,379	22,200	23,132
Utah	20,401	25,720	22,889	19,154	22,746
Vermont	20,988	29,496	25,425	18,429	23,147
Virginia	22,919	26,455	27,221	23,660	27,345
Washington	23,237	32,864	26,871	21,093	27,158
West Virginia	21,268	28,340	20,632	18,036	21,713
Wisconsin	21,293	28,046	24,782	18,681	25,201
Wyoming	20,049	24,551	21,106	14,773	22,106

*top 5 paying states for all industries indicated in boldface.

APPENDIX 9

SMALL BUSINESS ADMINISTRATION FIELD OFFICES

Office	Address	Officer in Charge	Telephone
REGION I			
Augusta, ME (DO)	Rm. 512, 40 Western Ave., 04330	Leroy G. Perry	207-622-8378
Boston, MA (RO)	9th Fl., 155 Federal St., 02110	Susan Collins	617-451-2023
Boston, MA (DO)	Rm. 265, 10 Causeway St., 02222-1093	Joseph D. Pelligrino	617-565-5590
Concord, NH (DO)	Rm. 210, 55 Pleasant St., 03302-1257	William K. Phillips	603-225-1400
Hartford, CT (DO)	2d Fl., 330 Main St., 06106	Carol White	203-240-4700
Montpelier, VT (DO)	Rm. 205, 87 State St., 05602	Kenneth Silvia	802-828-4474
Providence, RI (DO)	380 Westminister Mall, 02903	Joseph Loddo	401-528-4561
Springfield, MA (BO)	Rm. 212, 1550 Main St., 01103	Harold Webb	413-785-9484
REGION II			
Buffalo, NY (DO)	Rm. 1311, 111 W. Huron St., 14202	Franklin J. Sciortino	716-846-4305
Camden, NJ (PD)	2600 Mt. Ephrain, 08104	Cesar A. Ballester	609-757-4511
Elmira, NY (BO)	333 E. Water St., 14901	James J. Cristofaro	607-734-1571
Hato Rey, PR (DO)	Rm. 691, Federal Bldg., Carlos Chardon Ave., 00918	Carlos E. Chardon	8-809-766-5003
Melville, NY (BO)	Rm. 102E, 35 Pinelawn Rd., 11747	(Vacancy)	516-454-0764
New York, NY (RO)	Rm. 31-08, 26 Federal Plz., 10278	Michael Forbes	212-264-1450
New York, NY (DO)	Rm. 3100, 26 Federal Plz., 10278	(Vacancy)	212-264-1318
Newark, NJ (DO)	4th Fl., 60 Park Pl., 07102	Stanley Salt	201-645-3580
Rochester, NY (BO)	Rm. 601, 100 State St., 14614	Peter Flihan	716-263-6700
St. Croix, VI (PD)	Rm. 7, United Shopping Plz., 4C&D State Sion Farm Christiansted, 00820	Carl Christensen	809-778-5380
St. Thomas, VI (PD)	Rm. 283, Federal Office Bldg., Veterans Dr., 00801	Lionel Baptiste	809-774-8530
Syracuse, NY (DO)	Rm. 1071, 100 S. Clinton St., 13260	J. Wilson Harrison	315-423-5371
REGION III			
Baltimore, MD (DO)	3d Fl., 10 N. Calvert St., 21202	Charles J. Gaston	301-962-2054
Charleston, WV (BO)	Rm. 309, 550 Eagan St., 25301	Bill Durham	304-347-5220
Clarksburg, WV (DO)	5th Fl., 168 W. Main St., 26301	Marvin P. Shelton	304-623-4317
Harrisburg, PA (BO)	Rm. 309, 100 Chestnut St., 17101	Kenneth J. Olson	717-782-3846
King of Prussia, PA (RO)	Suite 201, 475 Allendale Rd., 19406	Catherine Killian	215-962-3710
King of Prussia, PA (DO)	Suite 201, 475 Allendale Rd., 19406	(Vacancy)	215-962-3801

(RO: Regional Office; DO: District Office; BO: Branch Office; PD: Post of Duty)

Office	Address	Officer in Charge	Telephone
Pittsburgh, PA (DO)	5th Fl., 960 Penn Ave., 15222	Joseph M. Kopp	412-644-4306
Richmond, VA (DO)	Rm. 3015, 400 N. 8th St., 23240	Dratin Hill, Jr.	804-771-2741
Washington, DC (DO)	6th Fl., 1111 18th St. NW., 20036	James O. Gordon	202-634-1805
Wilkes-Barre, PA (BO)	Rm. 2327, 20 N. Pennsylvania Ave., 18701	Frank H. Hamilton	717-826-6446
Wilmington, DE (BO)	Rm. 412, 920 N. King St., 19801	Fred B. Trescher, Jr.	302-573-6295

REGION IV

Office	Address	Officer in Charge	Telephone
Atlanta, GA (RO)	5th Fl., 1375 Peachtree St. NE., 30367	June Nichols	404-347-4999
Atlanta, GA (DO)	6th Fl., 1720 Peachtree Rd. NW., 30309	Wilfred A. Stone	404-347-4749
Birmingham, AL (DO)	Suite 200, 2121 8th Ave. N., 35203	James C. Barksdale	205-731-1341
Charlotte, NC (DO)	200 N. College St., 28202	Gary A. Keel	704-371-6561
Columbia, SC (DO)	Rm. 358, 1835 Assembly St., 29202	Elliott Cooper	803-253-5339
Coral Gables, FL (DO)	Suite 501, 1320 S. Dixie Hwy., 33136	Charles Anderson	305-536-5533
Gulfport, MS (BO)	Suite 1001, 1 Hancock Plz., 39501	Charles Gillis	601-863-4449
Jackson, MS (DO)	Suite 322, 101 W. Capitol St., 39269	Jack K. Spradling	601-965-4363
Jacksonville, FL (DO)	Suite 100-B, 7825 Bay Meadows Way, 32202	Thomas Short	904-443-1900
Louisville, KY (DO)	Rm. 188, 600 M.L. King, Jr., Pl., 40202	William Federhofer	502-582-5976
Nashville, TN (DO)	Suite 201, 50 Vantage Way, 37228	Robert M. Hartman	615-736-5850
Statesboro, GA (PD)	Rm. 225, 52 N. Main St., 30458	Ralph T. Clark	912-489-8719
Tampa, FL (PD)	Rm. 104, 501 E. Polk St., 33602-3945	Earl N. Moore	813-228-2594
West Palm Beach, FL (PD)	Suite 402, 5601 Corporate Way, 33407	Roderick Young	305-689-3922

REGION V

Office	Address	Officer in Charge	Telephone
Chicago, IL (RO)	Rm. 6 1975, 300 S. Riverside Plz., 60606-6611	(Vacancy)	312-353-0359
Chicago, IL (DO)	Rm. 1250, 500 W. Madison St., 60661	John L. Smith	312-353-4528
Cincinnati, OH (BO)	Suite 870, 525 Vine St., 45202	David E. Gray	513-684-2814
Cleveland, OH (DO)	Rm. 317, 1240 E. 9th St., 44199	Norma Nelson	216-522-4180
Columbus, OH (DO)	Rm. 512, 85 Marconi Blvd., 43215	Frank D. Ray	614-469-7310
Detroit, MI (DO)	Rm. 515, 477 Michigan Ave., 48226	Raymond L. Harshman	313-226-7240
Indianapolis, IN (DO)	Suite 100, 429 N. Pennsylvania St., 46204-1873	Robert D. General	317-226-7275
Madison, WI (DO)	Rm. 213, 212 E. Washington Ave., 53703	Curtis A. Charter	608-264-5268
Marquette, MI (BO)	228 West Washington St., Suite 4, 49855	Paul Jacobson	906-225-1108

Office	Address	Officer in Charge	Telephone
Milwaukee, WI (BO)	Suite 400, 310 W. Wisconsin Ave., 53203	(Vacancy)	414-291-1094
Minneapolis, MN (DO)	610-C Butler Sq., 100 N. 6th St., 55403	Edward A. Daum	612-370-2306
Springfield, IL (BO)	Suite 302, 511 W. Capitol St., 62704	D.I. Brookhart	217-492-4232

REGION VI

Office	Address	Officer in Charge	Telephone
Albuquerque, NM (DO)	Suite 320, 625 Silver Ave. SW., 87102	Tommy W. Dowell	505-262-6339
Austin, TX (PD)	Rm. 520, 300 E. 8th St., 78701	Arvan Holder	512-482-5288
Corpus Christi, TX (BO)	Suite 1200, 606 N. Caranc-ahua, 78476	Gail Goodloe	512-888-3301
Dallas, TX (RO)	Bldg. C, 8625 King George Dr., 75235	Lejeune Wilson	214-767-7611
Dallas, TX (DO)	Rm. 3C-36, 1100 Commerce St., 75242	James S. Reed	214-767-0600
El Paso, TX (DO)	Suite 320, 10737 Gateway W., 79935	John Scott	915-540-5676
Fort Worth, TX (BO)	Rm 10A27, 819 Taylor St., 76102	(Vacancy)	817-334-3673
Harlingen, TX (DO)	Suite 500, 222 E. Van Buren, 78550	Miguel Cavazos	512-427-8533
Houston, TX (DO)	Suite 112, 2525 Murworth St., 77054	Rodney Martin	713-660-4401
Little Rock, AR (DO)	Suite 601, 320 W. Capitol Ave., 72201	Donald Libbey	501-378-5277
Lubbock, TX (DO)	Suite 200, 1611 10th St., 79401	Walter Fronstin	806-743-7462
Marshall, TX (PD)	Rm. 103, 505 E. Travis St., 75670	George Lewis	214-935-5257
New Orleans, LA (DO)	Suite 2000, 1661 Canal St., 70112	Abby Carter	504-589-2744
Oklahoma City, OK (DO)	Suite 670, 200 NW. 5th St., 73102	(Vacancy)	405-231-5237
San Antonio, TX (DO)	Suite 200, 7400 Blanco Rd., 78216	(Vacancy)	512-229-4501
Shreveport, LA (PD)	Rm. 8A-08, 500 Fannin St., 71101	Bobby Boling	318-226-5196

REGION VII

Office	Address	Officer in Charge	Telephone
Cedar Rapids, IA (DO)	Rm. 100, 373 Collins Rd. NE., 52402	James Thomson	319-399-2571
Des Moines, IA (DO)	Rm. 749, 210 Walnut St., 50309	Conrad E. Lawlor	515-284-4567
Kansas City, MO (RO)	13th Fl., 911 Walnut St., 64106	Gary Nodler	816-426-3316
Kansas City, MO (DO)	Suite 501, 323 W. 8th St., 64105	(Vacancy)	816-374-6760
Omaha, NE (DO)	11145 Mill Valley Rd., 68154	Glenn Davis	402-221-3620
Springfield, MO (BO)	Suite 110, 620 S. Glenstone St., 65802	Dean Cotton	417-864-7670
St. Louis, MO (DO)	Rm. 242, 815 Olive St., 63101	Robert L. Andrews	314-539-6600
Wichita, KS (DO)	1st Fl., 110 E. Waterman St., 67202	Gary Cook	316-269-6566

Office	Address	Officer in Charge	Telephone
REGION VIII			
Casper, WY (DO)	Rm. 4001, 100 East B St., 82602	James Gallogly	307-261-5761
Denver, CO (RO)	Suite 701, 999 18th St., 80202	Gilbert M. Cisneros	303-294-7021
Denver, CO (DO)	Rm. 407, 721 19th St., 80201	Dratin Hill, Jr.	303-844-6501
Fargo, ND (DO)	Rm. 218, 657 2d Ave. N., 58108	James L. Stai	701-239-5131
Helena, MT (DO)	Rm. 528, 301 S. Park, 59626	John R. Cronholm	406-449-5381
Salt Lake City, UT (DO)	Rm. 2237, 125 S. State St., 84138	Stan Nakano	801-524-5804
Sioux Falls, SD (DO)	Suite 101, 101 S. Main Ave., 57102	Chester Leedom	605-330-4231
REGION IX			
Agana, GU (BO)	Rm. 508, 238 Archbishop F.C. Flores St., 96910	Jose M.L. Lujan	671-472-7277
Fresno, CA (DO)	2719 N. Air Fresno Dr., 93727	Peter Bergin	209-487-5791
Honolulu, HI (DO)	Rm. 2213, 300 Ala Moana, 96850	Charles Lum	808-541-2990
Las Vegas, NV (DO)	301 E. Stewart, 89125	Patrick Allison	702-388-6611
Los Angeles, CA (DO)	Suite 1200, 330 N. Brand Blvd., Glendale, 91203	(Vacancy)	213-894-2977
Phoenix, AZ (DO)	5th Fl., 2005 N. Central Ave., 85004	James P. Guyer	602-379-3737
Reno, NV (PD)	P.O. Box 3216, Rm. 238, 50 S. Virginia St., 89505	Art Ereckson	702-784-5268
Sacramento, CA (BO)	Suite 215, 660 J St., 95814	Roberta L. Conner	916-551-1445
San Diego, CA (DO)	Suite 4-S-29, 880 Front St., 92188	George P. Chandler, Jr.	619-557-7252
San Francisco, CA (RO)	20th Fl., 71 Stevenson St., 94105	Oscar Wright	415-774-6402
San Francisco, CA (DO)	4th Fl., 211 Main St., 94105	Michael R. Howland	415-744-6801
Santa Ana, CA (DO)	Rm. 160, 901 W. Civic Center Dr.	John S. Waddell	714-836-2494
Tucson, AZ (PD)	Rm. 3V, 300 W. Congress St., 85701	Ivan P. Hankins	602-629-6715
Ventura, CA (PD)	Suite 10, Bldg. C-1, 6477 Telephone Rd., 93003	Teddy Lutz	805-642-1866
REGION X			
Anchorage, AK (DO)	Rm. A36, No. 67, 222 W. 8th Ave., 99501	Frank Cox	907-271-4022
Boise, ID (DO)	Suite 290, 1020 Main St., 83702	Thomas Bergdoll	208-334-9641
Portland, OR (DO)	Suite 500, 220 SW. Columbia St., 97204	John L. Gilman	503-326-5221
Seattle, WA (RO)	Rm. 440, 2615 4th Ave., 98121	(Vacancy)	206-553-5534
Seattle, WA (DO)	Rm. 1792, 915 2d Ave., 98174	Robert P. Meredith	206-553-2786
Spokane, WA (DO)	10th Fl. E., W. 601 1st Ave., 99210	Robert Wiebe	509-353-2807

APPENDIX 10

U.S. GOVERNMENT PRINTING OFFICE BOOKSTORES

City	Address	Telephone
Washington, DC, area:		
Main Bookstore	710 N. Capitol St. NW.	202-512-0132
Farragut West	1510 H St. NW.	202-653-5075
Retail Sales Outlet	8660 Cherry Lane, Laurel, MD	301-953-7974
Atlanta, GA	Rm. 100, 275 Peachtree St. NE.	404-331-6947
Birmingham, AL	2021 3d Ave. N.	205-731-1056
Boston, MA	Rm. 179, 10 Causeway St.	617-720-4180
Chicago, IL	Rm. 124, 401 S. State St.	312-353-5133
Cleveland, OH	Rm. 1653, 1240 E. 9th St.	216-522-4922
Columbus, OH	Rm. 207, 200 N. High St.	614-469-6956
Dallas, TX	Rm. 1C50, 1100 Commerce St.	214-767-0076
Denver, CO	Rm. 117, 1961 Stout St.	303-844-3964
Detroit, MI	Suite 160, 477 Michigan Ave.	313-226-7816
Houston, TX	801 Travis St.	713-228-1187
Jacksonville, FL	Rm. 100, 100 W. Bay St.	904-353-0472
Kansas City, MO	120 Bannister Mall, 5600 E. Bannister Rd.	816-767-8225
Los Angeles, CA	C-Level, ARCO Plaza, 505 S. Flower St.	213-239-9844
Milwaukee, WI	Rm. 190, 517 E. Wisconsin Ave.	414-297-1304
New York, NY	Rm. 110, 26 Federal Plz.	212-264-3825
Philadelphia, PA	100 N. 17th St.	215-597-0677
Pittsburgh, PA	Rm. 118, 1000 Liberty Ave.	412-644-2721
Portland, OR	1305 SW. 1st Ave.	503-221-6217
Pueblo, CO	720 N. Main St.	719-544-3142
San Francisco, CA	Rm. 1023, 450 Golden Gate Ave.	415-252-5334
Seattle, WA	Rm. 194, 915 2d Ave.	206-553-4271

APPENDIX 11

COUNTRY DESK SPECIALISTS OF THE INTERNATIONAL TRADE ADMINISTRATION OF THE U.S. DEPARTMENT OF COMMERCE (see Part II, p. 503).

Country	Desk Officer	Phone (202) 482-	Country	Desk Officer	Phone (202) 482-
A			Central African		
Afghanistan	Timothy Gilman	2954	Rep	Phillip Michelini	4388
Albania	Lynn Fabrizio	4915	Chad	Phillip Michelini	4388
Algeria	Jeffrey Johnson	1870	Chile	Roger Turner	1495
	Claude Clement		Colombia	Laurie MacNamara	1659
	Chris Cerone		Comoros	Chandra Watkins	4564
Angola	Finn Holm-Olsen	4228	Congo	Debra Henke	5149
Anguilla	Michelle Brooks	2527	Costa Rica	Laura Subrin	2527
Argentina	Randolph Mye	1548	Cuba	Rodrigo Soto	2527
Aruba	Michelle Brooks	2527	Cyprus	Ann Corro	3945
ASEAN	George Paine	3875	Czechoslovakia	Mark Mowrey	2645
Antigua/Barbuda	Michelle Brooks	2527			
Australia	Gary Bouck (Bus.)	3646	**D**		
	William Golike (Policy)	3646	Denmark	Maryanne Lyons	3254
Austria	Philip Combs	2920	D'Jibouti	Chandra Watkins	4564
			Dominica	Michelle Brooks	2527
B			Dominican Republic	Rodrigo Soto	2527
Bahamas	Rodrigo Soto	2527			
Bahrain	Claude Clement	5545	**E**		
	Chris Cerone		East Caribbean	Michelle Brooks	2527
Baltics Republic	Pam Green		Ecuador	Laurie MacNamara	1659
Desk			Egypt	Thomas Sams	4441
	Susan Lewens	3952		Corey Wright	
Bangladesh	Cheryl McQueen	2954	El Salvador	Helen Lee	2527
Barbados	Michelle Brooks	2527	Equatorial Guinea	Debra Henke	4228
Belgium	Simon Bensimon	5041	Ethiopia	Chandra Watkins	4564
Belize	Michelle Brooks	2527	European Community	Charles Ludolph	5276
Benin	Debra Henke	4228			
Bermuda	Michelle Brooks	2527			
Bhutan	Timothy Gilman	2954	**F**		
Bolivia	Herbert Lindow	2521	Finland	Maryanne Lyons	3254
Botswana	Finn Holm-Olsen	4228	France	Elena Mikalis	6008
Brazil	Larry Farris	3871			
Brunei	Raphael Cung	3875	**G**		
Bulgaria	Lynn Fabrizio	4915	Gabon	Debra Henke	5149
Burkina Faso	Phillip Michelini	4388	Gambia	Philip Michelini	4388
Burma (Myanmar)	George Paine	3875	Germany	Brenda Fisher	2434
Burundi	Phillip Michelini	4388		Joan Kloepfer	2841
			Ghana	Debra Henke	5149
C			Greece	Ann Corro	3945
Cambodia	Hong-Phong B. Pho	3875	Grenada	Michelle Brooks	2527
Cameroon	Debra Henke	5149	Guadeloupe	Michelle Brooks	2527
Canada	Jonathan Don	3101	Guatemala	Helen Lee	2527
Cape Verde	Philip Michelini	4388	Guinea	Philip Michelini	4388
Caribbean Basin	Jay Dowling	1648	Guinea-Bissau	Philip Michelini	4388
Caymans	Michelle Brooks	2527	Guyana	Michelle Brooks	2527

Country	Desk Officer	Phone (202) 482-	Country	Desk Officer	Phone (202) 482-
H			Maldives	John Simmons	2954
Haiti	Rodrigo Soto	2527	Mali	Philip Michelini	4388
Honduras	Helen Lee	2527	Malta	Robert McLaughlin	3748
Hong Kong	Sheila Baker	3932	Martinique	Michelle Brooks	2527
Hungary	Brian Touhey	2645	Mauritania	Philip Michelini	4388
			Mauritius	Chandra Watkins	4564
I			Mexico	Rebecca Bannister	0300
Iceland	Maryanne Lyons	3254	Mongolia	Jenell Matheson	2462
India	John Simmons	2954	Montserrat	Michelle Brooks	2527
	John Crown		Morocco	Claude Clement	
	Tim Gilman			Chris Cerone	5545
Indonesia	Karen Goddin	3875	Mozambique	Finn Holm-Olsen	5148
Iran	Kate Fitzgerald-Wilks	1810			
	Paul Thanos		**N**		
Iraq	Thomas Sams		Namibia	Finn Holm-Olsen	4228
	Corey Wright	4441	Nepal	Timothy Gilman	2954
Ireland	Boyce Fitzpatrick	2177	Netherlands	Simon Bensimon	5401
Israel	Kate Fitzgerald-Wilks	1870	Netherlands		
	Paul Thanos	1870	Antilles	Michelle Brooks	2527
Italy	Boyce Fitzpatrick	2177	New Zealand	Gary Bouck (Bus.)	
Ivory Coast	Phillip Michelini	4388		William Golike (Policy)	3647
			Nicaragua	Laura Subrin	2527
J			Niger	Philip Michelini	4388
Jamaica	Rodrigo Soto	2527	Nigeria	Debra Henke	4228
Japan	Cantwell Walsh	2425	Norway	James Devlin	4414
	Edward A. Leslie				
	Eric Kennedy		**O**		
	Cynthia Campbell		Oman	Kate Fitzgerald-Wilks	1870
	Allan Christian			Paul Thanos	
Jordan	Kate Fitzgerald-Wilks				
	Paul Thanos	1857	**P**		
			Pacific Islands	Gary Bouck (Bus.)	
K				William Golike (Policy)	3647
Kenya	Chandra Watkins	4564	Pakistan	Cheryl McQueen	2954
Korea	Jeffrey Donius	4957	Panama	Laura Subrin	2527
	Renato Amador		Paraguay	Randolph Mye	1548
	Dan Duvall		People's Rep of	Robert Chu	2462
Kuwait	Corey Wright	1860	China	Laura McCall	3583
	Thomas Sams		Peru	Herbert Lindow	2521
			Philippines	George Paine	3875
L			Poland	Audrey Zuck	2645
Laos	Hong-Phong B. Pho	3875	Portugal	Mary Beth Double	4508
Lebanon	Corey Wright	4441	Puerto Rico	Rodrigo Soto	2527
	Thomas Sams				
Lesotho	Finn Holm-Olsen	4228	**Q**		
Liberia	Phillip Michelini		Qatar	Kate Fitzgerald-Wilks	1870
	Chris Cerone	4388		Paul Thanos	
Libya	Claude Clement	5545			
Luxembourg	Simon Bensimon	5401	**R**		
			Romania	Lynn Fabrizio	2645
M			Russia, NIS	Jack Brougher	0354
Macao	JeNelle Matheson	2462		Susan Lewens	
Madagascar	Chandra Watkins	4564		Tim Smith	
Malawi	Finn Holm-Olsen	4228		Peter Johnson	
Malaysia	Raphael Cung	3875		Russel Johnson	
			Rwanda	Phillip Michelini	4388

Country	Desk Officer	Phone (202) 482-	Country	Desk Officer	Phone (202) 482-
S			Thailand	Jean Kelly	3875
Sao Tome &			Togo	Debra Henke	5149
Principe	Phillip Michelini	4388	Trinidad & Tobago	Michelle Brooks	2527
Saudi Arabia	Jeffrey Johnson	4652	Tunisia	Corey Wright	1860
	Claude Clement			Thomas Sams	
Senegal	Philip Michelini	4388	Turkey	Heidi Lamb	5373
Seychelles	Chandra Watkins	4564	Turks & Caicos		
Sierra Leone	Philip Michelini	4388	Islands	Rodrigo Soto	2527
Singapore	Raphael Cung	3875			
Somalia	Chandra Watkins	4564	**U**		
South Africa	Emily Solomon	5148	Uganda	Chandra Watkins	4564
Spain	Mary Beth Double	4508	United Arab	Claude Clement	5545
Sri Lanka	John Simmons	2954	Emirates	Chris Cerone	
St. Bartholemey	Michelle Brooks	2527	United Kingdom	Robert McLaughlin	3748
St. Kitts-Nevis	Michelle Brooks	2527	Uraguay	Roger Turner	1495
St. Lucia	Michelle Brooks	2527			
St. Martin	Michelle Brooks	2527	**V**		
St. Vincent-			Venezuela	Herbert Lindow	4303
Grenadines	Michelle Brooks	2527	Vietnam	Hong-Phong B. Pho	3875
Sudan	Chandra Watkins	4564	Virgin Islands (UK)	Michelle Brooks	2527
Suriname	Michelle Brooks	2527	Virgin Islands (US)	Rodrigo Soto	2527
Swaziland	Finn Holm-Olsen	5148			
Sweden	James Devlin	4414	**Y**		
Switzerland	Philip Combs	2920	Yemen, Republic of	Kate Fitzgerald-Wilks	1870
Syria	Corey Wright			Paul Thanos	
	Thomas Sams	4441	Yugoslavia	Jeremy Keller	2645
T					
Taiwan	Ian Davis	4957	**Z**		
	Paul Carroll		Zaire	Debra Henke	5149
	Dan Duvall		Zambia	Finn Holm-Olsen	4228
Tanzania	Finn Holm-Olsen	4228	Zimbabwe	Finn Holm-Olsen	4228

APPENDIX 12

DISTRICT OFFICES OF THE INTERNATIONAL TRADE ADMINISTRATION (U.S. AND FOREIGN COMMERCIAL SERVICE) OF THE U.S. DEPARTMENT OF COMMERCE (see Part II, p. 503).

District/Address	Director	Telephone
Anchorage, AK (319 World Trade Ctr., Alaska, 4201 Tudor Ctr. Dr., 99508)	Charles Becker	907-271-6237
Atlanta, GA (4360 Chamblee-Dunwoody Rd., 30341)	George T. Norton, Jr.	404-452-9101
Baltimore, MD (413 U.S. Customhouse, 40 S. Gay St., 21202)	David Earle	301-962-3560
Birmingham, AL (Rm. 302, 2015 2d Ave. N., 35203)	(Vacancy)	205-731-1331
Boston, MA (Suite 307, World Trade Ctr., Commonwealth Pier Area, 02210)	Francis J. O'Connor	617-565-8563
Buffalo, NY (Rm. 1312, 111 W. Huron St., 14202)	George Buchanan	716-846-4191
Charleston, WV (Suite 807, 405 Capitol St., 25301)	Roger L. Fortner	304-347-5123
Chicago, IL (1406 Mid-Continental Plaza Bldg., 55 E. Monroe St., 60603)	(Vacancy)	312-353-4450
Cincinnati, OH (9504 Federal Office Bldg., 550 Main St., 45202)	Gordon B. Thomas	513-684-2944
Cleveland, OH (Rm. 600, 668 Euclid St., 44114)	Toby Zettler	216-522-4750
Columbia, SC (Suite 172, 1835 Assembly St., 29201)	Edgar L. Rojas	803-765-5345
Dallas, TX (2050 N. Stemmons Fwy., S. 170, 75242)	Donal Schilke	214-767-0542
Denver, CO (Suite 680, 1625 Broadway, 80202)	Neil Hesse	303-844-3246
Des Moines, IA (Rm. 817, 210 Walnut St., 50309)	John H. Steuber	515-284-4222
Detroit, MI (1140 McNamara Bldg., 477 Michigan Ave., 48226)	(Vacancy)	313-226-3650
Greensboro, NC (Suite 400, 400 W. Market St., 27401)	Samuel P. Troy	919-333-5345
Hartford, CT (Rm. 610-B, 450 Main St., 06103)	Carl Jacobsen, *Acting*	203-240-3530
Honolulu, HI (P.O. Box 50026, 300 Ala Moana Blvd., 96850)	George Dolan	808-541-1782
Houston, TX (Rm. 2625, 515 Rusk St., 77002)	James Cook	713-229-2578
Indianapolis, IN (Suite 520, 1 N. Capitol St., 46204)	Andrew W. Thress	317-226-6214
Jackson, MS (328 Jackson Mall Office Ctr., 300 Woodrow Wilson Blvd., 39213)	Mark E. Spinney	601-965-4388
Kansas City, MO (Rm. 635, 601 E. 12th St., 64106)	John Kupfer	816-426-3141
Little Rock, AR (Suite 811, 320 W. Capitol Ave., 72201)	Lon J. Hardin	501-324-5794
Los Angeles, CA (Rm. 9200, 11000 Wilshire Blvd., 90024)	Stephen Arlinghaus	310-575-7101
Louisville, KY (Rm. 636B, 601 W. Broadway, 40202)	John Autin	502-582-5066
Miami, FL (Suite 224, 51 SW. 1st Ave., 33130)	Ivan A. Cosimi	305-536-5268
Milwaukee, WI (Rm. 596, 517 E. Wisconsin Ave., 53202)	Johnny Brown	414-297-3473
Minneapolis, MN (Rm. 108, 110 S. 4th St., 55401)	Ronald E. Kramer	612-348-1638
Nashville, TN (Suite 1114, Parkway Towers, 404 James Robertson Pkwy., 37219)	James Charlet	615-736-5161
New Orleans, LA (432 World Trade Ctr., 2 Canal St., 70130)	Paul L. Guidry	504-589-6546
New York, NY (Rm. 3718, 26 Federal Plz., 10278)	Joel Barkan	212-264-0634
Oklahoma City, OK (6601 Broadway Extension, 73116)	Ronald L. Wilson	405-231-5302
Omaha, NE (11133 O St., 68137)	George H. Payne	402-221-3664
Philadelphia, PA (Suite 202, 475 Allendale Rd., King of Prussia, 19406)	Ted Rosen	215-962-4980
Phoenix, AZ (Rm. 3412, 230 N. 1st Ave., 85025)	Donald W. Fry	602-379-3285
Pittsburgh, PA (Rm. 2002, 1000 Liberty Ave., 15222)	John McCartney	412-644-2850
Portland, OR (Suite 242, 1 World Trade Ctr., 121 SW. Salmon St., 97204)	William Schrage	503-326-3001
Reno, NV (1755 E. Plumb Lane, No. 152, 89502)	Joseph J. Jeremy	702-784-5203
Richmond, VA (Rm. 8010, 400 N. 8th St., 23240)	Philip A. Ouzts	804-771-2246
Salt Lake City, UT (Suite 105, 324 S. State St., 84111)	Stephen P. Smoot	801-524-5116
San Diego, CA (Suite 230, 6363 Greenwich Dr., 92122)	(Vacancy)	619-557-5395
San Francisco, CA (14th Fl., 250 Montgomery St., 94104)	Betty D. Neuhart	415-705-2300
San Juan, PR (Hato Rey) (Rm. G-55, Federal Bldg., 00918)	J. Enrique Vilella	809-766-5555
Savannah, GA (Rm. A-107, 120 Barnard St., 31401)	Barbara Prieto	912-652-4204
Seattle, WA (Suite 290, 3131 Elliot Ave., 98121)	Charles Buck	206-553-5615
St. Louis, MO (Suite 610, 7911 Forsyth Blvd., 63105)	Donald R. Loso	314-425-3302
Trenton, NJ (Suite 100, Bldg. 6, 3131 Princeton Pike, 08648)	Rod Stuart, *Acting*	609-989-2100

APPENDIX 13

INDUSTRY SPECIALISTS OF THE INTERNATIONAL TRADE ADMINISTRATION OF THE U.S. DEPARTMENT OF COMMERCE

Industry	Contact	Phone (202) 482-	Industry	Contact	Phone (202) 482-
A			Airlines	Johson, C. William	5012
Abrasives	Presbury, Graylin	5158	Airport Equipment		
Accounting	Chittum, J. Marc	0345	(Market Support)	Driscoll, George	1228
Adhesives/Sealants	Prat, Raimundo	0128	Airport Equipment		
Advertising	Chittum, J. Marc	0345	(Trade Promo)	Vacant	1228
Aerospace Financing			Airports, Ports,		
Issues	Bender, Juliet	4222	Harbors (Major		
Aerospace Industry			Proj)	Piggot, Deboorne	3352
Analysis	Walsh, Hugh	4222	Air Traffic Control		
Aerospace Industry			(Market Support)	Driscoll, George	1228
Data	Walsh, Hugh	4222	Alcoholic Beverages	Kenney, Cornelius	2428
Aerospace Information			Alum Sheet, Plate/Foil	Cammarota, David	0575
& Analysis	Walsh, Hugh	4222	Alum Forgings, Electro	Cammarota, David	0575
Aerospace Market			Aluminum Extrud Alum		
Development	Vacant	1228	Rolling	Cammarota, David	0575
Aerospace Market			Analytical Instrument		
Promo	Vacant	1228	(Trade Promo)	Manzolino, Frank	2991
Aerospace-Space			Analytical Instruments	Nealon, Marquarite	3411
Market Support	Vacant	1228	Animal Feeds	Janis, William V.	2250
Aerospace Marketing			Apparel	Dulka, William J.	4058
Support	Driscoll, George	1228	Artificial Intelligence	Kader, Victoria	0571
Aerospace Policy &			Asbestos/Cement		
Analysis	Bath, Sally H.	4222	Prod	Pitcher, Charles	0132
Aerospace-Space			Assembly Equipment	Abrahams, Edward	0312
Programs	Pajor, Pete	2122	Audio Visual Services	Siegmund, John	4781
Aerospace Trade			Auto Ind Affairs Motor		
Policy Issues	Bender, Juliet	2124	Vehicles	Warner, Albert C.	0699
Aerospace Trade			Auto Ind Affairs		
Promo	Vacant	1228	Parts/Suppliers	Reck, Robert O.	1419
Agribusiness (Major			Auto Ind Affairs (Trade		
Proj)	Bell, Richard	2460	Promo)	White, John C.	0671
Agricultural Chemicals	Maxey, Francis P.	0128	Auto Industry Affairs	Keitz, Stuart	0554
Agricultural Machinery	Weining, Mary	4708	Aviation and Helicopter		
Air Conditioning			Services	Johnson, C. William	5012
Eqpmt	Vacant	3509	Avionics Marketing	Driscoll, George	1228
Air, Gas Compressors	McDonald, Edward	0680			
Air, Gas Compressors			**B**		
(Trade Promo)	Heimowitz, Leonard	0558	Bakery Products	Janis, William V.	2250
Air Pollution Control			Ball Bearings	Reise, Richard	3489
Eqpmt	Jonkers, Loretta	0564	Banking	Candilis, Wray O.	0339
Aircraft & Aircraft			Basic Paper & Board		
Engines (Market			Mfg	Smith, Len	0375
Support)	Driscoll, George	1228	Bauxite, Alumina, Prim		
Aircraft & Aircraft			Alum	Cammarota, David	0575
Engines (Trade			Belting & Hose	Prat, Raimundo	0128
Promo)	Vacant	1228	Beryllium	Duggan, Brian	0575
Aircraft Auxiliary			Beverages	Kenney, Cornelius	2428
Equipment (Market			Bicycles	Vanderwolf, John	0348
Support)	Driscoll, George	1228	Biotechnology	Arakaki, Emily	3888
Aircraft Parts (Market			Biotechnology (Trade		
Support)	Driscoll, George	1228	Promo)	Gwaltney, Geoffrey	3090
Aircraft Parts/Aux			Blowers and Fans	Jonkers, Loretta	0564
Eqpmt (Trade			Boat Building (Major		
Promo)	Vacant	1228	Proj)	Piggot, Deboorne	3352

Industry	Contact	Phone (202) 482-	Industry	Contact	Phone (202) 482-
Boats			Computers & Business		
Pleasure			Eqpmt (Office of)	McPhee, John E.	0572
Craft	Vanderwolf, John	0348	Confectionery		
Books	Lofquist, William S.	0379	Products	Kenney, Cornelius	2428
Books (Export Promo)	Kimmel, Edward	3640	Construction, Domestic	MacAuley, Patrick	0132
Builders Hardware	Williams, Franklin	0132	Contruction Machinery	Heimowitz, L.	0558
Builders Materials			Consumer Goods	Bodansky, Harry	5783
(Trade Policy)	Smith, Mary Ann	0132	Conventional Fossil		
Building Materials &			Fuel Power (Major		
Construction	Pitcher, Charles B.	0132	Proj)	Dollison, Robert	2733
Business Forms	Bratland, Rose Marie	0380	Converted Paper Prod	Stanley, Gary	0375
			Conveyors/Conveying		
C			Eqmt	Wiening, Mary	4708
CAD/CAM/CAE			Copper/Brass Mills	Duggan, Brian	0575
Software	Swann, Vera A.	0396	Copper Wire Mills	Duggan, Brian	0575
Cable Broadcasting	Siegmund, John	4781	Copper	Duggan, Brian	0575
Canned Goods	Hodgen, Donald A.	3346	Corn Products	Janis, William V.	2250
Capital Goods (Trade			Cosmetics	Hurt, William	0128
Promo)	Brandis, Jay	0560	Cosmetics (Export		
Carbon Black	Prat, Raimundo	0128	Promo)	Kimmel, Edward K.	3640
Case	Swann, Vera	4936	Costume Jewelry	Harris, John	1178
Cement	Pitcher, Charles	0132	Trade Promotion	Beckham, R.	5478
Cement Plants (Major			Cotton Seed Oil	Janis, William V.	2250
Proj)	White, Barbara	4160	Courier Services	Elliot, Fred	1134
Ceramics (Advanced)	Shea, Moira	0128	Current-Carrying		
Ceramics Machinery	Shaw, Eugene	3494	Devices	Whitley, Richard A.	0682
Cereals	Janis, William V.	2250	Cutlery	Harris, John	1178
Chemicals	Kelly, Michael J.	0128			
Chemical Plants			**D**		
(Major Proj)	Haraguchi, Wally	4877	Dairy Products	Janis, William V.	2250
Chemicals & Allied			Data Base Services	Inoussa, Mary C.	5820
Products	Siesseger, Frederic	0128	Data Processing		
Chinaware	Harris, John	1178	Services	Atkins, Robert G.	4781
Chromium	Presbury, Graylin	5158	Desalination/Water		
Civil Aircraft			Reuse	Wheeler, Fredrica	3509
Agreement	Bender, Juliet	1228	Diamond, Industrial	Presbury, Graylin	5158
Civil Aviation	Johnson, C. William	5012	Direct Mail	Elliott, Fred	3574
Coal Exports	Oddenino, Charles	1446	Disc Drives, Diskettes	Kader, Victoria	0571
Coal Exports	Yancik, Joseph J.	1466	Dolls	Vacant	0338
Cobalt	Cammarota, David	0575	Drilling Mus/Soft		
Columbium	Persbury, Garylin	5158	Compounds	Vacant	0564
Commercial Aircraft			Drugs	Hurt, William	0128
(Trade Policy)	Bath, Sally	4222	Durable Consumer		
Commercial Lighting			Goods	Ellis, Kevin M.	1176
Fixtures	Whitley, Richard A.	0682			
Commercial/Indus			**E**		
Refrig Eqpmt	Bodson, John	3509	Earthenware	Harris, John	1178
Commercial Printing	Lofquist, William	0379	Education Facilities		
Composites, Advanced	Manion, James	5157	(Major Proj)	White, Barbara	4160
Computer and DP	Atkins, Robert G.	4781	Educational/Training	Chittum, J. Marc	0345
Services	Inoussa, Mary	5820	Electric Industrial		
Computer Consulting	Atkins, Robert	4781	Apparatus Nec	Whitley, Richard A.	0682
Computer, Midrange	Hoffman, Heidi M.	2053	Elec/Power Gen/		
Computer Networks	Spathopoulos, Vivian	0572	Transmission &		
Computer, Personal	Woods, R. Clay	3013	Dist Eqt (Trade		
	Miles, Timothy O.	2990	Promo)	Brandes, Jay	0560
Computer, Portable	Hoffman, Heidi M.	2053	Electrical Power		
Computer, Professional			Plants (Major Proj)	Dollison, Robert	2733
Services	Atkins, Robert	4781	Electronic Components/		
Computer, Super	Streeter, Jonathan P.	0572	Prod & Test Equip.		
Computers (Trade			(Trade Promo)	Ruffin, Marlene	0570
Promo)	Fogg, Judy A.	4936			

Industry	Contact	Phone (202) 482-	Industry	Contact	Phone (202) 482-
Electronic Mail	Atkins, Robert G.	4781	Forest Products (Trade		
Electronic Prod. & Test	Finn, Erin	3360	Policy)	Hicks, Michael	0375
Electronic Prod. & Test			Forgings Semifinished		
(Export Promo)	Ruffin, Marlene	0570	Steel	Bell, Charles	0609
Electricity	Sugg, William	1466	Fossil Fuel Power		
ElectroOptical			Generation (Major		
Instruments (Trade			Proj)	Dollison, Robert	2733
Promo)	Gwaltney, G. P.	2991	Foundry Eqmt	Kemper, Alexis	5956
Electronic (Legislation)	Donnelly, Margaret	5466	Foundry Industry	Bell, Charles	0609
Electronic Components	Mussehl, Judy	2946	Frozen Fruits,		
	Blouin, Dorothea	1333	Vegetables &		
Electronic Components/			Specialties	Hodgen, Donald A.	3346
Production & Test			Fur Goods	Byron, James E.	4034
Equip	Burke, Joseph J.	5014	Furniture	Vacant	0338
Electronic Database			Fuzzy Logic	Kader, Victoria	0571
Services	Inoussa, Mary	5820			
Elevators, Moving			**G**		
Stairways	Weining, Mary	4708	Games & Children's		
Energy & Environ.			Vehicles	Vanderwolf, John	0348
Sys.	Greer, Damon	5456	Gaskets/Gasketing		
Energy (Commodities)	Yancik, Joseph J.	1466	Materials	Reiss, Richard	3489
	Oddenino, Charles L.		General Aviation		
Energy, Renewable	Rasmussen, John	1466	Aircraft (Industry		
Engineering/Construction			Analysis)	Walsh, Hugh	4222
Services (Trade			General Aviation		
Promo)	Ruan, Robert	0359	Aircraft (Market		
Entertainment			Support)	Driscoll, George	1228
Industries	Siegmund, John	4781	Gen. Indus. Mach.		
Explosives	Maxey, Francis P.	0128	Nec, Exc 35691	Shaw, Eugene	3494
Export Trading			Generator Sets/Turbines		
Company Affairs	Muller, George	5131	(Major Proj)	Dollison, Robert	2733
Express Delivery			Glass, Flat	Williams, Franklin	0132
Service	Elliott, Fred	1134	Glassware	Harris, John	0348
			Gloves (work)	Byron, James E.	3459
F			Giftware (Export		
Fabricated Metal			Promo)	Beckham, Reginald	5478
Construction			Grain Mill Products	Janis, William V.	2250
Materials	Williams, Franklin	0132	Greeting Cards	Bratland, Rose Marie	0380
Farm Machinery	Weining, Mary	4708	Ground Water		
Fasteners (Industrial)	Reise, Richard	3489	Exploration and		
Fats and Oils	Janis, William V.	2250	Development	Wheeler, Frederica	3509
Fencing (Metal)	Shaw, Robert	0132	Guns & Ammunition	Vanderwolf, John	0348
Ferroalloys Products	Presbury, Graylin	5158			
Ferrous Scrap	Sharkey, Robert	0606	**H**		
Fertilizers	Maxey, Francis P.	0128	Hand Saws, Saw		
Filters/Purifying Eqmt	Jonkers, Loretta	0564	Blades	Shaw, Eugene	3494
Finance & Management			Hand/Edge Tools Ex		
Industries	Candilis, Wray O.	0339	Mach Tl/Saws	Shaw, Eugene	3494
Fisheries (Major Proj)	Bell, Richard	2460	Handbags	Byron, James E.	4034
Flexible Mftg Systems			Hard Surfaced Floor		
Flour	Janis, William V.	2250	Coverings	Shaw, Robert	0132
Flowers	Janis, William V.	2250	Health	Francis, Simon	2697
Fluid Power	McDonald, Edward	0680	Heat Treating		
Food Products			Equipment	Kemper, Alexis	5956
Machinery	Shaw, Gene	3494	Heating Eqmt Ex		
Food Retailing	Konnoy, Cornelius	2428	Furnaces	Bodson, John	3509
Footwear	Byron, James E.	4034	Helicopter Services	Johnson, C. William	5012
Forest Products	Smith, Len	0375	Helicopters	Walsh, Hugh	4222
Forest Products,			Helicopters (Market		
Domestic			Support)	Driscoll, George	1228
Construction	Kristensen, Chris	0384			

Industry	Contact	Phone (202) 482-	Industry	Contact	Phone (202) 482-
Helicopters (Trade Promo)	Vacant	1228	Lasers (Trade Promo)	Mazolillo, Frank	2991
High Tech Trade, US Competitiveness	Hatter, Victoria L.	3913	Lawn & Garden Equipment	Vanderwolf, John	0348
Hoists, Overhead Cranes	Wiening, Mary	4708	Lead Products	Larrabee, David	0575
Hose & Belting	Prat, Raimundo	0128	Leasing: Eqmt & Vehicles	Shuman, John	3050
Hotel & Restaurant Eq. (Export Promo)	Kimmel, Edward K.	3640	Leather Tanning Products	Byron, James E.	4034
Hotels and Motels	Sousane, J. Richard	4582	Legal Services	Chittum, J. Marc	0345
Household Appliances	Harris, John M.	0348	LNG Plants (Major Proj)	Thomas, Janet	4146
Household Furniture	Vacant	0338	Logs, Wood	Hicks, Michael	0375
Housewares	Harris, John	1178	Luggage	Byron, James E.	3034
Housing Construction	Cosslett, Patrick	0132	Lumber	Wise, Barbara	0375
Housing & Urban Development (Major Proj)	White, Barbara	4160			
Hydro Power, Plants (Major Proj)	Healey, Mary Alice	4333	**M**		
			Machine Tool Accessories	McGibbon, Patrick	0314
I			Magazines	Bratland, Rose Marie	0380
Industrial Controls	Whitley, Richard A.	0682	Magnesium	Cammerota, David	0575
Industrial Drives/Gears	Reiss, Richard	3489	Mainframes	Miles, Tim	2990
Industrial Gases	Kostalas, Anthony	0128	Major Projects	Thibeault, Robert	5225
Industrial Organic Chemicals	Hurt, William	0128	Management Consulting	Chittum, J. Marc	0345
			Manganese	Presbury, Graylin	5158
Industrial Process Controls	Nealon, Marguerite	0411	Manifold Business Forms	Bratland, Rose Marie	0380
Industrial Process Controls (Export Promo)	Manzolillo, Frank	2991	Manmade Fiber	Dulka, William	4058
			Margarine	Janis, William V.	2250
Industrial Structure	Davis, Lester A.	4924	Marine Insurance	Johnson, C. William	5012
Industrial Trucks	Wiening, Mary	4608	Marine Recreational Equipment (Export Promo)	Beckham, Reginald	5478
Information Services	Inoussa, Mary C.	5820	Maritime Shipping	Johnson, C. William	5012
Inorganic Chemicals Pigments	Kostalas, Anthony	0128	Marketing Promo (Basic Ind)	Trafton, Donald R.	2493
Insulation	Shaw, Robert	0132	Materials, Advanced	Cammarota, David	0575
Insurance	McAdam, Bruce	0346	Meat Products	Hodgen, Donald A.	3346
Intellectual Property Rights (Services)	Siegmund, John E.	4781	Mech Power Transmission Eqmt, Nec	Reise, Richard	3489
International Commodities	Siesseger, Fred	5124	Medical Facilities (Major Proj)	White, Barbara	4160
International Major Projects	Thibeault, Robert	5225	Medical Instruments	Fuchs, Michael	0550
Investment Management	Muir, S. Cassin	0346	Medical Instruments (Trade Promo)	Keen, George B.	2010
Irrigation (Major Proj)	Bell, Richard	2460	Mercury, Flourspar	Manion, James J.	5157
			Metal Building Products	Williams, Franklin	0132
J			Metal Cookware	Harris, John	0348
Jams & Jellies	Hodgen, Donald A.	3346	Metal Cutting Machine Tools	Vacant	
Jewelry	Harris, John	1178	Metal Cutting Tools Fr Mach Tools	Vacant	
Jewelry (Export Promo)	Beckham, Reginald	5478	Metal Forming Machine Tools	Vacant	
K			Metal Powders	Duggan, Brian	0575
Kitchen Cabinets	Auerbach, Mitchel	0375	Metals, Secondary	Manion, James J.	5157
			Metalworking	Mearman, John	0315
L			Metalworking Eqmt Nec	McGibbon, Patrick	0314
Laboratory Instruments	Nealon, Marguerite	3411			
Laboratory Instruments (Trade Promo)	Gwaltney, G. P.	3090	Mica	Presbury, Graylin	5158

Industry	Contact	Phone (202) 482-	Industry	Contact	Phone (202) 482-
Millwork	Wise, Barbara	0375	**P**		
Mineral Based Construction Materials (Clay, Concrete, Gypsum, Asphalt, Stone)	Pitcher, Charles B.	0132	Packaging Machinery	Shaw, Gene	3494
			Paints/Coatings	Prat, Raimundo	0128
			Paper	Stanley, Gary	0375
			Paper and Board Packaging	Smith, Leonard S.	0375
Mining Machinery	McDonald, Edward	0680	Paper Industries Machinery	Abrahams, Edward	0312
Mining Machinery (Trade Promo)	Zanetakos, George	0552	Pasta	Janis, William V.	2250
Mobile Homes	Cosslett, Patrick	0132	Paving Materials (Asphalt & Concrete)	Pitcher, Charles	0132
Molybdenum	Cammarota, David	0575			
Monorails	Wiening, Mary	4708	Pectin	Janis, William V.	2250
Motion Pictures	Siegmund, John	4781	Pens/Pencils, etc.	Vacant	0338
Motor Vehicles Auto Ind Affairs	Gaines, Robin	0669	Periodicals	Bratland, Rose Marie	0380
			Pet Food	Janis, William V.	2250
Motor Vehicles	Warner, Albert T.	0669	Pet Products (Export Promo)	Kimmel, Edward K.	3640
Motorcycles	Vanderwolf, John	0348			
Motors, Elect	Whitley, Richard A.	0682	Petrochem, Cyclic Crudes	Hurt, William	0128
Music	Siegmund, John	4781	Petrochemicals	Hurt, William	0128
Musical Instruments	Harris, John	0348	Petrochemicals Plants (Major Proj)	Haraguchi, Wally	4877
Mutual Funds	Muir, S. Cassin	0343			
			Petroleum, Crude & Refined Products	Gillet, Tom	1466
N			Pharmaceuticals	Hurt, William	0128
Natural Gas	Gillett, Tom	1466	Pipelines (Major Proj)	Bell, Richard	2460
Natural, Synthetic Rubber	Hurt, William	0128	Photographic Eqmt & Supplies	Watson, Joyce	0574
Newspapers	Bratland, Rose Marie	0380	Plastic Construction Products (Most)	Williams, Franklin	0132
Nickel Products	Presbury, Graylin	5158			
Non-alcoholic Beverages	Kenney, Cornelius	2428	Plastic Materials	Shea, Moira	0128
			Plastic Products	Prat, Raimundo	0128
Noncurrent Carrying Wiring Devices	Whitley, Richard A.	0682	Plastic Products Machinery	Shaw, Eugene	3494
Nondurable Goods	Simon, Leslie B.	0341	Plumbing Fixtures & Fittings	Shaw, Robert	0132
Nonferrous Foundries	Duggan, Brian	0610			
Nonferrous Metals	Manion, James J.	0575	Plywood/Panel Products	Wise, Barbara	0375
Nonmetallic Minerals Nec	Manion, James J.	0575	Point-of-Use Water Treatment	Vacant	0564
Nonresidential Constr (Domestic)	MacAuley, Patrick	0132	Pollution Control Equipment	Jonkers, Loretta	0564
Nuclear Power Plants (Major Proj)	Dollison, Robert	2733	Porcelain Electrical Supplies (Part)	Whitley, Richard A.	2213
Numerical Cntrls Fr Mach Tools	McGibbon, Patrick	0314	Pottery	Harris, John M.	0348
			Poultry Products	Hodgen, Donald A.	3346
Nuts, Edible	Janis, William V.	2250	Power Hand Tools	Abrahams, Edward	0312
Nuts, Bolts, Washers	Reise, Richard	3489	Precious Metal Jewelry	Harris, John M.	1178
			Prefabricated Buildings (Wood)	Cosslett, Patrick	0132
O					
Ocean Shipping	Johnson, C. William	5012	Prefabricated Buildings (Metal)	Williams, Franklin	0132
Oil & Gas Development & Refining (Major Proj)	Bell, Richard	2460	Prepared Meats	Hodgen, Donald A.	3346
			Printing & Publishing	Lofquist, William S.	0379
Oil & Gas (Fuels Only)	Gillet, Tom	1466	Printing Trade Services	Brattland, Rose Marie	0380
Oil Field Machinery	McDonald, Edward	0680			
Oil Field Machinery (Trade Promo)	Zanetakoo, George	0552	Printing Trades Mach/Eqmt	Kemper, Alexis	5956
Oil Shale (Major Proj)	Bell, Richard	2460	Process Control Instruments	Nealon, Marguerite	3411
Organic Chemicals	Hurt, William	0128			
Outdoor Lightning Fixtures	Whitley, Richard A.	0682			
Outdoor Power (Export Promo)	Beckham, Reginald	5478			

Industry	Contact	Phone (202) 482-	Industry	Contact	Phone (202) 482-
Process Control Instruments (Trade Promo)	Manzolillo, Frank	2991	Semiconductor Prod Eqpmt & Materials	Finn, Erin	2795
Pulp and Paper Mills (Major Proj)	White, Barbara	4160	Semiconductor Prod Eqmt & Materials (Export Promo)	Ruffing, Marlene	0570
Pulpmills	Stanely, Gary	0375	Services, DAS	Powers, Linda F.	5261
Pumps, Pumping Eqmt	McDonald, Edward	0680	Shingles (Wood)	Wise, Barbara	0375
Pumps, Valves, Compressors (Trade Promo)	Heimowitz, Leonard	0558	Silverware	Harris, John	1178
			Small Business Trade Policy	Burroughs, Helen	4806
R			Snackfood	Janis, William V.	2250
Radio & TV Broadcasting	Siegmund, John	4781	Soaps, Detergents, Cleaners	Hurt, William	0128
Radio & TV Broadcasting Eqmt	Rettig, Theresa	4466	Soft Drink	Kenney, Cornelius	2428
Railroad Services	Sousane, J. Richard	4582	Software	Hijikata, Heidi C.	0571
Recreational Eqmt (Export Promo)	Beckham, Reginald	5478		Smolenski, Mary	2053
Refractory Products	Duggan, Brian	0610	Software (Export Promo)	Fogg, Judy	4936
Renewable Energy Eqpmt	Garden, Les	0556	Solar Cells/Photovoltaic Devices/Small Hydro	Garden, Les	0556
Research & Development	Price, James B.	4781	Solar Eqmt Ocean/ Biomass/Geoth	Garden, Les	0556
Residential Lighting Fixtures	Whitley, Richard A.	0682	Soy Products	Janis, William V.	2250
Retail Trade	Margulies, Marvin J.	5086	Space Policy Development	Pajor, Pete	4222
Rice Milling	Janis, William V.	2250	Special Industry Machinery, Nec	Shaw, Eugene	3494
Roads, Railroads, Mass Trans (Major Proj)	Smith, Jay L.	4642	Speed Changers	Reise, Richard	3489
Robots	Vacant	0314	Sporting & Athletic Goods	Vanderwolf, John	0348
Roofing, Asphalt	Pitcher, Charles	0132	Sporting Goods (Export Promo)	Beckham, Reginald	5478
Roller Bearings	Reise, Richard	3489	Steel Industry Products	Bell, Charles	0608
Rolling Mill Machinery	Abrahams, Edward	0312	Storage Batteries	Larrabee, David	0575
Rubber	Prat, Raimundo	0128	Supercomputing	Streeter, Jonathan P.	0572
Rubber Products	Prat, Raimundo	0128	Superconductors	Chiaredo, Roger	0402
Saddlery & Harness Products	Byron, James	3034	Switchgear & Switchboard Apparatus	Whitley, Richard A.	0682
Safety & Security Equip (Trade Promo)	Umstead, Dwight	2410	System Integration	Atkins, Robert G.	4781
Satellites, Communications	Cooper, Patricia	4466	**T**		
			Tantalum	Presbury, Graylin	5158
S			Tea	Janis, William V.	2250
Scientific Instruments (Trade Promo)	Manzolillo, Frank	2991	Telecommunication Services	Atkins, Robert G.	4781
Scientific Measurement/ Control Eqmt	Nealon, Marguerite	3411	Telecommunications	Stechschulte, Roger	4466
Screw Machine Products	Reise, Richard	3489	Telecommunications (CPE)	Edwards, Dan	4466
Screws, Washers	Reise, Richard	3489	Telecommunications (Cellular)	Gossack, Linda	4466
Security & Commodity Brokers	Muir, S. Cassin	0347	Telecommunications (Fiber Optics)	Judge, Paul	4466
Semiconductors	Mussehl-Aziz, Judee	2846	Telecommunications (Major Projects)	Paddock, Rick	4466
Semiconductors (Export Promo)	Ruffin, Marlene Scott, Robert	0570 2795	Telecommunications (Network Equip)	Henry, John	4466
Semiconductors (Japan)	Scott, Robert Blouin, Dorothea	3360 1333	Telecommunications (Radio)	Gossack, Linda	4466
			Telecommunications (Satellites)	Cooper, Patricia	4466

Industry	Contact	Phone (202) 482-	Industry	Contact	Phone (202) 482-
Telecommunications (Services)	Shefrin, Ivan	4466	Vanadium	Presbury, Graylin	5158
Telecommunications (Trade Promo)	Rettig, Theresa E.	4466	Vegetables	Hodgen, Donald A.	3346
			Video Services	Seigmund, John	4781
Telecommunications (TV Broadcast Equip.)	Rettig, Theresa E.	4466	Videotex Services	Inoussa, Mary C.	5820
Teletext Services	Inoussa, Mary	5820	**W**		
Textile Machinery	Vacant	0679	Wallets, Billfolds, Flatgoods	Byron, James E.	4034
Textiles	Dulka, William J.	4058	Warm Air Heating Eqmt	Vacant	3509
Textiles (Trade Promotion)	Molnar, Ferenc	2043	Wastepaper	Stanley, Gary	0375
Tin Products	Presbury, Graylin	5158	Watches	Harris, John	1178
Tires	Prat, Raimundo	0128	Water and Sewerage Treatment Plants (Major Proj)	Vacant	4643
Tobacco Products	Kenney, Cornelius	2428	Water Resource Eqmt	Vacant	3509
Tools/Dies/Jigs/Fixtures	Vacant		Welding/Cutting Apparatus	Kemper, Alexis	5956
Tourism (Major Proj)	White, Barbara	4160	Wholesale Trade	Margulies, Marvin	5086
Tourism Services	Sousane, J. Richard	4582	Windmill Components	Garden, Les	0556
Toys	Vanderwolf, John	0348	Wire & Wire Products	Vacant	0606
Toys & Games (Export Promo)	Beckham, Reginald	5478	Wire Cloth, Industrial	Reise, Richard	3489
Trade Related Employment	Teske, Gary R.	2056	Wire Cloth	Williams, Franklin	0132
Transformers	Whitley, Richard A.	0682	Wood Containers	Hicks, Michael	0375
Transportation Industries	Alexander, Albert	4581	Wood Preserving	Hicks, Michael	0375
Travel & Tourism	Sousane, J. Richard	4582	Wood Products	Stanley, Gary	0375
Trucking Services	Sousane, J. Richard	4581	Wood Products, Misc	Stanley, Gary	0375
			Wood Working Machinery	McDonald, Edward	0680
U			Workstations	Miles, Tim	2990
Uranium	Sugg, William	1466			
			Y		
V			Yeast	Janis, William V.	2250
Valves, Pipe Fittings Ex Brass	Reise, Richard	3489			

APPENDIX 14

U.S. AND FOREIGN COMMERCIAL SERVICE
Overseas Commercial Sections of the International Trade Administration of the U.S. Department of Commerce (see Part II, p. 503).

ALGERIA Algiers
Post: American Embassy
Senior Commercial Officer: Andrew Tangalos
Telephone: 011-213-2-60-39-73
Fax: 011-213-2-603-979
Workweek: Saturday–Wednesday
Street Address: 4 Chemin Cheich Bachir Brahimi
Mailing Address: U.S. Dept of State (Algiers)
  Washington, DC 20521-6030

ARGENTINA Buenos Aires
Post: American Embassy
Senior Commercial Officer: Ralph Fermoselle
Telephone: 011-54-1-773-1063
Fax: 011-54-1-775-6040
Street Address: 4300 Colombia 1425
Mailing Address: Unit 4326
  APO AA 34034

AUSTRALIA Sydney
Post: American Consulate General
Senior Commerical Officer: Michael Hand
Telephone: 011-61-2-261-9217
Fax: 011-61-2-261-8148
Street Address: Hyde Park Tower—36th Floor
  Park and Elizabeth Streets
Mailing Address: Unit 11024
  APO AP 96554-0002

Brisbane
Post: American Consulate
Commerical Assistant: Keith Sloggett
Telephone: 011-61-7-839-8955
Fax: 011-61-7-832-6247
Street Address: 383 Wickham Terrace
Mailing Address: Unit 11018
  APO AP 96553-0002

Melbourne
Post: American Consulate General
Commerical Officer: Daniel Young
Telephone: 011-61-3-526-5923
Fax: 011-61-3-510-4660
Street Address: 553 St. Kilda Road
Mailing Address: Unit 11011
  APO AP 96551-0002

Perth
Post: American Consulate General
Commerical Assistant: Marion Shingler
Telephone: 011-61-9-231-9400
Fax: 011-61-9-231-9444
Street Address: 16 St. George's Terrace, 13th Floor
Mailing Address: Unit 11021
  APO AP 96553-0002

AUSTRIA Vienna
Post: American Embassy
Senior Commerical Officer: Benjamin Brown
Telephone: 011-43-222-31-55-11
Fax: 011-43-222-34-12-61
Street Address: Boltzmanngass 16, A-1091
Mailing Address: APO AE 09108

BELGIUM Brussels
Post: American Embassy
Senior Commerical Officer: Jerry Mitchell
Telephone: 011-32-2-513-3830
Fax: 011-32-2-512-6653
Street Address: 27 Boulevard du Regent
Mailing Address: PSC 82, Box 002
  APO AE 09724-1015

Post: US Mission to the European
  Community (Brussels)
Senior Commerical Officer: James Blow
Telephone: 011-32-2-513-445
Fax: 011-32-2-513-1228
Street Address: 40 Blvd du Regent, B-1000
Mailing Address: PSC 82, Box 002
  APO AE 09724

BRAZIL Sao Paulo
Post: American Consulate General
Senior Commerical Officer: Richard Ades
Telephone: 011-55-11-853-2011
Fax: 011-55-11-853-2744
Street Address: Av. Paulista 2439
Mailing Address: APO AA 34040-0002

Brasilia
Post: American Embassy
Commercial Attache: Dar Pribyl
Telephone: 011-55-61-321-7272
Fax: 011-55-61-225-3981
Street Address: Avenida das Nocoes, Lote 3
Mailing Address: Unit 3502
  APO AA 34030

Belem
Post: American Consular Agency
Commerical Officer: Raymundo Teixiera
Telephone: 011-55-91-223-0800
Mailing Address: APO AA 34030

Belo Horizonte
Post: American Consular Agency
Commerical Assistant: Jose M. de Vasconcelos
Telephone: 011-55-31-335-3250
Fax: 011-55-31-335-3054
Mailing Address: APO AA 34030

Rio de Janeiro
Post: American Consulate General
Senior Commerical Officer: Walter Hage
Telephone: 011-55-21-292-7117
Fax: 011-55-21-240-9738
Street Address: Avenida Presidente Wilson, 147
Mailing Address: APO AA 34030

BULGARIA Sofia
Post: American Embassy
Commerical Officer: John Fogarasi
Telephone: 011-359-2-88-48-01
Fax: 011-359-2-80-38-50
Street Address: One Bulgaria Square
Sofia 1000
Mailing Address: Unit 2540
APO AE 09213-5740

CAMEROON Douala
Post: American Consulate General
Commerical Assistant: Jean Marie Sumo
Telephone: 011-237-425-331
Fax: 011-237-427-790
Street Address: 21 Avenue du General de Gaulle
Mailing Address: U.S. Dept. of State (Douala)
Washington, DC 20521-2530

CANADA Ottawa
Post: American Embassy
Commerical Officer: Robert Marro
Telephone: 1-613-238-5335
Fax: 1-613-233-8511
Street Address: 100 Wellington Street
Mailing Address: P.O. Box 5000
Ogdensburg, NY 13669

Calgary
Post: American Consulate General
Commerical Officer: Randall LaBounty
Telephone: 1-403-265-2116
Fax: 1-403-264-6630
Street Address: Room 1000,
615 MacLeod Trail S.E.
Mailing Address: c/o AmEmbassy Ottawa
P.O. Box 5000
Ogdensburg, NY 13669

Halifax
Post: American Consulate General
Commerical Representative: Richard Vinson
Telephone: 1-902-429-2482
Fax: 1-902-423-6861
Street Address: Suite 910, Cogswell Tower
Scotia Square
Halifax Nova Scotia B3J 3K1
Mailing Address: c/o AmEmbassy Ottawa
P.O. Box 5000
Ogdensburg, NY 13669

Montreal
Post: American Consulate General
Commerical Officer: Edward Cannon
Telephone: 1-514-398-9695
Fax: 1-514-398-0711
Street Address: Suite 1122, South Tower
Place Desjardins
Mailing Address: P.O Box 847
Champlain, NY 12919-0847

Toronto
Post: American Consulate General
Commerical Officer: Dan Wilson
Telephone: 1-416-595-5413
Fax: 1-416-595-5419
Street Address: 480 University Avenue, Ste. 602
Mailing Address: P.O. Box 135
Lewiston, NY 14092

Vancouver
Post: American Consulate General
Commerical Officer: Jere Dabbs
Telephone: 1-604-685-3382
Fax: 1-604-687-6095
Street Address: 1095 West Pender Street
20th Floor
Mailing Address: P.O. Box 5002
Point Roberts, Washington 98281

CHILE Santiago
Post: American Embassy
Senior Commerical Officer: Ricardo Villalobos
Telephone: 011-56-2-671-0133
Fax: 011-56-2-697-2051
Street Address: Codina Building
1343 Agustinas
Mailing Address: Unit 4111
APO AA 34033

CHINA Beijing
Post: American Embassy
Senior Commerical Officer: Mel Searls
Telephone: 011-86-1-532-3831
Fax: 011-86-1-532-3297
Street Address: Xiu Shui Bei Jie 3
Mailing Address: PSC 461 Box 50
FPO AP 96521-0002

Guangzhou
Post: American Consulate General
Commercial Officer: Dennis Barnes
Telephone: 011-86-20-67-8742
Fax: 011-86-20-666-409
Street Address: Dong Fang Hotel
Mailing Address: PSC 461 Box 100
FPO AT 96521-0002

Shanghai
Post: American Consulate General
Commerical Officer: David Murphy
Telephone: 011-86-21-433-2492
Fax: 011-86-21-433-1576
Street Address: 1469 Haui Hai Middle Road
Mailing Address: PSC 461 Box 200
FPO AP 96521-0002

Shenyang
Post: American Consulate General
Commerical Officer: (Vacant)
Telephone: 011-86-24-220-057
Fax: 011-86-24-290-074
Street Address: 40 Lane 4, Section 5
Sanjing Street, Heping District
Mailing Address: PSC 461 Box 45
FPO AP 96521-0002

COLOMBIA Bogota
Post: American Embassy
Senior Commerical Officer: Richard Lenahan
Telephone: 011-157-232-6550
Fax: 011-57-1-285-7945
Street Address: Calle 38, No. 8-61
Mailing Address: Unit 5120
 APO AA 34038

COSTA RICA San Jose
Post: American Embassy
Senior Commerical Officer: Sheri Lanza
Telephone: 011-506-20-3939
Fax: 011-506-314783
Street Address: Avenida O, Calle 120, PAVAS
Mailing Address: APO AA 34020

COTE D'IVOIRE Abidjan
Post: American Embassy
Senior Commerical Officer: Catherine Houghton
Telephone: 011-225-21-4616
Fax: 011-225-22-3259
Street Address: 5 Rue Jesse Owens
Mailing Address: U.S. Dept of State (Abidjan)
 Washington, DC 20521-2010

CZECHOSLOVAKIA Prague
Post: American Embassy
Senior Commerical Officer: Dan Harris
Telephone: 011-42-2-532-470
Fax: 011-42-2-532-457
Street Address: Trziste 15-12548, Praha
Mailing Address: Box 5630
 APO AE 09213-5630

Bratislava
Post: American Consulate General
Commerical Officer: (Vacant)
Telephone: 011-42-7-330-861
Fax: 011-42-7-335-439
Street Address: Hviezdoslavovo Namesite 4
 81102 Bratislava
Mailing Address: Box 5630
 Unit 25402
 APO AE 09213-5630

DENMARK Copenhagen
Post: American Embassy
Senior Commerical Officer: Stephen Helgesen
Telephone: 011-45-31-423144
Fax: 011-45-31-420175
Street Address: Dag Hammarskjolds Alle 24
Mailing Address: APO AE 09176

DOMINICAN REPUBLIC Santo Domingo
Post: American Embassy
Commerical Officer: Larry Eisenberg
Telephone: 1-809-541-2171
Fax: 1-809-688-4838
Street Address: Corner of Calle Cesar Nicolas Penson
 & Calle Leopoldo Navarro
 Unit 5515
Mailing Address: APO AA 34041-0008

ECUADOR Quito
Post: American Embassy
Senior Commerical Officer: Vicki Simon

Telephone: 011-593-2-561-404
Fax: 011-593-2-504-550
Street Address: Avenida 12 de Octubre y Avenida
 Patria
Mailing Address: Unit 5334
 APO AA 34039-3420

Guayaquil
Post: American Consulate General
Commerical Assistant: Gloria Ron
Telephone: 011-593-4-323-570
Fax: 011-593-4-324-558
Street Address: 9 de Octubre y Garcia Moreno
Mailing Address: APO AA 34039

EGYPT Cairo
Post: American Embassy
Senior Commerical Officer: Laron Jensen
Telephone: 011-20-2-357-2340
Fax: 011-20-2-355-8368
Workweek: Sunday–Thursday
Street Address: 3 Lazoghli Street
 Garden City, Cairo
Mailing Address: Unit 64900 Box 11
 APO AE 09839-4900

Alexandria
Post: American Consulate General
Commercial Specialist: Hanna Abdelnour
Telephone: 011-20-3-482-1911, 357-2291
Fax: 011-20-3-482-9199
Street Address: 100 Avenue Horreya
Mailing Address: Unit 64904
 FPO AE 09839-4904

FINLAND Helsinki
Post: American Embassy
Senior Commerical Officer: Maria Andrews
Telephone: 011-358-0-171-931
Fax: 011-358-0-635-332
Street Address: Itainen Puistotie 14ASF
Mailing Address: APO AE 09723

FRANCE Paris
Post: American Embassy
Senior Commerical Officer: Peter Frederick
Telephone: 011-33-1-4296-1202
Fax: 011-33-1-4266-4827
Street Address: 2 Avenue Gabriel
Mailing Address: APO AE 09777

Post: US Mission to the OECD (Paris)
Senior Commerical Officer: Robyn Layton
Telephone: 011-33-1-4524-7437
Fax: 011-33-1-4524-7410
Street Address: 19 Rue de Franqueville 75016 Paris
Mailing Address: APO AE 09777

Bordeaux
Post: American Consulate General
Commerical Assistant: Valerie DeRousseau
Telephone: 011-33-56-526595
Fax: 011-33-56-51-60-42
Street Address: 22 Cours du Marechal Foch
Mailing Address: c/o American Embassy Paris
 APO AE 09777

Lyon
Post: American Consulate General
Commerical Assistant: Alain Beullard
Telephone: 011-33-72-40-59-20
Fax: 011-33-72-41-71-81
Street Address: 7 Quai General Sarrail
Mailing Address: c/o American Embassy Paris
APO AE 09777

Marseille
Post: American Consulate General
Commerical Assistant: Igor Lepine
Telephone: 011-33-91-549-200
Fax: 011-33-91-550-947
Street Address: 12 Boulevard Paul Peytral
Mailing Address: c/o American Embassy Paris
APO AE 09777

Nice
Post: U.S. Commercial Office
Commerical Assistant: Reine Joguet
Telephone: 011-33-93-88-89-55
Fax: 011-33-93-87-07-38
Street Address: 31 Rue de Marechal Joffre
Mailing Address: c/o American Embassy Paris
APO AE 09777

Strasbourg
Post: American Consulate General
Commerical Assistant: Jacqueline Munzlinger
Telephone: 011-33-88-35-31-04
Fax: 011-33-88-24-06-95
Street Address: 15 Avenue d'Alsace
Mailing Address: c/o American Embassy Paris
APO AE 09777

GERMANY Bonn
Post: American Embassy
Senior Commerical Officer: John W. Bligh, Jr.
Telephone: 011-49-228-339-2895
Fax: 011-49-228-334-649
Street Address: Deichmannsaue, 5300
Mailing Address: Unit 21701 Box 370
APO AE 09080

Berlin
Post: American Embassy Office
Commerical Officer: James Joy
Telephone: 011-49-30-251-2061
Fax: 011-49-30-238-6296
Street Address: Neustaedtische Kirchstrasse 4-5
1080 Berlin
Mailing Address: Unit 26738
APO AE 09235-5500

Dusseldorf
Post: U.S. Commercial Office
Commerical Specialist: Barbara Ernst
Telephone: 011-49-211-596-798
Fax: 011-49-211-594-897
Street Address: Emmanual Lutz Str. 1B
Mailing Address: Unit 21701 Box 370
APO AE 09080

Frankfurt
Post: American Consulate General

Commerical Officer: Donald Businger
Telephone: 011-49-69-7535-2453
Fax: 011-49-69-748-204
Street Address: Siesmayerstrasse 21
6000 Frankfurt
Mailing Address: APO AE 09213

Hamburg
Post: American Consulate General
Commercial Officer: Hans Amrheim
Telephone: 011-49-40-4117-1304
Fax: 011-49-40-410-6598
Street Address: Alsterufer 27/28
Mailing Address: APO AE 09215-0002

Leipzig
Post: American Consulate General
Commercial Officer: B. Lehne
Telephone: 011-37-41-211-7866
Fax: 011-37-41-211-7865
Street Address: Karl Touchnitz Strasse
15/151 0-7010
Mailing Address: APO AE 09235-5100

Munich
Post: American Consulate General
Commercial Officer: Ed Ruse
Telephone: 011-49-89-2888-748
Fax: 011-49-89-285-261
Street Address: Koeniginstrasse 5
Mailing Address: APO AE 09108

Stuttgart
Post: American Consulate General
Commercial Officer: Camille Sailer
Telephone: 011-49-711-214-5238
Fax: 011-49-711-236-4350
Street Address: Urbanstrasse 7
Mailing Address: APO AE 09154

GREECE Athens
Post: American Embassy
Senior Commercial Officer: John Priamou
Telephone: 011-30-1-723-9705
Fax: 011-30-1-721-8660
Street Address: 91 Vasilissia Sophias Blvd.
Mailing Address: PSC 108 Box 30
APO AE 09482

GUATEMALA Guatemala
Post: American Embassy
Senior Commercial Officer: Henry Nichol
Telephone: 011-502-2-348-479
Fax: 011-502-2-317-373
Street Address: 7-01 Avenida de
la Reforma
Mailing Address: Unit 3306
APO AA 34024

HONDURAS Tegucigalpa
Post: American Embassy
Senior Commercial Officer: Eric Weaver
Telephone: 011-504-32-3120
Fax: 011-504-38-2888
Street Address: Avenido La Paz
Mailing Address: APO AA 34022

HONG KONG   Hong Kong
Post: American Consulate General
Senior Commercial Officer: Lee Boam
Telephone: 011-852-521-1467
Fax: 011-852-5-845-9800
Street Address: 26 Garden Road
Mailing Address: PSC 464 Box 30
  FPO AP 96522-0002

HUNGARY   Budapest
Post: American Embassy
Senior Commercial Officer: Gary Gallagher
Telephone: 011-36-1-122-8600
Fax: 011-36-1-142-2529
Street Address: V. Szabadsag Ter 12
Mailing Address: APO AE 09213-5270

INDIA   New Delhi
Post: American Embassy
Senior Commercial Officer: Jon Bensky
Telephone: 011-91-11-600651
Fax: 011-91-11-687-2391
Street Address: Shanti Path, Chanakyapuri 110021
Mailing Address: U.S. Dept. of State (New Delhi)
  Washington, DC
  20521-9000

Bombay
Post: American Consulate General
Commercial Officer: John Wood
Telephone: 011-91-22-262-4590
Fax: 011-91-22-262-3851
Street Address: 4, New Marine Lines
Mailing Address: U.S. Dept. of State (Bombay)
  Washington, DC
  20521-6240

Calcutta
Post: American Consulate General
Commercial Specialist: Nargiz Chatterjee
Telephone: 011-91-33-22-3611
Fax: 011-91-33-225-994
Street Address: 5/1 Ho Chi Minh Sarani
Mailing Address: U.S. Dept. of State (Calcutta)
  Washington, DC
  20521-6250

Madras
Post: American Consulate General
Commercial Specialist: Raj Dheer
Telephone: 011-91-44-475-947
Fax: 011-91-44-825-0240
Street Address: Mount Road
Mailing Address: U.S. Dept. of State (Madras)
  Washington, DC
  20521-6260

INDONESIA   Jakarta
Post: American Embassy
Senior Commercial Officer: Ted Villinski
Telephone: 011-62-21-360-360
Fax: 011-62-21-385-1632
Street Address: Medan Merdeka Selatan 5
Mailing Address: Box 1
  APO AP 96520

Medan
Post: American Embassy
Commercial Clerk: Zulhava Luthfi
Telephone: 011-62-61-322-200
Street Address: Jalan Imam Bonjol 13
Mailing Address: APO AP 96520

Surabaya
Post: American Embassy
Commercial Assistant: Midji Kwee
Telephone: 011-62-31-67100
Street Address: Jalan Raya Dr. Sutomo 33
Mailing Address: APO AP 96520

IRAQ   Baghdad
Post: American Embassy
Senior Commercial Officer: (Vacant)
Telephone: 011-964-1-719-6138
Fax: 011-964-1-718-9297
Workweek: Sunday–Thursday
Street Address: Opp. For. Ministry Club (Masbah
  Quarter)
Mailing Address: U.S. Dept. of State (Baghdad)
  Washington, DC
  20521-6060

IRELAND   Dublin
Post: American Embassy
Senior Commercial Officer: Gene Harris
Telephone: 011-353-1-687-122
Fax: 011-353-1-682-840
Street Address: 42 Elgin Rd., Ballsbridge
Mailing Address: U.S. Dept. of State (Dublin)
  Washington, DC
  20521-5290

ISRAEL   Tel Aviv
Post: American Embassy
Senior Commercial Officer: Judith Henderson
Telephone: 011-972-3-517-4338
Fax: 011-972-3-658-033
Street Address: 71 Hayarkon Street
Mailing Address: PSC 98 Box 100
  APO AE 09830

ITALY   Rome
Post: American Embassy
Senior Commercial Officer: Keith Bovetti
Telephone: 011-39-6-4674-2202
Fax: 011-39-6-4674-2113
Street Address: Via Veneto 119/A
Mailing Address: PSC 59
  APO AE 09624

Florence
Post: American Consulate General
Commercial Assistant: Alessandra Gola
Telephone: 011-39-55-211-676
Fax: 011-39-55-283-780
Street Address: Lungarno Amerigo Vespucci 38
Mailing Address: APO AE 09624

Genoa
Post: American Consulate General
Commercial Specialist: Erminia Lezzi
Telephone: 011-39-10-247-1412
Fax: 011-39-10-290-027
Street Address: Banca d'Americae d'Italia Building
  Piazza Portello
Mailing Address: PSC 58 Box G
  APO AE 09624

Milan
Post: American Consulate General
Commercial Officer: Peter Alois
Telephone: 011-39-2-498-2241
Fax: 011-39-2-481-4161
Street Address: Centro Cooperazione 20149 Milano
Mailing Address: PSC 59 Box M
  APO AE 09624

Naples
Post: American Consulate General
Commercial Assistant: Christiano Sartario
Telephone: 011-39-81-761-1592
Fax: 011-39-81-761-1869
Street Address: Piazza della Republica
Mailing Address: PSC 810 Box 18
  FPO AE 09619-0002

JAMAICA Kingston
Post: American Embassy
Senior Commercial Officer: Larry Eisenberg
  (Resident in Santo Domingo)
Telephone: 1-809-929-4850
Fax: 1-809-926-6743
Street Address: Jamaica Mutual Life Center
  2 Oxford Road 3rd Floor
Mailing Address: U.S. Dept. of State (Kingston)
  Washington, DC
  20521-3210

JAPAN Tokyo
Post: American Embassy
Senior Commercial Officer: George Mu
Telephone: 011-81-3-3224-5000
Fax: 011-81-3-3589-4235
Street Address: 10-1 Akasaka 1-chome
  Minato-ku (107)
Mailing Address: Unit 45004 Box 204
  APO AP 96337-0001

Tokyo
Post: U.S. Trade Center
Director: Thomas Moore
Telephone: 011-81-3-3987-2441
Fax: 011-81-3-3987-2447
Street Address: 7th Fl. World Import Mart
  1-3 Higoshi Ikebukuro 3-chome
  Toshima-ku, Tokyo 170
Mailing Address: Unit 45004 Box 258
  APO AP 96337-0001

Fukuoka
Post: American Consulate
Commercial Assistant: Yoshihiro Yamamoto
Telephone: 011-81-92-751-9331

Fax: 011-81-92-713-922
Street Address: 5-26 Ohori 2-chome Chuo-ku
  Fukuoka-810
Mailing Address: Box 10
  FPO AP 98766

Nagoya
Post: Representative Office
Commercial Officer: Todd Thurwachter
Telephone: 011-81-52-203-4011
Fax: 011-81-52-201-4612
Street Address: 10-19 Sakae 2-chome Naka-ku,
  Nagoya 460, Japan
Mailing Address: c/o AmEmbassy Tokyo
  Unit 45004, Box 280
  APO AP 96337-0001

Osaka-Kobe
Post: American Consulate General
Commercial Officer: Patrick Santillo
Telephone: 011-81-6-315-5957
Fax: 011-81-6-361-5978
Street Address: 9th Fl. Sankei Bldg.
  4-9 Umeda 2-chome
  Kita-ku Osaka (530)
Mailing Address: Unit 45004 Box 239
  APO AP 96337

Sapporo
Post: American Consulate
Commercial Specialist: Kenji Itaya
Telephone: 011-81-11-641-1117
Fax: 011-81-11-641-0911
Street Address: Kita 1-Jo Nishi 28-chome
  Chuoku Sapporo 064
Mailing Address: APO AP 96503

KENYA Nairobi
Post: American Embassy
Senior Commercial Officer: Richard Benson
Telephone: 011-254-2-334-141
Fax: 011-254-2-216-648
Street Address: Moi/Haile Selassie Ave.
Mailing Address: Unit 64100 Box 51
  APO AE 09831-4100

KOREA Seoul
Post: American Embassy
Senior Commercial Officer: Robert Connan
Telephone: 011-82-2-732-2601
Fax: 011-82-2-739-1628
Street Address: 82 Sejong-Ro Chongro-Ku
Mailing Address: Unit 15550
  APO AP 96205-0001

KUWAIT Kuwait
Post: American Embassy
Senior Commercial Officer: William Yarmy
Telephone: 011-965-242-4151
Fax: 011-965-244-7692
Workweek: Saturday–Wednesday
Street Address: Safat, Kuwait
Mailing Address: Unit 6900 Box 10
  APO AE 09880-9000

MALAYSIA Kuala Lumpur
Post: American Embassy
Senior Commercial Officer: Paul Walters
Telephone: 011-60-3-248-9011
Fax: 011-60-3-242-1866
Street Address: 376 Jalan Tun Razak
Mailing Address: APO AP 96535-5000

MEXICO Mexico
Post: American Embassy
Senior Commercial Officer: Roger W. Wallace
Telephone: 011-52-5-211-0042
Fax: 011-52-5-207-8938
Street Address: Paseo de la Reforma 305
Mailing Address: P.O. Box 3087
    Laredo, TX 78044-3087

Mexico
Post: U.S. Trade Center
Director: Robert Miller
Telephone: 011-52-5-591-0155
Fax: 011-52-5-566-1115
Street Address: Liverpool 31, 06600
Mailing Address: P.O. Box 3087
    Laredo, TX 78044-3087

Guadalajara
Post: American Consulate General
Commercial Officer: Americo Tadeu
Telephone: 011-52-36-25-0321
Fax: 011-52-5-36-26-3576
Street Address: Jal. Progreso 175
Mailing Address: P.O. Box 3098
    Laredo, TX 78044-3098

Monterrey
Post: American Consulate General
Commercial Officer: (Vacant)
Telephone: 011-52-83-452-120
Fax: 011-5-25-83-425-172
Street Address: N.L. Avenida Constitucion
    411 Poniente
Mailing Address: P.O. Box 3098
    Laredo, TX 78044-3098

MOROCCO Casablanca
Post: American Consulate General
Senior Commercial Officer: Samuel Starrett
Telephone: 011-212-26-45-50
Fax: 011-212-22-02-59
Street Address: 8 Blvd. Moulay Youssef
Mailing Address: APO AE 09718

Rabat
Post: American Embassy
Commercial Assistant: Asma Benghhalem
Telephone: 011-212-7-622-65
Fax: 011-212-7-656-61
Street Address: 2 Ave de Marrakech
Mailing Address: APO AE 09718

NETHERLANDS The Hague
Post: American Embassy
Senior Commercial Officer: Michael Hegedus
Telephone: 011-31-70-310-9417
Fax: 011-31-70-363-2985
Street Address: Lange Voorhout 102

Mailing Address: PSC 71 Box 1000
    APO AE 09715

Amsterdam
Post: American Consulate General
Commercial Officer: Bert Englehardt
Telephone: 011-31-20-664-5661
Fax: 011-31-20-675-2856
Street Address: Museumplein 19
Mailing Address: APO AE 09715

NEW ZEALAND Auckland
Post: American Consulate General
Senior Commercial Officer: (Vacant)
Telephone: 011-64-9-303-2038
Fax: 011-64-9-366-0870
Street Address: 4th Floor Yorkshire General Bldg.
    Shortland and O'Connell Streets
Mailing Address: PSC 467 Box 99
    FPO AP 96531-1099

Wellington
Post: American Consulate General
Commercial Assistant: Janey Coulthart
Telephone: 011-64-4-722-068
Fax: 011-64-4-781-701
Street Address: 29 Fitzherbert Ter. Thorndon
Mailing Address: PSC 467 Box 1
    FPO AP 96531-1001

NIGERIA Lagos
Post: American Embassy
Senior Commercial Officer: Fred Gaynor
Telephone: 011-234-1-616-477
Fax: 011-234-1-619-856
Street Address: 2 Eleke Crescent
Mailing Address: U.S. Dept. of State (Lagos)
    Washington, DC
    20521-8300

Kaduna
Post: American Consulate General
Commercial Specialist: Mathias Mgbeze
Telephone: 011-234-201070
Street Address: 2 Maska Road
Mailing Address: U.S. Dept. of State (Kaduna)
    Washington, DC
    20521-2260

NORWAY Oslo
Post: American Embassy
Senior Commercial Officer: Scott Bozek
Telephone: 011-47-2-44-85-50
Fax: 011-47-2-55-88-03
Street Address: Drammensveien 18
Mailing Address: PSC 69 Box 0200
    APO AE 09085

PAKISTAN Karachi
Post: American Consulate General
Senior Commercial Officer: Daniel Devito
Telephone: 011-92-21-568-5170
Fax: 011-92-21-568-1381
Workweek: Sunday–Thursday
Street Address: 8 Abdullah Haroon Road
Mailing Address: Unit 62400 Box 137
    APO AE 09814-2400

Lahore
Post: American Consulate General
Commercial Officer: Shalla Malik
Telephone: 011-92-42-365-530
Fax: 011-92-42-368-901
Workweek: Sunday–Thursday
Street Address: 50 Zafar Ali Road,
Gulberg 5
Mailing Address: Unit 62216
APO AE 09812-2216

PANAMA Panama
Post: American Embassy
Senior Commercial Officer: Peter Noble
Telephone: 011-507-27-1777
Fax: 011-507-27-1713
Street Address: Avenida Balboa Y Calle 38
Apartado 6959
Mailing Address: Unit 0945
APO AA 34002

PERU Lima
Post: American Embassy
Senior Commercial Officer: (Vacant)
Telephone: 011-51-14-33-0555
Fax: 011-51-14-33-4687
Street Address: Larrabure y Unanue 110
Mailing Address: Unit 3780
APO AA 34031

PHILIPPINES Manila
Post: American Embassy
Senior Commercial Officer: Jon Bensky
Telephone: 011-63-2818-6674 or 521-7116
Fax: 011-63-2818-2684
Street Address: 395 Buendia Ave.
Extension Makati
Mailing Address: APO AP 96440

POLAND Warsaw
Post: American Embassy
Senior Commercial Officer: Joan Edwards
Telephone: 011-48-22-21-45-15
Fax: 011-48-22-21-63-27
Street Address: Aleje Ujazdowskle 29/31
Mailing Address: c/o AmConGen (WAW)
APO AE 09213-5010

PORTUGAL Lisbon
Post: American Embassy
Senior Commercial Officer: Miguel Pardo de Zela
Telephone: 011-351-1-726-6600
Fax: 011-351-1-726-8914
Street Address: Avenida das Forcas Armadas
Mailing Address: PSC 83 Box FCS
APO AE 09726

Oporto
Post: American Business Center
Commercial Assistant: Adolfo Coutinho
Telephone: 011-351-2-63094
Fax: 011-351-2-600-2737
Street Address: Apartado No. 88 Rua Julio Dinis 826,
3rd Floor
Mailing Address: c/o AmEmbassy Lisbon
APO AE 09726

ROMANIA Bucharest
Post: American Embassy
Senior Commercial Officer: Kay Kuhlman
Telephone: 011-40-0-104-040
Fax: 011-40-0-120-395
Street Address: Strada Tudor Arghezi 7-9
Mailing Address: APO AE 09213-5260

RUSSIA Moscow
Post: American Embassy
Senior Commercial Officer: Dale Slaght
Telephone: 011-7-502-224-1106
Fax: 011-7-502-224-1105
Street Address: Ulitsa Chaykovskogo 15
Mailing Address: APO AE 09721

St. Petersburg
Post: American Consulate General
Commercial Officer: Karen Zens
Telephone: 011-7-812-274-8235
Fax: N/A
Street Address: Ulitsa, Petra Lavrova St. 15
Mailing Address: Box L
APO AE 09723

SAUDI ARABIA Riyadh
Post: American Embassy
Senior Commercial Officer: Kevin Brennan
Telephone: 011-966-1-488-3800
Fax: 011-966-1-488-3237
Workweek: Saturday–Wednesday
Street Address: Collector Road M,
Diplomatic Quarter
Mailing Address: Unit G1307
APO AE 09803-1307

Dhahran
Post: American Consulate General
Commercial Officer: Thomas Moore
Telephone: 011-966-3-891-3200
Fax: 011-966-3-891-8332
Workweek: Saturday–Wednesday
Street Address: Between Aramco Headquarters and
Dhahran International Airport
Mailing Address: Unit 66803
APO AE 09858-6803

Jeddah
Post: American Consulate General
Commercial Officer: Renato Davia
Telephone: 011-966-2-667-0040
Fax: 011-966-2-665-8106
Workweek: Saturday–Wednesday
Street Address: Palestine Road, Ruwais
Mailing Address: Unit 62112
APO AE 09811-2112

SINGAPORE Singapore
Post: American Embassy
Senior Commercial Officer: George Ruffner
Telephone: 011-65-338-9722
Fax: 011-65-338-5010
Street Address: 1 Columbo Ct., #05-12
Mailing Address: APO AP 96534-0006

SOUTH AFRICA Johannesburg
Post: American Consulate General
Senior Commercial Officer: George Kachmar
Telephone: 011-27-11-331-3937
Fax: 011-27-11-331-6178
Street Address: 11th Floor Kine Center
Commissioner and Kruis Streets
Mailing Address (Pouch): U.S. Dept. of State
(Johannesburg)
Washington, DC
20521-2500
Mailing Address (Int'l): P.O. Box 2155
Johannesburg 2000, South Africa

Cape Town
Post: American Consulate General
Commercial Assistant: Sylvia Frowde
Telephone: 011-27-21-214-280
Fax: 011-27-21-254-151
Street Address: Broadway Industries Center
Herrengracht, Foreshore
Mailing Address: U.S. Dept. of State (Cape Town)
Washington, DC
20521-2480

SPAIN Madrid
Post: American Embassy
Senior Commercial Officer: Robert Kohn
Telephone: 011-34-1-577-4000
Fax: 011-34-1-575-8655
Street Address: Serrano 75
Mailing Address: PSC 61 Box 0021
APO AE 09642

Barcelona
Post: American Consulate General
Commercial Officer: Ralph Griffin
Telephone: 011-34-3-310-0442
Fax: 011-34-3-319-5621
Street Address: Via Layetana 33
Mailing Address: PSC 64
APO AE 09646

SWEDEN Stockholm
Post: American Embassy
Senior Commercial Officer: Harrison Sherwood
Telephone: 011-46-8-783-5346
Fax: 011-46-8-660-9181
Street Address: Strandvagen 101
Mailing Address: U.S. Dept. of State (Stockholm)
Washington, DC
20521-5750

SWITZERLAND Bern
Post: American Embassy
Senior Commercial Officer: Kay Kuhlman
Telephone: 011-41-31-43-73-41
Fax: 011-41-31-43-73-36
Street Address: Jubilaeumstrasse 93
Mailing Address: U.S. Dept. of State (Bern)
Washington, DC
20521-5110

Post: US Mission to the GATT (Geneva)
Senior Commercial Officer: Andrew Grossman

Telephone: 011-41-22-749-5281
Fax: 011-41-22-749-4885
Street Address: Botanic Building
1-3 Avenue de la Paix
Mailing Address: U.S. Dept. of State (Geneva)
Washington, DC
20521-5130

Zurich
Post: American Consulate General
Commercial Specialist: Paul Frei
Telephone: 011-41-1-552-070
Fax: 011-41-1-383-9814
Street Address: Zollikerstrasse 141
Mailing Address: U.S. Dept. of State (Zurich)
Washington, DC
20521-5130

THAILAND Bangkok
Post: American Embassy
Senior Commercial Officer: Herbert Cochran
Telephone: 011-66-2-253-4920
Fax: 011-66-2-255-2915
Street Address: "R" Floor Shell Building
140 Wireless Road
Mailing Address: APO AP 96546

TURKEY Ankara
Post: American Embassy
Senior Commercial Officer: David Katz
Telephone: 011-90-4-467-0949
Fax: 011-90-4-467-1366
Street Address: 110 Ataturk Blvd
Mailing Address: PSC 93 Box 5000
APO AE 09823

Istanbul
Post: American Consulate General
Commercial Officer: Russell Smith
Telephone: 011-90-1-251-1651
Fax: 011-90-1-252-2417
Street Address: 104-108 Mesrutiyet
Caddesi, Tepebasl
Mailing Address: PSC 97 Box 0002
APO AE 09827-0002

Izmir
Post: American Consulate General
Commercial Specialist: Berrin Erturk
Telephone: 011-90-51-849-426
Fax: 011-90-51-830-493
Street Address: 92 Ataturk Caddesi (3rd Fl)
Mailing Address: APO AE 09821

UKRAINE Kiev
Post: American Embassy
Senior Commercial Officer: Stephan Wasylko
Telephone: 011-7-044-279-0188
Fax: 011-7-044-279-1485
Street Address: 10 Yuria Kotsyubinskovo
252053 Kiev 53
Mailing Address: U.S. Dept. of State (Kiev)
Washington, DC
20521-5850

UNITED ARAB EMIRATES Dubai
Post: American Consulate General
Senior Commercial Officer: Paul Scogna
Telephone: 011-971-4-378-584
Fax: 011-971-4-375-121
Workweek: Saturday–Wednesday
Street Address: Dubai International Trade Center
Mailing Address: U.S. Dept. of State (Dubai)
Washington, DC
20521-6020

Abu Dhabi
Post: American Embassy
Commercial Attache: Sam Dhir
Telephone: 011-971-2-345-545
Fax: 011-971-2-331-374
Workweek: Saturday–Wednesday
Street Address: 8th Floor Blue Tower Building,
Shaikh Khalifa Bin Zayed St.
Mailing Address: U.S. Dept. of State
(Abu Dhabi)
Washington, DC
20521-6010

UNITED KINGDOM London
Post: American Embassy
Senior Commercial Officer: Kenneth Moorefield
Telephone: 011-44-71-499-9000
Fax: 011-44-71-491-4022
Street Address: 24-31 Grosvenor Square
Mailing Address: PSC 801 Box 33
FPO AE 09498-4033

VENEZUELA Caracas
Post: American Embassy
Senior Commercial Officer: Edgar Fulton
Telephone: 011-58-2-285-2222
Fax: 011-58-2-285-0336

Street Address: Avenida Francisco de Miranda
y Avenida Principal de la Floresta
Mailing Address: Unit 4958
APO AA 34037

The American Institute in Taiwan
An important non-US&FCS commercial office:

Location: Taipei Office
Head, Commercial Unit: Ying Price
Telephone: 011-886-2-720-1550
Fax: 011-886-2-757-7162
Street Address: 600 Min Chuan East Road, Taipei
Mailing Address (letters): American Institute in Taiwan
Commercial Unit
P.O. Box 1612
Washington, DC 20013
Mailing Address (packages): American Institute in
Taiwan Commercial Unit
Dept. of State (Taipei)
Washington, DC 20521

Location: Kaohsiung Office
Head, Commercial Unit: Robert Strotman
Telephone: 011-886-7-224-0154
Fax: 011-886-7-231-8237
Street Address: 3d Fl.
#2 Chung Cheng
3d Road
Kaohsiung
Mailing Address (letters): American Institute in
Taiwan
Commercial Unit
P.O. Box 1612
Washington, DC 20013
Mailing Address (packages): American Institute in
Taiwan
Commercial Unit
Dept. of State (Kaohsiung)
Washington, DC 20521

APPENDIX 15

GUIDE TO STATE STATISTICAL ABSTRACTS

Source: Statistical Abstracts of the United States.
The bibliography includes the most recent statistical abstracts for states and Puerto Rico published since 1980 plus those that will be issued in late 1992 or early 1993. For some states, a near equivalent has been listed in substitution for, or in addition to, a statistical abstract. All sources contain statistical tables on a variety of subjects for the state as a whole, its component parts, or both. The page counts given for publications are approximate.

Alabama

University of Alabama, Center for Business and Economic Research, P.O. Box 870221, Tuscaloosa 35487, 205-348-6191

Economic Abstract of Alabama. 1992. 600 pp.

Alaska

Department of Commerce and Economic Development, Division of Economic Development, P.O. Box 110804, Juneau 9981, 907-465-2017

The Alaska Economy Performance Report. 1988–1989.

Arizona

University of Arizona, Economic and Business Research, College of Business and Public Administration, Tuscon 85721, 602-621-2150

Arizona Statistical Abstract: A 1992 Data Handbook. 600 pp.

Arizona Economic Indicators. Biannual. 52 pp.

Arkansas

University of Arkansas at Little Rock, regional Economic Analysis, Library 512, Little Rock 72204

Arkansas State and County Economic Data. Revised annually. 18 pp.

University of Arkansas at Little Rock, State Data Center, Library 508, Little Rock 72204, 501-569-8530.

Arkansas Statistical Abstract. Revised biennially. 500 pp.

California

Department of Finance, 915 L Street, 8th Floor, Sacramento 95814, 916-322-2263

California Statistical Abstract. 1992. 210 pp.

Pacific Data Resources, P.O. Box 1911, Santa Barbara, CA 93116-9954, 800-422-2546

California Almanac. 5th ed. Biennial. 645 pp.

Colorado

University of Colorado, Business Research Division, Campus Box 420, Boulder 80309, 303-492-8227

Statistical Abstract of Colorado, 1987. 600 pp.

Connecticut

Connecticut Department of Economic Development, 1990–1991 87 pp. No charge for single copy. 865 Brook St., Rocky Hill 06067-3405

Connecticut Market Data.

Delaware

Delaware Development Office, 99 Kings Highway, P.O. Box 1401, Dover 19903, 302-739-4271

Delaware Data Book, 1992. 146 pp.

District of Columbia

Office of Planning, Data Management Division, Presidential Building, Suite 500, 415 12th St., N.W., Washington 20004, 202-727-6533

Population Estimates and Housing Units. Annual.

Office of Policy and Program Evaluation, Executive Office of the Mayor, District Building, Room 208, 1350 Pennsylvania Ave., NW., Washington 20004, 202-727-4016

Indices—A Statistical Index to DC Services, 1990. Annual. 422 pp.

Florida

University of Florida, Bureau of Economic and Business Research, Gainesville 32611-2017, 904-392-0171

Florida Statistical Abstract, 1990. 25th ed. 1991. 736 pp.

National Data Consultants, P.O. Box 6381, Athens, Georgia 30604, 404-548-8460

45-Florida County Perspectives: 1991. Annual. 110 pp.

Georgia

University of Georgia, Selig Center for Economic Growth, Terry College of Business, Athens 30602-6269, 706-542-4085

Georgia Statistical Abstract, 1990–91. 1990. 483 pp.

University of Georgia, College of Agriculture, Cooperate Extension Service, Athens 30602, 404-542-8940

The Georgia County Guide, 1991. 10th ed. Annual. 190 pp.

Office of Planning and Budget, 254 Washington St., S.W., Atlanta 30334-8501, 404-656-0911

Georgia Descriptions in Data. 1990–91. 249 pp.

Hawaii

Hawaii State Department of Business, and Economic Development & Tourism, P.O. Box 2359, Honolulu 96804. Inquiries 808-586-2482; Copies 808-586-2404

The State of Hawaii Data Book 1990: A Statistical Abstract. 24th ed. 1990. 667 pp.

Idaho

Department of Commerce, 700 West State St., Boise 83720, 208-334-2470

County Profiles of Idaho, 1992.

Idaho Community Profiles, 1992.

Idaho Facts, 1992.

Idaho Facts Data Book, 1989.

Illinois

University of Illinois, Bureau of Economic and Business Research, 428 Commerce West, 1206 South 6th Street, Champaign 61820, 217-333-2330

Ilinois Statistical Abstract, 1991. 445 pp.

Department of Commerce and Community Affairs, 620 Adams St., Springfield 62701, 217-782-1438

Illinois State and Regional Economic Data Book—1989. 419 pp.

Indiana

Indiana University, Indiana Business Research Center, School of Business, Indianapolis 46202-5151, 317-274-2204

Indiana Factbook, 1985. 420 pp.

Indiana Factbook, 1989. 165 pp.

Indiana Factbook, 1992. 413 pp.

Iowa

Iowa Department of Economic Development Research Bureau, 200 East Grand Ave., Des Moines 50309

1991 Statistical Profile of Iowa. 111 pp.

Kansas

University of Kansas, Institute for Public Policy and Business Research, 607 Blake Hall, Lawrence 66045-2960, 913-864-3701

Kansas Statistical Abstract, 1990–91. 26th ed. 1992.

Kentucky

Department of Existing Business and Industry, Capital Plaza Office Tower, Frankfort 40601, 502-564-4886

Kentucky Deskbook of Economic Statistics. 28th ed. 1992.

Louisiana

University of New Orleans, Division of Business and Economic Research, New Orleans 70148, 504-286-6248

Statistical Abstract of Louisiana. 8th ed. 1990.

Maine

Maine Department of Economic and Community Development, State House Station 59, Augusta 04333, 207-289-2656

Maine: A Statistical Summary. Updated periodically.

Maryland

Department of Economic and Employment Development, 217 E. Redwood St., Baltimore 21202. Inquiries 410-333-6953; Copies 410-333-6955

Maryland Statistical Abstract, 1990–91. Biennial. 274 pp. (1993–1994 available in Spring 1993.)

Massachusetts

Massachusetts Institute for Social and Economic Research, 128 Thompson Hall, University of Massachusetts at Amherst 01003, 413-545-3460; FAX 413-545-3686

Projected Total Population and Age Distribution for 1995 and 2000: Massachusetts Cities and Towns. March 1992. 62 pp.

Michigan

Wayne State University, Bureau of Business Research, School of Business Administration, Detroit 48202

Michigan Statistical Abstract. 20th ed. 1986–87. 629 pp.

Minnesota

Department of Trade and Economic Development, Business Development and Analysis Division, 900 American Center Building, St. Paul 55101, 612-296-8283

Compare Minnesota: An Economic and Statistical Factbook, 1992–93. 165 pp.

Economic Report to the Governor: State of Minnesota, 1992. 148 pp.

Office of State Demographer, State Planning Agency, 300 Centennial Bldg., St. Paul 55155, 612-296-2557

Minnesota Population and Household Estimates, 1988. 74 pp.

Mississippi

Mississippi State University, College of Business and Industry, Division of Research, Mississippi State 39762, 601-325-3817

Mississippi Statistical Abstract. 1991. 750 pp.

Missouri

University of Missouri, Business and Public Administration Research Center, Columbia 65211, 314-882-4805

Statistical Abstract for Missouri, 1991. Biennial. 350 pp.

Montana

Montana Department of Commerce, Census and Economic Information Center, 1424 9th Ave., Helena 59620, 406-444-2896

Montana County Database. (Separate county and state reports; will be avavilable by subject section as well as complete reports by county and state, updated periodically, available in paper, microfiche, and diskette.)

Nebraska

Department of Economic Development, Division of Research, Box 94666, Lincoln 68509, 402-471-3779

Nebraska Statistical Handbook. 1990–91. 300 pp.

Nevada

Department of Administration, Planning Division, Capitol Complex, Carson City 89710, 702-687-4065

Nevada Statistical Abstract. 1992. Biennial. 405 pp.

New Hampshire

Office of State Planning, $2\frac{1}{2}$ Beacon St., Concord 03301, 603-271-2155

Current Estimates and Trends in New Hampshire's Housing Supply. Update: 1990. 22 pp.

Selected Economic Characteristics of New Hampshire Municipalities. 1992. 12 pp. (Other series available on population estimates and projections, and taxation.)

New Jersey

New Jersey State Data Center, NJ Department of Labor, CN 388, Trenton 08625-0388, 609-984-2593

New Jersey Statistical Factbook, 1992. 115 pp.

Statistical Source Directory for New Jersey State Government, 1992. 100 pp.

New Mexico

University of New Mexico, Bureau of Business and Economic Research, Albuquerque 87131, 505-277-2216

New Mexico Statistical Abstract. 1989. 215 pp.

County Profiles. Updated continuously.

New York

Energy Association of New York, 111 Washington Avenue, Suite 601, Albany 12210, 518-449-3440

New York at a Glance, 1989–90. 230 pp.

Nelson Rockefeller Institute of Government, 411 State Street, Albany 12203, 518-443-5522

New York State Statistical Yearbook, 1992. 17th ed. 536 pp.

North Carolina

Office of Governor

Office of State Planning, 116 West Jones Street, Raleigh 27603-8003, 919-733-4131

Statistical Abstract of North Carolina Counties, 1991. 6th ed.

North Dakota

University of North Dakota, Bureau of Business and Economic Research, Grand Forks 58202, 701-777-3365

The Statistical Abstract of North Dakota. 1988. 700 pp.

North Dakota Department of Economic Development and Finance, 1833 E. Bismark Expressway, Bismark 58504, 701-221-5300

North Dakota Economic Data Book. 1988. 100 pp.

Ohio

Department of Development, Ohio Data Users Center (ODUC), P.O. Box 1001, Columbus 43266-0101, 614-466-2115

ODUC Products and Services. Updated continuously.

Ohio County Profiles, 1992.

The Ohio State University, School of Public Policy and Management, 1775 College Road, Columbus 43210-1399, 614-292-8696

Benchmark Ohio, 1991. Biennial. 300 pp.

Oklahoma

University of Oklahoma, Center for Economic and Management Research, 307 West Brooks Street, Room 4, Norman 73019, 405-325-2931

Statistical Abstract of Oklahoma, 1992. Annual. 626 pp.

Oregon

Secretary of State, Room 136, State Capitol, Salem 97310

Oregon Blue Book, 1991–1992. Biennial. 488 pp.

Pennsylvania

Pennsylvania State Data Center, Institute of State and Regional Affairs, Penn State, Harrisburg, 777 West Harrisburg Pike, Middleton, Pennsylvania 17057-4898

Pennsylvania Statistical Abstract, 1992. 30th ed. 1992. 249 pp.

Rhode Island

Department of Economic Development, 7 Jackson Walkway, Providence 02903, 401-277-2601

Rhode Island Basic Economic Statistics. 1992. 145 pp. $5.00.

South Carolina

Budget and Control Board, Division of Research and Statistical Services, R. C. Dennis Building, Room 425, Columbia 29201, 803-734-3781

South Carolina Statistical Abstract: 1992. 392 pp.

South Dakota

University of South Dakota, State Data Center, Vermillion 57069, 605-677-5287

Handbook of Manpower Statistics for South Dakota. 294 pp.

1990 South Dakota Community Abstracts. 400 pp.

Tennessee

University of Tennessee, Center for Business and Economic Research, Knoxville 37996-4170, 615-974-5441

Tennessee Statistical Abstract, 1992-93. 14th ed. Annual. 700 pp.

Texas

Dallas Morning News, Communications Center, P.O. Box 655237, Dallas 75265, 214-977-8261

Texas Almanac, 1992–1993. 1991. 656 pp.

University of Texas, Bureau of Business Research, Austin 78712, 512-471-5180

Texas Fact Book, 1989. 6th ed. 250 pp.

Utah

University of Utah, Bureau of Economic and Business Research, 401 Kendall D. Garff Building, Salt Lake City 84112, 801-581-6333

Statistical Abstract of Utah. 1993. Triennial.

Utah Foundation, 10 West 100 South 323, Salt Lake City 84101-1544, 801-364-1837

Statistical Review of Government in Utah. 1991. 101 pp.

Vermont

Office of Policy Research and Coordination, Department of Employment and Training, Montpelier 05602, 802-229-0311 ext. 323

Demographic and Economic Profiles. Periodically issued.

Virginia

University of Virginia, Center for Public Service, Dynamics Building, 4th Floor 2015 Ivy Road, Charlottesville 22903, 804-924-3921

Virginia Statistical Abstract, 1992–93. Biennial. 850 pp.

Washington

Washington State Office of Financial Management, Forecasting Division P.O. Box 43113 Olympia 98504-3113, 206-753-5617

Washington State Data Book, 1991. Biennial. 306 pp.

Population Trends for Washington State. Annual. 128 pp.

West Virginia

West Virginia Chamber of Commerce, P.O. Box 2789, Charleston 25330, 304-342-1115

West Virginia: Economic-Statistical Profile, 1987–1988. Biennial. 750 pp.

West Virginia Research League, Inc., 405 Capitol Street, Suite 414, Charleston 25301, 304-346-9451

Economic Indicators. 1988. 110 pp.

The 1991 Statistical Handbook. 86 pp.

Wisconsin

Wisconsin Legislative Reference Bureau, P.O. Box 2037, Madison 53701-2037, 608-266-0341

1991–1992 Wisconsin Blue Book. Biennial. 1,000 pp.

Wyoming

Department of Administration and Information, Division of Economic Analysis, 327 E. Emerson Building, Cheyenne 82002, 307-777-7504

Wyoming Data Handbook, 1991. 310 pp.

Puerto Rico

Planning Board, Area of Economic and Social Planning, Bureau of Economic Analysis and Bureau of Statistics, Santurce 00940, 809-722-2070

Economic Report to the Governor, 1990. (In Spanish.)

Historic Series of Employment, Unemployment and Labor Force, 1988. 98 pp. (In Spanish.)

Social Statistics Abstract, 1987. 258 pp. (In Spanish.)

Socioeconomic Indicators by Municipios, 1989. (In Spanish.)

APPENDIX 16

GUIDE TO INTERNATIONAL STATISTICAL ABSTRACTS

Source: Statistical Abstracts of the United States.
This bibliography presents recent statistical abstracts for Mexico, the former Soviet Union, and member nations of the Organization for Economic Cooperation and Development. All sources contain statistical tables on a variety of subjects for the individual countries. Many of the following publications provide text in English as well as in the national language(s). For further information on these publications, contact the named statistical agency which is responsible for editing the publication.

Austria
Osterreichisches Statistisches Zentralamt, P.O. Box 9000, A-1033 Vienna

Statistisches Handbuch for die Republik Osterreich. Annual. 1991 592 pp. (In German.)

Australia
Australian Bureau of Statistics, Canberra

Yearbook Australia. Annual. 1991 790 pp. (In English.)

Belgium
Institut National de Statistique, 44 rue de Louvain, 1000 Brussels

Annuaire statistique de la Belgique. Annual. 1988 783 pp. (In French and Dutch.)

Canada
Statistics Canada, Ottawa, Ontario, KIA OT6

Canada Yearbook: A review of economic, social and political developments in Canada. 1990. Irregular. (In English and French.)

Denmark
Danmarks Statistik, Postboks 2550 Sejrogade 11, DK 2100, Copenhagen 0

Statistical Yearbook. 1990. Annual. 541 pp. (In Danish with English translations of table headings.)

Finland
Central Statistical Office of Finland, Box 504 SF-00101 Helsinki Centraal

Statistical Yearbook of Finland. Annual. 1991 598 pp. (In English, Finnish, and Swedish.)

France
Institut National de la Statistique et des Etudes Economiques, Paris 18, Bld. Adolphe Pinard, 75675 Paris (Cedex 14)

Annuaire Statistique de la France. Annual. 1989 864 pp. (In French.)

Greece
National Statistical Office, 14-16 Lycourgou St., 101-66 Athens

Statistical Yearbook of Greece. Annual. 1988 240 pp. (plus 7 pages of diagrams). (In English and Greek.)

Iceland
Hagstofa Islands/Statistical Bureau, Hverfisgata 8-10, Reykjavik.

Statistical Abstract of Iceland. 1991. Irregular. 267 pp. (In English and Icelandic.)

Ireland
Central Statistics Office, Earlsfort Terrace, Dublin 2

Statistical Abstract. Annual. 1991 400 pp. (In English.)

Italy
ISTAT (Instituto Centrale di Statistica), Via Censare Balbo 16, 00100 Rome

Annuario Statistico Italiano. Annual. 1991 701 pp. (In Italian.)

Japan
Bureau, Management & Coordination Agency, 19-1 Wakamatsucho, Shinjuku Tokyo 162

Japan Statistical Yearbook. Annual. 1991 842 pp. (In English and Japanese.)

Luxembourg
STATEC (Service Central de la Statistique et des Etudes), P.O. Box 304, L-2013, Luxembourg

Annuaire Statistique. Annual. 1991 529 pp. (In French.)

Mexico

Instituto Nacional de Estadistica Geografia y Informatica, Avda. Insurgentes Sur No. 795-PH Col. Napoles, Del. Benito Juarez 03810 Mexico, D.F.

Anuario estadistico de los Estados Unidos Mexicanos. Annual. 1986 706 pp. (In Spanish.)

Netherlands

Bureau voor de Statistiek. 428 Prinses Beatrixlaan P.O. Box 959, 2270 AZ Voorburg

Statistical Yearbook of the Netherlands. Annual. 1990 491 pp. (In English.)

New Zealand

Department of Statistics, Wellington

New Zealand Official Yearbook. Annual. 1990 707 pp. (In English.)

Norway

Central Bureau of Statistics, Skippergate 15, P.B. 8131 Dep. N-Oslo 1

Statistical Yearbook. Annual. 1988 502 pp. (In English and Norwegian.)

Portugal

INE (Instituto Nacional de Estatistica), Avenida Antonio Jose de Almeida, P-1078 Lisbon Codex

Anuario Estatistico: Continente, Acores e Madeira. Annual. 1990 336 pp. (In Portuguese.)

Soviet Union

Central Statistical Board, Moscow

Narodnoe Khoziaistvo SSSR: Statisticheskii ezhegodnik. Annual. 767 pp. (In Russian.)

Spain

INE(Instituto Nacional de Estadistica), Paseo de la Castellana, 183, Madrid 16

Anuario Estadistico de España. Annual. 1989 895 pp. (In Spanish.)

Anuario Estadistico. 1988. (Edicion Manual.) 976 pp.

Sweden

Statistics Sweden, S-11581 Stockholm

Statistical Abstract of Sweden, Annual. 1988 561 pp. (In English and Swedish.)

Switzerland

Bundesamt fur Statistik, Hallwylstrasse 15, CH-3003, Bern

Statistisches Jahrbuch der Schweiz. Annual. 1991 420 pp. (In French and German.)

Turkey

State Institute of Statistics, Prime Ministry, 114 Necatibey Caddesi, Bakanliklar, Yenisehir, Ankara

Statistical Yearbook of Turkey. Published on odd numbered years. 1988 497 pp. (In English and Turkish.)

Statistical Pocketbook of Turkey. Published on even numbered years. 1986 294 pp. (In English and Turkish.)

United Kingdom

Central Statistical Office, Great George Street, London SW1P 3AQ

Annual Abstract of Statistics. Annual 1991 349 pp. (In English.)

West Germany

Statistische Budnesamt, Postfach 5528, 6200 Wiesbaden

Statistisches Jahrbuch fur die Bundesrepublic Deutschland. Annual. 1990 740 pp. (In German.)

Yugoslavia

Savesni Zavod za Statistiku, P.O. Box 203, 11000 Belgrade

Statisticki Godisnjak Jugoslavije. Annual. 1991 779 pp. (In Serbo-Croatian with English, French, and Russian translations of table headings.)

Statistical Pocketbook of Yugoslavia. 1991. 161 pp. (In English.)

APPENDIX 17

FEDERAL INFORMATION CENTER PROGRAM LIST OF TOLL-FREE NUMBERS

If your state or metropolitan area is not listed, call 301-722-9098. Users of telecommunications devices for the deaf (TDD/TTY) may call 1-800-326-2996.

State/City	Telephone	State/City	Telephone
ALABAMA		MISSOURI	
Birmingham	800-366-2998	St. Louis	800-366-2998
Mobile	800-336-2998	From elsewhere in Missouri	800-735-8004
ALASKA		NEBRASKA	
Anchorage	800-729-8003	Omaha	800-366-2998
ARIZONA		From elsewhere in Nebraska	800-735-8004
Phoenix	800-359-3997	NEW JERSEY	
ARKANSAS		Newark	800-347-1997
Little Rock	800-366-2998	Trenton	800-347-1997
CALIFORNIA		NEW MEXICO	
Los Angeles	800-726-4995	Albuquerque	800-359-3997
Sacramento	916-973-1695	NEW YORK	
San Diego	800-726-4995	Albany	800-347-1997
San Francisco	800-726-4995	Buffalo	800-347-1997
Santa Ana	800-726-4995	New York	800-347-1997
COLORADO		Rochester	800-347-1997
Colorado Springs	800-359-3997	Syracuse	800-347-1997
Denver	800-359-3997	NORTH CAROLINA	
Pueblo	800-359-3997	Charlotte	800-347-1997
CONNECTICUT		OHIO	
Hartford	800-347-1997	Akron	800-347-1997
New Haven	800-347-1997	Cincinnati	800-347-1997
FLORIDA		Cleveland	800-347-1997
Ft. Lauderdale	800-347-1997	Columbus	800-347-1997
Jacksonville	800-347-1997	Dayton	800-347-1997
Miami	800-347-1997	Toledo	800-347-1997
Orlando	800-347-1997	OKLAHOMA	
St. Petersburg	800-347-1997	Oklahoma City	800-366-2998
Tampa	800-347-1997	Tulsa	800-366-2998
West Palm Beach	800-347-1997	OREGON	
GEORGIA		Portland	800-726-4995
Atlanta	800-347-1997	PENNSYLVANIA	
HAWAII		Philadelphia	800-347-1997
Honolulu	800-733-5996	Pittsburgh	800-347-1997
ILLINOIS		RHODE ISLAND	
Chicago	800-366-2998	Providence	800-347-1997
INDIANA		TENNESSEE	
Gary	800-366-2998	Chattanooga	800-347-1997
Indianapolis	800-347-1997	Memphis	800-366-2998
IOWA		Nashville	800-366-2998
From all points	800-735-8004	TEXAS	
KANSAS		Austin	800-366-2998
From all points	800-735-8004	Dallas	800-366-2998
KENTUCKY		Ft. Worth	800-366-2998
Louisville	800-347-1997	Houston	800-366-2998
LOUISIANA		San Antonio	800-366-2998
New Orleans	800-366-2998	UTAH	
MARYLAND		Salt Lake City	800-359-3997
Baltimore	800-347-1997	VIRGINIA	
MASSACHUSETTS		Norfolk	800-347-1997
Boston	000-347-1997	Richmond	800-347-1997
MICHIGAN		Roanoke	800-347-1997
Detroit	800-347-1997	WASHINGTON	
Grand Rapids	800-347-1997	Seattle	800-726-4995
MINNESOTA		Tacoma	800-726-4995
Minneapolis	800-366-2998	WISCONSIN	
		Milwaukee	800-366-2998

Index

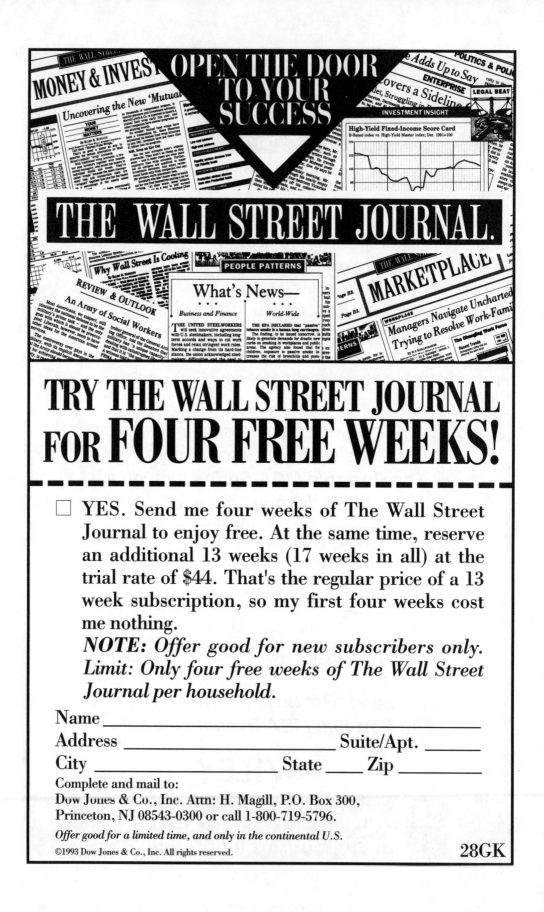